Industrial Marketing Management

A Strategic View of Business Markets

Second Edition

Industrial Marketing Management

A Strategic View of Business Markets

Second Edition

Michael D. Hutt
Arizona State University

Thomas W. Speh
Miami University

The Dryden Press
Chicago   New York   Philadelphia   San Francisco   Montreal   Toronto
London   Sydney   Tokyo   Mexico City   Rio de Janeiro   Madrid

Acquisitions Editor: Mary Glacken
Project Editor: Cate Rzasa
Managing Editor: Jane Perkins
Design Director: Alan Wendt
Production Manager: Claire Roth

Cover Designer: Alan Wendt
Copy Editor: Anne Grant
Indexer: Sheila Ary
Compositor: G&S Typesetters, Inc.
Text Type: 10/12 Baskerville

Library of Congress Cataloging in Publication Data

Hutt, Michael D.
  Industrial marketing management.

  Includes bibliographical references and index.
  1. Industrial marketing—Management.   I. Speh,
Thomas W.   II. Title.
HF5415.13.H87   1984   658.8'04   84-1668
ISBN 0-03-069307-1

Printed in the United States of America
567-038-98765432

Address orders:
383 Madison Avenue
New York, NY 10017

Address editorial correspondence:
One Salt Creek Lane
Hinsdale, IL 60521

CBS College Publishing
The Dryden Press
Holt, Rinehart and Winston
Saunders College Publishing

Cover Description:
A graphic representation of an experimental bubble-
memory microchip, which can store large amounts of
information.

To Rita
and
To Michele, Scott and Michael

The Dryden Press Series in Marketing

Preface

Special challenges and opportunities confront the marketer who intends to serve the needs of industrial or organizational customers. Commercial enterprises, institutions, and government at all levels constitute a lucrative but complex market worthy of separate analysis. The past several years have witnessed a rich and growing body of literature and thought in this special marketing area. Since the first edition of *Industrial Marketing Management* was published in 1981, an increasing level of research attention has been invested in studies of industrial or business marketing, and a growing number of collegiate schools of business in the United States and Canada have added industrial marketing to their curricula. The establishment of the Institute for the Study of Business Markets at Pennsylvania State University further illustrates the rising importance of this distinctive area of marketing in the academic and business communities. The expanding literature devoted to organizational buying behavior and the strategic dimensions of industrial marketing management provide the foundation for an integrated treatment of this area. A comprehensive treatment of industrial marketing management is particularly appropriate since more than half of all business school graduates enter industrial product/service firms.

Three objectives guided the development of this volume:

1. *To highlight similarities between consumer-goods and industrial-goods marketing and to scrutinize the points of departure.* Particular attention is given to industrial market analysis, organizational buying behavior, and the ensuing adjustments in marketing strategy required to reach industrial customers.

2. *To present a managerial rather than a descriptive treatment of industrial marketing.* While some descriptive material is required to convey the dynamic nature of the industrial marketing environment, the goal of the material is linked to industrial marketing management decision making.

3. *To integrate the growing body of literature into an operational treatment of industrial marketing management.* Here, we draw upon studies of or-

ganizational buying behavior, procurement, organizational behavior, logistics, strategic planning, and the behavioral sciences, as well as specialized studies of the components of industrial marketing strategy.

The book is structured to provide a complete treatment of industrial marketing while minimizing the degree of overlap with other courses in the marketing curriculum. A basic marketing principles course or relevant managerial experience provides the needed background for this text.

Organization of the Second Edition

The goal of the second edition is to present a clear, interesting, and integrative examination of industrial marketing management. To this end, each chapter provides an overview, highlights key concepts, and includes carefully chosen examples of contemporary industrial marketing practices, a cogent summary, and provocative discussion questions.

Although the objectives, approach, and style of the first edition have been maintained, changes and additions have been made to reflect both the growing body of literature and the emerging trends in industrial marketing management. The book is divided into six parts with a total of 17 chapters. Part I introduces the distinguishing features of the industrial marketing environment and examines each of the major types of industrial customers. Organizational buying behavior establishes the theme of Part II, which analyzes the many forces that impact upon the organizational buying process. The second edition of *Industrial Marketing Management* has been updated to incorporate the substantial amount of organizational buying behavior research that has been conducted since the first edition was published.

Once this important background is established in the organizational buying behavior area, Part III considers the industrial marketing intelligence function and effective techniques for assessing market opportunities. Part III includes a new chapter—"Industrial Marketing Intelligence"—and updated chapters on organizational market segmentation, measuring industrial market potential, and sales forecasting.

Part IV draws on recent research in strategic planning in discussing industrial marketing planning and the design of industrial marketing strategy. The treatment emphasizes competitive analysis and the interface of marketing with other key functional areas, such as manufacturing, research and development, and customer service. This functionally integrated planning perspective is a focal point in the analysis of how industrial marketing strategy is developed. In Part IV, each component of the marketing mix is examined from an industrial marketing perspective.

Part V examines techniques for evaluating industrial marketing strategy and performance, using marketing control systems and marketing profitability analysis. Emerging trends in buyer–seller relationships, organizational buying behavior research, manufacturing technology, international market analysis, strategic planning, and other areas are assessed. Part VI consists of a collection of cases tailored to the industrial marketing environment.

Cases

Of 18 cases in the second edition, 11 are new. This section provides a blend of cases of varying lengths, each of which isolates one or more industrial marketing problems. A case planning guide keys the cases to relevant text chapters and provides an organized structure to Part VI.

Teaching Package

A comprehensive instructor's manual is available which includes suggestions for course design, supporting teaching materials for each chapter, and transparency masters. Guidelines are provided for end-of-chapter discussion questions, as well as suggestions for case use and analysis. A large bank of objective questions is also provided in the manual.

Acknowledgments

The development of a textbook draws upon the contributions of many individuals. First, we would like to thank our students and former students at Arizona State University, Miami University, the University of Alabama, and the University of Vermont. They provided important input and feedback when selected concepts or chapters were class tested. Second, we express our gratitude to several distinguished colleagues who carefully reviewed the manuscript at various stages and provided incisive comments and valuable suggestions that improved the second edition. They include Jon M. Hawes, University of Akron; Wesley J. Johnston, Ohio State University; Gary L. Lilien, Pennsylvania State University; Paul McDevitt, Sangamon State University; Bruce Newman, University of Wisconsin-Milwaukee; and William S. Penn, Jr., San Jose State University. We also wish to acknowledge the contributions of Brian H. Long, Western Michigan University; Daniel H. McQuiston, Ohio State University; Lindsay N. Meredith, Simon Fraser University; Wayne A. Nero, University of Wisconsin-Stout; Richard E. Plank, Rutgers University; Marti Rhea, North Texas State University; and Joseph W. Thompson, Michigan State University. We would also like to express our continuing appreciation to others who provided important suggestions for the first edition: Paul F. Anderson, Virginia Polytechnic Institute; John J. Burnett, Texas Tech University; and John A. Czepiel, New York University.

A number of industrial marketing practitioners, including several participants at past management development seminars, provided valuable suggestions and interesting examples. We are especially indebted to Bruce Anderson and Raymond Hall, Electronic Representatives Association; Jeffrey A. Coopersmith, Distribution Centers, Inc.; Gerry Daley, The Black-Clawson Company, Shartle-Pandia Division; Patrick W. Fitzgerald, Cincinnati Electric Equipment Company; William Goldblatt, L. M. Berry Co.; Rod O'Connor, Motorola, Inc., Government Electronics Group; Edward Sauer, Industrial Products Division, Procter and Gamble; and Cap Stubbs, Raychem Corporation.

The talented staff of The Dryden Press displayed a high level of enthusiasm and professionalism throughout the project. In particular, Mary Glacken, Cate Rzasa, and Jill Spillone deserve special praise. We would also like to acknowledge the suggestions and encouragement provided by our colleagues at Arizona State University and Miami University.

Finally, but most importantly, our overriding debt is to our wives, Rita and Michele, whose encouragement, understanding, and support were vital to the completion of this volume. Their involvement and dedication are deeply appreciated.

Michael D. Hutt
Thomas W. Speh
October 1984

Case Contributors

William B. Ayars, *California State College, Bakersfield*
Danny Bellenger, *Texas Tech University*
Kenneth L. Bernhardt, *Georgia State University*
James D. Blaser, *Cleveland Consulting Associates*
Jay H. Coats, *West Virginia University*
William P. Dommermuth, *Southern Illinois University*
Dan T. Dunn, Jr., *Northeastern University*
George B. Glisan, *Illinois State University*
Thomas V. Greer, *University of Maryland*
Thomas Ingram, *University of Kentucky*
Roger Kerin, *Southern Methodist University*
J. W. Leonard, *Miami University*
David McConaughy, *University of Southern California*
Roger More, *University of Western Ontario*
Stuart U. Rich, *University of Oregon*
Howard F. Rudd, Jr., *California State College, Bakersfield*
Stanford Business Cases, *Stanford University*
Bill Stearns, *Texas Instruments*
W. Wayne Talarzyk, *The Ohio State University*
John Thanopoulos, *University of Akron*
Dan R. E. Thomas, *Thomas & Company*
Carolyn Vose, *University of Western Ontario*

Contents

C·H·A·P·T·E·R
2

The Industrial Market: Perspectives on the Organizational Buyer   **29**

P·A·R·T
II

The Organizational Buying Process   55

C·H·A·P·T·E·R
3

Dimensions of Organizational Buying   57

C·H·A·P·T·E·R
4

P·A·R·T
III

C·H·A·P·T·E·R
5

C·H·A·P·T·E·R

6

Segmenting the Organizational Market 147

C·H·A·P·T·E·R
7

Organizational Demand Analysis:
Measuring Market Potential   167

C·H·A·P·T·E·R
8

Organizational Demand Analysis:
Sales Forecasting   195

C·H·A·P·T·E·R
10

C·H·A·P·T·E·R
11

C·H·A·P·T·E·R
12

Industrial Marketing Channels: Design and Management 309

C·H·A·P·T·E·R
13

Industrial Marketing Channels:
The Logistical Interface   333

C·H·A·P·T·E·R
14

C·H·A·P·T·E·R
15

C·H·A·P·T·E·R
16

Industrial Marketing Communications: Managing the Personal Selling Function

P·A·R·T
V

Evaluating Industrial Marketing Strategy and Performance 453

C·H·A·P·T·E·R
17

Controlling Industrial Marketing Strategies 455

P·A·R·T
VI

P · A · R · T
I

The Environment of
Industrial Marketing

C·H·A·P·T·E·R
1

An Industrial Marketing Perspective

The industrial market poses special challenges and significant opportunities for the marketing manager. This chapter introduces the complex forces that are unique to the industrial marketing environment. After reading this chapter, you will understand:

1. *the dynamic nature of the industrial marketing environment as well as the basic similarities and differences between consumer and industrial marketing;*
2. *the underlying factors that influence the demand for industrial goods;*
3. *the types of customers in this important market;*
4. *some important dimensions of the processes that customers use in buying industrial goods;*
5. *the basic characteristics of industrial products and services.*

Industrial Marketing

Industrial buyers constitute the largest market of all; the dollar volume of transactions involved in industrial buying significantly exceeds that of the ultimate consumer market. Over *14 million* different industrial buying organizations, employing over *87 million workers*, generate an annual national income of over *one trillion dollars*.[1] All formal organizations, public or private, profit or not-for-profit, participate in the exchange of industrial products and services.

Industrial or business marketing is the process of (1) determining the needs and requirements of commercial enterprises, governments and institutions, and (2) developing the appropriate products, services, prices, distribution channels and communications to satisfy those requirements. An industrial marketer, as opposed to a consumer goods marketer, concentrates on meeting the needs of organizations (businesses, governments, institutions) which purchase goods and services that are incorporated into a finished product, used to produce a finished product, or used to facilitate a production process. A consumer goods marketer, by contrast, is concerned with understanding final consumer needs and developing products to be purchased by individuals for their own consumption. The factors that distinguish industrial from consumer marketing are the nature of the customer and how that customer uses the product. In industrial marketing, the customers are organizations rather than individuals; they purchase products and services for making other products or services rather than for personal consumption.

Business firms buy industrial goods to form or facilitate the production process or as components for other goods and services. Government agencies and private institutions buy industrial goods to maintain and deliver services to *their* market—the public. Industrial marketing accounts for well over half the economic activity in the United States, Canada, and most other nations. Over 50 percent of all business school graduates enter industrial product/service firms. The heightened interest in high technology markets—and the sheer size of the industrial market—has spawned increased emphasis on industrial marketing management in universities and corporate executive training programs.[2]

This book is designed to provide an operational treatment of industrial marketing management, by drawing on the literature of organizational buying behavior, procurement, organizational behavior, logistics and strategic planning, as well as specialized studies of industrial marketing strategy. The integrating questions are: What are the similarities and differences between the marketing of consumer products and the marketing of industrial products? What customers comprise the

---

[1] Wesley J. Johnston and Robert E. Spekman, "Special Section on Industrial Buying Behavior: Introduction," *Journal of Business Research* 10 (June 1982), pp. 133–134.

[2] Richard E. Plank, "Industrial Marketing Education: Present Conditions and Future Prospects," working paper, Montclair State College, Upper Montclair, N.J., July 1982.

industrial market? How can the multitude of industrial goods be classified into manageable categories? What forces influence the behavior of
industrial market demand? These questions establish the theme of this
first chapter.

Industrial Marketing Management

We are concerned with the *marketing of products and services to commercial
enterprises, government, and not-for-profit institutions, either for resale to other
industrial consumers or for use in the production of their own products or services.*[3] Many large industrial firms that produce products like steel, production equipment, or computer-memory chips cater exclusively to
organizational customers and never come into direct contact with ultimate consumers. Other firms participate in both the consumer-goods
and industrial-goods markets. The introduction of personal computers
brought IBM, historically an industrial marketer, into the consumer
market. Conversely, lagging consumer markets prompted Sony Corporation to expand to the industrial market by introducing office automation products.[4] Both companies had to dramatically reorient their
marketing strategies because of the significant differences in buying behavior in the consumer and the industrial markets.

    Purchases like calculators or personal computers may be both con-
sumer and industrial. What distinguishes industrial from consumer-
goods marketing is the intended use of the product, and the intended
consumer. Sometimes, the products are identical, but a fundamentally
different marketing approach is needed to reach the industrial buyer.

Marketing Concept

The basic task of management cuts across both consumer-goods and
industrial-goods marketing. Marketers serving both sectors can benefit
by rooting their organizational plan in the *marketing concept*, which holds
that the central aim of any organization is to define the needs of a target
market and to adapt products or services to satisfy these needs more
effectively than competitors.[5] Consumer-goods marketers seem to have
embraced this concept more completely than have their industrial counterparts.[6] Some industrial marketers are more concerned with the speci-

---

[3] Industrial Marketing Committee Review Board, "Fundamental Differences Between Industrial and Consumer Marketing," *Journal of Marketing* 19 (October 1954), p. 153.

[4] Urban C. Lehner, "Japan Electronic Firms Like Matsushita, Sony Push Into Computers," *Wall Street Journal* (March 8,
1983), p. 1.

[5] Philip Kotler, *Marketing Management: Analysis, Planning, and Control*, 5th ed. (Englewood Cliffs, N.J.: Prentice-Hall, Inc.,
1984), p. 14.

[6] Frederick E. Webster, Jr., "Management Science in Industrial Marketing," *Journal of Marketing* 42 (January 1978). p. 23;
see also, Grandhi Balakrishna, "Better Use of the Industrial Marketing Concept," *Industrial Marketing Management* 7
(January 1978), pp. 71–76.

fications of products than with how these specifications respond to customer needs.[7]

Like consumer-goods marketers, industrial marketers must design a product or service offering (including a communication program, and pricing and distribution system) that reaches and satisfies the needs of a target market segment. Philip Kotler's definition of marketing management captures the essence of the problem: *"Marketing management is the analysis, planning, implementation, and control of programs designed to create, build, and maintain mutually beneficial exchanges and relationships with target markets for the purpose of achieving organizational objectives."*[8]

Industrial Marketing and Consumer Goods Marketing Are Different
A common body of knowledge, principles, and theory applies to both consumer and industrial marketing, but because their buyers and markets function quite differently, they merit separate attention. The hope of capturing a share of a large, but unfamiliar, market leads many consumer-goods companies into the industrial arena. Surprises often follow. These firms are often frustrated in attempting to pinpoint specific markets; they are confused by the organizational buying process; many of their traditional marketing approaches turn out to be irrelevant in the industrial market. There are differences in the nature of markets, market demand, buyer behavior, buyer–seller relationships, environmental influences (economic, political, legal), and market strategy. Yet, the potential payoffs are high for the firm that can successfully penetrate the industrial market.

Industrial Demand

The nature of the demand for industrial products poses unique challenges—and opportunities—for the marketing manager.

Derived Demand   Demand for industrial products is derived from ultimate consumer demand. Industrial customers like commercial firms, governments, and not-for-profit institutions buy goods and services in order to produce other goods and/or services for their own customers. Car and truck manufacturers account for 25 percent of U.S. steel consumption, 65 percent of rubber consumption, and 30 percent of aluminum consumption.[9] General Motors alone purchases 7 percent of domestic steel.[10] As this example illustrates, demand for an industrial product is derived from the buying organization's customers (car buyers), *not* from the buying organization itself (General Motors).

[7] G. B. Thayer, Jr., "Industrial High Tech Positioning: How to Choose the Competitive Battlefield," *Industrial Marketing* 67 (June 1982), pp. 60–68.

[8] Cf. Kotler, *Marketing Management*, p. 22.

[9] "A Troubled Auto Industry—Impact on U.S.," *U.S. News & World Report* (August 27, 1979), p. 21.

[10] "Steel: The Prospect of Major Bankruptcies," *Business Week* (January 17, 1983), p. 64.

Table 1.1   Selected Suppliers of Component Parts for a Ford Car

Industrial Supplier	Component Part
TRW	Power-Steering Pump
Motorola	Electronic Engine Controls
Toyo Kogyo	Manual Transaxles
Dayco	Drive Belts
Harman Automotive	Outside Mirrors
Hamill	Seat Belts
Kelsey-Hayes	Front Disk-Brake Calipers
ITT	Door Hinges
Motor Wheel	Rear Brake Drums
Superior Industries	Cast-Aluminum Wheels
Hurd Lock	Door Locks
Firestone	
Goodyear	Tires
Michelin	

Source: "Are U.S. Cars Really Getting Better?" *U.S. News & World Report* (August 29, 1983), p. 57.

Consider that of the 12,000 parts of a typical Ford car, outside industrial firms produce half. Table 1.1 highlights selected suppliers of key component parts of a particular Ford product. In purchasing a car, the Ford customer is stimulating demand for products produced by Dayco, TRW, Goodyear, and uncounted other industrial firms.

Since demand is derived, the industrial marketing manager must carefully monitor demand patterns and changing buying preferences in final consumer markets. If automakers forecast that sales will climb or fall next year, the industrial marketer must make corresponding changes in the forecast for this segment of the market. Any changes in styling, design, or composition dictated by car buyers, competitive pressure, economic conditions, or government agencies may create opportunities for some industrial marketers, and problems for others.

Some industrial marketers must not only monitor final consumer markets but also develop a marketing program that reaches the ultimate consumer directly. Aluminum producers use television and magazine ads to point up the convenience and recycling opportunities that aluminum containers offer to the consumer—because the ultimate consumer *influences aluminum demand* by purchasing soft drinks in aluminum rather than plastic containers. DuPont and TRW advertise to ultimate consumers to stimulate the sales of consumer goods that incorporate their products.

Demand elasticity refers to the responsiveness of the quantity demanded to a change in price. Demand is elastic if a given percentage change in price brings about an even larger percentage change in the quantity demanded. Inelasticity results when demand is insensitive to price; for example, the percentage change in demand is less than the percentage change in price. Consider the demand for electronic components stimulated by companies making electronic video games in the early 1980s. As long as final consumers continue to purchase video games and are generally insensitive to price, manufacturers of the games are relatively insensitive to the price of electronic components. At the opposite end of the spectrum, if consumers are price-sensitive in regard to the purchase of soup and other canned grocery products, manufacturers of soup will be price-sensitive about the purchase of metal cans. Thus, the derived demand indicates that the demand for metal cans is price elastic.

Final consumer demand has a pervasive impact on the demand for industrial products. By being sensitive to trends in the consumer market, the industrial marketer can often identify both impending problems and opportunities for growth and diversification.

Environmental Forces Influence Demand   In monitoring and forecasting demand, the industrial marketer must be alert to factors in the competitive, economic, political, and legal environment that directly or indirectly influence demand. A mild recession cuts deeply into some segments of the industrial market while leaving other segments unscathed. Rising interest rates alter both the purchasing plans of home buyers and commercial enterprises contemplating expansion. Federal legislation targeted to improve gas mileage increases demand for lightweight materials like aluminum. Ecological concerns that render some industrial products and processes obsolete create challenging replacement opportunities. Foreign markets that offer lucrative potential to some industrial marketers may pose a serious challenge to domestic producers like the steel industry. Constant surveillance of these and other environmental forces is fundamental to accurate industrial demand analysis.

Monitoring International Competition   The relevant unit of analysis in an increasing number of industries today is not domestic but worldwide market share. The accelerating demand for industrial goods in the international market and the dramatic rise in competition from Western Europe, Japan, and from a new list of third-world multinationals demands a global perspective on competition.[11]

Kotler and Singh contend that "Companies now have to choose markets whose needs they can satisfy and whose competitors they can handle."[12] A thorough competitive assessment must involve an analysis of formidable competitors in distant markets.[13]

[11] David A. Heenan and Warren J. Keegan, "The Rise of Third World Multinationals," *Harvard Business Review* 57 (January/February 1979), pp. 101–109.

[12] Philip Kotler and Ravi Singh, "Marketing Warfare in the 1980s," *Journal of Business Strategy* 1 (Winter 1981), reprinted in Richard Wendel, ed., *Marketing 83/84* (Guilford, Conn.: The Dushkin Publishing Group, Inc., 1983), pp. 12–22.

[13] Lindsay N. Meredith and Michael D. Hutt, "Toward an International Perspective of Market Analysis," *Journal of Marketing Education*, in press.

Figure 1.1   An Industrial Ad Emphasizing the Global Nature of Competition

Source: Courtesy, Motorola, Inc.

A global orientation is especially important to industrial firms competing in rapidly changing industries like telecommunications and electronics or, at the other end of the continuum, in basic commodity industries like steel and forest products. Japanese steelmakers are formidable competitors and now have roughly a $100-per-ton edge in labor costs over their major U.S. counterparts.[14] In turn, many U.S.-based industrial firms like IBM, Cincinnati Milacron, and Motorola have moved to establish a position of strength for selected products in Japan.[15] The dynamic nature of competition in the industrial market is aptly illustrated in the advertisement in Figure 1.1.

Industrial and Consumer Marketing: A Contrast

Many consumer products companies with a strong reputation in the consumer market decide to capitalize on perceived opportunities in the industrial market. The move is often prompted by a maturing product

---

[14] "Time Runs Out for Steel," *Business Week* (June 13, 1983), p. 85.

[15] Craig M. Watson, "Counter-Competition Abroad to Protect Home Markets," *Harvard Business Review* 60 (January–February 1982), pp. 40–42.

line, a desire to diversify operations, or the strategic opportunity to profitably apply research and development or production strength in a rapidly growing industrial market. Procter and Gamble Company (P&G), departing from its packaged consumer goods tradition, is using its expertise in oils, fats, and pulps to diversify into fast-growing industries.[16] Hershey Foods Corporation may use P&G's cocoa butter in some of its candy products.[17]

The J. M. Smucker Company operates successfully in both the consumer and the industrial market. Smucker, drawing upon its consumer product base (jellies and preserves), produces filling mixes used by manufacturers of yogurt and dessert items. Marketing strawberry preserves to ultimate consumers differs significantly from marketing a strawberry filling to a manufacturer of yogurt. Key differences are highlighted below.

Smucker: A Consumer and Industrial Marketer

Smucker reaches the consumer market with a line of products sold through a range of retail outlets. New products are carefully developed, tested, targeted, priced, and promoted for particular segments of the market. To secure distribution, the firm employs food brokers who call on both wholesale and retail buying units. The company's own sales force reaches selected larger accounts. Achieving a desired degree of market exposure and shelf space in key retail food outlets is essential to any marketer of consumer food products. Promotional plans for the line include media advertising, coupons, special offers, and incentives for retailers. Pricing decisions must reflect the nature of demand, costs, and the behavior of competitors. In sum, the marketer must manage each component of the marketing mix: product, price, promotion, distribution.

The marketing mix takes on a different form in the industrial setting. Now the market consists of manufacturers that could potentially use Smucker products to produce other goods. The Smucker product will lose its identity as it is blended into yogurt, cakes, or cookies. Once all the potential users of the product are identified (e.g., large food processors, bakeries, yogurt producers), the industrial marketing manager attempts to identify meaningful market segments that Smucker can profitably serve. A specific marketing strategy is developed for each market segment.

When a potential organizational consumer is identified, the company's sales force calls directly on the account. The salesperson *may* begin by contacting a company president but generally spends a great deal

16 Damon Darlin and Bill Abrams, "New Ingredients: Procter & Gamble Co. Starts to Reformulate Tried-and-True Ways," *Wall Street Journal* (March 3, 1983), p. 1.

17 "P&G's New New-Product Onslaught," *Business Week* (October 1, 1979), pp. 76–81.

of time at first with the research and development director or the product development group leader. The salesperson is thus challenged to identify the *key buying influentials.*

Armed with product specifications, the salesperson returns to the research and development department at Smucker to develop samples. Several months may pass before a mixture is finally approved. Next, attention turns to price, and the salesperson's contact point shifts to the purchasing department. Because large quantities (truckloads or drums rather than jars) are involved, a few cents per pound can be significant to both parties. Quality and service are also vitally important.

Once a transaction is culminated, the product will be shipped directly from the Smucker warehouse to the manufacturer's plant. The salesperson will follow up frequently with the purchasing agent and the plant manager. How much business can Smucker expect from this account? The performance of the new consumer product in the marketplace will determine this: The demand for industrial goods is, as noted, derived from ultimate consumer demand. Note also the importance of developing a close and continuing working relationship with industrial customers, and of understanding the requirements of the total range of buying influentials in the target company.

Distinguishing Characteristics

This illustration spotlights some of the features that differentiate industrial marketing strategy from consumer-goods marketing strategy. The industrial marketer emphasizes *personal selling* rather than advertising (TV, newspaper) to reach potential buyers. Only a small portion of the industrial marketer's promotional budget is likely to be invested in advertising, most commonly through trade journals or direct mail. This advertising, however, often establishes the foundation for a successful sales call. The industrial salesperson must have a technical understanding of the organization's requirements and how those requirements can be satisfied as well as a detailed understanding of who influences the buying decision and why.

The industrial marketer's product also includes an important *service component.* The organizational consumer evaluates the quality of the physical entity and the quality of the attached services. Price *negotiation* is frequently an important part of the industrial buying/selling process. Products made to particular quality or design specifications must be individually priced. Industrial firms generally find that direct distribution to larger customers strengthens relationships between buyer and seller. Smaller accounts can be profitably served through intermediaries— manufacturer's representatives or industrial distributors.

As this example has illustrated, industrial marketing strategies differ from consumer goods marketing strategies in the relative emphasis given to certain elements of the marketing mix. Importantly, the ex-

---

Table 1.2   Industrial Marketing vs. Consumer Goods Marketing: Selected Distinguishing Characteristics

	Industrial Marketing	Consumer Goods Marketing
Product	More technical in nature; exact form often variable; accompanying services very important.	Standardized form; service important, but less so.
Price	Competitive bidding for unique items; list prices for standard items.	List prices.
Promotion	Emphasis on personal selling.	Emphasis on advertising.
Distribution	Shorter, more direct channels to market.	Passes through a number of intermediate links en route to consumer.
Customer Relations	More enduring and complex.	Less frequent contact; relationship of a shorter duration.
Consumer Decision-Making Process	Involvement of diverse group of organizational members in decision.	Individual or household unit makes decision.

---

ample also highlights fundamental differences between the buyers in each market. In an organization, a variety of individuals influence the purchase decision. Several major questions confront the Smucker industrial marketing manager: Who are key participants in the purchasing process? What is their relative importance? What criteria does each apply to the decision? Thus, the industrial marketer must understand the *process* that an organization follows in purchasing a product and which organizational members have roles in this process. Depending on the complexity of the purchase, this process may span many weeks or months and may involve the participation of several members of the organization. The industrial marketer who becomes involved early in the purchase process may have the greatest chance for success.

Industrial marketing is fundamentally different from consumer marketing because of how organizations purchase products. The industrial goods firm must respond not to a single consumer but to a much wider group of buying influentials, all of whom may bring different criteria to bear on the purchase decision.

While selected industrial product/market situations closely resemble those found in consumer-goods marketing, Table 1.2 emphasizes the common distinguishing characteristics of consumer-goods versus industrial marketing. Clearly, industrial marketers can often benefit from using some of the creative marketing strategies found in consumer-goods marketing. Making sound industrial marketing management decisions, however, requires knowledge of the fundamental traits that typify the industrial marketing environment.

Organizational Customers

Any attempt by the marketing strategist to isolate the similarities and differences among groups of industrial (or organizational) customers must begin with a definition of customer type. Industrial customers can be broadly classified into three categories: (1) commercial enterprises, (2) governmental organizations, and (3) institutions. Each represents a sizable market with many diverse parts.

Commercial Enterprises

Commercial enterprises can also be divided into three categories: (1) users, (2) original equipment manufacturers (OEMs), and (3) dealers and distributors.

Users   Users purchase industrial products or services to produce other goods or services that are, in turn, sold in the industrial or consumer markets. User customers purchase goods to form the manufacturing process. To illustrate, user customers may, for instance, purchase injection-molding machines, grinding wheels, lathes, and related items. When purchasing machine tools from General Electric Company, an auto manufacturer is a user. These machine tools do not become part of the automobile but instead help to produce it.

Original Equipment Manufacturers   The original equipment manufacturer (referred to as an OEM) purchases industrial goods to incorporate into other products sold in the industrial or ultimate consumer market. For example, Intel Corporation produces the microprocessors that constitute the heart of IBM's personal computer.[18] In purchasing these microprocessors, IBM would be classified as an OEM.

Dealers and Distributors   Dealers and distributors include those commercial enterprises that purchase industrial goods for resale in basically the same form to users and OEMs. The distributor accumulates, stores, and sells a large assortment of goods to industrial users, taking title to the goods purchased. Handling billions of dollars worth of transactions each year, industrial distributors are growing in size and sophistication. The strategic role assumed by distributors in the industrial market is examined in detail later in the volume.

Overlap of Categories   The three categories of commercial enterprises are not mutually exclusive. The classification of commercial enterprises

---

[18] "IBM and Intel Link Up to Fend off Japan," *Business Week* (January 10, 1983), p. 96.

Figure 1.2   Tracing an Industrial Product to Commercial Customers

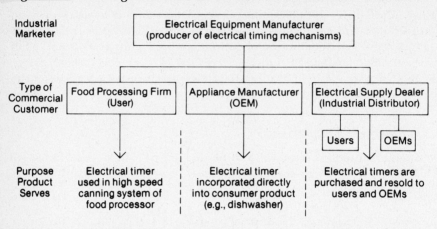

rests upon the intended purpose that the product serves for the customer. Ford Motor Company purchasing a machine tool for the manufacturing process is a user, but is an OEM purchasing radios to be incorporated into the ultimate consumer product.

A marketer requires a good understanding of the diverse organizational consumers in the industrial market. Properly classifying commercial customers as users, OEMs, and dealers or distributors is an important first step to a sharpened understanding of the *buying criteria* that a particular commercial customer uses in evaluating an industrial product.

Understanding Buying Motivations   Figure 1.2 depicts the different types of commercial customers for a particular industrial product—electrical timing mechanisms. Each class of commercial customers views the product differently because each purchases the product for a different reason.

The food-processing firm buys electrical timers for use in a high-speed canning system. For this customer, quality, reliability, and prompt and predictable delivery are critical. The appliance manufacturer, an OEM who incorporates the industrial product directly into consumer appliances, is concerned with the impact of the timers on the quality and dependability of the final consumer product. Since the timers will be needed in large quantities, the appliance manufacturer is also concerned about the producer's production capacity and delivery reliability. Finally, the electrical supply dealer, an industrial distributor, is most interested in matching the capability of the timing mechanisms to the needs of customers (users and OEMs) in a specific geographical market.

Governmental Organizations as Consumers

The government, whether federal, state, or local, is the largest consumer in the United States—the federal government alone purchases over $250 billion of products and services annually.[19] Governmental units purchase from virtually every category of goods—office supplies, missiles, fire engines, fuel, desks, lumber, grease, concrete, furniture. Governmental units as consumers can be a lucrative market for the astute industrial marketer.

Governmental buying procedures are highly specialized and sometimes frustrating. Typically, the government develops detailed specifications and invites bids from qualified suppliers. For more complex projects, the agency may negotiate directly with the few suppliers known to have the required knowledge or technical capability. Always, the emphasis is on competitive procurement. While some consideration may be given to the supplier's reputation or past performance, the low bidder usually has the edge.

To reach this important group, the marketer must understand government procurement procedures and locate the individuals who make or influence decisions. This market is explored in detail in Chapter 2.

Institutions as Consumers

Public and private institutions constitute another class of industrial customers. Churches, hospitals, nursing homes, colleges, and universities all require goods and services. Some institutional customers, such as public universities, have specific purchasing procedures that are rigidly followed; others follow less standardized approaches. Industrial marketers often find it profitable to establish a separate division to respond to the unique needs of institutional buyers.

The Organizational Buying Process

We broadly classify industrial consumers as commercial enterprises, governmental organizations, and institutions. Each customer type offers profitable opportunities and special challenges for the marketer. To create satisfied customers, the industrial marketer must respond to the needs of organizational buyers in each component of the marketing mix: product, price, promotion, and distribution strategy. Organizational buying behavior is defined as "the decision-making process by which formal organizations establish the need for purchased products

---

[19] *Statistical Abstract of the United States*, U.S. Department of the Census, 1982, p. 247.

and services, and identify, evaluate, and choose among alternative brands and suppliers."[20]

Multiple Buying Influences[21]

The organizational buying process often involves not one but several people. Buying responsibility may be delegated to a specialist, the purchasing agent, but others may also play an active role. To illustrate, representatives from production, quality control, marketing, finance, and other areas are involved to varying degrees in selecting machine tools for a new product line. Each brings a different perspective to purchasing situations. In addition, buying may be influenced by outsiders such as consulting engineers. Multiple buying influences are a noteworthy characteristic of organizational buying.

Buying Motives

Since norms, rules, and established procedures typify organizations, organizational buyers must be more rational than ultimate consumers. This is *not* always the case. Organizational buyers appear to be no more rational in making purchasing decisions than are consumers.[22] Organizational buyers are influenced by both rational and emotional motivations. Rational motives include such economic factors as cost, quality, and service. By contrast, emotional factors are more subjective; they might include status, security, or fear. In sum, organizational buyers are human. Organizational buyers do, however, (see Chapter 3) follow more formalized purchasing procedures than consumers.

On Selling Corporate Jets

In selling a $3 million business jet, a salesperson who relies exclusively on product specifications and depreciation schedules is overlooking the psychological and emotional components of the buying process. "For the chief executive," observes an experienced salesperson, "you need all the numbers for support, but if you can't find the kid inside the CEO and

---

[20] Frederick E. Webster, Jr. and Yoram Wind, *Organizational Buying Behavior* (Englewood Cliffs, N.J.: Prentice-Hall, Inc., 1972), p. 2; see also, Wesley J. Johnston and Robert E. Spekman, "Industrial Buying Behavior: A Need for an Integrative Approach," *Journal of Business Research* 10 (1982), pp. 135–146.

[21] The discussion of these characteristics is based on Webster and Wind, *Organizational Buying Behavior*, pp. 5–8.

[22] Jagdish N. Sheth, "Recent Developments in Organizational Buying Behavior," in A. Woodside, J. Sheth, and P. Bennett, eds., *Consumer and Industrial Buying Behavior* (New York: Elsevier North-Holland, Inc., 1977), p. 30.

excite him or her with the raw beauty of the new plane, you'll never sell the equipment. If you sell the excitement, you sell the jet."

Source: Thomas V. Bonoma, "Major Sales: Who Really Does the Buying?" *Harvard Business Review* 60 (May–June 1982), p. 112.

Technical Complexity

Major technical complexities influence many organizational buying decisions. The stakes can be high. The products and services acquired may influence the organization's performance for years. Specifications for equipment, materials, or services are developed meticulously, and alternative offerings are examined thoroughly.

Time Lags

Another distinctive feature of organizational buying is that the decision process can span a considerable period of time. The technical complexity of many decisions, the large financial outlays involved, and the corresponding risks and uncertainties all contribute to an elaborate review process that can easily consume several months or more. For the industrial marketer, significant time periods can intervene between the application of marketing effort (e.g., personal sales calls) and a particular organizational customer's decision.

Organizations Vary

Each buying organization possesses characteristics that make it unique. Potential organizational customers are likely to vary significantly because of differing objectives, resource bases, abilities, and experience. The five characteristics in Figure 1.3 provide some valuable initial insights into the nature of the organizational buying process and the motivations of the participants in that process. Knowledge of organizational buying behavior is necessary to formulate responsive industrial marketing strategy.

Classifying Industrial Goods

Having classified the customers that constitute the industrial market, we must now ask what type of goods they require, and how each type is marketed. One useful method of classifying industrial goods is to ask: How

Figure 1.3   Key Characteristics of the Organizational Buying Process

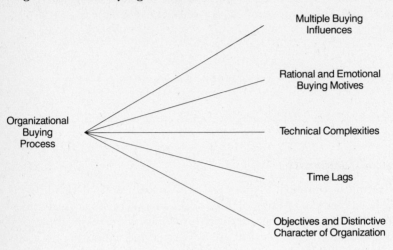

does the industrial good or service enter the production process and enter the cost structure of the firm?[23] The answer allows the marketer to find those who are influential in the organizational buying process and to understand how to design an effective industrial marketing strategy. In general, industrial goods can be divided into three broad categories (see Table 1.3).

Entering Goods

Entering goods are those which become part of the finished product. This category of goods consists of raw materials and manufactured materials and parts. Their cost is an *expense item* that is assigned to the manufacturing process.

Raw Materials   Observe from Table 1.3 that raw materials include both farm products and natural products. Raw materials are processed only to the level required for economical handling and transport; they enter the production process of the buying organization basically in their natural state.

Shortages or rapid changes in the price of raw materials can trigger problems for producers who are heavily dependent on particular raw materials. To illustrate, each year Kodak purchases over 50 million ounces of silver on the open market to be used for photofinishing

[23] Kotler, *Marketing Management*, p. 172.

Table 1.3   Classification of Industrial Goods

I. Entering Goods

A. Raw materials
  1. Farm products (examples: wheat, cotton, livestock, fruits, and vegetables)
  2. Natural products (examples: fish, lumber, crude petroleum, iron ore)
B. Manufactured materials and parts
  1. Component materials (examples: steel, cement, wire, textiles)
  2. Component parts (examples: small motors, tires, castings)

II. Foundation Goods

A. Installations
  1. Buildings and land rights (examples: factories, offices)
  2. Fixed equipment (examples: generators, drill presses, computers, elevators)
B. Accessory equipment
  1. Portable or light factory equipment and tools (examples: hand tools, lift trucks)
  2. Office equipment (examples: typewriters, desks)

III. Facilitating Goods

A. Supplies
  1. Operating supplies (examples: lubricants, coal, typing paper, pencils)
  2. Maintenance and repair items (examples: paint, nails, brooms)
B. Business services
  1. Maintenance and repair services (examples: window cleaning, typewriter repair)
  2. Business advisory services (examples: legal, management consulting, advertising)

Source: Adapted from Philip Kotler, *Marketing Management: Analysis Planning and Control*, 4th ed. (Englewood Cliffs, N.J.: Prentice-Hall, Inc., 1980), p. 172, with permission of Prentice-Hall, Inc.

and industrial/medical X-ray film products.[24] Unexpected surges in the price of silver will require swift changes in Kodak's pricing and product strategy.

Manufactured Materials and Parts   In contrast to raw materials, manufactured materials and parts undergo more initial processing. Component materials like textiles or sheet steel have been processed before reaching a clothing manufacturer or automaker but must be processed further before becoming part of the finished product that the consumer buys. Component *parts*, on the other hand, include small motors, motorcycle tires, and automobile batteries; they can be installed directly into another product with little or no additional processing.

Foundation Goods

The distinguishing characteristic of foundation goods is that they are *capital items*. As capital goods are used up or worn out, a portion of their original cost is assigned to the production process as a depreciation ex-

---

[24] Charles J. Elia, "Profit Forecasts for Kodak, a Big User of Silver, Are Scaled Back as the Metal's Price Skyrockets," *Wall Street Journal* (September 21, 1979), p. 39.

pense. The foundation goods category includes installations and accessory equipment.

Installations   Installations include the major long-term investment items that underlie the manufacturing process, such as *buildings and land rights* and *fixed equipment*. Large computers and machine tools are examples of fixed equipment.

Accessory Equipment   These products are generally less expensive and shorter-lived capital items than installations, and not considered part of the fixed plant. Accessory equipment can be found in the plant as well as in the office. Portable drills and typewriters illustrate this point.

Facilitating Goods

Facilitating goods are the supplies and services (see Table 1.3) that support organizational operations. Because these goods do not enter the production process or become part of the finished product, their costs are handled as *expense items*.

Supplies   Virtually every organization requires *operating supplies* like typing paper or business forms, and *maintenance and repair items* like paint and cleaning materials. These items generally reach a broad cross-section of industrial users. In fact, they are very similar to the kinds of supplies that consumers might purchase at a hardware or discount store.

Services   An organization often turns to an outside specialist to perform specific functions. This specialist possesses a level of expertise or efficiency that the organization can profitably tap. Business services include *maintenance and repair* support (e.g., machine repair) and *advisory* support (e.g., management consulting). Like supplies, services are considered expense items.

Industrial Marketing Strategy

The significance of an industrial goods classification system comes to light on examination of how marketing patterns differ by goods category. A marketing strategy appropriate for one category of goods may be entirely unsuitable for another. Often, entirely different promotional, pricing, and distribution strategies are required. The physical nature of the industrial good and its intended use by the organizational customer dictate to an important degree the requirements of the marketing program.

Illustration 1: Manufactured Materials and Parts

Recall that manufactured materials and parts enter the buying organization's own product. Whether a part is standardized or customized will often dictate the nature of marketing strategy. For custom-made parts, personal selling activities assume an important role in marketing strategy. The salesperson must link the engineering departments of the buying and selling firms. Though the product is the critical factor in making a sale, once the account is sold, reliable delivery becomes primary. Standardized parts are typically purchased in larger quantities on a contractual basis, and the marketing strategy centers on providing a competitive price and reliable delivery. Frequently, industrial distributors are used to achieve responsive delivery service to smaller accounts.

Personal selling is pivotal for many customized materials and parts; advertising is more important for many standardized items. The role of the salesperson is to call not only on purchasing agents but also on other key buying influentials (engineers and production managers) who develop product specifications. Sometimes components marketers will utilize manufacturer's representatives—intermediaries who are independent salespersons representing a variety of suppliers of noncompeting products. The manufacturer's representative is paid a commission on sales and provides a cost-effective way to secure a quality selling effort in markets where demand is low. Advertising supplements personal selling activities. The basic advertising appeals focus on product quality, delivery reliability, price, and service. Many producers of component parts and materials attempt to gain a differential advantage based on their ability to design unique parts for specific applications as well as their ability to provide the parts on a timely basis to meet production requirements.

The challenge for the marketer is to locate and accurately define the unique needs of diverse customers, uncover key buying influences, and adjust the marketing program to profitably serve these consumers. For example, observe in Table 1.4 the special needs of the customers that

Table 1.4   Conrad Spring Company: Serving Diverse Customers and Unique Needs

Selected Customers	Manufactured Part Required	Application
Ford Motor Company	Piston Spring	Automatic Transmission
Kenner Toys	Springs and Wire Forms	Star Wars Toys
International Telephone and Telegraph Corp.	Springs	Telephone Dials
Kees Surgical Specialty Company	Torsion Spring	Surgical Device Used by Brain Surgeons

Source: Tom Hayes, "Rising Costs Plague Plucky Spring Company," *The Cincinnati Enquirer* (June 4, 1978), p. D-7.

make up part of the market for springs. As a manufacturer of component parts, the Conrad Spring Company develops springs that are incorporated into products ranging from telephone dials to surgical equipment.

Illustration 2: Installations

Installations were classified earlier as foundation goods because they are capital assets that affect the buyer's scale of operations. Here the product itself is the central force in marketing strategy, and direct manufacturer-to-user channels of distribution are the norm. Less costly, more standardized installations, like lathes, may be sold through marketing middlemen.

Once again, personal selling is the dominant promotional tool. The salesperson works closely with prospective organizational buyers. Negotiations can span several months and involve the top executives in the buying organization, especially for buildings or custom-made equipment. Multiple buying influences complicate the selling task. Each executive may be applying slightly different criteria to the decision process. Trade advertising and direct mail advertising supplement and reinforce personal selling.

Buying motives center on economic factors, such as the projected performance of the capital asset, and emotional factors, such as industry leadership. A buyer may be quite willing to select a higher-priced installation if the projected return on investment supports the decision. To illustrate, a packaging machine that saves the using organization one gram of plastic per-unit-produced would yield substantial cost savings over its productive life, and would be preferred over lower-priced alternatives that did not offer such savings. In summary, the focal points for the marketing of installations include a strong personal selling effort, effective engineering and product design support, and the capability to offer a product which provides a higher return-on-investment than competing products. Initial price, distribution, and advertising play lesser roles.

Strategy Profile: Cincinnati Milacron

Machine tool firms, like Cincinnati Milacron, Inc. sell manufacturing technology.

Robots   The shift in this technology has been toward computer-controlled machine tools or robots; these are triggering what some call "a new age in manufacturing." Industrial robots can be programmed to perform painting, welding, machine loading, and numerous other assembly operations. The greatest potential benefit of this new manufacturing technology lies in its capacity to allow the production of goods cheaply *in small volumes*. Changes in production can be made by reprogramming the machine tools rather than investing in new equipment. Milacron forecasts that 100,000 robots will be installed in the United States by 1990.

Competition   The expected rapid growth of the market has spawned stiff competition which includes IBM, General Electric Company, Bendix Corporation and General Motors (previously one of Milacron's largest customers). Strong competition in the robot market is also coming from Japan and Europe. In fact, the new manufacturing technology is diffusing much faster in Japan than in the United States: Japan has more than twice the number of robots in use. Milacron has one-third of the U.S. market but only a fraction of the world market.

Marketing Strategy   Personal selling constitutes the dominant promotional tool; Milacron also reaches potential customers through displays at machine tool trade shows. Given the significant capital investment involved, potential machine tool customers carefully analyze the payback (number of years until the machine tool will pay for itself), maintenance costs, technical and training assistance provided by the supplier after-the-sale, and numerous other factors. The salesperson works closely with potential buying organizations, addressing the needs and varying perspectives of different departments. Top management, engineering, production managers, purchasing, machine operators, and shop foremen are among the organizational members who may take part in the robot purchasing decision. A Milacron executive noted, "IBM is the powerhouse in computers, they've never dealt with the guys on the shop floor. We know the guys who wear the bowling shirts and the baseball caps."

Source: Paul Ingrassi and Damon Darlin, "Cincinnati Milacron, Mainly a Metal-Bender, Now Is a Robot Maker," *Wall Street Journal* (April 7, 1983), p. 1. Also, *Robots: A Manager's Guide*, © 1982 Cincinnati Milacron Marketing Company.

Illustration 3: Supplies

The final illustration centers on a facilitating good—supplies. Again we find different marketing patterns. Most supply items reach a horizontal market of organizational customers from many different industries. Although some large users are serviced directly, a wide variety of marketing middlemen are required to adequately cover this broad and diverse market.

The purchasing agent plays the dominant role in the choice of suppliers and evaluates alternative suppliers on dependability, breadth of assortment, convenience, and price. While always searching for value, the purchasing agent lacks the time to carefully evaluate all available alternatives each time a purchase requirement surfaces. Dependable sources have the edge.

For supplies, the marketer's promotional mix includes catalog listings, advertising, and, to a lesser extent, personal selling. Advertising is directed to resellers (industrial distributors) and final users. Personal selling is less important for supplies than it is for other categories of goods, such as installations, that have a high unit value. Thus, personal selling efforts may be confined to resellers and large users of supplies. The degree of emphasis given to personal selling depends on the size of the company, the length of the firm's product line, and the amount of potential demand concentrated in large accounts or particular geographic areas. For example, a large industrial firm that produces a wide assortment of supply items is better equipped to develop a direct sales force than smaller firms with narrow product lines.

In general, then, the marketing strategy for supplies centers on developing the proper assortments of products to match the needs of diverse groups of customers. Often, the selection of an effective group of industrial distributors is fundamental to the marketing strategy. Price may be critical in the marketing strategy, since many supply items are undifferentiated. By providing the proper product assortment, timely and reliable delivery, and competitive prices, an industrial marketer of supply items may be able to develop a long-term contractual relationship with a customer.

The focus and direction of marketing strategy change from one category of industrial goods to another. Yet in every case, the marketer's ultimate concern must be on how potential organizational customers view a particular product, which may be quite different from customer to customer. Potential buyers have varying levels of experience with specific products in addition to having distinct organizational objectives and requirements. The successful industrial marketer recognizes unique organizational needs and satisfies them.

Strategy Profile: American Hospital Supply

American Hospital Supply (AHS) can provide a hospital with more than 60 percent of supply items needed to sustain operations, from bandages to bed linens to blood oxygenators. The firm produces over 28,000 products and distributes countless others. Competitors have much narrower product lines. Employing over 4,500 salespersons, AHS has been extremely successful in an industry where competing firms offer only slightly differentiated products.

Strong Customer Service Focus   One key to the firm's marketing success centered on improving the purchasing and inventory control procedures used by its customers—hospitals. AHS installed thousands of computer terminals in hospitals, allowing customers to order its products directly without bothersome paperwork. The company also has over 150 warehouses in its distribution network (far more than competitors) and can provide a prompt and reliable response to customer orders.

Source: Anne B. Pillsbury, "The Hard-Selling Supplier to the Sick," *Fortune* 106 (July 26, 1982), pp. 56–61.

A Look Ahead

The chief components of the industrial marketing management process are shown in Figure 1.4. Industrial marketing strategy is formulated within the boundaries established by the corporate mission and objectives. A corporation determining its mission must define its business and purpose, assess environmental trends, and evaluate its strengths and weaknesses. Corporate objectives provide guidelines within which specific marketing objectives are formed.

The industrial marketing management framework (Figure 1.4) provides an overview of the five major parts of this volume. This chapter introduced some of the features that distinguish industrial from consumer-goods marketing. The remaining chapter in Part 1 examines in more detail the nature of industrial market organizations. Major types of industrial customers—commercial enterprises, governmental units, and institutions—are examined closely.

Organizational buying behavior constitutes the theme of Part Two, which first examines the organizational buying process and the myriad

Figure 1.4   A Framework for Industrial Marketing Management

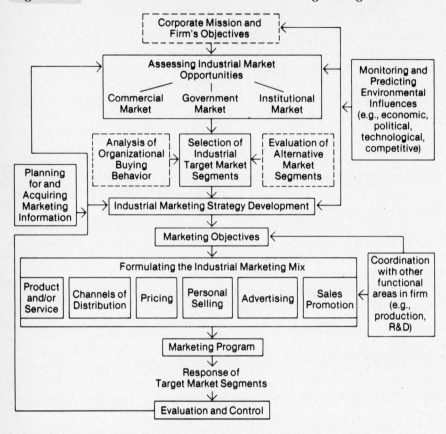

Source: Adapted from David W. Cravens, Gerald E. Hills, and Robert B. Woodruff, *Marketing Decision Making: Concepts and Strategy* (Homewood, IL: Richard D. Irwin, Inc., 1976), p. 20.

forces that affect the organizational decision maker. Part Three turns to the measurement of industrial market opportunities, demonstrating specific techniques for measuring the relative attractiveness of alternative sectors of the market and for selecting target segments.

Part Four centers on designing industrial marketing strategy. Each component of the marketing mix is treated from an industrial marketing perspective. Formulation of the industrial marketing mix (see Figure 1.4) requires careful coordination with such functional areas in the firm as research and development and production. Monitoring and controlling the marketing program are analyzed in Part Five. Industrial marketing management seeks to minimize discrepancy between planned and actual results in target markets by planning for and acquiring relevant and timely marketing information—a central theme of Part Five.

Summary

The industrial market offers significant opportunities and special challenges for the marketing manager. Although a common body of knowledge and theory spans all of marketing, important differences exist between consumer and industrial marketing, among them the nature of markets, demand patterns, buyer behavior, and products.

The diverse organizations that make up the industrial market can be broadly divided into: (1) commercial enterprises, (2) governmental organizations, and (3) institutions. Since purchases made by these industrial consumers are linked to goods and services that they, in turn, generate, derived demand is an important and often volatile force in the industrial market.

To penetrate the industrial market effectively, the marketer must understand the organizational buying process, which is affected by multiple buying influences, technical specifications, time lags, and complex buying motives. How the decision is made may vary with the type of industrial product under consideration. Industrial goods can be classified into three categories, based on how the product enters the cost structure and production process of the buying organization: (1) entering goods, (2) foundation goods, and (3) facilitating goods. Specific categories of goods may require unique marketing programs.

Discussion Questions

1. Du Pont, one of the largest industrial producers of chemicals and synthetic fibers, spends millions of dollars annually on advertising its products to final consumers. For example, over one million dollars was recently invested in a TV advertising blitz which emphasized the comfort of jeans made of Du Pont's stretch polyester-cotton blend. Since Du Pont does not produce jeans or market them to final consumers, why are large expenditures made on consumer advertising?

2. What are the chief differences between consumer goods marketing and industrial goods marketing? Use the following matrix as a guide in organizing your response:

	Consumer Goods Marketing	Industrial Goods Marketing
Customers		
Buying Behavior		
Buyer/Seller Relationship		
Product		
Price		
Promotion		
Channels		

3. Explain how a company such as General Electric might be classified by some industrial marketers as a "user" customer but by others as an OEM.

4. Illustrate the concept of derived demand using a product with which you are familiar.

5. Consumer products are frequently classified as convenience, shopping, or specialty goods. This classification system is based upon how consumers shop for particular products. Would this classification scheme apply equally well in the industrial environment? Explain.

6. Compare and contrast the marketing program that would be required for an entering good versus a facilitating good. Focus your discussion on an example of each product type.

7. Evaluate this statement: "The buying decisions that an organizational buyer makes in the office are much more rational than those that the same individual makes in a supermarket or department store."

8. Evaluate this statement: "The demand for major equipment (foundation good) is likely to be less responsive to shifts in price than that for materials, supplies, and components." Agree or disagree? Support your position.

C·H·A·P·T·E·R
2

The Industrial Market: Perspectives on the Organizational Buyer

The industrial marketer requires an understanding of the needs of a diverse mix of organizational buyers drawn from three broad sectors of the industrial market: commercial enterprises, government (all levels), and institutions. After reading this chapter, you will understand:

1. *the nature and central characteristics of each of these market sectors;*
2. *how the purchasing function is organized in each of these components of the industrial market;*
3. *the need to design a unique marketing program for each sector of the industrial market.*

The vast industrial market is characterized by tremendous diversity. In fact, many goods that are commonly viewed as final consumer products claim a large industrial market. To illustrate, microcomputers (personal computers) are bought by *commercial firms*—manufacturers, professional groups, service firms (Ford Motor Company planned to buy 1,500 micro-computers in 1983[1]); *institutions*—schools, hospitals and colleges (U.S. schools purchased over 50,000 personal computers during 1981–1982[2]); and *governments*—federal, state, and local. (Most issues of *Commerce Business Daily*, a listing of federal procurement invitations, include requests for personal computers by agencies like Social Security, the Internal Revenue Service, and the Army.)

The distribution channels for personal computers reflect the diversity of industrial and organizational customers and their requirements: computer stores account for 50 percent of total microcomputer sales, followed by direct sales from manufacturers (14 percent), system houses (13 percent), mail order (9 percent) and office product suppliers and industrial distributors (7 percent each).[3] A 50 percent annual growth rate in the industrial demand for microcomputers suggests that companies like IBM which are well-positioned in both the direct-from-manufacturer sales channel and the computer store channel, will gain significant advantages over competitors like Tandy and Apple, whose strength lies only in the computer store channel. Computer stores cater to individuals and small commercial, government, and institutional buyers, but a significant shift to the direct channel will be necessary to reach the large corporate buyers. Large government contracts demand understanding of and a careful response to the formal bidding process, conformance to specifications, and extensive paperwork.

A significant first step in creating successful marketing strategy is to isolate the unique dimensions of each of the major sectors of the industrial market. How much market potential does each sector represent? Who makes the purchasing decision? The answers provide a foundation upon which the marketing manager can formulate industrial marketing programs that respond to the specific needs and characteristics of each sector.

Commercial Enterprises

Commercial enterprises include manufacturers, construction companies, service firms (e.g., hotels), transportation companies, selected professional groups (e.g., dentists), and resellers (wholesalers and retailers

---

[1] William M. Bulkeley, "Microcomputers Gaining Primacy, Forcing Changes in the Industry," *Wall Street Journal*, LXIII (January 13, 1983), p. 37.

[2] "The Computer Moves In," *Time*, 121 (January 3, 1983), p. 23.

[3] Bob Davis, "Newcomers in Personal Computers Have Trouble Breaking Into Market," *Wall Street Journal*, LXIII (February 19, 1983), p. 37.

purchasing equipment and supplies for use in the operations). Manufacturers are the most important commercial customers; they purchased $1,093 billion of materials in 1980.[4]

Unique Characteristics: Distribution by Size

A startling fact about the study of manufacturers is that there are so few of them. In 1977 there were only 360,000 manufacturing firms in the United States.[5] And though only some 36,000 manufacturing firms (10 percent) employ more than 100 workers each, this handful of firms provides almost 80 percent of all value added (i.e., economic value created) by manufacturing in the United States.[6] Clearly, these large buyers can be very important to the industrial marketer. Because each large firm has such vast sales potential, the industrial marketer will often tailor a marketing strategy for each customer. Smaller manufacturing firms also constitute an important segment for the industrial marketer. Interestingly, over half of all manufacturers in the United States have fewer than 20 employees. Here the organizational buyer has different needs and, often, a different orientation. Again, the astute marketer will adjust the marketing program to the needs of this segment of the market.

Geographical Concentration   Concentration of industrial firms by size is not the only form of concentration important to the industrial supplier; manufacturers are also concentrated geographically (Figure 2.1). Primary areas of industrial concentration include the Midwest (Ohio, Indiana, Illinois, and Michigan) and the Middle Atlantic states (New Jersey, Pennsylvania, and New York). However, there has been significant industrial growth and concentration in the Southeast and Southwest over the past two decades. In 1973 the Southwest accounted for 5.8 percent of all shipments by manufacturers; by 1982 their share had risen to 9.76 percent.[7] In 1982, the ten states of California, Illinois, Texas, Ohio, Pennsylvania, Michigan, New York, New Jersey, Indiana, and North Carolina accounted for 57 percent of all U.S. shipments; the 50 largest manufacturing *counties* accounted for 37 percent.[8] Most large metropolitan areas are lucrative industrial markets. Concentration of industry only means, however, that a large potential volume exists in a given area; the requirements of each buyer may still vary significantly.

Geographic concentration has some important implications for the formulation of marketing strategy. First, firms can concentrate their marketing efforts in areas of high market potential, and make effective

---

[4] *Statistical Abstract of the United States*, U.S. Department of the Census, 1982, p. 768.

[5] *Ibid*, p. 768.

[6] *Ibid*, p. 779.

[7] "Survey of Industrial Purchasing Power," *Sales and Marketing Management*, 130 (April 25, 1983), p. 9.

[8] *Ibid*, pp. 9, 10.

Figure 2.1   The United States in Proportion to Value of Manufactured Products

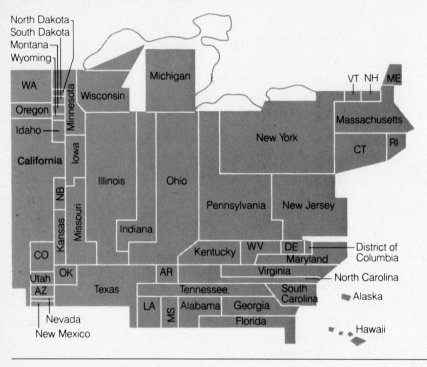

use of a full-time personal sales force in these markets. Second, distribution centers in large volume areas can insure rapid delivery to a large proportion of customers. Finally, firms may not be able to tie their salespeople to specific geographic areas because many large industrial buyers entrust to one individual the responsibility for purchasing certain products and materials for the entire company. For example, the Kroger Company, a huge supermarket chain, has centralized purchasing in Cincinnati for store supplies and fixtures. Thus, everything from paper bags to display cases are purchased in Cincinnati for distribution to individual stores. A paper bag salesperson whose territory included all retail stores in Tennessee and Arkansas could not be very effective against a competitor who maintains a sales office in Cincinnati. The marketer requires an understanding of how a potential buyer's purchasing organization is structured.

The Purchasing Organization

Every firm, regardless of its organizational characteristics, must procure the materials, supplies, equipment, and services necessary to successfully operate the business. How goods and services are purchased depends upon such factors as the nature of the business, the size of the firm, and the volume, variety, and technical complexity of items purchased. Rarely do individual departments within a corporation do their own buying. Procurement is usually administered by an individual called the manager of purchasing, purchasing agent, director of purchasing, or materials manager.

Purchasing in Large Firms   In large firms purchasing has become quite specialized, with the work typically divided into five categories:

1. *Administrative.* Purchasing administration involves management tasks, emphasizing the development of policies, procedures, controls, and mechanics for coordinating purchasing operations with those of other departments.

2. *Buying.* This includes reviewing requisitions, analyzing specifications, doing informal research, investigating vendors, interviewing salespeople, studying costs and prices, and negotiating.

3. *Expediting.* This order follow-up activity involves vendor liaison work such as reviewing the status of orders, writing letters, telephoning and telegraphing vendors, and occasionally visiting vendors' plants.

4. *Special staff work.* Any well-developed purchasing operation has an unending number of projects and studies requiring specialized knowledge and uninterrupted effort, including economic and market studies, special cost studies, vendor investigations, and systems studies.

5. *Clerical.* Every department must write orders, and maintain working files, catalog and library materials, and records for commodities, vendors, and prices.[9]

The purchasing manager is responsible for administering the purchasing process and, on occasion, may be involved in the negotiations of a small number of important contracts.

The day-to-day purchasing function is carried out by *buyers*; each buyer responsible for a specific group of products. Organizing the purchasing function in this way permits buyers to acquire a high level of

---

[9]Lamar Lee, Jr. and Donald W. Dobler, *Purchasing and Materials Management* (New York: McGraw-Hill Book Company, 1977), p. 440.

Figure 2.2   Typical Purchasing Organizing

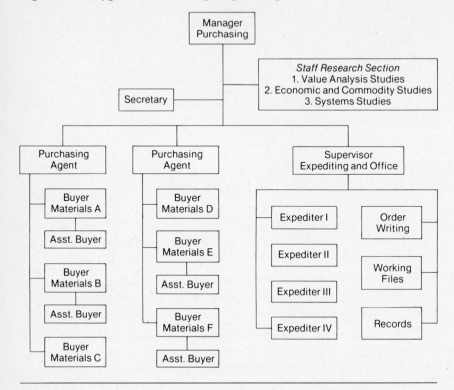

Source: Lamar Lee, Jr., and Donald W. Dobler, *Purchasing and Materials Management, Text and Cases* (New York: McGraw-Hill Book Company, 1977), p. 442. Reprinted by permission of McGraw-Hill Book Company.

technical expertise on a limited number of items. As products and materials become more sophisticated, buyers must become more knowledgeable about material characteristics, manufacturing processes, and design specifications. In some cases the salesperson requires significant knowledge of competing products to effectively respond to a buyer's probing questions.

The typical purchasing department is organized by type of product to be procured. If the firm is large, buyers will not report directly to the purchasing manager but to an intermediate level manager, usually with the title of purchasing agent or buying department manager.[10] Figure 2.2 shows the typical organization structure for a medium-sized purchasing department. The buyers are specialized by type of product. In

[10] Paul V. Farrell, coordinating ed., *Aljian's Purchasing Handbook*, 4th ed. (New York: McGraw-Hill Book Company, 1982), pp. 2–37.

this organization, each expediter works with a specific buyer. This company can afford the luxury of a staff research section (the influence of staff research on the purchasing process can be substantial) to conduct technical, in-depth research on complicated purchases and to administer the routine value analysis program.

Value Analysis   Value analysis is a method of weighing the comparative value of materials, components, and manufacturing processes from the standpoint of their purpose, relative merit, and cost in order to uncover ways of improving products, lowering costs, or both. Figure 2.3 provides some examples of how value analysis is used to evaluate the function and design of component parts, to result in lower product cost. Note that rather straightforward design/manufacturing alternatives can produce spectacular cost savings. Prudent industrial marketers will often participate in value analysis with their customers to better understand customer needs and to provide the exact level of product design and performance required. An industrial supplier might suggest value analysis to illuminate for potential customers the merits of his or her product.

Value analysis projects are usually sponsored or coordinated by the purchasing department, but often include other departments. A product may be value-analyzed several times with savings realized each time. Why? Over the years, new components or materials become available, new manufacturing methods evolve, or new ways of looking at the product or the production process emerge. In 1983, Westinghouse Electric introduced a "Get 60" program to cut annual material costs by $60 million, using teams of personnel from design engineering, purchasing, and manufacturing engineering. Each team was assigned a commodity or material and charged to reduce costs by 12 percent. Cost reductions on some materials exceeded 40 percent.[11]

The team for a particular project might consist of a purchasing specialist, a design engineer, a production engineer, and representatives from marketing and accounting. For other projects, a purchasing manager might work with a technical salesperson of a supplier. Clearly, the industrial salesperson can play an active role by supplying technical assistance, relevant data, and valuable recommendations. In fact, the salesperson of the industrial marketer is often pivotal in stimulating the purchasing organization to conduct a value analysis study, convincing purchasing or other organizational members that the potential benefits from a particular study exceed its costs.

The Marketer's Role   The nature and size of the purchasing department will have an important bearing on the formulation of marketing strategy. Considering the large number of small companies in the United

[11] Dale C. Weisenstein, "Westinghouse Teams Up For Quality and Productivity," *Purchasing World*, 27 (May 1983), p. 48.

Figure 2.3   How Value Analysis Slashes Costs

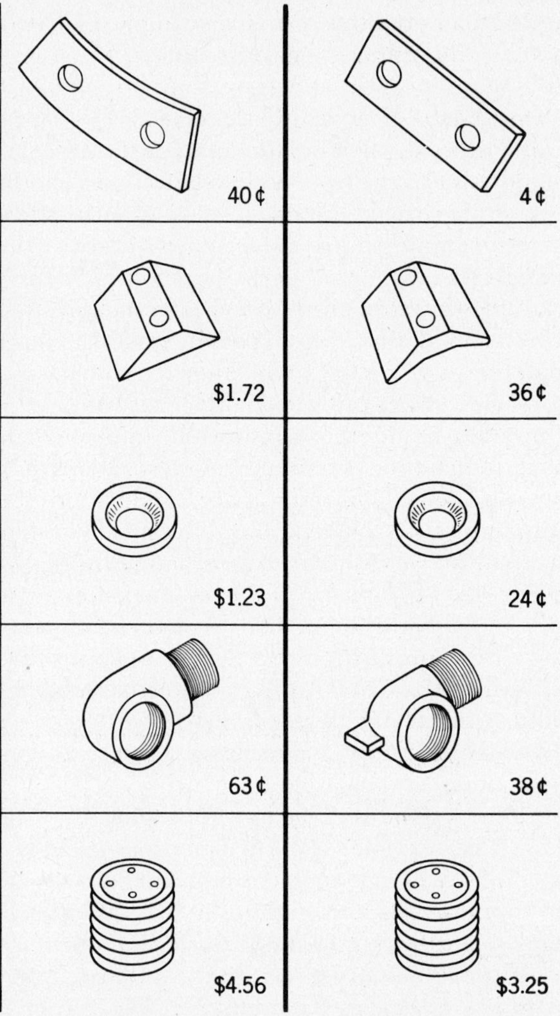

Weights mounted on a rotor ring were curved to match the ring curve. Did it need this feature? No. Using a straight piece, the cost dropped from 40¢ to 4¢.	40 ¢	4 ¢
Field coil supports were machined from stock, but the original design blended nicely into a casting operation. The change resulted in lowering the cost from $1.72 to 36¢ each.	$1.72	36 ¢
This insulating washer was made from laminated phenolic resin and fiber. Machined from individual pieces of material, it cost $1.23. A supplier with specialty equipment now fly-cuts the parts, nesting them on full sheets, at 24¢ each.	$1.23	24 ¢
Standard nipple and elbow required special machining to fit a totally enclosed motor. Casting a special street "L" with a lug eliminated machining and a special assembly jig. The cost dropped from 63¢ to 38¢.	63 ¢	38 ¢
An insulator costing $4.56 was originally porcelain, leaded extra heavy. Now molded from polyester and glass, it is lighter and virtually indestructible. New cost: $3.25.	$4.56	$3.25

Source: Lamar Lee, Jr., and Donald W. Dobler, *Purchasing and Materials Management, Text and Cases* (New York: McGraw-Hill Book Company, 1977), p. 265. Reprinted by permission of McGraw-Hill Book Company.

States, most purchasing departments are one- or two-person operations. The purchasing agent may report to the president, general manager, controller, or production manager. The purchasing agent in the small firm may lack detailed knowledge and expertise. In this case, the industrial salesperson should be viewed as an extension of the customer's purchasing department, acting as a consultant and providing assistance wherever required.

In dealing with the large corporation, where specialized buyers assigned to limited product categories have achieved sophistication in purchasing, the salesperson must be able to respond to very specific questions about product quality, performance, and costs. Purchasing units in large organizations are likely to use computer technology that significantly expands their ability to gather, process, and store information on the attributes and performance history of alternative suppliers. Techniques for serving the computer-assisted buyer, as well as the impact of computer technology on the nature of the buyer–seller relationship, are explored in more detail in Chapters 3 and 4.

Some large corporations that have geographically dispersed manufacturing facilities with relatively similar requirements for supplies and materials, coordinate a significant volume of their purchases through a centralized headquarters procurement unit. Mead Corporation's Dayton, Ohio headquarters directs the flow of equipment and materials to plant locations in Tennessee, Michigan, Wisconsin, and other locations. In response to centralized purchasing, many industrial marketers have developed a *national accounts sales force*, assigning one or more salespersons the responsibility of meeting the needs of a single large customer with sizable sales potential. The strategic implications of centralized buying and national accounts selling are explored in Chapter 4. Sales personnel and marketing managers who can effectively adapt to the purchasing conditions in each market segment are generally the leading marketers in their industry.

Materials Management: Integrating Purchasing into the Business Operation

A relatively new idea in the organization of the purchasing function is the concept of *materials management*, where all activities, including determination of manufacturing requirements, production scheduling, and procurement, storage, and disbursement of materials, are handled by a materials manager.[12] By giving the materials manager overall authority, the activities of various departments can be coordinated to insure that the total cost of materials to the organization is minimized. Without this central authority, savings in one function, such as purchasing, may add cost in another, such as inventory control. The materials management approach is expected to be implemented by as many as 75 percent of all U.S. manufacturers during the 1980s.[13] Large firms with geographically

---

[12] Farrell, *Aljian's Purchasing Handbook*, pp. 2–29.

[13] Gary J. Zenz, "Materials Management and Purchasing: Projections for the 1980's," *Journal of Purchasing and Materials Management*, 17 (Spring 1981), p. 20.

dispersed manufacturing facilities integrate their centralized materials management with operational materials management activities at plant and division levels. On-line computer systems combine and integrate all aspects of the materials management function.

GM to Suppliers: We Need It "Just-in-Time"

It is becoming increasingly difficult to qualify as a General Motors' parts supplier as a result of GM's adoption of the Japanese "kan-ban" or "just-in-time" parts supply and inventory system. The new approach basically calls for delivery of only those parts needed to support production on a particular day. The new system calls for closer working relationships with fewer suppliers, each holding long-term contracts.

The company stated that "most Japanese auto companies use fewer than 250 parts suppliers; GM, by contrast, had at one time about 3500 suppliers for its assembly operations alone! The intent is to reduce and simplify our supplier network—perhaps cutting the figure of 3500 in half."

At one plant where the system is operational, parts requirements for the next day are determined and telephoned to suppliers in the morning. Such parts as axles, frames and transmissions are then shipped by truck that same day to support the company's immediate production needs.

Source: Paul V. Farrell, "Expect More, Get More From Suppliers," *Purchasing World*, 26 (May 1982), p. 32.

Materials management has made purchasing personnel aware of the need to evaluate the total flow of purchased materials—including net delivered price, inventory control, traffic, receiving, and production control. The result places an extremely heavy burden on the industrial marketing strategist. Industrial marketing managers must coordinate all activities that affect the materials management function of their customers, including sales management, credit, traffic, expediting, warehousing, and production—and must be able to secure the necessary distribution support from their own logistics department. In the General Motors "just-in-time" inventory system, the distribution capabilities of GM parts suppliers is critical. Suppliers that can manage their own production, inventory, and distribution systems so as to match GM's requirements have the best chance to participate in sizable, long-term GM contracts. Thus, the advent of the materials management concept will stimulate a more systematic approach to industrial marketing strategy and a closer working relationship between buyers and sellers.

The Expanding Role of Materials Management   The materials management approach to purchasing will likely expand in scope and importance. A study by Edward Bonfield and Thomas Speh reveals that both chief operating officers and purchasing managers of large industrial corporations expect purchasing's involvement in the following areas to increase dramatically:

1.   raw materials, components, and supplies inventory control;

2.   planning and forecasting future supply needs;

3.   maintaining supplier lists;

4.   securing price quotations.

The study also concludes that purchasing will become more sophisticated as computer applications and value analysis increase.[14] The implications for industrial marketers are clear.

Governments: Unique Characteristics

Like commercial enterprises, institutions and government purchasers are also enhancing the effectiveness of the purchasing function through the implementation of value analysis, materials management, and other techniques. As Chapter 1 indicated, the federal government is the largest consumer in the United States and its buying procedures are highly specialized and often very confusing. To compete effectively in the government market, the industrial marketer must develop a thorough comprehension of this complex buying process. A first step is to understand the variety of government units and their characteristics.

In 1982, there were 82,688 governmental units in the United States[15] (Table 2.1). Note that a vast majority of government units are local, providing the industrial marketer with a widely dispersed market. However, there is some market concentration, as 10 states account for 49 percent of all government units in the United States.[16] The numbers in the table are somewhat misleading as they indicate a ratio of state and federal to local units of 1 to 1500. In reality, many functional areas

---

[14] Edward H. Bonfield and Thomas W. Speh, "Dimensions of Purchasing's Role in Industry," *Journal of Purchasing and Materials Management*, 13 (Summer 1977), p. 15; see also, Robert I. Parket and Joseph Eisenberg, "The Industrial Purchaser: New Star on the Organizational Chart," *Business*, 32 (January–March 1982), pp. 27–32.

[15] *Government Units in 1982*, U.S. Department of Commerce, Preliminary Report #1, June 1982, p. 1.

[16] *Ibid.*, p. 2.

Table 2.1   Types of Governmental Units

Type of Unit		Number of Units
United States Government		1
State Government		50
Local Government		82,637
County	3,041	
Municipality	19,083	
Township	16,748	
School Districts	15,032	
Special Districts	28,733	
Total		82,688

Source: Government Units in 1982, U.S. Department of Commerce, Preliminary Report #1, June 1982, p. 1.

within state government (education, state police, highway) and agencies within the federal government (defense, space, interior, transportation, postal service) are responsible for a sizable procurement volume. Thus, federal and state governments have hundreds of people, agencies, and functional areas that have direct and indirect impacts on the purchasing process.

Expenditures by the federal government totaled $741 billion in 1982, of which $249 billion was for purchases of goods and services.[17] (The remainder was spent on wages, salaries, and social programs.) Approximately 70 percent, or $174 billion, of the goods and services procurement was for defense. State and local governments had total expenditures of $485 billion in 1981, 60 percent of which was by local government units.[18] Government units rival the commercial sector in terms of total market potential.

Influences on Government Buying

Another level of complexity is added to the governmental purchasing process by the array of influences on this process. In large city, state, and federal procurement, buyers will be responsible to or influenced by dozens of interested parties who specify, legislate, evaluate, and use the goods and services.[19] Clearly, the range of outside influences extends far beyond the originating agency.

---

[17] *Statistical Abstract of the United States*, p. 247.

[18] *Ibid.*, p. 273.

[19] Cecil Hynes and Noel Zabriskie, *Marketing to Governments* (Columbus, Ohio: Grid, Inc., 1974), p. 1.

Understanding Government Contracts

Government purchasing is also affected by goals and programs that have broad social overtones. Some of these include *compliance*, *set-asides*, and *minority subcontracting*. The compliance program requires that government contractors maintain affirmative action programs for minorities, women, and the handicapped. Firms failing to do so are barred from holding government contracts. In the set-aside program, a certain percentage of a given government contract is "set-aside" for small or minority businesses; no others can participate in that proportion of the contract. The minority subcontracting program may require that major contractors subcontract a certain percentage of the total contract to minority firms. For example, Ohio law requires that 7 percent of all subcontractors on state construction projects be minorities, and in 1982, $46.3 million of the $550 million in construction contracts in the state went to minorities.[20] The potential government contractor must understand these programs and how they apply to the firm.

Most government procurement, at any level of government, is based on laws that establish contractual guidelines.[21] The federal government has set forth certain general contract provisions as part of the Federal Procurement Regulations. These provisions include stipulations as to product inspection, payment methods, actions as a result of default and disputes, among many others.

Without a clear comprehension of the procurement laws, the vendor is in an unfavorable position during the negotiation phase. The vendor also needs to explore the advantages and disadvantages particularly of the two basic types of contract: (1) *fixed-price contracts*, in which a firm price is agreed to before the contract is awarded, and full payment is made when the product or service is delivered as agreed, and (2) *cost-reimbursement contracts*, where the vendor is reimbursed for allowable costs incurred in performance of the contract and is sometimes allowed a certain number of dollars above cost as profit. Each type of contract has incentives built in to control costs or cover future contingencies.

Generally, the fixed-price contract provides the greatest profit potential, but the risks are also greater if unforeseen expenses are incurred, inflation increases dramatically, or conditions change. A large defense contractor lost over $60 million on the production of the first 20 fighter planes it built for the Navy as a result of inflation and unanticipated development problems. However, if the seller can reduce costs significantly during the contract, profits may exceed those estimated when the contract was negotiated. Cost-reimbursement contracts are carefully administered by the government because of the minimal incentives for

---

[20] Allen Howard, "Minority Contract Program Attacked from Both Sides," *Cincinnati Enquirer* (March 27, 1983), p. 37.

[21] David E. Gumpert and Jeffery A. Timmons, "Penetrating the Government Procurement Maze," *Harvard Business Review*, 60 (May–June 1982), p. 15.

contractor efficiency. They are usually employed for contracts involving considerable developmental work when it is difficult to estimate efforts and expenses.

Telling Vendors How to Sell: Useful Publications

Unlike most customers, governments often go to great lengths to explain to potential vendors exactly how to do business with the government. For example, the federal government makes available such publications as *Selling to the Military* and *Selling to the U.S. Air Force*. Government agencies also hold periodic seminars to orient businesses to the buying procedures used by the agency. The objective is to encourage firms to seek government business.

Purchasing Organizations and Procedures: Government

Government and commercial purchasing are organized similarly. However, governments tend to emphasize clerical functions because of the more detailed procedures the law requires. Although the federal government is the largest single industrial purchaser, it does not operate like a single company, but like a combination of several large companies with overlapping responsibilities and thousands of small independent units.[22] Every government agency possesses some degree of buying influence or authority. Federal government procurement is divided into two categories: defense and nondefense.

Defense Procurement   Each military department—army, navy, and air force—and the Defense Department is responsible for its own major purchases. However, the Defense Logistics Agency (DLA) procures billions of dollars worth of supplies used in common by all branches. The purpose of the DLA is to obtain favorable prices through volume purchasing and to reduce duplication of purchasing within the military. Defense-related items may also be procured by other government agencies, such as the General Services Administration. Also, many supplies for military base operations are procured locally.

Nondefense Procurement   Nondefense procurement is administered by a wide variety of agencies including cabinet departments (e.g., HHS, Commerce), commissions (e.g., Federal Trade Commission), the executive branch (e.g., Bureau of Budget), agencies (e.g., the Federal Aviation Agency), and administration (e.g., General Services Administration). The Commerce Department centralizes the procurement of supplies and equipment for its Washington office and all local offices. The Department of Interior, on the other hand, instructs each area and district

[22] *Ibid*, p. 16.

office of the Mining Enforcement and Safety Administration to purchase mine-safety equipment and clothing locally.[23]

Like the DLA, the General Services Administration (GSA) centralizes the procurement of many general use items (like office furniture, pens, light bulbs) for all civilian government agencies. The Federal Supply Service of the GSA is like the purchasing department of a large diversified corporation because it provides a consolidated purchasing, storing, and distribution network for the federal government. The Federal Supply Service purchases many items in common use by other government agencies including office supplies, small tools, paint, paper, furniture, maintenance supplies, and duplicating equipment. The GSA has the market power to place orders for one item totaling over $500,000 at any one time! If the GSA has approved a supplier, departments within the government may purchase the particular item at specified retail outlets at the agreed-upon price. However, securing the initial GSA contract is difficult indeed.

Federal Specifications—Are They Worth It?

A fundamental problem of most firms attempting to do business with the federal government is to untangle the maze of federal procurement specifications. The government appears reluctant to just go out and buy something; rather, they draw up elaborate specifications for anything they buy—from aircraft carriers to toothpicks. It takes the military 24 pages to list the "specs" for T-shirts, 15 pages for chewing gum and 17 pages for Worcestershire sauce. The result—the Pentagon pays $10 a case for Worcestershire sauce versus $8 for a commercial brand. In another instance, the military paid $1,130 a piece for piston rings that civilian buyers could purchase for $100!

Conversely, to reduce the estimated cost of $83 per round for armor-piercing ammunition fired by the 30-mm cannon on board the A-10 Thunderbolt, the Air Force contract officer decided not to impose any product specifications on the two firms that manufacture the ammunition. Instead, the firms were requested to "produce 30-mm ammo that worked, for the lowest price." Average cost per shell: $15.

Source: "The Winds of Reform," *Time*, 128 (March 7, 1983), p. 23.

---

[23] *Ibid*, p. 18.

Federal Buying

The president may set the procurement process in motion when he signs a congressional appropriation bill, or an accountant in the General Accounting Office may initiate the process by requesting a new desk-top calculator. Once the need is documented, the government will follow one of two general procurement strategies: *formal advertising* (also known as open bid) or *negotiated contract*.

Formal Advertising   Formal advertising means the government will solicit bids from appropriate suppliers; usually, the lowest bidder is awarded the contract. This strategy is followed when the product is standardized and the specifications straightforward. The interested supplier must gain a place on a bidder's list. Then, each time the government requests bids for a particular product, the supplier will receive an invitation to bid. The invitation to bid specifies the item and the quantity to be purchased, detailed technical specifications, delivery schedules, warranties required, packing requirements, and other purchasing details. The bidding firm will base its bid on its own cost structure and the anticipation of competitive bid levels.

Procurement personnel review each bid for conformance to specifications. Western Electric was recently disqualified on a $70 million contract for base PBX systems. Although Western Electric complained that there was no functional need for digital technology in the systems, they were automatically disqualified for not meeting the mandatory bid specifications for a fully digital PBX system.[24] Thus, a critical aspect of marketing strategy for the firm soliciting government business is to develop procedures which ensure that all specifications are carefully met. Bid price is obviously another essential strategic dimension in doing business with the government. Contracts are generally awarded to the lowest bidder; however, the government agency may select the next to lowest bidder if it can document that the lowest bidder would not responsibly fulfill the contract.

The formal advertising approach is expensive and time-consuming for all parties, generating a substantial volume of paperwork. However, the process does allow free and open competition. In addition, the government has fairly good assurance that there is no collusion and that it has obtained the lowest possible price.

Negotiated Contract Buying   This buying strategy is employed for products and services that cannot be differentiated on the basis of price alone, such as complex scientific equipment or research and develop-

---

[24]"Western Electric: Air Force Overpays $40 Million on Northern Telecom PBX Pact," *Electronic News*, 27 (July 13, 1981), p. 7.

ment projects or when there are few suppliers. There may be some competition, since the contracting office can carry on negotiations with several suppliers simultaneously.

Reflections of a Shipbuilder

Newport News Shipbuilding, one of the most successful private shipyards in the United States, produces aircraft carriers, tankers, submarines, cruisers, and other military and commercial vessels. Edward J. Campbell, President and Chief Executive Officer, provides these reflections on the government as a customer.

On the plus side:

- The government builds in incentives to reward good performance.
- Government contracts can put a firm at the cutting edge of technology and provide many useful technological spin-offs.
- Government contracts provide solid cash flow. Bills are paid regularly if the paperwork is done properly.
- The government is willing to share some of the risks involved in major, long-term shipbuilding contracts.
- The government is becoming more of a partner than an adversary.

On the minus side:

- Compared to the commercial marketplace, buyer–seller relationships are different. Government procurement units are required to get bids—bids that they can share with others, even competitors.
- There's a constant "changing of the guard," as key buying influentials are transferred or promoted. Old rules receive new interpretations as these buying influentials change.
- Major government contracts require lengthy review by many committees. Years may pass before a decision is made and the specifications may change throughout this process as the technology changes.
- There are many quality control checkpoints (some of them redundant) throughout the fulfillment of a major government contract.

> ▪   Nothing compares to the amount of regulation and paperwork involved in a major government defense contract. Employees of the shipbuilding industry often quip: "We're not finished until the paperwork outweighs the ship."
>
> *Source*: Edward J. Campbell, President and Chief Executive Officer, Newport News Shipbuilding Company. Lincoln Lecture Series, College of Business Administration, Arizona State University, April 14, 1983.

Obviously, negotiation is a much more flexible procurement procedure; the government purchasing office may exercise considerable personal judgment. Procurement is based on the more subjective factors of performance and quality as well as on price. Here, the procurement decision for the government is much like that of the large corporation: Which is the best possible product at the lowest price and will the product be delivered on time? Usually, extensive personal selling by the potential contractor is required to convince the government that the firm can perform. The selling effort should include negotiating favorable terms and reasonable payment dates, and developing intelligence on future contracts for which the company may want to bid.

Selling to the government is involved, time-consuming, and paper-generating. Government markets are among the most sophisticated and complex environments within which the industrial marketer will be operating.

Federal vs. Commercial Buying

Table 2.2 compares important characteristics that differentiate the federal acquisition process (Department of Defense) from the commercial buying process. Note that much of the initiative for a major system acquisition originates with the buyer in the case of the defense purchase. In addition, there are rigid standards (some defined by law) as to costing, product specifications, completion dates, and technical procedures. As a result, an industrial marketer positioned to sell to the government will have a much different marketing strategy focus than a firm that concentrates on the commercial sector. The government seller will emphasize (1) understanding the complex rules and standards it must conform to; (2) developing an intelligence system to keep informed of each agency's procurement plans; (3) generating a product development and

Table 2.2   Defense Acquisition Process versus Commercial Buying Behavior

Characteristic	Defense Acquisition Process	Commercial Buying Behavior
Product Justification	Established by the agency's mission within overall national defense	Market/economic benefits
Goals and Objectives	Match technology to national defense needs at lowest cost; some concern for social goals—compliance, set-asides	Reduce operating cost, improve product quality, etc.
Relationship Initiatives	Mostly from the buyer; invited bids	Mostly from the seller
Major Product Need Ideas	Mostly from the buyer	Based on market research and technological innovation
Nature of Technical Procedures	Complex, regulated by law	Less complex, based on company policy
Complexity of Decision-Making Unit	Multiple agencies; defined roles	Single agency; less defined internal roles
Buyer Intrusion on Marketers' Methods	Considerable	Infrequent
Management Procedure for Sellers	Endless paperwork	Single contracts and "working agreements"
Level of Capital Expenditure	Agency mission, technology, congressional appropriation	Investment policy, retained earnings, cash position of buyer
Marketing Mix Focus	Communications and technical research and development	Full range of marketing mix elements
Communications Thrust	Correct technical capability to meet mission performance	Sales reps convert marketing plan to sales and profits
Pricing Methods	Based on customer cost, accounting standards (law)	Based on product life cycle, cash flow, customer financing, competition
Funding and Facilities	Often provided by buyer	Nearly always provided by the seller
Economic Risk	Largely underwritten by buyer	Underwritten by seller
Relationship	Contractual	Some by contract
Key Decision Criteria	Conformity to written technical specifications, project completion deadlines, bid price, performance	Full range of quality, price, performance, service criteria

Source: Adapted from: Ronald L. Schill, "Buying Process in the U.S. Department of Defense," *Industrial Marketing Management*, 9 (October 1980), p. 295.

research and development strategy that facilitates the firm's response to government product needs; (4) a communications strategy that focuses on how technology meets agency mission objectives; and (5) a negotiation strategy to secure favorable terms regarding payment, contract completion, and cost overruns due to changes in product specifications.

The Institutional Market: Unique Characteristics

The institutional market constitutes the third important market component. Institutional buyers make up a sizable market—in 1982 total expenditures on education alone exceeded $200 billion, and health care costs totaled over $312 billion.[25] Schools and health care facilities are important factors in the institutional market, which also includes penal institutions, colleges and universities, libraries, foundations, art galleries, and clinics. In one sense institutional purchasers are similar to governments in that the purchasing process is often constrained by political considerations and dictated by law. In fact, many institutions are administered by government units—schools, for example. Other institutions are privately operated and managed like corporations; they may even have a broader range of purchase requirements than their large corporate counterparts. Like the commercial enterprise, institutions are ever cognizant of the value of efficient purchasing. If a university can save $100,000 through purchasing efficiencies, and its endowment earns 10 percent, the $100,000 savings is equivalent to an endowment gift of $1,000,000! Because the institutional market is similar to the other markets, its characteristics will be presented very briefly.

Institutional Buyers: Purchasing Procedures

Diversity is the key element in the institutional market. For example, the institutional marketing manager must be ready to respond first to a school purchasing agent who buys in great quantity for an entire city's school system through a formal bid procedure and then to a former pharmacist who has been elevated to purchasing agent for a small rural hospital.

Health care institutions provide a good example of the diversity of this market. Some small hospitals delegate responsibility for food purchasing to the chief dietitian. Although many of these hospitals have purchasing agents, the agent cannot place an order unless approved by the dietitian. In larger hospitals, decisions may be made by committees composed of a business manager, purchasing agent, dietitian, and cook. In still other cases, hospitals may belong to buying groups consisting of many local hospitals, or meal preparation may be contracted out. Because of these varied purchasing environments, successful institutional marketers usually maintain a separate marketing manager, staff, and sales force to tailor marketing efforts to each situation.

For many institutions, once the budget for a department has been established, the department will attempt to spend up to that budget limit. Thus, institutions may buy simply because there are unused funds

---

[25] *1983 United States Industrial Outlook*, U.S. Department of Commerce, Washington, D.C., January 1983, p. 52.6.

in the budget. An industrial marketer should carefully evaluate the budgetary status of potential customers in the institutional segment of the market.

Multiple Buying Influences   The institutional market offers some unique applications of the multiple buying influence concept discussed in Chapter 1. Many institutions are staffed with professionals—doctors, professors, researchers, and others. In most cases, depending upon size, the institution will employ a purchasing agent, and in large institutions a sizable purchasing department. There is great potential for conflict between those responsible for the purchasing function and the professional staff for whom the purchasing department is buying. The purchasing staff is in constant contact with suppliers, and can challenge restrictive specifications, secure information on market availability, and arrange for product demonstrations from several major suppliers. However, many professionals resent the usurping of their authority to buy from whom they wish. Industrial marketing and sales personnel, in formulating their marketing and personal selling approaches, must understand these conflicts and be able to respond to them. Often, the salesperson must carefully cultivate the professional staff in terms of product benefits and service while developing a delivery timetable, maintenance contract, and price schedule to satisfy the purchasing department.

Group Purchasing   An important distinction of institutional purchasing is group purchasing. Hospitals, schools, and universities may join cooperative purchasing associations to obtain quantity discounts. Universities affiliated with the Education and Institutional Purchasing Cooperative enjoy favorable contracts established by the cooperative and can purchase a wide array of products directly from vendors at the low negotiated price. Cooperative buying allows institutions to enjoy lower prices, improved quality (through improved testing and vendor selection), reduced administrative cost, standardization, better records, and greater competition.[26]

Group purchasing poses special challenges for the industrial marketer. First, the marketer must be in a position to develop not only strategies for dealing with individual institutions but also unique strategies for the special requirements of cooperative purchasing groups. The buying centers—individual institution versus cooperative purchasing group—may vary considerably in composition, criteria, and level of expertise. For the purchasing groups, discount pricing will assume special importance. Vendors who sell through purchasing groups must also have distribution systems that effectively deliver products to individual

[26] Michael R. Leenders, Harold E. Fearon, and Wilbur B. England, *Purchasing and Materials Management* (Homewood, Illinois: Richard D. Irwin & Co., 1980), p. 490.

group members. And even though a vendor has a contract with a large cooperative association, he or she still must be able to communicate effectively and respond to each institution that places an order against the contract.

Institutional Purchasing Policies   Table 2.3 shows an excerpt from the purchasing policy manual of a large hospital. Note that in many respects the purchasing process is similar to that of a large commercial firm. However, the manual illustrates some important distinctions between in-

---

Table 2.3   Purchasing Policies of a Large Hospital

A. Basic Purchasing Policies

1. The Administrator has delegated the purchasing function to the Purchasing Department which shall provide service to all other departments. The Administrator may delegate purchasing authority to others.
2. Each department head shall establish the specifications and requirements for supplies and equipment for use in his department. Purchasing will give assistance when requested to do so.
3. Multiple sources of supply are considered for all purchases so as to encourage competition and insure availability of supply.
4. Purchasing through cooperative buying organizations will be pursued whenever an advantage is to be gained by the hospital in cost savings and/or in quality of product.
5. Participation in cost comparison surveys will be done to evaluate the prices we are paying.
6. All items and services not fixed to one source of supply may be subject to bid, negotiation, or contract.
7. All factors being equal, local vendors will be awarded the bid or contract and will always be the preferred source of supply when bids are better than or equal to their competitors.
8. The Product Evaluation Committee will review all requests for changes in supplies which have major cost implications, for example, a change from a reusable item to a disposable one, and make recommendations to the Administrator. Every effort will be made to standardize a given item used throughout the hospital.

B. Interdepartmental Relationships

1. The Director of Purchasing has been authorized to initiate, sign, and place all purchase orders for the hospital. Note these exceptions: The Director of Dietary Services purchases all food; the Director of Pharmacy purchases all pharmaceuticals; the Manager of the Hospitality Center purchases all items sold in the Center; the Assistant Administrator, Plant Services, purchases architectural and engineering services, contractors' services, and service agreements for major plant systems; and the Director of Public Relations purchases artwork/printing services.
2. Purchasing will receive and interview all supplier representatives. Other departments requiring information from supplier representatives should make their needs known to Purchasing which will make the necessary arrangements. Purchasing should be kept fully informed of progress by the department in discussions with supplier representatives because of the possibility of involvement in later negotiations.
3. The Director of Purchasing, working with the department head, shall negotiate all purchases or contracts. Purchasing may question quality, quantity, and kind of material requested in order that the best interests of the hospital may be served.
4. In interviews with supplier representatives, employees or staff members outside Purchasing should not commit themselves on preference for any product or on the hospital's source of supply for any product, or give information regarding performance or price. In fairness to all concerned, prices and specific information received from vendors are considered confidential.

Source: Frank J. Roth, Director of Purchasing, Christ Hospital, Cincinnati, Ohio. Christ Hospital Manual, Volume 4.

Figure 2.4   A Market-Centered Organization

stitutional and commercial purchasing. The policies regarding cooperative buying, preference to local vendors, and the delegation of purchasing responsibility for food, pharmaceuticals, and a variety of other items
are of particular importance. It is just these characteristics that the industrial marketer must understand in order to carefully develop a sales
and communication strategy for this prospective institutional customer.

Dealing with Diversity:
A Market-Centered Organization

Because each sector of the industrial market is unique, many firms have
built market specialization into the marketing organization. To illustrate, the industrial products area of the J. M. Smucker Company is
organized around market sectors. The institutional, military, and industrial markets are each managed by different individuals, each thoroughly knowledgeable about one particular market. Mack Hanan refers
to such a structure as market-centered.[27] He contends that the most
effective way to satisfy the needs of distinct customer groups is to build
the firm's divisions around major customer markets.

One form of a market-centered organizational scheme is illustrated in Figure 2.4. Observe that a markets manager supervises and coordinates the activities of three market specialists. Each market specialist
examines the buying processes, product preferences, and similarities
and differences among customers in one sector of the industrial market.

---

[27] Mack Hanan, "Reorganize Your Company Around Its Markets," *Harvard Business Review*, 52 (November–December
1974), pp. 63–74.

Such an analysis allows the market specialist to further categorize customers in a particular sector into meaningful market segments, and design specialized marketing programs for each segment. A market-centered organization provides the industrial marketer with a structure for effectively dealing with diversity in the industrial market.

Summary

A large market awaits the industrial marketing manager. The market can be divided into three major components: commercial enterprises, governments (federal, state, and local), and institutions. The marketer requires an understanding of the unique characteristics and the structure of the purchasing function in each sector.

Commercial enterprises include manufacturers, construction companies, service firms, transportation companies, selected professional groups, and resellers. Of these, manufacturers account for the largest dollar volume of purchases. Furthermore, although the majority of manufacturing firms are small, buying power is concentrated in the hands of a relatively few large manufacturing establishments, which are also concentrated geographically. Commercial enterprises like service establishments and transportation and utility companies are more widely dispersed. Often, the purchasing process is administered by a purchasing manager or purchasing agent. In larger firms, the purchasing function has become quite specialized, placing heavy demands on the industrial salesperson who must match the expertise of potential buyers. In smaller organizations, one person may be responsible for all buying activities. The materials management concept, while gaining importance as an approach for reducing material acquisition cost, requires the careful coordination of a vendor's total marketing and distribution operations.

Many marketers find dealing with the government sector of the industrial market frustrating. However, government is the largest consumer in the United States. The diligent marketer who acquires an understanding of the procurement laws and different types of contracts employed by the government can find a lucrative market. Federal buying follows two general procurement strategies: formal advertising or negotiated contract. The formal advertising approach frequently followed for standardized products involves the solicitation of bids from appropriate suppliers. Negotiated contract buying is employed for unique requirements and is typified by discussion and bargaining throughout all phases of the contract.

Diversity is the characteristic that typifies the institutional market. Institutional buyers are somewhere between commercial enterprise and government buyers in terms of their characteristics, orientations, and purchasing processes. Group cooperative purchasing—a unique aspect of this segment—necessitates special strategic response by potential suppliers. Many industrial firms have found that a market-centered organization provides the specialization required to meet the needs of each sector of the industrial market.

Discussion Questions

1. Research suggests that an increasing number of buying organizations have adopted the "materials management" concept. Describe this concept and outline the managerial implications that it raises for the industrial marketer.

2. Compare and contrast the two general procurement strategies employed by the federal government: (1) formal advertising and (2) negotiated contract.

3. Institutional buyers fall somewhere between commercial enterprises and government buyers in terms of their characteristics, orientation, and purchasing process. Explain.

4. Evaluate the wisdom of this personal selling strategy: the approach that is appropriate for large purchasing departments is equally effective in small purchasing departments.

5. Describe the role of value analysis in the contemporary purchasing organization. What steps can the industrial marketer take to benefit from a value analysis?

6. Explain how the decision-making process that a university might employ in selecting a new computer would differ from that of a commercial enterprise. Who would be the key participants in the process in each setting?

7. Fearing red tape and mounds of paperwork, Tom Bronson, President of B&E Electric, has always avoided the government market. A recent discussion with a colleague, however, has rekindled Tom's interest in this industrial market sector. What steps should B&E Electric take to learn more about this market?

8. Describe the key characteristics that differentiate the federal acquisition process (Department of Defense) from the commercial buying behavior process.

9. Why have some industrial firms moved away from product-centered organizations and toward market-centered organizations?

P·A·R·T
II

The Organizational Buying Process

C·H·A·P·T·E·R
3

Dimensions of
Organizational Buying

An understanding of the organizational buying process is fundamental to the development of sound industrial marketing strategy. After reading this chapter, you will understand:

1. *the importance of examining industrial marketing management as an exchange process between buyers and sellers;*
2. *the decision process that organizational buyers apply as they confront different buying situations;*
3. *the specific strategy implications of different types of buying situations for the industrial marketer;*
4. *the rational and emotional factors that influence organizational members in choosing among the offerings of competing industrial marketers;*
5. *the formal evaluation systems and buying technology that organizational buyers employ in evaluating supplier performance.*

An industrial salesperson might begin the day with a lengthy sales call on a manufacturing facility in the morning, calling on a large hospital and a city government account in the afternoon. The day is characterized by negotiation, bargaining, problem-solving, information-sharing, and other exchange processes. Knowledge of organizational buying behavior can help the salesperson to isolate common elements in the purchasing systems of many organizations. Likewise, examining the nature of exchange relationships between industrial buyers and sellers can provide valuable insights into industrial marketing management.

The buying procedures of organizations, although more formal, resemble the approach to buying of final consumers. The purchasing agent may automatically order an item just as a shopper routinely selects a preferred brand from the retailer's shelf. Little time, effort, or deliberation goes into the decision. Other decisions, however, involve an elaborate search for information and a careful consideration of alternatives. In such cases, many members of the organization provide input. The household might be considered a group decision-making unit that operates in a similar fashion when major family purchases (e.g., a new car, television) are being considered.

To be effective, the marketer must understand the decision-making process of industrial customers, the key participants in this process, and the criteria they use in making decisions. What process do industrial customers follow in selecting needed products and services? How do they evaluate competing offerings? Clearly, an understanding of the nature of exchange relationships in the industrial market, coupled with a knowledge of the mechanics of the purchasing system, provides the marketer with a firm base for building responsive industrial marketing strategy.

Buyer–Seller Interactions

The true nature of industrial marketing is captured by examining buyer–seller interactions. At its most basic level, selling can be viewed as an exchange process in which two individuals trade items of value.[1] The buyer receives a physical product with attached services, as well as certain psychological assets. In turn, the seller receives financial, as well as psychological, benefits.

---

[1] For example, see David T. Wilson, "Dyadic Interactions: Some Conceptualizations," pp. 31–48, and Thomas V. Bonoma, Richard Bagozzi, and Gerald Zaltman, "The Dyadic Paradigm with Specific Applications Toward Industrial Marketing," pp. 49–66, in Thomas V. Bonoma and Gerald Zaltman, eds., *Organizational Buying Behavior* (Chicago: American Marketing Association, 1978).

Figure 3.1   Exchanges in Industrial Marketing and Purchasing Interactions

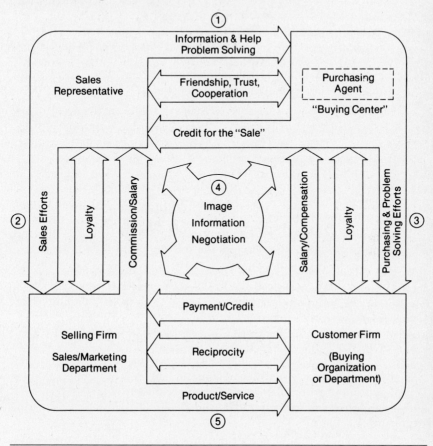

Source: Reprinted by permission of the publisher from "The Social Psychology of Industrial Buying and Selling," by Thomas V. Bonoma and Wesley J. Johnston, *Industrial Marketing Management*, 7 (October 1978), p. 216. Copyright © 1978 by Elsevier Science Publishing Co., Inc.

A Dyadic Exchange Model

Thomas Bonoma and Wesley Johnston assert that rich insights into industrial marketing can be gained by examining the smallest unit of analysis in marketing—the dyad.[2] Their exchange model of industrial marketing based on dyadic interactions (i.e., two parties, two firms) is presented in Figure 3.1. (Note the five important dyadic relations numbered in Figure 3.1.)

[2] Thomas V. Bonoma and Wesley J. Johnston, "The Social Psychology of Industrial Buying and Selling," *Industrial Marketing Management* 7 (July 1978), pp. 213–224.

1. *The sales representative–purchasing agent relationship.* Here, the seller exchanges information and assistance to solve a purchasing need of the buyer for the reward of a specific sale. Friendship, trust, and cooperation can develop in buyer–seller interactions.

2. *The sales representative–selling firm relationship.* Here, the salesperson exerts sales effort in return for a salary and/or commission from the industrial marketer. Psychological income (e.g., recognition, praise) is often exchanged for loyalty.

3. *The purchasing agent–buying organization relationship.* The purchasing agent exchanges talent at buying for a salary. Likewise, the purchasing specialist may receive psychological income (e.g., organizational status) and return loyalty.

4. *The seller's view of the buying firm; the buyer's view of the selling firm.* The image that each party has of the other helps establish the boundaries of the purchasing interaction. The salesperson and the buyer each have plans, goals, and intentions of their own. While these are often negotiable, they serve as the starting point for interaction.

5. *The buying firm–selling firm exchange.* Here the product/service is given in return for money or credit. Reciprocal trade agreements (each buying from the other) are often an outgrowth of this exchange.

To some degree, every transaction changes the selling firm and the salesperson, *and* the buying firm and its key participants in the purchasing process. Bonoma and Johnston contend that "it is only when all these complex flows of influence are managed effectively that maximal marketing response will be generated, and maximal customer satisfaction will result."[3]

The dyadic exchange model also provides a way to trace contemporary changes in buyer–seller relationships in the industrial market. Changes in the buying environment trigger corresponding adjustments in the selling environment.[4] These trends (highlighted in Chapter 2) reflect the growing sophistication and the rising organizational prestige and authority of the purchasing function in many firms. In the average firm, purchasing controls the allocation of more than half of the sales revenue; it can be the key force to maintaining profits and a favorable cash flow position.[5] If there is high inflation in material costs or shortages of basic raw materials, purchasing becomes even more strategic. In Table 3.1, such key trends in purchasing are linked to adjustments being

[3]*Ibid.,* p. 224.

[4]Wesley J. Johnston, "The Industrial Salesforce's Response to a Changing Environment," in Robert E. Spekman and David T. Wilson, eds., *Issues in Industrial Marketing: A View to the Future* (Chicago: American Marketing Association, 1982), pp. 56–68.

[5]Gregory D. Upah and Monroe M. Bird, "Changes in Industrial Buying: Implications for Industrial Marketers," *Industrial Marketing Management* 9 (May 1980), pp. 117–121.

Table 3.1   Changing Directions of Buyer–Seller Relationships

Trend in Purchasing/Procurement	Required Adaptation by Industrial Marketer
Increased status and authority of purchasing managers in the organization	Expand authority of industrial salesperson and utilize more sophisticated selling approaches
Increased use of value analysis procedures by purchasing organizations	Opportunity for creative applications of the same technique as a selling tool (for example, recommending cost-saving changes in the design of a component part)
Consolidation of purchasing, transportation, traffic, inventory control, and other departments into a materials management department	More careful synchronization of selling distribution activities (for example, order processing, inventory control, transportation) to meet customer requirements
Increased popularity and adoption of "kan-ban" (just-in-time) inventory control concept by purchasing managers	Improve logistical performance level (for example, delivery reliability) in order to match the production requirements of customers
Centralization of procurement at the headquarters level to consolidate purchasing power for geographically separated manufacturing facilities	Develop a separate sales force tailored to the special needs and selling requirements of these large national accounts
Increased use of computer technology by purchasing organizations	Increased need for knowledge of cost analysis and how computer technology can be used as a selling tool

made by industrial marketers. These changes highlight the dynamic and challenging nature of exchange relationships in the industrial market.

The Industrial Buying Process

To enhance their effectiveness as a party in the exchange process, industrial salespersons must understand *how* organizational buyers choose between the competing offerings of industrial marketers. Organizational buying behavior can best be understood from a decision process perspective. Here industrial buying is viewed as a *process* rather than as an isolated act or event. Tracing the history of a procurement decision in an organization uncovers critical decision points and evolving information requirements. Richard Cardozo contends that "organizational buying consists of several stages, each of which yields a decision."[6] Likewise, the composition of the decision-making unit can vary from one stage to the next as organizational members enter and leave the procurement process. The following eight-stage model describes the sequence of activities in the organizational buying process.[7]

[6] Richard N. Cardozo, "Modelling Organizational Buying as a Sequence of Decisions," *Industrial Marketing Management* 12 (February 1983), p. 75.

[7] The discussion in this section is based on Patrick J. Robinson, Charles W. Faris, and Yoram Wind, *Industrial Buying and Creative Marketing* (Boston: Allyn and Bacon, Inc., 1967), pp. 12–18.

Stage 1: Anticipation or Recognition of a Problem (Need)

Recognition of a problem or of a potential opportunity triggers the purchasing process: The firm's products become outmoded, equipment breaks down, or existing materials are unsatisfactory. A marketer can precipitate the need for a product by demonstrating opportunities for improving the organization's performance. Early involvement in the buying process provides the marketer with a clear understanding of the organization's needs and information requirements, and, therefore, a greater probability of success in securing the account.

Stage 2. Determination of the Characteristics of the Item and the Quantity Needed

Here, organizational members must determine specifically how the problem can be solved. These decisions generally are made within the using department where the needs invariably emerge. For example, members of the production department would primarily determine the characteristics needed in a high-speed packaging system. For technical products, performance specifications are prepared by the using department.

The development of performance specifications has a critical impact on the final choice of a product and a supplier. The decisions made in the early stages of the decision process inevitably limit and shape the decision making in the later stages of the process.[8]

Stage 3. Description of the Characteristics of the Item and the Quantity Needed

An extension of the second phase, step 3 involves a detailed and precise description of the needed item that can be readily communicated to others. This can be a critical stage for the marketer because key buying influences emerge here. Recognizing these buying influentials and their relative roles and importance can give the marketer a distinct advantage. A marketer who *triggers* the initial need has the benefit of a close working relationship with key organizational members throughout these formative stages in the procurement process.

Stage 4. Search for and Qualification of Potential Sources

Once the organization has defined the product that will satisfy its requirements, the search turns to sources of supply to determine which of the many possible suppliers can be considered potential vendors. The intensity of evaluation varies by organization and the particular buying

[8]Anita M. Kennedy, "The Complex Decision to Select a Supplier: A Case Study," *Industrial Marketing Management* 12 (February 1983), pp. 45–56.

situation. The organization will invest more time and energy in the evaluation process when the proposed product or service will have a strong bearing on organizational performance. (How organizational buyers evaluate potential vendors is treated in more detail later in the chapter.)

Stage 5. Acquisition and Analysis of Proposals

When the information needs of the buying organization are low, stages four and five occur simultaneously, especially when standardized items are under consideration. In this case the buying organization may merely check a catalog or update price information. For more complex goods like machine tools, many months may be consumed in the exchange of proposals and counterproposals. Stage five emerges as a distinct component of the buying process only when the information needs of the buying organization are high.

Stage 6. Evaluation of Proposals and Selection of Suppliers

Alternative proposals are analyzed, one or more of the offers is accepted, and the others are rejected. Negotiations may continue with the selected suppliers concerning the terms of the transaction.

Stage 7. Selection of an Order Routine

A marketer that survives the review process to be selected as a source of supply faces further tests. The using department will not view its problem as resolved until the specified product is available for its use. Concerning the order routine, a purchase order is forwarded to the vendor, status reports are forwarded to the using department, and inventory levels are planned. Thus, in this stage, procurement procedures are established for the item (e.g., the size and frequency of orders).

Stage 8. Performance Feedback and Evaluation

Did the purchased item solve the original problem? This constitutes the final stage in the procurement process. Feedback may flow through formal or informal channels. Feedback critical of the chosen supplier and supportive of rejected alternatives can lead members of the decision-making unit to reexamine their position.[9] If the product fails to meet the needs of the using department, vendors screened earlier in the procurement process may be given further consideration. To retain a new ac-

[9]David R. Lambert, Ronald J. Dornoff, and Jerome B. Kernan, "The Industrial Buyer and the Postchoice Evaluation Process," *Journal of Marketing Research* 14 (May 1977), pp. 246–251.

count, the marketer must insure that the needs of the buying organization have been completely satisfied. Failure to follow through at this critical stage leaves the marketer vulnerable.

Research on industrial purchaser satisfaction uncovered the importance of prompt response to customer complaints.[10] A prompt response that corrects the problem will enhance the probability of securing continuing orders. However, if a follow-up by the purchasing department is required to remedy the problem, the level of satisfaction diminishes even if actual results eventually are the desired results.

Strategy Implications

Some research suggests that the flow of stages in this eight-stage model of the procurement process may not progress sequentially and likely vary with the complexity of the purchasing situation.[11] However, the model provides important insights into the organizational buying process. Certain stages may be completed concurrently; the process may be reoriented at any point by a redefinition of the basic problem; it may be discontinued by a change in the external environment or in upper-management thinking. The organizational buying process is shaped by a host of internal and external forces like changes in economic or competitive conditions or a basic shift in organizational priorities.

Many small or incremental decisions are made during the procurement process that ultimately translate into the final selection of a supplier. For example, a quality control engineer might unknowingly establish specifications for a new production system that only supplier A can meet. This decision early in the buying process will dramatically influence the favorable evaluation and ultimate selection of supplier A.

Richard Cardozo demonstrates that industrial marketers can diagnose problems by examining the sequence of decisions.[12] A product manager for technically complex materials noticed that existing customers were consistently repurchasing the product but the firm had a very low success rate in securing business from the hundreds of prospective buyers who requested quotations and information. Further analysis revealed that the sales force was winning new accounts only where the prospective buyer had not formally established specifications. As a result, inquiries from prospective buyers were screened to identify organizations that were at the initial stages of the procurement process. In turn, the sales force was directed to concentrate on this segment of buyers. New business increased significantly.

---

[10] I. Fredrick Trawick and John E. Swan, "A Model of Industrial Satisfaction/Complaining Behavior," *Industrial Marketing Management* 10 (February 1981), pp. 23–30.

[11] See, for example, Wesley J. Johnston and Robert E. Spekman, "Industrial Buying Behavior: A Need for an Integrative Approach," *Journal of Business Research* 10 (1982), pp. 135–146.

[12] Cardozo, "Modelling Organizational Buying as a Sequence of Decisions," pp. 75–81.

Table 3.2   The Buygrid Framework for Industrial Buying Situations

	Buyclasses		
Buyphases	**New Task**	**Modified Rebuy**	**Straight Rebuy**
1. Anticipation or recognition of a problem (need) and a general solution.			
2. Determination of characteristics and quantity of needed item.			
3. Description of characteristics and quantity of needed item.			
4. Search for and qualification of potential sources.			
5. Acquisition and analysis of proposals.			
6. Evaluation of proposals and selection of supplier(s).			
7. Selection of an order routine.			
8. Performance feedback and evaluation.			

Note: The most complex buying situations occur in the upper left portion of the buygrid framework and involve the largest number of decision makers and buying influences.

Source: From the Marketing Science Institute Series, *Industrial Buying and Creative Marketing*, by Patrick J. Robinson, Charles W. Faris and Yoram Wind. Copyright © 1967 by Allyn and Bacon, Inc., Boston. Reprinted with permission.

Buying Situations Analyzed

The same product may elicit markedly different purchasing patterns in different organizations with different levels of experience and information. Therefore attention must be concentrated on "buying situations" rather than on "products." Three types of buying situations have been delineated: (1) new task, (2) modified rebuy, and (3) straight rebuy.[13] As illustrated in Table 3.2, each type of buying situation must be related to the eight-stage buying process.

New Task

Because in the new-task buying situation the problem or need is perceived by organizational decision makers as totally different from previous experiences, they require a significant amount of information in order to explore alternative ways of solving the problem and search for alternative suppliers.

When confronting a new-task buying situation, organizational buyers operate in a stage of decision making referred to as *extensive problem solving*.[14] The buying influentials and decision makers lack well-defined criteria for comparing alternative products and suppliers, but they also lack strong predispositions toward a particular solution.

[13] Robinson, Faris, and Wind, *Industrial Buying and Creative Marketing*, Chapter 1.

[14] John A. Howard and Jagdish N. Sheth, *The Theory of Buyer Behavior* (New York: John Wiley and Sons, Inc., 1969), Chapter 2.

The Direction of Marketing Effort   The industrial marketer, confronting a new-task buying situation, can gain a differential advantage by participating actively in the initial stages of the procurement process. Here the marketer should gather information on the problems facing the buying organization, isolate specific requirements, and offer proposals to meet the requirements. Ideas that lead to new products often originate not with the marketer but with the customer.[15]

Marketers who are presently supplying other items to the organization ("in" suppliers) have an edge over other firms; they can see problems unfolding and are familiar with the "personality" and behavior patterns of the organization. The successful industrial marketer carefully monitors the changing needs of organizations and is prepared to respond to the needs of new-task buyers.

Straight Rebuy

Where there is a continuing or recurring requirement, buyers have substantial experience in dealing with the need and require little or no new information. Evaluation of new alternative solutions is unnecessary and unlikely to yield appreciable improvements.

Routinized response behavior is the decision process approach organizational buyers employ in the straight rebuy.[16] Here, organizational buyers have well-developed choice criteria to apply to the purchase decision. The criteria have been refined over time as the buyers have developed predispositions toward the offerings of one or a few carefully screened suppliers.

The Direction of Marketing Effort   The purchasing department handles straight rebuy situations by routinely selecting a supplier from a list (formal or informal) of acceptable vendors and placing an order.[17] The marketing task appropriate in this situation depends on whether the marketer is an "in" supplier (on the list) or an "out" supplier (not among the chosen few). An "in" supplier must reinforce the buyer–seller relationship, meet the buying organization's expectations, and be alert and responsive to the changing needs of the organization.

The "out" supplier faces a number of obstacles. The nonsupplier must convince the organization that significant benefits can be derived from breaking the routine. This can be difficult because organizational buyers perceive risk in shifting from the known to the unknown. The organizational spotlight shines directly on them if an untested supplier

---

[15] Eric von Hippel, "Get New Products from Customers," *Harvard Business Review* 60 (March–April, 1982), pp. 117–122; see also, von Hippel, "Successful Industrial Products from Customer Ideas," *Journal of Marketing* 42 (January 1978), pp. 39–49.

[16] Howard and Sheth, *Theory of Buyer Behavior*, Chapter 2.

[17] Richard H. Evans, "Product Involvement and Industrial Buying," *Journal of Purchasing and Materials Management* (Summer 1981), pp. 23–28.

falters. Testing, evaluations, and approvals may be viewed by buyers as costly, time-consuming, and unnecessary.[18]

The marketing effort of the "out" supplier rests on an understanding of the basic buying needs of the organization; information gathering is essential. The marketer must convince organizational buyers that their purchasing requirements have changed or that the requirements should be interpreted differently. The objective is to persuade decision makers to reexamine alternative solutions and revise the preferred list to include the new supplier.

Modified Rebuy

In the modified rebuy situation, organizational decision-makers feel that significant benefits may be derived from a reevaluation of alternatives. The buyers have experience in satisfying the continuing or recurring requirement, but they believe it worthwhile to seek additional information, and perhaps consider alternative solutions.

Several factors may trigger such a reassessment. Internal forces include the search for quality improvements or cost reductions. A marketer offering cost, quality, or service improvements can be an external precipitating force. The modified rebuy situation is most likely to occur when the firm is displeased with the performance of present suppliers (e.g., poor delivery service).

Limited problem solving best describes the decision-making process for the modified rebuy. Decision makers have well-defined criteria, but are uncertain about which suppliers can best fit their needs.[19] For example, hydraulic pumps were purchased as a straight rebuy until an "out" supplier offered a substantially lower price, which stimulated a reevaluation of suppliers. The resulting chain of events is graphically outlined in Figure 3.2.

The Direction of Marketing Effort   In a modified rebuy, the direction of the marketing effort depends on whether the marketer is an "in" or an "out" supplier. An "in" supplier should make every effort to understand and satisfy the procurement need and move decision makers into a straight rebuy. The buying organization perceives potential payoffs from a reexamination of alternatives. The "in" supplier should ask why, and act immediately to remedy any customer problems. The marketer may be out of touch with the buying organization's requirements.

The goal of the "out" supplier should be to hold the organization in modified rebuy status long enough for the buyer to evaluate an alternative offering. Knowing the factors that led decision makers to reexamine alternatives could be pivotal.

---

[18] Robinson, Faris, and Wind, *Industrial Buying and Creative Marketing*, pp. 201–204.

[19] Howard and Sheth, *Theory of Buyer Behavior*, Chapter 2.

Figure 3.2   Example of a Modified Rebuy: Hydraulic Pump

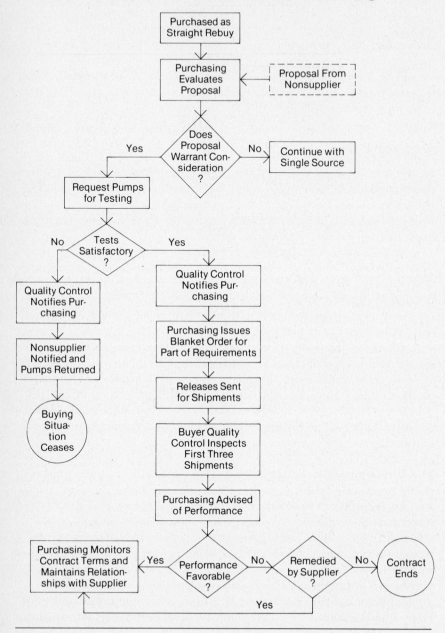

Hydraulic pumps were purchased as routine rebuys until an "out" supplier offered a substantially lower price which stimulated a reconsideration of sources. The resulting chain of events in the purchasing process is graphically outlined above.

Source: From the Marketing Science Institute Series, Patrick J. Robinson, Charles W. Faris, and Yoram Wind, *Industrial Buying and Creative Marketing*, p. 75. Copyright © 1967 by Allyn and Bacon, Inc., Boston. Reprinted by permission.

Table 3.3   Responding to Different Buying Situations: A Profile of Required Marketing Strategies

Buying Situation	Supplier Status	
	In Supplier	Out Supplier
New Task	Monitor changing or emerging purchasing needs in organization.	
	Isolate specific needs.	Isolate specific needs.
	If possible, participate actively in early phases of buying process by supplying information and technical advice.	If possible, participate actively in early phases of buying process by supplying information and technical advice.
Straight Rebuy	Reinforce buyer–seller relationship by meeting organization's expectations.	Convince organization that the potential benefits of reexamining requirements and suppliers exceed the costs.
	Be alert and responsive to changing needs of customer.	Attempt to gain a position on organization's preferred list of suppliers even as a second or third choice.
Modified Rebuy	Act immediately to remedy problems with customer.	Define and respond to the organization's problem with existing supplier.
	Reexamine and respond to customer needs.	Encourage organization to sample alternative offerings.

Source: From the Marketing Science Institute Series. Patrick J. Robinson, Charles W. Faris, and Yoram Wind, *Industrial Buying and Creative Marketing* (Boston: Allyn and Bacon, Inc., 1967), pp. 183–210.

Each buying situation requires a unique industrial marketing response. Strategies appropriate for each of the three buying situations are summarized in Table 3.3.

Buying Influentials and the Purchasing Task

Buying decisions typically involve not one but several members of the organization, whether the decisions are made by commercial enterprises, institutions, or governmental organizations. Thus, the relevant unit of analysis for the industrial marketer is the group decision-making unit or the buying center. The *buying center* includes all those individuals and groups that participate in purchasing decision making and share goals and risks arising from the decision.[20] The composition and the relative importance of individual members in the buying center change rapidly as a firm moves from phase to phase in the decision process.

[20] Frederick E. Webster, Jr., and Yoram Wind, *Organizational Buying Behavior* (Englewood Cliffs, N.J.: Prentice-Hall, Inc., 1972), p. 6; see also, Thomas V. Bonoma, "Major Sales: Who Really Does the Buying?" *Harvard Business Review* 60 (May–June 1982), pp. 111–119.

Locating Buying Influentials   Buyers have differing levels of experience and follow different problem-solving approaches as they move along the learning curve from extended to routine problem solving. To illustrate, the decision to purchase a lathe may be a new-task buying situation in one organization and a modified or straight rebuy in another.

Some research suggests that the number of participants in the buying center is smaller for firms in a straight rebuy situation.[21] Here the purchasing staff, following relatively routine procedures, handles the transaction. By contrast, new-task buying situations typically involve more participants in various stages of the purchasing process, sometimes including top management. Of course, top management will be more involved "where the results of the purchasing decision could substantially reduce the company's flexibility or ability to act in the future."[22] (For example, the addition of new fixed facilities for selected products may limit the firm's ability to respond to changing market conditions for other products.)

Strategy Implications   While past research provides some useful guidelines, great care must be exercised in forecasting the likely composition of the buying center for a particular purchasing situation.[23] The industrial marketer should attempt to identify purchasing patterns that apply to the firm.[24] To illustrate, the classes of industrial goods introduced in Chapter 1 (e.g., foundation goods versus facilitating goods) involve varying degrees of technical complexity and financial risk for the buying organization.

The industrial marketer, therefore, must look at the procurement problem or need as the buying organization does. How far has the organization progressed with the specific purchasing problem? How does the organization define the task at hand? The answers will direct and form the industrial marketer's response and also provide insight into the composition of the decision-making unit. Again, each type of buying situation could represent a different market segment that requires a specialized marketing strategy. Xerox, for example, deploys some sales teams that concentrate on servicing and penetrating existing customers, and others that specialize in obtaining new customers.[25]

To this point, the discussion has centered on three areas that provide a foundation for understanding organizational buying behavior:

---

[21] See, for example, Kennedy, "The Complex Decision to Select a Supplier: A Case Study," pp. 45–56; P. Doyle, A. G. Woodside, and P. Michell, "Organizational Buying in New Task and Rebuy Situations," *Industrial Marketing Management* 8 (1979), pp. 7–11; and Gordon T. Brand, *The Industrial Buying Decision* (London: Institute of Marketing and Industrial Market Research Ltd., 1972).

[22] Robinson, Faris, and Wind, *Industrial Buying and Creative Marketing*, p. 135.

[23] Joseph A. Bellizzi and Phillip McVey, "How Valid Is the Buy-Grid Model?" *Industrial Marketing Management* 12 (February 1983), pp. 57–62.

[24] Rowland T. Moriarty and Morton Galper, *Organizational Buying Behavior: A State-of-the-Art Review and Conceptualization* (Cambridge: Marketing Science Institute, 1978).

[25] Rowland T. Moriarty, *Industrial Buying Behavior* (Lexington, Mass.: Lexington Books, 1983).

(1) the buyer–seller exchange process; (2) the multi-stage procurement process; and (3) the classification of buying situations. A fourth factor is the buying motives of organizational buyers.

Buying Motivations of Organizational Buyers

The fate of the industrial marketer is determined by an organization's evaluation of potential suppliers. Suppliers screened out during the evaluation process may find it difficult to again get the buying firm's attention. The industrial marketer must understand how organizational buyers evaluate potential suppliers.

Organizational members are influenced by both rational and emotional factors in choosing among competing offerings. Rational motives are usually economic, like price, quality, and service; emotional motives are concerned with such human factors as job security or organizational status. The industrial marketer has to define the buying motives of the organizational members who will ultimately pass judgment on a product. This is particularly difficult because generalizations about the importance of selected buying motives cannot be made across all types of industrial buying decisions. Members of the buying center often use different criteria in evaluating suppliers.[26] For example, the purchasing agent may value maximum price economy, but engineers are primarily concerned with product quality. Also, the importance of the criteria varies with the product.[27]

The challenge for the marketer is to view the purchasing decision from the buying organization's perspective, to ascertain the roles of various members of the buying center, and to determine what motivates each member.

Rational Motives

Since commercial enterprises have profit objectives, and governmental units and not-for-profit organizations have budgetary constraints, rational or economic buying motives are significant.

Price   The professional buyer evaluates a quoted price from many perspectives. A buyer considering a new piece of capital equipment will analyze potential savings (return) in manpower, energy, and material and

---

[26] For example, see Jagdish N. Sheth, "A Model of Industrial Buyer Behavior," *Journal of Marketing* 37 (October 1973), pp. 50–56; see also J. Patrick Kelly and James W. Coaker, "Can We Generalize about Choice Criteria for Industrial Purchasing Decisions?" in Kenneth L. Bernhardt, ed., *Marketing: 1776–1976 and Beyond* (Chicago: American Marketing Association, 1976), pp. 330–333.

[27] Donald R. Lehmann and John O'Shaughnessy, "Difference in Attribute Importance for Different Industrial Products," *Journal of Marketing* 40 (April 1976), pp. 36–42; see also, Lehmann and O'Shaughnessy, "Decision Criteria Used in Buying Different Categories of Products," *Journal of Purchasing and Materials Management* 18 (Spring 1982), pp. 9–14.

relate these factors to the price (investment). Thus, a return on investment (ROI) calculation would be used to compare the offerings of competing equipment firms. In the case of a component part, the buyer might consider price in relation to ease of installation. A higher-priced component that was easier and less costly to install would have an edge over a less expensive model that posed cumbersome installation problems. Marketers often overestimate the importance of offering the lowest price. Frequently, the low bidder fails other tests.[28]

Quality   Organizational buyers do not want to pay for more quality than they need; at the same time, they are unwilling to compromise specifications for a reduced price. Uniformity or consistency of product quality is often the crucial factor. Such consistency can: (1) guarantee uniformity in the end product, (2) reduce the need for costly inspections of each incoming shipment, and (3) insure that the purchased material will mesh smoothly with the production process. Poor consistency in the quality of materials and components creates costly problems for the buying organization.

Service   All sectors of the industrial market (commercial enterprises, government, and institutions) require a broad range of services including technical assistance, information, delivery, repair capability, spare parts availability, and even financing. Service can be an important means of differentiation for the marketer. A marketer offering sound technical advice, reliable and speedy delivery, and an available supply of replacement parts may have an edge over competing suppliers. The buying organization must make a larger investment in inventory if the supplier's delivery is slow or unpredictable.

     The importance of physical distribution service to organizational buyers is vividly illustrated by William Perreault and Frederick Russ.[29] Their survey of industrial purchasing managers reveals that physical distribution service ranks second only to product quality in influencing industrial purchase decisions.

Continuity of Supply   Continuity of supply can be a critical concern of the purchasing manager. Any interruption in the flow of key materials or components can bring the production process to an abrupt halt, resulting in costly delays and lost sales. To guard against contingencies like an unanticipated strike in a supplier's plant, professional buyers are extremely reluctant to rely on a single source of supply; they choose to spread their business among two or more suppliers whenever possible. Continuity of supply is important not only during periods of shortages,

[28] Kelly and Coaker, "Can We Generalize about Choice Criteria?" pp. 330–333.

[29] William D. Perreault, Jr., and Frederick A. Russ, "Physical Distribution Service in Industrial Purchase Decisions," *Journal of Marketing* 40 (April 1976), pp. 3–10.

but also during times of plenty when shortages are anticipated. Concern with continuity of supply is greatest when the number of alternative suppliers is limited.[30]

Reciprocity   Because buyers and sellers often have close relationships in the industrial market, reciprocal trade possibilities emerge: "If you buy from me, I'll buy from you." The motivation for buying from each other is the key to whether an arrangement involves reciprocity: A relationship involves reciprocity when the *buyer–seller arrangement*, rather than economic or performance factors, influences the purchase decision.

Reciprocal trade relations can be based on friendly or highly coercive pressure: "If you don't buy X percent more from me, I'll reduce my purchases from you by Y percent!" Reciprocity is legal as long as the arrangement is not enforced through coercive power by one or more parties, and if the reciprocal agreement does not substantially lessen competition. One authority contends that anticompetitive and coercive reciprocity have been successfully checked by the government in recent years, but that friendship reciprocity continues to be a force in the industrial market.[31]

A new twist in buyer–seller relationships, *reverse reciprocity*, is also becoming more prevalent in the industrial market.[32] Operative during periods of resource shortages, reverse reciprocity involves buyers agreeing to sell one set of scarce resources to sellers in return for sellers agreeing to sell a different set of scarce resources to buyers. More simply: "If you'll sell to me, I'll sell to you."

Emotional Motives

A marketer concentrating exclusively on rational motives has an incomplete picture of the organizational buyer. Individuals, not organizations, make buying decisions.

Status and Rewards   Emotional motives include desires for status within the organization, promotion, salary increases, and increased job security. The industrial salesperson must understand the reward system of the organization and the projects or problems that have priority in the organization. Many firms periodically launch procurement projects geared to achieving significant cost savings during a 12-month period. In this environment, purchasing managers are particularly receptive to proposals from new or existing suppliers.

---

[30] Thomas V. Bonoma and Gerald Zaltman, "Introduction," in Bonoma and Zaltman, eds., *Organizational Buying Behavior* (Chicago: American Marketing Association, 1978), p. 8.

[31] F. Robert Finney, "Reciprocity: Gone but Not Forgotten," *Journal of Marketing* 43 (January 1978), pp. 54–59; see also, Reed Moyer, "Reciprocity: Retrospect and Prospect," *Journal of Marketing* 34 (October 1970), pp. 47–54.

[32] Upah and Bird, "Changes in Industrial Buying," pp. 117–121.

The Human Side of Buying . . . and Selling!

A producer of sophisticated graphics computers was having only limited success with large potential customers. Rather than following the industry practice of quoting high list prices and giving generous discounts for quantity purchases during negotiations with buyers, this firm priced their products 10–15 percent lower than competitors and gave smaller quantity discounts. While offering the lowest net price in the industry, buyers resisted. Why? Purchasing agents evaluated themselves and were evaluated by their superiors more on the basis of price concessions made during the negotiation process than on the net price actually paid.

Source: Thomas V. Bonoma, "Major Sales: Who Really Does the Buying," *Harvard Business Review*, 60 (May–June 1982), p. 111.

Perceived Risk   H. Lazo makes the provocative observation that "fear is one of the major influences in industrial buying. Fear of displeasing the boss. Fear of making a wrong decision . . . fear of losing status. Fear, indeed, in extreme cases, of losing one's job." [33] The marketer must ask how each buyer perceives and handles risk. [34] What happens if the product does not perform satisfactorily (functional risk), or if others in the organization view the decision negatively (psychological risk)? The perceived risk concept has two components: (1) *uncertainty* concerning the outcome of a decision and (2) the magnitude of the *consequences* associated with making the wrong choice.

The buyer will often reduce the level of risk by relying on familiar suppliers or by favoring suppliers with the best reputation. [35] Alternatively, an organizational buyer might reduce uncertainty by visiting the supplier's plant, or reduce the chances of unfavorable consequences by consulting top management before making the decision. [36]

[33] H. Lazo, "Emotional Aspects of Industrial Buying," in R. S. Hancock, ed., *Proceedings of the American Marketing Association* (Chicago: American Marketing Association, 1960), p. 265.

[34] Raymond A. Bauer, "Consumer Behavior as Risk Taking," in Hancock, ed., *Proceedings of the American Marketing Association, ibid.*, pp. 389–400; see also, James R. McMillan, *The Role of Perceived Risk in Vendor Selection Decisions*, unpublished Ph.D. dissertation (Columbus: The Ohio State University, 1972).

[35] Webster and Wind, *Organizational Buying Behavior*, p. 96.

[36] Timothy W. Sweeney, H. Lee Mathews, and David T. Wilson, "An Analysis of Industrial Buyers' Risk Reducing Behavior: Some Personality Correlates," *American Marketing Association Proceedings* (Chicago: American Marketing Association, 1973), pp. 217–221.

Friendship   Emotional motives often influence buying decisions in subtle ways. A purchasing manager may be known to select suppliers on the basis of competitive bids, but may work diligently with a friend "to get him competitive" on price level and product specifications.[37]

Emotional motives cannot be overlooked. An understanding of the buying motives (rational and nonrational) of the members of the buying center is vital in designing responsive marketing strategy.

How Organizational Buyers Evaluate Potential Suppliers

The rational and emotional buying motives of individual organizational buyers are ultimately reflected in the formal evaluation of suppliers. The buyer's knowledge of the suppliers, coupled with the organization's perception of the value and importance of the purchase, determine the problem-solving approach.

One of the most important developments in organizational purchasing is the application of computer technology to the procurement function. Declining costs have placed computerization within the reach of nearly all organizations—large and small. With a computer, purchasing units are better equipped to evaluate existing and potential suppliers.

The Computerized Purchasing Function

The objective of a computer-based purchasing system is to improve the quality of managerial purchasing decisions by improving the decision maker's ability to handle and process information.[38] The basic components of an automated purchasing system are sketched in Figure 3.3. Essentially, the computer system expands the memory of the buying organization by storing data that may be retrieved and profitably applied to future purchasing decisions. This includes:[39]

1. vendor price and address files;

2. purchase history data;

3. purchase usage data;

4. receiving and invoicing information; and

5. inventory control data.

---

[37] Bonoma and Zaltman, *Organizational Buying Behavior*, pp. 3–4.

[38] For example, see D. Larry Moore and Harold E. Fearon, "Computer Assisted Decision Making in Purchasing," *Journal of Purchasing* 9 (November 1973), pp. 5–25.

[39] Michael J. Timbers, "Status of Computer Development Activity in Purchasing," *Journal of Purchasing* 6 (November 1970), pp. 45–64.

Figure 3.3   Simplified Flow Chart of an Automated Purchasing System

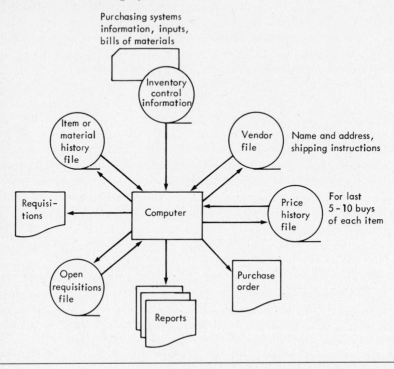

Source: Reprinted by permission from *Purchasing and Materials Management*, Seventh Ed., by Michael R. Leenders, Harold E. Fearon and Wilbur B. England, p. 85. Copyright © 1980 by Richard D. Irwin, Inc., Homewood, Illinois.

Although such information helps improve purchasing efficiency and performance, experts predict significant advancements in computer applications to purchasing. Once considered a luxury, computer assistance is now a necessity for a manufacturing firm producing complex products containing a significant amount of purchased material. The number of buying organizations employing electronic data processing in purchasing is expected to continue to increase.[40] What impact does computerization have on the purchasing function? Researchers have uncovered some interesting answers.[41]

First, the computer system is especially useful in highly repetitive buying tasks (straight rebuys). Routine purchases can be handled faster and more economically by the computer than by the purchasing staff. A computer program can be written to simplify inventory management

[40] Michael R. Leenders, Harold E. Fearon, and Wilbur B. England, *Purchasing and Materials Management*, 7th ed., (Homewood, Ill.: Richard D. Irwin, Inc., 1980), pp. 83–89.

[41] David T. Wilson and H. Lee Mathews, "Impact of Management Information Systems upon Purchasing Decision-Making," *Journal of Purchasing* 7 (February 1971), pp. 48–56.

and the automatic reordering of selected items. The marketer of standardized products will frequently confront computer-assisted buyers; researchers project, however, that the computerization of new-task buying situations is unlikely in the near future.

Second, computerized decision-making capability gives the purchasing agent time for a more thorough evaluation of possible vendors in more complex buying situations. Likewise, the purchasing agent can devote more time to direct negotiation with potential suppliers and assume an expanded role in interdepartmental activities in the organization. Often, these new roles of the purchasing agent lead to an upgrading of the purchasing function.

Third, the introduction of the computer into purchasing influences vendor selection. The computer-assisted buyer engages in a more intensive search for potential suppliers but concentrates orders with fewer vendors.[42] Thus, the addition of the computer to the purchasing function leads to a reduction in the number of suppliers utilized by the buying organization.

Marketing Strategy: Reaching the Computer-Assisted Buyer   The industrial marketer must be prepared to match wits with the computer-assisted buyer. As the buying organization expands its ability to store, retrieve, and analyze significant data on alternative suppliers, changes are necessary in selling strategies. Since the computer is employed predominantly for repetitive buying tasks, marketers of supplies and maintenance items should attempt to build long-term contractual relationships with buyers.[43] *Blanket ordering* might be encouraged by offering fast and reliable delivery service or lower prices for a range of selected items. Blanket ordering simplifies inventory control for the buyer, allows the marketer to strengthen customer loyalty, and achieves economies of scale for both. Blanket ordering also increases the likelihood that a buying organization will remain with a single supplier.[44] Buying organizations frequently prefer annual vendor contracts and review the vendor list at the end of each contract period.[45]

Evaluating Supplier Capability

A buying organization facing an important purchasing decision must carefully analyze the total capability of suppliers. Observe from Table 3.4 that this assessment covers technical, managerial, financial, and ser-

[42] H. Lee Mathews, David T. Wilson, and Klaus Backhaus, "Selling to the Computer Assisted Buyer," *Industrial Marketing Management* 6, No. 4 (1977), pp. 307–315.

[43] *Ibid.*, pp. 307–315.

[44] Leonard Groeneveld, "The Implications of Blanket Contracting for Industrial Purchasing and Marketing," *Journal of Purchasing* 8 (November 1972), pp. 51–58.

[45] H. Lee Mathews and David T. Wilson, "Industrial Marketing's New Challenge: A Computerized Buyer," Working Series in Marketing Research, Pennsylvania State University, No. 9 (October 1970), reported in Mathews, Wilson, and Backhaus, "Selling to the Computer Assisted Buyer," p. 309.

Table 3.4   Supplier Capability: Key Attributes Evaluated by Buyers

Attribute	Measure
Technical/Production Capability	Adequacy of equipment, production control, quality control, cost control.
Managerial Capability	The ability of supplier to plan, organize, and control operations.
Financial Condition	The financial stability of the supplier—profit record, cash flow, equity, working capital, credit rating.
Service Capacity	Supplier's ability to comply with promised product specifications, delivery dates, and technical assistance.

vice capabilities. Each provides a measure of ability to comply with promises made to the buying organization.

After the list of potential suppliers has been screened and narrowed, the buying organization generally conducts an on-site inspection of vendor facilities by representatives from purchasing, engineering, and, on occasion, production and finance. The trained observer can quickly appraise the production capability of a supplier: Is the equipment up-to-date? Are scheduling and production control properly organized to allow promised delivery dates to be met?

Buyers also evaluate the financial condition of potential suppliers. A solid financial position usually points to a well-managed operation. Financial stability is critical to continuity of supply and uniformity of product quality. A buyer consults such sources as Dun and Bradstreet (D&B) Reports, Moody's Industrials, or corporate annual reports in assessing the financial condition of a supplier.

The exact meaning of the term *service* varies with the nature of the product and the requirements of the buying organization. Service may encompass reliable delivery, technical assistance, innovative suggestions, credit arrangements, rapid support for special needs, and advance notice of impending price changes or shortages of supply. The marketer with strong service capabilities will be in a favorable position.

Evaluating Supplier Performance

Once a contract is awarded to a supplier, the evaluation process takes a different form. Actual performance must be evaluated. Buyers rate supplier performance in assessing the quality of past decisions, in making future vendor selections—and as a negotiating tool to gain leverage in buyer–seller relationships.[46] The National Association of Purchasing Management has examined the area of supplier evaluation in some

[46]David Bonneville, "Vendor Analysis Packs a Punch in Negotiations," *Purchasing World* 27 (March 1983), pp. 32–34.

depth.[47] The specific method and the scope of the rating system vary by industry and firm.[48] Three are briefly described below.[49]

Categorical Plan   Under this plan, supplier performance is evaluated by several departments that maintain informal records on each major vendor, perhaps including purchasing, engineering, quality control, receiving, and inspection. For every major supplier, each individual develops a list of significant performance factors. At a regularly scheduled meeting (usually monthly), each major supplier is tested against each set of criteria and given an overall group evaluation. Suppliers are then categorized as "preferred," "neutral," or "unsatisfactory." Ease of administration is the chief advantage of this highly subjective method.

Buyers Rate Salespersons: Likes and Dislikes

A sample of 300 purchasing managers was asked to identify the characteristics of outstanding and least desirable salespersons.

The characteristics attributed to the *outstanding* salesperson were:

- thoroughness and follow-through
- complete product knowledge
- willingness to pursue the best interests of the buyer within the supplier firm
- sound market knowledge and willingness to keep the buyer informed

Among the characteristics that can alienate buyers are:

- hard-selling, high-pressure tactics
- talking too long about unrelated matters
- exhibiting little interest in meeting the buyer's "real needs"

Source: Survey conducted by *Purchasing* magazine and reported in Larry Giunipero and Gary Zenz, "Impact of Purchasing Trends on Industrial Marketers," *Industrial Marketing Management*, 11 (February 1982), pp. 17–23.

---

[47] For example, see Douglas V. Smith, B. G. Lowe, D. H. Lyons, and William H. Old, *Evaluation of Supplier Performance* (New York: National Association of Purchasing Agents, 1963).

[48] C. David Wieters, "Influence in the Design and Use of Vendor Performance Ratings," *Journal of Purchasing and Materials Management* (Winter 1976), pp. 31–35; see also, Wieters, "The Design and Use of Supplier Performance Rating Systems in Selected Industries," unpublished D.B.A. dissertation (Arizona State University, 1976).

[49] Lamar Lee, Jr. and Donald W. Dobler, *Purchasing and Materials Management*, 3rd ed, (New York: McGraw-Hill, 1977), pp. 86–88.

The Weighted-Point Plan   Here the buying organization weights each performance factor according to its relative importance. Quality might be given a weight of 40, service 30, and price 30. This system alerts the industrial marketer to the nature and importance of the evaluative criteria used by a particular organization. The marketer's total offering can then be adjusted to more precisely fit the organization's needs.

One consumer products manufacturer "grades" suppliers on three criteria that are assigned the following weights:

- Delivery   40
- Quality   30
- Buyer Evaluation   30

A performance score is developed for each factor and the three factor scores are totaled to give the supplier's overall rating. For example, the performance score for quality is determined as follows:

Factor weight × Percentage of material received that passes inspection.

If 10 percent of supplier X's goods failed inspection, the quality performance score would be:

Factor	Weight	Actual Performance	Performance Score
Quality	30	10 percent rejects	$30 \times (1.00 - .10) = 27.0$

Performance measures and scores are developed for *delivery* and *buyer evaluation* and summed to give supplier X's overall evaluation. The performance of competing suppliers can then be compared quantitatively. The weighted-point plan is more objective and flexible than the categorical method. The buying organization can adjust the weights of various performance factors to meet particular needs. Likewise, the method forces the organizational buyer to define the key attributes of a supplier.

Some industrial customers send a regular report card to each of their suppliers. Such feedback reports can isolate supplier problems, stimulate improved performance, and strengthen buyer–seller relationships.

Cost-Ratio Plan   This method draws upon standard cost analysis. Under this plan, the buying organization evaluates quality, delivery, and service, assigning a minus (−) weight for favorable performance on a factor and a plus (+) weight for unfavorable performance. (That's right—a minus for good performance, a plus for bad performance. You will soon see why.) The weights for each performance factor are derived from standard cost calculations. For the delivery rating, the standard cost base might include the expense of factory downtime and rescheduling caused by a delinquent shipment as well as telephone follow-ups and associated costs. A penalty rating of +.02 might be assigned for a shipment received one week late and +.05 for a shipment delayed three weeks. Similar weights, based on standard costs, are made for quality and service and then combined into one final composite rating for each supplier. This composite rating is used to calculate an "adjusted price" for each major supplier. Supplier X will be evaluated using this approach.

An illustration   Assume that supplier X bids $80.00 and has a quality cost ratio of +1 percent, a delivery cost ratio of +5 percent, and a service cost ratio of −1 percent. The three cost ratios sum to +5 percent. Thus, the adjusted price for supplier X is $80.00 + (.05 × 80.00) = $84.00. The organizational buyer would select the vendor offering the most economical total package rather than the supplier with the lowest bid price. Poor delivery performance clearly damaged the position of supplier X. A competing supplier offering solid delivery performance and competitive quality and service would be selected even at a slightly higher bid price.

A computerized cost accounting system is needed to provide the cost estimates that form the core of the cost-ratio plan. While the method has generated widespread interest, many firms find the weighted-point plan simpler and more flexible. The quality of each method—categorical, weighted-point, and cost-ratio—depends on the accuracy and appropriateness of the underlying assumptions of the evaluator.

Vendor Analysis: Implications for the Marketer

Industrial marketers must be sensitive to the evaluation criteria of organizational buyers and to how these criteria are weighted. Many criteria may be factored into a buyer's ultimate decision: quality, service, price, company image, capability. Buyers' perceptions are also critical. When products are perceived as highly standardized, price assumes more importance. On the other hand, if products are perceived as unique, other criteria may dominate. The price of a product cannot be separated from the attached bundle of services and other intangible values.

Economic criteria assume significant importance in many industrial buying decisions,[50] especially the anticipated costs associated with buying, storing, and using the product. By contrast, product performance criteria evaluate the extent to which the product is likely to maximize performance. Economic criteria are important in the purchase of standard products of simple construction with standard applications. Performance criteria are more important in the evaluation of complex products or novel applications. By defining the type of vendor evaluation system used by existing or potential customers, the industrial marketer is better equipped to profitably satisfy their needs.

The marketer who secures a new account must be prepared to pass frequent performance tests. As purchasing departments increase their

[50] Lehmann and O'Shaughnessy, "Decision Criteria Used in Buying Different Categories of Products," pp. 9–14.

use of computers, purchasing becomes more centralized, the number of suppliers declines, and the performance of suppliers is subjected to increased quantitative scrutiny.[51]

Summary

Valuable insights into industrial marketing management can be secured by examining buyer–seller relationships from an exchange process perspective. Knowledge of the process that organizational buyers follow in making purchasing decisions is fundamental to responsive marketing strategy. As a buying organization moves from the problem recognition phase, where a procurement need is defined, to later phases, where suppliers are screened and ultimately chosen, the marketer can play an active role. In fact, the astute marketer often triggers initial awareness of the problem and aids the organization in effectively solving that problem. Incremental decisions made throughout the buying process narrow the field of acceptable suppliers and dramatically influence the ultimate outcome.

The nature of the buying process depends upon the organization's level of experience with similar procurement problems. It is thus crucial to know how the organization defines the buying situation: new task, modified rebuy, straight rebuy. Each buying situation requires a different problem-solving approach, involves different buying influentials, and demands a different marketing response.

Organizational buyers apply a wide range of rational and emotional buying motives to the purchasing decision process. After the decision is made, the buying organization monitors vendor performance often through the use of a formal rating system. Such systems key on supplier attributes that are important to the buying organization, such as quality, service, delivery, and price. Specific vendor rating systems range from the easily administered categorical plan to the complex cost-ratio method. Many firms have devised their own weighted-point plans. Vendor rating systems define the requirements that the industrial marketer must meet. Computer technology has markedly improved the ability of organizations to evaluate supplier performance.

Discussion Questions

1. The nature of industrial marketing is captured by examining buyer–seller interactions. Drawing upon the dyadic exchange model of industrial marketing, outline the flows of influence and information

---

[51] David T. Wilson and H. Lee Mathews, "Impact of Management Information Systems upon Purchasing Decision-Making," pp. 48–56, reported in Thomas V. Bonoma, Gerald Zaltman, and Wesley J. Johnston, *Industrial Buying Behavior* (Cambridge, Mass.: Marketing Science Institute, 1977), p. 114.

that are exchanged in buyer–seller relationships in the industrial market.

2. "Changes in the organizational buying environment trigger corresponding adjustments in the selling environment." Evaluate this statement.

3. What strategic advantage does the marketer gain by interfacing with the buying organization at the early rather than the late stages of the purchase decision process?

4. Jim Jackson, an industrial salesperson for Pittsburgh Machine Tool, will call on two accounts this afternoon. The first call will be on a buying organization that Jim has been servicing for the past three years. The second call, however, poses more of a challenge. This buying organization has been dealing with a prime competitor of Pittsburgh Machine Tool for five years. Jim, who has a good rapport with the purchasing and engineering departments, feels that the time may be right to penetrate this account. Recently, Jim learned that the purchasing manager was extremely unhappy with the poor delivery service provided by the firm's existing supplier. Define the buying situations confronting Jim, and outline the appropriate strategy that he should follow in each case.

5. Compare and contrast the weighted-point plan and the cost-ratio plan as used by organizational buyers in evaluating alternative suppliers.

6. Organizational buying decisions can be classified as new-task, modified rebuy, or straight rebuy. Each elicits a different problem-solving approach and involves different buying influentials. Explain.

7. Describe how the industrial marketer can profit by understanding the vendor rating system that a particular buying organization employs.

8. Assume that your career path takes you into purchasing rather than marketing. You are assigned the responsibility for purchasing an important component part of your firm's final consumer product—calculators. Describe the criteria that you would apply in evaluating the offerings of different industrial suppliers.

9. Mike Weber, the purchasing agent for Smith Manufacturing, views the purchase of widgets as a routine buying decision. What factors might lead him to alter this position? More importantly, what factors will determine whether a particular supplier, such as Albany Widget, will be considered by Mike?

10. How does the introduction of the computer into purchasing influence the vendor selection decisions of buying organizations?

C·H·A·P·T·E·R
4

Organizational Buying Behavior

The organizational buyer is influenced by a wide array of forces inside and outside the organization. Knowledge of these forces provides the marketer with a foundation on which to build responsive industrial marketing strategies. After reading this chapter, you will have an understanding of:

1. *the individual, group, organizational, and environmental variables that influence organizational buying decisions;*
2. *a model of organizational buying behavior that integrates these important influences;*
3. *how a knowledge of organizational buying characteristics allows the marketer to make more informed product design, pricing, and promotional decisions.*

Many questions must be addressed before industrial marketing strategy can be developed: What factors influence the purchasing plans of an organization? How and why do organizations, as well as individual organizational members, differ in their approach to buying? Why are some buying decisions made by a group, others by an individual? These issues strike at the core of organizational buying behavior. Understanding the dynamics of organizational buyer behavior is crucial to identifying profitable segments of the organizational market, locating buying influences within these segments, and reaching these organizational buyers efficiently and effectively with an offering that responds to their needs.

Each decision that the industrial marketer makes is based on a probable response of organizational buyers. A marketer who is sensitive to the forces that shape organizational buying decisions is best equipped to make sound decisions about product, price, distribution, and promotional strategy.

The last chapter provided a framework for analyzing buyer–seller exchange relationships, an eight-stage model of the buying process and a discussion of the salient characteristics of different purchasing situations. This chapter builds on that foundation to examine the myriad forces that influence organizational buyer behavior (Figure 4.1). These forces include environmental factors (e.g., health of the economy); organizational factors (e.g., size of buying organization); group factors (e.g., composition and roles of members); and individual factors (e.g., personal preferences).[1] Each of these areas constitutes a sphere of influence that encircles organizational buying decisions.

Environmental Forces

Organizational buyers do not make decisions in isolation; they are influenced by a broad range of forces in the external environment. A projected change in business conditions, a technological development, or a new piece of legislation can drastically alter organizational buying plans. Collectively, such environmental influences define the boundaries within which industrial buyers and sellers interact.

Types of Environmental Forces

Six types of environmental forces influence organizational buying behavior: economic, political, legal, cultural, physical, and technological.[2]

Economic Influences The general condition of the economy is reflected in economic growth, employment, price stability, income, and the

---

[1] Frederick E. Webster, Jr. and Yoram Wind, *Organizational Buying Behavior* (Englewood Cliffs, N.J.: Prentice-Hall, Inc., 1972), pp. 28–37.

[2] *Ibid.*, pp. 40–46.

Figure 4.1   Forces Influencing Organizational Buying Behavior

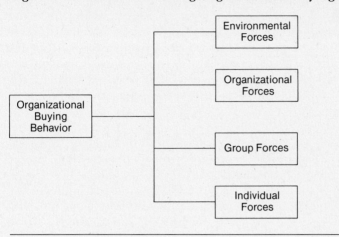

availability of resources, money, and credit. Because of the derived nature of industrial demand, the marketer must also be sensitive to the strength of demand in the ultimate consumer market. The demand for many industrial products fluctuates more widely than the general economy.

The economic environment influences an organization's ability and to a degree its willingness to buy. However, shifts in general economic conditions do not fall evenly on all sectors of the market. For example, a rise in interest rates may damage the housing industry (e.g., lumber, cement, insulation) but may have minimal effects on industries such as paper, hospital supplies, office products, and soft drinks. Marketers that serve broad sectors of the organizational market must be particularly sensitive to the differential impact of selective economic shifts on buying behavior. Compared to for-profit organizations, not-for-profit organizations are more likely to justify a purchase simply because funds were allocated for a particular item in their budget.[3] The rationale is that if the funds are not spent this fiscal year, the budget will be cut next year.

Political and Legal Influences   The political environment includes tariffs and trade agreements with other countries, government funding of selected programs (discussed in Chapter 2), and government attitudes toward business and social service activities. The legal environment in-

---

[3] Thomas V. Bonoma and Gerald Zaltman, "Introduction," in Bonoma and Zaltman, eds., *Organizational Buying Behavior* (Chicago: American Marketing Association, 1978), p. 23; see also, Kjell Gronhaug, "Exploring Environmental Influences in Organizational Buying," *Journal of Marketing Research*, 13 (August 1976), pp. 225–230.

cludes forces at the federal, state, and local levels that specify the boundaries of the buyer–seller relationship.[4]

The impact of governmental influences is illustrated by the results of the federal fuel-economy decision that 1985 model cars must average 27.5 miles per gallon. To achieve this goal, virtually every part of the automobile had to be redesigned. This in turn increased demand for machine tools, aluminum, lighter-weight steel, plastic, and related materials. The amount of aluminum alone in the average car could triple by the late 1980s.[5]

Culture   Culture can be thought of as methods of coping with the environment that are shared by people as members of society and passed on from one generation to another. "Culture as reflected in values, mores, customs, habits, norms, traditions and so on will influence the structure and functioning of the organization and the way members of the organization feel and act toward one another and various aspects of the environment."[6]

Physical Influences   The physical environment includes such factors as climate and geographical location of the organization. The availability of labor, selected raw materials, and transportation services often determine the initial selection of a location by an organization. In turn, nearby suppliers often have an advantage in the vendor selection process, particularly when procurement requirements necessitate a close buyer–seller relationship.[7]

Technological Influences   Rapidly changing technology can restructure an industry and dramatically alter organizational buying plans. The technological environment defines the availability of goods and services to the buying organization and, in turn, the quality of goods and services that the organization can provide to its consumers. Recall that computer-assisted buying was treated in detail in the preceding chapter.

The rate of technological change in an industry influences the composition of the decision-making unit in the buying organization.[8] As the pace of technological change increases, the importance of the purchasing manager in the buying process declines. Technical and engineering personnel tend to be more important to the organizational buying process where the rate of technological change is great.

In the face of rapidly changing technology, buying organizations often use technological procedures to help them forecast the time periods

[1] For an expanded treatment, see Reed Moyer and Michael D. Hutt, *Macro Marketing* (New York: John Wiley and Sons, Inc., 1978), Chapter 9.

[5] "Time Runs Out for Steel," *Business Week* (June 13, 1983), p. 85; see also, Leonard M. Apcar, "As Detroit Trims the Pounds Off Its Cars, Suppliers Scramble to Get New Contracts," *Wall Street Journal* (October 17, 1978), p. 40.

[6] Webster and Wind, *Organizational Buying Behavior*, pp. 45–46.

[7] *Ibid.*, pp. 42–43.

[8] Bonoma and Zaltman, "Introduction," p. 22.

in which major changes in technology might occur. The marketer must also actively monitor signs of technological change and be prepared to adapt marketing strategy to deal with new technological environments.[9]

A New Era in Manufacturing

Significant new developments in manufacturing technology have the potential for altering buyer–seller relationships. Some experts contend that *flexible manufacturing systems* will provide the foundation for the next industrial revolution. These systems consist of computer-controlled machinery centers that form complicated metal parts at high speed and with great reliability, robots that handle the parts, and remotely guided carts that deliver materials. These components are linked by electronic controls that dictate precisely what will happen at each stage of the manufacturing process. Importantly, flexible manufacturing systems have the capacity to produce products cheaply in *small volume*.

When an outside supplier of a component part failed to meet quality standards, flexible automation gave General Motors the opportunity to produce the item in-house. Using the flexible manufacturing system, the component was designed and built in just ten weeks—a task that would have taken up to a year using traditional manufacturing technology. A new era in manufacturing creates a new direction in buyer–seller relationships.

Source: Gene Bylinsky, "The Race to the Automatic Factory," *Fortune* (February 21, 1983), pp. 52–64.

Environmental Uncertainty

Robert Spekman and Louis Stern suggest that as the information needs of buying groups grow in response to higher environmental uncertainty (e.g., changes in company leadership, or in economic conditions), more people participate in making buying decisions.[10] Their research further indicates that the *influence* of the purchasing agent increases with the level of environmental uncertainty. Why? As a firm's external environ-

[9] For example, see James R. Bright, "Evaluating Signals of Technological Change," *Harvard Business Review*, 48 (January–February, 1970), pp. 62–70.

[10] Robert E. Spekman and Louis W. Stern, "Environmental Uncertainty and Buying Group Structure: An Empirical Investigation," *Journal of Marketing*, 43 (Spring 1979), p. 56.

ment becomes more unstable, "the information processing function of boundary role persons (here, the purchasing agent) becomes central to a firm's ability to effectively gather, analyze, and act on relevant environmental information,"[11] and purchasing agents thus become more influential.[12] This research highlights the importance of monitoring key environmental trends and tracing their impact on the organizational buying process.

Environmental Influences: Boundaries of the Organizational Buying Process

Collectively, these environmental influences define the general business conditions, the political/legal setting, the availability of products and services, and the values and norms that constrain buying actions. In addition, the environment provides a stream of information, including marketing communications, to the buying organization.[13]

Organizational Forces

Individual decision makers influence the functioning of organizations in several ways. A marketing strategist must know how organizational decision makers approach decisions, set priorities, search for information, resolve internal conflicts, and establish goals.

Since organizations have unique "personalities," the industrial salesperson must be sensitive to the climate or culture of an organization and also to where the purchasing function is positioned in the executive hierarchy. Both the organizational climate and the status of purchasing vary from firm to firm.

To unravel these complex organizational forces, a few key concepts, drawn from the behavioral theory of the firm, are particularly significant. Once the groundwork is established, the impact of the organizational climate on industrial buying behavior can be assessed. Finally, the influence of the organizational positioning of purchasing on buying behavior must be analyzed.

The Behavioral Theory of the Firm

The behavioral theory of the firm describes how organizations actually operate rather than prescribes how they should operate.[14] Drawing on empirical research on executive decision making, four concepts form the

---

[11] *Ibid.*, p. 60.

[12] Robert E. Spekman, "Information and Influence: An Exploratory Investigation of the Boundary Role Person's Basis of Power," *Academy of Management Journal*, 22 (March 1979), pp. 104–117.

[13] Webster and Wind, *Organizational Buying Behavior*, p. 41.

[14] Richard M. Cyert and James G. March, *A Behavioral Theory of the Firm* (Englewood Cliffs, N.J.: Prentice-Hall, Inc., 1963).

foundation of the theory: (1) quasi-resolution of conflict, (2) uncertainty avoidance, (3) problemistic search, and (4) organizational learning.[15] Each provides rich insights into the nature of the organizational buying process.

Quasi-Resolution of Conflict Latent conflict may exist among the goals of organizational members: purchasing agents may be concerned with economy, engineers with performance, and users with prompt delivery.[16] The goals reflect the decision makers' specialized interests and responsibilities within the organization, as well as their background and personal needs. Given these competing goals, how do organizational members ever achieve consensus? Richard Cyert and James March describe three mechanisms to reduce goal conflict:[17]

1. *Local rationality*—complex problems are broken down into sub-problems and handled by subunits, which are motivated by only some of the broader organizational goals;

2. *Acceptable-level decision rules*—the agreed solutions are not optimal decisions, but are simply acceptable within the constraints of organizational goals and subgoals;

3. *Sequential attention to goals*—conflicting goals are treated by approaching problems one at a time. (The purchasing manager might favor engineering's wishes this month and the goals of the production unit next month.)

Uncertainty Avoidance Organizational members are motivated by a strong desire to reduce uncertainty. Thus, decision makers concentrate on shorter-range problems that offer more immediate feedback; they tend to delay long-range problem solving and planning. The desire to reduce uncertainty also stimulates organizational members to seek a "negotiated environment," that is, a "set of relationships with the environment worked out through planning, procedures, contractual relationships with suppliers, and following traditional practices."[18]

To avoid uncertainty, organizational buyers may favor known suppliers, avoid the risks of innovation, and split orders between two or more vendors. The organizational buying process itself illustrates the attempt to avoid risk by creating a negotiated environment.[19]

[15] *Ibid.*, pp. 114–127; see also, James G. March, "Decision Making Perspective: Decisions in Organizations and Theories of Choice," in Andrew H. Van De Ven and William F. Joyce, eds., *Perspectives on Organization Design and Behavior* (New York: John Wiley & Sons, 1981), pp. 205–244.

[16] Jagdish N. Sheth, "A Model of Industrial Buyer Behavior," *Journal of Marketing*, 37 (October 1973). p. 53.

[17] Cyert and March, *A Behavioral Theory of the Firm.*

[18] Webster and Wind, *Organizational Buying Behavior*, p. 69.

[19] Yoram Wind, "Applying the Behavioral Theory of the Firm to Industrial Buying Decisions," *The Economic and Business Bulletin*, 20 (Spring 1968), pp. 22–28.

Problematic Search   The search for information is stimulated by the definition of a problem and directed toward solving that problem. This search process follows the simplest path, moving from the familiar to the less familiar until an acceptable alternative is found. The direction of the search reflects the decision maker's specialization, past experience, hopes and expectations, as well as any unresolved conflicts within the organization.

Organizational buyers do not consider new vendors unless their requirements change or problems emerge with existing vendors. Generally, the buyer will consider new suppliers only after all of the familiar alternatives have been screened. This search pattern poses a real challenge for the "out" supplier who is attempting to penetrate a straight rebuy situation.[20]

Organizational Learning   The concept of organizational learning provides additional insight into the behavior of organizations. Cyert and March identify three types of significant adaptive organizational behavior over time:[21]

1. *Adaptation of goals*—goals are shifted up or down in response to success or failure in previous periods.

2. *Adaptation in attention rules*—organizations learn to pay attention to some parts of the environment, to some comparable organizations, and to selected components of their performance and evaluative criteria, while ignoring other parts. An organization may be more sensitive to product-line modifications of competitors if they are well-known in their industry.

3. *Adaptation in search rules*—future search efforts generally begin in an area where a solution was found in the past.

Each of these adaptive mechanisms has been observed.[22] If an acceptable alternative cannot be identified, purchasing managers will adjust their goals to render an identified alternative "acceptable." Organizational buyers also devote their attention to the most urgent problems and rely on criteria in selecting alternatives that have yielded rewards in the past. Likewise, buyers turn first to suppliers that have performed well when new procurement requirements emerge.

The four dimensions of organizational decision making delineated in the behavioral theory of the firm advance our understanding of how and why organizational buying tasks occur.[23] Individual members of the

---

[20] Anita M. Kennedy, "The Complex Decision to Select a Supplier: A Case Study," *Industrial Marketing Management*, 12 (February 1983), pp. 45–56; see also Wind, *ibid.*

[21] Cyert and March, *A Behavioral Theory of the Firm*, pp. 114–127.

[22] Wind, "Applying the Behavioral Theory," pp. 22–28.

[23] Webster and Wind, *Organizational Buying Behavior*, p. 73.

Table 4.1   Selected Dimensions of Organizational Climate

Achievement Motivation	The degree to which the organization attempts to excel
Rules Orientation	The degree to which rules are revered and followed
Readiness to Innovate	The degree to which the organization encourages innovative activity
Industriousness	The degree to which hard work is expected of organizational members

Source: Adapted with modifications from Derek S. Pugh, "The Aston Program Perspective," in Andrew H. Van De Ven and William F. Joyce, eds., *Perspectives on Organization Design and Behavior* (New York: John Wiley & Sons, 1981), p. 155.

organization use mechanisms that partially resolve goal conflicts, reduce uncertainty, employ a narrow search for solutions to problems, and adapt their behavior in response to their experiences.

Organizational Climate

"In some organizations one may sense spontaneity, happiness, creativity—a place on the go. In other organizations the climate may crackle with tension. Organizational climate can provide one immediate indication of the health or sickness of an organization."[24] Two competitive organizations of comparable size may present markedly different organizational climates. One may encourage innovation and freely allow deviations from rules, the other may be rule-oriented and tradition-bound.

By understanding the climate of a potential buying organization (Table 4.1), the industrial salesperson can tailor a selling strategy to fit the particular "personality" of the organization.[25]

Organizational Positioning of Purchasing

An organization that centralizes procurement decisions will approach purchasing differently than a company where purchasing decisions are made at individual user locations. When purchasing is centralized, a separate organizational unit is given authority for purchases at a regional, division, or headquarters level. For example, Mead Corporation's centralized purchasing function serves as a central control point for the purchase of common materials used by Mead plants across the United States. A marketer who is sensitive to organizational influences can more accurately map the decision-making process, isolate buying in-

---

[24] Kenyon B. De Greene, *The Adaptive Organization: Anticipation and Management of Crisis* (New York: John Wiley & Sons, 1982), p. 31.

[25] Thomas S. Robertson and Yoram Wind, "Organizational Psychographics and Innovativeness," *Journal of Consumer Research*, 7 (June 1980), pp. 24–31.

fluentials, identify salient buying criteria, and target marketing strategy in both types of organization.

Centralization vs. Decentralization   Centralized and decentralized procurement differ substantially.[26] Centralization leads to specialization. Purchasing specialists for selected items develop comprehensive knowledge of supply/demand conditions, vendor options, supplier cost factors, and other information relevant to the supply environment. This knowledge, and the significant volume of business they control, enhances their buying strength and supplier options.

The priority given to selected buying criteria is also influenced by centralization or decentralization. By identifying the buyer's organizational domain, the marketer can generally identify the purchasing manager's objectives. Centralized purchasing units place more weight on long-term supply availability and the development of a healthy supplier complex. Decentralized buyers may be more concerned with short-term cost efficiency and profit considerations. Organizational buying behavior is greatly influenced by the monitoring system by which the performance of the unit is measured.

Personal selling skills and the brand preferences of users influence purchasing decisions more at user locations than at centralized buying locations. At user locations, "engineers and other technical personnel, in particular, are prone to be specific in their preferences, while nonspecialized, nontechnical buyers have neither the technical expertise nor the status to challenge them,"[27] as purchasing specialists at central locations can. Differing priorities between central buyers and local users often lead to conflict in the buying organization. In stimulating demand at the user level, the marketer should assess the potential for conflict and attempt to develop a strategy that can resolve any differences between the two organizational units.

The organization of the marketer's selling strategy should parallel the organization of the purchasing function of key accounts. To avoid disjointed selling activities and internal conflict in the sales organization, many industrial marketers have developed national account management programs to establish a close working relationship "which cuts across multiple levels, functions, and operating units in both the buying and selling organizations."[28] Thus, the trend toward the centralization of the procurement function on the buying side has been matched by

[26] Joseph A. Bellizzi and Joseph J. Belonax, "Centralized and Decentralized Buying Influences," *Industrial Marketing Management*, 11 (April 1982), pp. 111–115; Arch G. Woodside and David M. Samuel, "Observation of Centralized Corporate Procurement," *Industrial Marketing Management*, 10 (July 1981), pp. 191–205; and E. Raymond Corey, *The Organizational Context of Industrial Buying Behavior* (Cambridge, Mass.: Marketing Science Institute, 1978), pp. 6–12.

[27] Corey, *The Organizational Context*, p. 13.

[28] Benson P. Shapiro and Rowland T. Moriarty, *National Account Management: Emerging Insights* (Cambridge, Mass.: Marketing Science Institute, 1982), p. 8.

Table 4.2 Factors Contributing to the Centralization of Procurement

Commonality of Requirements	Two or more procuring units within the organization have common requirements (e.g., sugar and packaging material at General Foods).
Cost-Saving Potential	Opportunity to strengthen bargaining position, secure lower prices through the aggregation of a firm's total requirements, and achieve economies in inventory control.
Structure of Supply Industry	Opportunity to consolidate purchasing power and secure favorable terms and service when a few large sellers dominate the supply industry.
Involvement of Engineering in Purchasing	If high, purchasing group and engineering group must be in close organizational and physical proximity.

Source: Adapted from E. Raymond Corey, *The Organizational Context of Industrial Buying Behavior* (Cambridge, Mass.: Marketing Science Institute, 1978), pp. 9–12.

---

the development of national account management programs on the selling side.

Centralization of Procurement: Contributing Factors Why is there a trend toward centralizing purchasing? Factors that strongly contribute to this trend are highlighted in Table 4.2.

An organization with multiple plant locations can often achieve cost savings by pooling requirements. Before the procurement function was centralized at General Motors, 106 GM buying locations spent more than $10 million annually on nearly 24 million pairs of work gloves, buying over 200 different styles from 90 different sources. The cost savings generated from pooling the requirements for this item alone are substantial.

The nature of the supply environment also can determine whether purchasing is centralized. If the supply environment is dominated by a few large sellers, centralized buying may be particularly useful in securing favorable terms and proper service. If the supply industry consists of many small firms each covering limited geographical areas, decentralized purchasing may achieve better support.

Finally, note from Table 4.2 that the location of purchasing in the organization often hinges on the location of key buying influences. If engineering plays an active role in the purchasing process, the purchasing function must be in close organizational and physical proximity.

Marketing Implications Two organizations, with seemingly identical purchasing requirements, may have entirely different philosophies on the "proper" location of the purchasing function, using different operating procedures and markedly different criteria to evaluate suppliers. The marketer who recognizes such differences is best equipped to satisfy their needs.

Uncovering the Behavioral Styles of Buyers

What behavioral styles do buyers exhibit when interacting with industrial salespersons? Buyers can be classified into the following categories:

- "The hard bargainer" obtains several price quotations or uses several sources of supply for the same item; salespeople may find it difficult to make a sale.
- "The sales job facilitator" is amenable to salespersons' solicitations and even attempts to make the transaction go smoothly.
- "The straight shooter" behaves with integrity and propriety; these buyers rarely use their buying power to attain concessions.
- "The socializer" enjoys the personal interaction of the buyer–seller relationship.
- "The persuader" will attempt to market his or her own company to salespersons to stimulate a favorable impression of the buying firm.
- "The considerate" buyer displays compassion and concern for the industrial salesperson; these buyers may be willing to accept substitute products.

A mutually beneficial exchange relationship results when the industrial salesperson tailors selling strategy to buyer's behavior style.

Source: Alan J. Dubinsky and Thomas N. Ingram, "A Classification of Industrial Buyers: Implications for Sales Training," *Journal of Personal Selling and Sales Management*, 1 (Fall–Winter 1981–1982), pp. 46–51.

Group Forces

Purchasing managers rarely make a buying decision independent of the influence of others in the organization.[29] The organizational buying process typically involves a complex set of smaller decisions made or influenced by several individuals. Thus, multiple buying influences and group forces are critical in organizational buying decisions (see Chap-

[29] Robert J. Thomas, "Correlates of Interpersonal Purchase Influence in Organizations," *Journal of Consumer Research*, 9 (September 1982), pp. 171–182; see also, Yoram Wind, "Preference of Relevant Others and Individual Choice Models," *Journal of Consumer Research*, 3 (August 1976), pp. 50–57.

ter 3). The degree of involvement of group members in the procurement process varies from routine rebuys, where the purchasing agent
simply takes into account the preferences of others, to complex new-task
buying situations, where a group plays an active role throughout the decision process.

The industrial salesperson must address three questions.

- Which organizational members take part in the buying
  process?
- What is each member's relative influence in the decision?
- What criteria are important to each member in evaluating prospective suppliers?

The salesperson who can correctly answer these questions is ideally prepared to meet the needs of a buying organization and has a high probability of becoming the chosen supplier.

Buying Center

The concept of the buying center (see Chapter 3), provides rich insights
into the role of group forces in organizational buying behavior.[30] The
buying center, which includes all the organizational members involved
in the purchase decision, is an "informal, cross-departmental decision
unit in which the primary objective is the acquisition, impartation, and
processing of relevant purchasing-related information."[31] The size of
the buying center varies, but an average buying center will include more
than four persons per purchase;[32] the number of people involved in all
stages of one purchase may be as many as 20.[33]

The composition of the buying center may change from one purchasing situation to another and is not prescribed by the organizational
chart. A buying group evolves during the purchasing process in response to the information requirements of the specific purchase situation. Because organizational buying is a *process* rather than an isolated
act, different individuals are important to the process at different times.
A design engineer may exert significant influence early in the purchas-

[30] For a comprehensive review of buying center research, see: Wesley J. Johnston and Robert E. Spekman, "Industrial Buying Behavior: A Need for an Integrative Approach," *Journal of Business Research*, 10 (June 1982), pp. 135–146; Johnston and Thomas V. Bonoma, "The Buying Center: Structure and Interaction Patterns," *Journal of Marketing*, 45 (Summer 1981), pp. 143–156; Johnston, "Industrial Buying Behavior: A State of the Art Review," in Ben M. Enis and Kenneth J. Roering, eds., *Review of Marketing 1981* (Chicago: American Marketing Association, 1981), pp. 75–87; Yoram Wind, "The Organizational Buying Center: A Research Agenda," in Gerald Zaltman and Thomas Bonoma, eds., *Organizational Buying Behavior* (Chicago: American Marketing Association, 1978), pp. 67–76; and Robert E. Spekman, "An Alternative Framework for Examining the Industrial Buying Process," in Zaltman and Bonoma, *Organizational Buying Behavior*, pp. 84–90.

[31] Spekman and Stern, "Environmental Uncertainty and Buying Group Structure," p. 56.

[32] "Industrial Sales People Report 4.1—Buying Influences in Average Company," LAP Report 1042.2 (New York: McGraw-Hill Research, 1977).

[33] G. van der Most, "Purchasing Process: Researching Influences Is Basic to Marketing Plan," *Industrial Marketing* (October 1976), p. 120.

Table 4.3   The Involvement of Buying Center Participants at Different Stages of the Procurement Process

Buying Center	Stages of Procurement Process for a Medical Equipment Purchase			
	Identification of Need	Establishment of Objectives	Identification and Evaluation of Buying Alternatives	Selection of Suppliers
Physicians	High	High	High	High
Nursing	Low	High	High	Low
Administration	Moderate	Moderate	Moderate	High
Engineering	Low	Moderate	Moderate	Low
Purchasing	Low	Low	Low	Moderate

Source: Adapted by permission of the publisher from "An Empirical Study of Hospital Buying," by Gene R. Laczniak, *Industrial Marketing Management*, 8 (January 1979), p. 61. Copyright © 1979 by Elsevier Science Publishing Co., Inc.

ing process when product specifications are being established; others may assume a more dominant role in later phases. An industrial salesperson must define the buying situation and the information requirements from the organization's perspective in order to anticipate the size and composition of the buying center. Again, the composition of the buying center:

- evolves during the purchasing process,
- varies from firm to firm, and
- varies from one purchasing situation to another.

Composition   An important first step in defining the buying center is to define the buying situation and determine whether the firm is in the early or later stages of the procurement decision-making process. The buying center for a new-task buying situation in the not-for-profit market is presented in Table 4.3. The product, intensive-care monitoring systems, is a complex and costly purchase. Buying center members are drawn from five functional areas, each participating at varying degrees in the decision process. A marketer who concentrated exclusively on the purchasing function would be overlooking key buying influentials.

Because the purchasing function is an easily identifiable element in buying centers in all sectors of the organizational market, it often provides a convenient starting point for the industrial salesperson who is attempting to piece together the membership of the buying center. Company policy may dictate that the industrial salesperson must first touch base with the purchasing department before meeting with others. Purchasing managers frown on attempts to bypass purchasing and initiate contact at other points in the organization. The purchasing manager plays an important gatekeeping role, controlling the flow of information and the access of salespersons to other members of the buying center. Yet, although purchasing managers can readily identify the individuals of the buying center, they are often inaccurate in estimating the relative impact of each member on the purchasing decision.[34]

Tracing Communication Flows   Wesley Johnston provides a graphic description of the probable buying center for capital equipment.[35] In Figure 4.2, engineering, purchasing, and manufacturing interact with each other and are central to the buying process for capital equipment. Purchasing and, to a lesser extent, engineering communicate directly with potential industrial suppliers. Accounting and finance, sales and marketing, and receiving play minor supporting roles.

Manufacturing was the only functional area to interact heavily with top management within the buying center. Interestingly, very few industrial salespersons had made direct sales calls on top management or on manufacturing. From the industrial salesperson's perspective, "not going high enough in the buying organization to influence the decision could see many hours of marketing effort overruled."[36]

In approaching a particular buying organization, the industrial salesperson should attempt to:

1. define the functional areas that will be involved in a particular buying decision, identifying the organizational member(s) who will represent each area;

2. examine the patterns of communication within the buying center;

3. forecast the possible role of top management in the buying process.

Predicting Composition

A marketer can also predict the composition of the buying center by projecting the impact of the industrial product on different functional areas in the buying organization.[37] If the procurement decision will affect the marketability of a firm's product (e.g., product design, price), the marketing department will be active in the decision process. Engineering will be influential in decisions about new capital equipment, materials, and components, setting specifications, defining product performance requirements, and qualifying potential vendors. Manufacturing executives will be included in the buying center in procurement decisions that affect the production mechanism (e.g., the acquisition of ma-

---

[34] For a discussion of methodological issues that relate to buying center research, see: Alvin J. Silk and Manohar U. Kalwani, "Measuring Influence in Organizational Purchase Decisions," *Journal of Marketing Research*, 19 (May 1982), pp. 165–181; Rowland T. Moriarty and John E. G. Bateson, "Exploring Complex Decision Making Units: A New Approach," *Journal of Marketing Research*, 19 (May 1982), pp. 182–191; Johnston and Spekman, "Industrial Buying Behavior: A Need for an Integrative Approach," pp. 135–146; and Lynn W. Phillips, "Assessing Measurement Error in Key Informant Reports: A Methodological Note on Organizational Analysis in Marketing," *Journal of Marketing Research*, 18 (November 1981), pp. 395–415.

[35] Wesley J. Johnston, *Patterns in Industrial Buying Behavior* (New York: Praeger Publishers, 1981).

[36] Johnston and Bonoma, "The Buying Center," p. 154.

[37] Corey, *The Organizational Context of Industrial Buying Behavior*, pp. 28–36.

Figure 4.2   The Probable Buying Center for Capital-Equipment Purchases

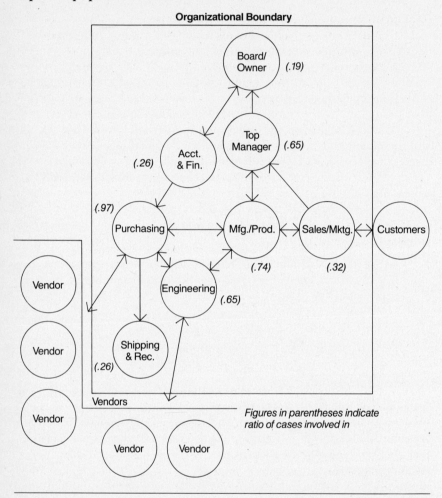

Source: Wesley J. Johnston, *Patterns in Industrial Buying Behavior* (New York: Praeger Publishers, 1981), p. 132. Reprinted by permission of Praeger Publishers, a division of CBS, Inc.

terials or parts used in production). When procurement decisions involve a substantial economic commitment or impinge on strategic or policy matters, top management will have considerable influence.

Influencing Composition   The marketer can sometimes influence the composition of the buying center. To illustrate, the desirable attributes of a new material handling system can best be understood and appreciated by a warehouse supervisor. By directing marketing communications (advertising and personal selling) to receptive users of the product, the marketer can draw them into the buying center and stimulate their active involvement in the procurement process.

Getting P&G's Attention

Flow Systems, Inc. produces a high-velocity, laser-like water tool that can be used to cut such materials as glass fiber and corrugated boxboard. Some 20 manufacturers in 14 countries use the tool in the manufacturing process for diapers. Thus, Procter and Gamble's (P&G) large disposable-diaper division represented a logical customer for Flow Systems.

Over a four-year period, despite numerous sales calls, the firm was unable to penetrate the organizational layers of P&G to reach key buying influentials. This changed, however, when the firm bought advertising space in regional editions of *Time*, *Newsweek* and other publications and led with the theme:

**"P&G, The Cleanest Way To Cut a Diaper
Can Also Pamper Your Bottom Line."**

Negotiations between Flow Systems and the purchasing department at P&G began shortly after the ads appeared.

Source: "All He Needs Is Luvs," *INC.* (February 1983), p. 24.

The Buying Committee   In some organizations, representatives from several departments comprise a committee charged to make a particular purchasing decision. The buying committee thus constitutes a more formalized buying center. Universities, hospitals, and industrial firms may assemble a temporary buying committee to choose a computer system; food retailers may use permanent buying committees meeting regularly for multiple decisions, such as which new food products should be given shelf space.[38] The philosophy underlying the committee concept is that (1) different viewpoints and a wider range of experience are applied to the decision-making process, (2) decisions are made more scientifically, and (3) the level of pressure in the buyer–seller relationship is lowered.

The industrial salesperson may not be given the opportunity to make a presentation before the full committee, but only to individual committee members. Here the salesperson must provide the accessible committee members with product-related information that may be salient for the inaccessible members. Questions and problems that may arise when the committee convenes should be anticipated and addressed.

[38] Michael D. Hutt, "The Retail Buying Committee: A Look at Cohesiveness and Leadership," *Journal of Retailing*, 55 (Winter 1979), pp. 87–97.

By working through a liaison to the buying committee, the sales-person attempts to create an advocate for the industrial firm's offering.[39] The marketer also should note that the most influential member of the buying group cannot necessarily be determined by comparing the organizational rank of committee members. Past product-related experience, technical expertise, personality traits, and other personal and organizational factors determine the structure of the decision-making unit and the relative influence of individual participants.

Buying Center Influence

Members of the buying center assume different roles throughout the procurement process (Table 4.4); they may be users, influencers, buyers, deciders, and gatekeepers.[40] One person could assume all roles in a purchase situation or each individual could assume a different buying role. To illustrate, as users, personnel from marketing, accounting, purchasing, and production all may have a stake in which new computer is selected. Thus, the buying center can be a very complex organizational phenomenon.

Identifying Patterns of Influence   Key influencers are frequently located outside of the purchasing department. James McMillan reports that the buying center for highly technical products includes the purchasing agent, scientists, engineers, and other managers—with the scientist having the greatest level of influence in the buying group.[41]

A study of the purchasing process for component parts found that only half of product or vendor selection decisions are made by the purchasing department.[42] Functional areas such as design and development engineering, research, and production engineering, dominate project initiation and the specification of requirements. Similar influence patterns emerge in the acquisition of materials and capital equipment. Wesley Johnston and Thomas Bonoma found that the typical capital equipment purchase involved an average of four departments, three levels of the management hierarchy (e.g., manager, regional manager, vice president), and seven different individuals.[43]

[39] Robert E. Krapfel, Jr., "An Extended Interpersonal Influence Model of Organizational Buyer Behavior," *Journal of Business Research*, 10 (June 1982), pp. 147–157.

[40] Webster and Wind, *Organizational Buying Behavior*, p. 77.

[41] James R. McMillan, "Role Differentiation in Industrial Buying Decisions," in *Proceedings of the American Marketing Association* (Chicago: American Marketing Association, 1973), pp. 207–211; see also, James R. Cooley, Donald W. Jackson, and Lonnie L. Ostrom, "Analyzing the Relative Power of Participants in Industrial Buying Decisions," in *Proceedings of the American Marketing Association* (Chicago: American Marketing Association, 1977), pp. 243–246.

[42] Scientific American, Inc., *How Industry Buys/1970* (New York: Scientific American, Inc., 1969), pp. 1–5.

[43] Johnston and Bonoma, "The Buying Center," pp. 143–156; see also Gary L. Lilien and M. Anthony Wong, "An Exploratory Investigation of the Structure of the Buying Center in the Metalworking Industry," *Journal of Marketing Research*, 21 (February 1984), pp. 1–11.

Table 4.4   Buying Center Roles Defined

Role	Description
Users	As the role name implies, these are the personnel who will be using the product in question. Users may have anywhere from inconsequential to an extremely important influence on the purchase decision. In some cases, the users initiate the purchase action by requesting the product. They may even develop the product specifications.
Gatekeepers	Gatekeepers control information to be reviewed by other members of the buying center. The control of information may be in terms of disseminating printed information or advertisements or through controlling which salesperson will speak to which individuals in the buying center. To illustrate, the purchasing agent might perform this screening role by opening the gate to the buying center for some sales personnel and closing it to others.
Influencers	These individuals affect the purchasing decision by supplying information for the evaluation of alternatives or by setting buying specifications. Typically, technical personnel, such as engineers, quality control personnel, and research and development personnel are significant influences on the purchase decision. Sometimes, individuals outside the buying organization can assume this role (e.g., an engineering consultant or an architect who writes very tight building specifications).
Deciders	Deciders are the individuals who actually make the buying decision, whether or not they have the formal authority to do so. The identity of the decider is the most difficult role to determine: buyers may have formal authority to buy, but the president of the firm may actually make the decision. A decider could be a design engineer who develops a set of specifications that only one vendor can meet.
Buyers	The buyer has *formal* authority for selecting a supplier and implementing all procedures connected with securing the product. The power of the buyer is often usurped by more powerful members of the organization. Often the buyer's role is assumed by the purchasing agent, who executes the clerical functions associated with a purchase order.

Source: Adapted from Frederick E. Webster, Jr., and Yoram Wind, *Organizational Buying Behavior* (Englewood Cliffs, N.J.: Prentice-Hall, Inc., 1972), pp. 77–80.

Understanding the Power Culture[44]   A key to identifying buying influentials rests on understanding the types of power that organizational members *have* or *appear to have*. Unfortunately, one cannot identify powerful buying center members by merely examining a company's organizational chart. Five major power bases are identified in Table 4.5. Note that organizational members can derive power from the rewards that they can provide (reward power) for compliance or withhold (coercive power) for noncompliance. Power can likewise accrue as a result of expertise, personal charm, or status in the organization.

By assessing the power culture of a buying organization, the salesperson can more readily identify buying center members, predict the

[44] This section is largely based on Thomas V. Bonoma, "Major Sales: Who *Really* Does the Buying?" *Harvard Business Review*, 60 (May–June 1982), pp. 111–119.

Table 4.5   Bases of Power

Type of Power	Description
Reward	Ability to provide monetary, social, political or psychological rewards to others for compliance.
Coercive	Ability to provide monetary or other punishments for noncompliance.
Attraction	Ability to elicit compliance from others because they like you.
Expert	Ability to elicit compliance from others because of technical expertise, either actual or reputed.
Status	Compliance-gaining ability derived from a legitimate position of power in a company.

Source: John R. P. French and Bertram Raven, "The Bases of Social Power," in Dorwin Cartwright, ed., *Studies in Social Power* (Ann Arbor, Mich.: University of Michigan Press, 1959), pp. 150–167, cited in Thomas V. Bonoma, "Major Sales: Who *Really* Does the Buying?" *Harvard Business Review*, 60 (May–June 1982), pp. 111–119.

role (e.g., influencer or decider) of each member in the buying process, and estimate the level of each member's influence on the final buying decision. Sensitivity to the power base of each buying center member can also help the salesperson to develop a personal selling strategy. A manufacturing executive may rely on expertise when new automated production equipment is being considered, thereby requiring a more technical sales presentation.

The Influence of Purchasing   Purchasing assumes a position of power in the buying center in procurement decisions "in a steady-state condition, that is, when the design of the purchased product is established and vendors have been qualified."[45] Likewise, purchasing is dominant in repetitive buying situations through technical expertise, knowledge of the dynamics of the supplying industry, and close working relationships with individual suppliers.[46]

Factors that contribute to purchasing's strength include: (1) its level of technical competence and credibility, (2) its base of relevant information, (3) its base of top management support, and (4) its organizational status as an authority in selected procurement areas.[47] Purchasing agents appear to be motivated by a strong desire to enhance their status and position within the organization.[48] The marketer cannot make sweeping generalizations concerning the "typical" level of power that purchasing

[15] E. Raymond Corey, *The Organizational Context of Industrial Buying Behavior*, p. 34; see also, Gloria P. Thomas and John F. Grashof, "Impact of Internal and External Environmental Stability on the Existence of Determinant Buying Rules," *Journal of Business Research*, 10 (June 1982), pp. 159–168.

[16] Corey, *ibid.*

[17] *Ibid.*, pp. 34–35.

[18] George Strauss, "Tactics of Lateral Relationship," *Administrative Science Quarterly*, 7 (September 1962), pp. 161–186.

possesses in the buying center, but must concentrate on the relative importance of purchasing in the particular buying situation and organizational context.[49]

Individual Forces

Individuals, and not organizations, make buying decisions. Each member of the buying center has a unique personality, a particular set of learned experiences, a specified organizational function, and perceptions of how best to achieve both personal and organizational goals. To understand the organizational buyer, the marketer should be aware of individual perceptions of the buying situation.

Different Evaluative Criteria

Evaluative criteria are specifications that organizational buyers use to compare alternative industrial products and services. These may conflict, however. Industrial product users generally value prompt delivery and efficient servicing; engineering values product quality, standardization, and pretesting; purchasing assigns the most importance to maximum price advantage and economy in shipping and forwarding.[50]

Jagdish Sheth contends that product perceptions and evaluative criteria differ among organizational decision makers as a result of differences in educational backgrounds, source and type of information exposure, interpretation and retention of relevant information (perceptual distortion), and level of satisfaction with past purchases.[51] Engineers have a different educational background from plant managers or purchasing agents; they are exposed to different journals, attend different conferences, and possess different professional goals and values. A sales presentation that is effective with purchasing may be entirely off the mark with engineering.

Understanding the Reward/Measurement System[52]   What factors motivate individual decision makers during the organizational buying process? According to Paul Anderson, they are motivated largely by:

1.   *Intrinsic rewards*, attained on a personal basis, such as feelings of accomplishment or self-worth;

---

[49] For example, see Wesley J. Johnston, "Communication Networks and Influence Patterns in Industrial Buying Behavior," unpublished doctoral dissertation (University of Pittsburgh, 1979).

[50] Jagdish N. Sheth, "A Model of Industrial Buyer Behavior," p. 51.

[51] *Ibid.*, pp. 52–54.

[52] Paul F. Anderson, "A Reward/Measurement Model of Organizational Buying Behavior," presentation to the American Marketing Association Faculty Consortium on Industrial Marketing (The Ohio State University, July 8, 1982); see also Anderson and Terry M. Chambers, "A Reward/Measurement Model," *Journal of Marketing*, in press.

Table 4.6   Issues of Importance in the Formation of Individual Preferences

	Key Importance	Less Importance
Production Engineers	Operating Cost Energy Savings Reliability Complexity	First Cost Field-Proven
Corporate Engineers	First Cost Field-Proven Reliability Complexity	Energy Savings Up-to-Date
Plant Managers	Operating Cost Use of Unproductive Areas Up-to-Date Power Failure Protection	First Cost Complexity
Top Managers	Up-to-Date Energy Savings Operating Cost	Noise Level in Plant Reliability
HVAC Consultants	Noise Level in Plant First Cost Reliability	Up-to-Date Energy Savings Operating Cost

Source: Jean-Marie Choffray and Gary L. Lilien, "Assessing Response to Industrial Marketing Strategy," *Journal of Marketing*, 42 (April 1978), p. 30. Reprinted from the *Journal of Marketing*, published by the American Marketing Association.

2.   *Extrinsic rewards*, distributed by the organization, such as salary increases or promotions.

Thus, the attributes individuals emphasize in evaluating alternative industrial suppliers are likely to reflect the reward and measurement systems of their primary work group. Also, individual expectations about the offerings of alternative suppliers will differ. Purchasing managers have been rewarded for one set of behaviors, such as reducing the cost of materials, while engineers have been rewarded for another, such as improving the quality of products. This will lead to conflicting advocacy positions within the buying group. How is this conflict resolved? Recall the conflict resolution mechanisms, drawn from the behavioral theory of the firm, examined earlier in the chapter.

Responsive Marketing Strategy   A marketer who is sensitive to differences in the product perceptions and evaluative criteria of individual buying center members is well-equipped to prepare responsive marketing strategy. To illustrate, a research study examined the industrial adoption of solar air-conditioning systems and identified the criteria of importance to key decision makers (Table 4.6)[53]: marketing com-

---

[53] Jean-Marie Choffray and Gary L. Lilien, "Assessing Response to Industrial Marketing Strategy," *Journal of Marketing*, 42 (April 1978), pp. 20–31.

munications directed at *production engineers* should center on operating costs and energy savings; *heating and air-conditioning consultants* (HVAC) should be addressed concerning noise level and initial cost of the system. Knowledge of the criteria that key buying center participants employ is of significant operational value to the marketer in designing new products and in developing and targeting advertising and personal selling presentations.

Information Processing

Volumes of information flow into every organization through direct-mail advertising, journal advertising, trade news, word-of-mouth, and personal sales presentations. What an individual organizational buyer chooses to pay attention to (or not), comprehend, and retain has an important bearing on procurement decisions.

Selective Processes   Information processing is generally encompassed in the broader term cognition, which refers to "all the processes by which the sensory input is transformed, reduced, elaborated, stored, recovered, and used."[54] Important to an individual's cognitive structure are the processes of selective exposure, attention, perception, and retention.

1. *Selective exposure* is the tendency to accept communication messages that are consistent with one's existing attitudes and beliefs. For this reason, a purchasing agent chooses to talk to some salespersons and not to others.

2. *Selective attention* is the filtering or screening of incoming stimuli in order to admit only certain ones to cognition. Thus, an organizational buyer will be more likely to notice a trade advertisement if it is consistent with his or her needs and values.

3. *Selective perception* is the tendency to interpret stimuli in terms of one's existing attitudes and beliefs. This explains why organizational buyers may modify or distort a salesperson's message to make it more consistent with their predispositions toward the company.

4. *Selective retention* is the tendency to store in memory only information pertinent to one's own needs and dispositions. An organizational buyer may retain information concerning a particular brand because it matches his or her criteria.

Each of these selective processes influences the way an individual decision maker will respond to marketing stimuli. Since the procurement

[54] U. Neisser, *Cognitive Psychology* (New York: Appleton, 1966), p. 4, quoted in James F. Engle, David T. Kollat, and Roger D. Blackwell, *Consumer Behavior*, 2d ed. (Chicago: Holt, Rinehart and Winston, 1973), p. 210.

process often spans several months and the marketer's contact with the buying organization is infrequent, marketing communications must be carefully designed and targeted. Poorly conceived messages will be "tuned out" or immediately forgotten by key decision makers.

Memory   Some memory theorists hypothesize that individuals possess three different types of memory storage systems:[55] a set of sensory stores (SS), a short-term memory store (STS), and a long-term memory store (LTS). According to this multiple-store theory, information passes from the sense organs to a sensory store, where information is lost in a fraction of a second unless attention is devoted to the stimulus. If, however, the information is processed, it moves into the STS, which has limited capacity. Here, information can be kept active by further processing. Active information in the STS can be retrieved quickly, and information in the LTS can be called upon as needed to interpret information. Thus, the STS is the center of current processing activity. Lastly, part of this information, if properly processed, is transferred to the LTS, which is hypothesized to have unlimited capacity.

What information is likely to be stored? Information that is deemed important to achieving goals or can be easily stored is likely assigned the highest priority.[56] The individual's expectation about how the information will be used also determines what is to be stored and how.

External Memory   The organizational buyer does have an external memory which can hold vast amounts of information. Catalogs, technical reports, and on-line computer systems are potential parts of this external memory. A purchasing agent may need to keep only a vendor's name in memory because extensive product-related information can be retrieved from external memory as the need arises. The marketer must thus provide relevant information in a form that can be assimilated into the buying organization's external memory. Pamphlets and technical reports provided by the industrial salesperson often are retrieved from storage weeks later at critical stages in the procurement process.

Risk-Reduction Strategies

Individuals are motivated by a strong desire to reduce the level of risk in purchase decisions. The perceived risk concept, introduced in Chapter 3, includes two components: (1) *uncertainty* about the outcome of a decision, and (2) the magnitude of *consequences* associated with making the wrong choice.

---

[55] R. C. Atkinson and Richard M. Shiffrin, "Human Memory: A Proposed System and Its Control Processes," in K. W. Spence and J. T. Spence, eds., *The Psychology of Learning and Motivation: Advances in Research and Theory, Vol 2* (New York: Academic Press, 1968), pp. 89–195, discussed in James R. Bettman, "Memory Factors in Consumer Choice: A Review," *Journal of Marketing,* 43 (Spring 1979), pp. 37–53.

[56] Richard M. Shiffrin and R. C. Atkinson, "Storage and Retrieval Processes in Long-Term Memory," *Psychological Review,* 76 (1979), pp. 179–193, discussed in James Bettman, *ibid.*

In confronting "risky" purchase decisions, how do organizational buyers behave? Organizational buyers appear to use four risk-reduction strategies: [57]

1. External uncertainty reduction (e.g., visit supplier's plant);

2. Internal uncertainty reduction (e.g., consult with other buyers);

3. External consequences reduction (e.g., multiple sourcing);

4. Internal consequences reduction (e.g., consult with company's top management).

Organizational buyers can also reduce the level of risk by relying on familiar suppliers.[58] Because source loyalty provides the organizational buyer with a convenient method of reducing risk, it constitutes a significant barrier to entry for an "out" supplier. This makes straight rebuy situations very hard for the new supplier to break. When an organizational buyer selects a particular supplier and is rewarded for the decision, the probability of selecting the same supplier again increases.

The reputation of the supplier also influences the perceived level of risk. Theodore Levitt reports that well-known companies, recognized as credible sources, tend to be favored by decision makers facing high-risk decisions.[59] The importance of source credibility appears to increase as the level of perceived risk increases. A first-time purchaser of a computer may feel "comfortable" in dealing with a large, well-known manufacturer such as IBM.

Anticipating Perceived Risk Level   Industrial marketers should carefully consider the level of risk that their product will elicit for a particular buying organization and for specific decision makers. When introducing new products, entering new markets, or approaching new customers, the marketing strategist should evaluate the impact of alternative strategies on perceived risk.

Individual vs. Group Decision Making

What factors determine whether a specific buying situation will be a group or individual decision? Jagdish Sheth theorizes that the following influence the structure of the decision-making unit:[60]

---

[57] Timothy W. Sweeney, H. Lee Mathews, and David T. Wilson, "An Analysis of Industrial Buyers' Risk Reducing Behavior: Some Personality Correlates," *American Marketing Association Proceedings* (Chicago: American Marketing Association, 1973), pp. 217–221.

[58] For example, see Richard N. Cardozo and James W. Cagley, "An Experimental Study of Industrial Buyer Behavior," *Journal of Marketing Research*, 8 (August 1971), pp. 329–334.

[59] Theodore Levitt, *Industrial Purchasing Behavior: A Study of Communication Effects* (Boston: Division of Research, Graduate School of Business Administration, Harvard University, 1965).

[60] Sheth, "A Model of Industrial Buyer Behavior," p. 54.

Product-Specific Factors

1.   *Perceived risk*—the higher the level of perceived risk, the greater the likelihood that the decision will be made by a group.

2.   *Type of purchase*—new-task buying situations are more likely to involve group decision making (e.g., a first-time purchase of a computer).

3.   *Time pressure*—with minimal time constraints, group decision making becomes more feasible.

Company-Specific Factors

1.   *Size*—large companies tend to use group decision making.

2.   *Degree of centralization*—the more decentralized an organization, the more likely decisions will be made by a group.

Sheth notes that these factors are supported by research conducted in the organizational behavior area, but need empirical verification in the industrial buying context.

The Organizational Buying Process: Major Elements

The behavior of organizational buyers is influenced by environmental, organizational, group, and individual factors. Each of these spheres of influence has been discussed in an organizational buying context, with particular attention to how the industrial marketer should interpret these forces and, more important, factor them directly into marketing strategy planning. A model of the organizational buying process is presented in Figure 4.3, which serves to reinforce and integrate the key areas discussed so far in the chapter.[61]

This framework focuses on the relationship between an organization's buying center and three major stages in the individual purchase decision process through:

1.   the screening of alternatives which do not meet organizational requirements;

2.   the formation of decision participants' preferences;

3.   the formation of organizational preferences.

---

[61] Choffray and Lilien, "Assessing the Response to Industrial Marketing Strategy," pp. 20–31. Other models of organizational buying behavior include Webster and Wind, *Organizational Buying Behavior*, pp. 28–37; Sheth, "A Model of Industrial Buyer Behavior," pp. 50–56; Thomas V. Bonoma, Gerald Zaltman, and Wesley J. Johnston, *Industrial Buying Behavior* (Cambridge: Marketing Science Institute, 1977), Chapter 2; Rowland T. Moriarty and Morton Galper, *Organizational Buying Behavior: A State-of-the-Art Review and Conceptualization* (Cambridge: Marketing Science Institute, 1978); Gene R. Laczniak and Patrick E. Murphy, "Fine Tuning Organizational Buying Models," in Charles W. Lamb and Patrick M. Dunne, Jr., eds., *Theoretical Developments in Marketing* (Chicago: American Marketing Association, 1980), pp. 77–80; and Manoj K. Agarwal, Philip C. Burger, and David A. Reid, "A New Model of Organizational Buying Behavior," unpublished working paper (Binghamton: State University of New York, School of Management, 1982).

Figure 4.3 Major Elements of Organizational Buying Behavior

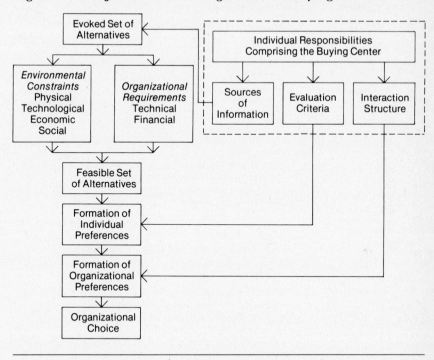

Source: Jean-Marie Choffray and Gary L. Lilien, "Assessing Response to Industrial Marketing Strategy," *Journal of Marketing*, 42 (April 1978), p. 22. Reprinted by permission of the American Marketing Association.

Observe that individual members of the buying center use different *evaluation criteria* and are exposed to different *sources of information*, which influence the industrial brands that are included in the buyer's *evoked set of alternatives*. The evoked set constitutes the alternative brands that a buyer calls to mind when a need arises and represents only a few of the many brands that may be available.[62]

Environmental constraints and organizational requirements influence the procurement process by limiting the number of product alternatives that satisfy organizational needs. For example, capital equipment alternatives that exceed a particular cost (initial or operating) may be eliminated from further consideration. The resulting brands become the *feasible set of alternatives* for the organization over which individual preferences are defined. The *interaction structure* of the members of the buying center, who have differing criteria and responsibilities, leads to

[62] John A. Howard and Jagdish N. Sheth, *The Theory of Buyer Behavior* (New York: John Wiley & Sons, 1969), p. 26; see also, Ronald P. LeBlanc, "Environmental Impact on Purchase Decision Structure," *Journal of Purchasing and Materials Management*, 17 (Spring 1981), pp. 30–36; and Lowell E. Crow, Richard W. Olshavsky, and John O. Summers, "Industrial Buyers' Choice Strategies: A Protocol Analysis," *Journal of Marketing Research*, 17 (February 1980), pp. 34–44.

Table 4.7   Organizational Buying Behavior: Forming the Foundation of Marketing Strategy

	Level	Illustrative Questions
Marketing Strategy Planning	Environmental	How will present economic projections for the industry and the economy affect the purchasing plans of this organization?
	Organizational	What are the unique *company attributes* (e.g., size, orientation) and *procurement attributes* (e.g., structure and organization position of purchasing) that will influence buyer behavior?
	Product-Specific	How far has the firm progressed in the *buying process* (early or late phase)?
		What type of *buying situation* does this purchase represent for the organization (new task, straight rebuy)?
		To what degree will organizational buyers perceive *risk* in purchasing this product?
	Group	Will the decision be made by an individual or a group?
		Who are the members of the buying center?
		What is each member's relative influence in the decision?
		What is the power base (e.g., status or expert power) of each member of the buying center?
	Individual	What criteria are important to each member of the buying center in evaluating prospective suppliers?
		How do potential suppliers rate on these criteria?

the formation of organizational preferences, and, ultimately, to organizational choice.[63]

An understanding of the organizational buying process allows the marketer to play an active rather than a passive role in stimulating market response.[64] The marketer who identifies organizational screening requirements and the salient evaluative criteria of individual buying center members can make more informed product design, pricing, and promotional decisions.

Organizational Buying Behavior: Marketing Strategy Implications

In probing the complex behavioral process of organizational buying, the marketer must systematically gather relevant market information by asking the right questions. Illustrative questions are presented in Table 4.7. They draw together the material of Part II, "The Organizational

[63] W. C. Buss, "A Comparison of the Predictive Performance of Group-Preference Models," *Proceedings of the American Marketing Association No. 47* (Chicago: American Marketing Association, 1981), pp. 174–177.

[64] Choffray and Lilien, "Assessing the Response to Industrial Marketing Strategy," pp. 20–31.

Buying Process." The industrial marketer can understand an individual decision maker only after examining the broader forces that form the decision-making process, and defining the context of the buying situation, which includes environmental, organizational, product-specific, group, and individual forces. Such analysis will allow the marketer to focus marketing strategy on profitable segments of the organizational market. As we will see in Chapter 6, key dimensions of organizational buying behavior, highlighted in Table 4.7, play a significant role in industrial market segmentation strategies.

Summary

Upon entering an organization, the marketer confronts a buyer who is constrained by several forces, or spheres of influence, which can be classified as environmental, organizational, group, and individual.

First, environmental forces define the boundaries within which buyers and sellers interact. Second, each organization develops a personality that makes it unique. The marketer must understand how organizational buyers approach decisions, set priorities, gather information, resolve conflicts, and establish and revise organizational goals. The location of the procurement function in the organizational hierarchy and the type of buying technology available to the purchasing staff directly influence marketing strategy requirements. Third, the relevant unit of analysis for the marketing strategist is the buying center. The composition of this group evolves during the buying process, varies from firm to firm, and changes from one purchasing situation to another. Fourth, ultimately the marketer must concentrate attention on individual members of the buying center. Each has a particular set of experiences and a unique personal and organizational frame of reference to bring to bear on the buying decision. The marketer who is sensitive to individual differences is best equipped to develop responsive marketing communications that will be retained by the organizational buyer.

Unraveling the complex forces that encircle the organizational buying process is indeed difficult. The goal of this chapter has been to provide a framework which allows the marketing manager to begin this task by asking the right questions. The answers will provide the base for effective and efficient industrial marketing strategy.

Discussion Questions

1. Environmental influences define the boundaries within which industrial buyers and sellers interact. Select a recent legal, political, or economic development that will affect demand patterns in a particular industry.

2. How does the rate of technological change in an industry influence the composition of the decision-making unit in the buying organization?

3. Fuel-economy, exhaust-emission, and safety standards are creating changes in the purchasing requirements of automobile manufacturers. In what way will such changes influence the demand for aluminum, steel, rubber, and related materials?

4. Since the composition of the buying center is often made up of individuals who perform different organizational functions (e.g., production vs. purchasing) and value different product and supplier attributes, how are decisions ever made? How is conflict within the buying center resolved?

5. An organization that centralizes procurement decisions at regional, division, or headquarters level will approach purchasing differently from a company that is decentralized with purchasing decisions made at individual user locations. Explain.

6. Explain how the composition of the buying center evolves during the purchasing process and varies from one firm to another, as well as from one purchasing situation to another.

7. The Kraus Toy Company recently decided to develop a new electronic game. Can an electrical parts supplier *predict* the likely composition of the buying center at Kraus Toy? What steps could an industrial salesperson take to *influence* the composition of the buying center?

8. Why does the influence of the purchasing manager appear to increase as the level of environmental uncertainty rises?

9. Carol Brooks, purchasing manager for Apex Manufacturing Co., read *The Wall Street Journal* this morning and carefully read, clipped, and saved a full-page ad by the Allen-Bradley Company. Ralph Thornton, the production manager at Apex, read several articles from the same paper but could not recall seeing this or, for that matter, any ads. How could this occur?

10. What factors determine whether a particular buying situation will be a group or an individual decision?

11. The industrial marketer who identifies organizational screening requirements and the salient evaluative criteria of individual buying center members can make more informed product design and advertising decisions. Explain.

P·A·R·T
III

Assessing Market Opportunities

C·H·A·P·T·E·R
5

Industrial Marketing Intelligence

The cornerstone of creative and effective marketing strategies is good information. Information about customers, competitors, and the environment, gathered continuously and organized to support decision making, allows the industrial marketing manager to base decisions on the realities of the marketplace rather than on hunch and intuition. The result is improved marketing performance. The system for capturing the necessary information for industrial marketing decision making is the marketing intelligence system. After reading this chapter, you will have an understanding of:

1. *the components of, and requirements for, an effective marketing intelligence system;*
2. *the need to develop the information base as a decision support system to ensure maximum managerial relevance;*
3. *how to use key secondary sources of information for industrial market planning;*
4. *the nature and function of marketing research in the industrial marketing environment.*

Marketing intelligence is a systematic process for generating the information needed to effectively manage industrial marketing strategy. Marketing strategy decisions will be based on information about market potential, customer requirements, industry and market trends, present and future competitive behavior, expected sales, market segment size and requirements, and sales and profit performance for customers, products, and territories. Marketing intelligence activities are thus focused on developing the research methodologies, data sources, and information-processing capabilities necessary to evoke this information in a form that supports marketing strategy development.

This chapter explores the strategic role of information in industrial marketing management. First, the key components of a marketing intelligence system are delineated. Here particular attention is devoted to the decision support system which is the core of the marketing intelligence function in the industrial firm. Next, the secondary sources of information available to the industrial marketer are described and evaluated. Third, the role and the unique characteristics of marketing research in the industrial market environment are analyzed.

The Role of Information: A Case Illustration

To illustrate the value of marketing intelligence in the marketing decision process, consider the case of an industrial firm that launched an aggressive marketing strategy. Distek, Inc., an integrated group of companies providing warehousing, telemarketing, computer software, and information, introduced a new program called "Cost MINUS." This is a new service of their public warehousing subsidiary which guarantees that the rate charged to customers for product handling will be lowered during the second and third years of the public warehouse contract. The customer agrees to lease warehouse space for three years; Distek provides productivity guarantees over the three-year period. What types of information were necessary to develop and implement this marketing program?

Gathering Required Market Information

First, secondary information (already published data) was thoroughly evaluated to address the following questions: Which industries are potential users of such a service? Which industries would benefit the most from the program? Who are the warehousing decision makers in the firms in these industries? The data from published sources was analyzed to develop target industries and specific target firms to whom the marketing program could be directed. However, to effectively develop strategy and properly target the program, an estimate of market potential by industry was required.

Market potential represents the total possible business available to all suppliers of warehousing. Primary and secondary research was conducted to determine market potential. Primary research is original data collection; telephone surveys were used to evaluate the requirements of potential users of the new service. Secondary research augmented the telephone surveys. In this way, Distek could concentrate marketing efforts on those industries and firms with the greatest potential. The analysis indicated that the greatest potential was offered by firms in the drugs, personal care, paper, and electrical and automotive parts industries. Research was also conducted on competitors; market analysts consulted annual reports, trade publications, industry contacts, and existing customers to determine whether competitors were presently offering or could offer similar programs.

Formulating Strategy

Once the market was delineated, specific facets of marketing strategy were formulated. Here, market intelligence was important. To develop the "product," it was necessary to learn how warehouse productivity would improve as Distek became familiar with an account. Past records relating to "cases handled per man-hour" were analyzed to evaluate performance over time so that Distek could determine the range of productivity improvement that could be guaranteed to a particular account. To develop an effective promotional plan, various trade publications were analyzed on the basis of circulation, readership, and target market coverage.

Evaluating Performance

Once the marketing program was implemented, the intelligence system provided immediate feedback on performance. Readers of the trade publications were surveyed by telephone to determine how well the advertising campaign had achieved desired objectives. Here attention centered on measuring the awareness, knowledge, and attitudes of potential users of the new service. Responses from each ad in each publication were monitored to compare media and message effectiveness. New business was also tracked, including the revenue, cost, and profit associated with each new account. Finally, customer service studies assessed customer satisfaction with the Distek program. This information allowed the firm to tailor their service offering to more precisely fit customer needs.

As this example suggests, marketing intelligence is a multi-faceted function that is the primary driving force behind all of the decisions made by industrial marketing managers. Note that Distek used a broad array of research methods to evaluate the market for their services. The information was used to identify target markets, determine market potential, analyze competitors, formulate marketing strategy, and finally, to evaluate the effectiveness of the strategies implemented. Valuable marketing information must be created systematically—data from a variety of sources is transformed into information to support executive decision making. The prudent industrial marketing manager will work to develop an intelligence system that provides the information necessary to make effective decisions.

Who Needs Market Research?

"About five years ago we hired an MBA from a prestigious eastern university. We manufacture heavy industrial machinery and felt we needed someone 'to do a little market research.' So we gave this MBA the title of Market Research Director—although we weren't sure exactly what he should do. He developed mountains of data and information—but it never seemed to be very useful. Actually, we didn't know what to do with the data or how to use it. After about five months we fired him!"

"Reflecting back on our experience I can now appreciate the value of that data. We recently adopted a formal marketing planning process and much of that information would be extremely useful today. I wish now that we had the benefit of a five-year-old data base—we are just beginning to develop similar data to enable us to implement our formal planning process."

Source: From a discussion with the Director of Marketing of an industrial machinery firm.

Industrial Marketing Intelligence Defined

Industrial marketing intelligence refers to the broad spectrum of information required to make decisions and effectively manage industrial marketing strategy. The manager for the marketing intelligence system would be responsible for designing and implementing systems and procedures to gather, record, analyze, and interpret all forms of pertinent marketing information. A comprehensive industrial marketing intelligence system would include:

1. *Formal Marketing Research Studies.* Marketing research may be conducted to determine buyer intentions, analyze primary demand, evaluate competitive behavior and performance, monitor the eco-

nomic and industry environment, evaluate customer satisfaction, analyze advertising effectiveness, determine price elasticity, evaluate distributor performance and satisfaction, or determine buying center composition and behavior.

2.   *Market Potential and Sales Forecasting.* Here the intelligence system must assemble data to determine market potentials and sales forecasts as well as appropriate methodologies.

3.   *Financial and Accounting Performance Analysis.* The intelligence system will coordinate the marketing needs with financial and accounting functions. The system should generate periodic reports on revenues, costs, and profits by customer, distributor, product, and territory. These results are compared with objectives set forth in the marketing plan.

4.   *New Product Research.* In many industrial markets, especially in high technology industries, success hinges on effective allocation of research and development expenditures. The marketing intelligence function develops procedures for generating new product ideas, monitoring customers, middlemen, and competitors for new product ideas, concept-testing new products, test marketing, and new product performance evaluation.

5.   *Secondary Data Files.* The sources of published information are diverse and include departments of federal and state governments, local governments, universities, institutes, trade associations, consulting firms, and private research organizations. The marketing intelligence function is responsible for determining which secondary data is relevant and then collecting, analyzing, and disseminating it regularly to the appropriate decision makers.

Marketing intelligence is clearly a broad and complex function whose effectiveness will dramatically affect the quality of industrial marketing decisions. Key components of the industrial marketing intelligence system are sketched in Figure 5.1.

Components of a Decision Support System

The heart of the marketing intelligence function is what John D. C. Little refers to as a "decision support system." A decision support system (DSS) is a coordinated collection of data, systems, tools, and techniques with the necessary software and computer hardware through which an organization gathers and interprets relevant information from the business and environment and turns it into information that can be acted upon.[1] The components of a DSS are shown in Figure 5.2; they include:

---

[1] John D. C. Little, Lakshmi Mohan, and Antoine Hatoun, "Using Decision Support Systems," *Industrial Marketing*, 67 (March 1982), p. 50. (This section is based on portions of this article.)

Figure 5.1   An Industrial Marketing Intelligence System

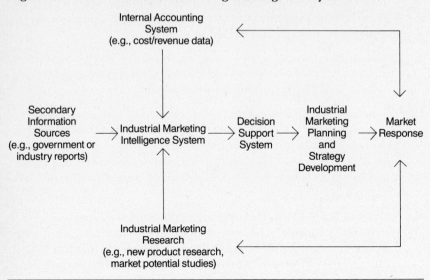

1. *Data Base.* The intelligence function develops and coordinates the flow of information from the multitude of external and internal sources. The primary task is to capture the data so that it can be used with the other components of the DSS to make decisions. A critical objective is to centralize all data in proper form and sufficient detail so that it is accessible for decision making.

2. *Models.* A model may be nothing more sophisticated than a rule of thumb, e.g. "for each 1 percent decline in territorial market share, trade promotion advertising should be increased by 5 percent." Or, models may be complicated computer-driven mathematical equations. In any case, models are quantitative or qualitative conceptualizations of how a system operates. The model expresses perceptions as to what data and variables are important and how the variables are related.

3. *Statistics and Manipulation.* This aspect of the DSS produces meaningful information by relating the data to the models. The typical operation involves segregating numbers into groups, aggregating them, taking ratios, ranking them, plotting, making tables, etc. General managerial models like pro forma profit and loss statements, budgeting and forecasting, and more complex models like marketing mix planning, product portfolio analysis, and new product tracking are aspects of data analysis performed in the statistical manipulation process.

4. *Display.* The display function is the interface between the industrial marketing manager and the DSS. Much of the communication is achieved through interactive, time-shared computing. Widespread

Figure 5.2   Decision Support System Components

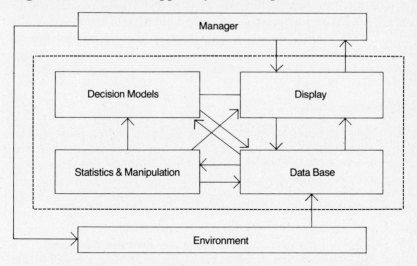

Source: John D. C. Little, Lakshmi Mohan, and Antoine Hatoun, "Yanking Knowledge from the Numbers," *Industrial Marketing*, 67 (March 1982), p. 46. Reprinted by permission.

use of CRTs (cathode ray tube) and microcomputer link-ups to mainframe computers enhances the manager's ability to interact with the DSS system. These developments facilitate the use of the information system for daily decision-making.

As John Little points out, industrial marketing is a fertile area for a DSS because it is complex, the markets are typically heterogeneous, the impact of technological change is significant, and pricing and sales force decisions are critical.[2] An effective DSS is especially relevant in the industrial sphere; many industrial firms find they have an overload of reports and data and significant shortfalls of *effective* information.

Required Decision Support System Attributes

To be effective, the DSS must incorporate three important attributes: managerial capability, analysis, and flexibility. First, the system should be able to provide managers with reports tailored to specific needs and market situations. Systems that impose a common format on all users and emphasize standardized rather than customized reports fail to meet the marketing manager's needs. Second, the system must be analytical rather than being simply report-generating. In addition to capturing historical information, the DSS should allow the evaluation of scenarios (e.g., "what would happen if . . ?").

[2]*Ibid*, p. 52.

The DSS should allow the manager to forecast the response of the market to alternative marketing strategies under a range of competitive and business environment scenarios. Third, the system must possess the flexibility and the speed to adapt quickly to changes in information requirements. Often, information is needed to provide the manager with a stronger and more relevant foundation for making a decision *today*!

Manipulating Data

A DSS is the core of the intelligence function in the industrial firm. The working DSS permits data aggregation at any level desired. For example, sales data would be stored by customer, product, and territory so that management can easily manipulate the data at any level of aggregation. Total sales, sales by top customers, sales by territory or large territories, or sales by product to specified customers in selected territories could be evaluated. In this way, the intelligence system is totally responsive to the level of analysis required for a specific industrial marketing decision. A focal point for any market intelligence system is the broad spectrum of secondary information available.

Secondary Information Sources

Information, whether developed through painstaking market research studies or gleaned from existing publications, exists to support business decisions. Secondary information gathered and published by government agencies, trade associations, trade publications, and independent research firms provides a valuable and often inexpensive start to building knowledge of the market. Of the many external sources of business information, secondary data is the principal source of information about a company's competitive and external environment.[3] Sources of secondary data abound; the real issue is to understand where to look for useful data in the face of so many possibilities.[4] The Standard Industrial Classification System is a vital source, as the vast majority of secondary information is reported on the basis of SIC codes.

The Standard Industrial Classification System

In order to develop meaningful data on United States businesses, the federal government has segmented all business activity into homogeneous categories. The classification system, known as the Standard Industrial Classification (SIC), facilitates the collection, tabulation, and

---

[3]James R. Fries, "Library Support for Industrial Marketing Research," *Industrial Marketing Management*, 11 (February 1982), p. 48.

[4]William E. Cox, Jr., *Industrial Marketing Research* (New York: John Wiley and Sons, 1979), p. 30.

analysis of a wide variety of economic data.[5] The *Standard Industrial Classification Manual*, published by the Office of Management and Budget and distributed through the U.S. Government Printing Office, describes the SIC fully.

The purpose of the SIC system is to identify groups of business firms that produce the same type of product. Every plant and business establishment in the United States is assigned a code that reflects the primary product produced at that location. The SIC coding system works in the following way:

First, the nation's economic activity is divided into 10 basic industries, *each of which is given a two-digit classification code. For example, codes 01–09 represent agriculture, 19–39 manufacturing, 70–89 services, and so on. Next,* major groups *are developed within each basic industry. Each major group has a specific two-digit code. Thus, manufacturing has 20 two-digit codes, each representing a major group such as SIC 34, which is fabricated metal products.*

Major groups are then further subdivided into three-digit industry groups. *There are 143 industry groups, including SIC 342, which represents hand tools and hardware. The next level of detail, four-digit codes, are* specific industries. *The SIC contains 454 specific industries, of which SIC 3423, hand and edge tools, is an example.*

The SIC system extends to additional levels of detail in some cases. Product classes *are defined by five-digit codes; the SIC contains 1,300 of these. Finally,* products *are assigned seven-digit codes; this subdivision contains 10,000 segments.*[6]

Figure 5.3 illustrates the basic elements of the SIC system, with hand tools as a specific example. As Figure 5.3 indicates, the more digits, the finer the classification. The most useful level of aggregation is the four-digit code, as there is little data published for five- and seven-digit codes. The *Census of Manufacturers* does assemble data at the five- and seven-digit levels, but the census is only published every five years.

The Design of the SIC System   To use SIC data effectively the industrial marketing manager must understand how the codes are developed and what their major limitations are. First, SIC codes are based on the product produced or the operation performed, with the final product as the major determining factor of classification. Second, codes are given to an "establishment," which refers to a single physical location such as a plant, factory, store, mine, farm, bank, office, or mill. Thus, a company may have many SIC codes, each applied to separate plants in the corporate system. Cincinnati Milacron, a billion-dollar producer of industrial manufacturing systems, operates plants in the Cincinnati area which have the following diverse SIC codes:

---

[5] *Standard Industrial Classification Manual*, 1982 (Washington, D.C.: U.S. Government Printing Office).

[6] Adapted from "Survey of Industrial Purchasing Power," *Sales and Marketing Management*, 120 (April 24, 1978), p. 32.

Figure 5.3   The Standard Industrial Classification

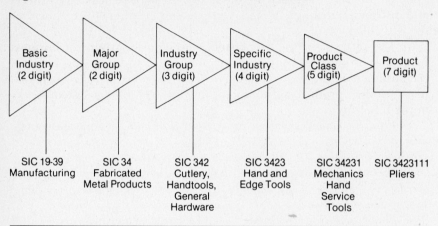

| SIC 19-39 Manufacturing | SIC 34 Fabricated Metal Products | SIC 342 Cutlery, Handtools, General Hardware | SIC 3423 Hand and Edge Tools | SIC 34231 Mechanics Hand Service Tools | SIC 3423111 Pliers |

- 2869   Industrial organic chemicals
- 2992   Lubricating oils and grease
- 3291   Abrasive products
- 3541   Screw machine products
- 3559   Special industry machinery
- 3622   Industrial controls
- 3679   Electronic components

The classification assigned to an individual establishment will depend on the "principal product" produced there. If two or more products are made, the principal product is determined by the one with the largest "value added."[7] However, sales or shipments are often used because of the difficulty in determining value added for individual products. All statistics for a particular plant will reflect activity associated with both the primary product and all secondary products. For example, if an electronics plant in Chicago manufactures $2.6 million of transformers (SIC 3612) and $5.9 million of electronic resistors (SIC 3676), an SIC code of 3676 would be assigned, and all data related to employment, investment, and value added are assigned to SIC 3676 because it is the primary product.

Finally, many companies have production facilities that manufacture items to be incorporated into the final product of their parent companies. In this situation, the data for the captive plant is assigned to the SIC of the parent plant's final product. The problem is that the output

[7] *Standard Industrial Classification Manual*, 1972, p. 646.

of the parent plant will thus be overstated, and the data for the industry to which the captive plant belongs will be understated.

Overcoming SIC Problems   In response to some of the difficulties associated with gathering data by "establishments" and assigning SIC by "primary product," the *Census of Manufacturers* has developed two corrective ratios. The *primary product specialization ratio* indicates the percentage of total shipments of a given four-digit industry accounted for by its primary product. For example, SIC 3011, tires and inner tubes, has a specialization ratio of 97 percent, while SIC 2812, alkalis and chlorine, has a ratio of 65 percent. Many firms in SIC 2812 apparently produce secondary products that make up a sizable portion of their total output. The specialization ratio indicates just how much of the production activity in an industry (four-digit SIC) is associated with its primary product. The higher the ratio, the more homogeneous the industry; as a rough rule of thumb, when ratios exceed 90 percent, data for the industry are very reliable.[8]

The *coverage ratio* compares the shipments of a primary product by a four-digit industry to the total shipments of that product by all SICs. SIC 3452, nuts, bolts, and washers, has a coverage ratio of 90 percent; SIC 2873, nitrogenous fertilizers, has a ratio of 69 percent. Thus, 31 percent of the nitrogenous fertilizer is made by establishments in other SIC groups. Obviously, if the manager is gathering data on a particular four-digit SIC industry with a low coverage ratio, it will be necessary to carefully investigate industries other than the SIC under scrutiny. As with the specialization ratio, a 90 percent coverage ratio indicates that the data is reliable.

The industrial marketing manager must use caution when using data based on the SIC, referring to the specialization and coverage ratios to assess the reliability of the information to be analyzed. Sometimes the manager will need to develop original data through market surveys to circumvent the problems associated with the classification system.

The limitations of the SIC, however, are in no way an indictment of the system. The process of classifying economic activity in an economy as vast and diverse as that in the United States is a tremendous undertaking. The SIC is an invaluable tool that industrial marketers can use to collect and analyze data about their markets from a variety of sources, knowing that the data is developed from a common base.

Using the SIC   Industrial firms are segmented by the products that they produce and the production processes that they employ. If the coverage and specialization ratios are high, each SIC group should be relatively homogeneous in terms of raw materials required, components

---

[8] Francis E. Hummel, *Market and Sales Potentials* (New York: The Ronald Press Company, 1961), p. 77.

used, manufacturing process employed, and problems faced. As a result, the SIC is often an excellent basis on which to segment markets. If the manager understands the needs and requirements of a few firms within an SIC category, requirements can be projected for all firms within that category. For example, most firms manufacturing truck trailers (SIC 3715) will need to purchase components such as wheels, tires, sheet steel, grease, oil, plastic parts, and electrical parts. Their requirements will be similar, and potential suppliers can evaluate the total market through a detailed analysis of a few SIC 3715 companies. Suppose a supplier of steel wheels determines through a sales analysis of present customers that SIC 3715 firms purchase $.08 of wheels per dollar of their final shipments. A market estimate of total wheel sales to SIC 3715 could be developed by reference to total shipments: The *Annual Survey of Manufacturers* for 1982 reveals that SIC 3715 shipped $1,223.1 million of trailers, which suggests a potential wheel sales volume of $1,223.1 million × .08 = $97.85 million.

Identifying New Customers   The SIC is useful for identifying new customers. The marketing manager can study a four-digit industry to evaluate whether the firms in it could use the marketer's product or service. Although this analysis will only provide rough estimates, it is very helpful in eliminating industries that are not potential product users. SIC groups that show promise of possible use can be singled out for evaluation in depth.

Segmentation   Since each SIC is relatively homogeneous in terms of problems and processes, segmentation on the basis of SIC is often very effective. An understanding of the SIC system is particularly relevant for gathering market information because so many government agencies, trade associations, and private research firms collect data on the basis of SIC codes.

Published Sources of Industrial Marketing Data

Marketing decisions are only as good as the data used to generate them. The breadth of data available to the industrial marketing manager provides both an opportunity and a challenge. The opportunity arises from the wealth of available industrial market data. Government at all levels, trade associations, trade publications, and private research companies publish a great deal of economic data on a national, state, and county basis. Most of this data is collected by SIC code, allowing for an analysis industry-by-industry and, sometimes, product-by-product. The challenge is to develop familiarity with secondary data sources, to understand the nature of the data in these sources, and to comprehend how the data can enhance industrial marketing. Table 5.1 provides a compact summary of prime data sources available for defining target segments in the organizational market, estimating market potential, forecasting sales, evaluating competitors, and providing an understanding of market needs.

Federal Government Data Sources   Some of the more important federal government sources are described in Table 5.1. Federal data is oriented to industries; the basic unit of analysis is a particular four-digit SIC category. For this reason, federal data sources are often the cornerstone for the determination of market and sales potentials by industry.

The most comprehensive set of federal data is the *Census of Manufacturers*. Every five years the Bureau of Census conducts a nationwide census of manufacturing establishments, surveying number of employees, value added, cost of materials, shipments, capital expenditures, etc. The data is summarized for four-digit SIC categories, geographic regions, and states. Thus, detailed economic statistics can be determined for every SIC category by state and region. Product shipments for five- and seven-digit SIC categories are also presented, allowing the marketing manager to focus on very specific industries within regions and states.

As Table 5.1 suggests, the *Census of Manufacturers* makes it possible to investigate, by geographic region, the size and scope of industries that are potential customers. The primary difficulty is the timeliness of the data—the *Census* is only published every five years. In addition, it takes one to three years from data collection to publication.

The problem of the timeliness of the *Census* is partially circumvented by the *Annual Survey of Manufacturers*. The *Annual Survey* is a probability sample of 70,000 manufacturers drawn from the *Census of Manufacturers* and supplemented by Social Security Administration lists of new establishments. All establishments with over 250 employees in the preceding *Census* are included in the sample.[9] The *Annual Survey* provides essentially the same data as the *Census*, but in less detail and to only the four-digit SIC code level. Survey data is usually published one to two years after collection.

County Business Patterns is an annual publication that provides employment statistics for all manufacturing establishments county-by-county. Statistics on taxable payrolls, number of employees, and number of reporting units, are reported by four-digit SIC group. *County Business Patterns* is especially valuable when demand for a company's product is highly correlated with the size of potential establishments as indicated by the number of employees. In such cases, market potential can be calculated on a county, region, state, or territorial basis in those industries deemed to be potential markets. A serious limitation of *County Business Patterns* is the nondisclosure rule, which prevents the Census Bureau

[9] U.S. Department of Commerce, "A Guide to Federal Data Sources on Manufacturing" (September 1977), p. 45.

Table 5.1 A Selection of Data Sources for Use in Industrial Market Analysis

Source	Title of Publication	Type of Data	Application	Frequency of Publication	Comments
Federal Government	*Census of Manufacturers* (U.S. Dept. of Commerce)	General data by 4-, 5-, 7-digit SIC on value added, employees, number of establishments, shipments, and materials consumed. Data shown by region, state, employment size, etc.	Provides comprehensive data to determine potential by area and for specific industries.	Every 5 years	Broadest array of industrial data; based on a census, may be dated.
	Annual Survey of Manufacturers (U.S. Dept. of Commerce)	Based on a sample of firms; yields current 4-digit SIC data similar to the *Census*.	Similar to the *Census*.	Annually	Less comprehensive and detailed than the *Census*; up to date.
	County Business Patterns (U.S. Dept. of Commerce)	Statistics on number of establishments and employment by 4-digit SIC for all counties in the U.S.	Used to estimate market potential by region; evaluate industry concentration by region.	Annually	Provides effective estimates of potential if number of employees is correlated to industry demand.
	Standard Industrial Classification Manual (U.S. Bureau of the Budget)	Complete description of the SIC system. Describes all 4-digit industries.	Used to evaluate possible industrial users based on products they produce.	Every 5 years	Lists each 4-digit SIC category and its primary products.
	U.S. Industrial Outlook (U.S. Dept. of Commerce)	Overall view of over 200 4-digit SIC industries with past and future growth rates in shipments and employment.	Project future market concentration and potential.	Annually	Reasonably current data; provides useful look at growth prospects in selected industries.
	Current Industrial Reports (U.S. Dept. of Commerce)	Series of over 100 reports covering 5000 products; usually based on 3-digit SIC, but may use 7-digit codes. Shipment and production data provided.	Provides in-depth analysis of potential by specific industry.	Monthly to Annually	Very timely data; published 4–8 weeks after data is collected.
	A Guide to Federal Data Sources on Manufacturing (U.S. Dept. of Commerce)	Describes nature and sources of all federal government data related to manufacturing.	A quick guide to locate appropriate government data.	Annually	Valuable source document for understanding government statistics.
State, Local Government	State and Local Industrial Directories	Type of data varies, but usually provides individual company data such as SIC code, sales, number of employees, products, and address.	Useful for defining specific potential customers by state and region.	Usually Annual	Provides data on firms of all sizes. Particularly useful when markets are concentrated in a few states.
Trade Associations	For example: National Machine Tool Builders Association, Glass Container Manufacturers Institute	Sales history of the industry; industrial, financial, and operating data.	Provide an evaluation of past and present growth potentials by industry.	Usually Annual	May provide useful industry data not contained in other sources, i.e., average age of equipment, etc.

			Updated	
Trade Publications	For example: S&MM "Survey of Industrial Purchasing Power."	Number of plants and shipments by SIC code by county; county percentage of total U.S. shipments by SIC.	Annually	Very timely source for quickly assessing potential by county and state.
	Iron Age: "Basic Marketing Data on Metal-Working."	Census of metalworking industry. Data on plants and employees on a regional basis.	Annual	Useful for easy estimation of potential for a particular industry.
Private Industrial Directories and Research (Fee) Companies	For example: Predicasts (Predicasts, Cleveland, OH)	Growth forecasts and market outlook for various industries by SIC.	Quarterly	Up-to-date information on growth trends by 7-digit SIC.
	Dun's Market Identifiers (Dun & Bradstreet, N.Y.)	Data on 3.5 million corporations relative to company SIC, address, locations, sales, and employees.	Continuous File	Timely information on specific firms can be obtained quickly.
	Standard & Poor's Industry Surveys' Basic Analysis (Standard & Poor's Corp., N.Y.)	Data on major industries and companies.	Weekly	Timely, general data on major industries.
International Data Sources	For example: The Yearbook of Industrial Statistics (United Nations Statistical Office)	Vol. 1: Basic country data and indicators showing global and regional trends in industrial activity	Annually	Largest compilation of international industrial data. Data covers a ten-year period for each volume.
		Vol. 2: Statistics for 500 industrial commodities and 200 countries		
	The Yearbook of International Trade Statistics (U.N. Statistical Office)	Quantity and value of exports and imports of various commodities over the past several years	Annually	Valuable for assessing trends in product and country imports and exports.
	Ulrich's International Periodicals Directory (R. R. Bowker Co., New York)	Covers 61,000 periodicals throughout the world	Annually	Market potential for various products by country
	Japan Company Handbook (Toyo Keizai Shinposha, LTD, Tokyo)	Covers 1,003 Japanese corporations	Biannually	Used to develop data base on international business activity
		Covers 1,003 Japanese corporations	Biannually	Evaluation of competition strength and market performance

from publishing data that could identify a specific firm. In such cases, the data for a particular county is not reported, which leads to underestimates of industrial activity there.

There are, of course, many additional federal data sources (see Table 5.1). Sources are more fully described in *A Guide to Federal Data Sources on Manufacturing*, published by the Department of Commerce.

Other Data Sources   The federal government collects primarily *industry* statistics; however, states, local governments, and private industrial directories provide data on individual firms. State and local governments publish annual directories of businesses within their jurisdiction. The directories generally include company name, address, SIC code, products produced, sales volume, and number of employees. The directories enable the marketing manager to evaluate market potential firm-by-firm by well-defined geographic areas.

Private industrial directories and research companies like Dun and Bradstreet and Standard and Poor's maintain up-to-date files on industrial firms. *Dun's Market Identifiers* provides current information on sales volume, products, employees, and location, for more than 3.5 million firms. It provides the manager with quick information on an individual company.

Trade associations often provide industry statistics that are not found in government sources (e.g., average age of capital equipment in the industry). Trade publications also report industry-oriented data. *Iron Age* annually does a census of the metalworking industry, which includes data on plants and employees. On a broader scale, *Sales and Marketing Management* publishes an annual *Survey of Industrial Purchasing Power*, which provides a quick reference to shipments by SIC groups by county. The *Survey* will be discussed further in Chapter 7.

International Data Sources   The United Nations is the primary source for international industrial data. The Statistical Office of the United Nations in New York publishes a vast array of statistics and reports. The two-volume *Yearbook of Industrial Statistics* annually reports on country and regional trends in business activity as well as statistics on more than 500 industrial products. Import and export data for a variety of commodities is reported by the *Yearbook of International Trade Statistics*. Private research companies are also active. Dun and Bradstreet publishes *Principal International Business*, which provides information on almost 50,000 large companies in 133 countries, arranged both geographically and by SIC number. The rapid ascension of Japan in world markets has spawned a variety of statistical publications on Japan alone. *Japan Company Handbook* supplies sales, financial data, and company outlook for over 1000 Japanese firms. As industrial marketing becomes global, the industrial marketing manager must be able to adapt the marketing intelligence system to capture secondary data world-wide.

So You Want to Sell to the Auto Industry?

Predicasts, a leading information and research firm, was asked to run a research study for a fictitious chair and sofa manufacturer who wished to enter the auto OEM market as a seat supplier. The response from Predicasts was fast and efficient. The customer, had it purchased Predicasts's on-line service, could have had a complete report almost instantly for $50, a full search for $375.

The information was substantial. Data gathered from hard copy publications, *Predicasts Forecasts* and *Basebook*, indicates market size for a variety of SIC industries dealing with the auto industry. Included are a time series of sales volume back to 1965 as well as the annual growth rate of the particular market and the source of the data. Further, the *Basebook* reveals that two-door sedans have an annual growth rate of 7.5 percent versus minus .1 percent for four-doors; small auto production grew at 20.9 percent annually compared to minus 1.2 percent for large autos. Bucket seats look good while the prediction for the big roomy back seats is pretty gloomy.

Forecasts reveals that the use of molded urethane seating is expected to drop 0.5 percent in the next 10 years. On the bright side, sales of foreign-made cars are expected to increase by as much as 12.3 percent in the next three years. Perhaps the export market offers the best opportunity.

A computer search of 2500 publications produces 10 feet of printout on the automotive seating market. The news is good and bad. Lear Siegler Automotive has already been chosen to produce a sizable portion of the seats in Ford and GM cars. Hoover Universal has secured a prominent position in the small car program for every major auto manufacturer—up to 40 percent of the domestic market. On the positive side, foreign markets are growing rapidly. Plastic seats are expanding in an effort to reduce weight. The sources also show the leading foreign manufacturers of seating as well as major seating contracts signed by various auto manufacturers.

Perhaps the automotive seating market doesn't look so good after all.

Adapted from: Philip Maher, "A Market Researcher's Basic Data Guide," *Industrial Marketing*, 67 (March 1982), p. 80.

Table 5.2   A Sample of Computer Data Bases

Data Base	Supplier	Cost	Nature of the Data Base
ABI/Inform	Lockheed's DIALOG	$73 per hour (of connect time)	Background information on industries, companies, products, current business topics. Four hundred trade and business periodicals are scanned.
Chemical Industry Notes	Lockheed	$80 per hour	Information from over 75 international business periodicals that cover the chemical industry. Biweekly update.
Dow Jones News	Dow Jones, Inc.	$80 per hour	Includes general business news from the *Wall Street Journal*, *Barrons*, and Dow Jones' Wire Service.
Frost & Sullivan Defense Market Measures System	Lockheed	$90 per hour	U.S. government contract awards, requests for proposals, sole-source negotiations, research and development sources sought, agency planning and procurement information. Quarterly updates.
Predicasts Terminal System	Predicasts, Inc.	$90 per hour	A variety of reports and forecasts with domestic and international coverage. Data can be extracted by SIC, companies, nations, and many other methods. Updated weekly.

Source: Adapted from James R. Fries, "Library Support for Industrial Marketing Research," *Industrial Marketing Management*, 11 (February 1982), p. 50.

Developing a Data Base from Secondary Sources

In creating a data bank of secondary data for decision making, industrial marketers are increasingly turning to on-line computer data base searching. The industrial marketer pays a fee (per hour of connect time to the computer) to an information service company such as Lockheed's DIALOG Information Service, Dow Jones, Inc., or Predicasts, Inc. The computer scans the periodical and publication base maintained by the information service company and provides output in the form of a report. On-line computer data base searching dramatically reduces the time-consuming and costly process of a library search of published information or first-hand gathering of the raw data itself.[10]

Computer data base searching has grown rapidly over the past ten years; there are over 450 computerized data bases available to the industrial marketer[11] (see Table 5.2 for types). Through the computerized data bases, industrial marketing managers can customize analyses for specific problems. The types of reports include bibliographies on almost any business topic; time series data on production, consumption, im-

[10] J. A. Roberts, "Marketing Research," *Industrial Marketing*, 70 (January 1981), p. 44–53.

[11] Walter Kiechel, "Everything You Always Wanted to Know May Soon Be On-line," *Fortune*, 101 (September 1980), p. 227.

ports, and exports of products and services; financial data on specific companies; or performance trends for industries.[12] Data base searching offers two important advantages for generating secondary information: (1) expediency—extensive library search time is totally eliminated; (2) custom-designed analyses—all available data bases can be scanned at the same time, or the search can be limited to specific topics, industries, companies, or countries.

The development of a secondary data base is one aspect of the marketing intelligence function. An equally important, and often more difficult, component is the market research function, the gathering of primary information.

Industrial Marketing Research

Industrial marketing research is a very broad area, defined as "the systematic gathering, recording, and analyzing of information and opportunities relating to the marketing of industrial goods and services."[13] It typically includes sales and market potential analysis, sales forecasting, market surveys, experiments, and observational studies. Formalized marketing research often provides the data used in planning and control. Industrial marketing research usually undertakes primary data studies—surveys, observation, or experiments—when conclusive research is needed or secondary data too limited for the decision at hand.

The terms marketing research and marketing intelligence are frequently confused by students and managers alike. Marketing research is more narrow in scope; it is but one component of the industrial marketing intelligence system. Marketing research is generally undertaken for unique projects with specific objectives. Marketing intelligence is an ongoing function designed to provide continuous information for decision making. One aspect is the design and implementation of marketing research projects to create an information base for making individual decisions. What are the distinguishing characteristics of industrial marketing research?

Industrial Marketing Research Is Different

Marketing research involves certain basic elements that apply generally. In any context, the research study must be planned, a data-gathering instrument designed, and a sampling plan designed. The data must then be gathered, processed, analyzed, and reported. However, because of the environment of the industrial market and the nature of organiza-

---

[12] Fries, "Library Support for Industrial Marketing Research," p. 49.

[13] Cox, *Industrial Marketing Research*, p. 3.

tional buying, industrial marketing research differs from consumer-goods research. Some of the more relevant differences are:[14]

1.   Greater reliance on exploratory studies, secondary data, and expert judgment data in industrial research. Because of demand concentration, market information tends to be concentrated among a few knowledgeable people, who may be surveyed when time and cost constrain large sample designs. The wealth of government and trade association data by SIC categories provides a valuable secondary data base for many industrial decisions.

2.   Industrial marketing research places more emphasis on surveys as opposed to experimental and observational primary data methods. Experimental and observational studies are not as effective in industrial as in consumer-goods markets.

3.   Personal interviewing is stressed in industrial marketing research. Usually, specific respondents can be identified in the industrial market (although they are sometimes difficult to reach) and the target population is smaller and more concentrated. Thus, specific individuals in the buying center can be singled out for in-depth interviews.

4.   Industrial marketing research is concerned with the determination of market size and potential, as opposed to the consumer research concern for psychological market segmentation.

5.   Surveys in industrial marketing frequently encounter different problems than those in consumer research; as a consequence, the survey process is often quite different. Figure 5.4 compares the survey research process in industrial and in consumer marketing research. Note the difficulties associated with respondent accessibility and cooperation on the industrial side. These are important, given the prevalence of personal interviewing.

Finally, industrial marketing research places increasing emphasis on systematic studies of the organizational buying process. Significant advances have been made over the past ten years, but refined marketing research approaches will be required to enable the industrial firm to more fully comprehend the buying decision center in target organizations.

The Tasks of Industrial Marketing Research

A survey by the American Marketing Association reports on the responsibilities of marketing research departments of industrial firms. It suggests that industrial research focuses on estimating potential, market

---

[14] The first four items are based on William E. Cox, Jr., and Luis V. Dominguiz, "The Key Issues and Procedures of Industrial Marketing Research," *Industrial Marketing Management*, 8 (January 1979), pp. 81–93.

Figure 5.4   Consumer vs. Industrial Marketing Research: What are the Differences?

	Consumer	Industrial
Universe/ Population	Large. Dependent on category under investigation but usually unlimited. 72.5 million U.S. households and 215 million persons.	Small. Fairly limited in total population and even more so if within a defined industry or SIC category.
Respondent Accessibility	Fairly easy. Can interview at home, on the telephone, or using mail techniques.	Difficult. Usually only during working hours at plant, office, or on the road. Respondent is usually preoccupied with other priorities.
Respondent Cooperation	Over the years has become more and more difficult, yet millions of consumers have never been interviewed.	A major concern. Due to the small population, the industrial respondent is being over-researched. The purchaser and decision makers in an industrial firm are the buyers of a variety of products and services from office supplies to heavy equipment.
Sample Size	Can usually be drawn as large as required for statistical confidence since the population is in the hundreds of millions.	Usually much smaller than consumer sample, yet the statistical confidence is equal due to the relationship of the sample to the total population.
Respondent Definitions	Usually fairly simple. Those aware of a category or brand, users of a category or brand, demographic criteria, etc. The ultimate purchaser is also a user for most consumer products and services.	Somewhat more difficult. The user and the purchasing decision maker in most cases are not the same. Factory workers who use heavy equipment, secretaries who use typewriters, etc., are the users and, no doubt, best able to evaluate these products and services. However, they tend not to be the ultimate purchasers and in many cases do not have any influence on the decision-making process.
Interviewers	Can usually be easily trained. They are also consumers and tend to be somewhat familiar with the area under investigation for most categories.	Difficult to find good executive interviewers. At least a working knowledge of the product class or subject being surveyed is essential. Preferably more than just a working knowledge.
Study Costs	Key dictators of cost are sample size and incidence. Lower incidence usage categories (for example, users of soft moist dog food, powdered breakfast beverages, etc.) or demographic or behavioral screening criteria (attend a movie at least once a month, over 65 years of age, and do not have direct deposit of social security payments, etc.) can up costs considerably.	Relative to consumer research, the critical element resulting in significantly higher per-interview costs are: the lower incidence levels, the difficulties in locating the "right" respondent (that is, the purchase decision maker), and securing cooperation (time and concentration of effort) for the interview itself.

Source: Martin Katz, "Use Same Theory, Skills for Consumer, Industrial Marketing Research," *The Marketing News* (January 12, 1979), p. 16. Reprinted by permission of the American Marketing Association.

share analysis, sales analysis, forecasting, and competitive product studies.[15] Many of these are discussed at length later in this book. Clearly, an effective marketing research department is a valuable asset in developing and controlling the industrial marketing program.

Research Methods

Although industrial marketers rely heavily on secondary data, primary data is often collected to gain firsthand knowledge of customer attitudes, motivations, and buying intentions. For all types of marketing research, the basic methods for gathering primary data are:

1. *Surveys*—questioning people believed to possess the information desired.

2. *Observation*—viewing people and behavior and recording the information without asking questions.

3. *Experimentation*—setting up a controlled situation in which the outcome of some test is evaluated, and one or more factors are varied to measure cause-and-effect relationships.

Surveys are the most common research method in industrial marketing research,[16] because they can provide the type of information industrial marketers seek.

Applications of Survey Research

Survey techniques are effective for gathering primary data of the following types:[17]

1. Awareness and knowledge

2. Attitudes and opinions

3. Intentions

4. Motivations

5. Demographic characteristics

6. Behavior

As this list suggests, the purpose of the survey is to understand the buying behavior of present and potential industrial customers in order to formulate appropriate marketing strategy. Figure 5.5 provides a rich example of the nature and use of survey data in industrial marketing. Although the situation is hypothetical, it does demonstrate the versatility

[15] *1973 Survey of Marketing Research* (Chicago: American Marketing Association, 1973), pp. 28–30.

[16] Cox, *Industrial Marketing Research*, p. 81.

[17] *Ibid*, p. 242.

Figure 5.5   Explaining Market Share Performance

Suppose an evaluation of desk-top copier sales reveals that market share for Xerox varies widely among the three primary market segments: commercial, industrial, and government. A survey among a sample from each segment can be utilized to explain the variance in performance.

First, each sample group would be queried on their general *awareness* and *knowledge* of Xerox desk copiers as well as competitive offerings in this product line. The goal here would be to ascertain whether market share performance is related to the job Xerox has done in communicating to the three market segments. A second phase of the survey would relate to assessing the decision-maker's *attitude* toward Xerox and its competitors in terms of company image, product characteristics, and service performance. Thus, although the segments may each be aware of Xerox, negative attitudes toward the firm or its product and service performance might explain the difference in sales penetration in the three segments.

A key feature of the survey in this case would be to develop a clear picture of the underlying *motivations* associated with the purchase of desk-top copiers. Part of the survey would be structured to elicit a ranking of key product and service attributes that different members of the buying center use in making a supplier choice. In this case, the survey might be able to show that Xerox has not focused their sales program on key product attributes that are important to the low-market share segments.

Most surveys include a section on *demographics*, that is, company characteristics (size, nature of business, location) and decision-maker characteristics (title, experience, job function, age). Evaluation of the demographic data relative to sales penetration may suggest important relationships between company and decision-maker characteristics and market share.

A final section of the survey may focus on *intention*, that is, an estimation of future buying plans for desk-top copiers. Although valid estimates of specific brand intentions would be difficult to obtain, the survey may be able to assess future product category expenditures. In this way a rough estimate of potential could be developed.

Source: Adapted from William F. Cox, Jr., *Industrial Marketing Research* (New York: John Wiley and Sons, Inc., 1979), p. 242.

---

of the survey method in generating primary data that would be unattainable from secondary sources. As the example demonstrates, survey data can be pivotal in evaluating performance and adjusting market strategies. Let us consider the different methods of applying survey research.

Survey Methods in Industrial Marketing

Three methods of contact with respondents prevail in industrial marketing: (1) personal interview, (2) telephone, and (3) mail.

Personal Interviews   Because industrial marketing research often uses relatively small samples and much of the information involves in-depth questioning and probing, personal interviewing is the dominant survey approach. Generally, the greater the complexity of the information sought, the more effective personal interviewing is. When technical data, graphs, and illustrations are required, personal interviews are the only choice.

Personal interviewing usually produces high response rates because the interviewer can locate and secure the attention of the correct respondent. In addition, more information can generally be elicited through personal interviews. But personal interviewing is the most expensive and time-consuming form of survey research, and the expense may limit its application.

Telephone Surveys　Telephone interviewing is useful in industrial marketing research particularly for evaluating advertising recall, assessing corporate image, and measuring company and brand awareness. If prior contact has been made with respondents with a shared vocabulary of technical terms, telephone surveys are a cost-effective way to obtain primary information. For telephone surveys to be effective, the researcher must be able to reach the correct respondent. Telephone interviews are clearly the fastest method for gathering information. Their major drawbacks are (1) limitations on the amount and kind of information that can be gathered, and (2) inability to detect and control interviewer bias. Telephone interviewers often have difficulty in gaining access to the respondent, as secretaries are adept at screening calls. Nevertheless, some firms find telephone surveys effective where advice or opinions are required to make a particular decision rapidly. In this case, a broad listing of firms can be maintained from which a sample can be quickly drawn.

Mail Surveys　Mail surveys are restricted in terms of the amount and complexity of information that can be gathered. The quality and quantity of data resulting from a mail survey depend on the respondent's interest in the topic and the degree of difficulty of the questions. The most severe problem associated with industrial mail surveys is nonresponse, particularly from large firms.[18] The nonresponse problem has two facets: (1) the original respondent simply fails to return the survey or (2) the survey is returned by someone other than the original respondent. The latter is often difficult to detect, but does reduce the validity of the survey. Generally, response rates to industrial mail surveys tend to be lower than for consumer surveys.[19] This is a continuing problem and one that industrial marketing researchers must address.

　　Mail surveys take more time to construct and administer than telephone surveys, but are not as demanding as personal interviews. Because of the impersonal nature of the contact and the complexity of the subject matter, the wording and structure of the questionnaire are extremely critical. To secure meaningful response rates, follow-up mailings are frequently required. As one might expect, mail surveys are generally the least expensive survey method.

　　Table 5.3 uses six criteria to compare the three survey techniques. The inherent tradeoffs among the three survey research methods must be evaluated in light of the type of information sought, time and re-

[18] T. L. Renschling and M. J. Etzel, "The Disappearing Data Source," *Business Horizons*, 16 (April 1963), p. 17.
[19] Cox, *Industrial Marketing Research*, p. 250.

Table 5.3   A Comparison of Industrial Survey Methods

Approach	Cost	Time	Criteria Information Quality	Information Quantity	Non-response Problem	Interviewer Bias
Personal Interview	Highest cost per respondent	Most time-consuming	Can elicit in-depth, complex information	Extensive	Few problems, as a result of face-to-face contact	Hard to detect and control
Telephone	Second highest cost	Least time-consuming	Complex information if prior contact established	Limited	Difficult to insure that contact is made with correct respondent	Hard to detect and control
Mail	Least cost	Moderate	Moderately complex information	Moderate; depends on respondent interest and effort required	Difficult to control who responds and how many will respond	Can be controlled by rigorous pretesting

Source: Adapted from William E. Cox, Jr., *Industrial Marketing Research* (New York: John Wiley and Sons, 1979), pp. 246–251.

search funds available, and the levels of reliability required. Only then can the appropriate method be selected.

Organizing for Research

The research function can be centralized, decentralized, or contracted out to specialized industrial marketing research companies. For maximum impact, research findings must be effectively integrated into the decision-making process. The organizational placement of the research function will have a definite effect on whether this goal is accomplished. Deciding how to organize the marketing research function requires consideration of several delicate organizational issues. Generally, marketing research should be free from the influence of those whom its work affects; have a location that is conducive to maximum operational efficiency; and have the wholehearted support of the executive to whom it reports.[20]

Two-Tier Research Staff   Large industrial firms often have a centralized corporate marketing research unit and smaller-scale divisional

[20] *Marketing, Business and Commercial Research in Industry*, Studies in Business Policy, No. 27 (New York: National Industrial Conference Board, 1955), p. 7, as reported in H. Robert Dodge, *Industrial Marketing* (New York: McGraw-Hill Book Company, 1970), p. 117.

marketing research units. The central research unit usually has a full-time staff whose major function is to gather broad-gauge data on the economy and the industry, and to conduct studies for product line alternatives, new product opportunities, and acquisitions. The centralized research staff may significantly contribute to the development of marketing plans and strategy. In general, central staff research activities affect more than one group or division—preparing economic forecasts, planning support, and researching management science and information systems.[21] The research conducted by the operating unit research staff is usually concerned with divisional performance areas such as product sales rates, advertising effectiveness, and market share studies.

Management Support   Regardless of how the industrial marketing research function is organized, the unit requires the support of top management. The central research department should report to a high-level executive or even to the president to ensure that: (1) marketing research information will be used properly in the decision-making process; and (2) the marketing research function will be given a fair hearing during the corporate budgeting process. The contribution of marketing research can be realized to its fullest extent when top management recognizes its role in the development and control of industrial marketing strategy.

Utilizing "Outside" Research Specialists

Many types of industrial marketing research require specialized skills. Studies on organizational buying behavior, company image evaluations, or strategic adjustments required by environmental conditions may require outside assistance. The range of alternatives is wide—from free advice provided by advertising agencies to expensive special-purpose studies conducted by management consultants or market research specialists. Some consulting and marketing organizations specialize in the industrial field.[22] The purpose and scope of the research needed and the research funds available determine which form of outside assistance is most appropriate.

   An important mode of industrial research is the multi-client study. A market research firm might propose to study the market for specialty steel products. The research firm circulates a written proposal to firms that might benefit from such a study. If enough firms are willing to participate, the cost of the research is shared by them. A company like Du Pont receives hundreds of such proposals every year.

---

[21] William P. Hall, "Marketing Research for Industrial Products," *Industrial Marketing Management*, 4 (1975), p. 211.
[22] For example, see *ibid.*, p. 211.

Industrial marketing research provides the data necessary to evaluate performance and plan future marketing strategies. The industrial marketing research process uses different techniques and tools from those employed in the consumer-goods market. However, sound research methods are equally necessary. The organization of the marketing research function will depend on the size, nature, and role of research in the industrial firm. However, for research to be effective, top management must understand that research plays a vital role in industrial marketing management.

Using Research in the Industrial Marketing Process

Market Potential and Sales Forecasting   The marketing intelligence function is responsible for maintaining the data base for estimating market potential and forecasting sales, as well as developing the appropriate methodologies and models for generating these estimates. Because of the importance of these estimation procedures, each will be discussed in a separate chapter.

New Product Research   Much of the research activity associated with new products is undertaken through formal market research studies. An important component of this type of research is the formulation of systematic procedures to gather new product ideas from customers, middlemen, sales personnel, competitors, and management. Without formal systems, many new product concepts will go unrecognized and significant opportunities for sales growth will be lost. Many of the issues associated with new product research will be treated in Chapter 10, "Managing the Industrial Product Line."

Marketing Control   The success of marketing strategy partially depends upon the ability of the marketing manager to understand the requirements of target customers and effectively develop the marketing mix to meet those requirements. Equally important is the system whereby the manager evaluates actual against planned performance and objectives, the *marketing control system*. Although the control process is vital in evaluating past performance, it is even more important to the future. Information generated by the marketing control system is an essential element in revising existing marketing strategies, formulating new strategies, and allocating funds to specific programs. The requirements of an effective control system are strict—data must be gathered continuously on the appropriate performance measures. Central to the industrial marketing intelligence system are systems and procedures for generating the required performance information and readily accessible information banks to continuously evaluate performance. Because the marketing control aspects of the marketing intelligence system are substantial and important, marketing control will be examined in detail in the final chapter.

The Cost of Primary Research

The substantial cost of collecting primary data must be balanced against its probable value to management. Managers must always take risks because of incomplete information; they cannot afford the luxury of sophisticated research every time a decision must be made. The cost of primary research can be more easily justified as the financial risk of a decision increases. If the level of risk is low, the cost of gathering more information may be greater than the financial loss associated with a poor decision. Primary research should be used when the manager believes that the risk can be greatly reduced at a reasonable cost.

Summary

A key aspect of marketing strategy formulation is the development of an information base that facilitates decision making, monitors the environment, and simplifies performance evaluation. The marketing intelligence system accomplishes these objectives. The marketing intelligence system is composed of models, information-gathering procedures, and analysis and marketing research techniques to provide a continuous information flow. This function includes marketing research studies, sales forecasting and market potential estimation, control systems, and secondary data files.

     The intelligence system is designed to provide management with a decision support system—data, models, manipulation, and displays that make information amenable to the decision-making process. Gathering and evaluating secondary data is another important dimension of marketing intelligence. The amount of secondary data available to the industrial marketing manager is staggering; many industrial firms are turning to on-line computer searches of secondary data as a means to more effectively gather, disseminate, and use such data.

     Marketing research refers to the techniques and procedures for gathering primary data for decision making. Industrial marketing research is unique as a result of the nature of the industrial market and the industrial buying process. Much primary research in the industrial setting is by surveys: personal, interviews, mail, or telephone. Gathering the necessary data to control marketing activities also falls within the domain of the intelligence system.

     Finally, sales forecasting and market potential estimates require significant data and extensive knowledge of market segments. Specific techniques for segmenting the industrial market constitute the theme of the next chapter.

Discussion Questions

1. Describe the key components of an industrial marketing intelligence system and the role that each component assumes in managing the marketing function in an industrial firm.

2. Some experts contend that industrial marketing is an especially fertile area for the application of a decision support system (DSS). First, describe the features of the industrial market that lend themselves to a DSS. Next, describe the attributes that a DSS should possess to aid the marketing manager.

3. The Tarlton Varnish Company would like to locate furniture manufacturers in Michigan that may be potential users of their product line. What sources of information could they consult in evaluating the potential demand for their products in Michigan? What sources could be used to identify potential customers by name and address?

4. To overcome some of the problems that arise in using SIC data for market planning, two ratios are particularly valuable: the primary product specialization ratio and the coverage ratio. Describe how an industrial marketer can improve the quality of segmentation decisions by applying these ratios.

5. What information can the industrial marketer draw from: (1) *Census of Manufacturers*, (2) *Annual Survey of Manufacturers*, and (3) *County Business Patterns*? How is the SIC system used in each?

6. The Alberg Machine Tool Company would like to evaluate the relative attractiveness of selected international markets. Suggest some international data sources that the firm might consult.

7. Compare and contrast marketing research in the industrial versus the consumer-goods sector.

8. Houston Electronics recently introduced a new component that appears to have significant potential among manufacturers of personal computers. The firm would like to use an industrial marketing research study to identify the composition of the buying centers for this product. Develop a research design.

9. Formulate an industrial marketing research problem that would lend itself to a telephone survey.

10. The marketing research function can be centralized at the corporate level or decentralized at the divisional level. Likewise, the marketing research function can be found in research and development or may be fully integrated into the marketing department. What factors must be considered in positioning the marketing research function in the corporate structure of the industrial firm?

C·H·A·P·T·E·R
6

Segmenting the
Organizational Market

The industrial seller faces a market made up of many different types of organizational customers with varying needs. Only when this aggregate market is broken down into meaningful categories can the industrial marketing strategist readily and profitably respond to unique needs. After reading this chapter, you will have an understanding of:

1. *the benefits of and requirements for segmenting the organizational market;*
2. *potential bases for segmenting the organizational market;*
3. *a procedure for evaluating and selecting market segments;*
4. *the role of market segmentation in the development of industrial marketing strategy.*

The organizational market consists of three broad sectors—commercial enterprises, institutions, and government. Whether marketers elect to operate in one or all of these sectors, they will encounter diversity in organizations, purchasing structures, and decision-making styles. Each sector has many different segments; each segment may have different needs and require a unique marketing strategy. The industrial marketer who recognizes the needs of the different segments of the market is best equipped to isolate market opportunities and respond with an effective marketing program.

The value of market segmentation to the industrial firm can be illustrated by briefly examining the mainframe computer market, where IBM is the market leader. General Electric, RCA, and Xerox failed in their attempts to compete head-on with IBM in this market. By targeting marketing strategies on particular segments or industry types (e.g., retailing), NCR, however, competes successfully.[1] This strategy builds upon NCR's traditional strengths in retailing. Specialized products are developed to fit the unique needs of the retail segment as well as the other market segments that NCR serves. Retail customers are encouraged to start in data processing on a small scale and gradually upgrade to more sophisticated NCR equipment. Salespersons assigned to a particular market segment like retailing are educated about the needs of that customer group and can provide consulting services for their customers. Similarly, the firm's technical service network is trained and organized to meet the special service requirements of different market segments. Rather than attempting a broad assault on the entire market, NCR develops marketing strategies for particular niches or segments of the computer market.

The goal of this chapter is to demonstrate how the manager can select and evaluate segments of the organizational market. First, the benefits of and requirements for successful market segmentation are delineated. Second, specific bases upon which the organizational market can be segmented are explored and evaluated. This section demonstrates the application of key buyer behavior concepts (examined in Chapter 4) and secondary information sources (Chapter 5) to market segmentation decisions. Third, a framework is provided for evaluating and selecting market segments. Here assessing the costs and benefits of entering alternative market segments and procedures for implementing a segmentation strategy are emphasized.

---

[1] Robert J. Thomas and Yoram Wind, "Toward Empirical Generalizations on Industrial Market Segmentation," in Robert E. Spekman and David T. Wilson, eds., *Issues in Industrial Marketing: A View to the Future* (Chicago: American Marketing Association, 1982), pp. 1–18; see also, John F. Grashof, "Comments on Industrial Marketing Segmentation," in Spekman and Wilson, *Issues in Industrial Marketing*, pp. 19–22.

Organizational Market Segmentation: Requirements and Benefits

A *market segment* is "a group of present or potential customers with some common characteristic which is relevant in explaining (and predicting) their response to a supplier's marketing stimuli."[2] Since virtually every market that is made up of more than one potential buying organization could conceivably be divided or segmented, the industrial marketer must understand the requisites for successful segmentation.

Requirements

An industrial marketer has four criteria for evaluating the desirability of potential market segments:[3]

1. *Measurability*, the degree to which information on the particular buyer characteristic exists or can be obtained;

2. *Accessibility*, the degree to which the firm can effectively focus its marketing efforts on chosen segments;

3. *Substantiality*, the degree to which the segments are large or profitable enough to be worth considering for separate marketing cultivation;

4. *Compatibility*, the degree to which the firm's marketing and business strengths match the present and expected competitive state of the market.

Thus, the art of market segmentation involves identifying groups of consumers that are sufficiently large, and sufficiently different, to justify a separate marketing strategy. The competitive environment of the market segment is a factor that must be analyzed.[4]

Evaluating the Competitive Environment

Although the concept of market segmentation is widely applied, a segmented marketing strategy is not always appropriate. One group of researchers isolates three product/market situations where a segmented marketing strategy is not appropriate:[5]

[2] Yoram Wind and Richard N. Cardozo, "Industrial Market Segmentation," *Industrial Marketing Management*, 3 (March 1974), p. 155.

[3] The first three of these four were advanced by Philip Kotler, *Marketing Management* (Englewood Cliffs, N.J.: Prentice-Hall, Inc., 1976), p. 143.

[4] Michael E. Porter, *Competitive Strategy* (New York: Free Press, 1980).

[5] Shirley Young, Leland Ott, and Barbara Feigin, "Some Practical Considerations in Market Segmentation," *Journal of Marketing Research*, 15 (August 1978), p. 405.

1.   Heavy users account for such a large proportion of the sales volume that they are the only relevant target.

2.   The market is so small that marketing to a portion of it is unprofitable (i.e., a brand must appeal in all segments).

3.   The brand holds the dominant position in the market (i.e., it draws from all segments of the market).

Thus, a careful analysis of the competitive environment is required to determine the appropriateness of segmentation.

Choosing a Competitive Environment   In selecting a market segment, the industrial marketer is also choosing a competitive environment. Many industrial firms now realize that they "have to choose markets whose needs they can satisfy and whose competitors they can handle."[6] Bruce Henderson, founder and chairman of the Boston Consulting Group, makes this astute observation:

> *For virtually all competitors the critical environment constraint is their interface with other competitors. Therefore any change in the environment that affects any competitor will have consequences that require some degree of adaptation. This requires continual change and adaptation by all competitors merely to maintain relative position.*[7]

Making a Commitment   Industrial market segments must be selected with care because of the close working relationship between buyer and seller after the sale.[8] While producers of consumer goods like toothpaste can shift from one demographic or life style segment to another relatively quickly, industrial firms may have to realign their entire marketing strategy (e.g., retrain salespersons) and alter the manufacturing process to meet the needs of a new market segment. Post-transaction service commitments to the new segment may continue for months or years. Thus, the decision to enter a particular market segment carries with it significant long-term resource commitments for the industrial firm.

Benefits

If the requirements for effective segmentation are met, several benefits accrue to the firm. First, the mere attempt at segmenting the organizational market forces the marketer to become more attuned to the unique needs of customer segments. While beneficial for firms of any size, mar-

---

[6] Philip Kotler and Ravi Singh, "Marketing Warfare in the 1980s," *Journal of Business Strategy*, 1 (Winter 1981), reprinted in Richard Wendel, ed., *Marketing 83/84* (Guilford, Conn.: The Dushkin Publishing Group, Inc., 1983), pp. 12–22.

[7] Bruce D. Henderson, "The Anatomy of Competition," *Journal of Marketing*, 47 (Spring 1983), p. 8.

[8] B. Charles Ames, "Marketing Planning for Industrial Products," *Harvard Business Review*, 46 (September–October 1968), pp. 100–111.

ket segmentation is crucial to the low market share firm. Often, segments are identified that are being neglected or inadequately served by competitors. "To be successful, a low market share company must compete in the segments where its own strengths will be most highly valued and where its large competitors will be most unlikely to compete."[9]

Second, knowledge of the needs of particular market segments helps the industrial marketer to focus product development efforts, develop profitable pricing strategies, select appropriate channels of distribution, develop and target advertising messages, and train and deploy the sales force. Thus, market segmentation provides the foundation for efficient and effective industrial marketing strategies.

Third, market segmentation provides the industrial marketer with guidelines that are of significant value in allocating marketing resources. Industrial firms often serve multiple market segments and must continually monitor the relative attractiveness and performance of these segments. Ultimately, the costs, revenues, and profits accruing to the firm must be evaluated segment by segment. As market or competitive conditions change, corresponding adjustments may be required in the firm's market segmentation strategy. Thus, market segmentation provides a basic unit of analysis for marketing planning and control.

Bases for Segmenting Organizational Markets

While the consumer-goods marketer is interested in securing meaningful profiles of individuals (demographics, life style, benefits sought), the industrial marketer profiles organizations (size, end use) and organizational buyers (decision style, criteria). Thus, the organizational market can be segmented on several bases,[10] broadly classified into two major categories, macro and micro.

Macro segmentation centers on the characteristics of the buying organization and the buying situation. Thus, macro bases divide the market by such organizational characteristics as size, geographic location, SIC category, or organizational structure. By contrast, *micro* bases require a higher degree of market knowledge; they focus on the characteristics of decision-making units within each macrosegment—buying decision criteria, perceived importance of the purchase, or attitudes toward vendors. Richard Cardozo and Yoram Wind recommend a two-stage approach to industrial market segmentation:[11] (1) identifying meaningful

[9] R. G. Hamermesh, M. J. Anderson, Jr., and J. E. Harris, "Strategies for Low Market Share Businesses," *Harvard Business Review*, 56 (May–June 1978), p. 98.

[10] For a comprehensive review of industrial market segmentation research, see Thomas and Wind, "Toward Empirical Generalizations on Industrial Market Segmentation," pp. 1–18.

[11] Wind and Cardozo, "Industrial Market Segmentation," p. 155; see also, Richard N. Cardozo, "Segmenting the Industrial Market," in Robert L. King, ed., *Marketing and the New Science of Planning* (Chicago: American Marketing Association, 1968), pp. 433–440; and Ronald E. Frank, William F. Massy, and Yoram Wind, *Market Segmentation* (Englewood Cliffs, N.J.: Prentice-Hall, Inc., 1971), Chapter 4.

Figure 6.1   A Hierarchy of Industrial Market Segmentation

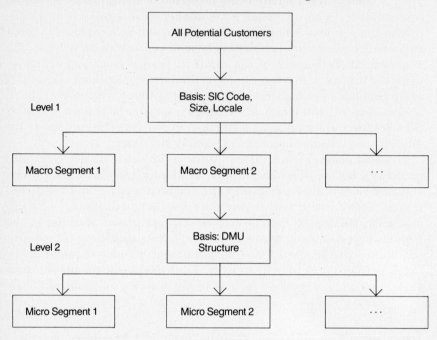

Source: Exhibit 9–11 (page 311) from *Marketing Decision Making: A Model Building Approach* by Gary L. Lilien and Philip Kotler. Copyright © 1983 by Harper & Row Publishers, Inc. Reprinted by permission of the publisher.

macro segments, and then (2) dividing the macrosegments into micro-segments (Figure 6.1).

In evaluating alternative bases for segmentation, the marketer is attempting to identify good predictors of differences in buyer behavior. Once such differences are recognized, the marketer can approach target segments with appropriate marketing strategy. Secondary sources of information (Chapter 5), coupled with data in company files, can be used to segment the market at the macro level. The concentration of the industrial market allows some marketers to monitor the purchasing patterns of *each* customer. For example, a firm that sells industrial products to paper manufacturers is dealing with hundreds of potential buying organizations in the United States and Canadian markets; a paper manufacturer selling to ultimate consumers is dealing with millions of potential customers. Such market concentration, coupled with rapidly advancing marketing intelligence systems, makes it easier for the industrial marketer to monitor the purchasing patterns of individual organizations.[12]

[12] Yoram Wind, "Industrial Marketing: Present Status and Future Potential," presentation to the American Marketing Association's Second Annual Faculty Consortium on Industrial Marketing, July 5, 1982.

Table 6.1   Selected Macro Bases of Segmentation

Variables	Illustrative Breakdowns
Characteristics of Buying Organizations	
Size (the scale of operations of the organization)	Small, medium, large—based on sales or number of employees
Geographical Location	New England, Middle Atlantic, South Atlantic, East North Central, etc.
Usage Rate	Nonuser, light user, moderate user, heavy user
Structure of Procurement	Centralized, decentralized
Product Application	
SIC Category	Varies by product
End Market Served	Varies by product
Characteristics of Purchasing Situation	
Type of Buying Situation	New task, modified rebuy, straight rebuy
Stage in Purchase Decision Process	Early stages, late stages

Macro Bases

Selected macro bases of segmentation are presented in Table 6.1. Recall that these are concerned with general characteristics of the buying organization, the nature of the product application, and the characteristics of the buying situation.

Characteristics of Buying Organizations   The marketer may find it useful to partition the market by size of potential buying organizations. Large buying organizations may possess unique requirements and respond to different marketing stimuli than smaller firms. The influence of presidents, vice presidents, and owners declines with an increase in corporate size; the influence of other participants, such as purchasing managers, increases.[13] Alternatively, the marketer may recognize regional variations and adopt geographical units as the basis for differentiating marketing strategies.

Usage rate constitutes another macro variable. Here, buyers are classified on a continuum ranging from nonuser to heavy user. While this scheme may be more appropriate for industrial rather than consumer-goods marketers, limited attention has been given to this segmentation dimension in the industrial marketing literature.[14] Clearly, a great deal

---

[13] Joseph A. Bellizzi, "Organizational Size and Buying Influences," *Industrial Marketing Management*, 10 (February 1981), pp. 17–21; see also, Jean-Marie Choffray and Gary L. Lilien, "Industrial Market Segmentation by the Structure of the Purchasing Process," *Industrial Marketing Management*, 9 (October 1980), pp. 331–342.

[14] Jagdish N. Sheth, "Recent Developments in Organizational Buying Behavior," in Arch Woodside, Jagdish N. Sheth, and Peter D. Bennett, eds., *Consumer and Industrial Buying Behavior* (New York: Elsevier-North Holland, Inc., 1977), p. 31.

of market knowledge is required to effectively implement this classification, but the potential payoff for distinguishing heavy users from light is high.

The structure of the procurement function constitutes a final macro characteristic of buying organizations. Firms with a centralized purchasing function behave differently from those with decentralized procurement (see Chapter 4). The structure of the purchasing function influences the degree of specialization of buyers, criteria emphasized, and the composition of the buying center. Centralized buyers place significant weight on long-term supply availability and the development of a healthy supplier complex. Decentralized buyers emphasize short-term cost efficiency.[15] Thus, the position of procurement in the organizational hierarchy provides a base for categorizing organizations and isolating specific needs and marketing requirements. Many industrial firms develop a national accounts sales force to meet the special requirements of large centralized procurement units.

Product Application   Because a specific industrial good often is used in different ways, the marketer can divide the market on the basis of specific product applications.[16] The manufacturer of a component like springs, may reach industries incorporating the product into machine tools, bicycles, surgical devices, office equipment, telephones, and missile systems. The SIC system and related information sources described in the previous chapter are especially valuable in segmenting the market on the basis of end use.

Purchasing Situation   A final macro base for segmenting the organizational market is the purchasing situation.[17] First-time buyers have different perceptions and information needs from repeat buyers. Therefore, buying organizations can be classified as in the *early* or *late* stages of the procurement process, or alternatively, as *new-task, straight rebuy*, or *modified rebuy* organizations (Chapter 3). The position of the firm in the procurement decision process or its location on the buying situation continuum dictates marketing strategy.[18]

These macro bases of segmentation illustrate those that industrial marketers can apply to the organizational market. Other macro bases may more precisely fit a specific situation. A key benefit of segmentation is that it forces the manager to search for bases that explain similarities and differences among buying organizations.

[15] E. Raymond Corey, *The Organizational Context of Industrial Buyer Behavior* (Cambridge, Mass.: Marketing Science Institute, 1978), pp. 6–12.

[16] For example, see Joel J. Barr, "SIC: A Basic Tool for the Marketer," in Donald E. Vinson and Donald Sciglimpaglia, eds., *The Environment of Industrial Marketing* (Columbus, Ohio: Grid, Inc., 1975), pp. 114–119.

[17] Patrick J. Robinson, Charles W. Faris, and Yoram Wind, *Industrial Buying and Creative Marketing* (Boston: Allyn and Bacon, Inc., 1967), Chapter 1.

[18] Richard N. Cardozo, "Modelling Organizational Buying as a Sequence of Decisions," *Industrial Marketing Management*, 12 (April 1983), pp. 75–81.

Macro Segmentation Illustrated   A producer of capital equipment which is sold to the food processing industry was successful in penetrating small- and medium-sized food manufacturers, but had little success with large buying organizations. The firm's marketing strategy centered on providing extensive technical assistance to potential customers planning plant modernization or expansion. Consistent with this strategy, the firm's application engineers would often spend days with customers analyzing technical requirements and proposing design modifications.

   While small- and medium-sized organizations, which often have a small engineering staff, responded favorably, large organizations did not. Potential customers with a large engineering staff preferred to handle the technical details in-house. In addition, the plant level technical staff was often augmented by direct engineering support from the corporate level in large capital projects.

   Thus, large customers wanted only manufacturing technology (capital equipment); small- and medium-sized organizations needed technical assistance as well. The industrial marketer responded by developing a marketing strategy consistent with the needs of each macro segment.

Micro Bases

Having identified macro segments, the marketer often finds it useful to divide each macro segment into smaller micro segments on the basis of the similarities and differences among decision-making units.[19] Often, several micro segments—each with unique requirements and unique responses to marketing stimuli—are buried in macro segments. To effectively isolate them, the marketer must move beyond secondary sources of information by soliciting input from the sales force or conducting a special market segmentation study. Selected micro bases of segmentation appear in Table 6.2.

Key Criteria   For some industrial goods, the marketer can divide the market according to which criteria are assigned the most importance in the purchase decision.[20] Criteria include product quality, prompt and reliable delivery, technical support, price, and supply continuity. The marketer also might divide the market based on supplier profiles that appear to be preferred by decision makers (e.g., high quality, prompt delivery, premium price vs. standard quality, less-prompt delivery, low price).

   The marketer can benefit by examining the criteria employed by decision-making units in different sectors of the organizational mar-

[19] Wind and Cardozo, "Industrial Market Segmentation," p. 155.

[20] Cardozo, "Segmenting the Industrial Market," pp. 433–440; see also, Donald R. Lehmann and John O'Shaughnessy, "Decision Criteria Used in Buying Different Categories of Products," *Journal of Purchasing and Materials Management*, 18 (Spring 1982), pp. 9–14; Lehmann and O'Shaughnessy, "Differences in Attribute Importance for Different Industrial Products," *Journal of Marketing*, 38 (April 1974), pp. 36–42; and Peter Gilmour, "Customer Service: Differentiating by Marketing Segment," *International Journal of Physical Distribution and Materials Management*, 12 (No. 3, 1982), pp. 37–44.

Table 6.2   Selected Micro Bases of Segmentation

Variables	Illustrative Breakdowns
Key Criteria	Quality, delivery, supplier reputation
Decision-Specific Conflict	High . . . . low
Purchasing Strategies	Optimizer, satisficer
Structure of Decision-Making Unit	Major decision participants, e.g., purchasing manager and plant manager
Importance of Purchase	High importance . . . . low importance
Attitude toward Vendors	Favorable . . . . unfavorable
Organizational Innovativeness	Innovator . . . . follower
Personal Characteristics	
Demographics	Age, educational background
Decision Style	Normative, conservative, mixed-mode
Risk	Risk taker, risk avoider
Confidence	High confidence . . . . low confidence
Job Responsibility	Purchasing, production, engineering

ket—commercial, governmental, and institutional. For example, the institutional market (hospitals, universities, etc.) represents a sector of growing significance in the United States economy. Do these noncommercial buyers employ the same criteria as their commercial counterparts? G. E. Kiser and C. P. Rao explore the similarities and differences between industrial purchasing agents and hospital buyers.[21] For standard product-buying situations, reliability (e.g., quality, fairness) and efficiency (e.g., delivery with required follow-up) are of utmost importance to both industrial and hospital buyers. Both buying groups identify "cost" as important. Hospital buyers, however, assign more importance to service and less to technical capabilities, past experience with suppliers, and direct source.[22] Thus, supplier attributes that are of considerable importance in the commercial sector have little value in the noncommercial segment. This kind of knowledge facilitates the development of differentiated marketing strategies.

Decision-Specific Conflict[23]   The organizational buying process involves not one but many decisions. Decision-specific conflict views a complex industrial exchange as a group of subdecisions across which the purchasing agent will experience different levels of conflict. The purchasing agent may merely provide input concerning the method of financing a proposed capital equipment purchase but may be responsible for resolv-

[21] G. E. Kiser and C. P. Rao, "Important Vendor Factors in Industrial and Hospital Organizations: A Comparison," *Industrial Marketing Management*, 6 (August 1977), pp. 289–296; see also, Kjell Gronhaugh, "Exploring Environmental Influences in Organizational Buying," *Journal of Marketing Research*, 13 (August 1976), pp. 225–229.

[22] Kiser and Rao, "Important Vendor Factors," pp. 289–296.

[23] Michael J. Ryan and Morris B. Holbrook, "Decision-Specific Conflict in Organizational Buyer Behavior," *Journal of Marketing*, 46 (Summer 1982), pp. 62–68.

Table 6.3   Consumption Segmentation Based on Conflict and Responsibility of Fleet Administrators

Decision Areas	Definitions
High Conflict	
Partial Responsibility	
Top/Bottom	Choice among fleet cars at the top, middle, and bottom of the line
Options	What options to include at the company's expense
Size	Size of fleet cars—small, mid-size, large
Replacement	Age or mileage at which to replace fleet vehicles
Low Conflict	
Complete Responsibility	
Timing	Timing of new car acquisition
Disposal	How to dispose of fleet—trade-in, auction, etc.
Maintenance	Arrangements for maintenance and repairs
Repair/Replace	Whether to repair or replace after an accident
Surplus	How to handle surplus vehicles
No Responsibility	
Insurance	How best to insure vehicles and drivers
Type Lease	Type of lease—finance, net, maintenance
Own/Lease	Whether to own or lease fleet vehicles
Lessor/Dealer	Choices of specific lessors or dealers

Source: Adapted, with modifications, from Michael J. Ryan and Morris B. Holbrook, "Decision-Specific Conflict in Organizational Buyer Behavior," *Journal of Marketing*, 46 (Summer 1982), p. 66. Reprinted by permission of the American Marketing Association.

ing conflicts between production and finance regarding technical attributes of the equipment. Throughout the purchasing process, different degrees of responsibility ranging from minimally to maximally responsible engender differing levels of conflict. The amount of conflict associated with each subdecision provides a basis for segmentation.

Michael Ryan and Morris Holbrook examined decision-specific conflicts in the fleet purchase of corporate automobiles (see Table 6.3). Fleet administrators account for several billion dollars worth of automobile demand each year.[24] The research study identified three roles for fleet administrators, each associated with a group of subdecisions: (1) joint decision maker (high conflict—partial responsibility); (2) sole decision maker (low conflict—complete responsibility); and (3) information source (low conflict—no responsibility). The fleet administrator in Table 6.3 has complete responsibility for the timing of new car acquisitions, partial responsibility for the size of cars, and no responsibility for the decision to own or lease.

[24] Amal Nag, "Auto Dealers Say They're Bypassed in Sales to Fleet Buyers and Move to Halt Practice," *Wall Street Journal* (June 21, 1983), p. 31.

By examining the roles assumed by a particular decision participant, the industrial salesperson can (1) locate buying influentials, (2) develop responsive personal selling strategies, and (3) offer proposals that respond to conflict-prone decisions.

Purchasing Strategies   Micro segments can be formed on the basis of the purchasing strategy employed by buying organizations. Two purchasing profiles that have been identified are *satisficers* and *optimizers*.[25]

Satisficers approach a given purchasing requirement by contacting familiar suppliers and placing the order with the first to satisfy product and delivery requirements. Optimizers consider numerous suppliers, familiar and unfamiliar, solicit bids, and examine all alternative proposals carefully, before selecting a supplier.

These purchasing strategies have numerous implications. A supplier entering the market would have a higher probability of penetrating a decision-making unit made up of optimizers than one consisting of satisficers who rely on familiar suppliers.

Identifying different purchasing patterns can help the marketer to understand differential responses to marketing stimuli. An organizational marketer of deep-frying shortening, for example, encounters both satisficers and optimizers. Large universities review and test alternatives carefully, consult with student committees, and analyze the price per unit cooked before selecting a supplier (optimizers). Restaurants and company cafeterias may follow a different pattern. Here the restaurant manager, consulting with the chef, selects a supplier that provides the required product quality and delivery (satisficer). Note that satisficing and optimizing are only two of many purchasing strategies of organizational buyers.

Structure of Decision-Making Unit   The structure of the decision-making unit or buying center likewise provides a means of dividing the industrial market into subsets of customers by isolating the patterns of involvement in the purchasing process of particular decision participants (e.g., engineering vs. top management). A comprehensive analysis of the commercial air conditioning market led to the identification of four micro segments (Table 6.4).[26] Note that the major decision participants in micro segment 3, which represents 32 percent of the potential market, are production engineers and heating ventilating and air conditioning (HVAC) consultants. These decision participants perceive a high level of risk in purchasing an unreliable system and a low to medium level of satisfaction with their current system. Such an analysis allows

[25] Richard N. Cardozo, "Situational Segmentation of Industrial Markets," *European Journal of Marketing*, 14 (5/6, 1980), pp. 264–276.

[26] For a complete discussion of the methodology used in the research, see, Jean-Marie Choffray and Gary L. Lilien, "A New Approach to Industrial Market Segmentation," *Sloan Management Review*, 19 (Spring 1978), pp. 23–24.

Table 6.4   Micro Segments for Industrial Air Conditioning Systems

Characteristics	Micro Segment 1	Micro Segment 2	Micro Segment 3	Micro Segment 4
Major Decision Participants	Plant Managers and HVAC Consultants	Production Engineers and Plant Managers	Production Engineers and HVAC Consultants	Top Management and HVAC Consultants
Satisfaction with Current System	Medium to High	Low	Low to Medium	High
Perceived Risk of Purchasing an Uneconomical System	Medium to High	Low	Low to Medium	High
Perceived Risk of Purchasing an Unreliable System	Medium to High	Low	High	Low to Medium
Percentage of Plant Area Requiring A/C	Medium to Large	Small	Large	Medium
Number of Separate Plants	Medium to Large	Small	Large	Small to Medium
Company Size	Medium	Large	Large	Small
Percentage of Potential Market	12%	31%	32%	25%

Source: Adapted from Jean-Marie Choffray and Gary L. Lilien, "A New Approach to Industrial Market Segmentation," *Sloan Management Review*, 19 (Spring 1978), pp. 23–24. Reprinted by permission of the publisher. Copyright © 1978 by the Sloan Management Review Association. All rights reserved.

the marketer to identify meaningful micro segments and respond with finely tuned marketing communications.

Importance of Purchase   Classifying organizational customers on the basis of the perceived importance of a particular product is especially appropriate when the product is applied in different ways by different customers. Buyer perceptions vary according to the impact of the product on the total mission of the firm. A large commercial enterprise may consider the purchase of an office machine as routine; the same purchase for a small manufacturing concern is "an event."

Attitudes toward Vendors   The attitudes of decision-making units toward the vendors in a particular product class provide a means of micro segmentation. An analysis of how various clusters of buyers view alternative sources of supply often uncovers opportunities in the form of vulnerable segments being neglected or not fully satisfied by competitors.

Organizational Innovativeness   Some organizations are more innovative and willing to purchase new industrial products than others. A study of the adoption of new medical equipment among hospitals found that psychographic variables can improve a marketer's ability to predict the adoption of new products.[27] These include such factors as an organization's level of change resistance or desire to excel. When these psychographic variables are combined with organizational demographic variables (e.g., size), accuracy in predicting organizational innovativeness increases.

Since products will diffuse more rapidly in some segments than others, microsegmentation on the basis of organizational innovativeness allows the marketer to identify segments that should be targeted first when new products are introduced. New product forecasting accuracy is also improved when diffusion patterns are estimated segment by segment.[28]

Personal Characteristics   Some micro segmentation possibilities deal with the personal characteristics of decision makers: demographics (age, education), personality, decision style, risk preference or risk avoidance, confidence, job responsibilities, and related characteristics. Although some interesting studies have shown the viability of segmentation on the basis of individual characteristics, further research is needed to explore its potential as a firm base for micro segmentation.[29]

Micro Segmentation Illustrated   A comprehensive analysis of buyer behavior in the nonintelligent data-terminal market provides a rich illustration of micro segmentation.[30] While IBM dominates, the market has more than 40 competitors. What factors distinguish IBM from non-IBM buyers? Research by Rowland Moriarty yielded the behavioral profiles in Table 6.5. Purchasers of IBM equipment are more concerned about software support and breadth of product line and less concerned about absolute price and price flexibility (i.e., willingness of suppliers to negotiate price).

The two micro segments also differed significantly in the importance of the industrial supplier's visibility among top management. "The IBM buyer's emphasis on visibility could also reflect the need of decision participants to minimize their risk in making the decision."[31] (Recall the concept of perceived risk!) Compared to a supplier unknown to top management, IBM is a risk-free choice.

[27] Thomas S. Robertson and Yoram Wind, "Organizational Psychographics and Innovativeness," *Journal of Consumer Research*, 7 (June 1980), pp. 24–31.

[28] Yoram Wind, Thomas S. Robertson, and Cynthia Fraser, "Industrial Product Diffusion by Market Segment," *Industrial Marketing Management*, 11 (February 1982), pp. 1–8.

[29] For example, see, David T. Wilson, "Industrial Buyers' Decision-Making Styles," *Journal of Marketing Research*, 8 (November 1971), p. 433; Wilson, H. Lee Mathews, and Timothy W. Sweeney, "Industrial Buyer Segmentation: A Psychographic Approach," *AMA Proceedings* (Chicago: American Marketing Association, 1971), pp. 327–331; and Timothy W. Sweeney, H. Lee Mathews, and David T. Wilson, "An Analysis of Industrial Buyers' Risk Reducing Behavior: Some Personality Correlates," *AMA Proceedings* (Chicago: American Marketing Association, 1973), pp. 217–221.

[30] Rowland T. Moriarty, *Industrial Buying Behavior* (Lexington, Mass.: Lexington Books, 1983).

[31] *Ibid.*, p. 101.

Table 6.5   Benefits Sought (*mean ratings*)*

Variable	IBM Buyers (204 respondents)	Non-IBM Buyers (285 respondents)
Speed	34.9	35.8
Operator	33.0	33.2
Aesthetics	27.9	27.2
Compatibility	39.0	39.2
Service	45.5	45.4
Delivery	37.4	37.0
Absolute price	33.3**	35.6**
Price flexibility	25.7**	29.3**
Software	40.8**	38.8**
Broad line	35.5**	33.2**
Visibility among top management	31.1**	26.5**
Manufacturer's stability	40.1	39.7
Sales competence	31.9	32.3
Reliability	43.2	43.5

*The higher the score, the greater the importance of the variable in the buying decision.

** Indicates statistically significant difference between the two groups at the 90-percent confidence level.

Source: Reprinted by permission of the publisher from *Industrial Buying Behavior*, p. 102, by Rowland T. Moriarty (Lexington, Mass.: Lexington Books, D. C. Heath and Company. Copyright 1983, D. C. Heath and Company).

In addition to isolating the behavioral profiles of IBM versus non-IBM buyers, the study also identified key benefit segments in the market. The distinguishing characteristics of the two largest benefit segments are that:

1. Segment 1 wishes to negotiate price, deal with a competent sales representative, and buy a terminal that is easy to operate.

2. Segment 2 assigns particular importance to software support, breadth of product line, and supplier visibility and financial stability.

A Model for Segmenting the Organizational Market

Macro bases of segmentation center on characteristics of buying *organizations* (e.g., size), product application (e.g., end market served), and characteristics of the purchasing situation (e.g., stage in the purchase decision process). Micro segmentation concentrates on characteristics of organizational decision-making *units*, for instance, choice criteria assigned the most importance in the purchase decision.

Identifying Market Segments

The model in Figure 6.2 combines these bases and outlines the steps required for effective segmentation. This approach to organizational market segmentation, developed by Yoram Wind and Richard Cardozo,

Figure 6.2   An Approach to Segmentation of Organizational Markets

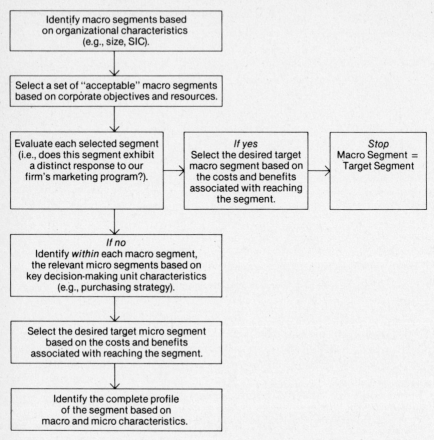

Source: Adapted by permission of the publisher from "Industrial Market Segmentation," by Yoram Wind and Richard Cardozo, *Industrial Marketing Management*, 3 (March 1974), p. 156. Copyright © 1974 by Elsevier Science Publishing Co., Inc.

begins with an analysis of key characteristics of the organization and of the buying situation (macro dimensions)[32] to identify, evaluate, and select meaningful macro segments. Note that the segmentation task is complete at this stage if *each* of the selected macro segments exhibits a *distinct* response to the firm's marketing stimuli. Since the information needed for macro basis segmentation can often be drawn from secondary information sources, the research investment is low.

[32] Wind and Cardozo, "Industrial Market Segmentation," pp. 153–166.

The cost of research increases, however, if a micro level of segmentation is required. Here a marketing research study is often needed to identify characteristics of decision-making units. At this level, chosen macro segments are divided into micro segments on the basis of similarities and differences among the decision-making units in order to identify small groups of buying organizations that each exhibit a distinct response to the firm's marketing strategy. Observe from Figure 6.2 that the desirability of a particular target segment depends upon the costs and benefits of reaching that segment. The costs are associated with marketing strategy adjustments, such as modifying the product, altering personal selling or advertising strategies, or entering new channels of distribution. The benefits include the short- and long-term opportunities that would accrue to the firm for tapping this segment. The marketer must evaluate the potential profitability of alternative segments before investing in separate marketing strategies.

Evaluating Market Segments

To evaluate the relative attractiveness of alternative market segments, the industrial marketer must assess company, competitive, and market factors.

Marketing Objectives   Industrial firms lack the flexibility of their consumer-goods counterparts in moving into and out of market segments. The strategic fit of a market segment with the firm's basic marketing objectives must be examined before resources are committed.

Interfunctional Coordination   The execution of industrial marketing strategy requires effective coordination of manufacturing, research and development, and finance.[33] The capabilities of these departments are blended with marketing strengths to form responsive industrial marketing strategy. Entry into market segment "A" may require a high level of manufacturing expertise and a strong research and development commitment; entry into segment "B" may require a responsive distribution and technical service network. Table 6.6 provides a framework for assessing the degree of fit between the company's functional strengths and the requirements of a given market segment.

Competitive Behavior   Note (Table 6.6) that a forecast should be made of the functional strengths of existing and likely competitors within the same market segment, including the number, size, and aggressiveness of domestic and foreign competitors.

[33] Yoram Wind and Thomas S. Robertson, "Marketing Strategy: New Directions for Theory and Research," *Journal of Marketing*, 47 (Spring 1983), pp. 12–25.

Table 6.6   Assessing Functional Requirements for Success in a Market Segment: Company vs. Competitors

Function	Company Strength High—Low	Requirements for Success in Segment High—Low	Competitor's Strength (estimates) High—Low
Manufacturing			
R & D			
Finance			
Technical Service			
Sales Force			
Advertising			
Distribution (e.g., delivery reliability)			

Market Size/Trends   A market segment must be large enough to warrant the development of a specialized marketing strategy. A marketer must estimate the size and growth rate of market demand and also investigate technological trends affecting the market segment. For example, a producer of raw materials or component parts should evaluate the potential threat of lower-cost or higher-quality substitutes.

Implementing a Segmentation Strategy

A well-developed segmentation plan will fail without careful attention to how the plan will be implemented.[34] The successful implementation of a segmentation strategy requires attention to such issues as:

- How should the sales force be organized?
- What special technical service requirements will organizations in the new segment have? Who will provide these services?
- Which media outlets can be used to target advertising to the new segment?
- Will adjustments be required in the physical distribution network to meet particular inventory requirements?

The astute industrial marketing strategist plans, coordinates, and monitors implementation details.

[34] Thomas V. Bonoma and Benson P. Shapiro, *Segmenting the Industrial Market* (Lexington, Mass.: Lexington Books, 1983); see also, Robert E. Spekman and Kjell Gronhaug, "Insights on Implementation: A Conceptual Framework for Better Understanding the Strategic Marketing Planning Process," in Patrick E. Murphy and Gene R. Laczniak, eds., *Proceedings of the AMA Educators' Conference* (Chicago: American Marketing Association, 1983).

Summary

The organizational market contains a complex mix of customers with diverse needs and objectives. The marketing strategist who analyzes the aggregate market and identifies neglected or inadequately served groups of buyers (segments) is ideally prepared for a market assault. Specific marketing strategy adjustments can be made to fit the unique needs of each target segment. Of course, such differentiated marketing strategies are feasible only if the target segments are measurable, accessible, compatible, and large enough to justify separate attention.

Procedurally, industrial market segmentation involves categorizing actual or potential buying organizations into mutually exclusive clusters (segments) which each exhibit a relatively homogeneous response to marketing strategy variables. To accomplish this task, the industrial marketer can draw upon two types of segmentation bases: macro and micro. Macro dimensions are the key characteristics of buying organizations and of the purchasing situation. The SIC system, together with other secondary sources of information, is valuable in macro level segmentation. Micro bases of segmentation center on key characteristics of the decision-making unit and require a higher level of market knowledge.

This chapter outlined a systematic approach for the organizational marketer to apply in identifying and selecting target segments. Before a final decision is made, the marketer must weigh the costs and benefits of a segmented marketing strategy. Here, the market potential of possible target segments is calculated and a careful assessment is made of company versus competitive strengths. Techniques for measuring market potential (opportunity) provide the theme of the next chapter.

Discussion Questions

1. Two years ago, Jackson Machine Tool selected four SIC categories as key market segments. A unique marketing strategy was then developed for each segment. In retrospect, they wonder if they are appealing to the right segments of the market. Again this year, sales were up slightly, profits were down rather sharply. They need your help. Outline the approach that you would follow in evaluating the appropriateness of their segmentation.

2. Critique this statement: "As an industrial-goods product manager, I am most concerned with sales and profits from the *total* market. I don't have time to worry about the advantages and disadvantages of little subcomponents in this overall market."

3. Define a *market segment*.

4. Explain why entry into a particular market segment by an industrial firm often entails a greater commitment than a comparable decision made by a consumer products company.

5. List some potential macro and micro bases of segmentation that a small manufacturer of printed packaging materials might employ.

6. Can the concept of market segmentation be applied to all sectors of the industrial market: commercial enterprises, institutions, government (state, federal, local)? Support your position.

7. What personal selling strategy would be most appropriate in dealing with an organizational buyer that is an optimizer? A satisficer?

8. How can the marketing strategist determine whether a particular basis of segmentation (e.g., SIC, company size) is appropriate and meaningful for the firm's product/market situation?

9. Some industrial firms follow a single-stage segmentation approach, using macro dimensions, others use both macro and micro dimensions. As an industrial marketing manager, what factors would you consider in making a choice between the two methods?

10. Describe the company, competitive, and market factors that an industrial firm should examine in evaluating the relative attractiveness of alternative market segments.

C·H·A·P·T·E·R
7

Organizational Demand Analysis: Measuring Market Potential

The industrial marketer confronts the difficult task of predicting the market response of organizational customers. The efficiency and effectiveness of the marketing program rests on the manager's ability to isolate and measure organizational demand patterns. Accurate projections of market potential and future sales are among the most significant and challenging dimensions of organizational demand analysis. After reading this chapter, you will have an understanding of:

1. *the importance of organizational demand analysis to industrial marketing management;*
2. *the role of market potential analysis and sales forecasting in the planning and control process;*
3. *specific techniques that can be effectively applied in measuring market potential.*

To successfully implement industrial marketing strategy, the industrial marketing manager must estimate the potential market for the firm's products. Accurate estimates of potential business enable the manager to allocate scarce resources to the customer segments, products, and territories that offer the greatest return. Estimates of market potential also provide the manager with a standard that can be used to assess the firm's performance in the product and market situations targeted. Market potential must be assessed accurately to effectively plan and control industrial marketing strategy.

Sales forecasting is likewise vital to marketing management. The sales forecast reflects management's estimate of the probable level of company sales, taking into account both potential business and the level and type of marketing effort demanded. Virtually every decision made by the marketer is based on a forecast, formal or informal.

This chapter explores the role of organizational demand analysis in the industrial marketing planning and control process. First, the nature and purpose of the market potential estimate and the sales forecast are contrasted. Once the groundwork is established, several methods of measuring market potential are described, illustrated, and evaluated. This discussion provides a base for understanding and applying sales forecasting techniques—the theme of the next chapter.

Organizational Demand Analysis

The industrial marketing manager must analyze organizational demand from two perspectives. First, what is the highest possible level of market demand that may accrue to all producers in this industry in a particular time period? This constitutes the *market potential* for a product. It is influenced by the level of *industry* marketing effort and the assumed conditions in the external environment. Second, what level of sales can the firm reasonably expect to achieve, given a particular level and type of marketing effort and a particular set of environmental conditions? This constitutes the firm's *sales forecast*. Note that the forecast depends upon the level of the *firm's* marketing effort. Thus, the marketing plan must be developed before the sales forecast. This section examines the significance of both components of organizational demand analysis for industrial marketing management.

The Role of Market Potential in Planning and Control

Market potential is "the maximum possible sales of all sellers of a given product in a defined market during a specified time period."[1] If the manager wishes to determine the maximum sales opportunities for a

---

[1] William E. Cox, Jr., and George N. Havens, "Determination of Sales Potentials and Performance for an Industrial Goods Manufacturer," *Journal of Marketing Research*, 14 (November 1977), p. 574.

product of an individual company, this is referred to as *sales potential.* Sales potential indicates the maximum share of market potential an individual company might expect for a specific product or product line.[2]

An example will clarify the nature of potentials. In 1982 manufacturers of aircraft engines and parts generated sales of $13.2 billion. What level of market potential would be expected for the industry in 1983? Based upon commercial and government contracts awarded for 1983, estimates of general economic growth, and commercial airline activity, total volume for the industry in 1983 might be projected to increase by 20 percent. Thus, the aircraft industry has a market potential of $15.8 billion in 1983 ($13.2B × 1.20). Of this, the aircraft engine division of General Electric in Cincinnati might expect to obtain 8 percent based on current market share, anticipated marketing efforts, production capacity, and other factors. General Electric's sales potential is therefore $1.26 billion for 1983 ($15.8B × .08).

Potential Represents Opportunity   In most instances, market potentials exceed total market demand and sales potentials exceed actual company sales volume. Market potential is just that—an *opportunity* to sell. In the aircraft engine and parts example, market potential may not be converted to demand for a number of reasons: the government may reduce aircraft defense spending; commercial airlines may postpone aircraft orders if passenger airline travel declines; a strike against major aircraft manufacturers could reduce their production of jet engines. Similarly, sales potentials are based upon an ideal set of circumstances: past market performance, a certain level of competitive activity, and a variety of events, both favorable and unfavorable to the firm. Clearly, a change in competitive actions, a decline in the general economy, or a reduction in the level and effectiveness of marketing may cause actual sales to fall short of sales potential.

Absolute vs. Relative Potential   The most common expressions of potentials are in terms of *absolute* and *relative.* Absolute potentials are measured in dollar or unit terms and indicate the total business available in the entire United States or within a certain market segment. Thus, the absolute potential for aircraft engines and parts is $15.8 billion for the United States market. A marketer of aircraft engines would analyze the regional pattern of potential demand, and thus determine important geographic locations for aircraft production. The absolute market potential for engines and parts might be $1.58 billion in Seattle, Washington (home base for the Boeing Corporation). The relative Seattle market potential, potential business in a given market segment or region compared with the total market, would be 10 percent (1.58 billion/15.8 bil-

---

[2] Francis E. Hummel, *Market and Sales Potentials* (New York: The Ronald Press Company, 1961), p. 8.

Figure 7.1   The Role of Potential in Marketing Planning and Control

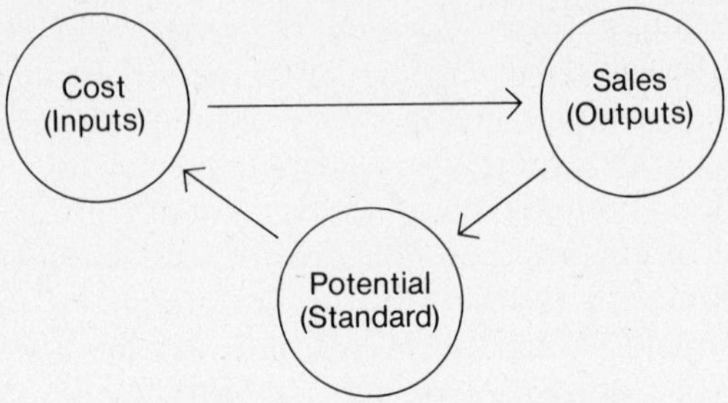

Source: Adapted from Richard J. Lewis and Leo G. Erickson, "Distribution System Costing: An Overview," in *Distribution Systems Costing: Concepts and Procedures*, Proceedings of the Fourth Annual James R. Riley Symposium on Business Logistics; Transportation and Logistics Foundation; The Ohio State University, 1972.

lion). Relative potentials facilitate the comparison of market segments on the basis of business available.

Potentials: Planning and Control by Segment   The primary application of market and sales potential information is clearly in the planning and control of marketing strategy by market segment. Recall from Chapter 6 that *segments* refer to homogeneous units—customers, products, territories, or channels—for which marketing efforts are tailored. Once sales potentials are determined for each segment, the manager can allocate expenditures on the basis of potential sales volume. There is little benefit to spending huge sums of money on advertising and personal selling in segments where the market opportunity is low. Sales in each segment can also be compared with potential sales to evaluate the effectiveness of the marketing program. Figure 7.1 illustrates the role of potentials in marketing planning and control.

A Systems View   If the marketing planning and control process is conceptualized as a system, inputs are the costs of various efforts and outputs are the sales in each segment. Potential serves as a *standard* for both input and output. Those segments with the largest potential are those where the corresponding marketing effort should be greatest. Segments which achieve the highest sales level relative to potential are those which are the most successful. Of course, the level of effort must also be considered if competition in a segment is intense. The marketing expenditures required to generate a certain share of the market may be so high as to negate the advantage of high potential. For this reason, profitability (sales minus marketing expenses) must also be considered.

    Consider the experience of a Cleveland manufacturer of quickconnective couplings for power transmission systems.[3] For more than 20

[3] Cox and Havens, "Determination of Sales Potentials," p. 578.

Table 7.1   Percentage of Total United States Shipments (Production) of Greeting Cards

County	Percent
Cuyahoga (Ohio)	12.2
Hamilton (Ohio)	9.2
Jackson (Missouri)	20.5
Cook (Illinois)	6.8

Source: "Survey of Industrial and Commercial Buying Power," *Sales and Marketing Management* (April 25, 1983).

years, one of their large distributors had been increasing its sales volume. In fact, this distributor was considered one of the firm's top producers. The firm then analyzed the sales potentials for each of their 31 distributors. The large distributor ranked thirty-first in terms of volume relative to potential, actualizing only 15.4 percent of potential! A later evaluation revealed that the distributor's sales personnel did not know how to sell couplings to their large accounts.

Assume that a company produces quality paper for use in the greeting card industry. Table 7.1 shows the percentage of United States shipments of greeting cards for a selected number of counties. In this case, the firm would allocate 20.5 percent of their sales budget to the Jackson County area in Missouri and 9.2 percent to Hamilton County in Ohio.

As this discussion demonstrates, market and sales potentials are pivotal in the marketing planning and control process. Therefore, great care must be taken in determining market and sales potential estimates. The industrial marketing manager must thoroughly understand the various techniques for developing potentials accurately.

The Role of the Sales Forecast

A second component of organizational demand analysis, sales forecasting, likewise poses a significant challenge. The sales forecast answers the question: "What level of sales do we expect next year, given a particular level and type of marketing effort?" Once potentials have been determined, the industrial marketing manager can allocate resources to the various elements of the marketing mix. Only after the marketing strategy is developed can expected sales be forecast. Many firms are tempted to use the forecast as a tool to decide on the level of marketing expenditures. Clearly, marketing strategy is a determinant of the level of sales and not vice versa! Figure 7.2 illustrates the position of market potential estimates and the sales forecast in the marketing planning process.

The sales forecast represents the firm's best estimate of the sales revenue expected to be generated by a given marketing strategy. The forecast will usually be less than sales potential. The firm may find that it

Figure 7.2   The Relationship of Potentials and Forecasts: A Planning Framework

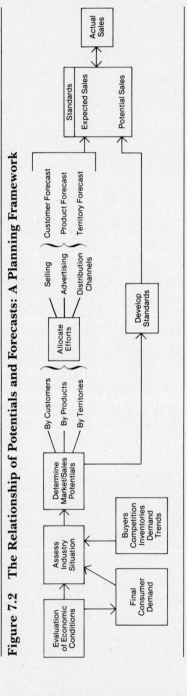

is uneconomical to try and capture all available business. Strong competitors within certain segments may preclude the achievement of total potential sales. Like sales potential data, the sales forecast is an aid in the allocation of resources and the measurement of performance.

Applying Market Potential and the Sales Forecast   Market potential estimates and sales forecasts complement each other in the marketing planning process. Market potential data is usually vital to sales forecasting: Market potential provides direction on which opportunities the firm should pursue and the sales forecast is generated once the level of resources to be applied to each opportunity has been decided. Market potential estimates are used to determine *where* the firm's attention should be focused; the total and relative levels of *expenditure* to apply to each opportunity; and benchmarks for evaluating performance. The sales forecast, in comparison, typically provides direction for making short-run, tactical decisions. Thus, estimates of actual sales over the next year guide management in planning production, estimating purchasing requirements, setting inventory levels, scheduling transportation and the warehouse work force, estimating working capital requirements, and planning short-term expenditures on promotion and advertising. Two-to-five-year projections of sales (based on the analysis of market potential) help guide decision making about plant and warehouse facilities and capital requirements, and channel strategy and structure. In summary, market potential provides guidelines for the general direction (in terms of markets and product opportunities) the firm will take, and for budget allocations to those opportunities. The sales forecast directs the timing of short-range tactical expenditures and longer-term capital spending.

There are specific tools for developing accurate estimates of market potential; the industrial marketer must understand the purposes of alternative techniques as well as their values and limitations.

Determining Market and Sales Potentials

The secondary data available, whether the product is new or established, the number of potential customers, and the extent of internal company information all play a role in estimating potentials. Estimating market potential requires analysis of variables which relate to, or cause, aggregate demand for the product. It is crucial to find the best measure of the underlying variables so that potential can be measured accurately. Methods of estimating potentials can be classified as (1) statistical series methods, (2) surveys, and (3) input/output analysis.

Statistical Series Methods

Statistical series methods presume a close correlation between the level of product demand and some statistical set, such as the number of production workers or the value added by manufacturing. The technique is not effective in those cases where its underlying logic does not hold. First, the manager must identify specific industries that use the firm's product or could use it. Second, a measure of economic activity is determined for each actual and potential consuming industry. The measure of economic activity is assumed to represent the relative sales volume of each industry. For example, the number of production workers is frequently used as the statistical series representing potential demand. The larger the work force in an industry, presumably the greater the potential need for a given industrial product, whether it is a component or capital equipment. Other statistical series used include value added, capital equipment expenditures, materials consumed, total value of shipments, and total employees and payrolls.

The rationale behind using the single series method is that many industrial products have a variety of applications in a multitude of consuming industries. It would be impractical, if not impossible, to directly estimate all the potential applications of the product as well as the total quantities involved. To make the task of estimating market potential manageable, the analyst turns to information that is easily available—a statistical series. The analyst relates one of these series to demand for the firm's product. Consider aluminum cans. Secondary data reveal that in a given year the beverage industry purchased $260 million of aluminum cans and had total shipments of $2 billion. Thus, a relationship between demand for cans and total dollar shipments (the statistical series) can be established. For every dollar of beverage sales, $0.13 of aluminum cans will be used. Potential for next year could be estimated for a given region (by determining estimated beverage sales in the region for next year) or another segment of the beverage industry (by estimating, say, beer sales for next year). Past relationships between demand for a product and a statistical series provide a reasonably firm basis for evaluating market potential in different market segments and regions.

Sales and Marketing Management's Survey of Industrial and Commercial Purchasing Power   *Sales and Marketing Management* (*S&MM*) magazine annually publishes the *Survey of Industrial and Commercial Buying Power* covering over 400 industries at the four-digit SIC level. The *Survey* is organized as follows:

1.   The four-digit SIC industries are presented sequentially, starting with SIC 1011, iron ore mining, and concluding with SIC 8221, colleges and universities.

2.   For each industry, the leading counties (those with 1,000 or more employees in that industry) are ranked according to their volume

of business. Also shown for each industry in each large county are the number of establishments, number of large establishments (100 or more employees), total employment, total shipments, and percent of total industry shipments produced.

3. The county data is followed by the industry's U.S. totals for establishments, large establishments, employment, and share of business accounted for by large establishments. Total establishments are the number of business plants with 20 or more employees (these generally account for 90–95 percent of an industry's activity). Total employment refers to the aggregate number of employees in establishments with 20 or more employees. The dollar value of goods produced or services provided indicates total shipments.[4]

Table 7.2 provides a sample of the type and format of data.

The statistical series in the *Survey* offers industrial marketing managers valuable insights into market potential by region and specific industry. Because the *Survey* lists all counties with 1,000 or more employees producing a particular good or service as well as the number of establishments employing 20 or more people, a manager can focus immediately on the relatively small number of counties where the bulk of production in a given industry is concentrated.[5] The counties shown in the *Survey* account for the vast majority of total employment for the 409 industries included. Drawing on *Survey* data, the industrial marketer can begin a market-by-market analysis of the relative attractiveness of alternative market segments.

Three statistical series are provided by the *Survey*: number of plants, total employment, and value of shipments. Separately or together, these data can be used to develop market potential: An industrial manufacturer of meat analyzers and formulators has recently developed a particular machine primarily for the meat packing industry. Studies by the firm's trade association reveal that if used by all meat packers, this specific machine would cost each packer approximately one-half cent on each sales dollar. The machine maker wants to estimate total market potential and forecast potential by geographic region. The *Survey* can be used for both.

First, total shipments for four-digit manufacturing industries are provided; the relevant SIC groups will include:

- SIC 2011   Meat packing plants
- SIC 2013   Sausages and prepared meats
- SIC 2016   Poultry and dressing plants

[4] Thayer C. Taylor, "For Marketers in Search of Critical Data, S&MM Offers Convenience Packaging," *Sales and Marketing Management*, 130 (April 25, 1983), p. 14.

[5] Jay Gould and Bentley Paykin, "S&MM's Survey Moves Into the 'Post-Industrial Era'," *Sales and Marketing Management*, 130 (April 25, 1983), p. 9.

Table 7.2   Example of Data in the *Survey of Industrial and Commercial Buying Power*

Rank County, State	No. Of Estab. Total	No. Of Estab. Large	Total Employ-ment	1982 Est. Total Shipments ($ Millions)	1982 Est. % Of U.S. SIC	1982 Est. % In Large Estab.
Manufacturing						
SIC 20 Food						
2011 Meat-Packing Plants						
1 Cook, IL	47	18	6,036	2,105.8	4.27	80
2 Dane, WI	1	1	4,000	1,395.2	2.83	100
3 Los Angeles, CA	31	15	3,967	1,384.0	2.81	82
4 Douglas, NE	19	7	3,281	1,144.8	2.32	81
5 Dakota, NE	1	1	2,500	872.1	1.77	100
5 Linn, IA	1	1	2,500	872.1	1.77	100
7 Wayne, MI	12	6	2,395	835.6	1.70	91
8 Lyon, KS	2	2	2,140	746.4	1.51	100
9 Dubuque, IA	2	1	2,075	723.8	1.47	96
10 Isle of Wight, VA	2	2	2,050	715.0	1.45	100
11 Mower, MN	1	1	2,000	697.6	1.42	100
12 Jefferson, KY	4	2	1,838	641.3	1.30	96
13 Bexar, TX	9	6	1,784	622.4	1.26	90
14 Gibson, IN	1	1	1,750	610.5	1.24	100
15 Hamilton, OH	7	2	1,745	608.8	1.24	85
16 Denver, CO	10	4	1,662	579.8	1.18	80
17 Potter, TX	3	1	1,650	575.6	1.17	91
18 Davidson, TN	5	4	1,531	534.1	1.08	96
19 Freeborn, MN	1	1	1,500	523.2	1.06	100
20 Black Hawk, IA	1	1	1,500	523.2	1.06	100
21 Clay, MS	1	1	1,242	433.2	.88	100
22 Buchanan, MO	4	4	1,220	425.6	.86	100
23 Webster, IA	2	2	1,200	418.6	.85	100
24 Philadelphia, PA	6	3	1,095	382.0	.78	91
25 Milwaukee, WI	5	2	1,050	366.2	.74	87
26 Albany, NY	2	2	1,039	362.4	.74	100
27 Dodge, NE	2	1	1,035	361.2	.73	97
28 Shelby, TN	6	4	1,032	360.0	.73	92
29 Stark, OH	1	1	1,000	348.9	.71	100
29 Thomas, GA	1	1	1,000	348.9	.71	100
U.S. Total	**1,004**	**327**	**141,245**	**49,280.8**	**100.00**	**80**

Source: *Sales and Marketing Management*, April 25, 1983, p. 57. Reprinted by permission from *Sales and Marketing Management* magazine, copyright 1983.

The *Survey* shows total shipments for each. Note from Table 7.2 that SICs 2011, 2013, and 2016 have 1982 shipments of $49.3 billion, $12.0 billion, and $9.4 billion, respectively. With this information, an estimate of total market potential can be calculated as shown in Table 7.3. Total dollar shipments of each four-digit industry SIC are multiplied by .005 (which represents a cost of one-half cent per sales dollar) to determine the market potential for each. In reality, each SIC may use more or less formulators per dollar of sales, and this fact can be accounted for by adjusting the "formulator per dollar of sales" figure applied to each SIC's shipment volume. Total market potential is $353.5 million, the majority accounted for by the meat packing industry—SIC 2011.

Rank County, State	No. Of Estab. Total	No. Of Estab. Large	Total Employ- ment	1982 Est. Total Shipments ($ Millions)	1982 Est. % Of U.S. SIC	1982 Est. % In Large Estab.
2013 Sausages & Other Prepared Meats						
1 Cook, IL	42	18	4,985	770.0	6.40	79
2 Minnehaha, SD	1	1	3,000	463.4	3.85	100
3 Oakland, MI	2	1	2,627	405.7	3.37	99
4 Philadelphia, PA	13	6	2,082	321.4	2.67	88
5 Los Angeles, CA	18	10	2,031	313.8	2.61	83
6 Suffolk, MA	8	4	1,669	257.6	2.14	81
7 Oklahoma, OK	5	2	1,445	223.1	1.85	90
8 Baltimore city, MD	11	2	1,302	200.8	1.67	66
9 Orange, CA	2	2	1,139	175.9	1.46	100
10 Dallas, TX	11	3	1,108	170.9	1.42	65
11 Wayne, MI	13	5	1,083	167.1	1.39	77
12 Stark, OH	2	1	1,075	166.0	1.38	93
13 Jefferson, KY	1	1	1,000	154.5	1.28	100
13 Waupaca, WI	1	1	1,000	154.5	1.28	100
U.S. Total	**766**	**208**	**78,003**	**12,037.9**	**100.00**	**70**
2016 Poultry-Dressing Plants						
1 Wilkes, NC	1	1	2,500	333.1	3.54	100
2 Marshall, AL	5	5	2,475	329.7	3.50	100
3 Hall, GA	7	5	2,304	307.0	3.26	96
4 Sussex, DE	4	3	1,612	214.8	2.28	98
5 Banks, GA	1	1	1,550	206.5	2.19	100
6 Rockingham, VA	4	4	1,480	197.2	2.09	100
7 Coffee, GA	2	2	1,327	176.7	1.88	100
8 Benton, AR	4	3	1,305	173.9	1.85	98
9 Washington, AR	4	2	1,260	167.8	1.78	91
10 Accomack, VA	2	2	1,211	161.3	1.71	100
U.S. Total	**299**	**215**	**70,704**	**9,420.1**	**100.00**	**95**
2017 Poultry & Egg Processing						
1 Lancaster, PA	1	1	1,186	42.8	2.93	100
2 Clarke, GA	2	2	1,130	40.9	2.80	100
3 Scott, MS	3	3	1,050	38.0	2.60	100

Potential for each geographic region may be determined by reference to the body of the *Survey*. Consider SIC 2011, meat packing plants. Let us assume that the formulator manufacturer presently has sales offices in Nebraska, Iowa, Illinois, and Texas, and desires an estimate of relative potential for these four states. Table 7.4 indicates how the *Survey* data would be used to calculate relative market potential.

Iowa (5.15 percent) has over twice the potential of Texas (2.43 percent); Illinois and Nebraska are almost equal in potential, but all the potential in Illinois is concentrated in one county. Dollar potential could be estimated for each state by multiplying relative potential by total dollar potential. Thus, the potential for SIC 2011 in Texas would be computed

Table 7.3 Market Potential for Meat Formulators

SIC	Total Dollar Shipments	Usage	Market Potential
2011	$49.3 Billion	.005	$246.5 Million
2013	$12.0 Billion	.005	60.0 Million
2016	$ 9.4 Billion	.005	47.0 Million
			$353.5 Million

Table 7.4 Relative Market Potential for Meat Formulators

State	County	Relative Potential: Percent of Total U.S. Shipments SIC 2011
Nebraska	Douglas	2.32
	Dakota	1.77
	Dodge	.73
	Nebraska Total	4.82
Iowa	Linn	1.77
	Dubuque	1.47
	Black Hawk	1.06
	Webster	.85
	Iowa Total	5.15
Illinois	Cook	4.27
	Illinois Total	4.27
Texas	Bexar	1.26
	Potter	1.17
	Texas Total	2.43

by multiplying $246.5 million by .0243 (2.43 percent), which equals $6.0 million.

S&MM's *Survey of Industrial and Commercial Buying Power* is most useful when the manager wants a quick estimate of potential by geographic region and by SIC category. To the extent that demand for a product is well correlated to either final shipments or total employment of the consuming industries, the *Survey* will generate valid estimates of potential. In addition, the *Survey* offers an advantage over *County Business Patterns* in that the *Survey* is not bound by the nondisclosure rule; the data in the *Survey* are not distorted by deletion of a single large plant in a particular county. However, the *Survey* data are developed only for counties with more than 1,000 employees in a particular industry in the county and only include plants that have at least 20 employees. As a result, not all industrial manufacturing activity is included in the *Survey*. For example, in 1983, shipments of *Survey*-listed counties represented

Table 7.5   Relative Market Potential for Illinois, 1980; Industrial Hand Soap Single Statistical Series Method

SIC (1)	Industry (2)	Number of Illinois Production Workers (3)	Total Number of U.S. Production Workers (4)	Proportion of U.S. Production Workers (5)	Subjective Weights (6)	Weighted Proportion of U.S. Workers (7)
2752	Commercial printing	23,484	260,904	.090	3	.270
2893	Printing ink	1,894	10,389	.182	2	.364
3312	Steel mills	36,447	430,033	.085	1	.085
3317	Steel pipe	1,553	31,036	.050	1	.050
3361	Aluminum foundries	4,141	58,751	.070	1	.070
3411	Metal cans	6,481	56,903	.114	2	.228
3469	Metal stampings	15,134	116,975	.129	2	.258
3537	Industrial trucks and tractors	4,537	34,468	.132	1	.132
3541	Machine tools	6,698	73,956	.091	3	.273
3561	Pumps and pumping	4,529	72,339	.063	2	.126
				Totals	18	1.856

Market Potential for Illinois = 1.856/18 = 10.31%

Source: *County Business Patterns*, 1980.

90 percent of the total output of SIC 3312 (blast furnaces and steel mills) and 85 percent of SIC 3573 (electronic computing equipment), but only 49 percent of SIC 2033 (canned fruits and vegetables).[6] Generally, if a product is consumed by industries made up of many small and medium-sized firms which are geographically dispersed, the *Survey* will not provide accurate estimates of geographic and total potentials.

Single Series Method   The single series method also calculates market potential on the basis of secondary data reflecting the relative buying power of industrial markets. To employ this procedure, management must have adequate knowledge of the SIC groups that are potential users of a product. Let us first consider how this approach may be used to analyze *relative market potential*.

Assume that a manufacturer of industrial hand soap wishes to determine the relative market potential in the state of Illinois. Production workers will be used as the statistical series because product usage is directly related to the size of the production work force. Past experience indicates that demand will be concentrated in SIC groups involving a significant degree of hand labor, and where the operations involve oiled, greased, or "dirty" raw materials, components, and parts. Table 7.5 lists the SIC groups that management feels have the greatest potential use

[6]"1983 Survey of Industrial and Commercial Buying Power," *Sales and Marketing Management*, 130 (April 25, 1983), pp. 58, 79, 88.

for the product. The SIC groups were determined by analyzing the full description of SICs in the *Standard Industrial Classification Manual*.

To calculate the relative potential for Illinois, management next refers to the Census Bureau's *County Business Patterns* to determine the number of production workers for each SIC group (Column 5 of Table 7.5). Column 6 indicates the subjective weights that management applies to each SIC group; these are an estimate of the relative consumption strength for each group. Finally, Column 7 is the weighted proportion of United States production workers in Illinois. Column 7 is then totaled and divided by the sum of the weights to show the relative market potential for Illinois. Similar analyses for other states (or by region or city) provide the data necessary for allocating sales efforts to various geographic areas.

Instead of relative potentials based on subjective weights, the industrial marketer may want to determine *absolute market potential* (in dollars or units) for the entire United States, various geographic areas, or specific SIC groups.

Estimates of absolute market potential can be determined with a statistical series using the following approach:

Step 1. Select a statistical series.

Step 2. Determine the relationship of the series to demand for the product for which potential is being estimated for each target SIC industry.

Step 3. Forecast the statistical series for the desired time frame.

Step 4. Determine market potential by relating demand to future values of the statistical series.

Selecting a Statistical Series To determine absolute potential using a statistical series, the analyst must first evaluate which statistical series is best related to demand for the product. The demand for some products may be highly correlated to the number of production workers—uniforms, hand soap, and some office products are good examples. In other cases, value added or the value of shipments is better correlated to demand. For example, the demand for metal cans by the beverage industry is more closely related to the value of beverage shipments than to the number of industry production workers, due to the high level of automation in the industry.

Important criteria in selecting a statistical series are that (1) data on the series are available and (2) future estimates of the series are easier to predict than would be product demand. Many of the statistical series reported by the Department of Commerce in the *Census of Manufacturers* and *County Business Patterns* can be forecast for one to three years with reasonable accuracy. Private research firms, such as Predicasts and Standard and Poor's, develop predictions on many of the series for various industries. In addition, *The U.S. Industrial Outlook*, published by the Department of Commerce, makes short- and long-term projections of employment, sales, and capital spending for a vast array of industries. Thus, if an industrial firm determines that consuming industries could use four units of a product per $1000 dollars of the consuming industry's output, an estimate of market potential for 1987 could be made by consulting a reference source that forecasts 1987 sales of the consuming industry. Market potential would equal 4 units times estimated 1987 sales (in thousands of dollars) of the consuming industry.

Determining the Demand and Statistical Series Relationship   Once the series has been selected, data on the series must be collected and related to demand for the product to develop what might be termed a "demand" or "usage" factor, that is, how much of the product would be demanded per unit of the statistical series.

One approach is to use the *Census of Manufacturers* or the *Survey of Industrial and Commercial Buying Power* to develop the data base for the statistical series, and then relate this to prior levels of demand for the product, either by SIC code or by geographic region. Assume we wish to estimate market potential for ball bearings in 1988, and SIC 3711 (motor vehicles) and SIC 3715 (truck trailers) are the primary target markets. The statistical series is value of shipments. To determine the usage or demand factor, we relate past ball bearing demand to the value of shipments in SIC 3711 and 3715 (Table 7.6).

Sales of bearings to the target industries would be gleaned from trade sources, while the statistical series, value of shipments, could be found in the *Survey of Industrial and Commercial Buying Power*. Thus, in SIC 3711, $.022 of bearings were purchased for each dollar of shipments. An estimate of market potential in 1988 would be developed by multiplying $.022 by the projected value of shipments by SIC 3711 in 1988.

Often data on total sales of a product to a specific industry are simply not available, or are proprietary. A significant problem for industrial marketers is to determine how much of a particular type of product would or could be consumed by a specific SIC industry. To overcome this difficulty, the marketer may have to survey a sample of firms. If the survey is conducted properly, the demand factors developed in this way may be more accurate than those developed through secondary sources.

Table 7.6   Usage Factor for Ball Bearings

Industry	Bearing Sales to the Industry— 198X (Millions)	Value of Shipments— 198X (Millions)	Demand Factor: Bearings/ $ of Shipments
SIC 3711	$1,680	$75,271	$.022
SIC 3715	$ 39	$ 2,767	$.014

Table 7.7   SIC 2065: Confectionery Products—Materials Consumed

Shipments: $4.49 billion
Cost of Materials: $2.17 billion
Value Added: $2.02 billion

Materials Consumed:	Quantity (Tons)	Dollar Value (Millions)
Sugar	523,500	$195.0
Cocoa beans	5,150	17.7
Chocolate coatings	105,350	240.0
Nuts, in shells	405,500	210.5
Nutmeats	361,000	393.0
Milk	—	87.0
Fat and oil	34,250	26.0
Corn Syrup	472,000	72.0
Cocoa butter	26,000	97.0
Flavors	—	17.0
Paper containers and packaging	—	245.0
Metal cans	—	34.0
Glass	—	25.0
Other materials	—	341.0
Materials, containers, suppliers, NSK	—	175.0

Source: Census of Manufacturers, 1977.

Suppose a manufacturer of plastic resins wants to analyze market potential in four SIC industries that the firm has never dealt with. There is no published data. A short survey of firms in each SIC group could be implemented to assess resin purchases and some other statistical series, say production workers. The results would be tallied for each SIC group, and a usage factor of resin (lbs.) per production worker calculated for each. The result could then be used to forecast market potential in each SIC industry by estimating total production workers in the relevant year and multiplying times the "usage or demand factor." The validity of this approach depends on how well the firms in the sample represent the target industries.

The "Materials Consumed" section of the *Census of Manufacturers* shows the quantity and value of materials, containers, and supplies consumed by specific SIC industries (see Table 7.7). A marketer of paper containers could determine from this section that firms in the confectionery industry would use $.0546 worth of paper containers for each dollar of shipments by the confectionery industry ($245 million of paper containers/$4.49 billion of shipments). Unfortunately, the level of detail for each industry varies. For some industries, specific components and raw materials are not detailed, but only total materials consumed. In the case of confectionery products, individual types of paper containers are not indicated. Thus, the manager must use caution in using this type of information.

Estimating a demand or usage factor this way must take into account the limitations of the approach. The analysis is based on averages; an average consumption of a given component per dollar of output or per production worker is computed. The average may or may not hold true for a particular target industry. Product usage may vary considerably between two firms even in the same SIC category. Further, the demand factor is based on historical relationships which may dramatically change, i.e., the industry may use more or less of the product as a result of the technological change, manufacturing system reconfigurations, or changes in final consumer demand. Nevertheless, carefully derived estimates of the relationship between demand and a statistical series can be powerful tools for measuring market potential.

Forecasting the Statistical Series   Once the relationship of demand and the series has been documented (the demand or usage factor has been determined), management will estimate future values of the series in one of two ways: they can independently forecast expected values, using their own estimated growth rates; or they can rely on forecasts made by government, trade associations, or private research firms. The goal is to project the series forward so that future market potential can be assessed by multiplying the demand factor by the estimated future value of the series.

The demand or usage factor expresses the relationship between demand and the series in terms such as "dollar of product/dollar of consuming industry sales" or "pounds of product/production worker." If we are estimating market potential two years into the future, we must ask whether usage of the product per production worker will change over that period. Management may want to adjust the demand or usage factor to reflect predicted changes in product usage among the targeted industries. An analysis of production processes, technology, competitive actions, and final consumer demand may be required to properly adjust the usage factor. A good example is found in the plastics industry: The move to lighten automobiles to enhance gas mileage would indicate a substantial increase in the "pounds of plastic/automobile" usage factor over the next five years.

Determining Market Potential   The final step is the easiest one—the demand or usage factor is multiplied by the forecasted value of the statistical series. Once this stage has been reached, the difficult data and estimation problems have been resolved, and the calculation is routine. Here, management must be sure that potential is calculated for all relevant market segments. For planning and control purposes, market potential estimates may be required for different customer segments, SIC groups, territories, and distribution channels. A comprehensive example is shown in Figure 7.3.

Figure 7.3   Estimating Market Potential with a Statistical Series

Problem: Estimate market potential for metal cans in SIC 2032, 2082, and 2086 for the State of California for 1987.

Product: Metal Cans

Market:

Region: California

SICs: 2032 Canned Fruits and Vegetables
2082 Malt Beverages
2086 Bottled and Canned Soft Drinks

Step 1: Select statistical series: Value of shipments, 1977

Step 2: Determine the relationship of demand and the statistical series (usage or demand factor)

Consuming Industries	Metal Cans Consumed, 1977 (Millions)	Value of Shipments, 1977[a] (Millions)	Usage Factor ($ Cans/$ Shipments)
2033 Canned Fruits and Vegetables	$ 942	$ 6,663	$0.1414
2082 Malt Beverages	1,660	6,653	0.2495
2086 Soft Drinks	1,222	10,007	0.1221

[a] *Source: Census of Manufacturers,* 1977.

Step 3: Forecast the series for the desired time frame

A. Estimate: Value of Shipments in California, 1987

SIC	Value of Shipments by California Industries, 1982[b]	Projected Annual Growth Rate[c]	Computation	Estimated Value of Shipments California 1987
2033	$1,657	1.1%	$1,657 $\times$ (1.01)^5	$1,742
2082	463	4.0%	463 (1.04)^5	563
2086	411	2.5%	411 (1.025)^5	465

Sources: [b] "Survey of Industrial Purchasing Power," *Sales and Marketing Management,* April 26, 1982.
[c] U.S. Industrial Outlook.

B. Adjust Usage Factor

SIC	Usage Factor	Estimated Usage Change[d], 1987	Adjusted Usage Factor
2033	$0.1414	No Change	$0.1414
2082	0.2495	(.5%)	0.2483
2086	0.1221	(2.5%)	0.1190

[d] Metal can usage forecasted to decline by 0.5% in the malt beverage industry over the next five years (*Standard and Poor's Industry Surveys,* January, 1983).

Metal can usage forecasted to decline by 2.5% in the soft drink industry (*Beverage Industry,* May 5, 1978).

Step 4: Determine market potential

SIC	Adjusted Usage Factor	Estimated Value of Shipments California, 1987 (Millions)	Market Potential California, 1987
2033	$0.1414	$1,742	$246.3
2082	0.2483	563	139.8
2086	0.1190	465	55.3

In summary, the effectiveness of the single series method of estimating market potential depends upon how well the demand or usage factor represents underlying demand, the quality of the data used, the ability to estimate future values of the series and usage factors, and the extent of distortion caused by using averages and gross estimates. This approach is well suited to industrial products that are in common use. For new products, unique items, and rarely used components, this approach is not appropriate because the data are insufficient. Modifications to the series and considerable management judgment are required to estimate potential. One way to develop better estimates is to use more than one statistical series.

Multiple Statistical Series Methods   The demand for a product depends on a host of factors; representation of demand by one variable is frequently insufficient. Industrial marketers often use sophisticated statistical techniques to measure the combined influence of a number of series on market potential. Those factors most closely associated with industry demand are given the highest weight or relative influence.

For example, a manufacturer of industrial cranes believes that product sales are related to the number of production workers and to customer expenditures on new plant and equipment (P&E). Data for these variables are secured from government sources. Analyzing the data using statistical regression yields an equation which relates crane sales to the number of production workers and to plant and equipment expenditures.[7] The regression equation indicates the nature of the relationship between a dependent variable (industry sales) and the independent variables (expenditures = x_1 and workers = x_2). The resulting equation might look like:

Potential crane sales = 7920 + 0.2363 (P&E expenditures)
                              − 1.024 (Production workers)

In this case, crane sales increase directly with plant and equipment expenditures, but decrease as the size of the work force expands (probably because there is less automation in plants with a large labor force).

Once the crane supplier determines the amount of P&E expenditures and production workers in any given market, total potential can be calculated. If Ohio has 9,000 production workers in user industries, and new P&E expenditures are estimated at $16 million, total potential crane sales in Ohio are:

Potential = 7920 + 0.2363 ($16 million) − 1.024 (9000)
          = $3,779,504

As with the single series method, great care must be taken in selecting the appropriate series. It may be necessary to experiment with

---

[7] For a discussion of regression analysis, see Morris Hamberg, *Statistical Analysis for Decision Making* (New York: Harcourt Brace Jovanovich, Inc., 1977), pp. 411 ff.

several series to see which combinations produce the best estimates. Comparison of sales potential estimates for prior years can be compared to actual sales in those years to evaluate which combination is most predictive.

Market Surveys

To avoid the problems inherent in historical statistical data, firms can use market surveys to gather primary information on future buyer intentions. Surveys are also used to generate data to be used with the statistical series. The techniques and procedures for conducting industrial market surveys were treated in Chapter 5. Here it is important to note the use of survey *results* for estimating market and sales potentials, as in determining the demand or usage factor to be used in the single statistical series approach.

The survey method is particularly useful for estimating market potential of new products. Surveys can provide information about whether specific plants are in the market for a new product, the extent of their needs, and the likelihood of purchase. Surveys are useful in determining potential product use by specific SIC groups, the percentage of plants in each SIC which have the greatest potential, and the relative importance of each SIC group to total sales. Surveys have also been utilized to evaluate the purchase potential of individual firms.

The National Lead Company conducted personal interviews with technical, marketing, and purchasing directors of major users to determine the usage factor of a new product. The company mailed questionnaires to small users, distributors, dealers, and jobbers who were too numerous for personal interviews.[8] In addition, National Lead annually surveys customers to determine their purchase intentions for the coming year.

A complete enumeration of the market can sometimes be made, and the potential volumes for each prospective customer summed to arrive at a total market potential. A complete census of the market is warranted where (1) the markets are very concentrated, (2) there is direct sales contact, (3) orders have a relatively high value, and (4) the unit volume is low.[9] The difficulty is collecting data for *all* potential users of the product. Typically, the sales force is assigned the task of collecting information. Developing information on existing customers is routine, but it becomes more difficult to solicit information from the user who is not a customer. Sales people often experience difficulties in reaching the individual in a noncustomer firm who has the information they need. They may also be reluctant to allocate a significant amount of time to collect-

---

[8] M. C. MacDonald, Jr., "Appraising the Market for New Industrial Products," *Conference Board Studies in Business Policy, No. 123* (New York: The Conference Board, 1967), pp. 77–80.

[9] William E. Cox, Jr., *Industrial Marketing Research* (New York: John Wiley and Sons, 1979), p. 158.

ing the data. However, in some industries, buyers are eager to share their annual raw material and component requirements with vendors in order to facilitate vendor planning and therefore assure a continuity of supply. The automobile industry, for example, provides steel suppliers with detailed estimates of its requirements for steel.[10]

Uses and Limitations   The survey method is appropriate in forecasting the market potential for new products and in providing estimates of potential based on objective facts and opinions rather than executive judgment. In addition, the survey can target specific industries that represent the greatest market potential for new or existing products. Its limitation is the one associated with any survey—the research method used. Nonrepresentative samples and nonresponse bias can distort findings, the wrong person in the respondent companies may fill out the questionnaire, and a small sample size may make sophisticated statistical analysis impossible. A particularly difficult problem is assessing who to contact.[11] The researcher will need to invest considerable effort to find the best source of data. It is the responsibility of the marketing manager to resolve the data collection problems and to insure that the survey research design will generate valid results.

Input/Output Analysis

Input/output (I/O) analysis constitutes a third approach to evaluating market potential. I/O analysis is based on the concept that the sales of one industry represent the purchases of another industry.[12]

The essence of I/O analysis is to provide an effective understanding of transactions between industries in the economy. Plastics, for instance, are used in thousands of products as well as being purchased directly by consumers. To effectively estimate total market demand, a plastics manufacturer must first comprehend all the potential applications of plastics. Consider all of the products—automobiles, washing machines, clothing, furniture, packaging, typewriters, among others—with plastic parts. For each application, the plastics supplier would want to know the expected sales volume for each product using plastic and the amount of plastic used in producing each product. To undertake separate studies of each product/market situation would be virtually impossible. Here I/O analysis makes its contribution.

I/O data expresses demand in terms of the amount of output (plastics) required to produce one unit of the using industry's output (automobiles). An I/O table might show that $185 of plastic is required to produce one automobile.

---

[10] *Ibid*, p. 159.

[11] Hummel, *Market and Sales Potentials*, p. 106.

[12] James Rothe, "The Reliability of Input-Output Analysis for Marketing," *California Management Review*, 14, No. 4 (1972), p. 75.

The United States I/O Tables   The most comprehensive I/O analysis is provided by the federal government in the United States Input/Output Tables developed by the Commerce Department's Office of Business Economics; these are published in the *Survey of Current Business*.[13] The tables show the internal productive structure of the entire United States economy by aggregating transactions among industries. Every sale by a selling industry is a purchase by a purchasing industry. Transactions among industries are organized into a flow matrix, where sales of each industry are shown horizontally and purchases by each are found by reading down the column.

One of the many types of I/O tables developed by the government is the basic "input and output flow" table illustrated with hypothetical data in Table 7.8. The row for an industry shows how its output was distributed to other industries. For example, Mining sold 80 units of output to Mfg. A and 60 units to Mfg. B. The columns, on the other hand, show purchases by an industry from every other industry. Services purchased 30 units of input from Mining and 120 units from Mfg. A.

The industrial marketer can use U.S. I/O tables to examine the interrelationship between producing and consuming industries and analyze how these relate to the demand for finished products by ultimate users and consumers. To estimate potential demand for plastics in the automobile industry, the plastics firm would estimate the amount of plastics required to produce one automobile. The "direct and indirect requirements coefficients" matrix in the U.S. Input/Output tables is designed for this purpose. Table 7.9 displays a hypothetical coefficients matrix.

The entries in each cell of the matrix represent what each industry in a column would have to purchase from each industry in a row to deliver one dollar of its output to final users or consumers. Assume that Mfg. A produces only plastics and that Mfg. B produces automobiles. The entry in Row 2, Column 3 is 0.1125. This means that for the auto-

Table 7.8   Example of a Hypothetical Input-Output Flow Table

Sales by:	Mining	Purchases by Mfg. A	Mfg. B	Services	Total Intermediate Output
Mining	20	80	60	30	190
Mfg. A	10	50	180	120	360
Mfg. B	—	200	20	100	320
Services	10	40	60	20	130
Total Inputs	40	370	320	270	1000

[13]"Input-Output Structure of the U.S. Economy," *Survey of Current Business* (February 1974).

Table 7.9   Sample of a Hypothetical Direct and Indirect Requirements Coefficients Matrix

	Mining	Mfg. A	Mfg. B	Services
Mining	1.2801	0.3142	0.1965	0.1258
Mfg. A	0.0894	1.3871	0.1125	0.4215
Mfg. B	0.1075	0.3016	1.2419	0.5924
Services	0.0209	0.0840	0.1867	1.1104

mobile industry to deliver $1000 worth of automobiles, plastics manufacturers must produce $112.50 worth of plastics.

I/O Analysis: Market Potential Estimation   The I/O coefficients data in Table 7.9 can be useful for estimating aggregate levels of market potential for a selected industry. First, an estimate of total demand for automobiles could be determined from industry estimates, trade association studies, or government estimates. Then, the entries in the coefficients table would be multiplied by expected final demand for automobiles. The result would show total plastics requirements for automobiles for the forthcoming year. Assume that automobile sales are estimated at $30 billion for next year. Reference to Table 7.9 indicates the requirements coefficient for the plastics industry to produce one dollar of output in the automobile industry is 0.1125. Total plastics requirements for the automobile industry for next year would be:

$30 billion × 0.1125 = $3.375 billion

Similar procedures could build up estimates for other plastics-using industries.

Realistically, the application of U.S. I/O tables is very difficult because of the aggregation of the data. The I/O tables function at the industry rather than the product level. As a result, the technique is most appropriate for estimates in very broad product categories. I/O analysis may also be applied to the evaluation of performance across market segments. Consider the plastics producer once again. The I/O tables show the broad industry groups that require plastics in their production process, and how much they require. The plastics producer can compare its sales in those segments to the total requirements for plastics. In this way, the firm can evaluate generally its relative performance in the various consuming industries. The I/O tables may also reveal new markets—industries to which the firm is not presently directing any of its marketing efforts.

I/O Analysis: Extent of Utilization   Although the I/O technique has been publicized as an effective means for locating new markets, applications have been limited.[14] A poll of Fortune 500 companies shows that only one in ten firms uses I/O analysis.[15] Celanese Corporation, however, used I/O techniques to pinpoint future markets, and American Metal Climax has used I/O in an attempt to improve projections of future demand.[16]

I/O Analysis: Limitations   I/O techniques are best suited to large firms producing relatively undifferentiated items like chemicals. Moreover, because data requirements are extensive, published I/O tables are frequently out of date. I/O analysis also presumes that all firms within an industry have the same production requirements and technology—a highly unlikely situation. Finally, I/O techniques cannot account for situations where there are either increasing or decreasing returns to scale. Where returns to scale exist, application of the I/O technique will result in demand estimates that are too high or too low.[17] The marketing manager must consider the strengths, weaknesses, and assumptions which underlie each technique for estimating market potential.

Evaluating Market Potential Estimates

The selection of the technique that best fits a particular product/market situation requires considerable judgment. Three alternative approaches have been examined in this chapter: (1) statistical series methods; (2) market surveys; and (3) input/output analysis. Since each could produce a different market potential estimate, the manager must evaluate the underlying assumptions and limitations of each technique. Estimating market potential involves considerable art—applying sound judgment to the method and its requirements. An important consideration is the quality of the data used to derive the market potential estimate. Information that is out-of-date or invalid for the situation will not produce viable estimates of demand, regardless of the sophistication and precision of the methodology used.

Summary

Estimating market potential and forecasting sales are the two most significant dimensions of organizational demand analysis. Each is fundamental to marketing planning and control. Knowledge of market potential enables the marketer to isolate market opportunity and efficiently

---

[14] Rothe, "The Reliability of Input-Output Analysis," p. 77.

[15] "After Many a Year Comes the Matrix," *Sales Management* (January 15, 1970), p. 54.

[16] "How Input-Output Helped Map the Marketing Strategy of Glass Containers Corp.," *Industrial Marketing*, 55 (January 1970), pp. 21–25.

[17] G. David Hughes, *Marketing Management, A Planning Approach* (Reading, Mass.: Addison-Wesley Publishing Company, 1978), p. 198.

allocate marketing resources to product and customer segments that offer the highest return. Measures of market potential also provide a standard against which the manager can monitor performance. Similarly, the sales forecast—the firm's best estimate of expected sales with a particular marketing plan—forces the manager to ask the right questions and to consider various strategies before allocating resources.

The methods for developing estimates of market potential fall into three categories: (1) statistical series methods, (2) market surveys, and (3) input/output analysis. The marketer must understand the strengths and weaknesses of each and their appropriateness to a particular marketing environment. The task of measuring market potential is always challenging. Accurate estimates facilitate the design of effective and efficient industrial marketing strategy.

Discussion Questions

1. Market potential can be used as a standard for planning and controlling marketing inputs (costs) and outputs (sales). Explain.

2. What is the underlying logic of statistical series methods used in measuring market potential?

3. What statistical series are provided in the *Survey of Industrial Purchasing Power*?

4. Distinguish between single and multiple statistical series methods for estimating market potential.

5. Why are market surveys favored over statistical series methods in measuring the market potential for new industrial products?

6. Before using input/output analysis, what limitations should be understood?

7. Define the following:

   a. Absolute potential
   b. Relative potential
   c. Direct technical coefficients (I/O analysis)

8. How could an industrial marketing manager use SIC information to determine demand potential in the Boston market? Be very specific—this manager is totally unfamiliar with the SIC system.

Exercises

1. The Thornton Company manufactures ink for use in all types of printing operations. The Midwest sales manager is confronted with the need to develop sales quotas for five salespersons located

in Pennsylvania, Ohio, Michigan, Indiana, and Illinois. The sales quotas are to be based on the market potential for printing ink in each state; preliminary analysis suggests that SIC 2711 (news-papers), SIC 2721 (periodicals), SIC 2732 (book printing), and SIC 2751 (letterpress commercial printing) are the primary ink-using industries. Historical sales records suggest that the cost of printing ink comprises about 0.1 percent of the sales dollar for the using industries. Using *Sales and Marketing Management's 1983 Survey of Industrial and Commercial Buying Power*, determine:

a. The total market potential for each SIC industry for the entire five-state area.
b. The total market potential for each state.
c. The relative market potential for each state.

2.   What cautions should the Thornton sales manager be aware of in applying market potential data to the formulation of sales quotas?

3.   The Simpson Company manufactures electronic controls for sale to a variety of industrial users. A primary market is New York State, where past sales volumes have not been up to management expec-tations. Last year, New York accounted for only 14 percent of total company sales volume. In an effort to evaluate that performance, management seeks to determine the relative market potential of New York. The market research department determines that the following SIC groups account for the vast majority of sales; the value added for New York and the entire United States is shown for each.

SIC	Value added—New York*	Value added—U.S.*
2992	$21,100	$142,600
3291	5,600	52,600
3541	46,500	420,300
3559	28,400	112,000
3662	12,500	205,400
3679	17,000	158,100

*In thousands of dollars.

Management estimates that the relative consumption strength (subjective weights) for each SIC in New York is 3 for SIC 2992 and 3662; 2 for SIC 3291, 3541, and 3679; and 1 for SIC 3559.

a. Use the single statistical series method to determine relative po-tential in New York.
b. How did the company perform last year in light of this infor-mation?

4.   The Simpson Company now requires an estimate of the total dollar market potential for the purpose of allocating advertising expendi-tures to the New York market. A small-scale study of a sample of

customers in each SIC group provides the following data on "electronic control purchases per dollar of value added":

SIC	Electronic Control Purchases Per Dollar of Value Added
2992	$.11
3291	.08
3541	.07
3559	.05
3662	.12
3679	.10

Determine the total dollar market potential for New York.

C·H·A·P·T·E·R
8

Organizational Demand Analysis: Sales Forecasting

The sales forecast has a pervasive influence on all facets of the industrial marketing plan. While it is inextricably linked to market potential analysis, sales forecasting is a separate and distinct component of organizational demand analysis. After reading this chapter, you will have an understanding of:

1. *the role of the sales forecast in industrial marketing management;*
2. *general approaches to sales forecasting;*
3. *the purpose of different forecasting time frames;*
4. *specific qualitative and quantitative techniques that can be applied in developing a sales forecast.*

The sales forecast is the manager's best estimate of the sales that will be generated if a particular marketing plan is adopted. Thus, the industrial marketer is challenged to predict how organizational customers will respond to alternative marketing strategies or to differing levels of marketing effort. The marketer has nearly unlimited options in blending the marketing mix and constructing the final marketing budget. Which products, customer segments, and territories should be emphasized in the marketing plan? Organizational demand analysis must be extended beyond market potential analysis to an actual forecast of sales.

This chapter examines the salient dimensions of sales forecasting. Selected sales forecasting techniques are described, illustrated, and evaluated.

The Essential Dimensions of Sales Forecasting

Selection of a sales forecasting technique depends on many factors, including the period for which the forecast is desired; the purpose of the forecast; the availability of data; the level of technical expertise possessed by the company; the accuracy desired; the nature of the product; and the extent of the product line. Evaluations of each factor will suggest the limits within which the firm must work in terms of forecasting methods.

General Approaches to Forecasting

Because all budgets in a company ultimately depend on how many units will be sold, the sales forecast often determines company-wide commitments for everything from raw materials and labor to capital equipment and advertising.[1] In marketing alone, forecasts are used to set sales quotas, evaluate advertising budgets, assess long-range product strategy, set inventory levels, determine transportation requirements, estimate personnel requirements, set sales compensation plans, and evaluate distribution channel alternatives. Because estimates of future sales are applied to so many activities, different types of forecasts are often required.

A forecast to determine inventory commitments for the next month has to be more precise than one used to set sales quotas, which may differ from expected sales due to their motivational value. A five-year forecast of machine tool industry growth will require a very detailed and sophisticated model incorporating numerous economic variables, while a six-month projection of No. 28 ball bearing sales may simply require the extrapolation of a trend line. The forecasting process may be administered *top-down* or *bottom-up*, or a combination of the two.

[1] Gordon J. Bolt, *Market and Sales Forecasting Manual* (Englewood Cliffs, N.J.: Prentice-Hall, Inc., 1982), p. 88.

Top-Down   In the top-down approach, estimates of the general economy and the industry first give managers a picture of the environmental conditions under which they will be operating. These estimates include evaluation of all economic and industry variables that would influence sales of their products. The data base necessary to develop these forecasts might include economic indicators like GNP, unemployment, capital expenditures, price indices, industrial production, and housing starts. A model (i.e., a mathematical equation) would be created to link the economic indicators to either industry or product sales. For example, Interroyal, a major supplier of commercial and institutional furniture, uses a forecasting model in which current GNP, construction starts 18 months earlier, and current plant and equipment expenditures are linked to expected sales of metal office furniture.[2] Eaton Corporation, a manufacturer of forklift trucks, used an overall economic forecast to build a five-year plan, then created an industry forecast of unit volume from which upper management sets market share targets.[3]

The top-down approach often will include *econometrics*, which refers to large, multivariable, computer-based models of the United States economy. Such models attempt to forecast changes in total U.S. economic activity or for specific industries by the use of complex equations which may number over 1000 for a single model. The equations mathematically represent the historical interworkings of the economy.

Econometric models are available from commercial, university, and bank sources, including Chase Manhattan Bank, the University of Michigan, Wharton School of Finance, Harris Trust, and Data Resources, Inc. Chase Econometric Associates, for example, provides clients with a monthly report on over 200 economic indicators plus current quarter data and data for the next ten quarters. In addition, Chase has supplemented its macroeconomic model with 80 industry models for making ten-year forecasts.[4] Some firms like General Electric develop their own econometric models. General Electric's model provides a long-range economic forecast to group and division managers to serve as a starting point for their own industry projections.

Bottom-Up   While the top-down approach begins with a macro view of the economy and industry and is initiated by upper management, the bottom-up method of sales forecasting originates with the sales force and marketing personnel. The logic behind the bottom-up approach is that sales personnel possess a good understanding of the market in terms of customer requirements, inventory situations, and general market trends. Salespeople can also procure economic data from corporate

[2]*Ibid.*, p. 11.
[3]*Ibid.*, p. 14.
[4]*Ibid.*, p. 34.

staff so that their projections will be based not only on historical sales data and customer needs, but also on economic and industry data.

The bottom-up approach works well where sales are limited to a well-defined industry. Jet aircraft is a good example. A firm supplying gaskets for jets knows that there are long lead times in the production of engines and a very limited number of producers. Thus, salespeople know almost exactly what will be built in the next one to three years, and by whom. Very specific estimates of gaskets required can be made. There is little need for an all-encompassing macroeconomic forecast.

Combination Approach   It is rare that either the top-down or bottom-up procedure will be used exclusively. The more common approach is to use both, with the marketing executive being responsible for coordinating the estimates. For example, at Interroyal, the national sales manager uses both estimates to project product line sales for the year. TRW combines economic projections for specific SIC codes made by Chase Econometric Associates with input from the field sales organization.[5] In the Rockwell Division of TRW, managers integrate the tailored econometric projections for each of their customer industries with the forecasts they receive from their forty-two salespersons.[6] To insure that all division managers and field personnel base their forecasts on the same assumptions, TRW's internal economic monitoring service evaluates the economic outlook for the next three years. The marketing manager will reconcile the various forecasts and develop appropriate sales estimates.

The Forecasting Time Frame

Sales forecasts may be prepared on a day-to-day basis for inventory control; or an estimate of sales ten years into the future may be needed to plan additional plant and warehouse capacity. The methodologies selected for each of these forecasts would probably differ; each forecasting method is suited for a specific forecasting time frame. In fact, the time horizon for which forecasts are prepared can often serve as a substitute for most of the criteria used to evaluate forecasting techniques.[7] Time horizons reflect such characteristics as the value of accuracy in forecasting, the cost of various methodologies, the timeliness of their results, and the types of data patterns involved in the sales data.[8]

Although the forecast time frame may range from a year to ten-to-fifteen years, four basic time frames are common:[9]

[5] *Ibid.*, p. 30.

[6] *Ibid.*, p. 31.

[7] Spyros Makridakis and Steven Wheelwright, "Forecasting: Issues and Challenges for Marketing Management," *Journal of Marketing*, 41 (October 1977), p. 30.

[8] *Ibid.*, p. 30.

[9] Adapted from R. A. Lomas and G. A. Lancaster, "Sales Forecasting for the Smaller Organization," *Industrial Management*, 20 (February 1978), p. 37.

1. *Immediate term.* Forecasts for this period range from daily to monthly. The purpose is to support operating decisions on such things as delivery scheduling and inventory.

2. *Short-term.* Short-term forecasts range from one month to six. The time frame may overlap with the immediate and intermediate terms. Short-term forecasts are necessary for planning merchandising and promotion, production scheduling, and cash requirements. The seasonal pattern of sales is generally the pattern of interest.

3. *Intermediate term.* This time frame generally ranges from six months to two years. Intermediate-term forecasts are used to set promotional levels, assess sales personnel needs, and set capital requirements. Seasonal, cyclical, and turning points in the sales data are of interest here.

4. *Long-term.* Long-term forecasts extend beyond two years to estimate trends and rates of sales growth for broad product lines. The results are used to plan product line changes, capital requirements, distribution channels, and plant expansion.

Forecasting Methods

As discussed, the sales forecast may be highly mathematical or based informally on sales force estimates. Two primary approaches to sales forecasting are recognized: (1) qualitative, and (2) quantitative, which includes time series and causal. Each category contains a variety of techniques; effective forecasting requires matching the marketing situation with an appropriate methodology.[10]

Qualitative Techniques

Qualitative techniques rely on informed judgment and rating schemes. The sales force, top-level executives, or distributors may be called upon to use their knowledge of the economy, the market, and the customers to create qualitative estimates of demand. Techniques for qualitative analysis are *executive panels*, *sales force composite*, and the *Delphi method*.

Industrial firms are more likely to employ qualitative techniques than are consumer-goods producers.[11] Their effectiveness depends on the close relationships between customers and suppliers that are typical in the industrial market. Qualitative techniques work well for items like heavy capital equipment, where the nature of the forecast does not lend itself to mathematical analysis. These techniques are also suitable for

[10] Makridakis and Wheelwright, "Forecasting: Issues and Challenges," p. 25.

[11] Douglas J. Dalrymple, "Sales Forecasting Methods and Accuracy," *Business Horizons*, 18 (December 1975), p. 70.

new product forecasts or in new technology areas where historical data are scarce or nonexistent.[12] An important advantage of qualitative approaches is that users of the forecast are brought into the forecasting process. The effect is usually increased understanding of the procedure and a higher level of commitment to the resultant forecast.

Executive Panels   The executive panel method and the sales force composite method have significantly greater usage than other forecasting procedures among a large sample of business firms.[13] The panel method is popular because it is easy to apply and understand. This method combines and averages top executives' estimates of future sales. Typically, executives from a variety of departments, such as sales, marketing, production, finance, and purchasing, are brought together to collectively apply their expertise, experience, and opinions to the forecast.

The primary limitation of the panel approach is that it does not systematically analyze cause and effect relationships. The resulting forecasts are only as good as the opinions of the panel members. The accuracy of the executive panel approach is also difficult to assess in a way that allows meaningful comparison with alternative techniques.[14]

The panel's "ball-park" estimates for the intermediate and long run are often used in conjunction with forecasts developed quantitatively. Where historical data is limited or unavailable, the panel approach may be the only approach available. The panel is sometimes used to assess and adjust forecasts based on mathematical projections.[15] Judgment and executive experience are used to check the credibility of the objective techniques.

Sales Force Composite   The rationale behind the sales force composite approach is that salespersons can effectively estimate future sales volume because they know customers, the market, and competition. In addition, participating in the forecasting process gives sales personnel an understanding of how forecasts are derived and a heightened incentive to achieve the desired level of sales.

Figure 8.1 shows the structure of a sales force composite approach used by a manufacturer of printing and packaging materials: Salespersons are asked to estimate sales for each target (large) account and total sales for all other accounts by evaluating three different scenarios: a favorable market outlook, a most likely or realistic market situation, and a depressed market. (Note that the sales personnel are required to list factors that will influence the performance of each account.) Forecasts are derived by assigning probabilities to each scenario, multiplying the

[12] John C. Chambers, Satinder K. Mullick, and Donald D. Smith, "How to Choose the Right Forecasting Technique," *Harvard Business Review*, 49 (July–August 1971), p. 46.

[13] Dalrymple, "Sales Forecasting Methods and Accuracy," p. 70.

[14] Makridakis and Wheelwright, "Forecasting: Issues and Challenges," p. 31.

[15] Bolt, *Market and Sales Forecasting Manual*, p. 278.

Figure 8.1 Example of a Sales Force Composite Approach

Bottom-Up Sales Forecast (year_____)

Sales Region _____   Sales Representative _____
Regional Manager _____   Product Line _____

1. Historical data – current year's sales performance

Target Account A (_____) ... $ _____
Target Account B (_____) ... $ _____
Target Account C (_____) ... $ _____
Other Accounts   (_____) ... $ _____
                                        Total ... $ _____

2. Relevant factors used in Scenario Analysis

Factors	Target Acct A	Target Acct B	Target Acct C	Other Accts.
Factor 1				
Factor 2				
Factor 3				
Factor 4				
Factor 5				

3. Next Year's Forecast – Currently Active Accounts

Account	Optimistic	Most Likely	Pessimistic	Expected
Target Account A	$_____	$_____	$_____	$_____
(probability)	(____)	(____)	(____)	(____)
Target Account B	$_____	$_____	$_____	$_____
(probability)	(____)	(____)	(____)	(____)
Target Account C	$_____	$_____	$_____	$_____
(probability)	(____)	(____)	(____)	(____)
Other Accounts	$_____	$_____	$_____	$_____
(probability)	(____)	(____)	(____)	(____)
			Total	$_____

4. Next Year's Forecast – New Business Generation

Conversion percentage (cold accounts), current year $_____
Dollar Sales volume generated from New accounts $ _____

Estimated Conversion percentage, next year:
                         (_____) .. optimistic $_____
.. probabilities (_____) .. most likely $_____
                         (_____) .. pessimistic $_____
Estimated Dollar volume from New Business:
                         (_____) .. optimistic $_____
.. probabilities (_____) .. most likely $_____
                         (_____) .. pessimistic $_____
Expected Level of New Business Generation ....$_____

5. Forecast for this Representative for this
   product line .... $_____

Source: Reprinted by permission of the publisher from "Bottom-up Sales Forecasting Through Scenario Analysis," by Cornelius A. deKluyver, *Industrial Marketing Management*, 9 (April 1980), p. 169. Copyright © 1980 by Elsevier Science Publishing Co., Inc.

probability times expected sales, and summing for all accounts. A similar procedure is used to estimate sales to new accounts; the result is added to expected sales from existing accounts to produce a total forecast for the salesperson.

Few companies rely solely on sales force estimates, but usually adjust or combine the estimates with forecasts developed by top management or other quantitative methods. The advantage of the sales force composite method is the ability to draw on the market and customer knowledge of the sales force. This advantage is particularly important in the industrial market where buyer–seller relationships are close and enduring. The salesperson often is the best source of information about customer purchasing plans and inventory levels. The method can also be executed relatively easily at a minimal cost.

Its problems are similar to those associated with the panel approach: It does not involve systematic analysis of cause and effect and it relies on informed judgment and opinions. Some sales personnel may overestimate sales to look good or underestimate them to generate a lower quota. All estimates must be carefully reviewed by management.

Salespeople can provide extremely valuable information for forecasting. Where good historical data is not available, the salesperson's experience and judgment become the primary input for forecasting. Sales force estimates are relatively accurate for immediate and short-term projections, but are not very effective long-range.

Delphi Method   In this approach to forecasting, the opinions of a panel of experts on future sales are converted into an informed consensus through highly structured multistage polling.[16] As in the executive panel technique, management officials are used as the panel, but each estimator remains anonymous. On the first round, written opinions are sought about the likelihood of some future event (e.g., sales volume, competitive reaction, or technological breakthroughs). The responses to this first questionnaire are used to produce a second. The objective is to provide feedback to the group so that first-round estimates and information available to some of the experts are made available to the entire group.

After each round of questioning, the analyst who administers the process will assemble, clarify, and consolidate information for dissemination in the succeeding round. Throughout the process, panel members are asked to reevaluate their estimates based on the new information from the group. Opinions are kept anonymous, eliminating "me-too" estimates and the need to defend a position. After continued reevaluation, the goal is to achieve a consensus. The number of experts will vary from six to hundreds, depending on how the process is organized and its purpose. The number of rounds of questionnaires will depend on how rapidly the group reaches consensus.

[16]David J. Luck and O. C. Ferrell, *Marketing Strategy and Plans* (Englewood Cliffs, N.J.: Prentice-Hall, Inc., 1979), p. 113.

Delphi Application   The Delphi technique is usually applied to long-range forecasting. The technique is particularly well suited to (1) new product forecasts, (2) estimation of future events for which historical data are limited, or (3) situations that are not suited to quantitative analysis. Where the market for a new product is not well-defined and the product concept is unique, the Delphi technique can produce some broad-gauged estimates. In technological forecasting, the objective is to predict areas where new product breakthroughs might occur. Corning Glass Works has used the procedure to estimate demand for unique industrial products like gas turbines, pollution measurement devices, and time-shared computer terminals.[17]

The Delphi technique suffers from the same problems as any other qualitative approach, but it may be the only way to develop certain types of estimates. However, there are some shortcomings specific to the approach. Assembling a panel of truly independent experts is extremely difficult. Officials in the same firm or individuals in the same profession tend to read the same literature, have similar training and background, and share the same attitudes on the phenomena under study. Some experts refuse to modify their views in light of feedback, thereby negating the consensus-forming process.

Qualitative forecasting is important in the forecasting process. The techniques can be applied to develop ball-park estimates where product uniqueness, data unavailability, and the nature of the situation preclude application of quantitative techniques. The accuracy of qualitative forecasts is difficult to measure due to lack of standardization. Typically, qualitative estimates will be merged with those developed quantitatively. Table 8.1 summarizes the qualitative approaches.

Table 8.1   Summary of Qualitative Forecasting Techniques

Technique	Approach	Application
Executive Panels	Combining and averaging top executives' estimates of future sales.	"Ballpark" estimates. New product sales estimates. Intermediate and long-term.
Sales Force Composite	Combining and averaging individual salespersons' estimates of future sales.	Effective when intimate knowledge of customer plans is important. Useful for short and intermediate term.
Delphi Method	Consensus of opinion on expected future sales volume is obtained by providing each panelist with the projections of all other panelists on preceding "rounds." Panelists modify estimates until a consensus results.	Appropriate for longer-term forecasting. Effective for projecting sales of new products or forecasting technological advances.

---

[17] Chambers, Mullick, and Smith, "How to Choose the Right Forecasting Techniques," p. 53.

Quantitative Techniques

Quantitative forecasting offers two methods: (1) time series, and (2) regression or causal. Time series techniques use historical data ordered in time to project the trend and growth rate of sales. The rationale behind time series analysis is that the past pattern of sales will apply to the future. However, to discover the underlying pattern of sales, the analyst must first understand all of the possible patterns that may affect the sales series. Thus, a time series of sales may include trend, seasonal, cyclical, and irregular patterns. Once the impact of each has been isolated, the analyst can then project the expected future of each pattern. Time series methods are well suited to short-range forecasting because the assumption that the future will be like the past is more reasonable over the short run than over the long run.[18]

Regression or causal analysis, on the other hand, takes an opposite view. Causal methods identify factors that have affected sales in the past and fit them together into a mathematical model.[19] Sales are expressed mathematically as a function of the items which affect it. Recall the earlier discussion of market potential in Chapter 7 where a regression equation was used to project potential based on production workers and on new equipment expenditures. A forecast is derived by projecting future values for each of the factors in the model, inserting these values into the regression equation, and solving for expected sales. Typically, causal models are more reliable for intermediate than long-range forecasts. The reason is that the magnitude of each factor affecting sales must first be estimated for some future time, which becomes difficult when estimating far into the future.

The remainder of the chapter will consider quantitative forecasting procedures.

Time Series Analysis   A time series is nothing more than a set of chronologically ordered data points. Company sales reported monthly for the past five years are an example. A time series is composed of measurable patterns, and the objective of the analysis is to identify these so that they may be projected. A time series has four components:

- T = Trend
- C = Cycle
- S = Seasonal
- I = Irregular

Figure 8.2 sets out the T, C, and S components.

The *trend* indicates the long-term general direction of the data. The trend may be a straight line of the form $y = a + bx$; or a curve, $y = ab^x$; or $y = a + bx + cx^2$. A straight line trend is displayed in Figure

[18] Spyros Makridakis, "A Survey of Time Series," *International Statistics Review*, 44, No. 1 (1976), p. 63.

[19] K. J. Rosier, "Sales Forecasts," *The Accountant*, 175 (December 9, 1976), p. 675.

Figure 8.2   Trend, Cycle, and Seasonal Components of Time Series

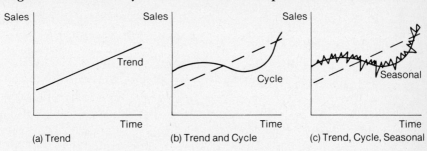

(a) Trend   (b) Trend and Cycle   (c) Trend, Cycle, Seasonal

8.2(a). The *cycle* represents intermediate term, regular upswings and downswings of the data around the trend. For example, the industrial chemical industry in England shows a fairly regular rise and fall in demand over four- or five-year periods. The cycle variations are shown in Figure 8.2(b). The cycle may originate from business cycle movements in the economy as a whole, from inventory swings in industry, or from a succession of new product introductions.[20] The cycle is extremely difficult to estimate because reversals need not occur at fixed intervals and, as a result, there may be no regularity to the pattern.

The *seasonal* pattern is depicted in Figure 8.2(c). These patterns represent regular, recurring movements within the year. Data expressed daily, weekly, monthly, and quarterly may show seasonal patterns. Seasonal patterns depend on such factors as seasonality of final consumption, end-of-period inventory adjustments, tax dates, business vacations, pipeline inventory adjustments, and the scheduling of special promotions.

The *irregular* component in a time series reflects short-term random movements in the data that do not conform to a pattern related to the calendar. Many factors contribute to such random swings in sales patterns (e.g., strikes, competitive actions). Generally, the assumption is that these short-term random effects will average out over a year.

In forecasting future sales volumes actual sales can be expressed as a combination of the four time series elements:

Actual sales = trend × seasonal × cycle × irregular

To develop a forecast, the analyst must determine each pattern and then extrapolate all four into the future. This requires a significant amount of historical sales information. The following illustration demonstrates how such a forecast would be derived.

Trend   A trend forecast fits the most appropriate line to a series of historical sales observations and projects the line into the future (Figure

Figure 8.3   "Freehand" Trend Line of Annual Sales

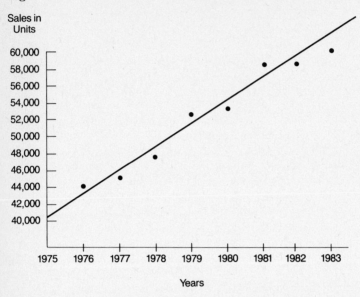

8.3). A relatively simple method for determining the trend line is to draw a straight line to describe the underlying, long-term movement in sales. This is referred to as a "freehand" trend line. The straight line in Figure 8.3 seems to approximate the general trend in sales.

A straight line equation that describes the trend takes the form $y = a + bx$, where a refers to the y intercept (value of sales at the origin or where $x = 0$), and b represents the slope of the line, or the annual change in sales volume. To determine a and b using Figure 8.3, $a = 41,000$ units at the origin (1975 in this case, i.e., at the y intercept), and b can be approximated by looking at the total change in the trend over the eight-year period. Thus, the trend line reflects sales of 41,000 units in 1975 and 60,000 units in 1983—an increase of 19,000 units. The average yearly change is therefore 19,000/8 or 2375. This means that $b = 2375$. With this information, the equation of the trend line can be summarized as:

sales (y) = 41,000 + 2375x

origin = 1975

x = 1 year

y = unit sales

To forecast sales for any year in the future, simply substitute the x value representing the year for which the trend is desired. For example, a forecast of sales for 1986 would be:

$$x = 11 \text{ in } 1986$$

$$\text{forecasted sales} = 41,000 + 2375(11)$$

$$= 67,125$$

The freehand method is the simplest way to determine trend lines, and a good trend line can often be located this way, particularly when there is little fluctuation around the trend line. However, a more precise method for calculating trend lines is often required, and the method of "least squares" is commonly used. The *least square method* mathematically derives the trend line that best fits the data. The actual procedures for developing the least squares trend line are comprehensively treated in many sources and will not be repeated here.[21] If, however, the least squares method were applied to the above example, the trend line would be:

$$\text{sales } (y) = 41,290 + 2483x$$

$$\text{origin} = 1975$$

$$x = 1 \text{ year}$$

$$y = \text{unit sales}$$

Although there is not much difference between this trend line and the one computed freehand, the least squares line will provide a better fit and the most accurate estimates. The greater the variability of the sales data around the trend, the more accurate the least squares line will be in estimating future sales values.

Of course, sales data do not always conform to straight line trends. Where the trend approximates a curve a curvilinear trend line will be required to forecast future sales trends accurately. The analyst may need to experiment with several types of trend lines (straight line, parabola, logarithmic) to determine which model best fits the data.[22]

Seasonal   Whenever sales data are expressed in time intervals of less than a year (quarterly, monthly, weekly), seasonal effects are intermixed with the trend and cycle influences and must be examined carefully.[23] Typically, seasonal patterns are expressed as index numbers. The index represents how far above or below "average" the sales are as a result of seasonal influence. Assume the seasonal index for quarterly sales of 5-HP gasoline engines is as listed on the next page.

---

[21] For example, see, John R. Stockton, *Introduction to Business and Economic Statistics* (Cincinnati: Southwestern Publishing Co., 1966), pp. 354–362.

[22] For example, see, Frank H. Eby, Jr., and William J. O'Neill, *The Management of Sales Forecasting* (Lexington, Mass.: Lexington Books, 1977), Chapter 5.

[23] For a more detailed discussion of procedures for estimating seasonal influences, see, John C. Chambers, Satinder Mullick, and Donald D. Smith, *An Executive's Guide to Forecasting* (New York: John Wiley and Sons, Inc., 1974), Chapter 10.

	Seasonal Index
1st Quarter	85
2nd Quarter	115
3rd Quarter	90
4th Quarter	110

The value of 85 in the first quarter means that engine sales are only 85 percent of what they would have been (average level) had there been no seasonal influence. Similarly, sales in the second quarter are 15 percent higher than normal as a result of seasonal influences. This pattern depicted above might result from increased production of lawnmowers in the winter and snowblowers in summer as manufacturers gear up in anticipation of the sales season.

If seasonal factors are reasonably constant from year to year, an average seasonal pattern can be computed. However, if seasonal patterns fluctuate widely, computations of an average seasonal pattern are much less reliable.

The seasonal pattern, if reasonably constant, can be merged with the trend estimation to forecast sales for periods less than one year. Assume the quarterly trend equation for gasoline engines is:

$$sales \ (y) = 400,000 + 22,000x$$

$$origin = 1979, \text{1st quarter}$$

$$x = 1 \text{ quarter}$$

$$y = \text{unit sales}$$

The trend forecast for third quarter, 1987 (34 quarters from origin) is:

$$sales \ (y) = 400,000 + 22,000(34)$$

$$= 1,148,000 \text{ units}$$

Recall that the seasonal index is 90 for the third quarter, and actual sales would be only 90 percent of "normal" sales because of seasonal influences. Thus, a forecast which considers the seasonal element would be: trend x seasonal, or

$$sales = 1,148,000 \times .90$$

$$= 1,033,200 \text{ units}$$

As the example demonstrates, seasonal patterns must be considered for short-term forecasts. If the forecast above had been based solely on trend projections, a rather substantial error would have resulted (i.e., 1,148,000 vs. 1,033,200). An important aspect of infusing seasonal elements into forecasting is to monitor the patterns for changes, gradual or abrupt. Because business practices constantly change, seasonal patterns can be expected to shift over the years, and reformulation of the seasonal indices may be required.

Cycle and Irregular   The sales history of a company is affected not only by long-term trends and short-term seasonal fluctuations, but also by intermediate-term variations in the business cycle and by random influences. Cycles in a particular industry or in the total economy may result in successive waves of expansion and contraction in a firm's sales volume. Such fluctuations can have damaging effects on forecasting because they are less predictable than other patterns. The length of a complete business cycle may vary from one year to twelve years. A machine tool firm found that the business cycle in their segments of the market lasts about four to five years. This cyclical pattern is used not only to forecast sales but also to time new product introductions for just before the upswing of the cycle.[24] The irregular component of time series is usually merged with the cycle to compensate for its basic inconsistency.

Unfortunately, no completely satisfactory method of directly measuring cyclical swings has been developed.[25] Cycles show wide variation in length as well as the amplitude of variations. Because of the cycle's inherently irregular nature, it is extremely difficult to find an average cycle to use as a pattern.

The most effective way to estimate the cycle pattern is a "backdoor" approach: A sales series reflecting trend, seasonal, cycle, and irregular forces is "decomposed"—first by removing seasonal variations and second by removing trend influences. The remaining variations are considered to be the cycle and irregular movements.

Consider sales data that have no seasonal variation, such as yearly sales of electric motors. To estimate the cyclical variation, all that must be done is to divide actual sales by the trend value of sales, expressing the cycle as a ratio of actual sales to trend sales. Variations around the trend line are assumed to be the result of business cycle forces.

Table 8.2 shows hypothetical data for electric motors, in which actual sales are expressed as a percentage of trend. Obviously, the actual cyclical pattern would not be as consistent. However, in this hypothetical case, a fairly regular cyclical pattern is evidenced by the percentage of trend figures. As with the seasonal index, it is possible to evolve an average index of cyclical variation. The procedure would be risky, though. The analysis of "percentage of trend" data does provide some limited insight into cyclical patterns. The reason for analyzing cyclical variations is to accurately project cyclical patterns forward. If the forecaster knew, for example, that the cycle (percentage of trend) would be 125 in 1987, a sales forecast could be derived by multiplying the trend projection for 1987 by 125. Unfortunately, the forecaster is never that confident of an estimate of cycle behavior.

Analysis of cycle patterns is sometimes useful for providing an early warning of slowdowns in sales before the raw data show a decline.

[24] Bolt, *Market and Sales Forecasting Manual*, p. 213.

[25] Stockton, *Introduction to Business*, p. 436.

Table 8.2   Hypothetical Sales Data for Electric Motors: Actual Sales as a Percentage of Trend

Year	Actual Sales	Trend Sales	Actual/ Trend (%)
1973	130	100	130
1974	99	110	90
1975	132	120	110
1976	104	130	80
1977	168	140	120
1978	150	150	100
1979	184	160	115
1980	179	170	105
1981	216	180	120
1982	171	190	90
1983	250	200	125

For example, low density polyethylene (LDPE), which is used to make garbage bags, bread wrappers and the like, was thought to be a growth industry throughout the 1970s and, as a result, immune to the general economic climate. A cycle analysis of LDPE sales revealed the definite impact that declines in the economy had upon LDPE sales. The underlying rate of growth masked the sensitivity to economic conditions (i.e., the business cycle).[26]

Time series analysis provides a means of evaluating past patterns in sales data and projecting these patterns to the future. Future estimates of each time series component can then be combined to develop the sales forecast.

Regression or Causal Techniques   Causal techniques have as their objective the determination of a relationship between sales and a variable presumed to be related to sales; knowledge of the "causal" variable can be used to determine expected future sales volumes. The method requires a significant amount of historical data to establish a valid relationship. The model mathematically expresses the causal relationship; the mathematical formula is usually referred to as a *regression equation*.

A critical aspect of regression analysis is to identify the economic variable(s) to which past sales are related. For forecasting purposes the *Survey of Current Business* is particularly helpful because it contains monthly, quarterly, and annual figures for hundreds of economic variables. The forecaster can test an array of economic variables from the *Survey* to find the variable(s) with the best relationship with past sales.

Two general rules should be followed in evaluating economic series. First, the economic series (variable) should be *logically* related to

[26]Peter H. Jedel, "Use of Cycle Analysis," *Business Economics*, 15 (March 1980), p. 15.

company sales.[27] Forecasters are often tempted to break this rule because they can easily "try out" any number of variables, many of which may not be logically related to company sales. A variable may be found to be highly correlated to past sales, but with no logical connection. Such spurious relationships are not effective for forecasting future sales as they are usually accidental and may not hold true. Second, it should be easier to forecast the economic variable than to project the sales level. The causal approach develops a sales forecast by establishing the relationship of sales and some other economic variable. Knowledge of this relationship is then used to estimate sales by determining future values of the economic variable and the correspondent sales level. If the variable is one for which future projections are either not available or of questionable validity, sales may as well be estimated directly.

Procedure   There are two important steps to forecasting with causal analysis: (1) determining the mathematical relationship of sales and a causal variable and (2) determining how "good" the relationship is, that is, the degree of association among the variables. For the first step, solving the regression equation, appropriate values for the coefficients in the equation must be determined. Although the regression equation may take many different functional forms, this treatment will deal with two-variable straight-line relationships. Hence, the regression equation is of the form:

$$Y_c = a + bX,$$

where Y_c is the dependent variable, or the variable to be estimated (sales), and X is the independent, or causal variable from which estimates are made. Where sales are related to more than one independent variable, a multiple regression equation would be used ($Y_c = a + bX + cX_2$). To estimate glass container sales, Owens-Illinois used the following multiple regression equation to forecast package beer consumption:[28]

$$\text{Beer} = 8959 + 70(\text{Yd}) + 1963(\text{Pop.}) - 23839(\text{Price})$$

where

Beer = Beer consumption (1000 barrels)

Y_d = Real disposable personal income

Pop. = Population, ages 21 to 34

$\text{Price} = \dfrac{\text{Consumer price index for beer}}{\text{Consumer price index for food}}$

---

[27] Frank H. Eby, Jr. and William J. O'Neill, *The Management of Sales Forecasting*, p. 145.

[28] Elmer Lotshaw, "All the Economics You Need for Industrial Market Planning—And No More," *Industrial Marketing Management*, 7 (1978), p. 4.

To simplify the discussion, we will look only at simple straight line regression.

As in estimating the linear trend line, determining the regression equation involves finding a line that best describes the relationship between sales and another variable. In this case, unlike trend analysis, the X variable represents not time but the causal variable.

Consider Figure 8.4: The scatter diagram plots investment in office telephone equipment in the United States against expenditures on new construction for the past ten years. Suppose the telephone company desires to use regression analysis to forecast sales of new equipment for the next five years. Management assumes that new construction expenditures can be used to predict new telephone equipment sales.

Figure 8.4 suggests a good relationship, as the two series appear to move in the same direction. To determine the precise relationship, the

Figure 8.4   Scatter Diagram of Investment in New Telephone Equipment and New Construction Expenditures

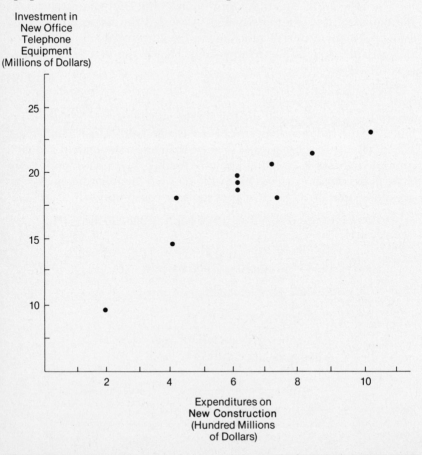

Table 8.3   Data to Calculate the Regression Equation

Year	Investment in Office Telephone Equipment (Millions) Y	New Construction Expenditures (Hundred Millions) X	XY	X^2	Y^2
1974	22	8	176	64	484
1975	23	10	230	100	529
1976	18	7	126	49	324
1977	9	2	18	4	81
1978	14	4	56	16	196
1979	20	6	120	36	400
1980	21	7	147	49	441
1981	18	6	108	36	324
1982	16	4	64	16	256
1983	19	6	114	36	361
	180	60	1159	406	3396

least squares method is used to develop a regression line that minimizes the squared deviations of the actual data points from the regression line. The mathematical equations necessary to determine the regression line are:

$$a = \bar{Y} - b\bar{X}$$

$$b = \frac{\Sigma XY - N\bar{X}\bar{Y}}{\Sigma X^2 - N\bar{X}^2}$$

Table 8.3 provides the data required to solve the equations.

Substituting the appropriate values into the equation we get:

$$\bar{X} = \frac{\Sigma X}{N} = \frac{60}{100} = 6 \text{ (hundred million)}$$

$$\bar{Y} = \frac{\Sigma Y}{N} = \frac{180}{10} = 18 \text{ (million)}$$

$$b = \frac{1159 - 10(6)(18)}{406 - 10(6)^2} = \frac{79}{46} = 1.717$$

$$a = 18 - 1.717(6) = 18 - 10.302 = 7.698$$

The least squares regression line is:

$$Y_c = 7.698 + 1.717X$$

and Figure 8.5 plots the line against the original data points. The b term in the regression equation indicates the slope of the line. In this case it is positive: for each $1000 increase in new construction expenditure, telephone equipment investment will increase by $17.17.

Figure 8.5   Regression Line Plotted Against the Original Data Points

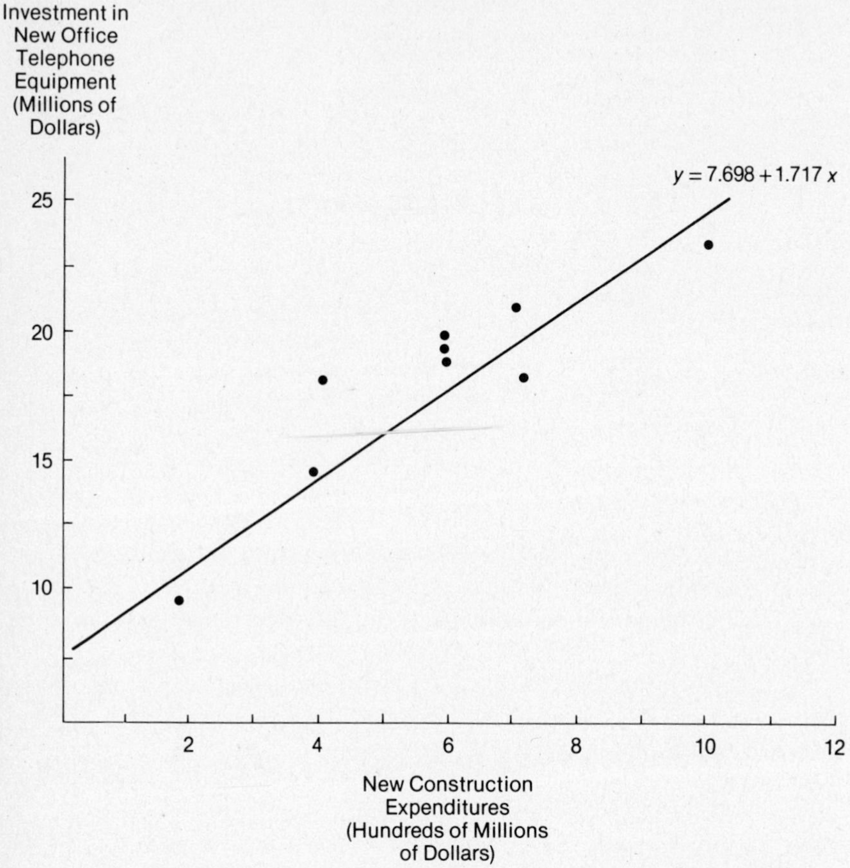

Investment in
New Office
Telephone
Equipment
(Millions of
Dollars)

$y = 7.698 + 1.717 x$

New Construction
Expenditures
(Hundreds of Millions
of Dollars)

How "good" is the relationship? Before the regression equation is employed, the second phase of the analysis, measuring the degree of association, should be completed. If the association between X and Y is high, the analyst will be more confident in predicting future sales with the equation. If the association is weak, further research should be undertaken to find causal variables more closely associated with sales, or the forecaster should consider multiple regression.

To measure the degree of association, variation in the actual Y (sales) values around the regression line ($Y - Y_c$) is compared to the total variation of the values around the mean of Y (i.e., $Y - \bar{Y}$). The smaller the variation of the Y values around the regression line ($Y - Y_c$), the better the regression line "fits" the data, and the better $Y_c = 7.698 + 1.717X$ is at predicting sales volume. A measure of the degree of association, the coefficient of determination, r^2, may be calculated from the above quantities:

$$r^2 = 1 - \frac{\Sigma(Y - Y_c)^2}{\Sigma(Y - \bar{Y})^2}$$

This indicates that as $(Y - Y_c)^2$ approaches zero (i.e., all Y values fall on the regression line), the value of r^2 approaches 1. If there were no association between X and Y, r^2 would equal 0. Since r^2 is interpreted as the percentage of the variation in Y associated with variation in X, then if $r^2 = 1$, *all* of the variation in Y is associated with variation in X. A formula to determine r^2, based on the quantities used to determine the regression line, is:

$$r^2 = \frac{a\Sigma Y + b\Sigma XY - N\bar{Y}^2}{\Sigma Y^2 - N\bar{Y}^2}$$

for our example:

$$r^2 = \frac{7.698(180) + 1.717(1159) - 10(18)^2}{3396 - 10(18)^2}$$

$$r^2 = .87$$

Thus, an interpretation of r^2 suggests that 87 percent of the variation in telephone equipment investment is associated with variations in new construction expenditures.

So, a good relationship exists, and the regression equation should produce relatively accurate estimates of sales. It was critical to reliably estimate the causal variable for 1986 before 1986 telephone equipment sales could be forecast. The federal government frequently projects variables like new construction one to ten years into the future and reference to such sources as *U.S. Industrial Outlook* may provide the necessary estimate of new construction expenditures. Regression analysis, however, will allow the analyst to create a variety of scenarios about future construction levels and then insert these values into the regression equation, thus producing a range of estimates of future telephone equipment volume. If federal sources project 1986 new construction at $1.1 billion, the regression forecast of telephone equipment sales would be:

$$Y_c = 7.698 + 1.717(11)$$

$$= 7.698 + 18.89$$

$$= 26.585$$

or $26.585 million. Regression estimates are rarely applied alone, but are tempered with qualitative estimates.

Use of Regression Techniques   Causal models are the most sophisticated forecasting tools. A recent study found that only 17 percent of firms regularly use regression techniques for forecasting, and 24 percent have never tried them.[29] Regression models are useful to industrial firms projecting final consumer demand for items of which their products become a part, as illustrated in the Owens-Illinois forecast of beer consumption. Similarly, American Can's projections of motor oil sales are based on a regression model that integrates auto registrations, average miles driven per car, average crank case size, and average interval between oil changes as causal variables. Further, an important dimension in forecasting is the ability to predict a turning point in the sales series. To the extent that turning points in causal variables can be foreseen, turns in company sales can be predicted.

Limitations   Although causal methods have measurable levels of accuracy, there are some important caveats and limitations. First, the fact that sales and some causal variables are correlated (associated) does not mean that the X or independent variable "caused" sales. The independent variable should be logically related to sales.

Second, because both X and Y have the same trend pattern, one may be, in effect, correlating only trends, while the other components (for example, cyclical and seasonal) are not highly correlated.[30] Thus, reliance on regression equations with high r^2's may be unsuitable for short-range projections where cyclical and seasonal factors are important.

Third, regression methods require considerable historical data if equations are to be valid and reliable, and the data required to establish stable relationships may not be available. Caution must always be used in extrapolating relationships into the future. The equation relates what *has* happened, and economic and industry factors may change in the future, making past relationships invalid.

The last, and probably the most crucial, limitation associated with causal methods is the problem of determining future values of independent or causal variables. Before the regression equation can be used to project future sales levels, future values of the independent variables must be determined. Thus, "what is actually done is to shift the burden of forecasting from that of directly predicting some factor of interest (sales) to another one which attempts to estimate several independent variables before it can forecast."[31] In the final analysis, the quality of the sales forecast generated by regression models will depend on the forecaster's ability to generate valid and reliable estimates of the independent variables. It is true that some excellent projections of a variety of economic series are provided by government sources, but management must face the fact that a direct estimate of sales may be more reliable than a regression model estimate.

---

[29] Dalrymple, "Sales Forecasting Methods and Accuracy," p. 70.

[30] Paul E. Green and Donald S. Tull, *Research for Marketing Decisions*, 3d ed. (Englewood Cliffs, N.J.: Prentice-Hall, Inc., 1975), p. 669.

[31] Makridakis, "A Survey of Time Series," p. 62.

Table 8.4   Summary of Quantitative Forecasting Techniques

Technique	Approach	Application
Time Series	Determination of past sales patterns and projection of these patterns to the future. Estimated patterns are combined to develop the sales forecast.	Provides reasonable estimates of short- and immediate-term sales. Assumes past sales patterns will hold in the future. May be the only available technique for long-term forecasts.
Causal	Past sales levels are correlated to another variable, which is presumed to be related to sales. A mathematical model of the relationship is determined. Forecasts are made by inserting reliable future estimates of the independent variable into the model to predict sales for any given future year.	Are effective for intermediate-term sales forecasts if reliable future estimates of the independent variables can be developed. Valuable in other respects as management is forced to consider all factors that have some effect on sales.

Time Series vs. Causal Methods   To what extent should each method be applied and to what situations is each best suited? The answers depend upon the criteria associated with forecast technique selection: time frame, accuracy, data requirements, cost, available expertise, and purpose of the forecast. Table 8.4 summarizes the two approaches. In general, the time series models seem to have done as well as, or better than, both the simple and complex regression models in accuracy.[32] The limitations of causal models do not necessarily negate their value but merely caution management to apply them carefully. A significant benefit associated with these models is the knowledge gained by management in attempting to link sales volumes quantitatively to underlying causative factors. The understanding gained in the causal procedure compared to the purely mechanistic time series approach may outweigh its limitations.

As we have reiterated, a forecast can be developed only after the marketing plan has been devised. Both time series and causal methods of forecasting seek to project sales into the future based on knowledge of past or current relationships. Thus, the forecast derived from quantitative approaches has to be adjusted to reflect marketing plans and strategy.

Role of the Computer in Sales Forecasting

Computers enable the industrial marketing manager to improve sales forecasting because they can store vast quantities of data, test and compare various forecasting methodologies, and evaluate the reliability of

[32] Makridakis and Wheelwright, "Forecasting: Issues and Challenges," p. 31.

the forecast. The computer is not a technique, but merely a means of making some techniques possible, of making others more effective and of making the results of some techniques more readily available.[33] The computer is not limited to the quantitative forecasting techniques. It can be useful, for example, in the sales force composite approach by maintaining data files for the sales force and by aggregating the forecasts of individuals.

Specifically, the computer can be used in sales forecasting to:

1.   *Search* for appropriate statistical forecasting models. Because it can process significant quantities of data, the forecaster can use the computer to test almost unlimited variations of statistical forecasting procedures. Many quantitative forecasting techniques could not be applied without a computer.

2.   Develop forecasts at almost any *level of detail* within acceptable cost and time constraints. Without computer processing, it might be too costly or time-consuming to generate separate sales forecasts for individual products, territories, customers, and channels.

3.   Analyze demand and *sales histories* maintained in computer files; the computer can be used to evaluate past sales patterns for trend, seasonal, and cyclical components.

4.   Evaluate the *relationship* of economic and business variables to past sales levels. The computer can search for factors that have a degree of correlation with the level of sales. The computer's ability to handle a large number of variables often makes it the best way, and sometimes the only way, of using multiple correlation techniques.

5.   *Audit* the sales forecast. The computer can monitor the accuracy of the forecast by comparing it with actual sales. Management can specify rules for when the sales forecast is outside acceptable error limits, and the computer can provide a built-in warning system so that action can be taken.

Management may use the computer in sales forecasting by developing their own forecasting programs or by purchasing existing software.[34] Most computer hardware manufacturers offer extensive libraries of software applicable to forecasting problems. Independent computer service organizations, including time-sharing firms, have canned programs that will effectively handle most of the popular time-series and regression techniques. Many general purpose software packages also include sales forecasting procedures.

Although the computer is a powerful tool for forecasting purposes, management must realize that it is only that—a tool. Computer-

[33] Bolt, *Market and Sales Forecasting Manual*, p. 270.

[34] Frank H. Eby, Jr. and William J. O'Neill, *The Management of Sales Forecasting*, p. 61.

generated forecasts are only as good as the data and techniques on which they are grounded. An inappropriate technique does not generate a valid forecast merely because the computer was used to create the forecast. As Gordon Bolt suggests, "Computer forecasts must be 'humanized' by being subjected to human intelligence and judgment."[35] Computers do not replace judgment; in fact they may necessitate higher levels of management judgment in selecting forecasting techniques, inputting correct data, and interpreting computer output.

A Final Note on Forecasting

The industrial marketer is faced with a difficult forecasting situation; an understanding of the characteristics of the available approaches is certainly paramount. In general, qualitative approaches to forecasting will continue to be of considerable importance in industrial marketing because of the close buyer-seller relationships, well-defined markets, importance of high unit-value sales, and sales force knowledge of customer product and inventory requirements. However, time series and causal approaches should be merged with qualitative estimates. John Chambers and his colleagues predict that quantitative and qualitative methods will be combined in future forecasting systems:

At the present time, most short-term forecasting uses only statistical methods, with little qualitative information. Where qualitative information is used, it is only used in an external way and is not directly incorporated into the computational routine. We predict a change to total forecasting systems, where several techniques are tied together, along with a systematic handling of qualitative information.[36]

Summary

The sales forecast is a projection of what the firm actually expects to sell if a particular marketing plan is followed. Forecasts are developed for different time periods ranging from the immediate term (daily or weekly) to the long-term (two or more years), depending on their purpose.

The forecasting techniques available to the industrial marketer are (1) qualitative, and (2) quantitative. Qualitative techniques rely on informed judgments of future sales and include executive panels, the sales force composite, and the Delphi method. By contrast, quantitative techniques have more complex data requirements and include time series and causal approaches. The time series method uses historical data ordered in time to project the future trend and growth rate of sales. Causal methods, on the other hand, seek to identify factors which have affected

---

[35] Bolt, *Market and Sales Forecasting Manual*, p. 270.
[36] Chambers, Mullick, and Smith, "How to Choose the Right Forecasting Technique," p. 73.

sales in the past and to incorporate these factors into a mathematical model. The computer is a valuable tool to facilitate the forecasting process for all methods.

Each technique is suited for certain situations and forecast time intervals; however, the essence of good forecasting is to effectively combine the forecasts provided by various methods. The processes of market potential estimating and sales forecasting are challenging; they require the industrial marketing manager to have a good working knowledge of available alternatives. This chapter has been structured to provide that knowledge.

Discussion Questions

1. The industrial marketing manager must develop not one but many forecasts over several time frames. Explain.

2. Compare and contrast the sales force composite and the Delphi method of developing a sales forecast.

3. While qualitative forecasting techniques are important in the sales forecasting process in many industrial firms, the marketing manager must understand the limitations of these approaches. Outline these limitations.

4. As alternative methods for sales forecasting, what is the underlying logic of (1) time series, and (2) regression or causal methods?

5. Briefly define the four components of a time series: (1) trend, (2) cycle, (3) seasonal, and (4) irregular.

6. What are the limitations that must be understood before applying and interpreting the sales forecasting results generated by causal methods?

7. What role does a computer have in facilitating the sales forecasting process?

8. What are the features of the industrial market that support the use of qualitative forecasting approaches? What benefits does the industrial market analyst gain by combining these qualitative approaches with quantitative forecasting methods?

Exercises

1. The Seibert Company manufactures V-belts and distributes them nationally through industrial distributors. The company requires a sales forecast for V-belts for 1989. The following information has been obtained from the market research department:

$$\text{Sales trend} = 1250 + 95X$$

$$X = \text{quarters}$$

$$\text{origin} = 1979, \text{1st quarter}$$

$$Y = \text{unit sales (hundreds)}$$

Seasonal Index:

Quarter	
1	75
2	150
3	110
4	65

a. Develop a forecast of trend sales for the third quarter, 1989.
b. Develop a sales forecast for the fourth quarter, 1989, showing the effect of trend and seasonal influences.
c. If actual unit sales in the first quarter 1989 are 380,000, what would they have been if there had been no seasonal influence?

2. A manufacturer of bearings wishes to estimate future sales over the next five years. The marketing manager is presented with the following historical data for the past ten years as well as data on the sales of heavy industrial equipment. The manager believes there is a good relationship between bearing sales and sales of heavy industrial equipment. In addition, future estimates of heavy industrial equipment sales are readily available from secondary sources.

Bearing Sales (Millions)	Heavy Equipment Sales (Billions)
12	30
19	45
10	10
12	24
8	10
8	9
17	41
13	30
12	27
10	20

a. Calculate the regression equation.
b. Determine whether there is a good relationship between bearing sales and sales of heavy industrial equipment.
c. Determine a sales forecast for 1989 if heavy equipment sales are projected to be $35 billion.

3. The following information on sales of electrical cable (Y) and an index of industrial supply prices (X) has been developed in preparation for determining a sales forecast for 1990. The data is based on 100 observations (Y in millions of dollars).

$$EX = 2,300$$
$$EY = 38,000$$
$$EXY = 850,000$$
$$EX^2 = 64,000$$
$$EY^2 = 14,500,000$$

a. Calculate the regression equation. Explain how cable sales vary with the price index.
b. Determine how good the relationship is. Interpret the measure you have calculated.
c. If the price index is forecast to be 1.10 by 1990, develop a sales forecast of electrical cable for 1990.
d. In evaluating the 1990 forecast, what limitations of this technique should the manager consider?

P·A·R·T
IV

Formulating Industrial
Marketing Strategy

C·H·A·P·T·E·R
9

Industrial Marketing Planning: Strategic Perspectives

To this point, the text has examined the techniques available to the industrial marketing manager for segmenting the organizational market, forecasting market potential, and forecasting sales. Likewise, you have developed an understanding of organizational buying behavior and the unique characteristics and strategic role of the industrial marketing intelligence system. All of this provides a perspective that is of fundamental importance to the industrial marketing planner.

After reading this chapter, you will have an understanding of:

1. *the role of strategic planning in corporate strategy development;*
2. *the special challenges of marketing planning in industrial organizations;*
3. *the essential components of the industrial marketing planning process;*
4. *the specific role of market segmentation and forecasting in the marketing planning process.*

To meet the challenges brought on by rising material costs, growing domestic and global competition, reduced profit margins, and limited cash reserves, marketers are increasingly recognizing the importance of formal strategic marketing planning.[1] Key product and market decisions made by the industrial marketer can influence the direction and fate of the firm for years to come. To illustrate, Alcoa sells aluminum to diverse manufacturers who, in turn, serve multiple end-use markets: automobiles, recreational vehicles, mobile homes, siding, cooking utensils, and packaging.[2] Growth potential, sales revenue, net income, and related performance characteristics vary by end-use segment. Likewise, the demand for aluminum used in some applications, such as recreational vehicles and campers, has strong seasonal variations. The demand for aluminum used in automobiles tends to be cyclical (i.e., moves in the same direction as GNP); the demand for aluminum used in utensils tends to be counter-cyclical (i.e., moves in the opposite direction of GNP).

Successful marketing strategy at Alcoa requires careful coordination between marketing and functional areas such as production and procurement. Similarly, a close working relationship between research and development and marketing is needed to respond to the changing needs of end-use market segments.

Planning encourages managers to think creatively about the future, to sharpen objectives, and to develop, coordinate, and control company efforts.[3] While few would question that benefits accrue to the planner, industrial marketing managers are often sadly disappointed with the results of formal planning efforts. The successful marketing planner analyzes market opportunity and assesses the firm's ability to take advantage of that opportunity. This chapter examines the nature and critical importance of planning in industrial marketing management.

First, we consider the role of strategic planning in designing long-run corporate strategies, properly matching the strengths of the corporation to attractive market opportunities. Second, we turn to the special requirements and problems of planning in the industrial marketing environment. A functionally integrated perspective of industrial marketing planning is provided. Third, the key components of the marketing planning process are examined, emphasizing the development of industrial marketing strategy. Thus, this chapter serves as a conceptual bridge to succeeding chapters where each component of the marketing mix is isolated and examined in depth.

[1] Yoram Wind and Thomas S. Robertson, "Marketing Strategy: New Directions for Theory and Research," *Journal of Marketing* 47 (Spring 1983), pp. 12–25; see also, Derek F. Abell and John S. Hammond, *Strategic Market Planning: Problems and Analytical Approaches* (Englewood Cliffs, N.J.: Prentice-Hall, Inc., 1979), pp. 3–15.

[2] Andris A. Zoltners and Joe A. Dodson, "A Market Selection Model for Multiple End-Use Products," *Journal of Marketing* 47 (Spring 1983), pp. 76–78.

[3] Melville C. Branch, *The Corporate Planning Process* (New York: American Management Association, 1962), pp. 48–49.

Strategic Planning

Many industrial firms have numerous divisions, product lines, products, and brands. Policies established at the corporate level provide the framework for strategy development in each business division to insure survival and growth of the entire enterprise. In turn, corporate and divisional policies establish the boundaries within which individual product or market managers develop strategy.

Assessing Opportunities

Strategic marketing management is the process that integrates "broadly defined sets of strategic and operating marketing decisions together for the purpose of directing resources toward opportunities consistent with enterprise capabilities to achieve predetermined outcomes."[4] One researcher emphasizes that only during limited periods is the match between the requirements of a market and the particular capabilities of a supplier at an optimum.[5] Thus, resources should be invested to coincide with periods when the "strategic window" is open. Likewise, resources should be withdrawn when the product/market fit erodes.

Large industrial firms are, in essence, a portfolio of different businesses. They must actively manage this portfolio by deciding which businesses should be expanded, which maintained, which phased out, and which new businesses would strengthen the portfolio by capitalizing on the organization's present or developing strengths.

Assessing the Competitive Environment

The state of competition, in particular industrial markets, ranges from intense in industries like steel or metal cans where no company earns spectacular returns on investment, to mild in industries like oil field services and equipment where there are opportunities for very high returns. To properly define the state of competition in a particular environment, the industrial marketing planner must understand the forces that shape competition in an industry.

Forces Shaping Competition[6]   Michael Porter contends that the state of competition in an industry is determined by the interplay of five basic forces (see Figure 9.1):

1.   The *seriousness of the threat of new entrants* depends on the barriers to entry which are present, and the reaction from existing competi-

[4] Roger A. Kerin and Robert A. Peterson, "The Strategic Marketing Management Process," in Kerin and Peterson, eds., *Perspectives on Strategic Marketing Management* (Boston: Allyn and Bacon, Inc., 1980), p. 5.

[5] Derek F. Abell, "Strategic Windows," *Journal of Marketing* 42 (July 1978), pp. 21–25.

[6] The discussion in this section is based on Michael E. Porter, "How Competitive Forces Shape Strategy," *Harvard Business Review* 57 (March–April 1979), pp. 137–145; see also, Porter, *Competitive Strategy* (New York: Free Press, 1980).

**Figure 9.1   Forces Governing
Competition in an Industry**

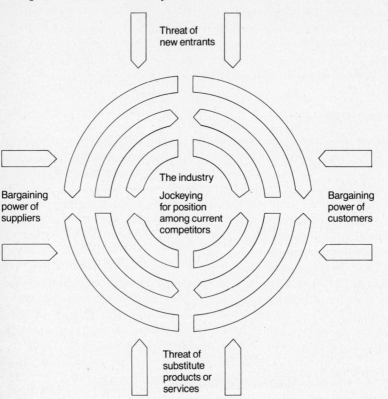

tors that the newcomer can expect. Barriers to entry include factors like high capital requirements or economies of scale in production, distribution, or service enjoyed by existing firms. Thus, the threat of new firms entering a particular industry is weak if barriers to entry are high and a new entrant can expect sharp retaliation from established competitors.

2.   The *threat of substitute products or services* that can or will be able to perform the same function also influences competition. Substitutes can limit the growth of an industry by placing a ceiling on prices. To illustrate, the profit potential of sugar producers has been limited by the commercialization of high-fructose corn syrup, a sugar substitute.

3.   The *bargaining power of suppliers* can have an impact on the profit potential of an industry. Powerful suppliers, by raising prices, can damage profitability if competitors are unable to recover cost increases by raising their own prices. Also, a powerful supplier can threaten *forward integration* into the industry's business. For example, IBM, a supplier to the computer-controlled machine tool industry, became a competitor in this industry through forward integration.

4.   The *bargaining power of buyers* can also constrain the profitability of an industry. High-volume buyers can force prices down and demand higher quality or more service. Likewise, large-volume buyers enhance their bargaining power by threatening *backward integration*. General Motors, a large user of computer-controlled machine tools, entered this market through backward integration.

5.   The *intensity of rivalry* (or jockeying for position) among existing participants relates to the presence of factors such as numerous competitors of roughly equal size and power, a slow rate of industry growth, and a product or service that lacks differentiation.

By examining the interplay of these five forces, the industrial marketer can gain insight into the present and future profitability of an industry and the strategic opportunities it offers to the firm. Because foreign competition is a potent force in many industries, the competitive assessment must encompass foreign as well as domestic competitors. A global perspective of competition is required even in industrial firms that choose not to operate in the international market.

The competitive analysis should also explore the strategy dimensions that particular competitors in the industry emphasize, such as product quality and technical service versus low price and broad product assortments. Here, the industrial marketer is extending the competitive assessment from the industry to the market segment level to estimate the strength of the firm vis-a-vis competitors by market segment.[7]

Defining Strategic Business Units

Competitive analysis that provides a foundation for assessing the quality of the firm's portfolio of businesses begins with *strategic business units* (SBUs). An SBU is a single business or collection of businesses that has a distinct mission, a responsible manager, and its own competitors, and is relatively independent of other business units.[8] An SBU could be one or more divisions of the industrial firm, a product line within one division,

---

[7] Wind and Robertson, "Marketing Strategy: New Directions," pp. 12–25.

[8] Philip Kotler, *Marketing Management: Analysis, Planning, and Control* (4th ed.; Englewood Cliffs, N.J.: Prentice-Hall, Inc., 1980), p. 76.

or, on occasion, a single product. SBUs may share resources, such as a sales force, with other business units to achieve economies of scale. An SBU may serve one or many product-market units.

Mead Corporation defined 24 SBUs and assigned 24 top executives to the new slots on the basis of a match between their expertise and business requirements. At Eaton Corporation, a five-year strategic plan is developed for the corporation, each of its 26 divisions, and 400 "product market segments."[9]

In identifying SBUs, two tests must be met.[10] First, the planning structure must be *strategically relevant* to the industrial firm and stimulate strategies that will yield a future competitive advantage. Those opportunities must be isolated that best match the distinctive strengths of the firm. Second, there are limits to the number of SBUs that can be effectively managed. Therefore, the number and structure of the SBUs must be *administratively feasible* and properly aligned with the organization's resources (e.g., manufacturing facilities).

General Electric's Business Screen

The industrial marketer must manage both resource generation and resource allocation. Some SBUs are well-positioned in attractive industries and should generate significant resources in the future; others, poorly situated, do not show promise. The first merit additional resources, the latter do not. To properly classify SBUs, General Electric set up a nine-cell strategic business screen.

Business Strength/Industry Strength   The business screen (Figure 9.2) matches the level of strength of a business to the level of attractiveness of the industry in which it operates. The functionally integrated planning perspective is fundamental in answering the question: What are the distinctive strengths of our firm? *Business strength* analysis rates market share, product quality, technological position, price competitiveness, and distribution effectiveness, among other management criteria. *Industry attractiveness* analysis rates market size, market growth rate, inflation vulnerability, industry profitability, and related dimensions.[11] The area of the circles in Figure 9.2 corresponds to the size of the industries in which the various businesses compete. The pie-shaped slices within the circles reflect a particular SBU's market share. G represents an SBU with a small market share in an industry of average size; in other words, G lacks business strength and competes in an unattractive industry.

[9]"Olin Shifts to Strategic Planning," *Business Week* (March 27, 1978), pp. 102–105.

[10]George S. Day, "Analytical Approaches to Strategic Market Planning," in Ben M. Enis and Kenneth J. Roering, eds., *Review of Marketing 1981* (Chicago: American Marketing Association, 1981), pp. 90–92.

[11]For a discussion of how to choose criteria, see, Charles W. Hofer and Dan Schendel, *Strategy Formulation: Analytical Concepts* (St. Paul: West Publishing Company, 1978), pp. 72–74.

Figure 9.2 General Electric's Business Screen

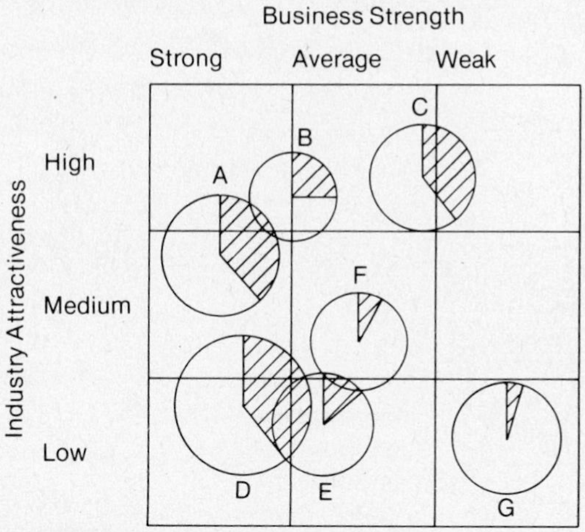

Business Strength

Strong   Average   Weak

Industry Attractiveness

High

Medium

Low

Source: Adapted from Charles W. Hofer and Dan Schendel, *Strategy Formulation: Analytical Concepts* (St. Paul: West Publishing Company, 1978), p. 32.

Projecting Future Positions Once SBUs are classified, management should plot the projected positions of these businesses, assuming no changes in basic strategies. Comparing current and projected position of the SBUs allows management to isolate problems and identify strategic alternatives. Through strategic planning, the Olin Corporation identified and sold a number of poorly performing businesses—a polyester film plant, a tent business, a propane camping equipment business. In turn, strategic planning suggested investments in businesses that better matched corporate expertise. Thus, Olin expanded its chlorine-caustic soda, hydrazine chemical, and copper-based alloy operations. These and other businesses are divided into more than 30 SBUs.[12]

Generic Strategy Alternatives

Various paths to profitable positioning in an industry have been proposed in recent years. Michael Porter, for example, sets out three generic strategies: industry-wide *cost leadership*; industry-wide product and/or marketing *differentiation*; and *focus*. Focus applies a strategy of cost leadership and/or product differentiation to a narrow target market.[13]

[12] "Olin Shifts to Strategic Planning," pp. 102–105.

[13] Michael E. Porter, *Competitive Strategy*. For a review of strategic planning perspectives, see, Ravi Singh Achrol and David L. Appel, "New Developments in Corporate Strategy Planning," in Patrick E. Murphy *et al.*, eds., *1983 AMA Educators' Proceedings* (Chicago: American Marketing Association, 1983), pp. 305–310.

Figure 9.3   Industry Position Relative to Competition: Key Supply and Demand Factors

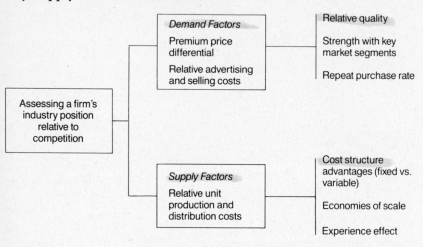

Source: Adapted by permission from the *Journal of Business Strategy*, Volume 4, Number 1, Summer 1983, "Gaining Insights Through Strategy Analysis," by George Day, p. 55. Copyright © 1983 by Warren, Gorham and Lamont, Inc., 210 South Street, Boston, Mass. All Rights Reserved.

George Day contends that "the distinctions between the various generic strategies boil down to a presumed choice between reducing costs versus building in more value to the customers. . . . What is sought is a perspective on relative competitive position that reflects both supply and demand factors."[14] Key supply and demand factors are highlighted in Figure 9.3. Different market definitions often illuminate the strategic balance of supply and demand factors.

Supply Factors   A supply perspective looks at broad market boundaries—often corresponding to conventional industry boundaries. Here the market definition should encompass products and activities that affect the ability to achieve economies of scale and gain advantages in production or distribution (Figure 9.3). Market share defined from a supply perspective is an indicator of relative unit production and distribution costs. The firm may gain a favorable industry position on the supply side through economies of scale or experience advantages.

Economies of scale reflect increased efficiency due to size. Large plants cost less per unit to build and operate than smaller plants. Scale effects also apply to many other cost elements such as sales, distribution, research and development, and purchasing. By contrast, the *experience*

[11]George Day, "Gaining Insights Through Strategy Analysis," *Journal of Business Strategy*, 4 (Summer 1983), p. 54; see also, George S. Day and Robin Wensley, "Marketing Theory with a Strategic Orientation," *Journal of Marketing* 47 (Fall 1983), pp. 79–89.

effect indicates that the per unit costs (measured in constant dollars) of producing and selling many products decline by a constant percentage each time accumulated experience (volume) is doubled. While the percentage value of this reduction will be constant each time experience is doubled, the usual decline is in the range of 20 to 30 percent. The concept of the experience effect is explored in the next chapter.

Demand Factors   A demand perspective relies on a customer-oriented market definition. Here, a differentiated competitive position is achieved by penetrating profitable target market segments. These segments are willing to pay a premium price for quality advantages that they perceive in a product or service. Through a focused promotion strategy, these customers can be reached efficiently. From a demand perspective, success is measured by the firm's relative share of these segments. A competitor without a strongly differentiated position will be unable to command a premium price and must emphasize a low-cost strategy.

Supply and demand factors often combine to determine a firm's relative position in an industry. Consider the central air conditioning market:

Manufacturers with high perceived quality and ability to provide continuing service support are in a particularly good margin position in the home modernization segment, which values these attributes and is willing to pay a premium for them. However, these manufacturers cannot avoid also serving the less profitable, highly price sensitive new construction market. Average unit manufacturing cost is determined by the combined volume of sales in the two end use segments.[15]

Several areas must be examined in assessing the relative importance of supply and demand in strategic planning, but the ability of competitors to match cost advantages or provide equivalent value on product or service dimensions is central to this analysis.

To this point, the discussion has centered on fundamental strategic planning concepts that apply generally. The industrial marketing environment presents special planning challenges.

Challenge the Fundamental Strategy Premises

In the past decade, a growing number of industrial firms have adopted formal strategic planning. Likewise, particular strategy analysis methods, such as the growth and market share matrix, have been widely accepted by industrial firms search-

---

[15] *Ibid.*, p. 54.

ing for tools to deal with the complex questions associated with strategic direction and resource allocation.

The growth-market share matrix judges business units by two criteria: relative market share and market growth rate. Based on a product's or business unit's position on these dimensions, strategy prescriptions like the following may be provided:

- withdraw from low-share businesses in a low-growth market;
- attempt to improve your position in a high-growth market where your position is viable but not dominant.

George Day suggests evaluating such strategy prescriptions with caution. If the underlying premises of the strategy analysis method do not fit the firm's situation, strategic signals can be grossly misleading. Two strategy premises worthy of particularly careful analysis are (1) the greater attractiveness of high-growth markets than low-growth markets, and (2) the positive relationship between market share and profitability. "Both premises are valid in general but often false in particular." Numerous variables can inhibit or enhance the relationship of market share and profitability: size of business, type of industry, stage of the product life cycle, shared experience, unionization, nature of competition.

The premises of various analysis methods must be scrutinized for their relevance to a given situation. Such an evaluation in itself significantly aids the strategic planning process.

Source: George Day, "Gaining Insights Through Strategy Analysis," *Journal of Business Strategy* 4 (Summer 1983), pp. 51–58.

Planning in the Industrial Marketing Environment

If marketing planning can be profitably applied by manufacturers of consumer goods like cake mixes and toothpaste, why not by producers of office equipment, chemicals, or machine tools? Industrial practitioners report, however, that this is often not the case. Why? Unique problems in industrial market planning are reported in a survey of 50 large industrial companies.[16]

[16] B. Charles Ames, "Marketing Planning for Industrial Products," *Harvard Business Review* 46 (September–October 1968), pp. 100–111.

Functional Interdependence

First, industrial marketing success depends to a large degree on such functional areas in the firm as engineering, research and development, manufacturing, and technical service.[17] Planning in the industrial setting thus requires more functional interdependence and a closer relationship to total corporate strategy than planning in the consumer-goods sector.[18] "Changes in marketing strategy are more likely to involve capital commitments for new equipment, shifts in development activities, or departures from traditional engineering and manufacturing approaches, any one of which would have companywide implications."[19] Some industrial companies have made the mistake of concentrating all planning in the marketing department, failing to recognize the need for an integrated effort across functional areas.

Diversity of Markets

A second problem that frustrates industrial marketing planners is the multitude and diversity of markets and channels.[20] For a manufacturer of insulation, such market segments as commercial contractors, small residential builders, large residential builders, and government agencies may each require a unique marketing strategy. As emphasized in Chapter 6, market segments must be selected with care because of the close working relationship between buyer and seller after the sale.

Production Orientation

Marketing planning often goes awry in the industrial setting because managers adopt a production rather than a consumer orientation.[21] Because a technical perspective prevails in industrial companies, marketers can become preoccupied with the technical capabilities of the product. Consumer needs—the central focus of marketing—are somehow forgotten. The industrial marketer must understand the costs of the customer's operations, the specific role of the product, and the competitive structure of the industry within which the customer operates.

In summary, the basic theory of marketing planning applies to both consumer-goods and industrial companies. However, successful implementation of marketing planning by the industrial marketer requires sensitivity to problems unique to industrial markets. First, planning must be functionally integrated. Second, the unique needs and

---

[17] *Ibid.*, pp. 101–102.

[18] Frederick E. Webster, Jr., "Management Science in Industrial Marketing," *Journal of Marketing* 42 (January 1978), p. 22.

[19] B. Charles Ames, "Trappings vs. Substance in Industrial Marketing," *Harvard Business Review* 48 (July–August 1976), pp. 95–96.

[20] Ames, "Marketing Planning," p. 101.

[21] Ames, "Trappings vs. Substance," pp. 93–102; see also, Webster, "Management Science," pp. 22–23.

Figure 9.4   Industrial Marketing Planning: A Functionally Integrated Perspective

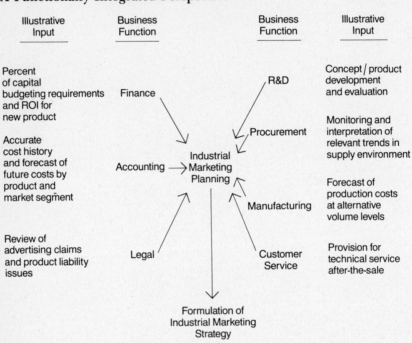

special marketing requirements of different market segments must be addressed. Third, a production orientation must be avoided.

Functionally Integrated Marketing Planning

Many marketing plans fail or are never implemented because the marketing manager developed them in isolation from other business functions.[22] All industrial marketing decisions—product, price, promotion or distribution—are affected, directly or indirectly, by other functional areas. In turn, business decisions in research and development (R&D), production and procurement, as well as the overall corporate strategy, are influenced by marketing considerations.

Industrial marketing planning must be coordinated and synchronized with corresponding planning efforts in R&D, procurement, finance, production, and other areas (Figure 9.4). For example, the marketing function gives procurement a sales forecast that facilitates

[22] Wind and Robertson, "Marketing Strategy: New Directions," p. 14.

material requirements planning. Procurement monitors and interprets supply trends that present opportunities or threats to marketing.[23] Industrial marketing plans must also be consistent with accounting and financial policies, personnel and procurement procedures, and short- and long-term corporate objectives.[24]

This section explores the interrelationships between marketing and three separate business functions: manufacturing, research and development, and customer service. Each assumes a particularly significant role in the development and execution of industrial marketing strategy.

Marketing–Manufacturing Interface

Manufacturing capabilities determine the volume and variety of products that can be marketed and influence the speed with which the industrial marketer can respond to changing market needs or competitive challenges. For efficient production, manufacturing relies heavily on marketing for an accurate sales forecast of the product line.

Defining Manufacturing Capabilities   Failure to align marketing strategy with manufacturing capability creates significant problems for the industrial firm. To select an appropriate strategic path, the industrial marketing manager must know the strengths and weaknesses of the production function.

One company found that its standardized product line was being challenged by competitors who were developing unique products targeted to specific market segments.[25] When this company responded by offering its own specialized products for each market segment, the result was disastrous. Its high-volume, standardized production processes were inefficient in producing low volumes of specialized products. Thus, competitors continued to capture market share because they had designed their production processes for the volume and product requirements of specific segments of the market.

Among the features of the manufacturing planning and control process that can directly shape marketing strategy are:[26]

1.   *Priorities*—how priorities are assigned. For example, an industrial firm that emphasizes customer service and fast delivery sets priorities based on customer needs rather than on least-cost produc-

[23] See, for example, John M. Browning, Noel B. Zabriskie, and Alan B. Huellmantel, "Strategic Purchasing Management," *Journal of Purchasing and Materials Management* 19 (Spring 1983), pp. 19–24.

[24] For a discussion of the marketing-finance interface, see, Paul F. Anderson, "The Marketing Management/Finance Interface," in Neil Beckwith *et al.*, eds., *Educators' Conference Proceedings* (Chicago: American Marketing Association, 1979), pp. 325–329.

[25] Robert H. Hayes and Steven C. Wheelwright, "The Dynamics of Process-Product Life Cycles," *Harvard Business Review* 57 (March–April 1979), pp. 127–136.

[26] Jeffrey G. Miller, "Fit Production Systems to the Task," *Harvard Business Review* 59 (January–February 1981), pp. 145–154.

tion. The latter system might fit a firm whose strategy emphasizes low prices.

2.   *Reflexes*—how quickly a production control system can shift direction. The reflexes of some manufacturing control systems are purposely slowed to protect production from costly changes. Other systems operate on short planning cycles to respond quickly to market-initiated changes.

3.   *Focus*—how well the manufacturing control system is adapted to the requirements of individual product lines or product groups. To meet the special needs of each of four market segments, a company might create four essentially independent order entry/assembly scheduling systems. Other firms may ignore focus to obtain economies of scale.

4.   *Technology*—how are computer technology and organizational technologies (i.e., regular meetings where department supervisors negotiate production plans) emphasized at various points in the manufacturing process. Some industrial firms use a computer system to centralize information about the current status of orders and the stage of completion of production projects. Other firms, while using the computer in production, rely more on organizational technologies where department supervisors negotiate production priorities. Top management tends to play a greater role in the manufacturing control system when the information system is centralized.

To properly match industrial marketing strategy with the manufacturing strengths of the firm, the industrial marketer must not only understand the manufacturing system but must also assume an active role in manufacturing system design decisions to insure that changing customer requirements and competitive challenges can be met. Unfortunately, many marketing managers fail to attend to the strategic role of manufacturing operations in gaining a competitive advantage.[27] Steven C. Wheelwright, an authority on manufacturing, notes that "American companies usually separate production decisions that are strategic from those that are merely operational. In Japan, no such separation occurs, for Japanese managers treat virtually all operational issues as strategic."[28]

Emerging Manufacturing Technology: Strategic Implications   By altering conventional manufacturing, new technology can alter industrial marketing strategy. Recent technological developments are briefly described in Table 9.1. Flexible manufacturing systems, the first step to-

---

[27] Robert Stobaugh and Piero Telesio, "Match Manufacturing Policies and Product Strategy," *Harvard Business Review* 61 (March–April 1983), pp. 113–120.

[28] Steven C. Wheelwright, "Japan—Where Operations Really Are Strategic," *Harvard Business Review* 59 (July–August 1981), pp. 67–74.

Table 9.1   Tracing Recent Trends in Manufacturing Technology

Technology	Description	Benefit
Computer-aided Manufacturing (CAM)	The linking of computers with manufacturing hardware to facilitate the handling of multiple tasks and rapid production changeovers at reasonable cost.	The ability to produce a variety of parts on the same machine at reasonable cost.
Computer-aided Design (CAD)	The use of the computer to evaluate alternative product characteristics and design dimensions.	Prompt, economic evaluation of alternative product designs.
Computer-aided Design/ Computer-aided Manufacturing (CAD/CAM)	Linking the above systems and drawing on a common data base, product design and production process decisions can be made at a CRT (an engineer can design the product and specify the process at the same time).	More accurate cost information and opportunities for improving machine productivity and lowering material costs.
Computer-integrated Manufacturing (CIM) (e.g., flexible manufacturing systems)	Building upon CAD/CAM, additional support aspects of manufacturing, such as inventory control, cost accounting, procurement, and physical distribution are integrated with the direct manufacturing control system.	Organization of massive amounts of information to produce goods economically in small volumes.

Source: Adapted from: Harry Thompson and Michael Paris, "The Changing Face of Manufacturing Technology," *The Journal of Business Strategy*, 3 (Summer 1982), pp. 45–52.

ward computer-integrated manufacturing systems, are a radical departure from the past where economies could be realized only at high levels of production.[29] Because a flexible system can be instantly reprogrammed, goods can be produced economically in small volumes. Flexible manufacturing extends the "reflexes" or diversity of manufacturing to a degree never before available. At its Sommerworth, New Hampshire plant, General Electric uses flexible manufacturing to produce 2000 different versions of its basic electric meter.[30]

Economies of Scope   The term, "economies of scope," describes the capacity of flexible automation to produce a small batch or even a single product as efficiently as a production line that manufactures the same items on a massive scale.[31] Because flexible automation allows the industrial firm to meet the special product requirements of small market segments or large individual customers, lower cost penalties for variety give

[29] Harry Thompson and Michael Paris, "The Changing Face of Manufacturing Technology," *The Journal of Business Strategy* 3 (Summer 1982), pp. 45–52.

[30] Gene Bylinsky, "The Race to the Automatic Factory," *Fortune* (February 21, 1983), p. 54.

[31] Thompson and Paris, "Manufacturing Technology," p. 49.

the industrial marketer more flexibility in the choice of product and market segmentation strategies.

Flexible manufacturing may also alter buyer–seller relationships in some markets because firms will have the option of producing components that they had previously purchased from suppliers. Dissatisfied with the quality of a purchased component part, General Motors, for example, turned to flexible automation to produce the item itself.[32]

Flexible manufacturing can also alter the nature of competition in selected industrial markets. Efficient production of products in small volumes broadens the scope of markets that competitors can serve. As flexible automation increases, "some companies will find themselves blind-sided by competitors they never imagined existed."[33] In monitoring the competitive environment, the industrial marketer should evaluate the marketing and manufacturing strengths of both existing and potential competitors.

How fast computer-integrated manufacturing systems like flexible automation will be adopted in particular industries is difficult to forecast. Some earlier users of the technology have encountered problems in making the transition from more conventional manufacturing.[34] However, computer-integrated manufacturing systems will constitute a potent force in the industrial market in the 1980s and 1990s.

Potential for Conflict   Many areas of conflict can potentially divide marketing and manufacturing. Table 9.2 highlights eight areas where there is strong probability of conflict in the marketing–manufacturing interface. The seeds for internal conflict or potential friction between manufacturing and marketing are rooted in such fundamental areas as sales forecasting, production scheduling, product distribution, and product planning. To increase the level of cooperation and decrease conflict between marketing and manufacturing, management must understand the causes of conflict.

Causes of Conflict   One researcher who has explored the marketing–manufacturing interface identifies three prime reasons for conflict.[35] First, different criteria are used to evaluate and reward the two areas. Marketing managers are evaluated on the basis of sales, profits, or market share, production managers on the basis of manufacturing efficiency and cost-effectiveness. Second, the inherent complexity of the two functions engenders conflict. The difficulty of accurately forecasting sales in marketing is matched by complexities emerging from frequent changes

[32] Bylinsky, "Automatic Factory," p. 63.

[33] *Ibid.*, p. 54.

[34] Carol Hymowitz, "Manufacturers Press Automating to Survive But Results Are Mixed," *Wall Street Journal* (April 11, 1983), pp. 1, 19.

[35] Benson P. Shapiro, "Can Marketing and Manufacturing Coexist?" *Harvard Business Review* 55 (September–October 1977), pp. 104–114.

Table 9.2   Marketing/Manufacturing: Areas of Necessary Cooperation but Potential Conflict

Problem Area	Typical Marketing Comment	Typical Manufacturing Comment
1. Capacity planning and long-range sales forecasting.	"Why don't we have enough capacity?"	"Why didn't we have accurate sales forecasts?"
2. Production scheduling and short-range sales forecasting.	"We need faster response. Our lead times are ridiculous."	"We need realistic customer commitments and sales forecasts that don't change like wind direction."
3. Delivery and physical distribution.	"Why don't we ever have the right merchandise in inventory?"	"We can't keep everything in inventory."
4. Quality assurance.	"Why can't we have reasonable quality at reasonable cost?"	"Why must we always offer options that are too hard to manufacture and that offer little customer utility?"
5. Breadth of product line.	"Our customers demand variety."	"The product line is too broad—all we get are short, uneconomical runs."
6. Cost control.	"Our costs are so high that we are not competitive in the marketplace."	"We can't provide fast delivery, broad variety, rapid response to change, and high quality at low cost."
7. New product introduction.	"New products are our life blood."	"Unnecessary design changes are prohibitively expensive."
8. Adjunct services such as spare parts inventory support, installation, and repair.	"Field service costs are too high."	"Products are being used in ways for which they weren't designed."

Source: Reprinted by permission of the *Harvard Business Review*. An exhibit from "Can Marketing and Manufacturing Coexist," by Benson P. Shapiro, 55 (September–October 1977), p. 105. Copyright © 1977 by the President and Fellows of Harvard College, all rights reserved.

in the production schedule. Third, marketing managers and production managers differ in orientation, education, career history, and life-style. The marketing/manufacturing interface is further complicated by budget constraints, rapid technological change, and speed of growth of the enterprise.

Managing the Conflict   Top management must create the atmosphere that fosters cooperation and a proper balance between manufacturing and marketing. Some degree of tension is constructive and promotes effectiveness and efficiency. Severe problems emerge when the conflict evolves into open warfare. An atmosphere of cooperation can be promoted by clear corporate policies, an evaluation and reward system that stresses interfunctional cooperation, and company activities that encourage interfunctional contact (e.g., inviting manufacturing managers to sales meetings). At the same time, marketers should analyze not only their customer needs, but also the operational strengths of the manufacturing unit.[36] The marketing program can then capitalize on the strengths of the manufacturing unit to meet the needs of target markets.

Marketing–R&D Interface

"Ignoring the R&D–marketing interface has resulted in many technology oriented firms developing products that are the engineer's and scientist's dream and the marketer's nightmare, since they meet no latent or overt consumer needs."[37] The importance of nurturing an effective marketing–R&D interface is reinforced by the sizable investments R&D commands in industrial firms. Xerox, Boeing, and General Electric each spend over $600 million annually on R&D, Du Pont over $800 million, and IBM over $2 billion.[38] Many small- and medium-sized firms make a significant investment as a percentage of sales in R&D.

New product development is the focus of the marketing–R&D interface, from idea generation to performance evaluation of the finished product. Successful new product developments depend heavily on marketing research regarding product features desired by target market segments and how potential organizational buyers view trade-offs among product attributes.[39] If marketing fails to provide adequate market and competitive information, R&D personnel will be in the precarious position of determining the direction of new product development without the benefit of market knowledge.[40] A successful relationship between marketing and R&D requires that each understand the strengths, weaknesses, and potential contribution of the other. For instance, a promising new product spawned by R&D may fail because the firm lacks the marketing strengths required to penetrate a particular market segment.

Potential for Conflict   Conflict can damage the effectiveness of both units as well as overall corporate strategy. The underlying causes of the marketing–R&D conflict are like those in the marketing–manufacturing interface. R&D managers often operate under a different reward system in the organization and bring a different orientation and background to the decision-making process. Selected problems that can undermine marketing–R&D relationships are outlined in Table 9.3. Any of these can severely hamper new product development projects. One research study identified 47 new product development projects where the marketing–R&D interface was characterized by distrust and lack of appre-

[36] *Ibid.*

[37] Yoram Wind, "Marketing and the Other Business Functions," in Jagdish N. Sheth, ed., *Research in Marketing*, vol. 5 (Greenwich, CT.: JAI Press, 1981), p. 244.

[38] "The U.S. Still Leads the World in R&D Spending," *Business Week* (June 20, 1983), p. 122.

[39] Yoram Wind, John F. Grashof, and Joel D. Goldhar, "Market Based Guidelines for the Design of Industrial Products," *Journal of Marketing* 42 (July 1978), pp. 23–37.

[40] Robert A. Linn, "A Sectoral Approach to Strategic Planning for R&D," *Research Management* 26 (January–February 1983), pp. 33–40.

Table 9.3   Signs of Disharmony in the Marketing–R&D Relationship

Problem Area	Characteristic Behaviors
Lack of Communication	Marketing is not fully informed of what R&D is working on until very late in the new product development cycle.
	Working documents, marketing research reports, and progress reports are not circulated between R&D and marketing personnel.
Lack of Appreciation	R&D fails to consult marketing concerning new product ideas.
	Marketing attempts to exercise close control over R&D whenever they work together.
Distrust	Marketing often goes outside the firm and uses subcontractors to meet its R&D needs.
	R&D and marketing personnel purposely avoid each other, sometimes refusing to sit down together at the same table.

Source: Adapted from William E. Souder, "Promoting an Effective R&D/Marketing Interface," Research Management, 23 (July 1980), pp. 11–12.

ciation.[41] Nearly two-thirds of these were commercial failures. In projects where there were no significant problems, the failure rate dropped to less than 15 percent.

Promoting Cooperation   New product development is successful in an organizational climate that stimulates innovation and encourages interaction between marketing and R&D. What steps can be taken to foster cooperation?

Some firms program regular exchanges of personnel between the two functions, frequent information meetings, periodic gripe-sessions, and an open invitation for marketers to visit the R&D laboratory.[42] Other industrial firms foster the entrepreneurial spirit in marketing, R&D, and other functional areas by creating mini-enterprises within the larger organization,[43] decentralizing the flow of information, decision-making responsibility, and authority, and providing incentives to reward successful new ventures. TRW, Inc., a diversified industrial products firm, has developed a bonus system to stimulate cooperation among its divisions.[44] TRW has also developed an index of its technological capabilities that allows managers working on over 250 independent space and defense contracts to share knowledge.

[41] William E. Souder, "Promoting an Effective R&D/Marketing Interface," Research Management 23 (July 1980), pp. 10–15.

[42] Ibid. For a discussion of measures for evaluating R&D effectiveness, see, A. Parasuraman and Linda M. Zeren, "R&D's Relationship with Profits and Sales," Research Management 26 (January–February 1983), pp. 25–28.

[43] Thomas J. Peters and Robert H. Waterman, Jr., In Search of Excellence, Lessons from America's Best-Run Companies (New York: Harper & Row, Publishers, 1982).

[44] "TRW Leads a Revolution in Managing Technology," Business Week (November 15, 1982), p. 130.

Capitalizing on R&D Strength: A Marketing Manager's View

Rod O'Connor, Marketing Manager, Commercial Communications Systems, for Motorola, Inc.'s Government Electronics Division, illustrates the strategic role of the marketing–R&D interface in a high-technology company.

In selling component parts to a major account like IBM, the Motorola salesperson identifies key buying influentials such as a circuit and systems design engineer and, when necessary, links them directly to engineers in the R&D group. This brings a strong customer orientation directly into our R&D efforts. The marketing function facilitates this communication flow and, of course, must serve as a control in managing the buyer–seller relationship.

In selling high-technology equipment to the government, there is also a close coupling between Motorola R&D and government R&D—engineer to engineer and program head to program head. We build these relationships by delivering on our promises and by never defaulting on a government contract. Again, the marketing function facilitates and controls the flow of communications, and identifies the problems that Motorola is best equipped to solve. By monitoring the communication flow and collating bits and pieces of data that arise out of the technical dialogue between buyer and seller, a significant amount of marketing research information can be gathered.

Industrial marketing managers are at a serious disadvantage in the marketplace if they fail to direct their R&D capabilities to solving customer problems.

Source: Interview with Rod O'Connor, Government Electronics Division, Motorola, Inc., Scottsdale, Arizona, June 27, 1983.

Marketing–Customer Service Interface

Since organizational buyers evaluate industrial suppliers on many service dimensions, the marketing–customer service interface is also vital to a successful marketing strategy. Two factors assigned particular importance in procurement decisions (see Chapter 3) are: (1) the speed and reliability of delivery service and (2) the quality and availability of technical service after-the-sale. The direct control of these activities often falls outside of the marketing function.

Many industrial firms have a separate department that manages physical distribution and still another that provides technical service. Others fully integrate these functions into marketing. Regardless of the organizational location of these functions, effective marketing strategy demands close coordination and open lines of communication among distribution, technical service, and marketing. Organizational buyers enter exchange relationships with industrial marketers to secure technical assistance, training, and responsive and reliable delivery service, as well as physical products. Carefully designed and coordinated service policies enable industrial firms to maximize the value of their total market offerings.

Functionally Integrated Planning: The Marketing Strategy Center[45]

Rather than operating in isolation from other functional areas, the successful industrial marketing manager is an integrator—one who understands the capabilities of manufacturing, R&D, and customer service and exploits their strengths in developing marketing strategies that are responsive to customer needs. Responsibility charting constitutes an approach that can be used to classify decision-making roles and to highlight the multifunctional nature of industrial marketing decision making. The structure of a responsibility chart is provided in Table 9.4. The decision areas (rows) illustrated in the matrix might, for example, relate to a planned product line expansion. The various functional areas that may assume particular roles in this decision process are listed in the columns of the matrix.

The alternative roles that can be assumed by participants in the decision-making process are defined below:[46]

1. *Responsible*—manager takes initiative for analyzing situation, developing alternatives, assuring consultation with others and makes initial recommendation. Upon approval of decision, the role ends.

2. *Approve*—manager accepts or vetoes decision before it is implemented, or chooses from alternatives developed by participant assuming "responsible" role.

3. *Consult*—manager is consulted or asked for substantive input prior to the approval of decision but does not possess veto power.

4. *Implement*—manager is accountable for the implementation of the decision, including notification of other relevant participants concerning decision.

[45] Michael D. Hutt and Thomas W. Speh, "The Marketing Strategy Center: Diagnosing the Industrial Marketer's Interdisciplinary Role," working paper, Arizona State University (January 1984).

[46] Joseph E. McCann and Thomas N. Gilmore, "Diagnosing Organizational Decision Making Through Responsibility Charting," *Sloan Management Review* 25 (Winter 1983), pp. 3–15.

Table 9.4   Interfunctional Involvement in Marketing Decision Making: An Illustrative Responsibility Chart

Decision Area	Organizational Function						
	Marketing	Manufacturing	R&D	Physical Distribution	Technical Service	Strategic Business Unit Manager	Corporate Level Planner
Product							
Design Specifications							
Performance Characteristics							
Reliability							
Price							
List Price							
Discount Structure							
Technical Service Support							
Customer Training							
Repair							
Physical Distribution							
Inventory Level							
Customer Service Level							
Sales Force							
Training							
Advertising							
Message Development							
Channel							
Selection							

Decision Role Vocabulary: R = Responsible; A = Approve; C = Consult; M = Implement; I = Inform; X = No role in decision.

5.   *Inform*—while not necessarily consulted before decision is approved, manager is informed of the decision once it is made.

Representatives of a particular functional area may, of course, assume more than one role in the decision-making process. The technical service manager may be "consulted" during the new product development process and may also be held accountable for "implementing" service support strategy. Likewise, the marketing manager may be "responsible" for and "approve" many of the decisions related to the product line expansion. For other actions, several decision makers may participate. To illustrate, the business unit manager, after "consulting" R&D, may "approve" (accept or veto) a decision for which the marketing manager is "responsible."

The members of the organization who become involved in the industrial marketing decision-making process constitute the organizational "selling" or strategy center. The composition or functional area representation of the strategy center evolves during the marketing strategy development process, varies from firm to firm, and varies from one strategy situation to another. Likewise, the composition of the marketing strategy center is not strictly prescribed by the organizational chart. The needs of a particular strategy situation, especially the information requirements, significantly influence the composition of the strategy center. Thus, the marketing strategy center concept shares certain parallels with the buying center (see Chapter 4).

The Industrial Marketing Planning Process

The industrial marketing planning process is inextricably linked to planning in other functional areas and to overall corporate strategy. It takes place within the larger strategic marketing management process of the corporation. To survive and prosper, the industrial marketer must properly balance the firm's resources with the objectives and opportunities of the environment. Marketing planning is a continuous process.

A model for the industrial marketing planning process is presented in Figure 9.5. The model has five main components: (1) situation analysis, (2) problems and opportunities, (3) master marketing strategy, (4) integrated marketing plan, and (5) measurement and evaluation of results. The marketing plan is the result of the planning process. The process should be global, with specific marketing plans for each country.

Situation Analysis

The process begins with situation analysis. To gain an understanding of the environment in which marketing effort will be expended, the industrial marketer (1) identifies the forces that have an impact on the present market situation, and (2) projects the forces that will shape the market

Figure 9.5   A Marketing Planning Model

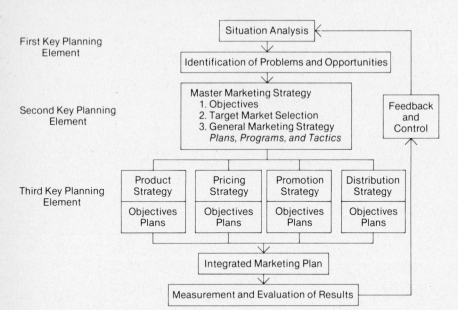

First Key Planning Element

Second Key Planning Element

Third Key Planning Element

Source: From *Marketing for Bankers* by Leonard L. Berry and James H. Donnelly, Jr., © 1975 by the American Bankers Association, 1120 Connecticut Avenue NW, Washington, D.C. 20036 U.S.A. Used with permission.

Table 9.5   Selected Components of the Situation Analysis

Areas of Analysis	Illustrative Questions
Environmental Climate	What are the relevant political, social, economic, and technological trends that will influence our product(s), industry, or customers?
Competitive Climate	What is the present and future structure and form of competition (e.g., number, aggressiveness, and anticipated retaliatory actions of competitors)?
Company Resources	What are the unique human skills and experience that qualify our organization to be in this business (e.g., marketing, research and development, production expertise)? Does our firm possess sufficient financial resources to support an effective marketing program?
Performance Profile	What level of sales, market share, and profitability did each of our products achieve in each of the last five years?
Market Potentials/ Market Description	What is the growth rate and market potential of each market? Describe the customer profiles of relevant market segments.
Performance Forecast	Assuming no changes in marketing strategy, what level of sales, market share, and profitability is anticipated? What are the key assumptions that underlie this forecast?

situation during the relevant planning period. The situation analysis develops the facts and assumptions on which the plan will be based (Table 9.5). The situation analysis assesses environmental, competitive, and company conditions; profiles past performance; and forecasts future performance. The industrial marketing intelligence system (see Chapter 5) provides valuable information for conducting the situation analysis.

Problems and Opportunities

The situation analysis inevitably uncovers both problems and opportunities. A particular product may enjoy a dominant market share, but in an unprofitable market (problem). Or the firm may discover that it has production and marketing skills uniquely suited to profitable and growing market segments (opportunity). Crown Cork & Seal, a large producer of metal cans and other items, had captured a large share of the sizable motor oil can business in 1958 by introducing the first one-quart aluminum oil can.[47] The firm later elected *not* to aggressively pursue this market because of the trend toward other packaging materials and toward container self-manufacture by large users. Instead, Crown Cork chose to concentrate on the beer, soft drink, and aerosol can markets—all with high growth rates, low risk of self-manufacture by users, and greater consistency with Crown Cork corporate capabilities.

Problems represent constraints that must be recognized; opportunities provide directions for growth. By ranking problems and opportunities in order of importance, the market planner is better able to define marketing objectives and design strategies.

Master Marketing Strategy

Here the industrial marketer makes decisions about how the controllable marketing mix variables will be blended to achieve predetermined goals through: (1) establishment of marketing objectives, (2) selection of market targets, and (3) development of the general marketing strategy required to achieve the established objectives.

Objectives   Marketing objectives are the results or ends that are sought. They should be expressed in qualitative and quantitative terms: To be operational, objectives must be specific and the degree of success or failure in reaching them must be measurable. Marketing objectives are often expressed in terms of: (1) sales volume (dollars or units), (2) market share, and (3) profit, or return on investment.

Besides setting concrete standards of performance, marketing objectives direct the organization toward a specific market level. Industrial

[47] E. Raymond Corey, "Key Options in Market Selection and Product Planning," *Harvard Business Review* 47 (September–October 1975), pp. 119–128.

marketers may have the option of concentrating on different levels of the manufacturing chain. For example, "the aluminum producer serving the residential housing market may have a choice whether to sell raw materials, semifabricated materials, components, or end products."[48] The choice becomes critical when the industrial marketing planner is selecting a target market.

Owens-Illinois: A Strategy Profile

Owens-Illinois, Inc., the largest producer of glass containers in the United States, is diversifying into new markets. While the firm derives $1.8 billion from glass containers, Owens-Illinois is moving into high technology plastic packaging and diversifying into health care management and supplies (in order to improve the firm's profit position, which has been eroded by the mature glass business). Planners forecast that glass will account for only 35 percent of the company's business by 1988, down from 50 percent in 1983.

Following corporate strategy, Owens-Illinois sold its Lily paper and plastic cup business and closed four glass container manufacturing facilities. The firm also invested over $500 million in a manufacturing modernization program that reduced labor costs to only 25 percent of manufacturing costs versus the 40 percent industry average.

To foster an entrepreneurial spirit, the firm's operations have been strategically divided into five autonomous product groups. Each is responsible for meeting profitability targets and funding its own research and development. To achieve profit goals, Owens-Illinois feels they must make a deep penetration into the higher-growth, high-technology plastics container market. Included here are flexible packages specifically designed for meat and containers that lock out oxygen and moisture. The firm has capitalized on long-standing relationships with such customers as Procter and Gamble and American Home Products. Also, they are negotiating with Brown-Forman Distillers Corporation to introduce spirits in plastic bottles.

The competition in the high-technology plastics market is extremely severe and Owens-Illinois does not enjoy the market leadership position to which they are accustomed in

---

[48]*Ibid.*, p. 122.

the glass container business. However, the firm has taken steps to realign its marketing strategy to meet competitive challenges. For example, separate sales organizations have been established to meet the needs of different segments of the plastic container market.

Source: "Owens-Illinois: A Cautious Venture Beyond Glass," *Business Week* (July 4, 1983), pp. 84–85.

Target Market Selection   In identifying a need of a target segment of organizational buyers and then directing the firm's resources toward satisfaction of that need, the marketer can draw upon information gathered in the situation analysis. A target market must be assessed objectively in terms of market potentials, competition, customer profiles, and company strengths and weaknesses. Industrial market segmentation (Chapter 6); market potential forecasting (Chapter 7); and sales forecasting (Chapter 8) are fundamental in evaluating alternative segments. Rather than merely describing possible target markets, the manager must analyze the nature of the market's need, the best means of satisfying that need, and the size and growth trend of the market segment.

Segment Positioning[49]   Figure 9.6 illustrates the importance of evaluating market opportunities and business strengths segment by segment. This framework includes four components:

- *Part A* is an assessment of the opportunities and threats offered by alternative market segments in a given country.
- *Part B* is an analysis of business strengths and weaknesses, incorporating valuable information gathered in the situation analysis.
- *Part C* is an evaluation of alternative market segment candidates and of positioning strategies for each segment. S_1P_3 represents the heavy-user market segment, satisfied with a particular product offering and motivated in purchasing by product performance.
- *Part D* is the evaluation of market opportunities in relation to company strengths. Observe that S_1P_3, the heavy user satisfied/performance segment, provides an attractive market opportunity (high) that matches the company's strength (high). The industrial firm has the manufacturing, R&D, and marketing skills required to satisfy the needs of the market segment. By following this procedure, the most attractive target markets can be identified.

[49] The following discussion is based on Wind and Robertson, "Marketing Strategy: New Directions," pp. 16–22.

Figure 9.6   Illustrative Market Opportunities and Business Strength Analysis by Segment Positioning

C   Segment by Positioning Analysis by Country
Expected Size and Characteristics of Selected
Segments/Positionings

Segmentation \ Positioning	P_1 Price	P_2 Convenience	P_3 Performance	P_4 Status, Image	P_5 Other
S_1: Heavy Users Satisfied					
S_2: Heavy Users Vulnerable					
S_3: Light Users Satisfied					
S_4: Light Users Potential					
S_5: Light Users Vulnerable					
S_6: Non-Users Potential					
S_7: Non-Users Limited Potential					

A   Opportunity–Threat Analysis
(Current & Projected Environmental Analysis by Country)

Likelihood of occurrence and impact of trends:

☐ Market demand
☐ Competitive behavior
☐ Market distribution
☐ Technological developments
☐ Legal/political environment
☐ Social/cultural environment
☐ Economic conditions

and their likely inter-dependency (cross-impact analysis). This analysis provides the framework for assessing the *market opportunities and threats.*

B   Analysis of Business Strengths and Weaknesses: Situation Analysis and Marketing Audit by Country

A comprehensive situation analysis evaluating the strengths and weaknesses of the firm and its businesses, including an audit of current and planned marketing objectives, strategies and operations. This analysis should include a projected risk/return analysis of the expected return of the current strategies. This analysis provides the framework for assessing the company's and business' *strengths and weaknesses.*

Opportunities and Threats

	Segments/Positioning	
	S_1P_1	S_2P_2 ...
Opportunities ======		
Threats ======		

Strengths and Weaknesses

	Segments/Positioning	
	S_1P_1	S_2P_2 ...
Strengths ======		
Weaknesses ======		

D   Evaluation of Segment/Positioning Units on Their Market Opportunities/ Company's Strength by Country

Company's Strength	H	S_1P_N S_1P_3
		S_2P_3 S_3P_4
	L	S_4P_3
		L H
		Market Opportunities

Source: Yoram Wind and Thomas S. Robertson, "Marketing Strategy: New Directions for Theory and Research," *Journal of Marketing*, 47 (Spring 1983), p. 18. Reprinted by permission of the American Marketing Association.

The approach recognizes the interdependence of marketing and other business functions, allows the industrial marketing manager to link company strengths directly to market segment needs—and establishes a foundation for assessing the risks and expected returns of alternative marketing strategies.

General Marketing Strategy   Once the planner defines the target market, specific decisions must be made, using the segment position analysis, about each controllable marketing variable: product, promotion, price, and distribution. Objectives, plans, and tactics for each marketing variable must be developed and coordinated into a total marketing program. *Strategy* prescribes *what* will be done; *tactics* prescribe how it will be accomplished. Of course, any decisions made will be consistent with budgetary constraints.

Formulating industrial marketing strategy is complex. To maximize the impact of the total strategy, the marketing planner must determine the function and assign a relative weight to each marketing variable. Clearly, the variations and combinations are unlimited. In evaluating marketing strategies, the manager should estimate the likely market response of market segments under different sets of environmental conditions. The industrial firm may be more vulnerable to competition in some segments than in others; alternatively, a recession might damage the firm's sales and profit performance in some segments, but not in others.

Integrated Marketing Plan

The master marketing strategy should be a written plan, formally documenting the marketing strategy and including all supporting plans and tactics. This plan should coordinate all the components of the marketing strategy—markets to be served, products/services to be marketed, price schedules, distribution methods, and so on. The plan clearly defines objectives and specifies courses of action to achieve these goals.

Measurement and Evaluation of Results

The marketing plan covers only a specified time period, but marketing planning is continuous. A plan cannot be forgotten until the next period. A central mechanism is required to compare actual to planned results and to insure that the firm's strategy and tactics are achieving their objectives. A serious gap between actual results and performance standards demands a change in strategy or objectives. Thus, the marketing planning model must contain a feedback and control mechanism.

Implementing Industrial Marketing Strategy

Well-conceived strategic plans fail if they are not properly implemented. Strategies may fail because marketing managers are out of touch with the marketplace—they have little direct contact with customers and they neglect to gather information from the sales force.[50] Other industrial

---

[50] Walter Kiechel III, "Three (or Four, or More) Ways to Win," *Fortune* (October 19, 1981), pp. 181–188.

marketing planning efforts may be irreparable if they are developed without recognizing important internal functional interrelationships. A research and development scientist who works on a product modification, a shop supervisor who sets priorities for the production schedule, a physical distribution manager who expedites the order, a technician who trains customers on product use after the sale—all are part of the implementation of marketing strategy.

Summary

Planning in the industrial marketing environment raises special problems. First, the high degree of functional interdependence required is often difficult to achieve. Top management must be sensitive to the interface between marketing and other functional areas. Industrial marketing planning may also be complicated by the diversity of industrial markets and by the tendency of managers to follow a technical rather than a customer orientation.

Strategic marketing management provides the means by which the particular capabilities of the company can be matched with attractive market opportunities. Policies established at the corporate level provide the framework for strategy development in each SBU.

Industrial marketing planning is that part of the larger strategic marketing management process which allows the industrial marketer to develop an integrated marketing program targeted at defined market segments to achieve performance goals. To be successful, the industrial marketer must be attuned to internal as well as external requirements. A continuous process, marketing planning involves five successive stages: (1) situation analysis, (2) evaluation of problems and opportunities, (3) formulation of a master marketing strategy, (4) development of an integrated marketing plan, and (5) measurement and evaluation of results. The end result of the planning process is the marketing plan, the formal written description of the marketing strategy. The succeeding chapters will analyze each marketing mix variable.

Discussion Questions

1. The evaluation of new or existing markets requires an analysis of competition. Michael Porter contends that the state of competition in an industry is determined by the interplay of five basic forces. Explain.

2. Explain how an industrial firm organized around four product lines might benefit by redesigning the organization around nineteen strategic business units.

3. An industrial marketer is considering entry into one of four indus-
    tries. What procedures could the industrial marketer follow to
    measure the relative attractiveness of these industries?

4. Various strategic paths to a profitable position in an industry have
    been proposed in recent years. Often, the distinction between al-
    ternative strategies boils down to a presumed choice between re-
    ducing costs (supply factors) versus building in more value to the
    customer (demand factors). First, describe the supply and demand
    factors that may contribute to a position of strength in a particular
    industry. Second, explain why different market definitions are
    needed to measure the success of a marketing strategy that empha-
    sizes supply versus demand factors.

5. While the need for careful planning and coordination cuts across
    both consumer-goods and industrial-goods companies, marketing
    planning in the industrial environment has special requirements.
    Explain.

6. What are the factors underlying the common conflict between mar-
    keting and manufacturing in the industrial firm? Describe the steps
    management can take to foster an atmosphere of cooperation.

7. Describe how each of the following features of the manufacturing
    and control process can shape industrial marketing strategy: pri-
    orities, reflexes, focus, and technology.

8. Compare and contrast the relevance of "economies of scale" and
    "economies of scope" to the industrial marketing strategist.

9. John S. Painter, President of Eagle-Picher, a Fortune 500 industrial
    firm, stated: "Unless we see that we are now No. 1 or have a strong
    chance of becoming No. 1 in a short period of time, it is not a prod-
    uct line we want to be in." How will this clear statement of corpo-
    rate objectives influence marketing objectives and, in turn, master
    marketing strategy?

10. Once a master marketing strategy is implemented, when should the
    industrial marketer first begin to compare actual versus planned
    results? At the end of the first quarter? At the end of the year?

C·H·A·P·T·E·R
10

Managing the Industrial
Product Line

The industrial product constitutes the central force in the marketing mix. The ability of the firm to put together a line of products and services that respond to the needs of customers is the heart of industrial marketing management. After reading this chapter, you will have an understanding of:

1.   the concept of the "total product";
2.   the different types of industrial product lines;
3.   a strategic approach for managing the existing product line;
4.   the process of developing and managing new industrial products.

An industrial marketer's identity in the marketplace is established through the products and services offered. Without careful product planning and control, marketers often are guilty of introducing products that are inconsistent with market needs, arbitrarily adding items that contribute little to existing product lines, and maintaining weak products that could be profitably eliminated.

Industrial product management is directly linked to market analysis and market selection. As Figure 10.1 illustrates, product policy is a circular process: Products are developed to fit the needs of the market and modified as those needs change. Drawing upon such tools of demand analysis as organizational market segmentation and market potential forecasting, the marketer evaluates opportunities and selects viable market segments, which in turn determines the direction of product policy. Product policy cannot be separated from market selection decisions.[1] In evaluating potential product/market fits, the firm must evaluate market opportunities and the number and aggressiveness of competitors, and gauge its own strengths and weaknesses.

This chapter examines the product management function in the industrial environment. First, we provide a perspective on the definition of an "industrial product." Second, since industrial goods can assume several different forms, we describe the industrial product line options. Third, we discuss how to manage existing product lines. The final section of the chapter is concerned with managing development of the new industrial product.

Figure 10.1   The Role of Product Policy in Market Analysis

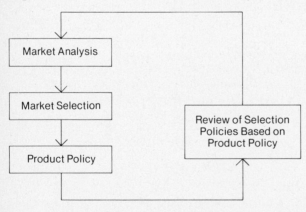

Source: Benson P. Shapiro, *Industrial Product Policy: Managing the Existing Product Line* (Cambridge, Mass.: Marketing Science Institute, 1977), p. 30. Reprinted by permission.

[1] E. Raymond Corey, "Key Options in Market Selection and Product Planning," *Harvard Business Review* 53 (September–October 1975), pp. 119–128; see also, Yoram Wind and Thomas S. Robertson, "Marketing Strategy: New Directions for Theory and Research," *Journal of Marketing* 47 (Spring 1983), pp. 12–25.

The Industrial "Product"

What is a product? A marketer can only respond from the viewpoint of a consumer: A product is all of the value satisfactions that a customer derives at both an organizational and a personal level.[2] The purchaser of cold rolled steel is buying physical specifications (thickness, chemical composition), a particular package, technical advice, and delivery reliability.[3] The seller may be able to satisfy more personal needs of the buyer by reducing risk, improving the buyer's organizational status, or merely breaking the monotony of a day with a pleasant discussion about outside interests. Thus, the physical attributes of the product can be augmented in many ways which add extra value to the product. The seller's identity in the market is established not only by the product or service, but also by the value satisfactions provided to the buyer.

Integrated Effort

The development of marketing strategy in general, and product policy in particular, requires a high degree of functional coordination within the enterprise. As explored in the previous chapter, manufacturing, research and development, engineering, inventory control, technical service, and marketing together create and deliver the total product with its customer value satisfactions.[4] If perceived benefits like strong technical support are not provided, the marketer's reputation may be irreparably damaged.

Decisions about modifications or extensions in the product line often cause conflict in the industrial firm. Manufacturing personnel are interested in short product lines with long and smooth production runs. Marketers may prefer to extend rather than cut product lines in the face of competition or changing market requirements.[5] The discussion of organizational buying behavior in Chapter 4 described the kind of interfunctional conflict that often emerges in the buying organization. Such conflict also affects product planning in the selling organization and stems from the same roots: differing backgrounds, perspectives, and departmental objectives.

Organizing the Industrial Product Management Function

Implementing corporate strategy for either industrial or consumer goods requires a coordinated effort. The need is particularly acute in industrial marketing. The industrial product management function can-

---

[2] Theodore Levitt, *The Marketing Mode: Pathways to Corporate Growth* (New York: McGraw-Hill, Inc., 1969), pp. 2–3.

[3] Benson P. Shapiro, *Industrial Product Policy: Managing the Existing Product Line* (Cambridge, Mass.: Marketing Science Institute, 1977), pp. 37–39.

[4] B. Charles Ames, "Marketing Planning for Industrial Products," *Harvard Business Review* 46 (September–October 1968), pp. 100–111.

[5] Benson P. Shapiro, "Can Marketing and Manufacturing Coexist?" *Harvard Business Review* 55 (September–October 1977), pp. 107–114.

not remain isolated within the organization, but must instead interface with other functional areas. Technical service and research and development groups are part of the product offering. The capability of manufacturing (low cost or high quality) may become a marketing weapon. Cost accounting is important to product management, providing accurate data on the profitability of the product mix.

The product management function must link product plans to overall corporate objectives and planning. Firms that overlook this, placing product planning in a vacuum, are often disappointed when the resulting plans clash with corporate goals and capabilities.

The design of the product management function depends upon company and market characteristics. Some industrial firms are organized around products, others around markets.

An industrial firm offering several products to the same general market might choose the *product manager form* of organization. A *market-centered form* of organization might be more appropriate for a firm that offers the same product to a number of different industry or market segments. With either form, the responsibilities of product management are the same: to plan, coordinate, and control the firm's product mix. Top management must foster the proper environment for product planning.[6]

Industrial vs. Consumer Goods Product Managers: A Comparative Profile

Compared with their consumer goods counterparts, industrial product managers:

1. have more experience and also are responsible for more products;

2. report greater levels of contact with distribution, sales, and final consumers, but interface less with marketing research, advertising, and advertising agencies;

3. are more involved in decisions about pricing and distribution and somewhat less in promotion and marketing research decisions.

---

[6] For a comprehensive discussion of organizational design see B. Charles Ames, "Dilemma of Product/Market Management," *Harvard Business Review* 49 (March–April 1971), pp. 66–74; see also, Barton Weitz and Erin Anderson, "Organizing the Marketing Function," in Ben M. Enis and Kenneth J. Roering, eds., *Review of Marketing 1981* (Chicago: American Marketing Association, 1981), pp. 134–142.

> Industrial goods product managers do not differ from consumer goods product managers on role conflict, job tension, and job satisfaction. Product managers with industrial goods responsibilities do, however, report a lower level of role clarity—the extent to which they receive and understand information needed to perform their assigned function.
>
> Role clarity for these managers may be enhanced by increasing the level of contact with marketing research and reducing the number of products that the typical manager handles.

Source: J. Patrick Kelly and Richard T. Hise, "Industrial and Consumer Goods Product Managers Are Different," *Industrial Marketing Management*, 8 (November 1979), pp. 325–332.

Industrial Product Policy

Product policy involves "the collection of decisions concerning the products and services which the company offers."[7] Three levels of decisions fall into the product policy area: (1) item, a specific version of the product; (2) product line, a group of related items; and (3) product mix, a collection of all items and product lines marketed by the company.[8]

This section is concerned with management of the existing industrial product line. First, different types of industrial product lines are described. Second, decisions about the management of the existing product line are examined. Determining the length of the product line and the strategic position of specific items in the line are emphasized.

Types of Product Lines Defined

Since product lines of industrial firms differ from those of consumer firms, classification is useful. There are four types of industrial product lines:[9]

1.   *Proprietary or catalog items* are offered only in certain configurations and produced in anticipation of orders. Product line decisions concern the addition, deletion, or repositioning of products within the line.

---

[7] Shapiro, *Industrial Product Policy*, p. 17.

[8] Philip Kotler, *Marketing Management: Analysis, Planning and Control*, 2d ed. (Englewood Cliffs, N.J.: Prentice-Hall, Inc., 1972), p. 439, reported in Shapiro, *ibid.*, p. 1.

[9] Shapiro, *ibid.*, pp. 17–21.

2. *Custom-built items* are offered as a set of basic units, with numerous accessories and options. A lathe manufacturer may offer several basic sizes, with a range of options (such as different motor sizes) and accessories for different applications. Here the marketer offers the organizational buyer a set of building blocks. Product line decisions center on offering the proper mix of options and accessories.

3. *Custom-designed items* are created to meet the needs of one or a small group of customers, perhaps a unique unit, such as a power plant or a specific machine tool. Some items produced in relatively large quantities, such as an aircraft model, may fall into this category. The product line is described in terms of the company's capability, and the consumer buys that capability. Ultimately, this capability is transformed into a finished good.

4. *Industrial services* do not include an actual product. The buyer is purchasing a company's capability, in an area like maintenance, technical service, or management consulting.

All types of industrial firms confront product policy decisions, whether they offer physical products, pure services (no physical product), or a product/service combination. Each product situation presents unique problems and opportunities for the marketer; each draws upon a different type of capability. Industrial product strategy rests on the intelligent utilization of corporate capability.[10]

Services: Special Marketing Requirements

Services are a special marketing case. First, the marketer must not only stimulate demand for the service, but also manage the buyer–seller interaction. Often, the services are rendered by personnel not assigned to the marketing function. The interactions between buyer and seller during the consumption process critically influence the client's perception of both the quality of the service rendered and the service company. Thus, the marketing of services in the industrial setting requires an interactive marketing function.[11] Such buyer–seller interactions are equally important to marketers whose product offering is augmented with services (technical support). The relationship between representatives of buyer and seller influences the client's image of the total "product."

Second, the marketing of services requires closer management of supply and demand than the marketing of products. While products can

[10] *Ibid.*, pp. 18–20.

[11] Christian Gronroos, "An Applied Theory for Marketing Industrial Services," *Industrial Marketing Management* 8 (January 1979), pp. 45–50; see also, Albert L. Page and Michael Siemplenski, "Product Systems Marketing," *Industrial Marketing Management* 12 (April 1983), pp. 89–99.

be held in inventory, services, not being storable, can only be produced when they are demanded. Kenneth Uhl and Gregory Upah note:

> *Demand for service must be met or lost. Demand that is met increases reve-nue; demand that is missed contributes no revenues. Service capacity that is avail-able at the wrong time or place and, in turn, is idle continues to incur costs, but not revenues. This is the essence of managing without storage.*[12]

Developing Service Strategies By focusing exclusively on the product, many industrial firms overlook the potential of service in gaining a strong competitive advantage. As emphasized, the industrial marketer must examine the total "product"—which includes any supplementary services. Post-purchase service is especially important to buyers in such industrial product categories as computers, machine tools, and custom-designed components. Responsibility for service support, however, is often diffused through departments like application engineering, cus-tomer relations, or service administration. Significant benefits accrue to the industrial marketer who can design the product service support in-dustrial buyers need.

Segmentation via Service[13] The benefits of segmentation based on product service support can be isolated in the office automation market. The servicing needs of a small business buying a new word processor are quite different from those of a corporate office buying several. At the single machine office, equipment failure spells disaster. Work ceases and the office staff invests precious time locating a replacement. This market segment demands a low equipment failure rate and minimum downtime per failure. Support costs are of secondary importance.

The multi-machine office, by contrast, is equipped to handle a "reasonable" equipment failure rate. Disruptive costs are low when a ma-chine fails because another word processing unit can be used to maintain the work flow. Support costs, however, are more important to this market segment. Here procurement managers are interested in minimizing maintainence and repair costs over the life of the office equipment.

A service strategy that emphasizes responsive on-site field repair would be especially important to the single-machine segment; the multi-machine segment might prefer a lower cost service support system such as remote diagnosis plus modular exchange. Industrial marketers using the latter system might set up a central service center that users can call toll free for help in diagnosing equipment problems. Once the problem is identified, the user can make the repairs by exchanging defective modules with functioning modules.

---

[12] Kenneth P. Uhl and Gregory D. Upah, "The Marketing of Services: Why and How Is it Different?" in Jagdish N. Sheth, ed., *Research in Marketing*, Vol. 6 (Greenwich, Conn.: JAI Press, Inc., 1983), pp. 231–257.

[13] This section is largely based on Milind M. Lele, "Product Service: How to Protect Your Unguarded Battlefield," *Business Marketing* (June 1983), pp. 69–76.

Figure 10.2   Product Map for a Paper Product

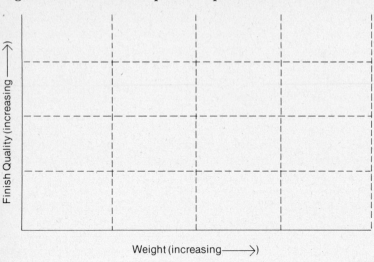

Source: Benson P. Shapiro, *Industrial Product Policy: Managing the Existing Product Line* (Cambridge, Mass.: Marketing Science Institute, 1977), p. 99. Reprinted by permission.

Blending Product and Service Strategies   Because product service support can be vital to industrial marketing strategy, it must be considered early in the new product development process. A firm that plans to emphasize remote diagnosis service must design the product in modules with "user-friendly" diagnostics. That is, the design of the product must match the design of the service support system. Unfortunately, many industrial firms fail to consider service strategies until just before the market introduction of a new product.

Managing the Existing Product Line [14]

Two important questions challenge the manager of an existing product line: (1) How many items should be in the line? and (2) How should the products be positioned? The concept of a product space (mapped in Figure 10.2) is particularly valuable in dealing with these questions. Product attributes of importance to buyers form the boundaries of the space. Once the most important attributes are identified, a product space is shaped to exhibit the positions of company and competitor products in the lines. Benson Shapiro's model for managing the existing product line draws on the concepts of "product space" and "product position-

[14] Shapiro, *Industrial Product Policy*, pp. 5–10.

Figure 10.3   Product Map for a Paper Product

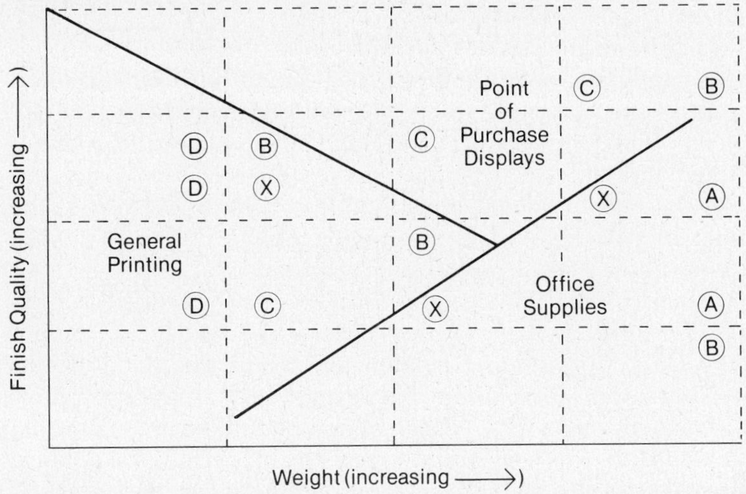

Source: Benson P. Shapiro, *Industrial Product Policy: Managing the Existing Product Line* (Cambridge, Mass.: Marketing Science Institute, 1977), p. 101. Reprinted by permission.

ing."[15] *Product positioning* represents the place that a product occupies in a particular market; it is found by measuring organizational buyers' perceptions and preferences for a product in relation to its competitors.[15] The product map for a paper product (Figure 10.2) has two dimensions (product attributes): weight and finish quality.

The product-space map forces the manager of the existing product line to identify the product attributes of central importance to customers and to evaluate the position of individual items in the line relative to competitors. This deepens the manager's understanding of the firm's existing product market position. Figure 10.3 presents a more detailed product map showing: (1) existing items in the product line, (2) the items in competitors' product lines, and (3) market segments or prospects. Firm D's product line converges on the general printing market segment and includes low weight papers with low to moderately high finish quality.

Product Line Length   The product map helps answer the question of product line length. Should an item be added at a particular point in the product space? Deleted? According to Benson Shapiro, "the line is, in essence, viewed as a collection of separate items, with the length deter-

15 Yoram J. Wind, *Product Policy: Concepts, Methods, and Strategy* (Reading, Mass.: Addison-Wesley Publishing Company, 1982), pp. 74–81.

mined intuitively on an item-by-item basis."[16] The industrial product manager seeks a group of items that capitalizes on the firm's capabilities and has meaning in the marketplace.

To facilitate the analysis of individual items, the product manager should gather the data on price, direct cost, output per unit time, and place in the production cycle within the industrial marketing intelligence system.[17] The manager may add data on production, marketing costs, and demand patterns. By subjectively estimating the impact of a new item or the effect of the elimination of an item on the rest of the product line, the decision support system (see Chapter 5) can be used to simulate the profit results of product line changes.[18]

Once a model is developed and refined, it can be extended. For example, the relationships between the product line and other components of the marketing mix can be analyzed. Thus, the model begins with simple, but important, building blocks and, through testing and refinement, evolves in stages to be of high operational value to the product planner. In addition to its conceptual appeal, the model also has political value; it deals with issues that often create conflict between manufacturing and marketing.[19]

Planning Industrial Product Strategy

Formulating a strategic marketing plan for an existing product line is the most vital part of the company's marketing planning efforts. Having identified product attributes of importance to organizational buyers, and having compared the firm's product offerings with those of competitors, the planner now considers the current and projected performance of the total product mix. Two tools for planning industrial product line strategy are: (1) experience curve analysis and (2) the product evaluation matrix. Each is of value in illuminating the firm's current product/market position as well as establishing clear strategy directions.

Experience Curve Analysis

The experience curve is based on the discovery that costs (measured in constant dollars) decline (usually from 10 to 30 percent) by a predictable and constant percentage each time *accumulated* production experience (volume) is doubled.[20] The experience curve effect encompasses a broad

---

[16] Shapiro, *Industrial Product Policy*, p. 102.

[17] *Ibid.*, pp. 102–103.

[18] For a comprehensive discussion of decision support systems, see John D. C. Little, "Decision Support Systems for Marketing Managers," *Journal of Marketing* 43 (Summer 1979), pp. 9–25.

[19] Shapiro, *Industrial Product Policy*, p. 103.

[20] William J. Abernathy and Kenneth Wayne, "Limits of the Learning Curve," *Harvard Business Review* 52 (September–October 1974), pp. 109–119; see also, Staff of the Boston Consulting Group, *Perspectives on Experience* (Boston: Boston Consulting Group, Inc., 1972).

Figure 10.4   A Typical Experience Curve (85 percent)

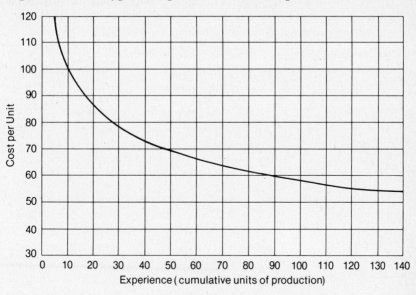

Source: Adapted from *Perspectives on Experience* (Boston: Boston Consulting Group, Inc., 1968), p. 13. Reprinted by permission.

range of costs—manufacturing, marketing, distribution, and administrative. Clearly, a manager thinking to extend the product line must examine whether the item will converge on the firm's manufacturing and marketing experience.

The curve illustrated in Figure 10.4 is an 85 percent experience curve: With every doubling of experience, costs per unit drop to 85 percent of their original level—a 15 percent reduction in costs for every doubling of cumulative production. Different products and industries experience different "learning" rates (75 percent, 80 percent, 85 percent). The experience curve phenomenon has been supported in studies of numerous industries, including chemical, steel, paper, and electronics. The concept appears to be especially relevant in high technology markets such as semiconductors and computer memories.[21]

Sources of the Experience Curve Effect   To capitalize on the experience effect, the industrial product manager must understand *why* costs decline with accumulated experience. George Day and David Montgomery isolate three major sources of the experience effect:[22]

[21] George S. Day, "Analytical Approaches to Strategic Market Planning," in Ben M. Enis and Kenneth J. Roering, eds., *Review of Marketing 1981* (Chicago: American Marketing Association, 1981), pp. 92–94.

[22] George S. Day and David B. Montgomery, "Diagnosing the Experience Curve," *Journal of Marketing* 47 (Spring 1983), pp. 44–58.

1.   *Learning by doing* encompasses the increased efficiency of labor as workers of all types become more adept at a job as they repeat it. Similarly, learning includes the discovery through greater job specialization of better methods to organize work flows.

2.   *Technological improvements* include economies derived from new production processes, product standardization, product redesign, or changes in resource mix, such as automation replacing labor.

3.   *Economies of scale* arise from increased efficiency due to size. "Seldom does an increase in throughput require an equivalent increase in capital investment, size of sales force, or overhead functions."[23] Scale also creates the potential for other cost reductions such as volume discounts and the division of labor.

The experience curve is strategically relevant to the industrial product manager only when these three effects are influential features of the environment.[24] The fact is that as experience is gained, costs do not necessarily decline. Costs that are not carefully managed will inevitably rise. Experience merely gives management the opportunity to seek cost reductions and efficiency improvements. A thorough effort must be made to exploit the benefits of experience. Product standardization, new manufacturing processes, labor efficiency, work specialization—these are a few of the many areas that must be examined to capitalize on the experience curve effect.

Experience curve analysis is also of value when product line modifications are being considered. Often, two or more products in the firm's line share a common resource or involve the same production or distribution activity. Such shared experience is significant because the costs of one item in the product line can be reduced even more because of accumulated experience with other product line items.[25]

Experience Curve Analysis and the Product Life Cycle[26]   Experience curve analysis helps the industrial marketer to project costs and prices. Here the experience curve can be linked to the product life cycle to provide a base for developing industrial product strategy. The life cycle of a product is often described in terms of stages: introduction, growth, maturity, and decline. The product life cycle shows trends in primary demand and patterns of competition.

Selected stages of the product life cycle are joined with an industry price experience curve in Figure 10.5. It shows, not a single company,

---

[23] *Ibid.*, p. 47.

[24] *Ibid.*, pp. 44–58.

[25] Derek F. Abell and John S. Hammond, *Strategic Market Planning: Problems and Analytical Approaches* (Englewood Cliffs, N.J.: Prentice-Hall, Inc., 1979), pp. 125–127.

[26] This section is largely based on Day and Montgomery, "Diagnosing the Experience Curve," pp. 50–52. For a related discussion, see Hans B. Thorelli and Stephen C. Burnett, "The Nature of Product Life Cycles for Industrial Goods Businesses," *Journal of Marketing* 45 (Fall 1981), pp. 97–108.

Figure 10.5   Product Life Cycle Stages and the Industry Price Experience Curve

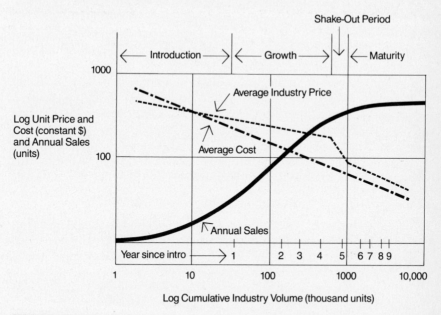

Source: George S. Day and David B. Montgomery, "Diagnosing the Experience Curve," *Journal of Marketing*, 47 (Spring 1983), p. 51. Reprinted by permission of the American Marketing Association.

but the industry cumulative experience across a hypothetical product life cycle. In the introductory stage, the average industry price is below current costs. The demand stimulus generated by a low price, together with experience-based cost declines, leads to a level of profitability much higher than a price policy oriented to covering all costs immediately.[27]

Experience curve analysis also provides insights into the relative ease or difficulty with which competitors can enter a product market. If early entrants into a market have significant cost advantages, the experience effect could create substantial entry barriers. In fact, moderate experience slopes seem to create a greater entry barrier than very small or very large slopes.[28] (Consistent with our earlier discussion, a large slope might reflect that costs per unit decline by 40 percent with each doubling of experience, while a small slope reflects a decline of 10 percent.) Small experience effects provide only a minor advantage to the innovator;

[27] Bruce Robinson and Chet Lakhani, "Dynamic Price Models for New Product Planning," *Management Science* 21 (June 1975), pp. 1113–1122; see also, Robert J. Dolan and Abel P. Jeuland, "Experience Curves and Dynamic Demand Models: Implications for Optimal Pricing Strategies," *Journal of Marketing* 45 (Winter 1981), pp. 52–73; and Louis E. Yelle, "Industrial Life Cycles and Learning Curves: Interaction of Marketing and Production," *Industrial Marketing Management* 9 (October 1980), pp. 311–318.

[28] Michael A. Spence, "The Learning Curve and Competition," *The Bell Journal of Economics* 12 (Spring 1981), pp. 49–69.

large experience effects often make it relatively easy for late entrants to catch up with early entrants, perhaps by learning from the innovator's mistakes or by carefully analyzing the design of the innovator's product. Where there was a moderately sloped experience curve, entry tended to cease after three or four firms entered. Of course, competitive entry patterns are also shaped by the growth rate of the market and the average margins available to new entrants.

As illustrated in Figure 10.5, a shake-out period can occur between the growth and maturity stages of the product life cycle, triggering a sharp break in the industry price trend. Among the factors that can spawn a shake-out of competitors are: a slowing growth rate; a market leader cutting prices to stem erosion of market share; or aggressive late entrants relying on price cuts as the prime force in their marketing strategy. Overall, competitive cost differentials steadily narrow as the market matures.

Strategic Relevance   An astute industrial marketing manager must understand the strengths and limits of particular strategic planning tools. Experience curve analysis and the product life cycle concept are useful in exploring the underlying dynamics of a market and in evaluating alternative product strategy scenarios. They cannot be used to prescribe simple strategies. They are organizing frameworks.

First, experience curve analysis, as emphasized, is relevant when learning, technology, and economies of scale are important features of the environment. If these are present, the industrial product manager can use experience curve analysis to capitalize on opportunities for improved efficiency within the firm, or to better understand competitive behavior.

Second, the product life cycle is a versatile framework for organizing hypotheses about strategy alternatives and "directing management attention toward anticipation of the consequences of the underlying dynamics of the served market."[29] The concept does not provide generalized universal industrial marketing strategies.

High and Low Market Share Success   The analysis of experience curves and product life cycles inevitably raises questions about the value of market share to profitability, whether of a firm or a single product. The rationale for using market share as a performance measure rests on the growing body of research finding that market share is positively and strongly related to product profitability.[30] Increases in market share are accompanied by a decline in marketing costs as a percentage of sales, a

---

[29] George S. Day, "The Product Life Cycle: Analysis and Applications Issues," *Journal of Marketing* 45 (Fall 1981), p. 65; see also, Charles W. Hofer, "Toward a Contingency Theory of Business Strategy," *Academy of Management Journal* 18 (December 1975), pp. 784–810.

[30] Robert D. Buzzell, Bradley T. Gale, and Ralph G. M. Sultan, "Market Share—A Key to Profitability," *Harvard Business Review* 53 (January–February 1975), pp. 97–106; and Robert D. Buzzell and Frederik D. Wiersema, "Successful Share-Building Strategies," *Harvard Business Review* 59 (January–February 1981), pp. 135–144.

higher profit margin, and higher-quality products that demand a higher price. It also appears that market share is even more significant for industrial products than for consumer products, especially for infrequently purchased goods like capital equipment.[31]

Does the research evidence spell doom for the low market share business? No. A study of successful low market share firms makes it clear that failure to be a market leader need not damage a company's financial position.[32] Over 600 manufacturing companies with a pretax return on investment of at least 20 percent were identified. Most produced frequently purchased components or supplies for the industrial market. The competitive strategies followed by these successful low market share firms had the following common characteristics:

1. selectivity—rather than copying the market share leader or trying to serve everyone, these firms concentrated on particular market segments and particular bases of competition, such as product quality and price;

2. a reputation for high quality;

3. medium to low relative prices complementing high quality;

4. low total costs, achieved by producing only a narrow line of products for a particular market segment and spending less than competitors on R&D, advertising, new product introductions, and related activities.

Clearly, the strategy of an industrial firm must be tailored to its distinctive capabilities and the requirements of its competitive environment.

In this section we have discussed a strategic planning tool of value to the industrial product strategist: experience curve analysis. Drawing on recent research, we then moved to an analysis of the significance of market share as a product performance measure. We now consider a procedure for developing a marketing strategy for an industrial product.

Pitney Bowes, Inc.: Shifting Product Line Focus

After unsuccessful diversification into high technology businesses such as electronic cash registers, Pitney Bowes, Inc. is placing renewed emphasis on the product line that the firm

---

[31] Buzzell, Gale and Sultan, "Market Share," pp. 97–106. For a comprehensive review of market share research studies, see, Yoram Wind and Vijay Mahajan, "Market Share: Concepts, Findings and Directions for Future Research," in Ben M. Enis and Kenneth J. Roering, eds., *Review of Marketing 1981* (Chicago: American Marketing Association, 1981), pp. 31–42.

[32] Carolyn Y. Woo and Arnold C. Cooper, "The Surprising Case for Low Market Share," *Harvard Business Review* 60 (November–December 1982), pp. 106–113.

knows best: mailing equipment. Over 50 percent of the firm's annual revenues (over $1 billion) is derived from mailing equipment, including electronic scales which weigh mail, and mail inserting and folding equipment.

These products are sold to a diverse array of commercial accounts and the postal service by 7,000 salespersons. Pitney Bowes has attempted to capitalize on its market leadership in mailing equipment by entering the copier, word processing, and dictaphone businesses. Facing formidable competition, the firm abandoned the manufacturing of copiers in favor of marketing cheaper Japanese models. Likewise, stiff competition faced the firm's entry into the word processing market. Management concedes that the new office equipment businesses will be sold if they fail to become profitable.

The new emphasis on traditional product lines is evidenced by the dominant share of the R&D budget being devoted to mailing equipment products and the significant proportion of capital expenditures going into automated manufacturing systems for the mailing business. The United States and European sales organizations are being realigned to further capitalize on Pitney Bowes' traditional product lines.

Source: "Pitney Bowes: Betting on Postal Equipment to Deliver Future Profits," *Business Week* (January 10, 1983), pp. 91–92.

Product Evaluation Matrix

Once the strategic position of a product in a particular industry environment has been examined with the help of the experience curve, the manager of an existing line has at hand a second planning aid—a matrix approach developed by Yoram Wind and Henry Claycamp.[33] The matrix is a comprehensive tool integrating three product performance measures: sales, market share, and profitability. As with any other strategic planning tool, a strong market focus is needed; each product must be examined in relation to the segment it serves.

The approach has five levels providing increasingly specific guidance to product management decisions (Table 10.1). The first step is to

[33] Yoram Wind and Henry J. Claycamp, "Planning Product Line Strategy: A Matrix Approach," *Journal of Marketing* 40 (January 1976), pp. 2–9; see also, Yoram Wind, *Product Policy*, pp. 129–132.

Table 10.1   Levels of Analysis and Specificity of Guidance

Specificity of Guidance	Nature of Analytical Operation
Lowest	1. Current product position on industry sales, company sales, market share, and profitability.
	2. Projected product position on sales, market share, and profitability, assuming no major changes in the firm's marketing activities, competitive action, and environmental conditions.
	3. Projected product position on sales, market share, and profitability under alternative marketing strategies (conditional forecast), assuming no major changes in competitive action and environmental conditions.
	4. The above plus diagnostic insights into the competitive structure and the effectiveness of the firm's marketing activities.
Highest	5. Projected product position on sales, market share, and profitability under alternative marketing strategies, anticipated competitive action, and alternative environmental conditions (based on computer simulation).

Source: Yoram Wind and Henry J. Claycamp, "Planning Product Line Strategy: A Matrix Approach," *Journal of Marketing* 40 (January 1976), p. 8. Reprinted by permission of the American Marketing Association.

profile the product in terms of industry sales, company sales, market share, and profitability. The analysis then proceeds through an evaluation of alternative product strategies under different competitive and external conditions. The approach forces a manager to ask the right questions about the product's current and future position.[34]

Using the Matrix   The approach is operationalized using the product evaluation matrix illustrated in Figure 10.6. Company sales are illustrated on the horizontal scale and industry sales on the vertical scale. Each is divided into three categories: growth, stable, or decline. Then profitability is classified as below-target, target, or above-target, and market share as dominant, average, or marginal. The categories for sales, market share, and profitability are merely illustrative and can be varied as company and industry situations vary. The manager also must define the intervals for each category, for example, for market share: less than 10 percent—*marginal*; 10 to 24 percent—*average*; over 25 percent—*leading*. The appropriate intervals are heavily dependent upon the standards for the firm and the industry.[35]

Two products are positioned in the evaluation matrix in Figure 10.6. Product A enjoys a solid performance position, a dominant market share, growing company sales, and profitability at target in a growing industry. Product B, on the other hand, occupies a place in a stable industry with marginal market share, stable company sales, but profits below

[34] Wind and Claycamp, *ibid.*, pp. 3–4.
[35] *Ibid.*, p. 4.

Figure 10.6   The Product Evaluation Matrix

Company Sales Industry Sales	Profit-ability Market Share	Decline			Stable			Growth		
		Below Target	Target	Above Target	Below Target	Target	Above Target	Below Target	Target	Above Target
Growth	Dominant								A	
	Average									
	Marginal									
Stable	Dominant									
	Average						B₁			
	Marginal				B					
Decline	Dominant									
	Average									
	Marginal									

Source: Structure provided by Yoram Wind and Henry J. Claycamp, "Planning Product Line Strategy: A Matrix Approach," *Journal of Marketing*, 40 (January 1976), pp. 2–9. Reprinted by permission of the American Marketing Association.

target. The appropriate marketing strategy for product A would be to maintain the favorable market position. For product B, however, alternative strategies must be considered. The performance of product B should be considered under a number of different marketing strategy scenarios. The sales, market share, and profitability of product B next year are conditional upon the strategy decisions that are made now. Thus, a conditional forecast of product performance should be made for each alternative marketing strategy. The decision support system, the heart of the industrial marketing intelligence system, facilitates the evaluation of these for each market segment.

In search of the most desirable marketing strategy, the industrial marketer would also consider potential competitive behavior and projected external conditions. This comprehensive analysis of strategy options and likely external events may lead to a strategy that improves the market position of product B, as illustrated as product B₁ in Figure 10.6.

Developing a Strategy   Wind and Claycamp identify five strategy options that might be appropriate for a particular product or for an entire line.[36]

1.   Maintain the product and its marketing strategy in the present form.

[36]*Ibid.*, p. 8.

2.   Maintain the present form of the product but change its marketing strategy.

3.   Change the product and alter the marketing strategy.

4.   Drop the product or the entire product line.

5.   Add one or more new items into a line or add new product lines.

The product evaluation matrix allows the industrial product manager to systematically address two basic questions: "Where are we now?" and "Where should we go from here?" The product evaluation matrix provides management with the information required to analyze each product's performance; the combined analyses constitute the firm's current product portfolio. The tool can likewise be applied to assess competitive products, using the same procedure to monitor competitive strategy and performance.

Monitoring Competition   A particular product strategy will stimulate a response from the market, and a corresponding response from competitors. Failure to give proper attention to the competitive environment can severely damage the accuracy of product performance forecasts.

Based on an empirical analysis of management decision variables in over 1,200 business components, Craig Galbraith and Dan Schendel developed a typology of strategies for both the consumer and industrial firms in the sample.[37] Their research suggests that four strategies best fit the nature of competition in the industrial market:

- Strategy Type 1 (Low Commitment—17 percent of sample): These firms are unwilling to commit significant resources to their products, relative to both current and expected market growth rates; they give little or no attention to strengthening their strategy positions by improving product quality or increasing promotional expenditures.
- Strategy Type 2 (Maintenance—49 percent of sample): These firms follow a cost-minimizing strategy, attempting to reduce the overall costs of manufacture and distribution while maintaining market position.
- Strategy Type 3 (Growth—25 percent of sample): These firms have a strong commitment to their products, making significant investments in promotion and product line extensions. Prices are above the industry norm.
- Strategy Type 4 (Niche—9 percent of sample): These firms have a specialized strategy geared to a particular market segment, and emphasize a high product quality, narrow product line, and high pricing policies.

[37] Craig Galbraith and Dan Schendel, "An Empirical Analysis of Strategy Types," *Strategic Management Journal* 4 (April–June 1983), pp. 153–173.

Of course, the nature of competition can vary by industry, country, geographical region within a country, or product. However, by examining the strategy posture of key competitors, industrial product managers customize their own strategies to fit the competitive environment. The product evaluation matrix provides not only a framework for developing product strategy, but also a structure for tracing the strategy followed by competitors.

To this point, we have concentrated on managing the firm's existing product line using two strategic planning tools of particular value: experience curve analysis and the product evaluation matrix. Often, the analysis of existing products uncovers market opportunities that could be profitably tapped with new products.

The New Product Development Process

The high expectations ascribed to new products are often not fulfilled. Worse, many new industrial products fail.[38] While the definitions of "failure" are somewhat illusive, research suggests that 30 to 40 percent of industrial products do fail.[39] While there may be some debate over the number of failures, there is no debate over the fact that a new product rejected by the market constitutes a substantial waste to the firm and to society.

Spotting a Technological Winner

Eastman Kodak, Lockheed, IBM, and the management teams of other corporations all failed to recognize the major technological opportunity that xerographical copying presented. These firms were among the many that turned down the chance to participate with the small and unknown Haloid Company in refining and commercializing this technology. In the end, Haloid pursued it alone and transformed this one technological opportunity into the Xerox Corporation. Among the "tales of high tech," this will remain a classic.

What steps can managers take to improve their chances of spotting a technological winner? George White and Margaret Graham suggest that the central determinants of innova-

---

[38] See, for example, Robert G. Cooper, "New Product Success in Industrial Firms," *Industrial Marketing Management* 11 (July 1982), pp. 215–223.

[39] *Ibid.* See also, David S. Hopkins, *New Product Winners and Losers* (New York: The Conference Board, 1980).

tion success are technological potency and business advantage, and that a strategic assessment of a particular innovation strategy must consider four criteria.

■ *Inventive merit*—a truly significant inventive concept will employ a new combination of scientific principles to relieve or avoid major constraints inherent in the previous art. Example: the transistor allowed the elimination of the heated cathode of a vacuum tube, permitting reductions in the size and weight of portable radios.

■ *Embodiment merit*—this constitutes the value of the physical form given to an inventive concept. Substantial engineering is required to shape a concept into a product. Thus, the embodiment of an invention can often provide as many opportunities for improvement as the invention itself. Example: Boeing capitalized on jet engine technology by embodying a swept-wing design in its planes, thus allowing maximum jet speed advantage.

■ *Operational merit*—the more innovative the technology in question, the more likely that existing business operations will be superseded. Example: the small size of transistor radios, coupled with improved product reliability, removed the need for a franchised dealer service network. New marketing channels were created.

■ *Market merit*—by comparing the advantages of the innovation with direct product competitors, the market merit of technology can be assessed. Example: jet aircraft offered significant revenue opportunities for purchasers because airline passengers overwhelmingly preferred the fast, quiet, vibration-free jet over piston engine planes. This triggered increased demand for long-range travel.

Source: George R. White and Margaret B. W. Graham, "How to Spot a Technological Winner," *Harvard Business Review*, 56 (March–April 1978), pp. 146–152.

Since new product ventures can represent a significant risk as well as an important opportunity, new product development requires systematic thought. This section examines key components of that process: (1) organization of the new product development effort, (2) sources of new product ideas, (3) new product review and evaluation, and (4) determinants of new product success and failure.

Table 10.2   Interfunctional Involvement in the New Product Development Process

Stages in New Product Development Process	Organizational Function					
	Top Management	Marketing	Finance	R&D	Manufacturing	Other (Legal, Procurement, Personnel, etc.)
1. Setting objectives or selection of internal vs. external development	Primary responsibility	Inputs	Inputs	Inputs		
2. Idea generation		Primary responsibility	Inputs	Primary responsibility	Inputs	Inputs
3. Idea/concept screening	Approval	Primary responsibility	Primary responsibility		Inputs	Inputs
4. Concept/product development	Approval	Primary responsibility		Primary responsibility	Inputs	Inputs
5. Concept/product evaluation	Approval		Primary responsibility			Inputs
6. Final product evaluation & development of marketing strategy	Approval	Primary responsibility	Primary responsibility	Inputs	Inputs	Inputs
7. Continuous evaluation of product performance	Approval	Primary responsibility	Inputs	Inputs	Inputs	Inputs
8. Product introduction		Primary responsibility			Primary responsibility	

Source: Yoram Wind, "Marketing and Other Business Functions," in Jagdish N. Sheth, ed., *Research in Marketing*, Vol. 5 (Greenwich, CT: JAI Press, Inc., 1981), pp. 256–257. Reprinted by permission of the publisher.

New Product Organizational Arrangements

The strong need for integrated effort between marketing, production, engineering, and other functional areas in developing industrial marketing strategy has been emphasized throughout this volume. Highlighting the interfunctional nature of the new product development process, Table 10.2 describes the role of key functional areas in bringing a new industrial product to fruition.

While the specific design of the new product function is dependent on many factors, such as company size and structure, three are worthy of some consideration.[40]

1. *New product committee*—a top management committee of representatives from marketing, production, accounting, engineering, and other areas who review new product proposals. While not involved in actual development, the committee must evaluate new product plans.

2. *New product department*—a department created in many large firms to generate and evaluate new ideas, direct and coordinate development, and implement field testing and precommercialization of the new product. The department head generally has substantial authority and access to top management.

3. *New product venture team*—"a group specifically brought together from various operating departments and charged with the responsibility of bringing a specific product to market or a specific new business into being."[41] The composition of the venture team changes as the venture passes through various stages of development. The venture team may be dissolved once a product is established.

Regardless of the particular organizational scheme adopted, careful coordination and control are needed during and after the development process.

Sources of New Product Ideas

The industrial marketer should be alert to new product ideas, sources both within and outside the company. Internally, new product ideas may flow from salespersons who are close to customer needs, research and development specialists who are close to new technological developments, and top management who know the company strengths and weaknesses. Externally, ideas may come from channel members like distributors, customers, or an assessment of competitive moves.

[40] Philip Kotler, *Marketing Management: Analysis, Planning and Control*, 3d ed. (Englewood Cliffs, N.J.: Prentice-Hall, Inc., 1976), pp. 199–201.

[41] *Ibid.*, p. 200.

Ideas from Customers   Eric von Hippel challenges the traditional view that marketers typically introduce new products to a passive market.[42] His research suggests that industrial customers often develop the idea for a new product and even select the supplier to make that product. The customer is responding to the perceived *capability* of the industrial marketer, rather than to a specific physical product. This points up the need for involving the customers in new product development and promoting corporate capability to consumers (idea generators).

Some computer manufacturers have devised approaches to seek, evaluate, and sell user-developed software products. Once potentially marketable software packages are evaluated, the computer firm negotiates an agreement with the customer (developer) that often involves a one-time flat fee payment. The software product is then marketed to other customers who may find it valuable to their operations.[43]

Screening New Product Ideas

Before committing resources to the costly process of transforming an idea into a finished industrial product, the idea must be scrutinized. Firms that fail to properly assess market needs, the level of demand potential, production requirements, the nature of the buying process, the aggressiveness of competitors, the extent of technical service requirements, and related factors are doomed to failure. To guard against such omissions, many industrial marketers have developed elaborate screening procedures to evaluate new products from several perspectives.

New Product Profile Chart   Monsanto Corporation uses a new product profile chart (Table 10.3). The major points for analysis include: (1) financial aspects, (2) marketing and product aspects, (3) production and engineering aspects, and (4) research and development.[44] The chart analyzes the profit, sales, and cash requirements of a venture, and the degree to which the potential product fits with the production, research and development, and marketing capabilities of the firm. The quality of this review often rests squarely on the firm's knowledge of market needs; it is often necessary to examine each potential application separately.[45] Each application may represent a distinct market segment with special requirements.

To implement the new product profile chart, firms may rate each dimension on a scale, for example, the dimension of "marketability to present customers":

---

[42] Eric von Hippel, "Get New Products from Customers," *Harvard Business Review* 60 (March–April 1982), pp. 117–122; see also, von Hippel, "Successful Industrial Products from Customer Ideas," *Journal of Marketing* 42 (January 1978), pp. 39–49; and von Hippel, "Has Your Customer Already Developed Your Next Product?" *Sloan Management Review* 18 (Winter 1977), pp. 63–74.

[43] von Hippel, "Get New Products from Customers," p. 118.

[44] John S. Harris, "New Product Profile Chart," *CHEMTECH* (September 1976), pp. 554–562.

[45] For example, see Pierre Chenu and David L. Wilemon, "A Decision Process for New Product Selection," *Industrial Marketing Management* 3 (1973), pp. 33–46.

Table 10.3   A New Product Profile Chart

Financial Aspects	Return on investment (before taxes)
	Estimated annual sales
	New fixed capital payout time
	Time to reach estimated sales volume
Marketing and	Similarity to present product lines
Product Aspects	Effect on present products
	Marketability to present customers
	Number of potential customers
	Suitability of present sales force
	Market stability
	Market trend
	Technical service
Production and	Required corporate size
Engineering Aspects	Raw materials
	Equipment
	Process familiarity
Research and	Research investment payout time
Development Aspects	Development investment payout time
	Research know-how
	Patent status

Source: Reprinted with permission from "New Product Profile Chart," by John S. Harris, CHEMTECH (September 1976), p. 559. Copyright © 1976 the American Chemical Society.

-2 entirely different customers

-1 some present customers

$+1$ mostly present customers

$+2$ all present customers

The assignment of numerical values provides a visual indication of the level of desirability of the venture on each criterion. Since the selected criteria are not equally important and vary by project, this weighting system does not replace the need for managerial judgment. Management must weigh the relative importance of each criterion to a specific project before evaluating the project on that dimension.

Determinants of New Product Success and Failure

A prime limitation of the new product checklist approach is that neither the screening criteria nor their relative importance are empirically derived. Which factors are most important in determining the success or failure of the new product?

The Determinants of Success   According to Robert Cooper, three factors appear to be crucial to new product success.[46] The *level of product*

---

[46] Robert G. Cooper, "The Dimensions of Industrial New Product Success and Failure," *Journal of Marketing* 43 (Summer 1979), pp. 93–103; see also, Cooper, "Identifying Industrial New Product Success: Project NewProd," *Industrial Marketing Management* 8 (April 1979), pp. 124–135; and Cooper, "Why New Industrial Products Fail," *Industrial Marketing Management* 4 (1975), pp. 315–326.

uniqueness and superiority is the most important. Highly innovative products that improve on competing offerings gain a strong differential advantage. They offer clear benefits, such as reduced customer costs, and are of a higher quality (e.g., more durable) than the products of competitors.

Market knowledge and marketing proficiency are pivotal in new product outcomes. As might be expected, industrial marketers with a solid understanding of market needs, buyer behavior, and market potential, who combine this with a well-conceived launch promotion, are likely to succeed.

Technical and production synergy and proficiency emerge as the third important new product dimension. When industrial firms can draw upon a compatible technical and production resource base and proficiently pass through the stages of the new product development process (e.g., product development, prototype testing, pilot production, and production start-up), their products succeed.

A Good Idea—But?

A large supplier of industrial grease developed a novel approach for delivery, storage, and use by customers. Manufacturers typically purchase grease in 400-pound drums, and buy the drums ten at a time. The drums are bulky and nonreturnable, thus creating a disposal problem. Used on the production line, a significant amount of grease is wasted because supervisors like to begin each shift with a full drum to avoid stopping a production line mid-shift to replace an empty.

The supplier's functional innovation involved the delivery of grease in bulk by a specially designed delivery truck capable of pumping grease directly into the customer's plant. The customer would have to install some relatively inexpensive equipment to use the system—several 5,000-pound capacity tanks, plus piping from the reservoirs to greasing stations on the production line. Substantial savings would accrue— lower purchase cost, reduced drum-handling and waste, and reduced production line shut-downs.

The new system failed. Why? Salespersons were poorly trained in describing the advantages and cost savings of the system. Customers were uneasy about making the low-cost plant alterations required. The industrial marketer had failed to understand the buying motives and potential objections of buyers. The delivery truck remains idle.

Source: Peter M. Banting, "Unsuccessful Innovation in the Industrial Market," *Journal of Marketing*, 42 (January 1978), pp. 99–100.

Barriers to Success   Three barriers to success uncovered by Cooper are likewise worthy of emphasis:

1.   a high-priced product, relative to competition, with no economic advantage to the customer;

2.   a dynamic market with many new product introductions;

3.   a competitive market, where customers are already well-satisfied.[47]

Overall, this research points up the critical importance of the *product* in industrial marketing strategy. Likewise, new industrial product success is heavily dependent upon a strong market orientation blended with strong technical/production capability.

The New Industrial Product Adoption Process

The industrial product adoption process has been conceptualized as having two basic stages: (1) the initiation stage and (2) the implementation stage.[48] Each has important substages, briefly described in Table 10.4.

What is the importance of various information sources throughout the adoption process? In general, trade journals or mass communication tends to be the most significant information source in triggering awareness of a new industrial product. Salespersons and the proposals they provide dominate the remaining phases.[49] The organizational buyer's need for information of all types increases as the product moves from initiation to implementation, particularly when a buyer perceives great risk in adoption.

As informal information sources, opinion leaders within the organization are important, especially in the later stages of the process.[50] In contrast to other organizational members, opinion leaders tend to have more exposure to trade journals.

In designing promotional support for a new industrial product, the marketer must recognize the specific roles of advertising and personal selling. Technical and trade journals stimulate awareness; personal selling identifies the key buying influences and satisfies their information needs. Both are fundamental to successful launching of a new product.

---

[47] Cooper, "The Dimensions of Industrial New Product Success and Failure," p. 101.

[48] Gerald Zaltman, Robert Duncan, and Jonny Holbek, *Innovations and Organizations* (New York: Wiley-Interscience, 1973), p. 158; see also, Urban B. Ozanne and Gilbert A. Churchill, "Adoption Research: Information Sources in the Industrial Purchasing Decision," in Robert L. King, ed., *Marketing and the New Science of Planning* (Chicago: American Marketing Association, 1968), pp. 352–359.

[49] Frederick E. Webster, Jr., "Informal Communication in Industrial Markets," *Journal of Marketing Research* 7 (May 1970), pp. 186–189; see also, Ozanne and Churchill, *ibid.*, pp. 352–359.

[50] John A. Martilla, "Word-of-Mouth Communications in the Industrial Adoption Process," *Journal of Marketing Research* 8 (May 1971), pp. 173–178. For related research, see, John A. Czepiel, "Word-of-Mouth Processes in the Diffusion of a Major Technological Innovation," *Journal of Marketing Research* 11 (May 1974), pp. 172–180.

Table 10.4   Stages of Innovation Adoption Process in Organizations

Stage	Description
I. Initiation Stage	
1. Knowledge-awareness substage	Organizational decision makers perceive that there is a discrepancy between desired and actual performance.
2. Formation of attitudes toward the innovation substage	Important attitudinal dimensions include the openness of organizational decision makers to the innovation and their perception of the potential for innovation.
3. Decision substage	Information concerning the potential innovation is evaluated. If organizational members are highly motivated to innovate or their attitudes are highly favorable toward innovation, implementation is likely.
II. Implementation Stage	
1. Initial implementation substage	Organization makes first attempt to utilize the specific innovation.
2. Continued-sustained implementation substage	A successful and relatively trouble-free initial implementation increases the likelihood that the innovation will be further utilized by the organization.

Source: Adapted from Gerald Zaltman, Robert Duncan, and Jonny Holbek, *Innovations and Organizations* (New York: Wiley Interscience, 1973), p. 158.

Formulating New Industrial Product Strategy[51]

Market knowledge and marketing proficiency characterize industrial firms that launch successful new products. Before a commitment is made to a particular product design, the industrial product planner must know the key buying criteria or specifications that target market segments use in purchasing such products. Unless the new product has those specifications, it will not be accepted by the market.

The Industrial Market Response Model

Jean-Marie Choffray and Gary Lilien provide a model for dealing with new product strategy decisions. Their approach, the industrial market response model, has four components, each directly relating organizational buying behavior to a key product strategy area:

1.   *Awareness model*—relates the level of marketing effort invested in an industrial product to the probability that an individual in an organization will be aware of the product.

---

[51] This section is largely based on Jean-Marie Choffray and Gary L. Lilien, "Assessing Response to Industrial Marketing Strategy," *Journal of Marketing* 42 (April 1978), pp. 20–31; see also, Jerome E. Scott and Stephen K. Keiser, "Forecasting Acceptance of New Industrial Products with Judgment Modeling," *Journal of Marketing* 48 (Spring 1984), pp. 54–67.

2.   *Acceptance model*—relates product "design characteristics to the likelihood that an organization will find the product feasible."[52] Of the organizations surveyed about the purchase of industrial air conditioning systems 50 percent require that the cost per ton be less than $988.

3.   *Individual evaluation models*—"relate evaluation of product characteristics to the preferences of each category of decision participants."[53] The criterion of key importance to those evaluating industrial air conditioning systems varied by job category. Plant managers were most interested in operating costs, top managers in up-to-date technology, and heating and air conditioning consultants in noise level in the plant.

4.   *Group decision model*—relates group choice to the preference of the members composing the group.

Estimating Market Share and Sales

By using this model as a framework for gathering market information, the industrial marketer can forecast market share and sales for the new product:

Market Share =

> Fraction of potential buying organizations aware of the new product

> × Fraction of organizations for whom the product is feasible (given that they are aware)

> × Fraction of organizations who prefer the product to other alternatives (given that they are aware and the product is feasible for them)

Sales =

> Market potential (opportunity) × Projected market share

Evaluating Product Design Scenarios

The marketer can also use the industrial market response model to evaluate the impact of alternative product designs on market share and sales. By comparing competitive product designs to the specifications preferred by key market segments, the industrial marketer can isolate

[52] *Ibid.*, p. 24.
[53] *Ibid.*, p. 25.

market segments that are inadequately served.[54] Furthermore, customer perceptions of possible product design trade-offs can be examined. Consider the case of a marketer planning a new high-speed packaging system. The marketer must ask how much potential buyers would be willing to pay for incremental improvements in processing speed.

Designing New Product Strategy

This approach can also be used to improve pricing decisions and to develop and target advertising and sales presentations. Advertising messages might emphasize the particular product benefits sought by each member of the buying center. Recall from our discussion in Chapter 4 that messages consistent with the organizational buyer's frame of reference are much more likely to be retained. Clearly, the development of sound industrial marketing strategy rests on knowledge of organizational buying behavior. By linking the two, the industrial market response model makes an important contribution.

Summary

The product is usually the most important component of the industrial marketing mix. Conceptualizing a "product" must go beyond mere physical description to include all of the benefits and services that provide consumer satisfaction. Industrial product lines can be broadly classified into: (1) proprietary or catalog items, (2) custom-built items, (3) custom-designed items, and (4) industrial services. Industrial product management can best be described as the management of capability.

Managing the existing industrial product line involves two considerations: (1) How many items should be in the line? (2) How should they be positioned in the market? The concepts of *product space* and *product positioning* facilitate analysis of these strategic questions. In monitoring product performance and formulating marketing strategy, the industrial marketer can profitably use two planning aids: the *experience curve analysis* and the *product evaluation matrix*.

Sustained growth is dependent on innovative products that respond to existing or emerging consumer needs. Before committing substantial resources to a new product idea, the proposed venture must be carefully screened. An idea that successfully passes the screening must progress through a well-organized and integrated development process. In turn, marketers must understand that innovative products are carefully evaluated by consumers before they are adopted. The *industrial*

---

[54] For a comprehensive discussion of the supporting methodology, see Jean-Marie Choffray and Gary L. Lilien, "DESIGNOR: A Decision Support Procedure for Industrial Product Design," *Journal of Business Research* 10 (June 1982), pp. 185–197.

market response model is a valuable tool in isolating appropriate product design features and developing responsive marketing strategies.

Discussion Questions

1. Robots with programmed mechanical arms can be used to perform monotonous, uncomfortable, or dangerous production tasks. Robots can pour molten aluminum, load and unload heavy stacks of laminated parts for motors, paint refrigerators as they move down the assembly line, and perform related functions. Yet acceptance of these machine tools has been slow. As a new industrial product, what steps could the industrial marketer take to speed the rate of adoption of this technology? What barriers would the marketer of robots face, in your view?

2. Distinguish among catalog items, custom-built items, custom-designed items, and services. Explain how marketing requirements vary across these classifications.

3. Illustrate how the concept of product space can be used by the industrial marketer to determine the composition and length of the product line.

4. Experience curve analysis and the product life cycle concept are useful tools in exploring the dynamics of a market but cannot be used to derive simple strategy prescriptions. Explain.

5. Valves play an important role in American industry. They control the flow of liquids in refineries, chemical plants, and electric power facilities. Thus, valve manufacturers serve many users, including chemical-petrochemical complexes, refineries, pipelines, and electric power plants. How much effort should be invested in the development of special valves for the nuclear power market? Given the political, legal, and general uncertainties that surround this potentially large market, what steps should the product planner take?

6. In your position as product manager for the Bronson Machine Tool Company, you must develop a marketing program for existing product X. In determining how much to spend and where to spend it, you are given information on the sales, profitability, and market share of product X for the past five years. You are also provided with a forecast of general economic conditions. Describe how you would develop a strategy for product X.

7. The Los Angeles Motor Works Company has had numerous new products fail in the industrial market. As a marketing consultant, you have been asked to develop a new product review guide for screening new product ideas. To be useful, this checklist or guide

should be relatively concise and highlight priority areas in order of importance. Present your recommendations.

8. The ultimate criterion in adding a new item to an industrial firm's existing product line should be that product's contribution to overall company profits. Agree or disagree? Support your position.

9. Critique this statement: "Industrial products and consumer products fail for the same basic reasons."

10. Some industrial product managers argue that their prime function is to market the "capability" of their firm, rather than physical products. Do you agree or disagree? Explain.

C·H·A·P·T·E·R
11

Industrial Marketing Channels:
Channel Participants

The channel of distribution is the marketing manager's bridge to the market. In managing the industrial channel, many decisions made directly influence the effectiveness and efficiency of marketing strategy. The appropriateness and quality of these decisions often hinge on an understanding of the role and function of various industrial channel participants.

After reading this chapter, you will have an understanding of:

1. *the alternative forms of industrial distribution channels;*
2. *the nature and function of industrial distributors;*
3. *the role of manufacturers' representatives;*
4. *the special problems and opportunities that these and other types of channel members present for the industrial marketer.*

The marketing channel is the primary means through which the industrial firm finds new prospects for its products, communicates with existing customers, and physically delivers the product. The selection of the best channel to accomplish these ends is challenging because: (1) the alternatives are numerous; (2) marketing goals differ; and (3) the variety of industrial market segments often means that separate channels must be employed concurrently.

Motorola, a supplier of semiconductors, added an additional channel—manufacturers' representatives—to their distribution network.[1] The company already used two distinct channels: (1) its own sales force to call on large accounts where the volume justifies the selling expense; and (2) a vast system of franchised distributors that maintain local market inventories, service repeat orders, and provide credit. The reps were added in an attempt to penetrate the market of small- and medium-sized accounts. The rep, who works on a fixed commission and can spread costs over a range of complementary products, allows Motorola to reach certain markets where the market potential would not justify a direct sales force.

How many channels is just one of the many decisions to be made about this aspect of industrial marketing. Other questions are whether to use intermediaries; if so, how many and what kind; how to effectively administer the channels; and how to design an efficient physical distribution network. This chapter will focus on channel participants, exploring the role of intermediaries in industrial channels, the nature of their operations, and some of the trends expected to develop with intermediaries. The discussion will concentrate on industrial distributors and manufacturers' representatives, because they are the primary industrial intermediaries. Chapter 12 will examine the design of industrial channels and the nature of the management process required to achieve channel objectives. Chapter 13 concentrates on physical distribution. Together they provide a comprehensive treatment of distribution management.

The Industrial Channel

The link between manufacturers and customers is the channel of distribution. The channel accomplishes all the tasks necessary to effect a sale and to physically deliver products to the customer. These tasks include *making contact* with potential buyers, *negotiating*, *contracting*, *transferring* title, *communicating*, *arranging financing*, *servicing* the product, and providing local *inventory*, *transportation*, and *storage*. These tasks may be performed entirely by the manufacturer, entirely by intermediaries, or shared between them. The customer may even undertake some of these

[1] Denny Mosier and Richard Bombrick, "Distributors Evaluate Motorola Rep Network," *Electronic News*, 22 (December 9, 1977), p. 26.

Figure 11.1   Channel Alternatives in the Industrial Market

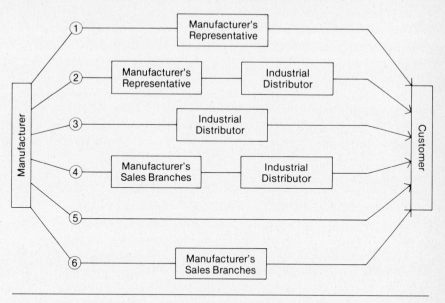

Source: Adapted from William M. Diamond, Distribution Channels for Industrial Products (Columbus, Ohio: Bureau of Business Research, College of Administrative Sciences, The Ohio State University, 1963), p. 56.

functions; for example, customers granted certain discounts may agree to accept larger inventories, and the associated storage costs. One of the most challenging aspects of industrial marketing is to allocate the tasks so as to insure effective performance. The tasks *must always be performed* as the product moves from manufacturer to customer. Figure 11.1 shows the different ways that industrial channels can be structured. The first four channel structures are *indirect*; that is, some type of intermediary is involved in selling and/or handling the products. Channels five and six are *direct*: here the manufacturer must accomplish all the marketing functions necessary to create a sale and deliver products to the customer.

The basic issue in channel management then is how to structure the channel so that the tasks are performed optimally. One alternative is for the manufacturer to do it all.

Direct Distribution

Direct distribution, very common in industrial marketing, is a channel strategy that does not use intermediaries. The manufacturer's own sales force deals directly with the customer, and the manufacturer has full responsibility for performing all the necessary channel tasks. Direct distribution is often required in industrial marketing because of the nature of the selling situation. A case in point is Rockwell International's Municipal and Utility (M&U) Division.[2] The M&U Division markets water, gas, and parking meters to local municipalities and gas utilities through a direct sales organization. The direct sales approach is viable because the customers are large and well-defined; the customers often insist upon direct sales; sales involve extensive negotiations with high level utility management; and control of the selling job is necessary to insure proper implementation of the total product package and to guarantee a quick response to market conditions. In fact, using a direct sales force allowed the company to change its price schedule five times in six months and to negotiate all the important contracts required by those price changes.

Changing Markets = Changing Channels

Prior to the mid-1970s, Ingersoll-Rand sold most of its heavy duty tools direct to customers, most of whom were "heavy industry." However, broader acceptance of pneumatic tools for a variety of maintenance and production applications began to be evidenced in the mid-1970s and since that time, the firm has marketed their air tool product line through distributors. The distributors are able to effectively provide fast local service to the broadened market.

— market acceptance + knowledge of product

Source: Ronald D. Michman, "Trends Affecting Industrial Distributors," *Industrial Marketing Management*, 9 (July 1980), p. 214.

Indirect Distribution

Indirect distribution uses one or more types of intermediaries. Industrial channels typically include fewer types of intermediaries than do consumer-goods channels. In a study of 156 industrial manufacturers in 220 product lines, six types of channels accounted for 100 percent of sales.[3] *Manufacturers' representatives* and *industrial distributors* account for most of the business handled through indirect industrial channels.

Many Channels Often Required

As Figure 11.1 indicates, various combinations of intermediaries and direct selling may be employed in the industrial channel. In fact, one manufacturer may use various combinations. The need to use more than one

[2] P. H. Luckett, "Industrial Marketing Channels: Direct or Indirect?" in Bruce J. Walker and Joel B. Haynes, eds., *Marketing Channels and Institutions, Selected Readings* (Columbus, Ohio: Grid Publishing, Inc., 1978), p. 53.

[3] Robert J. Haas, *Industrial Marketing Management* (Boston: Kent Publishing Company, 1982), p. 201.

channel arises from the different marketing tasks demanded either by product variety or market segmentation.

Timeplex, a manufacturer of time division multiplexes, sells through manufacturers' reps.[4] Reps offer low cost distribution, expertise in data communications, and complementary product lines that facilitate the sale of Timeplex products. The key buying influence in the end-user firm, to which reps direct their attention, is the data communications manager. As Timeplex commercializes products now on the drawing board, the key buying influence will be the electronic data processing manager. The president of Timeplex says that "there is an iron wall between the data communications manager and the electronic data processing manager. Because our reps may be unable or reluctant to call on the EDP manager, we'll probably have to consider building a parallel direct sales organization." The buying process in customer and potential user firms determines the most effective channels.

Use of indirect channels of distribution is common for a wide variety of industrial products. The quality and performance of the intermediaries have a critical impact on whether the industrial marketer achieves his or her goals. An important first step in designing and managing industrial marketing channels is to fully comprehend the nature and role of industrial intermediaries.

Participants in the Industrial Channel

The types of industrial intermediaries are distributors, manufacturers' agents (reps), jobbers, brokers, and commission merchants. Distributors and reps handle the vast preponderance of industrial sales made through intermediaries. This section of the chapter will emphasize the role of each in the industrial channel, the nature of their operations, and some of the trends expected to occur for both.

Distributors

Industrial distributors are the most pervasive and important single force in industrial distribution channels. They number close to 12,000 and in 1982 accounted for almost $43 billion in sales volume.[5] A recent study of plant purchasing agents and other buying influences revealed that few, if any, deal with fewer than five industrial distributors and over 50 percent buy from between 30 and 100.[6] What accounts for the unparalleled position of the distributor in the industrial market? What role do distributors play in the industrial distribution process?

[4] Thayer C. Taylor, "A Line Turn for Timeplex," *Sales & Marketing Management*, 117 (February 5, 1979), p. 5.

[5] "37th Annual Survey of Distributor Operations," *Industrial Distribution*, 73 (July 1983), p. 37.

[6] "Distributor Image: '79—How the Buyer Sees It," *Industrial Distribution*, 69 (February 1979), p. 54.

Table 11.1   Profile of an Industrial Distributor

Annual Sales:	$2,057,000
Gross Profit:	27%
Net Profit:	2.5%
ROI:	7.0%
Average Inventory:	$300,000–400,000
Sales per Employee:	$140,000
Number of Employees:	15
Number of Outside Salespersons:	4
Number of Inside Salespersons:	3
Warehouse Square Feet:	12,000
Number of Branch Locations:	1
Ownership:	Independent
Average Salary*:	
Outside Salesperson	$27,400
Inside Salesperson	$16,500

*"NIDA/SIDA Survey Shows Pay Scales Among Distributors," *Industrial Distribution*, 72 (February 1982), p. 14.

Source: "'82 Sales Down Sharply, Profits Flat," *Industrial Distribution*, 73 (July 1983), pp. 37–45.

Industrial Distributor Profile

Table 11.1 provides a concise view of the "typical" industrial distributor. Distributors are generally small, independent businesses serving narrow geographic markets. Sales average about $2.1 million, although some top $200 million. Net profits are relatively low as a percentage of sales (2.5 percent); return on investment averages 7.0 percent. The typical order is small. Orders are generated by a sales force of four "outside" and three "inside" salespersons. Outside salespersons make regular calls on customers and handle normal account servicing and technical assistance. Inside salespersons complement these efforts, processing orders and scheduling delivery. Their primary duty is to take telephone orders. Most distributors operate from a single location, but some approach the "supermarket" status with as many as 130 branches.

The Distributor's Responsibilities

Contact and Product Availability   The industrial distributor's primary responsibility to the manufacturers represented is to contact present and potential customers and to make the product available—with all required supporting activities like delivery, credit, order processing, and technical advice—as quickly as economically feasible.[7] The products distributors sell—cutting tools, power tools, pipe, bearings, handling equipment, fasteners, electric equipment, welding equipment, maintenance,

[7] Frederick E. Webster, Jr., "The Role of the Industrial Distributor in Marketing Strategy," *Journal of Marketing*, 40 (July 1976), p. 13.

repair, and operating supplies, and contractor supplies—are generally those that buyers need quickly to avoid production disruptions. Thus, the distributor is vital in informing customers of product availability and ensuring that the products are available when needed.

Industrial users who buy through distributors, like the manufacturers who sell through distributors, recognize the importance of the distributor. As *Purchasing* magazine says, "The 'middlemen' image that for years haunted industrial distributors is vanishing—at least in the eyes of professional buyers. Purchasing execs now view distributors more as extensions of their buying arms than as conduits from prime manufacturers."[8] An effective distributor can provide the user with valuable technical advice, suggest substitute products, promote standardization of operating and maintenance supplies, and help in negotiating price and credit terms with the manufacturer. Table 11.2 shows how a group of purchasing agents rated the importance of various services provided by distributors. Note the importance assigned to the distributor's ability to provide adequate inventories, reliable delivery, and reasonable prices.

Repair Service   With complex equipment like construction and mining machines, repair service is crucial to the customer–supplier relationship. The local distributor is in the best position to provide this service. Because of the cost of repair facilities and the distance from manufacturer to customer, the local industrial distributor can economically supply the vital repair service required for many industrial products.

Marketing through distributors may be the only cost-effective sales method for many manufacturers. Escalation in the cost of gasoline, hotels, and on-the-road meals has made the cost of a direct sales force prohibitively high for many industrial firms.[9] The response has been to shift increasing business and selling responsibilities to the industrial distributor.

Distributor Assembly and Light Manufacturing   Bulk transportation of sheet steel, tubing, or pipe is much less expensive than shipment of finished products. In addition, inventory costs can be reduced substantially by maintaining unfinished inventory in bulk rather than in individual inventories of finished products. As a result, many distributors buy in bulk, and do assembly and manufacturing as product orders are received. One saw manufacturer now ships rolled band saw stock to distributors who cut, weld, and finish the product to customer specifications.[10] Distributor assembly and manufacturing reduces distribution costs and allows for more careful tailoring of the final product to customer requirements. *— depending on sophistication of prod.*

[8]"Middlemen Are Out, Problem Solvers Are In," *Purchasing*, 78 (September 13, 1978), p. 62.

[9]Ronald H. Michman, "Trends Affecting Industrial Distributors," *Industrial Marketing Management*, 9 (July 1980), p. 214.

[10]Webster, "Perceptions of the Industrial Distributor," *Industrial Marketing Management*, 4 (1975), p. 260.

Table 11.2   How Purchasing Agents Rate Distributor Services

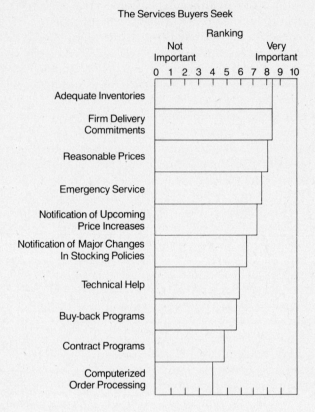

The Services Buyers Seek

Using Distributors in Industrial Channels

The role of industrial distributors, and why they are used, is well illustrated by James Hlavacek and Tommy McCuistion. Some considerations in deciding how best to use industrial distributors are:

1.   *Is the product suitable to distribution by industrial distributors?* Suitable products enjoy a large customer base, require local stocking and delivery, involve small-quantity sales,

are purchased at low management levels, and require rapid delivery and service.

2. *Does the distributor match the target market?* Different distributors should be used to reach different target industries; the language, requirements, and applications of the product in each segment are different.

3. *How will industrial distribution job change over the product life cycle?* Introduction demands distributors with excellent selling skills and high-level technical assistance. As the product matures, becoming more standardized and better-known, delivery time and price become more important than specialized knowledge; expanding the number of general distributors in nonexclusive territories should then be considered.

4. *How will product specification be achieved?* Manufacturers must assign their own personnel to getting the company's products specified or qualified at an OEM's headquarters, government office, or buying agency's headquarters. Once the product is specified, distributors can take the orders.

Source: James D. Hlavacek and Tommy J. McCuistion, "Industrial Distributors—When, Who and How?" *Harvard Business Review,* 61 (March–April 1983), pp. 96–101.

In summary, the industrial distributor is a full-service intermediary who takes title to the products sold, maintains inventories, provides credit, delivery, wide product assortment, and technical assistance, and may even do light assembly and manufacturing. Although the distributor is primarily responsible for contacting and supplying present customers, industrial distributors also solicit new accounts and work to expand the market. Products handled by industrial distributors are generally established products—typically used in manufacturing operations, repair and maintenance—with a broad and large demand.

Classification of Distributors

To select the most appropriate distributor for a particular channel, the marketing manager must understand the diversity in distributor operations. Industrial distributors vary according to product lines handled and user markets served. Firms may be ultraspecialized (e.g., selling only to municipal water works) or carry a broad line of generalized industrial products. Generally, however, three primary distributor classifications are recognized.

General Line Distributors   General line distributors cater to a broad array of industrial needs. They stock an extensive variety of products and could be likened to the supermarket in consumer-goods markets. Some general line distributors maintain separate departments, such as abrasives and power tools, to meet specific needs of certain important accounts.

Specialists   Specialists focus on one or a few related lines. Such a distributor may handle only power transmission equipment—belts, pulleys, and bearings. The most common specialty is fasteners, while specialization also occurs in cutting tools, power transmission equipment, pipe, valves, and fittings. There is a trend toward increased specialization as a result of increasing technical complexity of products and the need for higher levels of precision and quality control.

Combination House   A combination house operates in two markets: industrial and consumer. Such a distributor might carry electric motors for industrial customers and hardware and automotive parts to be sold through retailers to final consumers.

   The selection of a distributor will depend upon the manufacturer's requirements. The general line distributor offers the advantage of "one-stop" purchasing to the manufacturer's potential customers. If a high level of service and technical expertise is not required, the general line distributor is a strong choice. The specialist, on the other hand, provides the manufacturer with a high level of technical capability and a well-developed understanding of complex user requirements. Fasteners, for instance, are handled by specialists because of the strict quality control standards users impose.

The Distributor as a Valuable Asset

The quality of a firm's distributors often is the difference between a highly successful marketing strategy and an ineffective one. Good distributors are prized by customers, making it all the more necessary to continually strive to engage the best in any given market. Distributors often provide the only economically feasible way of obtaining comprehensive market coverage.

Industrial Distributors: Selected Problems

Although industrial distributors are a vital part of the channel for many industrial products and offer significant benefits to suppliers, marketing through them may raise important problems. Because many distributors are small—a great many have sales volumes under $2 million—they often do not employ sophisticated management practices. This makes it difficult to maintain a workable partnership between supplier and distributor.

Some manufacturers have found their distributors to be overly committed to their customers, so that the distributor substitutes a less expensive competitive brand for their own brand. Distributors view themselves as *independent* entrepreneurs, with their main obligation being to their customers (regardless of how their actions affect a particular manufacturer).[11] Manufacturers, on the other hand, view the end-user/customer as *their* customer, and distributors as only a facilitating link.

Sources of Conflict   The difference in perceptions is manifested in other areas. One constant source of controversy involves competing lines carried by the distributor. Another is large accounts, which the manufacturer often prefers to serve directly. Distributors feel cheated if they are not allowed to reap the economic rewards associated with these large accounts. Inventory commitments are still another area of friction. The manufacturer views inventory as essential to good customer service, while the distributor is sensitive to the impact of inventory on profitability.

Toward a Manufacturer–Distributor Partnership

The manufacturer–distributor relationship is not always a smooth one. The potential for channel conflict is sometimes high. The manufacturer has no single solution to the problem.

The manufacturer–distributor relationship should be viewed as a partnership, and the manufacturer should provide all the assistance that is economically feasible to enhance the distributor's performance. Increased margins or financial assistance may be necessary to stimulate the distributor to increase inventory levels. Some manufacturers give distributors a percentage commission on sales to large accounts in their territory—easing the "large account" conflict.

Manufacturers must also know how their sales force can aid distributors' performance. Holo-Krome, a manufacturer of fasteners and couplers, practices the partnership philosophy by pledging to distributors that it will supply practically everything in its catalog immediately from factory stocks.[12] If a distributor phones in an order before 10 a.m., it will be shipped the same day. As a result, distributors can reduce inventories as well as improve service to the end user.

The supplier's salespeople can be used to strengthen the distributor's operations through joint sales calls or supplemental technical support. Training programs for distributor personnel may not only improve distributor effectiveness, but also strengthen the bond between distribu-

---

[11] Webster, "Perceptions of the Industrial Distributor," p. 261.

[12] "What About the Vendor Behind the Distributor?" *Purchasing*, 89 (November 6, 1980), p. 63.

tor and manufacturer. The partnership will be made more effective through the coordinated efforts of the manufacturer to strengthen and support distributors in their weak areas.

Distributor Dynamics: The Future

One of the great challenges of industrial marketing is to understand the dynamics of a market and forecast its directions. This is particularly true for industrial distributors in a time of change. A gradual evolution in distributor operations has begun (Table 11.3). From the manufacturer's perspective—size, chain operations, and specialization—pose important questions for future channel management strategies. Each trend suggests that a higher level of distributor sophistication, market power, and customer loyalty will result, making careful distributor selection even more important for manufacturers.

Industrial distributors are a powerful force in industrial channels and all indications point to an expanded role for them. The manufacturer's representative is an equally viable force in the industrial channel.

Table 11.3 New Directions in Distributor Operations

Changes in Distributor Operations	Impacts on the Manufacturer
Increased Size	Larger, more sophisticated distributors are emerging.* By utilizing only a few, well-managed distributors, a manufacturer can reduce logistics costs and enhance effectiveness of dollars spent on training and support. However, fewer effective uncommitted distributors will be available.
Distributor "Supermarkets"	A growing force in the industrial field is the distributor chain operation—a chain of distributor outlets with regional or nationwide coverage, owned and managed by a single corporation.** Chains may carry multiple brands as opposed to exclusive brand coverage; offer private labels in some product categories; use price discounting; provide wide and deep inventories. The net result will probably be a shift of market power to the chain.
Specialization	The tendency to concentrate efforts in restricted product lines appears to be growing. Specialist distributors offer buyers expert knowledge, effective service and a variety of brands in a narrow line. From the manufacturer's viewpoint, these factors may serve to link the end-user customer more closely to the distributor. Again, a shift of market power and control to the specialist distributor is a likely result. Since the manufacturer's brand may be only one of several carried by the specialist, the industrial marketer may be forced to provide price concessions, heavy advertising, or direct sales controls to the end user to maintain a viable market position.

*Ronald H. Michman, "Trends Affecting Industrial Distributors," *Industrial Marketing Management*, 9 (July 1980), p. 214.

**J. G. Main, "The Chain Reaction That's Rocking Industrial Distribution," *Sales and Marketing Management*, 114 (February 23, 1976), pp. 41–45.

Table 11.4   Profile of a Manufacturers' Representative

Company:	Alcon Company
Location:	Middle Village, N.Y.
End-User Market:	Bottling and Brewery Industry
Estimated Average Commission:	10–14 percent
Geographic Market Coverage:	New England states, New York, New Jersey, Pennsylvania, Maryland, Delaware, eastern Virginia
Products Handled:	Bottle filler replacement parts: conveyors, case packers, uncasers, warmers and reusers, empty bottle inspectors, plastic cases, decappers.
Companies Represented:	P. T. Barkmann & Sons, Hamrich Manufacturing, McQueen Technology Corp., Bacmis Volckening, Inc., Kyowa America Corp.

Manufacturers' Representatives

For many industrial marketers who need a strong selling job with a technically complex product, manufacturers' representatives, or reps, are the only cost-effective answer. Reps are salespeople who work independently, representing several different companies in the same geographic area, selling noncompeting but complementary products. Table 11.4 provides a concise sketch of a typical rep.

The Rep's Responsibilities

A rep is a knowledgeable salesperson who works independently (or for a rep company) and neither takes title to nor holds inventory of the products handled. (Some reps do, however, keep a limited inventory of repair and maintenance parts.) The rep's forte is expert product knowledge coupled with a keen understanding of the market and customers covered. Reps are usually limited to defined geographical areas; thus, a manufacturer seeking nationwide distribution will usually work with several rep companies.

The Rep–Customer Relationship   Reps are the selling arm for manufacturers—making contact with customers, writing orders, following up the orders, and linking the manufacturer with the industrial end users. While paid by the manufacturer, the rep is also important to the customers served. Often, the efforts of a rep during a customer emergency (e.g., an equipment failure) mean the difference between continuing or stopping production. Most reps are thoroughly experienced in the industries that they serve; they can offer technical advice while enhancing the customer's leverage with suppliers in securing parts, repair, and delivery. The rep also provides customers with a continuing flow of information on innovations and trends in equipment, as well as in the industry as a whole.

Table 11.5   Manufacturers' Representatives' Commission

| | 1982 Commissions | |
Industry	Average High	Average Low
Automotive, OEM	6.7%	3.8%
Chemicals	11.8%	7.2%
Computers	14.7%	9.7%
Controls and Instrumentation	17.5%	9.2%
Electronic Products	15.1%	8.1%
Fasteners	7.2%	4.9%
Office Supplies and Equipment	15.0%	6.3%
Paper	9.0%	4.3%
Steel Mills	6.7%	4.1%

Source: "S&MM's 1983 Survey of Selling Costs," *Sales and Marketing Management* (February 21, 1983), p. 74.

Commission Basis   Reps are paid a commission on sales; the commission varies by industry and by the nature of the selling job. Table 11.5 provides a sample of average rep commission percentages for various industries in 1982. They range from a low of 3.8 percent for automotive to 17.5 percent for controls and instrumentation. Percentage commission compensation is very attractive to manufacturers because they have few fixed sales costs. Reps are paid only when orders are generated. Because reps are paid on commission, they are motivated to generate high sales levels—another fact appreciated by the manufacturer.

Experience and an Expanding Role   Reps possess sophisticated product knowledge and typically have extensive experience in the markets they serve. Most reps develop their field experience while working as a salesperson for a manufacturer. They are motivated to become reps from a desire to be independent, and to reap the substantial monetary rewards possible on commission. The number of reps appears to be growing. Based on trade association membership, the number of manufacturers' representatives has grown from 2000 in 1970 to 5000 in 1978.[13]

When Reps Are Used

Large and Small Firms   Small- and medium-sized firms generally have the greatest need for a rep, although many large firms—for example, Dow Chemical and W. R. Grace—use them. The reason is primarily economic: Smaller firms could not justify the expense of maintaining their own sales force. The rep provides a very efficient means to obtain total

[13]Loel Kuzela, "How to Work with a Manufacturer's Rep," *Industry Week*, 197 (April 17, 1978), p. 40.

market coverage, with costs incurred only as sales are made. The quality of the selling job is often very good as a result of the rep's prior experience and market knowledge.

Limited Market Potential   The rep also plays a vital role where the manufacturer's market potential is limited. A manufacturer may use a direct sales force in heavily concentrated industrial markets where the demand is sufficient to support the expense, and cover less dense markets with reps. Because the rep carries several lines, expenses can be allocated over a much larger sales volume.

Servicing Distributors   Reps may also be employed by a firm that markets through distributors. When a manufacturer sells through hundreds of distributors across the United States, reps may sell and service the distributors. Here again, the use of reps eliminates the need for a direct sales force.

Reducing Overhead Costs   Sometimes the commission rate paid to reps exceeds the cost of a direct sales force, yet the supplier continues to use reps. This policy is not as irrational as it appears. Assume, for example, that costs for a direct sales force approximate 8 percent of sales, while a rep's commission rate is 11 percent. The use of reps in this case is often justified because of the hidden costs associated with a sales force. First, the manufacturer does not provide fringe benefits or a fixed salary to reps. Second, the costs of training a rep are usually limited to those required to provide product information. Thus, the use of reps eliminates rather significant overhead costs.

The cost advantage associated with reps would appear to be increasing as the costs associated with making a sales call escalate. McGraw-Hill's study of selling costs indicates that the cost of a sales call for industrial firms in 1981 reached $178.[14] Expenses associated with the sales call include salary, commissions, bonuses, travel, and entertainment. The variable nature of the rep's commission enhances the position of the rep versus a company's own sales force in this kind of cost environment. Of course, using reps instead of a direct sales force is not without pitfalls.

Sources of Conflict

Degree of Effort   The use of any intermediary by a manufacturer involves a loss of control over the marketing of the product. Reps are independents, carrying a line of products to satisfy their customers. Their allegiance is to their customers, and to those products in their line that are most lucrative. Obviously, the overall sales effectiveness of reps usually does not match that of a direct sales force. A constant source of fric-

---

[14] "Sales Call Costs Explode," *Industrial Marketing*, 67 (July 1982). p. 9.

tion between the manufacturer and the rep is the amount of attention the rep is devoting to the firm's product. The rep often carries products that are easier to sell or have a higher commission rate than a particular manufacturer's product. The marketer has little control over the rep's effort.

— need to give reps support and high commissions

A Rep's Tale of Two Manufacturers

"We have represented two manufacturers for many years. Both of them are principals whose lines we took on at about the same time. The president of manufacturer A always calls when he's in town. He's in touch with me at least once a month. The national sales manager talks to me at least every other week, and the regional sales manager is in touch at least twice a week, if not more often.

"They send all of my people (including myself) birthday cards, notes of congratulations, condolences, and other communications that show us their interest and concern. There are small quota-busting gifts. We are called in to sit on their Rep Advisory Council—they involve us in the decision-making process to some degree. They exercise strong leadership, and they give us good reasons why they can't do something. They praise us when we do well; they're on our backs when we do poorly, but in a constructive way.

"I've only met the president of manufacturer B on two occasions. The national sales manager has never worked the territory, and I'm lucky if I get to see him at a show. The regional sales manager is in touch with us perhaps once a month. When I was in the hospital, I never got a card from them. We only see official correspondence and directives.

"Now I ask you. Which manufacturer am I going to drop everything for and respond to, should they both call with an emergency need? Which manufacturer is going to get more of my time?" (Based on a conversation the author had with a rep.)

Source: Edwin E. Bobrow, "Suddenly, An Urge to Boost Their Potential," *Sales and Marketing Management*, 8 (June 7, 1982), p. 38.

Commission Rate   The commission rate itself is a source of conflict between manufacturers and reps. The commission rate is critical because it influences the quality of the rep's performance. In one case in the electronic industry, a low commission rate on sales to distributors forced reps to accept small orders from end users (higher commission rate) that should have been processed through distributors. The result is that the small orders must be processed by the manufacturer, and these orders are extremely expensive. Thus, an increase in rep commissions for distributor sales would focus the rep's attention on serving distributors rather than soliciting small end-user orders.

Manufacturer's Attitudes   A final area of concern is the manufacturer's attitude toward the rep's function. Unfortunately, some firms will use a rep to develop a new territory, and as soon as sales volume is sufficient assign the territory to a direct salesperson. This does not promote long-term goodwill with reps. Although the situation may be inevitable, the long-term policy should be agreed upon in advance by the manufacturer and the rep. The dialog will strengthen the relationship between the parties and reduce the level of uncertainty that often surrounds such channel arrangements.

As with distributor relationships, the manufacturer-rep association should be viewed as a partnership. Whatever the manufacturer can do to increase the effectiveness of reps will be reflected in the long-term sales and profits of the company. The manufacturer may sometimes have to compromise on commission rates and be willing to accept whatever level of sales effort the rep can devote to the firm's products—especially if the rep is the only viable selling alternative.

Other Industrial Intermediaries

The importance of distributors and reps far outshadows that of industrial intermediaries. Jobbers, brokers, and commission merchants may, however, be a vital cog in the distribution network for certain manufacturers.

Jobbers

Jobbers typically obtain orders from industrial customers and pass them along to the manufacturers that they represent. The distinguishing feature of jobbers is that they take title to the products that they sell but do not physically handle, stock, or deliver them. The jobber's niche in the industrial marketplace is in marketing products so bulky that additional handling would be prohibitively expensive and only add to the risk of damaging the product. Thus, jobbers deal with products like coal, iron ore, lumber, and chemicals where bulk shipments in carload quantities do not necessitate any grouping and sorting by the intermediary.

Commission Merchants

Commission merchants deal with bulk commodities—usually raw materials. Typically, they do not have a permanent arrangement with their suppliers, but perform a one-time selling function. An industrial company involved in mining might ship its output to a large central market where buyers inspect the material before purchase. In this case, the commission merchant makes the product available for inspection; although commission merchants do not take title, they can negotiate prices and execute the sale for the supplier. Commission merchants provide sellers with representation in the marketplace, physical handling of goods, and completion of the transaction.

Brokers

Brokers facilitate transactions between buyers and sellers by providing information on what is demanded and what is available. Like the commission merchant, the broker operates on a more-or-less irregular arrangement. A firm desiring to sell used machinery might employ a broker to seek out potential buyers and complete negotiations leading to eventual sale. The party that engages the broker pays the commission. The broker's role is particularly important where product and market information is nonexistent or inadequate.

Summary

Industrial intermediaries can be vital to the success of the marketing strategies for many industrial products. A clear understanding of their functions, operating characteristics, and limitations is necessary to make effective decisions about their employment. Distributors and reps are the key intermediaries in most industrial channels.

Distributors provide the full range of marketing services for their suppliers, although customer contact and product availability are the functions of particular value. The trend in industrial distribution points to the growth of large distributors with multiple branch locations. Likewise, there are trends toward growing specialization and toward the use of marketing techniques previously confined to consumer-goods marketing.

Manufacturers' representatives specialize in the selling side of marketing—providing their suppliers with quality representation in the market and extensive product and market knowledge. The rep is not involved with physical distribution, leaving that burden to the manufacturers.

The relationship between the manufacturers and their intermediaries often determines the success or failure of the marketing program, but conflict often surfaces. The treatment of large accounts, the emphasis given to the supplier's products, and the termination of the relationship are often the major points of friction. An enlightened view of the channel—as a partnership—is necessary for success.

Brokers, commission merchants, and jobbers complete the tally of industrial intermediaries. These channel intermediaries are usually employed only in special situations. Comprehension of the industrial intermediary's role in the industrial channel sets the stage for the development of industrial channel strategy. Chapter 12 will examine the channel design and management process.

Discussion Questions

1. Explain how a direct channel of distribution may be the lowest cost alternative for one industrial marketer and the highest cost alternative for another competing in the same industry.

2. Why do some industrial firms find it necessary to put together a number of separate channels, using direct distribution for some sectors of the market and indirect for others?

3. Compare and contrast the functions performed by industrial distributors and manufacturers' representatives.

4. Since both industrial marketers and distributors are interested in achieving profit goals, why are manufacturer–distributor relationships characterized by conflict? What steps can the marketer take to reduce the level of conflict and thus improve channel performance?

5. What product/market factors lend themselves to the use of manufacturers' representatives?

6. Manufacturers' representatives often offer this complaint: "If I do an excellent job in building demand for the manufacturer's products in my market area, I will be replaced by a company salesperson. The uncertainty makes it difficult for me to commit too much time to any one industrial firm." What steps can the industrial marketer take to remove this uncertainty and strengthen the relationship with reps?

7. Describe the functions performed by: (a) jobbers, (b) commission merchants, and (c) brokers in the industrial channel of distribution.

8. Given the rising cost of recruiting, training, and deploying a company sales force, will industrial firms give more emphasis to industrial distributors and manufacturers' representatives in the years ahead? Support your position.

C·H·A·P·T·E·R
12

Industrial Marketing Channels: Design and Management

Designing and managing the industrial channel is a challenging and ongoing task. The industrial marketer must insure that the firm's channel is properly aligned to the needs of important market segments, yet must also satisfy the needs of channel members, whose support is crucial to the success of industrial marketing strategy.

After reading this chapter, you will have an understanding of:

1. *the central components of channel design;*
2. *managerial aids that can be used to evaluate alternative channel structures;*
3. *requirements for managing the existing channel;*
4. *methods for monitoring channel performance.*

In designing marketing strategy, the industrial marketing manager's primary objective is to maximize the chance that customers will respond favorably to the firm's product offerings. The way to do this is to make contact with buyers, insure that the product is available as needed, and provide all the required services before and after the sale. The channel of distribution is probably the single most important component to providing these services. It is the industrial channel that creates communication and physical supply linkages with existing and potential customers.

The channel component of industrial marketing strategy has two important, and related, dimensions. First, the channel structure designed must accomplish desired marketing objectives. Among the challenges in the design of a distribution channel are specifying channel goals, evaluating constraints on the design, analyzing channel activities, and specifying channel alternatives. Each requires evaluation. Once the channel structure has been specified, the industrial marketer must then manage the channel to achieve prescribed goals. To effectively administer channel activities, the manager must develop procedures for selecting intermediaries, motivating them to achieve desired performance, mediating conflict among channel members, and evaluating performance.

Channels are pivotal in the overall scheme of industrial marketing. The purpose of this chapter is to provide a structure for designing and administering the industrial channel.

Channel Design

Channel design is a dynamic process of developing new channels where none existed and modifying existing channels.[1] The industrial marketer usually deals with modification of existing channels. New products and customer segments may require entirely new channels. Regardless of whether the manager is dealing with a new channel or modifying an existing channel, channel design is an active rather than a passive task. Effective distribution channels do not simply evolve; they are developed by management action on the basis of a well-conceived plan which reflects overall marketing goals.

Channel design is best conceptualized as a series of stages that must be completed so that the industrial marketing manager is assured that all important channel dimensions have been evaluated (Figure 12.1).

The result of the channel design process is to specify the structure that provides the highest probability of achieving the firm's objectives. Note that the process focuses on channel *structure* and not on channel participants. Channel structure refers to the underlying framework: the

[1] Bert Rosenbloom, *Marketing Channels, A Management View* (Hinsdale, Ill.: The Dryden Press, 1978), p. 105.

Figure 12.1   The Channel Design Process

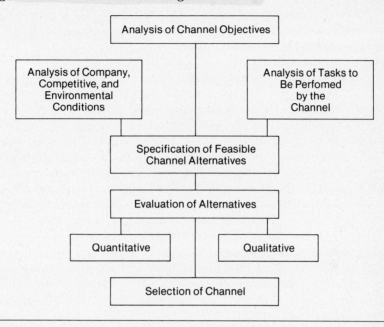

Source: Adapted from Michael D. Hutt and Thomas W. Speh, "Realigning Industrial Marketing Channels," *Industrial Marketing Management*, 12 (July 1983), pp. 171–177.

number of channel levels, the number and types of intermediaries, and the linkages among channel members. Selection of individual intermediaries is indeed important; it will be examined later in the chapter.

Stage 1. Channel Objectives

Industrial firms formulate their marketing strategies to appeal to selected market segments, to earn targeted levels of profits, to maintain or increase sales and market share growth rates, and to achieve all this within specified resource constraints. Each element of the marketing strategy has a specific purpose. Thus, whether the industrial marketer is designing a totally new channel or redesigning an existing one, the first phase of channel design is to fully comprehend marketing goals and formulate corresponding channel objectives.

Structure Based on Profits and Strategy Integration   Profit considerations and asset utilization must be reflected in channel objectives and design. For example, the cost of maintaining a salesperson in the field, including lodging, meals, and auto rental, has increased dramatically over the past decade. McGraw-Hill reports that the cost of one sales call for an industrial firm averaged \$178 in 1981.[2] For the manufacturer, these costs are somewhat fixed in the short run. Working capital committed to these costs might be eliminated by switching from a direct sales force to manufacturer's reps, whose compensation as a percentage of sales is totally variable. Of course, many other factors, such as the quality of the selling job, must also be evaluated. Channel structure must be compatible with all marketing strategy elements.

Channel Objectives Reflect Marketing Goals   Specific distribution objectives are established on the basis of broad marketing objectives. Distribution objectives force the manager to relate channel design decisions to broader marketing goals. A manufacturer of industrial cleaning products might have a distribution objective to "provide product availability in every county in the Midwest with over \$5 million in market potential." The distribution objective of a supplier of air conditioning units might be "to make contact with industrial plant architects once every month and industrial contractors once every two months."

Marketing and distribution objectives guide the channel design process and actually limit the range of feasible channel structures. However, before the alternative channel structures can be evaluated, the industrial marketing manager must evaluate other limitations on the choice of channel structures.

Scoring With the Right Distribution

"The largest mating ritual in the business world happens annually in Las Vegas—it's called Comdex, and each year hundreds of microcomputer manufacturers flock there to strut their wares, hoping to meet their perfect distribution channel. There is nothing in the business world to match this awesome sight because in no other industry is the search for distribution so paramount. The companies who pair up with the right partners will be winners in a market that is expected to triple to \$15 billion in the next five years. But those who choose poorly face extinction—according to some experts only a fraction of the roughly 150 microcomputer manufacturers today will dominate the business in 1987.

"In the microcomputer industry, says one expert, 'the success of the enterprise is directly related to the effectiveness of its distribution system.' However, the search for effective

---

distribution is frustrating—there are dozens of possible routes to reach would-be buyers. Reaching business buyers—the most profitable part of the market—is particularly difficult. Vendors selling to businesses may go through direct sales, dealers, distributors, OEM's, wholesalers, retail stores, company-owned stores, systems vendors, trade marts, or dozens of variations on those themes. One consultant concludes, 'It's an incredible mess, no one knows what is the best way to reach their buyers, and you see continual competition between vendors and their own channels.'"

Source: Philip Maher, "Scoring With the Right Distribution," *Business Marketing*, 68 (June 1983), p. 54.

Stage 2. Channel Design Constraints

Frequently, the manager has little flexibility in the selection of channel structures because of trade, competitive, company, and environmental factors. In fact, the decision on channel design may be imposed on the manager. The variety of constraining factors is almost limitless.[3] Figure 12.2 summarizes those factors most relevant to the industrial marketer.

Stage 3. Pervasive Channel Tasks

Each channel structure will be evaluated on its ability to effectively and efficiently perform the required channel activities. The concept of a channel as a sequence of activities to be performed, rather than as a set of channel institutions, is essential to channel design. The industrial marketing manager must creatively structure the tasks necessary to meet customer requirements and company goals rather than merely accepting existing channel structures or traditional distribution patterns.

Manufacturers' reps typically carry no inventory of their suppliers' products. A manufacturer of semiconductors and microcircuits, upon a careful analysis of required channel activities, may decide that, although reps can provide the level of sales service needed, large accounts need emergency local inventories of a few selected microcircuits. The solution in this case would not be to abandon the rep as a viable channel, but to compensate the rep for carrying a limited inventory of emergency circuits. Thus, analysis of required tasks and a view of the channel as a se-

---

[3] See Bert Rosenbloom, *Marketing Channels*, pp. 119–127; Louis W. Stern and Adel I. El-Ansary, *Marketing Channels*, 2nd ed. (Englewood Cliffs, N.J.: Prentice-Hall, Inc., 1982), pp. 243–250; and Philip Kotler, *Marketing Management, Analysis, Planning and Control*, 4th ed. (Englewood Cliffs, N.J.: Prentice-Hall, Inc., 1980), pp. 431–433.

Figure 12.2   Factors Limiting Industrial Channel Choice

---

1. *Availability of Good Intermediaries*

   Competitors often "lock-up" the better intermediaries

   Established intermediaries are not always receptive to new products

2. *Traditional Channel Patterns*

   Established patterns of distribution are difficult to violate

   Large customers may demand direct sales

3. *Product Characteristics*

   Technical complexity dictates direct distribution

   Extensive repair requirements may call for local distributors to service the product line

4. *Company Financial Resources*

   Capital requirements often preclude direct distribution

5. *Competitive Strategies*

   Direct service by competitors may force all firms to sell direct

6. *Geographic Dispersion of Customers*

   A widely dispersed market of small customers often requires low-cost representation afforded by intermediaries

---

quence of activities would lead the firm to a creative solution to the inventory problem.

The backbone of channel design is the analysis of objectives, constraints, and channel activities. Once these are understood, channel alternatives can be evaluated.

Stage 4. Channel Alternatives

Specification of channel alternatives involves four primary issues:

1.   the number of levels to be included in the channel (i.e., the degree of "directness");

2.   the number of channel intermediaries at each level of the channel;

3.   the types of intermediaries to employ;

4.   the number of channels to employ.

The decisions made for each are predicated upon the objectives, constraints, and activities previously analyzed.

Degree of "Directness"   Industrial channels may be one-step distribution, in which the manufacturer sells direct to the customer, or elaborate systems with various levels of different types of intermediaries. Level, in the channel context, refers to each separate type of marketing institution used by the manufacturer to bring about a sale and deliver the product to the customer. A multilevel industrial channel might include manufacturer, sales rep, distributor, and customer. This type of structure prevails for a product like abrasives, where as many as 1000 general line distributors might be needed to secure adequate market coverage and product availability. Reps would be used to sell to the distributor.

Assessing Product/Market Factors   The number of channel levels depends on a host of company, product, and market variables. The "length" of channels used to market industrial products was studied by Donald Jackson, Robert Krampf, and Leonard Konopa.[4] Their study of 300 industrial firms suggested that industrial channel length is influenced by availability of capable intermediaries, market factors, and customer characteristics. Market factors included number of customers, geographic concentration of customers, and industry concentration. Customer characteristics included significance of the purchase as perceived by the customer and volume potential of a customer. Channel length increases with greater availability of effective intermediaries and with number of customers; it decreases when the purchase becomes more significant, customer potential increases, and market and industry concentration increases.

Gary Lilien reports the results of a study of marketing mix decisions for industrial products.[5] Part of the study dealt with the channel component of the marketing mix. In addition to customer and market characteristics, he found that technical product complexity, product life cycle stage, and size of the selling firm influence the length of industrial channels. Direct distribution is used for technically complex products, mature markets, and larger sellers.

There is a greater tendency in industrial than in consumer-goods marketing to sell directly to the customer. However, direct selling is often not feasible. For products like tools, abrasives, fasteners, pipes, valves, materials-handling equipment, and wire rope, as much as 97 percent of the annual volume moves through industrial distributors only.[6] These products are typically bought frequently, repetitively (straight rebuy), and in small quantities. Instantaneous availability is fundamental; industrial distributors handle such products efficiently.

The Number of Intermediaries   How many intermediaries of each type are required to effectively cover a particular market? The answer is sometimes easy—for example, when a firm distributes through reps.

---

[4] Donald M. Jackson, Robert F. Krampf, and Leonard J. Konopa, "Factors That Influence the Length of Industrial Channels," *Industrial Marketing Management*, 11 (October 1982), pp. 263–268.

[5] Gary L. Lilien, "Advisor 2: Modeling the Marketing Mix Decision for Industrial Products," *Management Science*, 25 (February 1979), pp. 191–204.

[6] Frederick E. Webster, Jr., "Perceptions of the Industrial Distributor," *Industrial Marketing Management*, 4 (1975), p. 259.

Since reps act as the firm's sales force, there would be no point to using more than one rep to call on a specific customer. (Unless, of course, each rep specialized in a different part of the company's product line.) Thus, the industrial marketer would select the single best rep organization in each of the geographical areas to be covered.

In the case of distribution through industrial distributors, the company may require two, three, or even more carefully selected distributors in a geographic market to ensure adequate market coverage. The policy of carefully choosing channel members in a particular geographical area is referred to as *selective distribution*. The nature of the product and the purchasing process usually dictate a selective policy. Materials-handling equipment, electric motors, power transmission equipment, and tools typically fall into the category of straight or modified rebuy situations. The time spent in evaluating sources for these products is not great, yet the purchase is not always simple and repetitive. The buyer needs advice about applications, maintenance, and repair, and the buyer usually demands rapid product delivery, repair, and service. The manufacturer wants to be represented by a distributor that can satisfy these customer requirements. To ensure that distributors will perform the job required and provide proper emphasis to the manufacturer's line, the number of distributors will be limited to a few in a given market.

Generally, the more standardized the products, the more frequently they are purchased, and the smaller their unit value, the greater the number of distributors in a given market. The abrasives manufacturer who requires up to 1000 general line distributors is following an intensive rather than a selective distribution policy. An *intensive distribution* policy is especially appropriate when availability is a requirement. Customers must have a product source in close proximity to their plants.[7]

The number of intermediaries to use depends on the types to be included in the channel. The type of institution to use must also be examined.

Type of Intermediary   Intermediaries are selected on the basis of the tasks they perform. The types of industrial intermediaries and the functions they perform were discussed at length in Chapter 11. The question here is whether more than one type of intermediary will be needed to satisfy all target markets.

The primary reason for using more than one distribution channel for the same product is that different market segments require different channel structures. Motorola works through three distinct channels. Large accounts are called on by the firm's own sales force, distributors handle small repeat orders, and now manufacturers' reps develop the market made up of medium-sized firms.

[7] For a comprehensive discussion of distributor/market coverage, see Frederick E. Webster, Jr., "The Role of the Industrial Distributor in Marketing Strategy," *Journal of Marketing*, 40 (July 1976), pp. 10–16.

Like size of accounts, differences in purchase behavior may also dictate more than one channel system. If a firm produces a wide line of industrial products, some may require high caliber selling to a multitude of buying influences within a single buyer's firm. In this case, the firm's own sales force would focus on the more complex buying situations, while distributors sell standardized products from local stocks.

Some products in a line well need [handwritten annotation]

When One Channel is Not Enough—Diamond Tool Comments from the Sales Vice President

"We make hand tools and horseshoes. We're medium-sized, with 15 factory salesmen covering the entire U.S. and manufacturer's agents on the west coast and in New York City. We find that we need heavy concentration in these two areas and haven't enough of our own staff people to handle the assignment. It would not be profitable, for example, to replace our several west coast reps with factory men. It would entail too costly a travel budget to use our own men here. The agents do a highly satisfactory job for us in the areas they cover. We can trust them to do a job for us. They've been doing it, most of them, for many years. We select them on the basis of recommendations by industrial distributors, who rarely steer us wrong. We find that the distributor's recommendation is the most effective way to get in touch with good agencies. Of course, before we hire one, we examine it carefully to see that it meets our needs and will give us ample attention. Our success record here has been excellent. I would say that our agents stack up favorably in performance with our own factory salesmen."

Source: "How Good Are Manufacturers' Agents?" *Industrial Distribution*, 72 (May 1982), p. 120. Courtesy, *Industrial Distribution* Magazine.

Legal Issues   Maintaining more than one channel is not without problems. Some accounts may be double-covered, or different channel members may find themselves competing for business. Industrial marketers often want to reserve large accounts for their own sales force or restrict certain territories for "selected" distributors.

There are complex legal issues associated with such restrictions. Although Supreme Court rulings on territorial restrictions have been contradictory and confusing over the past thirty years, a manufacturer may be in violation of the Sherman Act if it restricts the territory of distributors who take title to the goods.[8] Thus, industrial marketers may not be able to prevent distributors from calling on large accounts, although they can try to reach an agreement with distributors on general channel policy about the treatment of large accounts. Distributors may even *force* a manufacturer to distribute through them. In a recent case, the courts ruled that a supplier could not refuse to sell to a qualified distributor, even though the supplier had an acceptable exclusive agreement with another distributor.

The manufacturer is not so confined in dealings with reps because reps do not take title to the products. This gives the manufacturer the right to impose territorial restrictions.[9] A dual channel policy may be dictated by customer and market conditions, but its implementation can be fraught with behavioral and legal difficulties.

The careful analysis of company objectives, channel goals, design constraints, and required channel tasks is basic to the evaluation of industrial channel alternatives. In addition, most channel design decisions are modification decisions—the structure is to be slightly altered, rather than totally redesigned. Here the alternatives are much more limited. The task before the industrial marketing manager is to select the most effective channel structure from among the feasible alternatives.

Stage 5. Channel Selection

Most channel design decisions are only slight modifications of the channel structure, in response to changing markets, expanding geographic coverage, new customer requirements, or new products. Selection of the appropriate modification in channel structure might be rather straightforward. In fact, the range of choice may be quite limited.

Complex Channel Selection Decisions   The total redesign of an existing channel system or the initiation of a totally new one generally requires a more thorough analysis of alternatives. The alternatives are more numerous, as are the influencing variables. Although the manager seeks to design the optimal channel for maximum long-run profit, this is nearly impossible. Why?

First, the cost and revenue data to support the decision may not be available. So many factors influence the channel decision that it is often impossible to assess their future impact on channel costs and revenues. Second, channels are dynamic, while the design decision is made at a

---

[8] John F. Cady, "Reasonable Rules and Rules of Reason: Vertical Restrictions on Distributors," *Journal of Marketing*, 46 (Summer 1982), p. 29; see also, "Never Say No to a Distributor," *Sales and Marketing Management*, 117 (February 5, 1979), pp. 16–17.

[9] "Clemmer Moving and Storage vs. North American Van Lines and Louderback Transportation Co.," *Journal of Marketing*, 34 (April 1970), p. 84.

Table 12.1   Channel Shift toward the Public Warehouse: Analyzing Efficiency and Effectiveness

Efficiency Dimensions	Effectiveness Dimensions
Cost of shifting selling function to sales force or available reps	*Environmental fit*, e.g.: —Impact of business conditions on channel structure
Cost of shifting storage function and related activities (e.g., billing)	*Organizational fit*, e.g.: —Quality of sales force or available reps
Cost of providing required level of customer service	*Market fit*, e.g.: —Quality/quantity of required selling effort at time of sale —Entrenchment of customer buying patterns —Impact of shift on customer satisfaction
Cost of providing auxiliary services (e.g., minor maintenance)	*Competitive fit*, e.g.: —Competitive norms for comparable product line *Strategic fit*, e.g.: —Impact of shift on longer term strategy plans in market segment
Analyzing cost/service level trade-offs	Analyzing cost/revenue trade-offs

Source: Reprinted by permission of the publisher from "Realigning Industrial Marketing Channels" by Michael D. Hutt and Thomas W. Speh, *Industrial Marketing Management*, 12 (July 1983), p. 173. Copyright © 1983 by Elsevier Science Publishing Co., Inc.

single point in time. The optimal channel today may not be optimal in five years, or even one year. Channel design is a process, not a decision. Lastly, the chance of finding all the relevant alternatives is slim.

Nevertheless, existing channels must be continually monitored to determine whether a total or a partial change in channel structure is necessary to meet corporate profitability goals. Any change in the channel structure should consider the net impact on channel effectiveness and efficiency.[10] To illustrate, a manufacturer is considering a shift in channel structure from industrial distributors to public warehousing. (A public warehouse performs the distribution functions of product-handling, order-processing, storage, and delivery, but does not sell and does not take title.) Table 12.1 shows factors to be evaluated when assessing the effectiveness and efficiency of the shift. The manager must analyze the direct costs associated with the channel functions to be shifted (selling, storage, service) and the longer time horizon, and consider how potential changes in the channel fit with overall marketing strategy.

[10] Michael D. Hutt and Thomas W. Speh, "Realigning Industrial Marketing Channels," *Industrial Marketing Management*, 12 (July 1983), pp. 171–177.

Techniques for Evaluating Alternative Channels

Recognizing these constraints, the industrial marketer must approach the decision systematically to achieve the optimal channel structure. We will examine three approaches for structuring this process that have relevance to industrial channels: (1) weighted factor, (2) cost/revenue, and (3) capital budgeting.

Weighted Factor Approach

The essence of this approach is to use the analysis of company objectives, distribution tasks, and constraints to evaluate each alternative channel structure.[11] In Table 12.2, a manufacturer of materials-handling equipment seeks to expand distribution to the New England states. Analysis reveals the following variables to be important:

1.　higher-level personal selling;

2.　maintenance of local spare parts inventories;

3.　intensive market coverage;

4.　manufacturer control of marketing;

5.　relatively low selling costs;

6.　knowledge of user/customer requirements;

7.　low investment.

The feasible alternatives are selling through distributors or through manufacturers' reps.

The weighted factor approach has five steps. First, factors important in achieving channel objectives are defined. Seven factors were identified by the materials-handling manufacturer. Second, each factor is assigned a weight to reflect its relative importance. (The sum of these factor weights should always equal 1.0.) Third, each factor is rated on a 0.0 to 1.0 scale for each channel alternative. Distributors were assigned a factor score of 0.3 for the *selling ability* factor, and reps 0.9. Fourth, each factor weight is multiplied by each factor score. For example, distributors achieve a score for *selling ability* of 0.03 (0.10 × 0.3); reps = 0.09 (.10 × 0.9). Fifth, a composite score for each channel alternative is calculated by summing the individual scores.

In Table 12.2, the distributor alternative has the higher score and, in the absence of other data, should be selected, for two primary reasons: (1) superiority in maintaining inventory and (2) lower relative

[11] Philip Kotler, *Marketing Decision Making: A Model Building Approach* (New York: Holt, Rinehart and Winston, 1971), p. 293.

Table 12.2 Weighted Factor Method of Channel Selection

Factor (1)	Factor Weight (2)	Factor Score* (3)											Distributor Rating (x) (2 × 3)	Rep Rating (y) (2 × 3)
		.0	.1	.2	.3	.4	.5	.6	.7	.8	.9	1.0		
1. Selling Ability	0.10				x						y		0.03	0.09
2. Inventory	0.15	y									x		0.135	0.00
3. Market Coverage	0.20							y			x		0.18	0.12
4. Control	0.05		x					y					0.005	0.03
5. Selling Costs	0.05							x				y	0.03	0.05
6. Customer Knowledge	0.25							x		y			0.15	0.20
7. Investment	0.20	y								x			0.16	0.00
	1.00								Total Score =				0.690	0.490

*x = Distributor's Rating

y = Rep's Rating

investment requirements. If there were more than two alternatives, this approach would allow management to rank them all.

The advantage of the weighted factor approach is that it forces management to consider explicitly the important variables in the channel decision and then to evaluate each alternative quantitatively. Of course, the approach has limitations. The results are only as good as management's estimate of the relative importance of channel variables and of each alternative's likely performance on each variable. This approach does not estimate the profit or risk associated with each alternative; an approach that does may be necessary in its own right or to complement the weighted factor method.

Cost/Revenue Approaches

Cost/revenue approaches evaluate the profit and return on investment dimensions of each channel alternative. It must be stressed that estimating future channel costs and revenues is not easy. Although internal cost information necessary for analysis is usually available from a firm's accounting system, the information often is not readily available to managers making channel decisions.[12] Research also indicates that the contribution of individual channel members to corporate profitability is often not considered by marketing managers. Thus, systems for gathering extensive internal and external channel cost and revenue data will be required for management to effectively evaluate the profit and return-on-investment (ROI) consequences of channel alternatives.

Capital Budgeting Approach

Eugene Lambert offers a capital budgeting approach to channel evaluation.[13] The industrial marketing manager begins by evaluating the stream of earnings and investment requirements for each alternative channel. The ROI can then be compared to the firm's cost of capital. By comparing the ROI of various channel options to the returns that might accrue to other company projects, the firm can isolate the most profitable venture. A firm might decide that funds saved by using intermediaries rather than a direct sales force could be profitably invested in a new product.

The value of Lambert's approach is that it forces management to consider channel financial dimensions, such as capital investment requirements, future earning streams, and estimated future cost streams. Unfortunately, the approach is severely constrained by the difficulties of

---

[12] Douglas M. Lambert, "The Distribution Channels Decision: A Problem of Performance Measurement," *Management Accounting*, 60 (June 1978), p. 63.

[13] Eugene A. Lambert, Jr., "Financial Considerations in Choosing a Marketing Channel," *MSU Business Topics*, 14 (Winter 1966), pp. 17–26.

forecasting investment requirements and future cost/revenue streams for something as dynamic as a distribution channel.

The weighted point, cost/revenue, and capital budgeting approaches are just three of a range of quantitative methods to aid in decision making when evaluating channel structure alternatives. When data and cost requirements are met, computer simulations can also be applied to distribution planning.[14]

Qualitative Dimensions

The channel decision maker must consider qualitative as well as quantitative factors. Given two channels with nearly similar economic performance, the critical factor may be the degree of *control* that the industrial marketer can exercise over the channels. A rep as opposed to a distributor channel generally gives the manager higher control because the manufacturer maintains title and possession of the goods. The manufacturer may be willing to trade off short-run economic benefits to gain long-term control over channel activities.

Adaptation by channel members may have long-run importance. Small, undercapitalized distributors may not be able to respond effectively to new competitive thrusts or to problems caused by economic downturns. The viable alternatives then will be to sell direct or use reps and make products available through a system of public warehouses.

Such factors as intermediary *image, financial capacity, sales*, and *merchandising ability* must also be analyzed. And once the channel is designed, it must be administered.

Channel Administration

Once a particular industrial channel structure is selected, channel participants must be selected, and arrangements made to ensure that all obligations are assigned. Next, channel members must be motivated to perform the tasks necessary to achieve channel objectives. Third, conflict within the channel must be properly controlled. Lastly, performance must be controlled and evaluated.

Selection of Intermediaries

Why is the selection of channel members part of channel management rather than an aspect of channel design? The primary reason is that intermediary selection is an ongoing process—some intermediaries choose to leave the channel and others are terminated by the supplier. Thus, selection of intermediaries is more or less continuous. Performance

---

[14] For example, see Stern and El-Ansary, *Marketing Channels*, pp. 235–238.

of individual channel members must be evaluated continuously. The manufacturer should be prepared to move quickly, replacing poor performers with potentially better ones. Including the selection process in ongoing channel management puts the process in its proper perspective.

Selection Criteria   Because all firms do not have the same channel objective or activities to be performed, there is no single set of criteria with universal application. Some firms find it impossible to reduce the selection of intermediaries to a rigid procedure, but some means for objectively comparing potential channel members is vital. Ideally, the industrial marketing manager wants to examine objective factors concerning the channel situation and sensibly temper these evaluations with personal impressions, opinions, and judgment.

Each industrial marketer will have to develop criteria that are relevant to the firm's own product/market situation. Many companies use checklists to compare prospective distributors or reps. The form used by the McGraw-Edison Company is shown in Figure 12.3. The criteria that McGraw-Edison feels are important are market coverage, product lines, personnel, growth, and financial standing.

Securing Good Intermediaries   The marketer can identify prospective intermediaries through discussions with company salespeople and existing or potential customers, or through trade sources, such as *Industrial Distribution* magazine or the *Verified Directory of Manufacturers' Representatives*. Once the list of potential intermediaries is reduced to a few names, the manufacturer will use the selection criteria to evaluate them.

The formation of the channel is not at all a one-way street. The manufacturer now must induce the intermediaries to become part of the channel system. Some distributors evaluate potential suppliers just as rigorously, and on many of the same dimensions, as the manufacturers rate them. Manufacturers often must demonstrate the sales and profit potential of their product and be willing to grant the intermediaries some territorial exclusivity. Massey-Ferguson, a large industrial equipment concern, provides prospective distributors with a six-page analysis of the distributor's potential sales and profit opportunities, personnel requirements, estimated expenses, market potentials by product and market, and estimated operating expenses.[15]

Motivating Channel Members

Distributors and reps are independent and profit-oriented. They are oriented toward their customers and the means necessary to satisfy customer needs for industrial products and services. Their perceptions and

---

[15] Roger M. Pegram, *Selecting and Evaluating Distributors* (New York: The National Industrial Conference Board, Inc., 1965), p. 95.

Figure 12.3   Distributor Evaluation Form

LINE MATERIALS INDUSTRIES
A Division of MC GRAW-EDISON COMPANY

Distributor Evaluation Form

In any business arrangement, the parties must know each other well. We have told you all about ourselves and would, in return, like to know about you. Please furnish the requested information so we can judge each other on an equal basis. Thank you.

Company Name _____
Address _____
City and State _____
Telephone Number _____

1. Geographic and Market Coverage
   a. What is present geographic coverage (list counties)? _____
   b. Is geographic expansion planned in near future? Yes _____ No _____.
      If yes, please list additional counties to be covered. _____
   c. What is present market coverage and how frequently are calls made in these markets?

   | | | APPROXIMATE SALES |
MARKET	CALL FREQUENCY	VOLUME – DOLLARS

2. Present Product Lines
   What major product lines (competitive as well as compatible) are presently handled?

PRODUCT OR PRODUCT LINE	MANUFACTURER

3. Products and Markets – Historical Performance
   a. What, if any, major products were previously carried, but have been dropped? Why?

PRODUCT LINE	WHY DISCONTINUED?

   b. What markets, if any, were covered, but are no longer contacted? Why?

MARKET	REASON

4. Personnel
   Total number of employees? _____
   Number of inside sales personnel? _____
   Number of outside salesmen? _____

   Do you have a lighting engineer? Yes _____ No _____.
   Do you have technically trained employees familiar with electrical power apparatus? Yes _____ No _____.
   If yes, how many? _____

5. Financial Information
   a. Sales volume last year? _____
   b. Sales volume this year to date? _____
   c. Financial Statements: Please attach balance sheets and profit and loss statements for past two years. In addition, please include any information showing financial soundness and growth that you desire.
   d. Comments: _____

6. Current Dun & Bradstreet rating? _____

7. Growth Outlook
   a. What are your plans for future growth? _____
   b. Do you plan any building expansions in the near future? Yes _____ No _____. If yes, please indicate plans.
      _____

8. Do you feel that the addition of L-M products will appreciably increase your sales volume? Yes _____.
   No _____. If yes, what annual sales increase would you feel acceptable? $_____

9. Additional Comments: _____

                                          Signed _____
                                          Title _____
                                          Date _____

Source: Roger Pegram, *Selecting and Evaluating Distributors*, Business Policy Study No. 116 (New York: The National Industrial Conference Board, 1965), p. 51. Reprinted by permission of The Conference Board.

outlook may vary substantially from those of the manufacturers they represent. As a consequence, marketing strategies can fail because managers at the manufacturer's level do not tailor their programs to the capabilities and orientation of their intermediaries. To effectively manage the industrial channel, the marketer must understand the intermediaries' perspective and devise methods for motivating them to perform so as to enhance the manufacturer's long-term success. The manufacturer must continually seek support from intermediaries and the quality of that support will depend on the motivational techniques employed.

A Partnership   Channel member motivation begins with the understanding that the channel relationship is a *partnership*. Manufacturers and intermediaries are in business together; whatever expertise and assistance the manufacturer can provide to the intermediaries will improve total channel effectiveness. Some industrial firms recognize the partnership concept by preparing formal contracts to be signed by both parties. Columbus McKinnon Corporation, a large industrial firm, makes the following agreement with its distributors:

The distributor will maintain an inventory that gives four turns based on last year's sales; will purchase at least $15,000 a year from the supplier; will actively promote the sale of the supplier's products. The supplier (Columbus McKinnon), in turn, extends the latest discount service and freight; contributes a specific amount to joint advertising; works a specified length of time with each distributor salesman; and helps develop annual sales targets.[16]

Both company and distributors agree that a formal contract is the only effective way to operationalize the partnership idea and avoid potential misunderstandings.

As industrial buyers develop more effective purchasing procedures, the partnership concept will assume increasing importance. A case in point is the emergence of *systems contracting*, a procedure by which an industrial buyer arranges for a single source for MRO (maintenance, repair, operating) supplies under a stockless purchasing concept where the industrial distributor carries the required inventory. The buyer is able to reduce the high cost of buying and holding low value, repetitive-use MRO items; the distributor (and manufacturer) have the advantage of being single source suppliers. To effect such contracts, the manufacturer and distributor must synchronize their production scheduling, inventory, delivery, finance, and selling. Systems contracts change the channel of distribution fundamentally—the industrial distributor's power is strengthened because customers are tied to the distributor and the distributor becomes a more important customer to the manufac-

---

[16] Duffy Marks, "Post Carborundum: Distributors Evaluate Their Vendor Relations," *Industrial Distribution*, 7 (June 1983), p. 35.

turer.[17] Good relations and close cooperation between the manufacturer and distributor become even more important.

Management Aids   Manufacturers often have the size and skill to develop sophisticated management techniques for areas of purchasing, inventory, order processing, and the like which can be passed on to channel members. Some firms may provide elaborate cost accounting and profitability measurement systems for their distributors to assist them in tracking product performance.

Dealer Advisory Councils   Distributors or reps may be brought together with management personnel of the manufacturer periodically to review distribution policies. Intermediaries can voice their opinions on policy matters and are brought directly into the decision-making process for channel operations. To be effective, dealer councils must allow meaningful input to channel policy decisions.

Margins and Commissions   In the final analysis, the primary motivating device will be compensation. The surest way to lose intermediary support is with compensation policies that do not meet industry and competitive standards. Reps or distributors who feel cheated on commissions or margins will shift their selling attention to products generating a higher profit. The manufacturer must be current with prevailing compensation rates in the industry and adjust its rates as conditions change. Inflation in travel, lodging, and entertainment expenses force many reps and distributors to seek higher commissions and margins. Although such increases are painful to the manufacturer, if rates are not adjusted fairly, suppliers can expect a marked reduction in sales effort.

The compensation provided to intermediaries should reflect the marketing tasks performed. If the manufacturer seeks special attention for a new industrial product, most reps will require higher commissions. Requiring distributors to hold excess inventories in selected product lines will entail higher gross margins for those items. Ingersol-Rand's (I-R) program for pneumatic tools provides distributors with an extra 10 percent discount if they maintain inventory at one-third of the dollar volume of their previous year's I-R sales.[18] Compensation must always be geared to channel objectives to be achieved by the channel participants.

Market Protection   Most intermediaries want territorial protection from excessive competition with other distributors of the same product. Often, selective distribution will benefit both manufacturer and distribu-

---

[17]Marsha A. Scheidt, I. Fredrick Trawick, and John E. Swan, "Impact of Purchasing Systems Contracts on Distributors and Producers," *Industrial Marketing Management*, 11 (October 1982), p. 288.

[18]Somerby Dowst, "Manufacturers Turn More to Distributor Sales," *Purchasing*, 77 (February 22, 1977), p. 49.

tors. The manufacturer receives loyal commitment from the distributor, and the distributor enjoys limited product competition and a relatively large market potential.

Other tools may also be used to motivate industrial channel members. However, the success of the motivational program hinges on the overall quality of the firm's channel strategy *and* management's attitude toward channel members. An attitude of assistance, cooperation, and partnership is primary; this attitude should be reinforced by a well-conceived plan that provides support, training, and communication to the channel participants.

Conflict: The Need for Interorganizational Management

The very nature of a distribution channel—with each member dependent upon another for success—carries the seeds for conflict among the members. Although realizing the need for cooperation, individual members seek to maximize their autonomy and, hence, their profitability.[19] *Channel conflict* occurs when one channel member A perceives another channel member B to be preventing or impeding A from achieving important goals.[20] The opportunities for conflict in industrial channels are limitless—for example, a manufacturer's refusal to increase reps' commissions, a distributor's refusal to maintain required inventory levels, a manufacturer's insistence on a nonexclusive distribution policy. Thus, because channel participants have different goals, different perceptions of their roles in the channel, and different evaluations of their spheres of influence, tensions develop which may cause them to perform in ways that damage channel performance.[21] The industrial marketer must manage conflict through interorganizational management approaches.[22] Interorganizational management improves overall channel performance by coordinating relationships among the organizations that make up the channel.

Is There Conflict?   Managers may not recognize a conflict situation until after the fact—when it may be too late to respond to the causes. Clearly, a device is needed to recognize a potential conflict situation before it occurs. Surveys of distributors and reps at periodic intervals can

---

[19] Stern and El-Ansary, *Marketing Channels*, pp. 265–302.

[20] *Ibid.*, p. 283.

[21] Louis W. Stern and James L. Heskett, "Conflict Management in Interorganizational Relations: A Conceptual Framework," in Louis Stern, ed., *Distribution Channels: Behavioral Dimensions* (Boston: Houghton-Mifflin Company, 1969), pp. 293–294.

[22] For example, see Robert F. Lusch, "Sources of Power: Their Impact on Intrachannel Conflict," *Journal of Marketing Research*, 13 (November 1976), p. 384; Stern and Heskett, "Conflict Management in Interorganizational Relations," p. 293; Larry J. Rosenberg and Louis Stern, "Conflict Measurement in the Distribution Channel," *Journal of Marketing Research*, 8 (November 1971), pp. 437–442; Louis Stern and Ronald H. Gorman, "Conflict in Distribution Channels: An Exploration," in Stern, ed., *Distribution Channels: Behavioral Dimensions*, p. 156; Larry J. Rosenberg, "A New Approach to Distribution Conflict Management," *Business Horizons*, 16 (October 1974), pp. 67–74; and Louis P. Bucklin, "A Theory of Channel Control," *Journal of Marketing*, 37 (January 1973), pp. 39–47.

uncover potential conflict areas by eliciting their perceptions of how the channel works. Open communication between the company's sales force and channel members is an informal method of assessing potential conflict. Whether using a formal or an informal approach, management must be alert to present or emerging areas of conflict.

Reducing Conflict   Larry Rosenberg recommends three interorganizational approaches for dealing with conflict:

1.   A *channel-wide committee* could periodically evaluate emerging problems. This provides a forum which considers the diverse viewpoints of the channel members.

2.   *Joint goal-setting* by the committee (or an advisory council) can help mitigate the effects of conflict. Although a consensus on goals may not always be possible, the dialogue is beneficial in reducing conflict.

3.   A *distribution executive* position could be established in each major organization in the channel to coordinate internal and external issues that spawn conflict.[23]

The results of conflict management are improved channel performance and enhanced channel solidarity.[24] The reduction of conflict may sometimes be the only means of preserving the channel system. The final aspect of channel management is evaluation.

Evaluating Channel Performance

An essential aspect of channel management is evaluation of intermediary performance against the manufacturer's channel objectives. The extent and frequency of performance evaluation depends to a great degree on the scope of the channel, the power of the manufacturer, the relative importance of intermediaries, and the type of product. Firms selling through thousands of distributors could not afford the time or expense of frequent, comprehensive distributor reviews, though the manufacturer with extensive market power and a popular product can usually demand detailed information. By the same token, firms that use intermediaries for only a small portion of their total volume would have little need for frequent and comprehensive evaluation. Firms producing repeat-purchase, low unit-value industrial products generally need limited evaluation. Each situation will differ, and the review and evaluation process will be expanded or decreased as the situation dictates.

[23] Larry J. Rosenberg, "A New Approach to Distribution Conflict Management," *Business Horizons,* 17 (October 1974), pp. 67–74.

[24] Stern and El-Ansary, *Marketing Channels,* p. 266.

Criteria

The criteria used to evaluate distributor and rep performance should be similar to those used in selecting the intermediaries, and specified by the channel objectives. Although the types of evaluative criteria are vast, certain factors have broad applications. These include total sales compared to market potential, inventory turnover rate, selling ability (e.g., new accounts developed), financial performance, and end-user/customer evaluation.

Taking Action

The industrial marketing manager must now use the evaluation data to make adjustments in channel operations. Some intermediaries may be terminated and replaced by stronger ones. In other cases, corrective steps will be taken to improve performance in weak areas. The performance evaluation also allows the industrial marketer to identify high-performance channel members. Their performance should be reinforced.

The annual evaluation may even suggest the need for a change in channel structure. Reps may be replaced by a direct sales force where potential appears to be far outstripping sales. Thus, intermediary performance evaluation enables the manufacturer to continually adjust the channel to changing market conditions.

Summary

Channel strategy is an exciting and challenging aspect of industrial marketing. The challenge comes from the number of alternatives available to the manufacturer in distributing industrial products. The excitement is there because markets, user needs, and competitors are always changing.

Channel strategy involves two primary management tasks: designing the overall structure and managing the operation of the channel. Channel design includes the evaluation of distribution goals, activities, and potential intermediaries. Channel structure includes the number, types, and levels of intermediaries to be used in the channel. The primary participants in industrial channels are distributors and reps; both perform key marketing functions for suppliers.

Channel management is the ongoing task of administering the channel structure to achieve distribution objectives. Selection and motivation of intermediaries are two management tasks vital to channel success. In addition, the industrial marketing manager may need to apply interorganizational management techniques to resolve channel conflict. The final phase of channel management is the evaluation of the intermediary. Evaluation provides the feedback necessary to adjust channel operations to accomplish goals.

Logistical or physical distribution performance is a key variable in determining the success or failure of industrial marketing strategy. This is the theme of the next chapter.

Discussion Questions

1. For many years, critics have charged that intermediaries contribute strongly to the rising prices of goods in the American economy. Would industrial marketers improve the level of efficiency and effectiveness in the channel by reducing as far as possible the number of intermediate links in the channel? Support your position.

2. Describe specific product, market, and competitive conditions that lend themselves to: (a) a direct channel of distribution, (b) an indirect channel of distribution.

3. Often, the industrial marketer may have very little latitude in selecting the number of channel *levels*. Explain.

4. The trend in industrial channels of distribution is toward an increased reliance on few, but larger, distributors. Why?

5. Explain how a change in segmentation policy (i.e., entering new markets) may trigger the need for drastic changes in the industrial channel of distribution.

6. Assume perfect information. What specific information would you desire in comparing channel alternatives? How would you use this information in making channel decisions?

7. The opportunities for conflict in the channel of distribution are limitless. What steps can the industrial marketer take to reduce the chances of conflict emerging in the channel?

8. Explain how two industrial distributors generating identical sales results for the industrial marketer might receive markedly different performance appraisals, one favorable, the other unfavorable.

C·H·A·P·T·E·R
13

Industrial Marketing Channels:
The Logistical Interface

If promised delivery performance is not provided, buyers will search for a new supplier. Organizational buyers assign high importance to responsive physical distribution, or logistical systems. Therefore, substantial resources are invested to service demand through the logistical system.

After reading this chapter, you will have an understanding of:

1. *the role of logistical management in industrial marketing strategy;*
2. *the importance of achieving the desired interface between logistics and the distribution channel;*
3. *the importance of cost and service trade-offs in creating effective and efficient logistical systems.*

Industrial marketers frequently delegate selling and other demand stimulation to intermediaries. Other functions of equal importance, however, must be performed to successfully implement marketing strategies and to satisfy customer needs. Products must be delivered *when* they are required, *where* they are required, and in *usable condition*. Unfortunately, an industrial marketer cannot totally shift the burden of these functions to intermediaries. Even if distributors are employed in the channel, manufacturers must be able to efficiently deliver products to the distributor. The industrial marketer's effectiveness in delivery will dramatically influence the distributor's ability to satisfy delivery requirements of the end user. Direct channels place even greater logistical burdens on the manufacturer.

This chapter will describe the role of logistical management in industrial marketing strategy in general and in channel performance in particular.[1] The discussion will be directed by such questions as: How do logistical activities interface with the distribution channel? What are the logistical variables that must be managed to create an effective interface with the channel? What role does logistical service play in the organizational purchase decision? What types of logistical services are sought by buyers? How can these services be designed and implemented most effectively and efficiently? Let us first examine the nature of logistical management.

Elements of Logistical Management

Logistics is an imposing and sometimes mysterious term that originated in the military. In business usage, *logistics* refers to the design and management of all activities (basically transportation, inventory, and warehousing) necessary to make materials available for manufacturing and to make finished products available to customers as they are needed in the condition required. Logistics thus embodies two primary product flows: (1) *physical supply*, or those flows which provide raw materials, components, and supplies to the production process; and (2) *physical distribution*, or those flows which deliver the completed product to customers and channel intermediaries (Figure 13.1). The physical supply and physical distribution flows must be coordinated to successfully meet delivery requirements of industrial customers. Although the physical supply dimension of logistics is important, we will concentrate in this chapter on the physical distribution component. Good industrial marketing demands efficient, systematic delivery of finished products to intermediaries and industrial users.

---

[1] For a comprehensive discussion of all facets of business logistics, see Ronald H. Ballou, *Business Logistics Management* (Englewood Cliffs, N.J.: Prentice-Hall, Inc., 1973); Donald J. Bowersox, *Logistical Management*. 2d ed. (New York: Macmillan Publishing Company, 1978); Douglas M. Lambert and James R. Stock, *Strategic Physical Distribution Management* (Homewood, Ill.: Richard D. Irwin, 1982).

Figure 13.1   The Industrial Logistics System

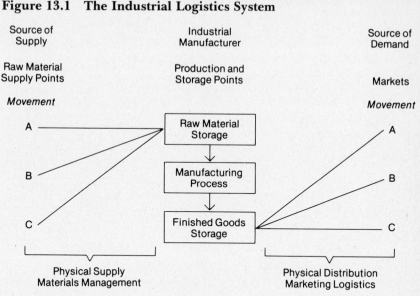

Source: Adapted from John J. Coyle and Edward J. Bardi, *The Management of Business Logistics* (New York: West Publishing Co., 1976), p. 6.

The physical supply aspect of logistics is where an industrial supplier's logistical system must interact with the customer's logistics and manufacturing process. A repair part delivered only five hours late may cost a manufacturer thousands of dollars in lost production time.

Creating Differential Advantage through Logistical Service

To compete effectively in any market requires some differential advantage over competitors and their product or service offerings. The differential advantage may be a distinctive product, image, or price. Logistics also can be used to develop a differential advantage; this strategy is particularly relevant when there is little real product differentiation, or where price competition would lead only to profit erosion.

   Xerox, the early market leader, realized that potential office copier customers perceived most competing copiers as offering the same benefits and that margins would not withstand price-cutting. Xerox turned to service—particularly logistics service for repair parts. A recent ad in the business press for Xerox copiers stated:

Because the best way to get new customers is to keep our current ones happy, Xerox offers the largest service force in the business. We have over 30,000 service people worldwide.

Parts inventories and parts distribution systems are all part of our job. That is why we have distribution centers around the globe.

So, chances are, our technical representatives will always have what you need where you need it. Whenever possible, we standardize parts so that they are interchangeable from country to country. That way we take better care of our copiers and our customers.

Similar approaches have been used by companies like Digital Equipment and Caterpillar which have built commanding positions in their markets and maintained them through effective use of customer service.

Source: Martin Christopher, "Creating Effective Policies for Customer Service," *International Journal of Physical Distribution and Materials Management*, 13, No. 2 (1983), p. 16.

Timely Logistical Support

Owens-Illinois, a major supplier of glass containers, shows how precisely a supplier must tailor its logistics system to customer needs. Owens-Illinois is a primary supplier to the J. M. Smucker Company, the jam and jelly manufacturer. Because of its vast container requirements, Smucker must carefully manage inventory and delivery of glass containers. To reduce container inventory, Smucker maintains only enough glass containers to run the production line for a *few hours*. The burden of this policy falls directly on the shoulders of Owens-Illinois. First, Owens-Illinois must schedule the production process at its Toledo plant to provide all the inventories Smucker requires. Then, warehouse systems and reliable motor carriers assure that deliveries match Smucker's inventory policy and avoid production interruptions. Consistent delivery performance to Smucker standards is surely an essential ingredient in this long-term supplier–customer relationship. Here logistical service may have created the differential advantage.

"Just in Time"   Many industrial marketers may soon have no choice but to provide almost immediate delivery of their products. The automobile industry is leading a campaign to introduce Japanese "just-in-time" inventory principles into U.S. manufacturing. Under this principle, all suppliers must carefully coordinate parts and supplies delivery with the automobile production schedule—often delivering products just hours before they are to be used. Some industrial marketers have already capitalized on this concept, gearing their production and logistical sytems to match customer needs. Hoover Universal, a manufacturer of steel frames, springs, and seats, delivers seats in specified sizes, colors, and numbers to a Nissan truck plant in Smyrna, Tennessee within three hours before they are bolted into Nissan trucks.[2] As such delivery requirements become industry standards, those industrial firms with effective and efficient logistical systems already in place will enjoy significant marketing advantages.

Elements of a Logistical System

The controllable variables of a logistical system are set out in Table 13.1. Almost no decision on a particular logistical activity can be made without evaluating its impact on the other areas.

The system of warehouse facilities, inventory commitments, and transportation linkages will determine the supplier's ability to provide timely product availability to industrial users. As a result of poor supplier performance, customers may have to bear the extra cost of higher inventories, institute expensive priority order expediting systems, develop secondary supply sources, or, worst of all, turn to another supplier.

Total Cost Approach

In the management of logistical activities, two performance variables must be considered: (1) total distribution costs and (2) the level of logistical service provided to customers. The logistical system must be designed and administered to achieve that combination of cost and service levels that yields maximum profits. First, let us consider the scope and behavior of logistical costs.

Logistical costs vary widely for industrial marketers depending on the nature of the product and the importance of logistical service to the buyer. However, logistical costs can assume 25 percent of each sales dollar at the manufacturing level and assets required by logistical activities can exceed 40 percent of total assets; logistics can have a significant impact on corporate profitability.[3] It is generally felt that opportunities for productivity gains in production, selling, and promotion have been exploited, and logistics can be considered "the last frontier of cost reduc-

[2] Bob Woods, "Selling Parts With Service," *Sales and Marketing Management*, 128 (July 4, 1983), p. 31.

[3] Douglas M. Lambert and James R. Stock, "Strategic Planning for Physical Distribution," *Journal of Business Logistics*, 3, No. 2 (1982), p. 42.

Table 13.1   Controllable Elements in a Logistics System

Elements	Key Aspects
Transportation	Represents the single most important activity in the creation of place-values and time-values; is the means of moving goods from the end of the production line to consumers in the marketplace.
Warehousing	Creates place-values and time-values by making goods available in the marketplace when needed.
Inventory Management	Insures that the right mix of products is available at the right place and at the right time, in sufficient quantity to meet demands; balances the risks of stockouts and lost sales against the risks of overstocks and obsolescence; facilitates production planning.
Protective Packaging	Protective packaging insures good condition of products when they arrive in the marketplace, and maximizes use of warehouse space and transport equipment cube.
Materials Handling	Maximizes speed and minimizes cost of: order-picking, moving to and from storage, loading of transportation equipment, and unloading at destination; relates to product protection.
Order Processing	Assists in creation of place-time values by communicating requirements to appropriate locations. Relates to inventory management by reflecting demands on current stocks and changes in inventory position.
Production Planning	Insures realization of place-time values by making goods available for inventory. Permits planning of warehouse facility utilization, transportation requirements.
Customer Service	Relates place-time values as seen by the company to place-time values as seen by its customers. Establishes levels of customer service consistent with marketing objectives as well as with cost limitations.
Plant Location: Warehouse Location, Facilities Planning	Maximizes place-time values by relating plant and warehouse location to transportation services and costs in terms of markets to be served. Facilities planning insures that capacity, configuration, and throughput of warehouse and shipping facilities are compatible with product flow.

Source: Adapted from "The Many Faces of PDM," (*Japan Airlines*, 1969), p. 10.

tion in American business."[4] How, then, can the marketer manage logistical costs?

The *total-cost or trade-off* approach to logistical management offers a guarantee that total logistical costs in the firm and within the channel are minimized. The assumption is that costs associated with individual logistical activities are interactive; that a decision about one logistical variable affects all or some of the other variables. Management is thus concerned with the efficiency of the entire system rather than with minimizing the

[1] Wendell M. Stewart, "Physical Distribution: Key to Improved Volume and Profits," *Journal of Marketing*, 39 (January 1965), pp. 65–70; see also, Thomas W. Speh and Michael D. Hutt, "The Other Half of Marketing: Lost or Found," in Robert S. Franz, Robert M. Hopkins, and Al Toma, eds., *Proceedings: Southern Marketing Association* (University of Southwestern Louisiana: Southern Marketing Association, 1978), pp. 332–335.

Figure 13.2   Cost Trade-Offs

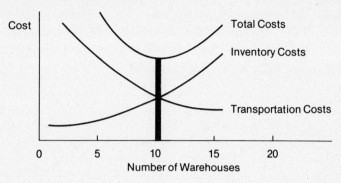

cost of any single logistical activity. The interactions among logistical activities (i.e., transportation, inventory, warehousing) are described as *cost trade-offs*, because a cost increase in one activity is traded for a large cost decrease in another activity, with the net result an overall cost reduction.

Evaluating Cost Patterns   Figure 13.2 shows costs associated with a change in the number of warehouses maintained by an industrial firm. As additional warehouses are added, transportation costs decline as a result of high-volume shipments at low rates into the warehouses and small-volume high-cost shipments moving only short distances to the customers. Total transportation costs decline with more warehouses as the high-cost small-volume shipments are moved over shorter and shorter distances. Conversely, *inventory costs* rise as more warehouses are added because more stock is required to maintain the same level of product availability than with fewer warehouses. Combining inventory and transportation costs, the least cost solution, where the trade-off of inventory for transportation is optimized, is to maintain ten warehouses. A warehouse decision based on inventory costs alone or transportation costs alone would not result in the least-cost total system (Figure 13.2).

　　　Cost tradeoffs occur among all logistical activities. Xerox at one time maintained large inventories of supplies, chemicals, and parts at 40 different warehouses. It was realized that 80 percent of the items were "slow movers." These slow movers were consolidated at one central warehouse and transported by air freight as needed. The trade-off of higher transportation costs for lower inventory costs saved Xerox millions of dollars annually.

Service-Cost Trade-Offs

The other half of the logistical equation is service. For many industrial products, the ability to deliver customer orders rapidly is more important than the logistical costs involved; different levels of service are capable of producing different demand responses.[5] However, each aspect of logistical service has a cost, and the cost must be evaluated in light of the revenue generated. Profitability, as measured by the difference between logistical revenue and cost, is the important control variable.

Total Channel System Orientation

Part of logistical management is the evaluation of the impact of logistical decisions on the channel members' operations. Manufacturer shifts in inventory policy, transportation modes, and warehouse locations directly affect channel members and end users. Reducing field warehouses from ten to two may require distributors to hold more inventory. Although the manufacturer's warehousing and inventory costs are diminished, distributor costs will rise, and customer service may be substantially curtailed. The result may dramatically reduce the overall performance of the channel system.

Channel Cooperation for Logistical Efficiency

AiResearch Industrial Division (AID) of the Garrett Corporation is a major OEM manufacturer of turbochargers for automobile, truck, construction, agricultural, and other engines. The life of a turbocharger itself is shorter than that of a turbocharged engine (due to the very high heats and revolutions per minute to which turbos are subjected). For example, a diesel engine in a semi-tractor may have a life of a million miles before a complete overhaul is required, while the life of the turbocharger on the engine might be 100,000 miles. Therefore, a system for stocking replacement turbos and for rebuilding turbos is required. Because the number of turbocharged engines is large, geographically dispersed, and varied by engine use, a manufacturer-distributor-dealer channel of distribution is required for the after-market sales of rebuilt and replacement turbos. Complete remanufacturing takes place at the manufacturing level; other types of repairs are made by both distributors and dealers.

To manage inventory in the channel at economic levels and to provide good service to engine owners, dealers stock "A" items, primarily rebuilt turbo units with high demand.

---

[5] Ernest B. Uhr, Ernest G. Hauck, and John C. Rogers, "Physical Distribution Service," *Journal of Business Logistics*, 2, No. 2 (1981), pp. 158–169.

Distributors stock these "A" items and also "B" items, which are high usage repair parts. The "C" (low turnover) items are stocked at the AID factory on the west coast of the United States or at a customer service center in the midwest. AID provides assistance to distributors and dealers by providing recommended target inventory levels and items to be stocked. The co-operative inventory concept was sold by AID in a series of distributor meetings held across the country.

Source: Lynn E. Gill and Robert P. Allerheiligen, "Co-operation in Channels of Distribution: Physical Distribution Leads the Way," *International Journal of Physical Distribution and Materials Management*, 11, No. 8 (1981), p. 64.

In summary, the total cost, total system, trade-off framework is a necessary point of departure for the management of industrial logistical strategy. Channel-wide performance can only be optimized through the systematic evaluation of logistical trade-offs.

Industrial Logistical Service

It was learned that purchasing managers in the forgings industry begin the vendor selection process by first calling suppliers with the *best delivery service* to see whether they are willing to negotiate prices.[6] Buyers with known low prices were not contacted to see if they would improve delivery service. Similar approaches to vendor selection are evidenced in other industries because logistical service is so important to the industrial buyer.

Definition of Customer Service

Logistical service relates to the availability and delivery of products to the customer, "the series of sales-satisfying activities which begins when the customer places the order and ends with the delivery of product to customers."[7] Logistical service thus includes whatever aspects of performance that are important to the industrial *customer* (Table 13.2). These service elements cover order cycle time, order accuracy, and expediting. Each of these has the potential for affecting production processes, final product output, costs, or all three.

[6] Patrick J. Robinson, Charles W. Faris, and Yoram Wind, *Industrial Buying and Creative Marketing* (Boston: Allyn and Bacon, Inc., 1967), pp. 170, 173–174.

[7] Warren Blanding, *11 Hidden Costs of Customer Service Management* (Washington, D.C.: Marketing Publications, Inc., 1974), p. 3.

Table 13.2   Elements of Logistics Service

Elements	Description
1. Order Cycle Time	The elapsed time from placement of the order to receipt of the order.
2. Consistency of Order Cycle Time	The variation of order cycle lengths from average or expected order cycle times.
3. Percent of Stockouts	Percentage of total items ordered from a supplier's warehouse which are unavailable from existing supplier inventory.
4. Order Accuracy	The degree to which items received conform to the specification of the order.
5. Percentage Fill Rate	The proportion of orders which are filled completely at the time of order placement.
6. Order Condition	The physical condition of the goods when received by the buyer.
7. Order Size and Frequency Constraint	Minimum order size requirements: maximum frequency of order placement limitations.
8. Billing Accuracy	The agreement of billing with the actual order received.
9. Back Orders, Expediting	Supplier's ability for handling back orders and expediting the delivery of products back ordered.

Source: Adapted from P. Ronald Stephenson and Ronald P. Willett, "Selling with Physical Distribution Service," *Business Horizons* 11 (December 1968), p. 78. Copyright © 1968 by the Foundation for the School of Business at Indiana University. Reprinted by permission.

Impacts of Supplier Logistical Service on Industrial Customers

All of this translates into product *availability*. For a manufacturer to produce or a distributor to resell, industrial products have to be available at the right time, at the right place, and in usable condition. The longer the supplier's order delivery time, the less available the product; the more inconsistent the delivery time, the less available the product.

For example, a reduction in the supplier's order cycle time period permits a buyer to hold less inventory because its needs can be met rapidly. The customer has reduced inventory carrying cost and less risk of interruptions in the production process. Consistent delivery performance allows the buyer to program more effectively or routinize the purchasing process, thus lowering its costs. A dramatic impact of consistent order cycle performance is the opportunity for the buyer to cut the level of buffer or safety stock maintained, and thereby the inventory cost. However, for many industrial products, most of which are low unit value and relatively standardized, the overriding concern is not inventory cost, but simply having the products. A malfunctioning $0.95 bearing could shut down a whole production line.

The Role of Logistical Service in the Industrial Buying Decision

Because the impacts of logistical service are so dramatic, it is not surprising that buyers rank logistical service above many other important supplier characteristics. William Perreault and Frederick Russ report that logistical services rate second only to product quality in influencing industrial purchasing decisions (Table 13.3).[8] These findings are reinforced by those from an earlier study of valve and pump manufacturers,[9] where delivery reliability for steel castings and forgings was rated the most important factor in influencing buyers' perceptions of suppliers. For a sizable group of purchasing managers, as reported in Table 13.3, if a supplier fails even once to respond to a rush order request, they would find a different supplier. The conclusion is clear: Industrial marketing managers must create effective systems to make products available to their industrial customers.

Table 13.3   Summary: A Study of How Industrial Purchasing Managers Evaluate Logistical Service

I. The importance of logistical service:

Supplier Characteristics	Mean Index of the Relative Importance of Supplier Characteristics in the Purchase Decision
Product Quality	0.176
Distribution Service	0.171
Price	0.161
Supplier Manager	0.152
Distance to Supplier	0.114
Required Order Size	0.108
Minority/Small Business	0.078
Reciprocity	0.046

II. What happens when you receive a stockout notice for a product?

32 percent of the time, purchasing managers switch to another supplier.

Over a prior two-year period, 50 percent of the purchasing managers stopped using a supplier because of slow or inconsistent service.

III. What would you do if the request for a rush order was not acted upon by the supplier?

42 percent of the purchasing managers would change suppliers after only *one* such inaction on a rush order.

54 percent would change suppliers if the problem occurred several times.

Source: William D. Perreault, Jr., and Frederick A. Russ, "Physical Distribution in Industrial Purchase Decisions." *Journal of Marketing* 40 (April 1976), pp. 5, 6. Reprinted by permission of the American Marketing Association.

[8] William D. Perreault and Frederick A. Russ, "Physical Distribution in Industrial Purchase Decisions," *Journal of Marketing*, 40 (April 1976), p. 3.

[9] Martin Christopher, "Logistics and the National Economy," *International Journal of Physical Distribution and Materials Management*, 11, No. 4 (1981), p. 16.

Determining the Level of Service

Obviously, not all products or all customers require the same level of logistical service. Many industrial products that are made to order—such as heavy machinery—have relatively low logistical service requirements. Others, such as replacement parts, components, and subassemblies, require extremely demanding logistical performance. Similarly, customers may be more or less responsive to varying levels of logistical service.

Some purchasing agents are far more sensitive to poor service than the majority of purchasing managers.[10] Market segments must be identified on the basis of logistical service sensitivity.[11] Buyers of scientific instruments were classified into groups—private firms, government, secondary schools, etc. Private firms viewed delivery time as more important than other groups did, secondary school buyers ranked ordering convenience more highly than others. Industrial marketing managers should attempt to isolate segments and adjust the logistical service offerings accordingly.

Profitability is the major criterion for evaluating the appropriate customer service levels. Information on alternative service levels and their associated sales results must be evaluated in relation to their costs.[12] Figure 13.3 demonstrates the cost–service relationship, showing that profit contribution varies with the service level. In this case, the optimal service level is at point x, where profits are maximized.

To reiterate, service level standards are developed by assessing customer service requirements. The sales and cost impacts of various service levels are analyzed to find the service level generating the highest profits. The needs of different customer segments will dictate different logistical system configurations. Where logistical service is critical, industrial distributors provide the vital product availability. Customers with less rigorous service demands can be served from factory inventories.

The Interface of Logistics in the Channel

Logistical activities, whether by manufacturer or intermediary, touch every phase of channel performance and are inherent to the success or failure of most industrial channel systems. The task of the industrial marketer is to first understand the impacts of supplier logistical performance on the intermediary's operations, and then to effect programs that will enhance the intermediary's performance and overall channel coordination.

---

[10] Perreault and Russ, "Physical Distribution in Industrial Purchase Decisions," p. 10.

[11] Peter Gilmour, "Customer Service: Differentiating by Market Segment," *International Journal of Physical Distribution and Materials Management*, 12, No. 3 (1982), pp. 37–44.

[12] For example, see David P. Herron, "Managing Physical Distribution for Profit," *Harvard Business Review*, 57 (May–June 1979), pp. 121–132; Harvey N. Shycon and Christopher Sprague, "Put a Price Tag on Your Customer Servicing Levels," *Harvard Business Review*, 53 (July–August 1975), pp. 71–78.

Figure 13.3   Cost–Service Relationship

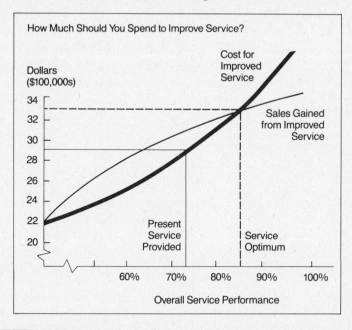

How much should a firm spend on customer service in order to gain extra sales? Graph shows how much a typical firm can improve its share of market for each $100,000 spent. Indicated too is the point of diminishing returns, at which additional expenditures will exceed the value of increased sales. Though the graph suggests a breakpoint of about 85 percent, a company can determine its own figure only by studying specific conditions in its field. The nature of the product, geographic circumstances, transport characteristics and other factors all affect the optimum service point.

Source: Illustration from *Traffic Management* Magazine, September 1982. Reprinted by permission.

Logistical Impacts on Industrial Intermediaries

A supplier's logistical system directly affects an intermediary's ability to control cost and service to end users. The order cycle time not only influences the customer's inventory requirements, but also the operations of channel members. If a supplier provides erratic delivery service to distributors, the distributor is forced to carry higher inventory in order to provide a satisfactory level of product availability to end users. The result of inefficient logistics service to the distributors is to increase their costs (larger inventories) or to create stockouts of the supplier's products at the distributor level. Neither result is good: in the first instance, distributor loyalty and marketing efforts will suffer; in the second, end users will eventually change suppliers.

Impact on Customer Service

Poor logistical performance is a double-edged sword. It constricts sales possibilities and antagonizes intermediaries. A 5 percent reduction in customer service can result in a sales decrease of 20 percent.[13] An industrial distributor will not long remain loyal to a manufacturer whose logistical performance reduces service levels to end users. Because inventories typically represent the single largest item among distributor assets and also the largest distribution expense, distributors are increasingly aware of the impact of supplier logistical service. Because distributors often pass freight charges along to their customers, abnormally high transportation costs can place the manufacturer's product at a price disadvantage in the marketplace.

Federal Mogul "FOCUSES" on Logistics

With the after-market for vehicular, construction, and aerospace markets contributing 80 percent of its corporate profits, Federal Mogul Corp. will pin its marketing efforts on new ways to reach and help these customers. Among recent approaches is a FOCUS (Field Operations and Customer Service) program, which is designed to assist distributors in inventory control and ordering. The automated inventory control and order system allows immediate ordering and inventory adjustments for all company products (friction bearings, oil seals, engine bearings, etc.) sold through its 38 U.S. and 5 Canadian distributors. The program will help the company to manage its own inventory within branches and, in turn, will allow distributors and customers to maintain minimal stock levels.

Source: Joseph Bohn, "Federal Mogul Tries Service Marketing Strategy," *Business Marketing*, 68 (April 1983), p. 25.

Improving Logistical Performance in the Channel

The industrial marketer can do much to improve channel-wide logistical performance. First, information systems can be developed to provide realistic sales forecasts for individual channel members, and their inventory control systems can be linked to the manufacturer's information system. Second, coordination of logistical activities can be facilitated, perhaps by standardization of packaging, handling, and palletization systems. Third, the manufacturer may perform certain functions (e.g.,

---

[13] Bernard J. LaLonde and Paul H. Zinszer, *Customer Service: Meaning and Measurement* (Chicago: National Council of Physical Distribution Management, 1976), p. 77.

warehousing) that contribute to improved efficiency for the entire channel. Finally, shipment consolidation is often effective in reducing channel-wide transportation costs. Distributors in a particular area might be encouraged to "pool" shipments into a truckload quantity, or to place all of their orders on the same day. In summary, logistics must be integrated channel-wide to effectively implement marketing strategy.

Industrial Logistical Management

Logistical management is the integration of transportation, inventory, facilities, and communications to provide the logistical service desired by customers and intermediaries at the lowest possible cost. The upper portion of Figure 13.4 focuses on determining customer service levels and their impact on revenues and profits. The remainder of the figure highlights the integration of the major logistical variables necessary to create the desired level of service. Particularly noteworthy is the need to consider both operating costs and the investment levels associated with the logistical system. The impact of logistics on the company's return on in-

Figure 13.4   Framework for Selecting the Optimum Logistics System

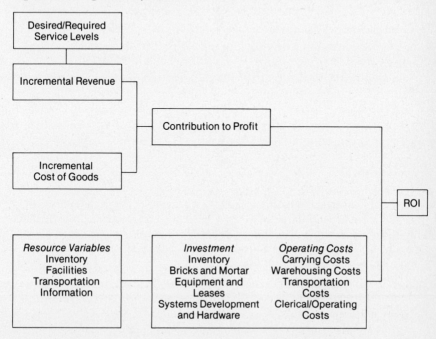

Source: Adapted from "A Logistics Hotseat: Customer Service Redefined," Cleveland Consulting Associates, Cleveland, Ohio, 1978. Reprinted by permission.

vestment is viewed in terms of revenue (customer service levels) minus the logistics operating costs and the required capital investments in the logistics system. This type of framework cues the industrial marketing manager to evaluate logistical system alternatives on the basis of all three aspects—revenue, cost, and capital investments. A modification that increases operating costs, yet leaves capital investment unchanged while more than proportionately expanding sales, would be highly favorable. An alternative where sales are unchanged, operating costs increase, yet the investment base is substantially reduced would also be viewed favorably.

While the basic approach is to discuss each area separately, decisions about facilities, transportation, and inventory are so intertwined that it is impossible to evaluate one without considering the other two.

Logistical Facilities

The strategic deployment of a warehouse provides the industrial marketer with the opportunity to increase the level of delivery service to buyers, or reduce transportation costs, or both. Industrial firms distributing repair, maintenance, and operating supplies often find that the only way to achieve desired levels of delivery service is to locate warehouses in key markets. The warehouse circumvents the need for premium transportation (air freight) and costly order processing by keeping products readily available in local markets.

Servicing Channel Members   The nature of the industrial channel affects the warehousing requirements of an industrial supplier. Where manufacturers' reps are utilized, the industrial supplier will often require a significant number of strategically located warehouses. On the other hand, a channel system involving distributors will offset the need for warehousing. Obviously, local warehousing is a real service for the distributor. Nevertheless, a few well-located supplier warehouses may be all that are required to effectively serve the distributors.

Private or Public   Operating costs, service levels, and investment requirements are essential considerations regarding the type of warehouse to use. The industrial firm may either own, rent, or lease warehousing space. At a *public warehouse*, space may be rented by the month or leased for a longer time. The advantage is flexibility—the firm can increase or decrease its use of space in a given market or move into or out of any market quickly. Public warehousing involves no fixed investment; user costs are totally variable. Where sales volume is seasonal, erratic, or generally low in a given market, the public warehouse is an economical means of providing excellent product availability.

Public warehousing may sometimes supplement or replace distributors in a market. Many public warehouses provide a variety of logistical services for their clients, including packaging, labeling, order processing, and some light assembly. Distribution Centers, Inc. (DCI), a public warehouse based in Columbus, Ohio, maintains warehouse facilities in a number of major markets. Clients can position inventories in all these markets while dealing with only one firm. DCI can also link its computer with the suppliers' to facilitate order-processing and inventory updating. They will also repackage products to the end-user's order, label, and arrange for local delivery. An industrial marketer could ship standard products in bulk to the DCI warehouse, gaining transportation economies, and still enjoy excellent customer delivery service. The public warehouse is a feasible alternative to the distributor channel when the sales function can be economically executed with a direct sales force or reps.[14]

The alternative to renting or leasing warehouse space is *private warehousing*. Here, the manufacturer makes a capital investment in the facility. Although the investment is substantial, private facilities can provide operating cost advantages when the facility is regularly used close to capacity. Often more important than the cost and investment aspects is the enhancement of customer service. For example, National Twist Drill and Tool Company's private warehouse in Rochester, Michigan, uses a computerized inventory location system that enables the company to ship all orders within 24 hours.[15] The private warehouse offers more control over the warehousing operation, permitting efficient levels of operation and delivery service.

Transportation

Transportation is usually the largest single logistical expense, and with the impact of continually rising fuel costs, its importance will probably increase. Typically, the transportation decision involves the evaluation and selection of a mode of transportation and the individual carrier(s) that will ensure the best performance at the lowest cost. *Mode* refers to the type of carrier—rail, truck, water, air, or some combination of the four. *Individual carriers* are evaluated on rates and delivery performance.[16] In this section we will consider: (1) the role of transportation in industrial channels; (2) criteria for evaluating transportation options; (3) the purpose of expedited logistical systems; and (4) the private carrier alternative.

Transportation and Logistical Service   An industrial marketer must be able to move finished inventory between facilities, to channel intermediaries, and to handle customers effectively. The transportation sys-

---

[14] Michael D. Hutt and Thomas W. Speh, "Realigning Industrial Marketing Channels," *Industrial Marketing Management*, 12 (July 1983), pp. 171–177.

[15] "The Nation's Newest Private Distribution Centers," *Handling and Shipping*, 13 (July 1972), pp. 71–75.

[16] See Marvin L. Fair and Ernest W. Williams, *Transportation and Logistics* (Dallas: Business Publications Inc., 1981); Robert C. Lieb, *Transportation: The Domestic System*. 2d ed. (Englewood Cliffs, N.J.: Prentice-Hall, Inc., 1982).

tem is the link that binds the logistical network together and ultimately results in timely delivery of products. Efficient warehousing has little impact on order cycle performance if transportation is inconsistent or inadequate.

Effective transportation service may be used in combination with warehouse facilities and inventory levels to generate the required customer service level or it may be used in place of them. Inventory maintained in a variety of market-positioned warehouses can be pulled back to one centralized warehouse if there is rapid transportation service from the central location to industrial customers. The Xerox situation cited earlier is an example of using premium air freight service to offset the need for high inventories and extensive warehouse locations. The decision on transportation modes and particular carriers will depend on the cost tradeoffs and service capabilities of each.

Effective Transportation at Boise Cascade Means Profits

Distribution is critical to Boise Cascade Corporation. Transportation costs alone absorbed 10 percent of every sales dollar in 1982, totaling more than $340 million.

"Effective transportation makes us more competitive," says John B. Frey, Chairman of the Board and CEO. "Better customer service is just one of the reasons for this. Another reason is that by holding down overall freight costs, we keep our products competitively priced. Furthermore, because goods in transit represent the greater share of our total inventory, close transportation control plays a big part in achieving sound asset management."

Source: Jack Farrell, "Transportation: An 'Active Partner' in the Business," *Traffic Management*, 22 (July 1983), p. 42.

Transportation Performance Criteria   *Cost of service* is the variable cost associated with moving products from origin to destination, including any terminal or accessory charges. The cost of service may range from 0.25 cents per ton-mile for water, 2.07 cents for rail, 4.59 cents for motor carrier, to 45.8 cents for air freight.[17] Although these figures are averages, they demonstrate the structure of costs among the modes. The important aspect of selecting the mode of transportation is not cost per se,

---

[17] Ronald H. Ballou, *Basic Business Logistics* (Englewood Cliffs, N.J.: Prentice-Hall, Inc., 1978), p. 134.

but cost relative to the objective to be achieved. Bulk raw materials generally do not require rapid delivery service, so the cost of anything other than rail or water transportation could not be justified. On the other hand, while air freight may be almost ten times more expensive than motor freight, when a customer needs an emergency shipment of spare parts, the cost is inconsequential. The cost of premium (faster) transportation modes may be justified by the resulting inventory reductions.

Speed of service refers to the elapsed time to move products from one facility (plant or warehouse) to another facility (warehouse or customer plant). Again, speed of service often overrides the cost of service. Rail, a relatively slow mode used for bulk shipments, requires inventory buildups at the supplier's factory and the destination warehouse. The longer the delivery time, the more inventory customers must maintain to service their needs while the shipment is in transit. The slower modes involve lower variable costs for product movement, yet result in lower service levels and higher investments in inventory. The faster modes produce just the opposite effect. Not only must an intermodal comparison be made in terms of service, but different carriers within a mode must be evaluated on their "door-to-door" delivery time.

Service consistency is usually more important than average delivery time, and all modes of transportation are not equally consistent. Although air provides the lowest average delivery time, generally it has the highest *variability* in delivery time relative to average. The wide variations in modal service consistency are particularly critical in industrial marketing planning. The choice of transportation mode must be made on the basis of cost, average transit time, and consistency if effective customer service is to be achieved.

Because industrial buyers often place a premium on effective and consistent delivery service, the choice of transportation mode is an important one—one in which cost of service is often secondary. However, the best decision on transportation carriers will result from a balancing of service, variable costs, and investment requirements. The manager must also consider the transportation requirements of everyday versus expedited or rush-order shipments.

Normal vs. Expedited Systems   Logistical systems in industrial marketing channels are often *two-tier*: The routine logistical requirements are satisfied through one system, while the rush order needs are met through a different system. The normal system is designed to provide low-cost delivery at required service levels. Transportation modes and carriers are selected on the basis of simple efficiency—lowest rates and average delivery performance. A manufacturer of brake shoes may find that rail shipments from factory to distributor or to customer warehouses provide very low cost transportation at a service level that is adequate for most customer orders. However, brake shoes may be rush ordered perhaps 5 percent of the time as a result of increased customer production or abnormally high breakdowns in a truck fleet. The backup system might entail air express shipments from a special warehouse or any of a number of small package express services.

Reliance Electric encourages distributors to order in fewer, but larger, orders to economize on freight rates, but uses United Parcel Service for rush orders under 50 pounds per package.[18] Often such carriers form the backbone of the second-tier, priority logistical system.

Decision Criteria   The decision to use a premium transportation mode depends on the unit cost of the item, the predictability of the demand, inventory carrying costs, cost of the premium mode, savings in transit time, and the importance of priority delivery to the customer. The alternative is maintaining inventories close to customers. David Herron's model, which explicitly evaluates these variables,[19] suggests that for items with high unit value, low sales, and unpredictable demand, low inventories should be maintained at the destination, and premium transportation modes should be used to expedite orders. Faster transportation modes are also profitable for high-cost items when delivery time by the normal carrier is inconsistent and demand is unpredictable. Herron concludes that

A two-tier combination of normal and expedited operations is the most profitable. The cheaper mode is used to ship products whose demand is predictable; the faster mode for expedited items whose inventories at the destination have been reduced. This arrangement results in savings in the sum of transportation and inventory-carrying costs compared with costs of using either transportation mode alone.[20]

Private Carriers   Sometimes the only way for a supplier to achieve the consistent delivery performance required by customers is with its own trucks. Service improvement is the primary justification for a company fleet, because the private fleet may be more expensive than for-hire transportation. The investment requirements are significant—vehicles, maintenance facilities, and the like, though this can sometimes be reduced by leasing equipment. The decision to operate the private fleet is a complex one.[21] However, private ownership and management of transportation service may effectively balance the cost, investment, and service aspects of transportation. Inventory, the third leg of logistical management, is very much interrelated with the transportation decision.

[18] "Closing the Transportation/Delivery Gap," *Industrial Distribution*, 68 (April 1978), p. 46.

[19] David P. Herron, "Managing Physical Distribution for Profit," *Harvard Business Review*, 57 (May–June 1979), p. 128.

[20] *Ibid.*

[21] For example, see "The Elements of Private Carriage," booklet reprinted from *Transportation and Distribution Management* magazine (Washington, D.C.: The Traffic Service Corporation, 1970); H. G. Becker, Jr., "Private Carriage: Facts and Trends. Some Reasons Why," *Handling and Shipping*, 17 (July 1976), p. 42.

Inventory Management

Inventory management is the "buffer" in the logistical system. Inventories are needed in industrial channels because: (1) production and demand are not perfectly matched; (2) operating deficiencies in the logistical system often result in product unavailability (e.g., delayed shipments, inconsistent carrier performance); and (3) industrial customers cannot predict their product needs with certainty (e.g., a machine breakdown or a sudden need to expand production). Inventory may be viewed in the same light as warehouse facilities and transportation: It is an alternative method for providing the level of service required by industrial users, and the level of inventory is determined on the basis of cost, investment, and service (revenue).

Inventory Costs Inventory costs are subtle and difficult to comprehend because they are often not segregated, but are found throughout a firm's system of accounts. Inventory costs include four basic cost categories: (1) capital costs; (2) inventory service costs (e.g., taxes and insurance); (3) storage space costs; and (4) inventory risk costs (e.g., damage and pilferage).[22]

Together these four cost categories are known as *inventory carrying costs*, typically stated as a percentage of the value of the products held in inventory. (A carrying charge of 20 percent means that the cost of holding one unit in inventory for one year is 20 percent of the value of the product.) Inventory carrying costs usually range from 12 to 35 percent; yet these percentages may be much higher if all relevant inventory-related costs are considered.[23] One company that historically had used a 19 percent carrying charge for making inventory decisions, was found to have a true carrying charge of 38 percent.[24]

The implications are clear. To make sound inventory decisions, industrial managers must be able to capture the true cost of holding inventories. Only after the true costs of inventory are known can management evaluate the cost/service and inventory transportation cost tradeoffs. Effective inventory policy also demands a product-by-product analysis.

The 80/20 Rule Most industrial marketers with extensive product lines are aware that the great bulk of their products do not turn over very rapidly. This is the 80/20 principle: 80 percent of the sales are generated by 20 percent of the product line.

The major implication of the 80/20 principle is that industrial marketers must manage their inventory selectively, treating fast- and

---

[22] Bernard J. LaLonde and Douglas M. Lambert, "A Methodology for Determining Inventory Carrying Costs: Two Case Studies," in James Robeson and John Grabner, eds., *Proceedings of the Fifth Annual Transportation and Logistics Educators Conference* (October 1975), p. 47.

[23] *Ibid.*, p. 47.

[24] *Ibid.*, p. 39.

slow-moving items differently. If a company has half its inventory committed to products that produce only 20 percent of the unit sales volume, significant gains can be made by reducing inventories of the slow sellers to the point where their turnover rate approximates that of the fast sellers.[25] This applies regardless of how the inventory function is handled in the channel. Thus, suppliers can develop more efficient channels and substantially reduce distributor inventory costs by allowing the distributor to cut back inventory on slow turnover items. Not only will distributor cost performance improve, but enhanced channel goodwill should result.

Selective Inventory Strategies   The evaluation of selective inventory strategies will depend on the cost and service trade-offs involved. First, inventory of slow movers can be reduced at all locations; the result, however, may be a marked reduction in customer service. As with transportation, one workable alternative is to centralize the slow-moving items at a single location, thereby reducing total inventories. The result is a higher sales volume per unit of product at a given location. In turn, inventories of fast-moving items can be expanded, enhancing their service levels.

A selective inventory policy must be applied cautiously. Typically, fast-moving items are standardized items that customers expect to be readily available; slow movers often are nonstandardized, and customers expect to wait to receive them.[26] However, there is no rule that all slow-moving items require low service levels. If a slow-moving item is critical in the production process or is needed to repair a machine, an extremely high level of service is required. Thus, a selective inventory policy mandates that turnover rates and how critical the product is to the customer be evaluated in determining the inventory-transportation system.

The Critical Role of Forecasting   Estimates of future sales are the primary variable in determining inventory levels throughout the industrial logistics system. Short-term sales forecasts for weekly, monthly, quarterly, or yearly sales are the heart of any inventory planning system; inventories throughout the channel will be based on expected demand. The approaches to forecasting developed in Chapter 8 are relevant to the inventory decision. However, it is often necessary to adapt the broad sales forecasts to logistical purposes. A general forecast used to plan sales and promotional efforts is usually not specific enough for logistical inventory planning. Product-by-product estimates for short intervals are needed so that inventories can be adjusted. These are often not included in general marketing-sales forecasts. Finally, forecasting must be inte-

---

[25] James L. Heskett, "Logistics—Essential to Strategy," *Harvard Business Review*, 56 (November–December 1977), p. 89.
[26] *Ibid.*, p. 29.

grated within the channel. Distributors and suppliers must work from the same sales estimates so that order timing and quantities can be accurately determined for the channel.

Inventory decisions are based on cost-service and transportation-inventory trade-offs. Inventory costs must be accurately calculated through accounting systems designed to capture all relevant inventory expenses. Often, the true costs are higher than expected. Analysis of product turnover and customer product usage will dictate the selectivity of the inventory policy and specify the type of transportation service required. Finally, short interval sales forecasting developed on a common basis for all channel members is essential to create channel-wide inventory policy.

Computer Inventory Controls: As Easy as "ABC"

Two years ago, Kaman Bearing & Supply Corp. East took stock of its assets and was dismayed. More than half of the Syracuse-based firm's assets were tied up in inventory.

Kaman's management agreed that the company needed to overhaul its entire inventory-management system. So the supplier of bearings, belts, and drive components contracted with Peat, Marwick, Mitchell & Co. to formulate a cost-effective, computerized inventory-control system.

The new inventory-management package gives Kaman up-to-the-minute information on stock levels and transactions. Within four months, the computer will develop a complete profile of all stock items, breaking them down into ABC volume categories. (A items are important, fast-moving products; B and C items are slower-moving.) To provide this inventory profile, the computer tracks the movement of every stock item and prints out complete volume breakdowns.

These data are helpful in forecasting order volumes. By tracking stock-transaction histories, the computer can establish seasonal demand patterns. The system tells the company when it will need replacement stock and how much it will need. If usage peaks in March, for example, the computer may tell management to order the needed materials in January so it will have them in stock on time.

Accurate status reports on inventory levels and improved forecasting capability allow Kaman to set product-by-product service levels and adjust stock accordingly. The company programs into the computer the level of service it wants for each category. A items, for example, may have a designated order fulfillment rate of 99 percent, while C items may be rated at 50 percent. This service level can be adjusted to reflect changes in Kaman's service policies or sales figures.

By computerizing its inventory-management procedures, Kaman expects to pinpoint stock needs more accurately, thus eliminating the cost of carrying unnecessary inventory. Management receives higher-quality information on all order transactions and can use this to tailor customer service levels.

Although no actual performance figures are available yet, the firm is confident that its inventories will drop by as much as 30 percent.

Source: Lisa Harrington, "Better Management Means Lower Costs," *Traffic Management*, 21 (November 1982), p. 43.

The System: Focal Point of Logistical Planning

The "systems" perspective in logistical management cannot be stressed enough—it is the only way that management can be assured that the logistical function will meet prescribed goals. Not only must each logistical variable be analyzed in terms of its impact on every other variable, but the sum of the variables must be evaluated in light of the service level provided to customers. Logistics elements throughout the channel must be integrated to assure smooth product flow.

The burden on management is to plan the system to meet desired objectives *and* monitor its performance against those objectives. Management must recognize the signs of *maldistribution*, that undesirable state where a firm provides poorer service than its competitors at higher costs.[27] Signs of maldistribution include slow inventory turnover, poor customer service, and excessive premium freight charges. Louis Stern and Adel El-Ansary suggest that one reason for maldistribution is that management is "technique-" or "equipment-"oriented rather than system-oriented in the approach to logistics management.[28]

[27] Stephen B. Oresman and Charles D. Scudder, "A Remedy for Maldistribution," *Business Horizons*, 17 (June 1974), p. 72.

[28] Louis W. Stern and Adel I. El-Ansary, *Marketing Channels*, 2nd ed. (Englewood Cliffs, N.J.: Prentice-Hall, Inc., 1982), p. 192.

Summary

Logistical service is critical in buyer evaluation of industrial suppliers. Logistical service seems to rank second only to product quality as a desired supplier characteristic. Industrial marketing managers are faced with a stern challenge to develop cost-efficient logistical systems that provide the necessary service levels.

Decisions in the logistical area must be based on cost trade-offs among the logistical variables, and on comparisons of the costs and revenues associated with alternative levels of service. The optimal system is one that produces the highest profitability relative to the capital investment required.

The major logistical variables are facilities, transportation, and inventory. Decisions are required on the number of warehouses, whether they are to be owned or rented, the transportation mode and specific carrier, the level and deployment of inventory, and the selectivity of inventory levels. The systems approach can structure these three variables effectively. Management must continually evaluate system performance, watching for signals of maldistribution. Finally, the industrial supplier must monitor the impact of logistics on channel members and on overall channel performance.

Discussion Questions

1. Adopting the perspective of an organizational buyer, carefully illustrate how the most economical source of supply might be the firm that offers the highest price, but also the fastest and most reliable delivery system.

2. Why is the logistical function often singled out as "the last frontier of cost reduction in American business?"

3. Describe a situation where *total* logistical costs might be reduced by doubling transportation costs.

4. A key goal in logistical management is to find the optimum balance of logistical cost and customer service which yields optimal profits. Explain.

5. Explain how consistent order cycle performance gives the organizational buyer the opportunity to cut the level of safety stock maintained.

6. Explain how the use of reps versus distributors influences the number of warehouses that the industrial marketer will need to employ in the logistical system.

7. Why is it often necessary for industrial marketers to have a two-tier logistical system: one for routine orders, one for rush orders?

8. Inventory decisions for the industrial marketer are based on cost-service and transportation-inventory trade-offs. Illustrate the nature of these trade-offs.

9. Frequent interwarehouse shipments and slow inventory turnover are two signs of maldistribution. If these danger signals appear, what steps should the industrial marketer take?

10. An increasing number of manufacturers are adopting a materials management philosophy (see Chapter 2) and more sophisticated inventory control systems. What are the strategic implications of these developments for industrial marketers wishing to serve these customers?

C·H·A·P·T·E·R
14

Managing the Industrial
Pricing Function

The price that an industrial marketer assigns to a product or service is one of many factors that will be scrutinized by the organizational buyer. Pricing decisions cannot be made in a vacuum; they must be in concert with other marketing strategy decisions. The diverse nature of the industrial market presents unique problems and opportunities for the price-setter.

After reading this chapter, you will have an understanding of:

1. *the role of price in the cost/benefit calculations of organizational buyers;*
2. *the central elements of the industrial pricing process;*
3. *how effective new product prices are established and the need for periodic adjustment of the prices of existing products;*
4. *strategic approaches to competitive bidding;*
5. *the strategic role of lease marketing.*

The industrial marketing manager has to blend the various components of the marketing mix into a total offering that responds to the needs of the market and provides a return consistent with the firm's objectives. Price must be carefully meshed with the product, distribution, and communication strategies of the firm. Organizational customers view price as an attribute of the product; thus, product and pricing policies must be closely coordinated. In turn, price decisions can influence channel relationships by altering the profit margins of distributors or manufacturers' representatives. Thus, pricing objectives are linked to marketing as well as overall corporate objectives. *quality image etc.*

The interdependence of price and other strategy components must be recognized before the pricing function can be isolated for analysis. Clearly, there is no one best way for establishing the price of a new industrial product or modifying the price of existing products. The price-setter must know the firm's objectives, markets, costs, competition, and customer demand patterns—not easy when time is short, information incomplete, and the competitive and business climate changing rapidly. Material shortages, growing competition (foreign and domestic), new technology, changing consumer requirements, and the changing fortunes of different business sectors—these forces call for an active rather than a passive approach to pricing.[1]

This chapter is divided into five parts. First, the special meaning of price is defined in an industrial marketing context. Second, key determinants of the industrial pricing process are analyzed, and, an operational approach to pricing decisions provided. Third, pricing policies for new and existing products will be examined, with emphasis on the need for actively managing a product throughout its life cycle. Fourth, we consider price administration (i.e., types of price adjustments). Last, we turn to two areas of particular importance to the industrial marketer—competitive bidding and leasing.

An Industrial Pricing Perspective

When organizational decision makers select a particular product, they are "buying" a given level of product quality, technical service, and delivery reliability. Other elements may be of importance—the reputation of the supplier, a feeling of security, friendship, and other personal benefits flowing from the buyer-seller relationship. Thus, the total "product" (as discussed in Chapter 10) is much more than its physical attributes. Likewise, the *cost* of an industrial good includes much more than the seller's *price*. Pricing decisions and product policy decisions are inseparable and must be balanced within the firm's market segmentation plan.[2]

[1] Kent B. Monroe, "Some Common Myths Concerning Industrial Pricing," in Robert E. Spekman and David T. Wilson, eds., *Issues in Industrial Marketing: A View to the Future* (Chicago: American Marketing Association, 1982), pp. 78–89.

[2] Benson P. Shapiro and Barbara B. Jackson, "Industrial Pricing to Meet Customer Needs," *Harvard Business Review* 56 (November–December 1978), p. 125.

Benefits

Different market segments, each with unique needs, base their evaluation of a product on dimensions of particular value to them. The benefits of a particular product can be functional, operational, financial, or
personal.[3] These benefits are of varying degrees of importance to different market segments and to different individuals within the buying center. Functional benefits are the design characteristics that might be attractive to technical personnel; operational attributes are durability and
reliability, desirable qualities to production managers. Financial benefits
are favorable terms and opportunities for cost savings, of importance to
purchasing managers and controllers. Organizational status, reduced
risk, and personal satisfaction are among the personal benefits that
might accrue to an individual from a particular supplier choice.

Costs

A broad perspective is likewise needed in examining the costs a particular alternative may present for the buyer. These costs include not only
price, but also transportation, installation, order-handling, and inventory carrying costs. Less obvious, but no less important, are the risks of
product failure and poor technical and delivery support.[4] — *if product has
reputation for quality charge more*

These costs are made especially vivid in buying organizations using
formal supplier evaluation programs (see Chapter 3). Systems like the
cost-ratio and the weighted-point methods allow the buyer to measure
the total cost of dealing with alternative suppliers.[5]

A buyer may find that the supplier offering the lowest price may be
the highest cost alternative in the long run. Clearly, the supplier with the
lowest price is not guaranteed an account. This was reinforced in a study
of purchasers of selected capital items (e.g., liquid transfer and control
systems). In an analysis of over 100 purchase decisions, the low bidder
was *not* selected in over 40 percent of the cases.[6]

The Industrial Pricing Process

There is no easy formula for pricing an industrial product or service.
The decision is multidimensional rather than one-dimensional. The interactive variables of demand, cost, competition, profit relationships,
and customer usage patterns each assume significance as the marketer

---

[3]*Ibid.*, pp. 119–127.

[4]*Ibid.*

[5]For an interesting discussion of supplier evaluation from a marketer's perspective, see C. David Wieters and Lonnie L.
Ostrom, "Supplier Evaluation as a New Marketing Tool," *Industrial Marketing Management* 8 (1979), pp. 161–166.

[6]J. Patrick Kelly and James W. Coaker, "Can We Generalize about Choice Criteria for Industrial Purchasing Decisions?"
in Kenneth L. Bernhardt, ed., *Marketing: 1776–1976 and Beyond* (Chicago: American Marketing Association, 1976),
pp. 330–333.

Figure 14.1   Key Components of the Industrial Pricing Process

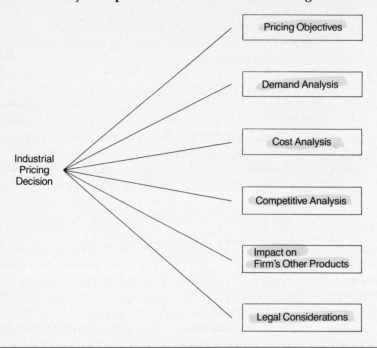

formulates the role that price will play in the firm's marketing strategy. Pertinent considerations illustrated in Figure 14.1, are (1) price objectives, (2) demand determinants, (3) cost determinants, and (4) competition. The product line and legal implications of a particular pricing decision are treated later.

Price Objectives

The pricing decision must be based on objectives congruent with marketing and overall corporate objectives. The marketer starts with principal, and adds collateral, pricing goals: (1) achieving a target return on investment; (2) achieving a market share goal; or (3) meeting competition. There are many other potential pricing objectives that go beyond profit and market share goals, and take into account competition, channel relationships, and product line considerations.

An example of pricing objectives, drawn from a classic study by Robert Lanzillotti, illustrates the nature of principal and collateral pricing goals.[7] United States Steel's principal pricing goal was to achieve an

[7] Robert F. Lanzillotti, "Pricing Objectives in Large Companies," *American Economic Review* 48 (December 1958), pp. 921–940; see also, J. Fred Weston, "The Myths and Realities of Corporate Pricing," *Fortune* 85 (April 1972), p. 85.

8 percent return on investment after taxes. Collateral pricing objectives were to achieve: (1) a target market share of 30 percent, (2) a stable price, and (3) a stable margin.

Pricing objectives must be established with care because they have far-reaching effects. Each firm faces unique internal and external environmental forces. Contrasting the strategies of Du Pont and the Dow Chemical Company illustrates the importance of a unified corporate direction.[8] Dow's strategy centers first on pricing low margin commodity goods low to build a dominant market share and then on maintaining that dominant share. Du Pont's strategy, on the other hand, emphasizes specialty products that carry a higher margin. Initially, these products are priced at a high level, and prices are reduced as the market expands and competition intensifies. Each firm requires explicit pricing objectives that are consistent with its corporate mission.

Demand Determinants

A strong market perspective is fundamental in pricing. The industrial market is diverse and complex. A single industrial product can be used in many different ways; each market segment may represent a unique application for the product and a separate usage level. The degree of importance of the industrial good in the buyer's end product also varies by market segment. Therefore, potential demand, sensitivity to price, and potential profitability can vary markedly across market segments. Once again, a sound market segmentation strategy is pivotal in effective marketing strategy development.

A Customer Focus   A sound industrial pricing perspective involves an analysis of the benefits and costs of the product from the standpoint of the customer.[9] In calculating the benefits of a product, the marketer can examine the physical attributes of a product (hard benefits) and the attached services (soft benefits). Hard benefits may be defined with a price-performance ratio. For example, one performance variable for a piece of earth-moving equipment may be dollars per horsepower or, better yet, yards of earth moved per hour. This approach forces the marketer to examine the product from the consumer's perspective and allows for a comparison of the firm's product offering with those of competitors. Soft benefits are more difficult to define precisely, but determining their degree of importance to various market segments should be attempted.

To the organizational customer, cost includes more dimensions than price. The "costs" of a new packaging machine, purchased by a

---

[8] "Pricing Strategy in an Inflation Economy," *Business Week* (April 6, 1974), pp. 42–49.

[9] Shapiro and Jackson, "Industrial Pricing to Meet Customer Needs," pp. 123–124.

manufacturer, begin with the price but also include transportation, installation, repair and maintenance, and energy usage. In calculating the customer costs of such a product, the marketer can apply *life cycle costing* to calculate the total cost of a product over its life span. It includes maintenance, repair, operating costs, and useful product life. Rising labor, energy, and material prices are among factors that have stimulated renewed interest in life cycle costing by government agencies, commercial enterprises, and institutions—and marketing managers.[10]

Although the concept has generally been applied to capital items, (e.g., computers, heavy industrial equipment, health facilities), it can also be applied to lighter industrial goods. In using life cycle costing as a marketing tool, the producer of a packaging machine may be able to justify a high initial price if there will be clear savings in energy, material, labor, and maintenance costs over the life of the asset.

Other costs are more difficult to quantify precisely.[11] The buyer of packaging equipment might be very concerned about the possibility of a production stoppage due to machine failure. Segments of the market that are sensitive to this risk will be interested in the benefit of reliability, and may be willing to pay a higher price to reduce the risk of system failure.

To recap, the industrial price-setter must examine how organizational buyers balance the costs and benefits of alternative offerings. This approach is useful, not only in determining an appropriate price, but also in facilitating the development of responsive product, advertising, and personal selling strategies.

Diagnosing Cost/Benefit Trade-Offs[12]   How organizational buyers will evaluate the cost/benefit trade-offs of the total offering determines the appropriateness of a particular industrial pricing strategy. Two competitors with similar products may ask different prices, because their total offerings are perceived to be different by buyers. In the eyes of the organizational buyer, one firm may provide more *value* than another.

A core pricing issue is: "Which attributes of the offering contribute most to its perceived value?" Several attributes of a total product offering are illustrated in Table 14.1. These attributes, which relate to a particular Du Pont product offering, were identified as those that have value to buyers and differ among competitors. Two levels of performance are provided for each attribute. Since higher costs are incurred in providing higher levels of performance on one or more of the attributes,

[10] Robert J. Brown, "A New Marketing Tool: Life Cycle Costing," *Industrial Marketing Management* 8 (April 1979), pp. 109–113.

[11] Shapiro and Jackson, "Industrial Pricing to Meet Customer Needs," pp. 119–127.

[12] Irwin Gross, "Insights from Pricing Research," in Earl L. Bailey, ed., *Pricing Practices and Strategies* (New York: The Conference Board, 1978), pp. 34–39.

Table 14.1   Attributes of a Total Product Offering: Some Trade-Offs

Attribute	High Level	Low Level
Quality	Impurities less than one part per million	Impurities less than ten parts per million
Delivery	Within one week	Within two weeks
System	Supply total system	Supply chemical only
Innovation	High level of R and D support	Little R and D support
Retraining	Retrain on request	Train on initial purchase
Service	Locally available	Through home office

Source: Irwin Gross, "Insights from Pricing Research," in Earl L. Bailey, ed., *Pricing Practices and Strategies* (New York: The Conference Board, 1978), p. 37. Reprinted by permission of The Conference Board.

Figure 14.2   Relative Perceived Value of Two Product Offerings

$$\begin{bmatrix} \text{Relative Perceived} \\ \text{Value of} \\ \text{Offering "A" vs.} \\ \text{Offering "B"} \end{bmatrix} = \begin{bmatrix} \text{Price Premium for} \\ \text{Indifference} \end{bmatrix} = \begin{bmatrix} \text{First} \\ \text{Attribute} \\ \text{Value} \end{bmatrix} \times \begin{bmatrix} \text{Perceived} \\ \text{Performance of} \\ \text{Offering "A" on} \\ \text{First Attribute} \end{bmatrix} - \begin{bmatrix} \text{Perceived} \\ \text{Performance of} \\ \text{Offering "B" on} \\ \text{First Attribute} \end{bmatrix} + \begin{bmatrix} \text{Second} \\ \text{Attribute} \\ \text{Value} \end{bmatrix} \times \begin{bmatrix} \text{Perceived} \\ \text{Performance of} \\ \text{Offering "A" on} \\ \text{Second Attribute} \end{bmatrix} - \begin{bmatrix} \text{Perceived} \\ \text{Performance of} \\ \text{Offering "B" on} \\ \text{Second Attribute} \end{bmatrix}$$

Source: Irwin Gross, "Insights from Pricing Research," in Earl L. Bailey (ed.), *Pricing Practices and Strategies* (New York: The Conference Board, 1978), p. 38. Reprinted by permission.

the strategist should assess the relative importance of the attributes to alternative market segments and the strength of the firm's offering on each of the important attributes vis-a-vis competitors.

The equation in Figure 14.2 highlights how the relative perceived values of two competing offerings are compared. Irv Gross contends that the relative perceived value of offering A versus B "can be thought of as the price differential at which the buyer would be indifferent between the alternatives."[13] As in Figure 14.2, the premium price differential, or perceived relative value, can be broken down into components based on each important attribute: (1) the value of the attribute to the buyer, and (2) the perception of how competing offerings perform on that attribute. By summing all of the component values, we reach the total relative perceived value of an offering. Thus, product offering A may have a total perceived value of $24 per unit, compared to $20 for offering B. The $4 premium might be derived from the value that buyers assign to a high level of product quality and a responsive delivery system, and the perceived advantage of A over others on these attributes.

Strategy Implications of the Cost/Benefit Analysis   By isolating the important attributes and the perceptions that enter into the cost/benefit

[13] *Ibid.*, p. 35.

calculations of organizational buyers, the industrial marketer is better equipped to establish a price and to shape other elements of the marketing strategy. First, if the firm's performance on a highly valued product attribute is truly higher than those offered by competitors, but the market perceives no differences, marketing communications must be devised to bring perceptions into line with reality. Second, marketing communications may also alter the values that organizational buyers assign to a particular attribute. The importance of an attribute like customer training might be elevated through marketing communications that emphasize the improved efficiency and safety that training affords the potential buying organization.

Third, the perceived value of the total product offering can be changed by improving the firm's level of performance on attributes that are assigned special importance by organizational buyers. Fourth, knowledge of the cost/benefit perceptions of potential customers presents market segmentation opportunities. For example, good strategy might target those market segments that value the particular product offering attributes that match the distinctive strengths of the firm.

Elasticity Varies by Market Segment   Price elasticity of demand is a measure of the degree to which customers are sensitive to price changes. Specifically, price elasticity of demand refers to the rate of percentage change in quantity demanded attributable to the percentage change in price.

Price elasticity of demand is not the same at all prices. An industrial marketer contemplating an alteration in price policy must understand the elasticity of demand. For example, total revenue (price × quantity) will *increase* if price is decreased and demand is price-elastic, whereas revenues will *fall* if the price is decreased and demand is price-inelastic. Many factors influence the price elasticity of demand—one of them may be buyer perceptions of price/quality relationships. Research suggests that organizational buyers do not associate higher quality with higher price or lower quality with lower price.[14]

Efforts to measure the demand patterns of an individual firm or even an entire industry are extremely difficult. "No one has yet developed a completely reliable method to measure the price elasticity of demand for a particular brand."[15] Since price is only one of many variables under the control of the marketing manager and only one component of the total product offering, other demand elasticities—promotion, distribution, service—also assume importance. However, recognizing that measurement of price elasticity is difficult should not deter the marketer

---

[14] Phillip D. White and Edward S. Cundiff, "Assessing the Quality of Industrial Products," *Journal of Marketing* 42 (January 1978), pp. 80–86.

[15] Alfred R. Oxenfeldt, "A Decision-Making Structure for Price Decisions," *Journal of Marketing* 37 (January 1973), p. 50.

from attempts to define buyer sensitivity to the price variable across market segments.

Elasticity and End Use   Important insights can be secured by answering this question: *How important is the industrial marketer's product as an input into the total cost of the end product?* If the industrial marketer's product has an insignificant effect on cost, demand is likely inelastic:

> *A manufacturer of precision transistors was contemplating an across-the-board price decrease to increase sales. However, an item analysis of the product line revealed that some of its low volume transistors had exotic applications. A technical customer used the component in an ultrasonic testing apparatus which was sold for $8,000 a unit. This fact prompted the transistor manufacturer to raise the price of the item. Ironically, the firm then experienced a temporary surge of demand for the item as purchasing agents stocked up in anticipation of future price increases.*[16]

Of course, the marketer must temper this estimate with an analysis of the costs, availability, and suitability of substitutes. Generally, if the industrial product constitutes an important but low cost input into the end product, price is less important than quality and delivery reliability.[17]

Where the industrial product input assumes a more substantial portion of the final product's total cost, changes in price may have an important effect on the demand of both the final product and the industrial product input. If demand in the final consumer market is price elastic, a reduction in price of the end item that is caused by a price reduction of an industrial product input would generate an increase in demand for the final product and, in turn, for the industrial product.

Because the demand for many industrial products is derived from the demand of the product of which they are a part, a strong end-user focus is needed. The marketer can benefit by examining the trends and changing fortunes of important final consumer markets. Different sectors of the market grow at different rates, confront different levels of competition, and face different short-run and long-run challenges. A downturn in the economy does not fall equally on all sectors. Pricing decisions demand a two-tier market focus—of organizational customers and final product customers. "All things being equal, an industrial supplier will have more success in passing on a price increase to customers who are prospering than to customers who are hard-pressed."[18]

The value that customers assign to a firm's offering can vary by market segment because the same industrial product may serve different purposes for different customers. This underscores the important role of market segmentation in the development of profitable pricing strategies.

---

[16] Reed Moyer and Robert J. Boewadt, "The Pricing of Industrial Goods," *Business Horizons* 14 (June 1971), pp. 27–34.

[17] *Ibid.*, p. 28.

[18] *Ibid.*, p. 30.

Forecasting Demand for Chips

Computer chips are the small electronic circuits that constitute the essence of a computer. These chips have many applications—defense products, telecommunications equipment, office automation equipment, toys, and automobiles. A manufacturer of computer chips, therefore, must forecast demand by application or market segment. During recession, demand for chips can decline sharply in some segments, such as the automobile industry. As the demand in consumer markets picks up, computer chip manufacturers often have trouble meeting demand and, at times, have been forced to restrict the amounts their customers can order. As a result, some computer manufacturers have entered into long-term agreements with computer chip manufacturers to assure supply continuity.

       Since the demand for industrial products like computer chips is derived from the demand for other products like personal computers and automobiles, sound industrial pricing decisions rest on an understanding of demand patterns by application.

Source: Erik Larson and Carrie Dolan, "Heavy Demand for Computer Chips Sets Suppliers, Buyers Scrambling," *Wall Street Journal* (July 15, 1983), pp. 21, 30.

Methods of Estimating Demand   How can the industrial marketer measure the price elasticity of demand? Some techniques rely on objective statistical data, others on the intuition and judgment of managers.

      Test marketing, as a rule, is considered appropriate only for consumer-goods manufacturers.[19] However, this technique should not be eliminated from the industrial marketer's repertoire. Industrial products that are sold to a large number of potential users, have short usage cycles (to analyze repurchase patterns), and have feasible test market sites, lend themselves to test marketing. While most high-priced capital items do not fit this profile, products like industrial paints and maintenance items do.

      The *survey approach* examined in Chapter 5 can also be used to measure price elasticity, testing for willingness to buy at various prices or price ranges. On occasion, joint research with a consumer goods cus-

[19]*Ibid.*, pp. 27–34.

tomer could survey final consumer demand. Since price is only one variable, the survey instrument must also probe for product and service perceptions. It would be useful to ascertain how organizational buyers view price in fundamental cost/benefit tradeoffs. This broader perspective is particularly useful in isolating market segments.

When, as often happens, the price-setter lacks time and resources, a more informal, subjective approach becomes practical. This technique, drawing upon executive experience, intuition, and judgment, analyzes the relationship of price to other marketing mix variables, like product, promotion, and distribution strategies and a particular competitive setting.[20]

Knowledge of the market is the cornerstone of industrial pricing. A strong market focus, which examines how consumers trade-off benefits and costs in their decision making, establishes a base for assigning prices. In this precarious task, the goal is to estimate as precisely as possible the probable demand curve for the firm's product. Knowledge of demand patterns must be augmented by knowledge of costs.

Cost Determinants

Industrial marketers often pursue a strong internal orientation; they base prices on their own costs, reaching the selling price by calculating unit costs and adding a percentage profit. A strict cost-plus philosophy of pricing overlooks customer perceptions of value, competition, and the interaction of volume and profit.

Costs do, however, establish the lowest pricing point. Since costs fluctuate with volume and vary over time, they must be considered in relation to demand, competition, and pricing objectives. The marketer must know which costs are relevant to the pricing decision and how these costs will fluctuate with volume and over time. Product costs are crucial in projecting the profitability of individual products as well as the entire product line. Proper classification of costs is essential.

Classifying Costs[21]   The goals of a cost classification system are to: (1) properly classify cost data into their fixed and variable components and (2) properly link them to the activity causing them. The manager can then analyze the effects of volume and, more importantly, identify sources of profit. The following cost concepts are instrumental in the analysis:

1.   *Direct traceable or attributable costs*—those costs, fixed or variable, incurred by and solely for a particular product, customer, or sales territory (e.g., raw materials).

[20] For example, see Bill R. Darden, "An Operational Approach to Product Pricing," *Journal of Marketing* 32 (April 1969), pp. 29–33.

[21] Kent B. Monroe, *Pricing: Making Profitable Decisions* (New York: McGraw-Hill Book Company, 1979), pp. 52–57.

2.   *Indirect traceable costs*—those costs, fixed or variable, that can be traced to a product, customer, or sales territory (e.g., general plant overhead may be indirectly assigned to a product).

3.   *General costs*—those that support a number of activities and that cannot be objectively assigned to a product on the basis of a direct physical relationship (e.g., the administrative costs of a sales district).

General costs will rarely change because an item is added or deleted from the product line. Marketing, production, and distribution costs all must be classified. In developing a new line or deleting or adding an item to an existing line, the marketer must grasp the cost implications:

- What proportion of the cost of the product is accounted for by purchases of raw materials and components from suppliers?
- How will costs vary at different levels of production?
- Based on the forecasted level of demand, can economies of scale be expected?
- Does our firm enjoy cost advantages over competitors?
- How does the experience effect impact our cost projections?

Experience Effect   The marketing strategist must also consider the behavior of costs over time, forecasting costs and, in turn, prices. The experience effect is a concept of strategic importance here.

Experience curve analysis was introduced in Chapter 10 as a tool to aid product management. The experience curve reflects the theory that costs (measured in constant dollars) decline by a predictable and constant percentage each time *accumulated* production experience (volume) is doubled. Thus, each time accumulated volume is doubled, the unit costs of many products fall, usually by 20 to 30 percent.[22] The experience curve effect encompasses a broad range of manufacturing, marketing, distribution, and administrative costs.

The three major sources of the experience effect are (1) learning by doing, (2) technological improvements, and (3) economies of scale.[23] Figure 14.3 traces the cost experience for steam turbine generators. The cost per megawatt (MW) of output of steam generators followed a 70 percent slope (alternatively, a 30 percent reduction in costs for every doubling in production). The sources of the decline in costs resulted from: (1) practice in producing units of each size, which followed an 87 percent slope; (2) scale economies derived from building larger units, 600 MW rather than 200 MW units; and (3) technological improvements

[22] William J. Abernathy and Kenneth Wayne, "Limits of the Learning Curve," *Harvard Business Review* 52 (September–October 1974), pp. 109–119; see also, Staff of the Boston Consulting Group, *Perspectives on Experience* (Boston: Boston Consulting Group, Inc., 1972).

[23] George S. Day and David B. Montgomery, "Diagnosing the Experience Curve," *Journal of Marketing* 47 (Spring 1983), pp. 44–58.

Figure 14.3   Cost Experience for Steam Turbine Generators

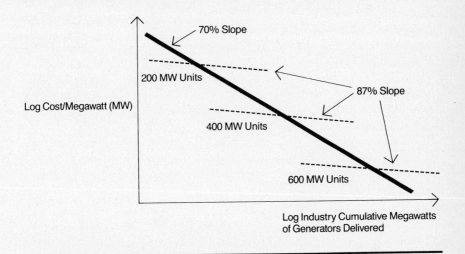

Source: George S. Day and David B. Montgomery, "Diagnosing the Experience Curve," *Journal of Marketing*, 47 (Spring 1983), p. 47. Reprinted by permission of the American Marketing Association.

in such areas as bearings and high strength steels, which permitted the design of larger units.[24]

Unfortunately, as experience is gained, costs do not automatically decline. In fact, costs that are not carefully managed will inevitably rise. Experience merely gives management the opportunity to seek cost reductions and efficiency improvements. A thorough effort is needed to exploit the benefits of experience. Product standardization, new production processes, labor efficiency, work specialization—these are only a few of the many areas that must be examined to capitalize on the experience effect.

The experience effect can raise a strategic dilemma for the industrial marketer. Often, the aggressive pursuit of a cost minimization strategy leads to a reduced ability to make innovative product changes in the face of competition.[25] Clearly, any firm following an efficiency strategy must insure that its product remains in line with the needs of the market. A product that is efficiently produced and carries a low price can only survive if there are significant market segments that emphasize low price as a choice criterion.

---

[24] Ralph Sultan, *Pricing in the Electrical Oligopoly*, Vols. I and II (Cambridge, Mass.: Harvard Graduate School of Business Administration, 1974), cited in Day and Montgomery, *ibid.*

[25] Abernathy and Wayne, "Limits of the Learning Curve," pp. 109–119.

The experience effect can be used to project costs and prices. The concept is also of value when product line modifications are being considered. Often, two or more products in the firm's line share a common resource or involve the same production or distribution activity. With such shared experience, the costs of one item in the product line are reduced even more because of the accumulated experience with the other product line item.[26] For example, the same production operations may be used to produce high torque motors for oil exploration and low torque motors for conveyor belts.[27] The marketer that has carefully classified costs is best equipped to take advantage of shared experience opportunities.

Experience curve analysis is relevant when learning, technology, and economies of scale are important in the environment.[28] Here the industrial marketer can use experience curve analysis to project potential cost reduction opportunities.

Break-Even Analysis   Break-even-point analysis, a basic financial tool, inevitably enters the pricing process. Break-even-point analysis allows the decision maker to determine the level of sales required to cover all relevant costs. The break-even-point can be calculated as follows:

$$BEQ = \frac{FC}{P - VC}$$

where

BEQ = break even sales quantity
FC = fixed costs
P = selling price
VC = direct variable costs

Assume that fixed costs are $200,000; direct variable costs are $15; and consideration is being given to a $20 selling price. Thus:

$$BEQ = \frac{200,000}{20 - 15} = \frac{200,000}{5} = 40,000 \text{ units}$$

From Figure 14.4, note that break-even analysis assumes that: (1) fixed costs remain constant as the volume of production increases, and (2) variable costs increase proportionately with increases in production. Break-even-point calculations are often based heavily on historical cost data when, in fact, projected costs and prices are more critical.

---

[26] Derek F. Abell and John S. Hammond, *Strategic Market Planning: Problems and Analytical Approaches* (Englewood Cliffs, N.J.: Prentice-Hall, Inc., 1979), pp. 125–127.

[27] Day and Montgomery, "Diagnosing the Experience Curve," p. 54.

[28] *Ibid.*, pp. 56–57.

Figure 14.4   Break-Even Analysis

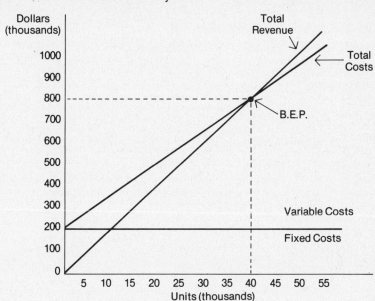

Competition

Competition establishes an upper limit on price. Industrial marketers seem to regard "competitive level pricing" as the most important pricing strategy.[29] The degree of latitude that the individual industrial firm has in its pricing decision depends heavily upon the level of differentiation that the product has in the perceptions of organizational buyers. Price is only one component of the cost/benefit equation of buyers; the marketer can gain a differential advantage over competitors on many dimensions other than physical product characteristics, such as reputation, technical expertise, delivery reliability, and related factors.

In addition to assessing the product's degree of differentiation in various market segments, one must ask how competitors will respond to particular pricing decisions.

Gauging Competitive Response   To predict the response of competitors, the marketer can first benefit by examining the cost structure of direct competitors and producers of potential substitutes. Here the marketer can draw upon public statements and records (e.g., annual reports) to form rough estimates. The experience effect can also be used to assess

[29] John G. Udell, *Successful Marketing Strategies* (Madison, WI: Mimir Publishers, Inc., 1972), p. 109.

**Table 14.2   Selected Cost Comparison Issues:
Followers vs. the Pioneer**

Why followers may have lower initial costs:

Technology/ Economies of Scale	Followers may benefit by using more current production technology than the pioneer or by building a plant with a larger scale of operations.
Product/Market Knowledge	Followers may learn from the pioneer's mistakes by analyzing the competitor's product, hiring key personnel, or identifying through market research problems and unfulfilled expectations of customers and channel members.
Shared Experience	Compared to the pioneer, followers may be able to gain advantages on certain cost elements by sharing operations with other parts of the company.
Experience of Suppliers	Followers, together with the pioneer, benefit from cost reductions achieved by outside suppliers of components or production equipment.

Source: Adapted from George S. Day and David B. Montgomery, "Diagnosing the Experience Curve," *Journal of Marketing*, 47 (Spring 1983), pp. 48–49.

the cost structure of competition. Competitors that have ascended the learning curve may have lower costs than those just entering the industry and beginning the climb. An estimate of the cost structure is valuable in gauging how well competitors can respond to price reductions and in projecting the pattern of prices in the future.

Under certain conditions, however, followers into a market may confront lower initial costs than the pioneer. Why? Some of the reasons are highlighted in Table 14.2. By failing to recognize potential cost advantages of late entrants, the industrial marketer can dramatically overstate cost differences.

The market strategy employed by competing sellers is also important here. Competitors will be more sensitive toward price reductions that threaten market segments that they deem important. They learn of price reductions earlier when their market segments overlap. Of course, competitors may choose not to follow a price decrease, especially if their products enjoy a differentiated position.

Industry Structure   Where there are few sellers (*oligopoly*), the actions of one seller produce reactions on the part of its competitors. Examples of oligopolistic industries are computers, aluminum, steel, automobiles, electrical equipment, and glass. In each case, a small number of manufacturers dominate total output. Oligopolies can be either pure or differentiated. In a pure oligopoly, competing firms offer homogeneous products (e.g., steel); a differentiated oligopoly contains producers of differentiated products (e.g., computers). As the extent of product differentiation in an oligopoly increases, the price differences also increase.

The *kinked demand curve* is characteristic of oligopolistic markets. The theory assumes that competing sellers will follow any decrease in

Figure 14.5   Kinked Demand Curve

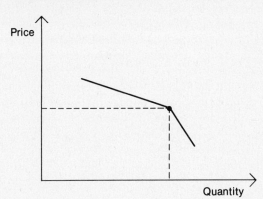

price in order to protect their market shares, but will refrain from following price increases, in order to capture part of the market share of the price-raiser. Thus, the individual firm's demand curve (Figure 14.5) is kinked at the current price-quantity combination. A price decrease results in a relatively small increase in sales. On the other hand, a price increase would lead to a significant reduction in quantity demanded and, in turn, total revenue, as customers shift to lower-priced competing firms.

There is often a recognized price leader in the industrial market. *Price leadership* results when one firm essentially serves as the industry spokesman and other sellers in the industry accept its pricing policy. This leadership position can result from technical superiority, size and strength, cost efficiency, power in the channel of distribution, market information, or a combination. The industry leader is presumed to bring profitability and stability to an industry by establishing a price that produces satisfactory profits for all sellers.

The manager requires a grasp of objectives, demand, cost, competition, and legal factors (discussed later) to approach the multidimensional pricing decision. Price-setting is not an act but an ongoing process.

A Price-Setter's Dilemma

The following scenario, provided by the president of an electrical equipment company, describes how costs and competitive forces can signal an end to the life of a product. The product is a component part for electric motors.

We began to get information back from the field that our prices were no longer competitive. On the other hand, an examination of costs indicated that if we lowered the price, the line would go from marginally profitable to significant loss.

We analyzed our manufacturing techniques and compared them with the reasonable knowledge that we had about our competition. It became apparent that without an expenditure of approximately $500,000 for new equipment, we would not be able to produce the product for a price that would approach that of our two major competitors.

At the time, we sold about $1 million worth of this product; and we projected that the increased investment in manufacturing would provide a profit of approximately $140,000 before taxes on this volume. We decided that a three-and-one-half-year payout was inadequate and phased out the line.

We have benefited from this decision. First, the capital was invested in other product lines, thus increasing their profitability. In addition, by focusing our strengths on fewer products, we were able to increase market penetration on those remaining products so significantly that our total sales today are probably much higher than they would have been had we continued to manufacture (that part).

Source: David H. Hopkins, *Business Strategies for Problem Products* (New York: The Conference Board, 1977), p. 32. Reprinted by permission of The Conference Board.

Pricing Across the Product Life Cycle

What price should be assigned to a distinctly new industrial product or service? When an item is added to an existing product line, how should it be priced in relation to products already in the line?

Pricing New Products

The strategic decision of pricing new products can be best understood by examining the policies at the boundaries of the continuum—from *skimming* (high initial price) to *penetration* (low initial price).

Consider again the pricing strategies of Du Pont and Dow Chemical. Du Pont assigns an initial high price to new products in order to generate immediate profits or to recover research and development expenditures, while Dow Chemical follows a low price strategy with the objective of gaining market share.

Skimming vs. Penetration   In evaluating the merits of skimming compared to penetration, the marketer must again examine price from the buyer's perspective. This approach "recognizes that the upper limit is the price that will produce the minimum acceptable rate of return on the investment of a sufficiently large number of prospects."[30] This is especially important in pricing new products, because the potential profits accruing to buyers of a new machine tool, for example, will vary by market segment, and these market segments may differ in the minimum rate of return that will induce them to invest in the machine tool.

Skimming   A skimming approach, appropriate for a distinctly new product, provides the firm with an opportunity to profitably reach market segments that are not sensitive to the high initial price. As a product ages, and as competitors enter and organizational buyers become accustomed to evaluating and purchasing the product, demand becomes more price-elastic. The policy of using skimming at the outset, followed by penetration pricing as the product matures, is referred to by Joel Dean as *time segmentation*.[31] A skimming policy allows the marketer to capture early profits, then reduce the price to reach segments that are more price-sensitive. It also allows the innovator to more quickly recover high developmental costs.

During the innovative firm's monopoly period, Robert Dolan and Abel Jeuland demonstrate that:[32]

1.   A skimming policy is optimal if the demand curve is stable over time (no diffusion) and production costs decline with accumulated volume;

2.   A penetration policy is optimal if there is a relatively high repeat purchase rate for nondurable goods or if a durable good's demand is characterized by diffusion.

Penetration   A penetration policy is appropriate when there is: (1) high price elasticity of demand, (2) strong threat of imminent competition, and (3) opportunity for a substantial reduction in production costs as volume expands. Drawing upon the experience effect, a firm that can quickly gain substantial market share and experience can gain a strategic advantage over competitors. The viability of this strategy increases with

---

[30] Joel Dean, "Pricing Policies for New Products," *Harvard Business Review* 54 (November–December 1976), p. 151.

[31] *Ibid.*, p. 152.

[32] Robert J. Dolan and Abel P. Jeuland, "Experience Curves and Dynamic Demand Models: Implications for Optimal Pricing Strategies," *Journal of Marketing* 45 (Winter 1981), pp. 52–62.

the potential size of the future market. By taking a large share of new sales, experience can be gained when there is a large market growth rate. Of course, the value of additional market share differs markedly between industries and often among products, markets, and competitors within a particular industry.[33] Factors to be assessed in determining the value of additional market share include the investment requirements, potential benefits of experience, expected market trends, likely competitive reaction, and short- and long-term profit implications.

Product Line Considerations   The contemporary industrial firm with a long product line faces the complex problem of achieving balance in pricing the product mix. Firms extend their product lines because the demands for various products are interdependent, the costs of producing and marketing those items are interdependent, or both.[34] A firm may add to its product line—or even develop a new product line—to fit more precisely the needs of a particular market segment. If both the demand and costs of individual product line items are interrelated, production and marketing decisions about one product line item inevitably influence both the revenues and costs of the others.

Are specific product line items substitutes or complements? Will a change in the price of one item enhance or retard the usage rate of this or other products in key market segments? Should a new product be priced high at the outset to protect other product line items (e.g., potential substitutes) and give the firm time to revamp other items in the line? Such decisions require a knowledge of demand, costs, competition, and strategic marketing objectives.

Announcements of new product introductions are often accompanied by revisions in the price schedule for other product line items. Technological advances have been bringing down the prices of computers for years. IBM's introduction of a less expensive, but more sophisticated, central processing unit was paralleled by a reduction in the price of older models.[35] Such product line pricing adjustments must be made with care, but are common in the industrial market.

Organizational buyers often screen out product alternatives that fall outside an acceptable price range to concentrate on a feasible set of alternatives. Kent Monroe suggests that if all products in a line are priced within the acceptable range, there is a higher probability that a buyer will purchase a product from that line.[36] Thus, success in penetrating a buying organization with one item often means success for other items in the product line.

---

[33] Yoram Wind and Vijay Mahajan, "Market Share: Concepts, Findings and Directions for Future Research," in Ben M. Enis and Kenneth J. Roering, eds., *Review of Marketing 1981* (Chicago: American Marketing Association, 1981), pp. 31–42; see also, Kent B. Monroe, "Some Common Myths," pp. 78–89.

[34] Monroe, *Pricing*, p. 143.

[35] Jeffrey A. Tannenbaum, "IBM Introduces New Processors for System 370," *Wall Street Journal* (January 31, 1979), p. 2.

[36] Monroe, *Pricing*, p. 153.

Price Administration

The industrial marketer deals with different types of customers (e.g., middlemen vs. original equipment manufacturers) in different geographical regions who buy in different quantities. Thus, there is a need to adjust prices to these conditions. This is the responsibility of price administration.

At the outset, it is important to understand a basic pricing tradition. Industrial sellers often provide a list price and a multiplier. The net price—the price of most importance to the organizational buyer— equals the list price times the multiplier. A product with a list price of $100 and a multiplier of 82 percent has a new price of $82. Why do industrial price-setters send their customers on such a circuitous route to the net price? Industrial manufacturers have many items in their product line and, often, many product lines described in a catalog. Rather than printing a new catalog each time the price of one or more items is adjusted, the firm merely prints a new price schedule and conveys the changes in adjusted multipliers. (For example, the multiplier for the $100 item might be changed to 80 percent, a two-dollar reduction.) Likewise, the list-price multiplier system makes it more difficult for competitors to detect price changes as they occur.

Discounts

Price administration requires a discount schedule, which in turn requires decisions about trade, quantity, and cash discounts. Each is defined and illustrated in Table 14.3.

Trade Discounts   Trade discounts, offered to intermediaries or particular classifications of customers, allow the marketer to adjust the price based on the costs and benefits of dealing with different classifications of customers. Trade discounts are offered to distributors because they are performing important services. Trade discounts for original equipment manufacturers could be justified by their high volume purchasing and low selling requirements. In establishing trade discounts, the marketer must recognize competitive norms and the relative importance of different channel members and customer types to overall marketing objectives.

Quantity Discounts   Table 14.3 defines two types of quantity discounts—cumulative and noncumulative. The choice of the type and specific schedule for quantity discounts depends on an assessment of demand, costs, and competition. In determining break points in the discount schedule, a strong customer focus is once again valuable, in terms of inventory carrying costs, order processing costs, transportation costs, and usage rates of different market segments. The marketer can also benefit from examining cost/service tradeoffs (see Chapter 13).

Table 14.3   Types of Discounts

Types	Characteristics
Trade Discounts	Those offered to different types of customers and or middlemen. Often consist of a chain of discounts, subtracted successively from each new net price. *Example*: An item with a $10 list price might be offered to distributors with a discount of 25 + 10 percent: $10.00 − .25(10.00) = $7.50, and $7.50 − .10(7.50) = $6.75.
Quantity Discounts	
Noncumulative	Those granted on the basis of the size (measured in dollars or units) of a single purchase, to encourage large orders. *Example*:

Size of Order	Percent Off
Less than 20 units	0
20–29 units	2
30 or more units	4

Cumulative	Those granted on the basis of the size (measured in dollars or units) of orders over a specified period of time. *Example*: Annual Customer

Purchases	Size of Discount
Less than $1,000	0%
1,000–1,999	3%
2,000–2,999	4%
3,000–3,999	5%

Cash Discounts	Those offered for payment of an invoice within a specified period of time. *Example*: 2 10, net 30 (i.e., a 2 percent discount may be taken by the buyer if paid within 10 days).

Cash Discounts   Cash discounts are offered to encourage prompt payment of invoices, thereby allowing the marketer to maintain a more favorable cash flow position. As illustrated in Table 14.3, a 2 percent discount might be offered if the bill is paid within 10 days. Often, cash discounts present a delicate problem for marketers. Large buyers pay their bills well beyond the 10-day period and still deduct the cash discount, especially during periods of high interest rates. The marketer's success in correcting this problem often depends on the power that the industrial firm brings into the buyer–seller relationship. This dilemma is compounded by the fact that the Robinson-Patman Act requires sellers to offer the same terms to all competing buyers, large or small.

Legal Considerations

Since the industrial marketer deals with different classifications of customers and middlemen and different types of discounts, an awareness of legal considerations in price administration is vital. The Robinson-Patman Act holds that it is unlawful to:

discriminate in price between different purchasers of commodities of like grade and quality . . . where the effect of such discrimination may be substantially to lessen competition or tend to create a monopoly, or to injure, destroy, or prevent competition. . . .

Price differentials are permitted, but they must be based on cost differences or the need to "meet competition."[37] Cost differentials are very difficult to justify, and clearly defined policies and procedures are needed in price administration. Such cost justification guidelines are useful not only in making pricing decisions, but also in providing a legal defense against price discrimination charges.

Geographic Pricing

An element in the ultimate price to the buyer is the transportation cost, so geography must play a role in overall price administration. Prices will differ according to whether buyer or seller assumes transportation costs. The price will vary according to the weight and bulk of the product, the nature and location of key market segments, the percentage of the total price represented by transportation costs, competitive conditions, and industry norms. Transportation is one factor in the buyer's cost/benefit equation, and organizational buyer sensitivity to different types of geographical price arrangements must be taken into account.

The industrial marketer cannot leave price administration to chance. Discounts must be aligned with the firm's pricing policies and related to the requirements of key market segments. Pricing policies are often based on a defensive, or risk-aversive, perspective rather than a positive one.[38] For example, industrial firms might offer larger quantity discounts to partially offset price increases; opportunities for revising discount schedules may emerge as costs change. Tradition-bound firms can easily overlook creative uses of pricing policies.

Competitive Bidding

A significant volume of business in the industrial market is transacted through competitive bidding. Rather than relying on a specific list price, the industrial marketer must develop a price, or bid, to meet particular product and/or service requirements of a customer.

The Buyer's Side of Bidding

Buying by government and other public agencies is almost exclusively by competitive bidding. Competitive bidding in private industry is less frequent and usually applied to the purchase of nonstandard materials,

---

[37] For a comprehensive discussion of the Robinson-Patman Act, see Monroe, *Pricing*, pp. 249–267.

[38] Joseph P. Guiltinan, "Risk-Aversive Pricing Policies: Problems and Alternatives," *Journal of Marketing* 40 (January 1976), pp. 10–15.

complex fabricated products where design and manufacturing methods vary, and products made to the buyer specifications.[39] The types of items procured through competitive bidding are ones for which there is no generally established market level. Competitive bids allow the purchaser to evaluate the appropriateness of the prices.[40] Competitive bidding may be either closed or open.

Closed Bidding

Closed bidding, often used by industrial and governmental buyers, involves a formal invitation to potential suppliers to submit written, sealed bids for a particular business opportunity. All bids are opened and reviewed at the same time, and the contract is generally awarded to the lowest bidder who meets desired specifications. The low bidder is not guaranteed the contract; buyers often make awards to the "lowest responsible bidder." The ability of alternative suppliers to perform remains part of the bidding process.

Open Bidding

Open bidding is more informal and allows suppliers to make offers (oral and written) up to a certain date. Here the buyer may deliberate with several suppliers throughout the bidding process. Open bidding may be particularly appropriate when specific requirements are hard to rigidly define, or when the products and services of competing suppliers vary substantially.

In selected buying situations, negotiated pricing may be employed. Complex technical requirements or uncertain product specifications may lead buying organizations to, first, evaluate the capabilities of competing industrial firms and then negotiate the price and the form of the product/service offering. Negotiated pricing is appropriate for procurement decisions in both the commercial and governmental sectors of the industrial market (see Chapter 2).

Strategies for Competitive Bidding

Careful planning is fundamental to success in competitive bidding. Planning has three important steps: (1) precise definition of objectives; (2) a screening procedure for evaluating alternative bid opportunities; and (3) a method for assessing the probability of success of a particular bidding strategy.

---

[39] Stuart F. Heinritz and Paul U. Farrell, *Purchasing, Principles and Applications* (Englewood Cliffs, N.J.: Prentice-Hall, Inc., 1971), p. 206.

[40] J. H. Westing, I. V. Fine, and Gary J. Zenz, *Purchasing Management* (New York: John Wiley and Sons, Inc., 1976), p. 198; for related research see Niren Vyas and Arch G. Woodside, "An Inductive Model of Industrial Supplier Choice Processes," *Journal of Marketing* 48 (Winter 1984), pp. 30–45.

Table 14.4   Evaluation of a Bid Opportunity

Prebid Factors	Weight	High 10	Rating of Medium 5	Low 0	Score
Plant Capacity	25	10			250
Degree of Experience	20	10			200
Follow-up Bid Opportunities	15			0	0
Competition	25	10			250
Delivery Requirements	15	10			150
Total	100				850

Ideal Bid Score: 1000
Minimum Acceptable Score: 750

Objectives   Before preparing a bid for any potential contract, the industrial firm must carefully define its objectives. This helps the firm to decide what types of business to pursue, when to bid, and how much to bid. The objectives may range from profit maximization to company survival. Other objectives might be to keep the plant operating and the labor force intact or to enter a new type of business. The marketer can also benefit by analyzing the objectives of likely bidding rivals.

Screening Bid Opportunities   Because developing bids is costly and time-consuming, contracts to bid on should be chosen with care. Contracts offer differing levels of profitability according to the related technical expertise, past experience, and objectives of the bidding firm. Thus, a screening procedure is required to isolate properly the contracts that offer the most promise (see Table 14.4).

Screening Procedure[41]   The use of a screening procedure to evaluate contracts has improved the bidding success of industrial marketers.[42] The procedure has three steps: First, the firm identifies criteria for evaluating contracts. While the number and nature of the criteria vary by firm and industry, five prebid factors are common:

1. The impact of the contract on plant capacity;

2. The degree of experience the firm has had with similar projects;

3. Follow-up bid opportunities;

4. Expected competition;

5. Delivery requirements.

---

[41] This method is adapted from Stephen Paranka, "Competitive Bidding Strategy," *Business Horizons* 14 (June 1971), pp. 39–43; see also, Stephen Paranka, "Question: To Bid or Not to Bid? Answer: Strategic Prebid Analysis," *Marketing News* (April 4, 1980), p. 16.

[42] For example, see "Evaluation System Boosts Job Shop's Bidding Average," *Steel* (September 21, 1964), p. 47.

Once identified, the prebid factors are assigned weights based on their relative importance to the firm (e.g., a weight of 25 of the total of 100 is assigned to plant capacity). The third step is to evaluate each factor, giving it a high (10), medium (5), or low (0) value. In Table 14.4, the contract is evaluated favorably on all factors except follow-up bid opportunities. Summing the product of each factor's weight and rating provides a total score. The industrial marketer can use this procedure to evaluate alternative potential contracts. The firm may wish to establish a minimum acceptable score before effort will be invested in preparing a bid. Since the bid opportunity evaluated in Table 14.4 yields a score above the cut-off point, a bid would be prepared.

Probabilistic Bidding Models   Having isolated a project opportunity, the marketer must now estimate the probabilities of winning the contract at various prices. Assuming that the contract is awarded to the lowest bidder, the chances of the firm winning the contract decline as the bid price increases. How will competitors bid? At what bid price will the firm optimize its chances of winning and its level of profit if it does win? Probabilistic bidding models help the firm to deal with such questions.[43] Firms that use probabilistic bidding models seem to be more successful in competitive bidding.[44]

Such models often assume that competitors will behave in the future as they have in the past. Clearly, new competitors may emerge, or existing competitors may alter their bidding strategies. However, probabilistic bidding models give the marketer an objective procedure for evaluating the success probabilities and potential profits of different bidding scenarios. These formalized bidding approaches do motivate managers to assess carefully the costs, competition, and potential profit opportunities of a particular project. Screening procedures also allow the marketer to isolate those projects that are most consistent with the firm's objectives and capabilities.

The Role of Leasing in the Industrial Market[45]

Leasing is assuming increased importance in the industrial market. A lease is essentially a contract through which the asset owner (lessor) extends the right to use the asset to another party (lessee) in return for

---

[43] For a more complete discussion of probabilistic bidding models, see Douglas G. Brooks, "Bidding for the Sake of Follow-On Contracts," *Journal of Marketing* 42 (January 1978), pp. 35–38; see also, Murphy A. Sewall, "A Decision Calculus Model for Contract Bidding," *Journal of Marketing* 40 (October 1976), pp. 92–98; and Wayne J. Morse, "Probabilistic Bidding Models: A Synthesis," *Business Horizons* 16 (April 1975), pp. 66–74.

[44] Stephen Paranka, "The Pay-Off Concept in Competitive Bidding," *Business Horizons* 12 (August 1969), pp. 77–81.

[45] This section is largely based on Paul F. Anderson and William Lazer, "Industrial Lease Marketing," *Journal of Marketing* 42 (April 1978), pp. 71–79; For additional research in the lease marketing area, see Paul F. Anderson, *Financial Aspects of Industrial Leasing Decisions: Implications for Marketing* (Division of Research, Graduate School of Business Administration, Michigan State University, East Lansing, Mich., 1977).

periodic payment of rent over a specified period. The value of industrial equipment on lease is projected to exceed $250 billion by the late 1980s. This section examines the strategic role that leasing can assume in the industrial market.

Financial Leases vs. Operating Leases

Leases can be divided into two broad categories: financial (full-payout) and operating leases. *Financial* leases are noncancellable contracts that are usually long-term and fully amortized. Lease payments over the contract period equal or exceed the original purchase price of the item. A food packaging machine might be purchased outright at a price of $21,000 or leased for five years with lease payments of $5800 per year. The organization leasing the equipment is generally responsible for operating expenses, but the marketer/lessor may attach benefits (e.g., maintenance) if competitive pressures dictate. A purchase option is frequently a part of financial leases. This option, which may be exercised at the termination of the contract, is usually the asset's fair market value at time of exercise. Operating leases (sometimes called rental agreements), by contrast, are shorter-term, cancellable agreements which are not fully amortized. Since the purpose is to provide equipment which is only needed for short periods, a purchase option is usually not included. Operating lease rates are usually higher than financial lease rates because the marketer is assuming the operating costs as well as the risks of obsolescence. Financial leasing will receive particular attention.

Lease vs. Purchase

As emphasized throughout the chapter, organizational buyers examine the cost/benefit tradeoffs of alternative offerings. Thus, buyers contemplating the purchase of capital equipment confront the "lease vs. purchase" decision. "A manufacturer's product and service mix is augmented by the additional benefits, largely economic in nature, available to customers through leasing."[46]

How do organizational customers evaluate the benefits and costs of a lease? Among the benefits and costs are:

Benefits	vs.	Costs
Avoidance of cash purchase cost		Cash outflow of lease payments
Avoidance of those operating costs absorbed by lessor		Foregone tax shields resulting from depreciation, interest, and operating expenses
Tax shield provided by lease payments		Sacrifice of asset's salvage value

[46] Anderson and Lazer, *ibid.*, p. 72.

Essentially, the decision should rest on the present value sum of the costs and benefits of the lease: Do the cash flow benefits of the lease exceed the cash flow costs?

At the same time, however, buyers may also enter into lease arrangements for reasons not reflected in the lease versus purchase cash flow equation.[47] Leasing can preserve credit capacity, minimize equipment disposal problems, allow for the acquisition of equipment when other financing sources are not available, avoid the dilution of ownership or control that accompanies debt or equity financing, and protect against the risks of equipment obsolescence. Thus, the ultimate decision to lease or purchase may depend on a balance between the quantifiable costs of leasing and both the quantifiable and nonquantifiable benefits.[48]

Industrial Lease Marketing: Strategic Implications

Many large industrial customers, when confronting the lease versus purchase decision, may be using financial techniques that fail to give appropriate weight to the economic benefits of leasing.[49] Paul Anderson and William Lazer contend that a bias against leasing can be overcome by creating a financial specialist position within the sales organization. This specialist would interface with financially-oriented influencers within the buying center and provide the customer with consulting services and financial, tax, and accounting information. Xerox Corporation caters to potential lessees through a marketing financial analyst known as a *consulting service representative*. Customers interested in outright purchase are served by another specialist—the *sold equipment representative*. Such specialization permits the marketer to respond to the particular needs and objectives of organizational customers. Such services increase the value of the firm's total offering in the minds of organizational buyers and often provide the marketer with a differential advantage over competitors.

Strategic leasing decisions cannot be isolated from product, pricing, and marketing communication decisions. A particularly delicate decision emerges in the development of pricing strategy. Here, a price *and* a lease rate must be established for the same product.

Pricing Strategy   Depending upon the firm's objectives, the marketer can establish the lease rate at a level which: (1) encourages leasing; (2) encourages outright purchase; or (3) achieves balance between the lease rate and the sales rate. To illustrate, a marketer might offer rates that

---

[47] Paul F. Anderson, "Industrial Equipment Leasing Offers Economic and Competitive Edge," *Marketing News* (April 4, 1980), p. 20, and Paul F. Anderson and Monroe M. Bird, "Marketing to the Industrial Lease Buyer," *Industrial Marketing Management* 9 (April 1980), pp. 111–116.

[48] Anderson and Bird, p. 115.

[49] Paul F. Anderson and John D. Martin, "Lease vs. Purchase Decisions: A Survey of Current Practice," *Financial Management* 6 (Spring 1977), pp. 41–47.

encourage leasing in order to link buying organizations to the firm's product line or to reach market segments that were previously inaccessible. New products that can be tried on a limited or experimental basis diffuse more rapidly than those that cannot.[50] By offering attractive leasing options, the industrial marketer provides potential adopters with the opportunity to experiment with the product on a limited basis.

Alternatively, the industrial marketer might wish to set relatively high lease rates in order to encourage customers to purchase the capital items outright. Leasing can cause a troublesome cash flow drain for the seller. Thus, marketers might wish to improve their cash flow position by encouraging customers to buy rather than lease. Xerox has provided loans to customers at interest rates two percentage points below the terms available through a bank, thus encouraging outright purchase.[51]

Regardless of the strategy followed, the price-setter must have a product line perspective. A change in the price or lease rate of one item may directly or indirectly influence the demand for other items. IBM cut the price of several small computer systems but left the leasing rates unchanged.[52] Such a strategy would encourage customers to purchase the equipment they are currently leasing. Likewise, new customers would be more inclined to purchase rather than lease. To stimulate demand for new items, the firm might prefer to offer attractive lease rates.

The marketer of industrial equipment must understand the benefits and costs of leasing to the customer in order to define the strategic role of leasing in the total industrial marketing program.

Summary

At the outset, the industrial marketer must assign pricing its role in the firm's overall marketing strategy. Giving a particular industrial product or service an "incorrect" price can trigger a chain of events that undermines the firm's market position, channel relationships, and pricing and personal selling strategies. Price is but one of the costs that buyers examine in the buying process. Thus, the marketer can profit by adopting a strong end-user focus which gives special attention to the way buyers tradeoff the costs and benefits of various products.

Price-setting is a multidimensional rather than one-dimensional decision. To establish a price, the manager must identify the firm's objectives and analyze the behavior of demand, costs, and competition. While this task is clouded with uncertainty, the industrial pricing decision must be approached actively rather than passively. Likewise, by isolating de-

---

[50] Everett M. Rogers with F. Floyd Shoemaker, *Communication of Innovations*, 2d ed. (New York: The Free Press, 1971), p. 155.

[51] Jeffrey A. Tannenbaum, "To Prop Sales, Xerox Gives Bargain Loans," *Wall Street Journal* (January 8, 1981), p. 19.

[52] "IBM Cuts Quotes for Buying Parts of Small Systems," *Wall Street Journal* (December 3, 1979), p. 5.

mand, cost, or competitive patterns the manager can gain insights into market behavior and opportunities that have been neglected.

Competitive bidding, a unique feature of the industrial market, calls for a different strategy. Again, carefully defined objectives are the cornerstone of strategy. These objectives, combined with a meticulous screening procedure, help the firm to identify projects that integrate with company capability. Probabilistic bidding models can be useful in determining the probability of winning and in gauging expected profit outcomes.

Leasing, an area of rising importance in the marketing of industrial equipment, creates numerous strategy options. Successful lease marketing requires a well-integrated marketing program that effectively conveys information on the benefits of leasing to potential customers. The marketer can adjust the relationship between the price and lease rate of a product to encourage or discourage leasing and to meet changing company or market conditions.

Discussion Questions

1. Explain why it is often necessary for the industrial marketer to develop a separate demand curve for different segments of the market. Wouldn't one total demand curve be better for making the industrial pricing decision? Explain.

2. The rising cost of labor has stimulated industrial marketers to develop machine tools that allow users to reduce production costs. Programmable robots are frequently the center of attention at machine tool trade shows. Many machine tool manufacturers contend that the robot will assume increasing importance in the workplace because of the opportunities it provides for cost-savings: the cost of labor (including fringe benefits) in the auto industry is over $14 per hour, while the cost per robot-hour is $4.80, including installations, maintenance, depreciation, and energy. Illustrate how the concept of life-cycle costing could be employed by machine tool producers in marketing high-priced but efficient "robots."

3. The XYZ Manufacturing Corporation has experienced a rather large decline in sales for its component parts. Mary Vantage, Vice President of Marketing, feels that a 10 percent price cut may get things going again. What factors should Mary consider before reducing the prices of the components?

4. Define the *experience effect* (behavior of costs) and explain why it occurs. Explain how the experience effect relates to strategic pricing decisions.

5. An industrial marketing manager often has great difficulty in arriving at the optimum price level for a product. First, describe the

factors that complicate the pricing decision. Second, outline the approach that you would follow in pricing an industrial product. Be as specific as possible.

6. Leasing is increasingly important in the marketing of capital equipment items. Describe the factors that the industrial marketer must consider in determining the relationship of the lease rate to the purchase price (e.g., low lease rate—high purchase price; high lease rate—low purchase price).

7. Explain how a change in the price of one item often contributes to the need for a change in price of other items in the product line.

8. Evaluate the competitive bidding strategy followed by a West Coast commercial air conditioning contractor: "To improve my chances of winning contracts, I bid on virtually every contract that comes up in our market area."

C·H·A·P·T·E·R
15

Industrial Marketing Communications: Advertising and Sales Promotion

Advertising supports and supplements personal selling efforts. A smaller share of the marketing budget is devoted to advertising in industrial than in consumer-goods marketing. A well-tailored industrial advertising campaign can, however, contribute to the increased efficiency and effectiveness of the overall marketing strategy.

After reading this chapter, you will have an understanding of:

1. *the specific role of advertising in industrial marketing strategy;*
2. *the decisions that must be made in forming an industrial advertising program;*
3. *industrial media options;*
4. *methods for measuring industrial advertising effectiveness.*

Communication with existing and potential customers is vital to industrial marketing success. Experience has taught marketing managers that
not even the best products sell themselves: The benefits, problem solutions, and cost efficiencies of those products must be effectively communicated to all of the individuals who influence the purchase decision. As
a result of the technical complexity of industrial products, the relatively
small number of potential buyers, and the extensive negotiation process,
the primary communication vehicle in industrial marketing is the salesperson. However, nonpersonal methods of communication, including
advertising, catalogs, and trade shows, have a unique and often critical
role in the communication process.

Consider the recent decision of a manufacturer of automotive
shock absorbers to purchase a component made of zinc rather than aluminum. The decision process involved 43 separate steps, in which 30
different individuals were involved.[1] Clearly, a salesperson may not
know that 30 individuals were involved, let alone effectively contact each
of them. However, it is possible to know that numerous specialists will be
involved in the decision and advertisements can be placed in selected industrial trade publications to reach these influencers. A very important
role for industrial advertising is to communicate to those buying influences inaccessible to the salesperson. Industrial advertising and promotion, of course, serve many other functions in the communication strategy as well.

The focus of this chapter is fourfold: (1) to provide a clear understanding of the role of advertising in industrial marketing strategy; (2) to
present a framework for structuring advertising decisions that integrates the decisions related to objectives, budgets, messages, media, and
evaluation; (3) to develop an understanding of each industrial advertising decision area; and (4) to evaluate supplementary forms of promotion, including catalogs, trade shows, and trade advertising.

The Role of Advertising

Integrated Communication Programs

Advertising and sales promotion are rarely employed alone in the industrial setting, but are intertwined with the total communications strategy—particularly personal selling. Personal and nonpersonal forms of
communication interact to inform key buying influences. The challenge
for the industrial marketer is to create an advertising and sales promotion strategy that effectively blends with personal selling efforts to
achieve sales and profit objectives. In addition, the advertising and sales

---

[1] John Lamson, "The 'Top Dog' Theory Has Holes in It," *Media Decisions*, 11 (November 1976), p. 88.

Table 15.1   Contacting the Unidentified Buying Influentials

Century Electric Co.	Century found that 12 individuals are typically involved in its own buying decisions. On the average, only 2 are ever contacted by salespersons.
Yale and Town	Nine individuals are involved in a typical Yale and Town buying decision; only an average of 1.3 were contacted by salespersons.
Chilton Company	Chilton interviewed 4420 buying influencers (each of whom had "purchasing influence" (on an average of 4.3 products) in eight major industries. Sixty-one percent of the respondents had not been called on by a salesperson in the past six months.
American Rubber Co.	Of 903 prospects, American Rubber salespeople knew only 169, or 19 percent. Of every five prospects, only one was known by the sales force.

Source: Adapted from Richard Manville, "Why Industrial Companies Must Advertise Their Products," *Industrial Marketing*, 63 (October 1978), p. 47.

promotion tools must be integrated; that is, a comprehensive program of media and sales promotion methods must be coordinated to achieve the desired results.

Nature of Organizational Buying Affects Industrial Advertising

To understand the role of advertising we must recognize the forces that shape and influence organizational buying decisions. These are typically joint decisions. The intricacies of the buying center were well documented in Chapter 4. Recall that an industrial marketer must focus on the full range of individuals involved in the buying center for a particular purchase. Salespeople are not able to make contact with all these; "the average salesperson does *not* reach six to seven out of every ten purchase decision influentials."[2] Table 15.1 shows the extent of the problem. Note the variety of industrial situations in which salespeople are unable to reach key purchase decision makers.

The point is clear: Industrial advertising fills the void.[3] Carefully targeted advertising extends beyond the salesperson's reach to unidentified buying influentials. Advertising is often the *only* means of communicating the existence of a product to the potential buyers. Advertising also increases recognition of the company's name and reputation, enhancing the salesperson's opportunity to create a sale.

[2] Richard Manville, "Why Industrial Companies Must Advertise Their Products," *Industrial Marketing*, 63 (October 1978), p. 47.

[3] Of studies documenting the ability of advertising to reach industrial buying influences not accessible to the salesperson, two of the most frequently cited are *The U.S. Steel/Harnischfeger Study: Industrial Advertising Effectively Reaches Buying Influences at Low Cost* (New York: American Business Press, 1969) and *The Evolution of a Purchase Study* (Bloomfield Hills, Michigan: Bromsom Publishing Co., 1967).

Advertising: Enhancing Sales Effectiveness

Effective advertising can make personal selling more productive. John Morrill examined nearly 100,000 interviews on 26 product lines at 30,000 different buying locations to study the impact of industrial advertising on salesperson effectiveness.[4] He concluded that dollar sales per salesperson call were significantly higher when customers had been exposed to advertising. Buyers who had been exposed to a supplier's advertisement also rated that supplier's sales personnel substantially higher on product knowledge, service, and enthusiasm.[5] A primary role of industrial advertising is to enhance the reputation of the supplier. Industrial advertising also contributes to increased sales efficiency. Increased expenditures on advertising lead to greater brand awareness of industrial products, which translates into larger market shares and higher profits.[6] Gamewell, a manufacturer of fire alarm and smoke detection systems, found that increasing the advertising budget by 12 percent led to a 12 percent rise in market share and a 25 percent increase in profits within a year.[7] Gamewell brand awareness rose over the period from sixth place to first.

Advertising: Increased Sales Efficiency

The impact of advertising on the overall efficiency of the industrial marketing program is evidenced in two ways: First, industrial suppliers frequently need to remind actual and potential buyers of their products or to make them aware of new products or services. Although these objectives could be partially accomplished through personal selling, the costs of reaching a vast group of buyers would be prohibitive. An advertisement properly placed can reach hundreds of buying influences for only a few cents each; the average cost of an industrial sales call is approaching $180.[8] The cost of a sales call is determined by the salesperson's wages, travel and entertainment costs, and fringe benefits costs. If these costs total $720 per day and a salesperson can make four calls per day, then each call costs $180.

Secondly, advertising appears to make all selling activities more effective; therefore, there may be economies of scale associated with industrial advertising. Gary Lilien and others reviewed research studies assessing the impact of industrial advertising expenditures on total marketing costs.[9] The general conclusion was that the larger the advertising

---

[4] John E. Morrill, "Industrial Advertising Pays Off," *Harvard Business Review*, 48 (March–April 1970), pp. 4–14.

[5] *Ibid.*, p. 6.

[6] "New Proof of Industrial Ad Values," *Marketing and Media Decisions*, 16 (February 1981), p. 64.

[7] *Ibid.*, p. 65.

[8] "Sales Call Costs Explode," *Industrial Marketing*, 67 (July 1982), p. 9.

[9] Gary L. Lilien, Alvin J. Silk, Jean-Marie Choffray, and Murlidhar Rao, "Industrial Advertising Effects and Budgeting Practices," *Journal of Marketing*, 40 (January 1976), pp. 20–21; see also, Gary L. Lilien and David Weinstein, "An International Comparison of the Determinants of Industrial Marketing Expenditures," *Journal of Marketing*, 48 (Winter 1984), pp. 46–53.

budget, the lower the total marketing expenses as a percentage of sales. However, since some studies have shown that economies of scale in advertising do not exist, it is well to avoid assuming that more advertising is necessarily better. Advertising effectively interacts with all communication and selling activities. It can result in higher levels of efficiency for the entire marketing expenditure.

Advertising: Creating Awareness

From a communications standpoint, the buying process can be viewed as taking potential buyers sequentially from unawareness of a product or supplier to *awareness*, brand *preference*, *conviction* that the particular purchase will fulfill their requirements, and, ultimately, to actual *purchase*.[10] Industrial advertising often creates awareness of the supplier and the supplier's products; it also may make some contribution to achieving preference for the product—all very cost-efficiently. Advertising also can create a corporate identity or image; broad media like *Business Week*, or even television, may be used to develop desired perceptions.

Creating a Corporate Image

Spot television on nightly newscasts, election coverage, TV specials, and sports programming is the vehicle used by TRW to heighten awareness of the company and lay a foundation for creating the firm's image.

In 1980 the firm tested the image campaign by surveying business decision makers. The test measured recall of the theme "A Company Named TRW" from the past few years of TV spots. Surprisingly, 43 percent of the executives surveyed could identify the phrase "A Company Named . . ." with TRW. An impressive result, to say the least!

Source: Theodore J. Gage, "Grooming the Image for a Real Impression," *Advertising Age*, 53 (June 14, 1982), p. m-16.

Buyers of machine tools were surveyed to ascertain the importance of five different communication channels in providing information about machine tool products and services[11]: (1) salespersons, (2) com-

---

[10] Robert J. Lavidge and Gary A. Steiner, "A Model for Predictive Measurement of Advertising Effectiveness," *Journal of Marketing*, 25 (October 1961), pp. 59–61.

[11] Charles H. Patti, "Buyer Information Sources in the Capital Equipment Industry," *Industrial Marketing Management*, 6 (1977), pp. 259–264; see also, Alicia Donovan, "Awareness of Trade-Press Advertising," *Journal of Advertising Research*, 19 (April 1979), pp. 33–35.

pany catalogs, (3) trade magazine advertising, (4) trade shows, and (5) direct mail. Industrial advertising was rated the primary source of information to these buyers.

Advertising: Self-Selection

It is often impossible to determine exactly which companies could be potential users of an industrial product. As a result, advertising can prompt unknown prospects to seek product information.[12] If a media or direct mail advertisement can effectively illustrate important product benefits, potential prospects will "self-select," that is, respond to the advertisement by requesting additional information. In this way, the industrial marketer can assist the prospect and also collect information about the prospect's product applications, product interests, and potential as a customer.

The Limitations of Industrial Advertising

To develop an effective communications program, the industrial marketing manager must blend all communication tools into an integrated program, using each tool for the purposes for which it is most effective. Industrial advertising quite obviously has limitations. Advertising cannot substitute for effective personal selling; it must supplement, support, and complement that effort. In the same way, personal selling is constrained by its costs, and should not be used to create awareness and disseminate information—tasks quite capably performed by advertising.

Generally, advertising cannot create product "preference"; this requires demonstration, explanation, and operational testing. Similarly, "conviction" and "purchase" can only be ensured by personal selling. Advertising has a supporting role creating awareness, providing information, and uncovering important leads for salespeople; that is how the marketing manager must use it to be effective.

Managing Industrial Advertising

The advertising decision model in Figure 15.1 shows the structural elements involved in the management of industrial advertising. First, advertising is only one aspect of the entire marketing strategy and must be integrated with other components to achieve strategic goals. The advertising decision process begins with the formulation of advertising objectives, which are derived from marketing goals. From this will follow a determination of expenditures necessary to achieve those goals. Then,

---

[12] John L. DeFazio, "An Inquiry-Based MIS," *Business Marketing*, 68 (August 1983), p. 55.

Figure 15.1   An Advertising Decision Model

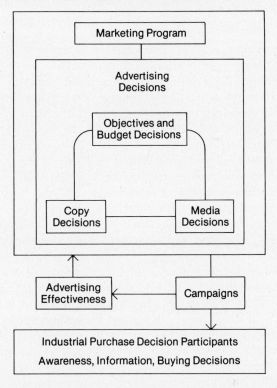

Source: Adapted from David A. Aaker and John G. Myers, *Advertising Management* (Englewood Cliffs, NJ: Prentice-Hall, Inc., 1975), p. 25. Reprinted by permission of Prentice-Hall, Inc.

specific communication messages are formulated to achieve the market behavior specified by the objectives. Equally important is the evaluation and selection of the media to reach the desired audience. The result is an integrated advertising campaign to elicit a specific attitude or behavior by the target group. The final, and critical, step is to evaluate the effectiveness of the campaign.

Advertising Objectives

Knowing what advertising must accomplish enables the manager to determine an advertising budget more accurately, and provides a yardstick against which advertising can be evaluated. In specifying advertising goals, the marketing manager must realize that (1) *the advertising mission flows directly from the overall marketing strategy*; advertising must fulfill a marketing strategy objective, and the goal set for advertising must reflect the general aim and purpose of the entire strategy; and (2) *the objectives of the advertising program must be responsive to the roles for which advertis-*

ing is suited: creating awareness, providing information, influencing attitudes, and reminding buyers of company and product existence.[13]

Written Objectives　An advertising objective is a concise statement of the intended outcome of a particular advertising action, phrased in terms of what should happen in the mind of the prospect as a result of reading the advertisement.[14] They must speak in unambiguous terms of a specific outcome. The purpose is to establish a single working direction for everyone involved in creating, coordinating, and evaluating the advertising program.[15] Correctly conceived objectives set standards against which the advertising effort can be evaluated. A specific objective might be:

> *To develop the awareness among at least 25 percent of chemical processing plant building and maintenance engineers of the use-benefit fact that our brand of industrial-maintenance paint stops metal corrosion.*

The objective directs the manager to create a message related to the major product benefit, using media that will reach building and maintenance engineers. The objective also provides a way to measure accomplishment (awareness among 25 percent of the target audience).

Industrial advertising objectives frequently bear no direct relationship with specific dollar sales targets. Although dollar sales results would provide a "hard" measure of advertising accomplishment, it is often impossible to directly link advertising to sales. Personal selling, price, product performance, and competitive actions have a more direct relationship to sales levels, and it is almost impossible to sort out the impact of advertising. Thus, advertising goals are typically stated in terms of "communication goals" like brand awareness, recognition, and buyer attitudes. These goals can be measured; it is presumed that achieving them will stimulate sales volume.

Target Audience　A final consideration is the specification of target audiences. Because a primary role of advertising is to reach buying influences inaccessible to the salesperson, the industrial marketing manager must define the buying influence groups to be reached. Generally, each group of buying influencers is concerned with distinct product and service attributes and criteria, and the advertising must focus on these. Thus, the objectives must specify the intended audience and its relevant decision criteria.

To plan an effective advertising campaign, one needs objectives upon which to structure media and measure results.

[13] W. H. Grosse, *How Industrial Advertising and Sales Promotion Can Increase Marketing Power* (New York: American Management Association, Inc., 1973), p. 41.

[14] Joseph A. Bellizzi and Julie Lehrer, "Developing Better Industrial Advertising," *Industrial Marketing Management*, 12 (February 1983), p. 19.

[15] "Preplanning the Advertising Campaign," *Industrial Marketing*, 59 (August 1974), p. 51.

Determining Advertising Expenditures

Typically, industrial companies use a blend of intuition, judgment, experience, and only occasionally, more advanced decision-oriented techniques to determine advertising budgets. Among the more common techniques are rules of thumb and objective-task methods.

Rules of Thumb   Often, because advertising is a relatively small part of the total marketing budget for industrial firms, the value of using sophisticated methods for advertising budgeting is not great. In these cases, managers tend to follow simple rules of thumb (e.g., "allocate 1 percent of sales to advertising" or spend "what competition spends"). Unfortunately, percentage-of-sales decision rules are all too pervasive throughout industrial marketing, even where advertising is an important expenditure.

The fundamental problem with percentage-of-sales decision rules is that they "implicitly make advertising a consequence rather than a determinant of sales and profits and can easily give rise to dysfunctional policies."[16] Percentage-of-sales decision rules suggest that the industrial advertiser reduce advertising when sales volume declines, when increased advertising may be more appropriate. Nevertheless, simple rules of thumb will continue to be applied in industrial budget decisions because they are easy to use, and familiar to management.

Objective-Task Method   The task method for budgeting advertising expenditures is an attempt to relate advertising costs to the objective it is to accomplish.[17] David Nylen capsulizes the dimensions of the task approach:

> While acknowledging that the ultimate objective of advertising is profitable sales, the task approach sees a series of intermediate objectives or profit-facilitating tasks assigned to advertising. The budgeting problem under the task approach becomes one of determining how much it will cost to accomplish each of the tasks assigned to advertising.[18]

Thus, the task method focuses on the communications effects of advertising, not the sales effects.

The task method is applied by evaluating the tasks to be performed by advertising, analyzing the costs associated with each task, and summing up the total costs to arrive at a final budget. The steps are to:

1. Establish specific marketing objectives for the product in terms of such factors as sales volume, market share, profit contribution, and market segments.

---

[16] Lilien et al., "Industrial Advertising Effects and Budgeting Practices," p. 22.

[17] Chuck Wingis, "Refining the Classic Task Method of Budgeting," *Industrial Marketing*, 67 (July 1982), p. 67.

[18] David W. Nylen, *Advertising: Planning, Implementation and Control* (Cincinnati: Southwestern Publishing Co., 1975), p. 230.

2.   Assess the communication functions that must be performed to realize the marketing objectives, and determine the role of advertising and other elements of the communications mix in performing these functions.

3.   Define specific goals for advertising in terms of measurable communication response required to achieve marketing objectives.

4.   Estimate the budget needed to accomplish advertising goals.[19]

The task method addresses the major problem of the rule of thumb methods—funds are applied to accomplish a specific goal so that advertising is a *determinant* of those results, not a consequence. Using the task approach, managers will allocate all the funds necessary to accomplish a specific objective, rather than allocating some arbitrary percentage of sales. The most troubling problem of the method is that management must have some instinct for the proper relationship between expenditure level and communication response. It is difficult to know what will produce a certain level of awareness among industrial purchase influencers. Will 12 two-page insertions in *Iron Age* over the next six months create the desired recognition level or will 24 insertions over one year be necessary?[20]

The ADVISOR Project: Guidelines for Industrial Advertising Budgets

The lack of specific guidelines for formulating industrial advertising budgets stimulated an extensive research project to determine the product and market factors that affect industrial advertising expenditures. The ADVISOR project of Gary Lilien and John Little resulted in a model that specifies the typical size and range of marketing budgets based on six product and market characteristics.[21] The ADVISOR project analyzed 66 products manufactured by 12 different companies.

ADVISOR Results   Six factors were judged to be predominant in describing the impact of product-market-customer characteristics on advertising and marketing budgets (Table 15.2).[22] The model developed in the ADVISOR project combines these effects to determine budget norms and ranges.

---

[19] Lilien et al., "Industrial Advertising Effects and Budgeting Practices," p. 22.

[20] Some industrial firms have developed quantitative models to relate advertising expenditures to profits or sales. For example, see David A. Aaker and John G. Myers, *Advertising Management* (Englewood Cliffs, N.J.: Prentice-Hall, Inc., 1975), Chapter 3, pp. 51–81.

[21] Gary L. Lilien and John D. C. Little, "The ADVISOR Project: A Study of Industrial Marketing Budgets," *Sloan Management Review*, 16 (Spring 1976), pp. 17–31.

[22] *Ibid.*, p. 23.

Table 15.2   ADVISOR: Variables Affecting Advertising and Marketing Budgets

1. Life Cycle Stage	As the life cycle progresses, the ratio of marketing expenditures (advertising and personal selling) to sales (M/S) decreases. The advertising expense to sales ratio (A/S) behaves differently: early in the life cycle it is high; later it tends to be low.
2. Frequency of Purchase	Frequency of purchase does not affect the M/S ratio but does impact the ratio of advertising expense to marketing expense (A/M). The greater the purchase frequency, the higher the A/M ratio. As a result, purchase frequency has a positive effect on the A/S ratio.
3. Product Quality, Uniqueness, and Identification with Company	Products with quality, uniqueness, and strong identification with company name have high A/M ratios. The conclusion is that these products have a "story to tell," and advertising is used to do it. More is spent on advertising, and the A/S ratio is larger.
4. Market Share	The M/S ratio tends to decrease as market share increases. So too with A/S, as advertising expenditures as a percentage of sales decrease with higher market shares.
5. Concentration of Sales	As sales are concentrated with fewer large customers, the M/S ratio declines. The net effect on the A/S is small.
6. Growth of Customers	As the percentage increase in the *number* of customers grows, all three ratios—M/S, A/M, A/S—will increase.

Source: Adapted from "The ADVISOR Project: A Study of Industrial Marketing Budgets," by Gary L. Lilien and John D. C. Little, *Sloan Management Review*, Vol. 17, No. 3 (Spring 1976) pp. 24–25, by permission of the publisher. Copyright © 1976 by the Sloan Management Review Association. All rights reserved.

An interactive computer program can be used by an industrial advertiser to evaluate appropriate *budget norms*.[23] The program asks the user a series of questions related to the product-market variables shown in Table 15.2. The data are analyzed by the computer model, which, based on the user's response to the product-market questions, produces budget and allocation guidelines. Industrial marketing managers may then adjust their budgets to conform to the guidelines prescribed by the ADVISOR model. ADVISOR does not tell the manager what to do; it only demonstrates what the typical industrial firm would do under the same conditions.[24]

ADVISOR Output   Table 15.3 illustrates the ADVISOR output. The company's M/S (marketing expenditures to sales) ratio is within guidelines, but advertising expenditures are below the dollar guideline limit. The A/M (advertising expense to marketing expense) ratio is acceptable, but in the lower range. So although marketing expenditures are within industry guidelines, the proportion allocated to advertising is not up

[23]*Ibid.*, p. 28.
[24]*Ibid.*

Table 15.3 ADVISOR Program Output for a Sample Company

	Actual Expenditure	Advisor Norms	
		Center	Range
Advertising (thousands)	$105	$330	$120–$745
Advertising/Marketing Ratio	0.0323	0.0600	0–0.1100
Marketing/Sales Ratio	0.0680	0.1100	0.0600–0.1400

to industry standards. The manager may wish to reallocate funds to advertising.

The ADVISOR project is a landmark effort to understand the advertising budget process and provide workable decision rules for allocating marketing expenditures. In a refinement and extension of the original ADVISOR project—ADVISOR 2—[25], the data base was expanded to additional companies and product situations, and many of the model equations were refined. The results of ADVISOR 2 confirm the consistency and validity of the earlier model. Also, the variables were refined: customer growth rate is better represented by product plans and number of users; purchase frequency was found to be ambiguous and was deleted. The ADVISOR studies provide a benchmark against which budget decisions can be evaluated.

Industrial firms seem to be accepting the objective-task method of budgeting but have not fully embraced other, more sophisticated quantitative approaches.[26] In a study of 64 of the top 100 industrial advertisers, 74 percent used the objective-task and 16 percent the percentage-of-sales method, 13 percent set budgets arbitrarily, and only 3 percent used a quantitative approach (other methods were also mentioned).

Because the budgeting process is so important to advertising effectiveness, managers must not blindly follow rules of thumb. Instead, they should evaluate the tasks required and their associated costs against industry norms. With clear objectives and proper budgetary allocations, the next step is to design effective advertising messages.

The Advertising Message

Message development is a complex, critical task in industrial advertising. Highlighting a product attribute that is unimportant to a particular buying group not only is a waste of advertising dollars, but also a lost oppor-

[25] Gary L. Lilien, "ADVISOR 2: Modeling the Marketing Mix for Industrial Products," *Management Science*, 25 (February 1979), pp. 191–204.

[26] Vincent J. Blasko and Charles H. Patti, "The Advertising Budgeting Practices of Industrial Marketers," *Journal of Marketing* (in press).

tunity. Both the appeal and the way that appeal is conveyed are vital to successful communication. Thus, creating industrial advertising messages involves evaluation of the buying criteria of the target audience and analysis of the most appropriate language, format, and style for presenting the message.

Perception   For a successful advertising message, first, an individual must be exposed to and pay attention to it, and then, once the individual has noticed the message, he or she must interpret it as the advertiser intended. Perceptual barriers often prevent a message from being perceived by a receiver. An industrial advertisement must be successful at catching the decision-maker's attention. Yet, even though the individual is "exposed" to an advertisement, there is no guarantee that the message will be processed. In fact, the industrial buyer may read every word of the copy, and find a meaning in it quite opposite to that intended by the advertiser.

The industrial advertiser must contend with two important elements of perception: *attention* and *interpretation*. Buyers tend to screen out messages that are inconsistent with their own attitudes, needs, and beliefs, and to interpret information in the light of those beliefs (see Chapter 4). Thus, unless advertising messages are carefully designed and targeted, they may be disregarded or interpreted improperly. Advertisers must put themselves in the position of the receivers to evaluate how the message will appear to them.

The Appeal: Benefits   An industrial buyer purchases benefits—a better way to accomplish some task, a less expensive way to produce a final product, the solution to a problem, faster delivery. Advertisers tend to concentrate on a physical product, forgetting that the physical product is useless to an industrial buyer unless it solves some problem. A public warehousing company analyzing advertising strategy in their industry discovered, to their horror, that many companies, themselves included, were concentrating their advertising messages on the "product": For example, "We offer 200,000 square feet of refrigerated space"; and "Our company has 17 delivery trucks."

To appeal more effectively to the concerns of warehouse users, the company developed a series of advertisements demonstrating the benefits provided to warehouse users (see Figure 15.2).

The advertisement designed for distribution executives, the primary decision makers in selecting a public warehouse, emphasized that the public warehouse (DCI) provides effective and professional service that meets the high standards of the user's own business operations. The message also emphasizes that these high standards of performance translate into cost reductions for warehousing over the years. The benefits to the potential user are clear and unambiguous; "product" features are hardly mentioned.

**Figure 15.2   An Industrial Advertisement
Focused on Important User Benefits**

Finally. A warehouse as smart as you are.

You build your product intelligently. And that's the way you wish you could warehouse it. You can, with DCI. Because whatever you find wrong with your current warehouses, you'll find right with DCI.

What makes DCI so different? We practice results management — not just in the executive suite, but on the warehouse floor. We emphasize on-time shipments. We don't even ask for a shrinkage allowance. And we're so productive, we can guarantee — in writing — your costs will decrease over the years.

What's more, sophisticated computerization allows us to offer more personalized service, because we develop programs to fit each client's needs. We're geared to handling emergencies. And we warehouse anywhere you need us.

If words like **trustworthy, cost efficient, flexible** and **responsive** don't come to mind when you think of your warehouses, you're not dealing with DCI. Speaking as one smart manager to another…call us. Soon.

DCI

Distribution Centers, Inc.

One of the Distek companies
229 Huber Village Boulevard • Westerville, OH 43081 • (614) 890-1730

Source: Reprinted courtesy of Distek, Inc.

Understanding Buyer Motivations   Which product benefits are important to each separate buying influence group? The industrial advertiser
cannot assume that a standard set of "classical buying motives" applies in
every purchase situation. Industrial advertisers often do not understand
the buying motives of important market segments.[27]

A methodology for determining the dimensions and benefits perceived by buying decision participants would be extremely useful to industrial advertisers. A very promising effort is the industrial marketing
strategy response model of Jean-Marie Choffray and Gary Lilien,[28] discussed in Chapter 10 in connection with product strategy development.
An application of the model to industrial cooling system purchases provided information useful for developing advertising messages. Product
attributes varied in importance for each of the six identified decision
participants. Production engineers were concerned with operating cost
and energy savings, heating and air conditioning consultants with noise
level in the plant and first cost.

Physical Characteristics of an Advertisement   Once the perception
process has been evaluated and user benefits identified, the industrial
advertiser must decide how the advertisement is to be structured. A wide
variety of factors must be considered including size of the ad, use of
color and illustrations, and media placement; recall and readership of
industrial advertisements are strongly related to mechanical and format
characteristics (size, color, placement, etc.) of the advertisement.[29]

McGraw-Hill analyzed five years of ad readership scores for nearly
3600 individual business advertisements to evaluate the impact of various elements on the effectiveness of industrial advertisements.[30] Table
15.4 shows which physical characteristics of an advertisement influence
effectiveness at various steps of the decision-making process. Note the
importance of color in the early phases of establishing contact and the
critical importance of copy and product display throughout the later
phases. "The copy factor of the reader relevance of an advertised propo-
sition contributes perhaps 80 percent of an ad's success or failure."[31]
Thus, although certain mechanical aspects help create awareness and interest in the advertisement, its ultimate success will depend on how well
the message is targeted to the benefits sought by the buying influencer.

In conclusion, to formulate industrial advertising messages one
must analyze the perceptual process, base the appeal on product bene-

[27] Gordon McAleer, "Do Industrial Advertisers Understand What Influences Their Markets?" *Journal of Marketing*, 38 (January 1974), pp. 15–23.

[28] Jean-Marie Choffray and Gary L. Lilien, "Assessing Response to Industrial Marketing Strategy," *Journal of Marketing*, 42 (April 1978), p. 29.

[29] Dominique Hanssens and Barton A. Weitz, "The Effectiveness of Industrial Print Advertisements Across Product Categories," *Journal of Marketing Research*, 17 (August 1980), p. 304.

[30] Bob Donath, "Q: What Makes the Perfect Ad? A: It Depends," *Industrial Marketing*, 67 (August 1982), pp. 89–92.

[31] *Ibid.*, p. 90.

Table 15.4   Characteristics of Industrial Advertisements that Favorably Affect Each Phase of the Decision-Making Process

Phase of Decision-Making Process	Ad Elements That Create an Effective Impact
1. Establishing Contact	Four-color; color with illustrations; color with product
2. Creating Awareness	Product shown by itself; four or more copy blocks, more than 300 words of copy
3. Arousing Interest	Product ad; product by itself; use of 800 incoming WATS number, tables, and charts; three to five illustrations
4. Building Preference	Product ad; product by itself; four or more copy blocks
5. Keeping Customers Sold	More than 300 words of copy; product by itself

Source: Bob Donath: "Q: What Makes a Perfect Ad? A: It Depends," *Industrial Marketing*, 67 (August 1982), pp. 89–92.

fits, differentiate the buying criteria of the various decision participants, and design the advertisement appropriately.

Industrial Advertising Media

Although the message is vital to advertising success, an equally important factor is the medium through which it is presented. Industrial media are selected by target audience—the particular purchase decision participants to be reached. Generally, the first decision is whether to use *trade publications, direct mail,* or both. Selection of particular media also involves budgetary considerations—where are dollars best spent to generate the customer contacts desired?

Business Publications   The American Business Press estimates that in 1982 there were more than 2725 business publications carrying advertising amounting to over $2.3 billion.[32] For those specializing in distribution, *Handling and Shipping, Distribution Worldwide, Traffic Management,* and *Modern Materials Handling* are a few of the publications available. *Iron Age* and *Steel* are aimed at individuals in the steel industry. Business publications are either *horizontal* or *vertical*. Horizontal publications are directed at a specific task, technology, or function whatever the industry. *Advertising Age, Purchasing,* and *Handling and Shipping* are horizontal. Vertical publications, on the other hand, may be read by everyone from foreman to president within a specific industry. Typical vertical publications are *Glass Industry* or *Manufacturing Confectioner*.

If an industrial marketer's product has applications only within a few industries, vertical publications are a logical media choice. Where

[32]"Largest Advertisers Spend $380 Million," *Business Marketing*, 68 (May 1983), p. 89.

many industries are potential users and well-defined functions are the principal buying influencers, a horizontal publication is effective.

Controlled circulation is another important aspect of trade publications. Controlled circulation is free, as opposed to paid subscriptions, to selected readers in a position to influence buying decisions. Subscribers must provide their title and function and buying responsibilities, among other information. Thus, the advertiser can tell whether each publication reaches the desired audience.

---

10 Largest Business Publication Advertisers in 1982

Company	Business Publication Ad Expenditure
AT&T	$17,336,260
IBM	14,332,838
General Motors	14,212,386
Ford	12,495,566
Xerox	11,639,471
Hewlett-Packard	9,640,777
3M	9,080,200
DuPont	8,527,150
General Electric	7,924,118
IT&T	7,893,291

Source: "Largest Advertisers Spend $380 Million," *Business Marketing*, 68 (May 1983), p. 90.

Obviously, publication choice is predicated on a complete understanding of the range of purchase decision participants and the industries where the product will be used. Only then can the target audience be matched to the circulation statements of alternative business publications.

Advertising Cost   Circulation is an important criterion in the selection of publications, but circulation must be tempered by cost. First, the total advertising budget must be allocated among the various advertising tools. Most studies indicate that the breakdown of expenditures among the types of advertising tools is approximately: [33]

---

[33] Lilien and Little report approximately the same distribution of budget dollars in their ADVISOR study; McGraw-Hill studies have shown similar results. See Phillip Burton and J. Robert Miller, *Advertising Fundamentals* (Columbus, Ohio: Grid Publishing, Inc., 1976), p. 364.

Trade Publications	40 percent
Sales Promotion	25 percent
Direct Mail	25 percent
Trade Shows	10 percent

Of course, these will vary with company situation and advertising mission. However, the 40 percent allocation appears fairly consistent from company to company.

Allocation of the trade publication budget among various journals will depend on their relative effectiveness and efficiency, usually measured in *cost per thousand*. The formula is:

$$\text{Cost per thousand} = \frac{\text{Cost per page}}{\text{Circulation in thousands}}$$

To compare two publications on their actual page rates would be misleading, because the publication with the lower circulation will usually be less expensive. The cost per thousand calculation should be based on circulation to the *target* audience, not the total audience. Although some publications may appear high on a cost per thousand basis, they may in fact be very cost-effective, with very little wasted circulation.

Some industrial firms are very sophisticated in their approach to media selection. The Timken Company has a computerized media fact file with information on 91 publications that reach industries targeted by Timken.[34] Circulation by SIC code and job function for over 80 percent of the publications are maintained, allowing media planners to determine, for example, the best circulation for the machine tool industry in the purchasing, design/engineering, administrative management, and production functions. Publications can be compared by cost per thousand, based on very specific targets—"cost per thousand purchasing agents in SIC 3341."

Frequency and Scheduling   Even the most successful business publication advertisements are seen by only a small percentage of the people who read the magazine; therefore, one-time ads are generally ineffective. Because a number of exposures are required before a message "sinks in," and because the reading audience varies from month to month, a schedule of advertising insertions is required. To build continuity and repetitive value, at least six insertions per year may be required in a monthly publication and 26 to 52 insertions, with a minimum of 13, in a weekly.[35]

---

[34]"No Substitute for the Truth," *Media Decisions*, 12 (July 1977), p. 108.

[35]Burton and Miller, *Advertising Fundamentals*, p. 354; see also, Stanton G. Cort, David R. Lambert, and Paula L. Garret, "Effective Business-to-Business Frequency: New Management Perspectives from the Research Literature," *Advertising Research Foundation Literature Review* (October 1983).

Direct Mail Advertising   Direct mail delivers the advertising message firsthand to selected individuals. Possible mailing pieces range from a sales letter introducing a new product to a lengthy brochure or even a product sample. Direct mail can accomplish all of the major advertising functions, but its real contribution is in delivering the message to a precisely defined prospect.

Direct mail is commonly used for:

1.   corporate image promotion;

2.   product and service promotion;

3.   sales force support;

4.   distribution channel communication;

5.   special marketing problems.[36]

In promoting corporate image, as NCR does, direct mail may help to establish a reputation of technological leadership. On the other hand, product advertising by direct mail can be used to put specific product information in the hands of buying influencers. Kaiser Aluminum booklets explain aluminum's advantages to industrial buyers and specifiers, while messages on how to work with aluminum and a quantity/weight calculator are sent to machine operators and shop foremen.[37] Kaiser tailors its messages to the exact needs of each buying influence group.

Direct Mail: Benefits and Requirements   Direct mail also supports the salespeople—providing leads from returned inquiry cards, paving the way for a first sales call. It can be used effectively to notify potential customers of the location of local distributors. New products are frequently introduced through a direct mail campaign. In a study by IBM Corporation, 60 percent of the executives queried preferred to hear about new office products by mail.[38] Finally, direct mail applies to a host of special situations, such as identifying new customers and markets, meeting competitor claims, and promoting items that are not receiving enough sales support.

Direct mail is a viable advertising medium when "potential buyers can be clearly identified and easily reached through the mail. It can be a wasteful medium if the prospect lists are so general in nature that it is difficult or impossible to find a common denominator among the prospects."[39]

---

[36] J. Taylor Sims and Herbert E. Brown, "Increasing the Role of Direct Mail Marketing in Industrial Marketing Strategy," *Industrial Marketing Management*, 8 (November 1979), p. 294.

[37] *Ibid.*, p. 295.

[38] Ann Helming, "Direct Mail Leaves Its Indelible Stamp," *Advertising Age*, 53 (June 14, 1983), p. m-12.

[39] Terry Quinn, "The Marketing Base for International Direct Marketing Programmes," in John Dillion, ed., *Handbook of International Direct Marketing* (London: McGraw-Hill Book Company, 1976), p. 2.

Direct Mail Builds Profits at Minolta

Although Minolta uses various forms of print advertising, Jolin Vacca, marketing director of Minolta Business Systems, claims "newspaper and other print advertising just doesn't do it for us. It's a pain in the neck [for a prospect] to cut out a coupon from a newspaper. Ninety-nine percent of our efforts go into direct mail. It's the only way to go to generate qualified sales leads."

A recent direct mail program used a narrowly targeted mailing list and a "unique mailing piece": A segmentation survey developed a list of companies that had bought Minolta equipment previously. The mailing piece included a two-color booklet titled "Copier Needs Analysis." The booklet was like a game: readers took blind tests to discover the type of copier they needed. They then turned to the back of the booklet to find the required brand name (from a list of 40 brands besides Minolta).

The response rate from the 375,000 prospect list reached 2.8 percent (excellent, compared to the typical 1–1.5 percent rate). Ten percent of the responses were turned into sales.

Source: Ann Helming, "Direct Mail Leaves Its Indelible Stamp," *Advertising Age*, 53 (June 14, 1982), p. m-14.

A direct mail advertisement typically gains the full attention of the reader, and therefore provides greater impact than a trade publication advertisement. Industrial buyers surveyed by the Business Advertising Research Council claimed to read or at least scan three-quarters of the direct mail promotions sent to them.[40] Timing is also flexible; a new price schedule or new service innovation can be communicated to the buyer as needed. Finally, direct mail makes it easy for the buyer to respond—usually a reply postcard is included or the name, address, and phone number of the local salesperson or distributor are provided.

A Planned Response Package　　Most direct mail programs seek some type of response. Often, the potential buyer is asked to return a reply card to receive additional information, such as a sample or a brochure

---

[40] Ann Helming, "Direct Mail Leaves Its Indelible Stamp," p. m-12.

explaining the benefits and applications of a product. Only 1 out of every 40 raw leads developed from a direct mail campaign may be actually worth a salesperson's attention.[41] As a result, there is often a tendency to adopt a casual approach for responding to sales leads. However, to realize the potential of direct mail, there must be a formal program to "qualify" each inquiry and respond promptly. Qualification may be accomplished by telephoning the respondent and assessing his or her authority and readiness to purchase. Once the respondent has been qualified, the response program might involve mailing literature to the prospect, referring the prospect to a salesperson, or calling to explain product details. A planned response "package" would aim to generate a sale, and should include a motivating cover letter; a descriptive brochure; and a reply card that makes it easy to respond.[42]

The Mailing List   The critical ingredient of a direct mail advertising campaign is the *list of buying influencers*. The selectivity of direct mail, although its primary advantage, is also its greatest challenge. There are literally hundreds of mailing lists available. Mailing lists for industrial advertising purposes may be: (1) circulation lists provided by trade publications; (2) lists provided by industrial directories; (3) lists provided by mailing list houses (e.g., firms specifically engaged in renting industrial mailing lists); and (4) self-generated lists of previous customers and prospects. Computers are playing an increasing role in maintaining mailing lists; 89 percent of respondents to one survey maintained their lists on the computer.[43] The computer also allows the advertiser to supplement the list with sales data and SIC codes. A catalog published by Standard Rate and Data Service inventories and describes most of the industrial mailing lists available. These often have names of individual executives. However, if the lists are even slightly out of date, a list by company and functional title should be used.

Telemarketing   Telemarketing not only supplements the personal sales call (see Chapter 16), but can also enhance the effectiveness of direct mail advertising. Increasingly, many firms initiate telemarketing by including a toll-free telephone number in their print and direct mail advertisements.[44] Honeywell's Process Control Division's direct mail features a toll-free number.[45] When a prospect responds, the telemarketing operator does preliminary qualifying directly onto a terminal linked to a Honeywell DPS-8 computer. The screen displays questions keyed to a given product in question, and the answers are entered and stored

---

[41] John L. DeFazio, "An Inquiry-Based MIS," p. 54.

[42] Robert W. Bly, "The Key to Great Inquiry Fulfillment," *Business Marketing*, 68 (April 1983), p. 96.

[43] Bob Donath, "More Evidence, Sort of, on the Direct Mail Boom," *Business Marketing*, 68 (April 1983), p. 102.

[44] Roy Voorhees and John Coppett, "Telemarketing in Distribution Channels," *Industrial Marketing Management*, 12 (April 1983), p. 105.

[45] Richard G. Webster, "High-Tech Telemarketing Scores for Honeywell Division," *Business Marketing*, 68 (June 1983), p. 102.

immediately. Once the prospect is qualified, the operator determines whether the response should be mailed information or a sales call. The computerized information is used to create a mailing list. The sales force is notified via electronic mail, so that the prospects can be contacted promptly (usually within a day). Telemarketing support for direct mail provides ease of response for the prospect, immediate reply while the idea is fresh, and interactive dialogue to more fully delineate customer needs.[46]

Media Selection: A Recap   In conclusion, selecting industrial advertising media is a matching of media with the target audience. The industrial advertiser must choose the specific purchase decision participants to which an advertising message will be directed, and then match these to the circulations of various journals. The final decision on media choice will depend on the budget, the cost per thousand of the medium, and the medium's circulation.

Advertising Effectiveness

The industrial advertiser rarely expects orders to result immediately from advertising. Advertising is designed to create awareness, stimulate loyalty to the company, or create a favorable attitude toward a product. Even though advertising may not directly precipitate a purchase decision, advertising programs must be held accountable. Thus, the industrial advertiser must be able to measure the results of current advertising in order to improve future advertising, and to evaluate the effectiveness of advertising expenditures against expenditures on other elements of marketing strategy.

Measuring Impacts on the Purchase Decision   Measuring advertising effectiveness means assessing advertising's impact on what "intervenes" between the stimulus (advertising) and the resulting behavior (purchase decision).[47] The theory is that advertising can affect awareness, knowledge, and other dimensions that more readily lend themselves to measurement. In essence, the advertiser attempts to gauge advertising's ability to move an individual through the purchase decision process. This approach assumes, correctly or not, that enhancement of any one phase of the decision process or movement from one step to the next increases the ultimate probability of purchase.

In summary, advertising effectiveness will be evaluated against objectives formulated in terms of the elements of the buyer's decision process. Advertising efforts will also be judged, in the final analysis, on cost

---

[46] Benson Shapiro and John Wyman, "New Ways to Reach Your Customers," *Harvard Business Review*, 59 (July–August 1981), p. 106.

[47] Aaker and Myers, *Advertising Management*, p. 89.

Table 15.5   The Five Primary Areas for Advertising Evaluation

Area	Pre-Evaluation	Post-Evaluation
1. Markets	Identifying the market targets at which the advertising is aimed	Measuring extent to which advertising succeeded in reaching its market targets
2. Motives	Determining what causes people to buy (as preparatory step toward constructing advertising message)	Measuring motivating factors after the action (such as a purchase) occurred
3. Messages	Determining the best ways to construct and communicate messages	Measuring extent to which the message registered
4. Media	Determining the best combination of media to reach the market with the messages	Measuring extent to which various media succeeded in reaching the market with the message
5. Overall Results	Identifying the specific results that advertising is uniquely qualified to perform	Evaluating extent to which advertising accomplished its objectives as a basis for deciding what to continue, what to change, how much to spend

Source: Maurice I. Mandell, *Advertising* (Englewood Cliffs, N.J.: Prentice-Hall, Inc., 1974), p. 610. Reprinted by permission of Prentice-Hall, Inc.

---

per level of achievement (e.g., dollars spent to achieve a certain level of awareness or recognition).

The Measurement Program   A good measurement program entails substantial advanced planning. Table 15.5 shows the basic areas of advertising evaluation. Each has a planning (pre-evaluation) and an evaluation aspect (post-evaluation). Thus, the manager must determine in advance what is to be measured, how, and in what sequence. The five primary areas for advertising evaluation are: (1) markets, (2) motives, (3) messages, (4) media, and (5) results.

The evaluation of industrial advertising is demanding and complex, but absolutely essential. Budgetary constraints are generally the limiting factors. Professional research companies are often called on to develop field research studies. In determining the impact of advertising on moving a decision participant from awareness of the product/company to a point of readiness to buy, the evaluations will usually measure knowledge, recognition, recall, awareness, preference, and motivation. Measurements of actual sales impacts are unfortunately not often possible.

Supplementary Promotional Tools

Media and direct mail advertising are the cornerstone of most nonpersonal industrial promotional programs. Industrial advertising funds are designated primarily for trade publication and direct mail, but these are reinforced by other promotional activities, like exhibits and trade shows, catalogs, and trade promotion.

Exhibits and Trade Shows

Most industries stage a business show or exhibition annually to display new advances and technological developments in the industry. Total attendance at 8000 trade shows in 1980 reached 31.5 million; firms were reported to have spent $7 billion to exhibit.[48] Generally, sellers present their products and services in booths visited by interested industry members. A trade show exhibit offers a unique opportunity to publicize a significant contribution to technology or to demonstrate new and old products. According to Thomas Bonoma, "For many companies, trade show expenditures are the major—and for more than few, the only—form of organized marketing communication activity other than efforts by the sales force and distributors."[49]

Through the trade show,

1.   An effective selling message can be delivered to a relatively large and interested audience at one time (for example, over 30,000 people attend the annual Plant Engineering Show).

2.   New products can be introduced to a mass audience.

3.   Customers can get hands-on experience with the product in a one-on-one selling situation.

4.   Potential customers can be uncovered, providing sales personnel with qualified leads.

5.   General goodwill can be enhanced.

6.   Often free publicity is generated for the company.

The cost of reaching a prospect at a trade show is approximately $70, while the cost of making an industrial sales call approaches $180.[50]

Trade Shows Are Effective   A study by the Trade Show Bureau found that eight weeks after an office equipment show, 53 percent of the visitors expected to make a purchase. One year later, 63 percent of them had actually made one purchase at an average cost of $255,000, and 75 percent of these said they had been influenced by what they had seen at the trade show.[51] Many potential buyers that visit a display booth often

---

[48] Joanne Cleaver, "You Don't Have to be a Star to be in This Show," *Advertising Age*, 53 (June 14, 1982), p. m-8.

[49] Thomas V. Bonoma, "Get More Out of Your Trade Shows," *Harvard Business Review*, 61 (January–February 1983), p. 76.

[50] Joanne Cleaver, "You Don't Have to be a Star to be in This Show," p. m-8.

[51] *Ibid.*, p. m-8.

have not been visited by the exhibitor's sales force in the preceding year. Among industrial promotion tools for influencing the purchase decision process, trade shows have been ranked third behind peer recommendations and personal selling,[52] and above both print advertising and direct mail. Finally, the Trade Show Bureau reports that the cost of developing and closing a trade-show-generated sales lead is 77 percent less than the cost of closing the average industrial sale.[53] Because trade shows can be extremely costly, while dramatically enhancing sales effectiveness, they must be carefully planned.

Planning Trade Show Strategy   To develop an effective trade show communications strategy, managers must address four questions:

1.   What functions should the trade show perform in the total marketing communications program?

2.   To whom should the marketing effort at trade shows be directed?

3.   What is the appropriate show mix for the company?

4.   What should the trade show investment-audit policy be? How should audits be carried out?[54]

Answering these questions will help management to crystallize their thinking about target audiences, results to be expected, and how funds should be allocated.

Trade Show Objectives   Some of the functions of trade shows in generating sales include identifying decision influencers, identifying potential customers, providing product, service and company information, learning of potential application problems, creating actual sales, and handling current customer problems. In addition to these selling-related functions, the trade show can be a valuable device for building corporate image, gathering competitive intelligence, and enhancing sales force morale. Specific objectives are needed to guide the development of trade show strategy and specify the activities of company personnel while there. Once specific objectives are formulated, the exhibitor must evaluate alternative trade shows in light of the target market.

Selecting the Shows   The challenge is to decide which trade shows to attend and how much of the promotional budget to expend.

---

[52] A. Parasuraman, "The Relative Importance of Industrial Promotion Tools," *Industrial Marketing Management*, 10 (October 1981), pp. 277–281.

[53] "Does Exhibiting Cut Your Selling Costs?" *Business Marketing*, 68 (July 1983), p. 106.

[54] Thomas V. Bonoma, "Get More Out of Your Trade Shows," p. 79; see also J. Steven Kelly and James Comer, "Research Lends Coherency to a Trade Show Marketing Plan," *Marketing News*, (March 2, 1984), p. 4–5.

Nippon Electric: Star of the Show

To make the trade show an effective aspect of corporate promotional activities, Nippon Electric plans trade show exhibits as carefully as product strategy. Consider the strategy used at the 1982 National Association of Broadcasters Show:

1. A preshow survey of customers evaluated specific likes and dislikes about trade show presentation styles. One "like" was new product information before the show. So, Nippon ran ads before the show to preview new products.

2. Current customers and important prospects were called and appointments were made to see them at the booth. Nearly 85 percent kept their appointments.

3. The sales staff was trained in techniques for making presentations at trade shows, including methods for screening prospects to qualify potential buyers.

4. Prospects were given buttons color-coded to the products they were interested in. The buttons helped the sales staff to direct visitors to the right displays and give them appropriate material.

5. The booth was designed to showcase new product demonstrations, improve traffic flow, and provide a private area for sales conferences.

How effective was the strategy? One initial objective was to generate 100 qualified leads for one system; the total was 200. Nippon sold out of the entire first year's scheduled production for a new product in 3½ days!

Source: Joanne Cleaver, "You Don't Have to be a Star to be in This Show," *Advertising Age*, 53 (June 14, 1982), p. m-9.

Clearly, the firm will want to be represented at those shows frequented by its most important customer segments. A useful service is the *Exposition Audit* provided by Business Publication Audit of Circulation, Inc. The audit reports registered attendance at trade shows and a complete profile of each registrant's business, job title, and function. Many firms make a preshow survey of target prospects to learn which shows they will attend and what they hope to gain from attending. In this way the exhibitor can prepare their trade show strategy to fit the needs of their potential customers.

Managing the Trade Show Exhibit   Nippon Electric, in an effort to generate interest in an exhibit, runs advertisements in trade publications profiling new products to be exhibited at the show. Many exhibitors will call prospects and customers before the show to make appointments at the show.

Sales personnel must be trained to perform in the trade show environment. The selling job differs from the typical sales call in that the salesperson may have only five to ten minutes to make a presentation. On a typical sales call, salespersons usually first sell themselves, then the company, and finally the product. At the trade show, the process is reversed.

Finally, there must be a system for responding effectively to inquiries generated at the show. Digital Equipment Corporation uses a computer at the show to transmit information to corporate headquarters electronically.[55] Headquarters staff then use word processing to generate a letter and mailing label, and send out the required information. When prospects return to their offices after a show, the material is on their desks.

The Trade Show Budget   How much to budget is hard to decide:

It is strange to find that so little is known about the usefulness of exhibitions, that they are so often an expression of faith rather than fact, with such factors as size of stand and budget determined intuitively by some senior executive.[56]

More money is probably wasted at exhibitions than in any other advertising medium. One reason seems to be the apparent need for competitors to outdo each other in creating grand displays.

Gary Lilien's ADVISOR studies shed some light on trade show budgeting. The level of spending on trade shows is likely to be greater if: a product is in the early stages of its life cycle; enjoys high sales volume; is backed by aggressive marketing plans; and has low customer concentration.[57] Thomas Bonoma recommends that a "full-base high-profile" show be used (if available shows mainly attract current customers) by companies whose promotion mix is poor for retaining customers although efficient at identifying and selling prospects.[58] On the other hand, shows that attract *potential* customers should be exploited by firms whose promotion is effective and efficient in keeping customers—but inefficient in getting them.

[55] "DEC Goes On-Line at Showtime," *Sales and Marketing Management*, 128 (February 8, 1982), p. 80.

[56] Norman Hart, *Industrial Advertising and Publicity* (New York: John Wiley and Sons, Inc., 1978), p. 56.

[57] Gary L. Lilien, "A Descriptive Model of the Trade-Show Budgeting Decision Process," *Industrial Marketing Management*, 12 (February 1983), p. 29.

[58] Thomas V. Bonoma, "Get More Out of Your Trade Shows," p. 79.

Budgeting for trade shows is more art than science. Trade shows are an inherently "sloppy" marketing problem to which sophisticated techniques or models will probably never be applied.[59] Nevertheless, industrial marketing managers must carefully evaluate each trade show and its associated expenses in terms of the likely sales and corporate image impacts. As with all other promotional vehicles, the planning and budgeting for trade shows must focus on specific objectives. Once these objectives have been determined, the rational approach will then identify the tasks that must be accomplished and the levels of expenditure required.

Catalogs

Because it is not possible for distributors to inventory all items, many manufacturers provide loose-leaf catalogs from which the distributor can order. Many suppliers of products mail extensive catalogs describing their products and potential applications to likely industrial buyers. Catalogs are an efficient way for office and computer supply companies, for example, to generate the relatively small dollar sales typical of their business.[60] Catalogs can be a powerful promotional device; if properly distributed, they will be on the shelves of every important potential buyer in the industry.

Catalogs are a form of direct marketing. They generally contain enough information for the reader to make a purchase. In effect, a good catalog is like having a salesperson in the buyer's office at all times. In addition, the catalog will supplement personal selling by providing information between sales calls. Some industrial marketers find that catalogs may in fact substitute for a salesperson or a rep in peripheral market areas.

If the supplier distributes the catalog, appropriate mailing lists must be developed. Catalog mailing lists need to be continually updated. Important potential buyers may be missed if efforts are not made to add new companies to the list. An industrial marketer can delegate the catalog distribution function to a firm specializing in such activities. Distributing companies, like Sweets, may collect catalogs from a number of firms, bind them together, and distribute them. Users find the compendium of catalogs reduces search time, and, the advertiser is assured of greater life and greater use of its section of the catalog file.[61]

Trade Advertising

Trade advertising refers to the promotional efforts of a supplier that are directed at intermediaries. The focus of advertising to customer/users is on communicating product benefits, but trade promotion stresses the

[59] *Ibid.*, p. 83.

[60] Benson Shapiro and John Wyman, "New Ways to Reach Your Customers," p. 107.

[61] Maurice I. Mandell, *Advertising*, 2nd ed. (Englewood Cliffs, N.J.: Prentice-Hall, 1974), p. 661.

profits associated with carrying the manufacturer's line. In addition, promotional pieces are made available to distributors and reps so they can associate their name with the manufacturer in a local advertising campaign. Suppliers often supply dealer aids, such as displays or sales kits, to intermediaries to enhance their effectiveness. The quality of promotion support provided to distributors can be important in solidifying an effective channel relationship.

Summary

Because of the nature of the industrial buying process, personal selling is primary in creating sales; advertising supports and supplements personal selling. Yet advertising does perform some tasks that personal selling simply cannot perform. Advertising is able to reach buying influences that sales personnel cannot.

Advertising supports personal selling by making the company and product known to potential buyers. The result is greater overall selling success. Effective advertising makes the entire marketing strategy more efficient, often lowering total marketing and selling costs. Finally, advertising can provide information and company/product awareness more efficiently than personal selling.

Managing the advertising program begins with the determination of advertising objectives. Advertising objectives need to be written, and directed to a specific audience. Once objectives are specified, funds must be allocated to advertising efforts. Rules of thumb, though common, are not the ideal approach to specifying advertising budgets. The task method, used with industry guidelines established by the ADVISOR studies, is more effective.

Advertising messages are created with the understanding that the potential buyer's perceptual process will influence receptivity to the message. The most effective appeal is one that projects product benefits sought by the targeted buying influencers.

Advertising media are selected on the basis of their circulation; that is, how well their audience matches the desired audience of purchase decision influencers. Direct mail places advertisements in the hands of precisely defined audiences. Finally, advertising effectiveness must be evaluated against the communication objectives established for the advertising campaign. Readership, recognition, awareness, attitudes, and intention-to-buy are typical measures of industrial advertising performance.

A variety of supplementary promotional tools are available. Trade shows are an effective way to reach large audiences with a single presentation, but funds must be allocated carefully. Catalogs may also lead to direct sales if effectively designed and distributed. Trade advertising emphasizes profitability to intermediaries and provides devices to enhance their effectiveness.

Discussion Questions

1. While the bulk of the promotional budget of the industrial firm is allocated to personal selling, advertising can play an important role in industrial marketing strategy. Explain.

2. The Hamilton Compressor Company increased advertising expenditures 15 percent in the Chicago market last year and sales increased 4 percent. Upon seeing the results, Mr. White, the president, turns to you and asks: "Was that increase in advertising worth it?" Outline your reply. (Feel free to include questions that you would ask Mr. White.)

3. Breck Machine Tool would like you to develop a series of ads for a new industrial product. Upon request, Breck's marketing research department will provide you with any data that they have concerning the new product and the market. Outline the approach that you would follow in *selecting media* and *developing messages* for the campaign. Specify the types of data that you would draw upon to improve the quality of your decisions.

4. Outline how you would evaluate the effectiveness and efficiency of an industrial firm's advertising function. They would like you to center on budgeting practices and performance results.

5. Explain how a message presented in an industrial advertisement may be favorably evaluated by the production manager, unfavorably evaluated by the purchasing manager, and fail even to trigger the attention of the quality control engineer.

6. Given the rapid rise in the cost of making industrial sales calls, should the industrial marketer attempt to substitute direct mail advertising for personal selling whenever possible? Support your position.

7. What is the role of trade advertising in the industrial marketer's promotional program?

8. It is argued that industrial advertising is not expected to precipitate sales directly. If industrial advertising does not persuade organizational buyers to buy brand A versus brand B, what does it do, and how can we measure its impact against expenditures on other marketing strategy elements?

C·H·A·P·T·E·R
16

Industrial Marketing Communications: Managing the Personal Selling Function

Industrial marketing communications consist of advertising, sales promotion, and personal selling. As explored in the last chapter, advertising and related sales promotion tools supplement and reinforce personal selling. Personal selling is the most important demand-stimulating force in the industrial marketer's promotional mix. Through the sales force, the marketer links the firm's total product and service offering to the needs of organizational customers.

After reading this chapter, you will have an understanding of:

1. *the role of personal selling in industrial marketing strategy;*
2. *the importance of viewing industrial marketing management as a buyer–seller interaction process;*
3. *the nature of the industrial sales management function;*
4. *selected managerial tools that can be applied to major sales force decision areas.*

Personal selling is dominant in industrial markets because the number of potential customers is relatively small compared to consumer markets, and the dollar purchases are large. The importance of personal selling in the marketing mix depends on such factors as the nature and composition of the market, the nature of the product line, and the company's objectives and financial capability. Industrial marketers have many potential links to the market. Some may rely on manufacturers' representatives and distributors, others exclusively on a direct sales force. Similarly, each firm must determine the relative importance of the various components of the promotional mix—advertising vs. sales promotion vs. personal selling.

Across all product categories, the cost of an industrial sales call averages $178,[1] though this varies with the method of distribution. Industrial companies selling directly to customers have an average sales call cost of $225, compared with $134 for those using distributors. Of course, these figures would vary, depending upon a host of company, product, and market conditions. They do point up, however, that significant resources are invested in personal selling in the industrial market. To maximize effectiveness and efficiency, the personal selling function must be carefully managed and integrated into the firm's marketing mix.

This chapter first considers industrial marketing management as a buyer–seller interaction process. Relevant aspects of organizational buying behavior (Chapters 3 and 4) will be related to the personal selling process. The chapter then turns to sales force management, and the need for defining personal selling objectives, structuring the sales organization, sales force allocation, and the evaluation and control of sales force operations.

Foundations of Personal Selling: An Organizational Customer Focus

Personal selling is the means through which industrial marketing strategy is executed. Once the marketer defines target market segments on the basis of organizational characteristics (macro) or the characteristics of decision-making units (micro), the sales force is deployed to meet the needs of these segments. The salesperson augments the total product offering and serves as a representative for both seller and buyer. The image, reputation, and need-satisfying ability of the seller firm is conveyed, to an important degree, by the sales force. By helping procurement decision makers to define requirements and match the firm's product or service to requirements, the salesperson is offering not just a

---

[1] "Sales Call Costs Explode," *Industrial Marketing* (July 1982), p. 9.

physical product but also ideas, recommendations, technical assistance, experience, confidence, and friendship. A large toy manufacturer, for example, evaluates suppliers on the basis of product quality, delivery reliability, price, and *the value of ideas and suggestions provided by the sales personnel.* This buying organization, in fact, openly solicits ideas, and evaluates suppliers formally on the number and quality of these recommendations.

As a representative for the buyer, the salesperson will often articulate the specific needs of a customer to research and development or production personnel in the industrial firm. Product specifications, delivery, and technical service are often negotiated through the salesperson. The salesperson serves as an uncertainty absorption point, reducing conflict in the buyer–seller relationship.

Organizational Buying Behavior

Successful personal selling relies heavily upon a recognition of the unique requirements of each organizational customer. Industrial products may have numerous applications; organizational buyers have varying levels of experience and information in purchasing certain products. A sensitivity to how buying organizations vary, coupled with a knowledge of organizational buying behavior, is the foundation for successful personal selling.

A salesperson can benefit by examining a potential buyer organization from several perspectives. First, how would the organization view this specific buying situation—new task, modified rebuy, or straight rebuy? As emphasized in Chapter 3, each buying situation calls for a different personal selling strategy—the exact form depending on whether the marketer is an "in" or an "out" supplier. Second, what are the environmental, organizational, group, and individual influences on the organizational buying process (Figure 16.1)?[2] Among the considerations that will form the personal selling task are:

1. *Environmental Factor Identification.* How are business conditions (e.g., growth, inflation) or political-legal trends (e.g., governmental regulation) affecting the industry within which this firm operates?

2. *Organizational Factor Identification.* Is procurement in this buying organization centralized or decentralized? To what extent does the procurement department use the computer in buying and in selecting and evaluating suppliers?

3. *Buying Center Identification.* Which organizational members will be included in the buying center?

[2] Richard E. Plank and William A. Dempsey, "A Framework for Personal Selling to Organizations," *Industrial Marketing Management* 9 (April 1980), pp. 143–149.

Figure 16.1   Identifying Key Features of the Organizational Buying Environment

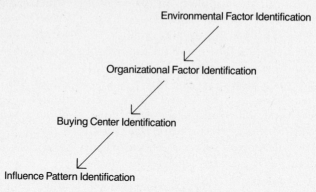

4.   *Influence Pattern Identification.* Which buying center members will exert the most power in the buying decision? What are the selection criteria of each?

Knowledge of the special competitive challenges that the buying firm faces, how the proposed product/service offering will be applied, how it will influence the cost structure and performance of different departments—these are the insights that allow the marketer to sharply focus personal selling strategy. Empathy with the buyer is the core of a mutually beneficial buyer–seller relationship.

Exploring Buyer–Seller Interactions

Industrial selling, at its most basic level, can be viewed as an exchange process in which two individuals or firms trade items of value. The dyadic exchange model, introduced in Chapter 3, provides rich insights into the nature of buyer–seller relationships in the industrial market.[3] Understanding the complex flows of influence in buyer–seller interactions is fundamental to successful industrial sales management.

A Dyadic Exchange Perspective

An exchange perspective of industrial marketing points up not only what the selling organization gains from a transaction, but also what the buying organization secures in return (Figure 16.2). Exchange relationships between the organizational selling center and the organizational

---

[3] Thomas V. Bonoma and Wesley J. Johnston, "The Social Psychology of Industrial Buying and Selling," *Industrial Marketing Management* 7 (1978), pp. 213–224.

Figure 16.2   Diagnosing Exchange Processes in Industrial Marketing

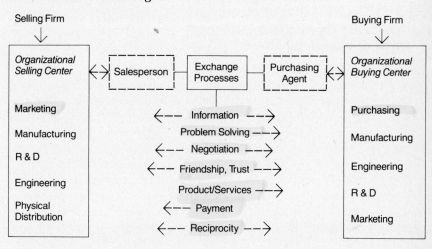

buying center are central. The members of the selling organization who participate, to some degree, in making a particular industrial marketing decision constitute the organizational selling or strategy center (see Chapter 9).[4] The needs of a particular selling situation, especially the information requirements, significantly influence the composition of the organizational selling center.

Assuming visible roles in the exchange process are the salesperson (selling center representative) and the purchasing agent (buying center representative). The salesperson and the buyer each begin the interaction with particular plans, goals, and intentions. The salesperson exchanges information and assistance in solving a purchasing problem for the reward of a sale given by the buyer or by members of the buying center.

In addition to external negotiations with members of the buying center, the industrial salesperson, acting on behalf of the potential customer, often is involved in internal negotiations with other members of the selling center, such as manufacturing or R&D, to insure a successful exchange relationship with a particular customer. Internal negotiations also occur within the buying center as various members represent the interests of their functional areas in the selection of suppliers. Complex flows of influence characterize buyer–seller interactions in the industrial market. To insure maximum customer satisfaction and the desired market response, Thomas Bonoma and Wesley Johnston contend that indus-

[4] Michael D. Hutt and Thomas W. Speh, "The Marketing Strategy Center: Diagnosing the Industrial Marketer's Interdisciplinary Role," *Journal of Marketing*, in press.

trial sellers must effectively manage the complex flows of influence that are exchanged in buyer–seller relationships.[5]

Buyer–Seller Interactions: Style and Content of Communication [6]

Jagdish Sheth theorizes that the content and style of communications strongly influence the quality of the interaction between buyer and seller. The *content of communication* refers to the substance of the interaction, the recommending, offering, or negotiating of a set of product-specific utilities, and the expectations of the participants. Content is concerned with the performance characteristics of a product or service and related utilities (e.g., social, organizational, and emotional).

The *style of communication* refers to the format, rituals, and mannerisms that the buyer and the seller use in their interaction. Common styles are: (1) task-oriented, highly purposeful; (2) interaction-oriented, socializing or personalizing; or (3) self-oriented, preoccupied with self-interests.

An ideal transaction requires compatibility on both style and content, and incompatibility on these two dimensions results in no transaction (Figure 16.3). The latter case may, in fact, lead to negative side effects, such as distrust or unfavorable word-of-mouth concerning one another. When the content is compatible and the style is incompatible, the process might be terminated, or, if a sale results, negative feelings will remain about how each handled the transaction. Finally, if the incompatibility centers on content rather than style, the interaction process will either cease or negotiations will continue with each attempting to alter the other's product expectations.

Knowledge of incongruity between the buyer and the seller with respect to style or content can signal problems for the marketer. If the incompatibility centers on content, adjustments may be needed in the firm's offering, or its market segmentation rationale may need to be reassessed. By contrast, if the interaction problems are style-related, corrective actions might include modifying personal selling approaches or retraining the sales personnel. The firm also might consider changes in the recruiting and selection of sales personnel.

A study of life insurance buyer–seller interactions found that there were greater attitudinal similarities between agents and sold prospects than between agents and unsold prospects. Further, "sales success in a dyadic encounter may be a function of the degree to which the prospect

[5] Bonoma and Johnston, "Social Psychology of Industrial Buying and Selling," pp. 213–224.

[6] This section is largely based on Jagdish N. Sheth, "Buyer–Seller Interaction: A Conceptual Framework," in B. B. Anderson, ed., *Advances in Consumer Research, Volume III* (Cincinnati: Association for Consumer Research, 1976), pp. 382–386.

Figure 16.3   Outcomes of Dyadic Interaction Processes: The Influence of Content and Style of Communication

	Compatible Style	Incompatible Style
Compatible Content	Ideal Transaction	Inefficient Transaction
Incompatible Content	Inefficient Transaction	No Transaction

Source: Adapted from Jagdish N. Sheth, "Buyer–Seller Interaction: A Conceptual Framework," in B. B. Anderson (ed.), *Advances in Consumer Research, Volume III* (Cincinnati, Ohio: Association for Consumer Research, 1976), p. 383. Used by permission of the Association for Consumer Research.

perceives the salesperson as fulfilling his attitudinal and behavioral expectations."[7]

The Industrial Salesperson: An Interorganizational Link[8]

Industrial salespersons provide a means by which firms are linked to critical elements in the environment of their enterprise. For example, the salesperson serves as an important link in the firm's communication with its customers, spanning boundaries by:

1. *Representing and transacting.* The salesperson represents the marketer but must balance the needs of two organizations—the industrial firm and the customer organization.

2. *Buffering.* The salesperson enhances environmental stability by smoothing irregularities between the production cycle of the marketer and the sales ordering cycle of customers.

3. *Information processing and monitoring.* The salesperson monitors environmental conditions and transfers relevant information back to organizational decision-makers.

4. *Linking and coordinating.* The salesperson initiates and guides informal coordination between seller and client firms or among the seller, a middleman, and a client firm.

[7] Edward A. Riordan, Richard L. Oliver, and James H. Donnelly, Jr., "The Unsold Prospect: Dyadic and Attitudinal Determinants," *Journal of Marketing Research* 14 (November 1977), p. 536.

[8] This section is based on Robert E. Spekman, "Organizational Boundary Behavior: A Conceptual Framework for Investigating the Industrial Salesperson," in Richard P. Bagozzi, ed., *Sales Management: New Developments from Behavioral and Decision Model Research* (Cambridge, Mass.: Marketing Science Institute, 1979), pp. 133–144; for related research see Stephen W. Clopton, "Seller and Buying Firm Factors Affecting Industrial Buyers' Negotiation Behavior and Outcomes," *Journal of Marketing Research* 21 (February 1984), pp. 39–53.

These boundary-spanning activities have great strategic importance and inherent strains and conflicts.

On Corporate Culture and Selling High-Tech Products

Raychem Corporation is a Fortune 500 producer of material science products such as electrical interconnect systems and high performance wire and cable. Cap Stubbs, Corporate Director of Marketing, offers these observations on corporate culture and the marketing of high tech products.

Fundamental to the success of an industrial firm is a corporate culture that emphasizes customer satisfaction. A strong customer orientation is fundamental at all levels in the strategic planning hierarchy and to all departments in the organization. R&D, design engineering, manufacturing, technical service, physical distribution, marketing—all are involved in creating and delivering customer satisfaction. The Raychem salesperson plays a key role in conveying this philosophy of customer satisfaction across organizational boundaries and in managing the buyer–seller relationship. The salesperson links key members of the selling organization, for example, R&D, to their counterparts in the buying organization. Frequently, engineers and other technical personnel find themselves directly involved in the industrial selling process. They must be prepared to assume a key selling role here. On other occasions, the salesperson, acting on behalf of the customer, negotiates technical design changes or an earlier delivery date with other departments in our firm.

A corporate culture that emphasizes customer satisfaction provides the foundation for developing profitable long-term buyer–seller relationships in the industrial market.

Source: Interview with Cap Stubbs, Corporate Director of Marketing, Raychem Corporation, Menlo Park, California, January 9, 1984.

Managing the Industrial Sales Force

Effective management of the industrial sales force is fundamental to the firm's success. Sales management is the planning, organizing, directing, and control of personal selling efforts (Figure 16.4).[9]

---

[9] A comprehensive treatment of all aspects of sales management is beyond the scope of this volume. For more extensive discussion, see Herbert W. Johnson, *Sales Management: Operations Administration Marketing* (Columbus, Ohio: Merrill Publishing Co., 1976); see also, Richard P. Bagozzi, ed., *Sales Management: New Developments*.

Figure 16.4   Sales Force Management Decision Process

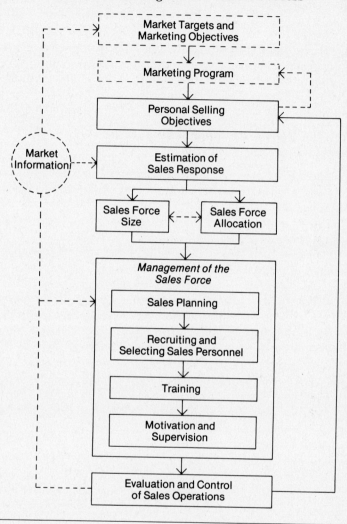

Source: David W. Cravens, Gerald E. Hills, and Robert B. Woodruff, *Marketing Decision Making: Concepts and Strategy* (Homewood, IL: Richard D. Irwin, Inc., 1976), p. 674 and 735. Reprinted by permission. Copyright © 1976 by Richard D. Irwin, Inc.

Sales force decisions are tempered by overall marketing objectives and must be integrated with the other elements of the marketing mix. Forecasts of the expected sales response guide the firm both in determining the total selling effort required (sales force size) and in allocating the sales force (perhaps to sales territories). The techniques for estimating market potential and forecasting sales (discussed in Part Three—Assessing Market Opportunities) are particularly valuable here. Sales management also involves the ongoing activities of sales planning, recruiting and selecting sales personnel, training, motivation, and supervision. Finally, sales operations must be monitored to identify problem areas and assess the efficiency, effectiveness, and profitability of personal selling units.

This section will consider (1) the role of personal selling in the marketing program; (2) methods for organizing the sales force; (3) the requirements for successful sales force administration; and (4) models that can be employed in deploying the industrial sales force.

Defining the Role of Personal Selling in the Industrial Marketing Program

The specific role of personal selling in the marketing program varies by company and product/market conditions. The following scenarios show two different personal selling roles.

Kim Kelly, a sales representative for Honeywell, Inc., had been competing with the sales personnel of four other firms for a large computer account. He made numerous sales calls to different individuals in the buying organization over a three-year period. In fact, for the last three months as the firm neared a decision, he had worked nearly full time on this account. His diligence and follow-up culminated in an $8 million order on which Kim received an $80,000 commission.[10]

Kim's prime personal selling function was *demand-stimulation*. Although supported by advertising, sales promotion, and technical personnel, personal selling is the dominant demand-stimulating force in the communications mix. This is often referred to as a *push strategy*.

Joe Smith is the sales representative for a major manufacturer of industrial accessory equipment. He travels several states calling on industrial distributors who are authorized dealers for his company's product line. These distributors sell the equipment to industrial users. Joe begins his day by stopping at a nearby distributor to solicit an order to replenish inventory levels. Joe checks the distributor's inventory, prepares an order, discusses it with the buyer, and gets it approved and signed. The order is placed in the outgoing mail.

After a 20-minute drive, Joe arrives at another distributor. He is informed that a shipment came in freight collect and should have been freight prepaid. Joe calls his traffic department and authorizes a credit memo for the amount of the shipping charges. With the problem resolved, Joe leaves.

On the third distributor call, Joe learns that a recent bid was lost to a competitor. He gathers all the available information on the missed sale, writes a brief report, and mails it to his sales manager.[11]

Joe's activities go beyond demand-stimulation into channel assistance, market intelligence, and strengthening buyer–seller relationships. This more passive role for personal selling is referred to as a *pull strategy*.

[10] "To Computer Salesmen, the 'Big-Ticket' Deal Is the One to Look For," *Wall Street Journal* (January 22, 1974), pp. 1, 35.

[11] Noel B. Zabriskie and John Browning, "Measuring Industrial Salespeople's Short-Term Productivity," *Industrial Marketing Management* 8 (April 1979), pp. 168–169.

The *push strategy* is more common in industrial marketing. Sales personnel may primarily work to stimulate demand while also providing a range of other customer services. Some industrial firms divide the sales force on the basis of a specific selling mission. Xerox has "new business" selling teams to obtain new accounts, while other selling teams service existing accounts.

Emerging Industrial Selling Styles   Industrial selling is becoming increasingly professional. Industrial selling styles that reflect this increased professionalism are: [12]

- *Consultative selling* occurs when the salesperson assumes the role of a consultant helping to improve the profitability of the client. The consultative salesperson, by becoming an expert on the client's business operations, providing analytical expertise and solving problems, attempts to offer a level of value beyond competitors.

- *Negotiation* describes a selling style designed to maximize the benefits of a transaction for both the buyer and seller. The goal is to form a salesperson-customer partnership with common objectives, mutually beneficial strategies, and a common defense against others outside the partnership.

- *Systems selling* has evolved to meet the rising sophistication and increased materials management concerns of organizational buyers. The salesperson for a business forms supplier might begin by defining a prospect's record and information needs, then prescribe a package of machines and forms, offer a recommended layout of facilities, establish a training program for employees, and design operating procedures and maintenance arrangements. [13]

- *Team selling* occurs when the industrial seller assembles a team of personnel with functional expertise that matches the specialized knowledge of key buying influences within the customer firm. The mode of operation adopted by the selling team varies by selling situation. On occasion, the entire sales team will take part in the presentation to the buying center, while in other cases, they are contacted at various points in the selling process when the salesperson requires technical expertise.

Telemarketing   The rising sophistication of telecommunications equipment and services has transformed telephone selling into telemarketing. Over 60 percent of industrial firms now use the telephone for selling or lead generation, or both. [14] The distinction between telephone selling

[12] Thomas R. Wotruba, "The Changing Character of Industrial Selling," *European Journal of Marketing* 14, (1980), pp. 293–302.

[13] *Ibid.*; see also, W. J. Hannaford, "Systems Selling: Problems and Benefits for Buyers and Sellers," *Industrial Marketing Management* 5 (1976), pp. 139–145.

[14] Murray Roman and Bob Donath, "Exclusive First-Ever Survey: What's Really Happening in Business/Industrial Telemarketing?" *Business Marketing* (April 1983), pp. 83–90.

and telemarketing centers on the use of trained personnel and meticulous quality control procedures. Only 30 percent of the firms sampled met these requirements.

As the average cost of an industrial sales call rapidly approaches $200, telephone sales calls, at $10–20 each, provide an economical substitute for personal visits to small accounts. Telemarketing can also be used to supplement personal sales calls.

Often the cost of the required call frequency is greater than the sales volume justifies and, in these cases, telephone calls can supplement personal visits. The visits might be made two to four times per year and the telephone calls eight to ten times per year for a total frequency of one per month—but at a cost substantially lower than twelve visits.[15]

While many industrial firms have used inside salespeople for years to handle routine transactions, creative applications of telemarketing are an emerging trend.

Organizing the Personal Selling Effort

How should the sales force be organized? The appropriate form depends upon many factors, including the nature and length of the product line, the role of intermediaries in the marketing program, the diversity of market segments served, the nature of buying behavior in each market segment, and the structure of competitive selling. The size and financial strength of the manufacturer often dictate, to an important degree, the feasibility of particular organizational forms. The industrial marketer can organize the sales force by geography, product, or market. Large industrial concerns that market diverse product lines may employ all three at different points throughout the organizational structure.

Geographical Organization The most common form of industrial sales organization is geographical. Here, each salesperson sells all of the firm's products in a defined geographical area. By reducing travel distance and time between customers, this method usually minimizes costs. Likewise, sales personnel know clearly the customers and prospects that fall within their area of responsibility.

The major disadvantage of the geographical sales organization is that each salesperson must be able to perform all of the selling tasks, for all of the firm's products, for all customers in a particular territory. If the products have diverse applications, this can be very difficult. A second disadvantage is that the salesperson has substantial flexibility in choosing which products and customers to emphasize. Sales personnel may emphasize those products and end-use applications with which they are

[15] Benson P. Shapiro and John Wyman, "New Ways to Reach Your Customers," *Harvard Business Review* 59 (July–August 1981), p. 106.

most familiar. Of course, this problem can be remedied through training and capable first-line supervision. Since the salesperson is crucial in operationalizing the firm's segmentation strategy, careful coordination and control are required to align personal selling effort with marketing objectives.

Product Organization   A product-oriented sales organization is one in which salespersons specialize in relatively narrow components of the total product line. This is especially appropriate when the product line is large, diverse, or technically complex and when a salesperson needs a high degree of application knowledge in order to meet customer needs. Furthermore, different products often elicit different patterns of buying behavior. The salesperson concentrating on a particular product becomes more adept at identifying and communicating with members of buying centers.

A prime benefit of this approach is that it allows the sales force to develop a level of product knowledge that enhances the value of the firm's total offering to customers. The product-oriented sales organization may also facilitate the identification of new market segments.

One drawback is the cost of developing and deploying a specialized sales force. A product must have the potential for generating a level of sales and profit that justifies individual selling attention. Thus, a "critical mass" of demand is required to offset the costs.

Market-Centered Organization   The industrial marketer may prefer to organize personal selling effort by customer type. The Xerox information system group, which markets copiers and duplicators, has shifted from geographical selling to vertical selling by industry type.[16] By learning the specific requirements of a particular industry or customer type, the salesperson is better prepared to identify and respond to buying influentials. Also, key market segments become more accessible, thus providing the opportunity for differentiated personal selling strategies. The market segments must, of course, be sufficiently large to warrant specialized treatment.

Organizing to Serve National Accounts

To serve very large and important customers, an increasing number of industrial firms are establishing a national accounts program. Here the activities of several functional areas in the selling firm, such as design engineering, manufacturing and logistics, can be carefully integrated to meet special customer needs.

---

[16] Mack Hanan, "Reorganize Your Company Around Its Markets," *Harvard Business Review* 52 (November–December 1974), pp. 63–75.

Figure 16.5　Traditional Sales, Major Accounts, and National Accounts

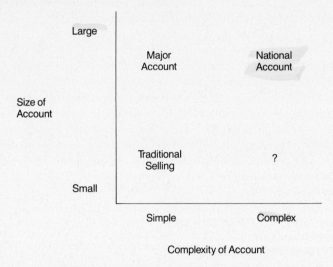

Source: Benson P. Shapiro and Rowland T. Moriarty, *National Account Management: Emerging Insights* (Cambridge, Mass.: Marketing Science Institute, 1982), p. 6. Used with permission.

National account management programs have been established by such corporations as Olin Corporation, Dow Chemical Company, Union-Carbide, Digital Equipment, and Westinghouse. Why? The concentration of the industrial market, the trend toward centralized procurement, the rising importance of materials management and the ensuing need for close buyer–seller coordination of inventory and logistical support, the increasing complexity of industrial products—these are among the forces that encourage the development of industrial national account management programs.[17]

National Account Management[18]　As illustrated in Figure 16.5, a distinction can be made between *major accounts* and *national accounts*. A major account represents a significant amount of potential business. Major accounts are often served through multi-level selling with participation by salespersons, sales and marketing managers, and general managers from the selling organization. National accounts are both large and complex, requiring an even more elaborate selling process. The complexity

[17] Benson P. Shapiro and Rowland T. Moriarty, *National Account Management: Emerging Insights*, Report No. 82-100 (Cambridge, Mass.: Marketing Science Institute, 1982).

[18] This section is largely based on Shapiro and Moriarty, *ibid.*

that requires a national accounts response can involve the following three customer dimensions:

- Geographical dispersion of customer buying points;
- Functional dispersion of customer buying influences—the involvement of two or more functional units in the purchasing process (e.g., procurement, engineering, manufacturing, etc.);
- Operating unit dispersion of customer purchasing activities (e.g., several different divisions within a company that operate with some degree of autonomy).

National account management provides a mechanism for responding to these three dimensions of customer complexity. For example, rather than reaching the geographically dispersed plants of the Mead Corporation through geographically dispersed sales offices, a national account management program might be devised to deal with Mead centrally. Such special attention would not be warranted for complex accounts that represent only limited potential business (thus the question mark in Figure 16.5).

Characteristics of National Account Programs   National account management programs depend on the company and industry environment, but do have some features in common: [19]

1.   National accounts are large, relative to other accounts served by the company, sometimes generating more than $50 million in sales revenue each.

2.   The national account manager's responsibility often spans multiple divisions in the selling company.

3.   The national account manager's team frequently includes support and operations personnel.

4.   The selling activities of the national account manager span several functional areas in the buying company and may involve highly conceptual financially-oriented systems sales.

How national account programs are structured and organized can vary by firm. For example, in some industrial firms the national account manager has line authority over a large, dispersed sales and support team, while in others these managers simply coordinate sales and support personnel. There can be a wide range in the number and size of accounts for which the manager is responsible. Although the organizational structure can vary across companies, the common objective of na-

---

[19] Shapiro and Wyman, "New Ways to Reach Your Customers," pp. 103–110.

Typical Job Titles

Top-level marketing management

Marketing vice president. Typically the top marketing executive in the company or division.

Sales vice president. Sometimes another title for marketing vice president but sometimes the top sales executive who will report to either the president or the marketing vice president.

Top-level line sales management

National sales manager. The top sales executive responsible for all sales-force-related activities.

General sales manager. Another title for national sales manager.

Middle-level line sales management

National account sales manager. Usually responsible for a separate, high-quality sales force which calls on national accounts. Often the only person in the national account sales force and responsible for actual selling, but the accounts are so large that the position needs a relatively high-level manager.

Regional, divisional, or zone sales manager. These are titles for high-level field sales managers to whom other field sales managers report. Occasionally, the titles are used for first-level sales management jobs in which salespeople are managed.

Market sales manager. A sales manager responsible for salespeople calling on a specific group of accounts. Often this position has marketing responsibility in addition to sales management and perhaps sales responsibility. A company which specializes its sales force by market will have one market sales manager to head each separate sales force.

Product sales manager. The same as market sales manager except that the job is organized around a product line instead of a customer category. Both positions are more likely to occur in industrial companies than in consumer-goods companies. The product sales managers are usually more involved with product-oriented decisions than are market managers.

Lower-level line sales management

District or field sales manager. The first line sales manager to whom the salespeople report.

Upper-level sales positions

Account executive, key account salesperson, national account salesperson, major account salesperson. These people are responsible for selling to major accounts. In the consumer-goods field, the title sometimes involves chain stores, meaning usually the three large national general merchandise chains (Sears, Penney, Montgomery Ward), food chains, or mass merchandisers such as discount department stores.

Typical sales positions

Salesperson, field salesperson, territory manager, account representative, sales representative. All are typical titles for the salesperson responsible for selling and servicing a variety of accounts.

Staff sales management

These positions are usually functionally oriented and include titles such as manager of sales training, sales analyst, etc. The typical staff responsibilities include training, recruiting, and sales analysis. More general staff positions include the title assistant to the national sales manager. Assistant national sales managers may be either line or staff managers. Staff positions may occur at any level in the organization. Some companies with divisional sales forces, for example, have a job of corporate vice president of sales who has no line sales management responsibility. Other companies have regional or area sales vice presidents responsible for aiding salespeople from various divisions with major account sales. This is found, for example, in some weapons marketers where various product-oriented divisions call upon the same buying organization.

Note: The titles and descriptions above are generalities. Different industries and different companies in many cases use different titles for the same job and organize job content differently.

Source: Benson P. Shapiro, *Sales Program Management: Formulation and Implementation* (New York: McGraw-Hill Book Company, 1977), p. 7. Reprinted by permission.

tional account management programs is "to provide incremental profits from large or potentially large complex accounts by being the preferred or sole supplier. To accomplish this goal, a supplier seeks to establish, over an extended period of time, an 'institutional' relationship, which cuts across multiple levels, functions, and operating units in both the buying and selling organization."[20]

Sales Administration

Successful administration of the sales force involves recruiting and selecting salespersons, training, motivation and supervision, and evaluation and control of the sales force. The industrial firm should foster an organizational climate that encourages the development of a successful sales force.

Recruiting and Selecting Salespersons   Today more emphasis is being placed on the recruiting process and on reducing salesperson turnover because:

Today's salesperson must have many talents: knowledge of business, current affairs, and organizational politics; social graces to mingle with company presidents and workers on the shop floor; patience, persistence, etc.[21]

The recruiting process presents numerous tradeoffs for the industrial marketer. Should experienced salespersons be sought or should inexperienced individuals be hired and trained by the company? The answer is situation-specific; it varies with the size of the firm, the nature of the selling task, the firm's training capability, and its market experience. Smaller firms often reduce training costs by hiring experienced and more expensive salespersons. By contrast, large organizations with a more complete training function, can hire less experienced personnel and support them with a carefully developed training program.

A second tradeoff is the quantity versus quality question.[22] Often, sales managers screen as many recruits as possible in selecting new salespersons. However, this can overload the selection process, thus hampering the firm's ability to identify quality candidates. Recruiting, like selling, is an exchange process between two parties. A poorly-organized recruiting effort that lacks closure leaves candidates with a negative impression. A well-organized recruiting effort insures that candidates fitting the position requirements are given the proper level of attention in the screening process. Thus, procedures must be established to insure

---

[20] Shapiro and Moriarty, *National Account Management*, p. 8.

[21] Ben M. Enis and Lawrence B. Chonko, "A Review of Personal Selling: Implications for Managers and Researchers," in Gerald Zaltman and Thomas V. Bonoma, eds., *Review of Marketing 1978* (Chicago: American Marketing Association, 1978), p. 291.

[22] Benson P. Shapiro, *Sales Management: Formulation and Implementation* (New York: McGraw-Hill Book Company, Inc., 1977), p. 457.

that inappropriate candidates are screened out early, so that the pool of candidates is reduced to a manageable size.[23]

Responsibility for recruiting and selecting salespersons may lie with the first-level supervisor, who often receives assistance from an immediate superior, or the personnel department or other executives at the headquarters level. The latter group tends to be more involved when the sales force is viewed as the training ground for marketing or general managers.

Training   To adequately prepare new industrial salespersons the training program must be carefully designed. Periodic training is required to sharpen the skills of experienced salespersons, especially when the firm's environment is changing rapidly. Changes in industrial marketing strategy (e.g., new products, new market segments) require corresponding changes in personal selling styles. The salesperson needs a wealth of knowledge about the company, the product line, customer segments, competition, organizational buying behavior, and effective communication skills. All these must be part of industrial sales training programs.

Effective training builds confidence and motivation in the salesperson, thereby increasing the probabilities of successful performance. In turn, training helps the industrial marketer by keeping personal selling in line with marketing program objectives. A successful training effort can reduce the costs of recruiting; many industrial firms have found that salesperson turnover declines as training improves. Clearly, a salesperson who is inadequately prepared to meet the demands of selling can quickly become discouraged, frustrated, and envious of friends who chose other career options. Much of this anxiety—which is especially prevalent in the early stages of many careers—can be removed by effective training and capable first-line supervision.

Supervision and Motivation   The sales force must be directed in a way that is consistent with the company's policies and marketing objectives. Critical supervisory tasks are continued training, counseling, assistance (e.g., time planning), and activities which help sales personnel to plan and execute their work. Supervision also sets sales performance standards, fulfills company policy, and integrates the sales force with higher organizational levels.[24]

Motivation can be viewed as the amount of effort the salesperson "desires to expend on each of the activities or tasks associated with his job, such as calling on potential new accounts, planning sales presenta-

[23] Wesley J. Johnston and Martha C. Cooper, "Industrial Sales Force Selection: Current Knowledge and Needed Research," *Journal of Personal Selling and Sales Management* 1 (Spring/Summer 1981), pp. 49–55.

[24] B. Charles Ames, "Building Marketing Strength into Industrial Selling," in Donald E. Vinson and Donald Sciglimpaglia, eds., *The Environment of Industrial Marketing* (Columbus, Ohio: Grid, Inc., 1975), pp. 310–329.

Figure 16.6   Determinants of Salesperson's Performance

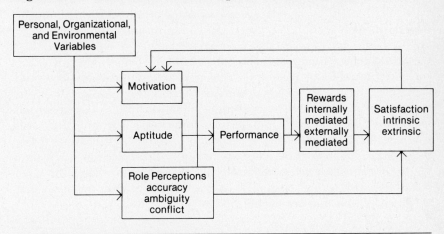

Source: Orville C. Walker, Jr., Gilbert A. Churchill, Jr., and Neil M. Ford, "Motivation and Performance in Industrial Selling: Present Knowledge and Needed Research," *Journal of Marketing Research*, 14 (May 1977), p. 158. Reprinted by permission of the American Marketing Association.

tions, and filling out reports."[25] The model presented in Figure 16.6 hypothesizes that a salesperson's job performance is a function of three factors: (1) the level of motivation; (2) aptitude or ability; and (3) perceptions about how his or her role should be performed. Each is influenced by personal variables (e.g., personality), organizational variables (e.g., training programs), and environmental variables (e.g., economic conditions). Sales managers can influence some of the personal and organizational variables through selection, training, and supervision.

Motivation to perform is thought to be related strongly to the individual's perceptions of the types and amounts of rewards that will accrue from various degrees of job performance, and to the value the salesperson places on these rewards. For a given level of performance, two types of rewards might be offered:

1. *Internally mediated rewards*, those that the salesperson attains on a personal basis, such as feelings of accomplishment or self-worth;

2. *Externally mediated rewards*, those controlled and offered by managers or customers, such as financial incentives, pay, or recognition.

The rewards strongly influence salesperson satisfaction with the job and the work environment. Job satisfaction is also influenced by the individual's role perceptions. It is theorized to *decline* if the salesperson's perception of the role (1) is *inaccurate* in terms of the expectations of superi-

[25] Orville C. Walker, Jr., Gilbert A. Churchill, Jr., and Neil M. Ford, "Motivation and Performance in Industrial Selling: Present Knowledge and Needed Research," *Journal of Marketing Research* 14 (May 1977), pp. 156–168.

ors; (2) is characterized by *conflicting* demands among role partners (company and customer) that the salesperson cannot possibly resolve; or (3) is surrounded by *uncertainty* due to a lack of information about the expectations and evaluation criteria of superiors and customers.[26]

Organizational Climate and Job Satisfaction[27]   Gilbert Churchill, Jr., Neil Ford, and Orville Walker, Jr., who contributed the model presented in Figure 16.6, also provide empirical support for some propositions that flow from the model. In examining job satisfaction in a cross-section of industrial salespersons, the authors found that role ambiguity and role conflict have a detrimental influence on job satisfaction. Salespersons are likely to experience anxiety and dissatisfaction when they are uncertain about the expectations of role partners or when they feel that role partners (e.g., customers, superiors) are making demands that are incompatible and impossible to satisfy.

Job Satisfaction: Managerial Implications   Salespersons tend to have a higher level of job satisfaction when: (1) they perceive that their first-line supervisor closely directs and monitors their activities; (2) management provides them with the assistance and support needed to meet unusual and nonroutine problems; and (3) they perceive themselves to have an active part in determining company policies and standards that affect them. Job satisfaction also appears to be related more to the substance of the contact between sales managers and salespersons than to the frequency of contact. Also, salespersons appear to be able to accept direction from a number of different departments in the organization without a significant negative impact on job satisfaction; unity of command does not appear to be a prerequisite for high morale.

Performance and individual differences in achievement motivation, self-esteem, and verbal intelligence may also affect job satisfaction. Richard Bagozzi notes:

Salespeople tend to be more satisfied as they perform better, but the relationship is particularly sensitive to the level of motivation and positive self-image of the person. Although management may have no direct control over the performance achieved by salespeople, they can influence the level of motivation and self-esteem through effective incentive and sensitive supervisor–employee programs and thereby indirectly affect both performance and job satisfaction.[28]

[26] *Ibid.*

[27] This section is based on Gilbert A. Churchill, Jr., Neil M. Ford, and Orville C. Walker, Jr., "Organizational Climate and Job Satisfaction in the Salesforce," *Journal of Marketing Research* 13 (November 1976), pp. 323–332. For a related discussion, see R. Kenneth Teas, "Supervisory Behavior, Role Stress, and the Job Satisfaction of Industrial Salespeople," *Journal of Marketing Research* 20 (February 1983), pp. 84–91; see also, Charles M. Futrell, "Measurement of Salespeople's Job Satisfaction: Convergent and Discriminant Validity of Corresponding INDSALES and Job Descriptive Index Scales," *Journal of Marketing Research* 16 (November 1979), pp. 594–597.

[28] Richard P. Bagozzi, "Performance and Satisfaction in an Industrial Sales Force: A Causal Modeling Approach," in Bagozzi, ed., *Sales Management: New Developments*, pp. 70–91. See also, Bagozzi, "Performance and Satisfaction in an Industrial Sales Force: An Examination of Their Antecedents and Simultaneity," *Journal of Marketing* 44 (Spring 1980), pp. 65–77.

While some of the areas that influence job satisfaction and performance are beyond the control of sales managers, this line of research points up the importance of responsive training, supportive supervision, and clearly-defined company policies that are congruent with the needs of the sales force.

Evaluation and Control   An ongoing sales management responsibility is the monitoring and control of the industrial sales force at all levels—national, regional, and district—to determine if objectives are being attained, to identify problems, recommend corrective action, and keep the sales organization in tune with changing competitive and market conditions.

The standards by which salespersons are evaluated are the means for comparing the performance of different salespersons or sales units (e.g., districts), as well as gauging the overall productivity of the sales organization. Managerial experience and judgment are important in developing appropriate standards.

Performance standards are usually related to sales, profit contribution, or activity (e.g., number of new accounts developed, number of prospects contacted). Often, quotas are used for evaluation and motivation. As discussed in Part Three, quotas are often derived from the sales forecast and estimates of market potential. These quotas can be expressed in terms of dollar sales volume, product-line sales, new accounts developed, new account sales volume, sales volume by customer type, and number of prospecting calls.[29] The standards must relate to overall marketing objectives, and they must take into account differences in sales territories, where the number and aggressiveness of competitors, the level of market potential, and the workload can vary markedly.

There is a positive relationship between goal clarity and task performance.[30] Thus, the nature and importance of goals should be clearly defined for salespersons, and feedback on the extent to which they are achieving these goals should be continuous. First-line supervisors are vital in providing salespersons with performance standings against preestablished goals. Supervisors also can help sales personnel take corrective action early.

Toward a Profit Focus   Both large and small industrial firms appear to be oriented toward sales volume in the evaluation and control of the sales force. "In the quotas they set, the job dimensions they evaluate during performance appraisal, and the bases they use to establish incentive pay (e.g., commission, bonus), the focus is extensively on sales volume generated by sales personnel, rather than on profit contribution or activ-

---

[29] For a more comprehensive discussion of sales quotas, see Shapiro, *Sales Management*, p. 308.

[30] Charles M. Futrell, John E. Swan, and John T. Todd, "Job Performance Related to Management Control Systems for Pharmaceutical Salesmen," *Journal of Marketing Research* 13 (February 1976), pp. 25–33.

ities/tasks performed."[31] Given the dominant role of personal selling costs in the industrial marketing budget, there is clearly a need for a stronger profit focus in the sales management function.

The Computer's Role[32]   The microcomputer can help sales managers to evaluate the performance of each sales representative, improve time management skills, and teach salespersons to operate their territories as profit centers.

    Table 16.1 provides a comparative income statement for a sales district using a VisiCalc program—one of the most popular spreadsheet programs for microcomputers. Each salesperson can be evaluated on several financial criteria, starting with his or her product contribution. Product contribution varies by account because some accounts purchase only low-margin products while others may purchase a mix of products that generate a higher profit margin. The costs incurred in serving accounts are captured in the comparative income statement. Some accounts require a disproportionate share of costs for freight, inventory, technical service, promotion, or interest on accounts receivable. The performance of each salesperson, as well as the district, can then be evaluated on financial terms including net contribution and return on assets managed. Observe the excellent performance of sales representative J. Taylor.

    This illustration deals with the district level, but comparable data could be generated to sharpen industrial selling strategies by account, by territory, or by region. Guidelines for structuring the control system for each level in the sales organization can be coordinated by general sales managers. Overall, the computer can help improve sales force productivity, control expenses, and refine goals and strategies. Computer technology can also be pivotal in solving complex deployment problems for the sales manager. To maximize profitability, how should the sales force be deployed across customers and territories?

Models for Industrial Sales Force Management

To this point, our discussion has been concerned with (1) recruiting and selection, (2) training, (3) motivation and supervision, and (4) evaluation and control. Poor decisions in one area can create a backlash in other areas. One critical sales management task remains—deploying the sales force. Here, the objective is to form the most profitable sales territories,

[31] Alan J. Dubinsky and Thomas E. Barry, "A Survey of Sales Management Practices," *Industrial Marketing Management* 11 (April 1982), pp. 133–141. See also, Donald W. Jackson, Jr., Lonnie L. Ostrom, and Kenneth R. Evans, "Measures Used to Evaluate Industrial Marketing Activities," *Industrial Marketing Management* 11 (October 1982), pp. 269–274.

[32] This section is largely based on G. David Hughes, "Computerized Sales Management," *Harvard Business Review* 61 (March–April 1983), pp. 102–112. For a related discussion, see James M. Comer, "Sales Management and the Computer: Prospects for the 1980's," *Journal of Personal Selling and Sales Management* 1 (Fall/Winter 1981–82), pp. 6–9.

Table 16.1 District Comparative Income Statement

	E. Martin		J. Taylor		W. Jones		District Totals	
1 Period(s)	$000	%	$000	%	$000	%	$000	%
Sales	2200	100	2500	100	2000	100	6700	100
Acct-Product Contb. Exh. 2	479	21.77	613	24.52	457	22.85	1549	23.12
Acct. Costs Exh. 3								
Freight	63	2.86	65	2.60	60	3.00	188	2.81
Inventory	44	2.00	30	1.20	39	1.95	113	1.69
Accts. Receivable	64	2.91	75	3.00	59	2.95	198	2.96
Tech. Services	18	0.82	18	0.72	17	0.85	53	0.79
Adv. & Prom.	21	0.95	35	1.40	18	0.90	74	1.10
Total Customer Costs	210	9.55	223	8.92	193	9.65	626	9.34
Personal Selling Costs								
Compensation	31.50	1.43	33.00	1.32	29.90	1.50	94.40	1.41
Transportation	6.00	0.27	5.00	0.20	7.00	0.35	18.00	0.27
Lodging & Meals	3.50	0.16	3.50	0.14	4.00	0.20	11.00	0.16
Telephone	1.35	0.06	1.70	0.07	1.20	0.06	4.25	0.06
Entertainment	3.00	0.14	1.00	0.04	2.50	0.13	6.50	0.10
Samples & Literature	2.00	0.09	2.00	0.08	1.50	0.08	5.50	0.08
Misc.	0.50	0.02	0.50	0.02	0.30	0.02	1.30	0.02
Total Pers. Selling Cst	47.85	2.18	46.70	1.87	46.40	2.32	140.95	2.10
Net Territory Contrib ($000)	221.15	10.05	343.30	13.73	217.60	10.88	782.05	11.67
Return on Assets Managed:								
Territory Assets ($000)	800		890		775		2465	
Asset Turnover (Sales/Assts)	2.75		2.81		2.58		2.72	
Add: Interest Inv.		2.00		1.20		1.95		1.69
Interest A/R		2.91		3.00		2.95		2.96
Total Contribution Percent		14.96		17.93		15.78		16.31
Return on Assets Managed		41.14		50.37		40.72		44.34
(% Contrib. × Turnover)								

Source: Reprinted by permission of the *Harvard Business Review.* An exhibit from "Computerized Sales Management" by G. David Hughes, 61 (March/April 1983), p. 109. Copyright © 1983 by the President and Fellows of Harvard College; all rights reserved.

Table 16.2   Deployment Decisions Facing Sales Organizations

Type of Decision	Specific Deployment Decisions
Set total level of selling effort	Determine sales force size
Organize selling effort	Design sales districts
	Design sales territories
Allocate selling effort	Allocate effort to trading areas
	Allocate sales calls to accounts
	Allocate sales calls to prospects
	Allocate sales call time to products
	Determine length of sales call

Source: Reprinted by permission of the publisher from "Steps in Selling Effort Deployment" by Raymond LaForge and David W. Cravens, *Industrial Marketing Management*, 11 (July 1982), p. 184. Copyright © 1982 by Elsevier Science Publishing Co., Inc.

deploy salespersons to serve potential customers in those territories, and allocate the time of the sales force effectively among those customers.

Deployment Analysis: A Strategic Approach

The size of the industrial sales force establishes the total level of selling effort that can be employed by the industrial firm. The selling effort is then organized by designating sales districts and sales territories. Allocation decisions determine how the selling effort is to be assigned to customers, prospects, and products. All these are illustrated in Table 16.2.

Proper deployment requires a multistaged approach to find the most effective and efficient means of assigning sales resources (e.g., sales calls, number of salespersons, percentage of salesperson's time) across all of the *planning and control units* (e.g., prospects, customers, territories, districts, products) served by the firm.[33] Thus, effective deployment means understanding the factors that influence sales in a particular planning and control unit such as a territory.

Territory Sales Response   What influences the level of sales that a salesperson might achieve in a particular territory? Eight classes of variables are outlined in Table 16.3. This list shows the complexity of estimating sales response functions. Such estimates are needed, however, to make meaningful sales allocations.

Three territory traits are worthy of particular attention in sales response studies: potential, concentration, and dispersion.[34] *Potential* (as discussed in Chapter 7) is a measure of the total business opportunity for

[33] Raymond LaForge and David W. Cravens, "Steps in Selling Effort Deployment," *Industrial Marketing Management* 11 (July 1982), pp. 183–194.

[34] Adrian B. Ryans and Charles B. Weinberg, "Territory Sales Response," *Journal of Marketing Research* 16 (November 1979), pp. 453–465.

Table 16.3   Selected Determinants of Territory Sales Response

1. Environmental Factors (e.g., health of economy)
2. Competition (e.g., number of competitive salespersons)
3. Company Marketing Strategy and Tactics
4. Sales Force Organization, Policies, and Procedures
5. Field Sales Manager Characteristics
6. Salesperson Characteristics
7. Territory Characteristics (e.g., potential)
8. Individual Customer Factors

Source: Adrian B. Ryans and Charles B. Weinberg, "Territory Sales Response," *Journal of Marketing Research* 16 (November 1979), pp. 453–465.

all sellers in a particular market. *Concentration* is the degree to which potential is confined to a few larger accounts in that territory. If potential is concentrated, the salesperson can cover with a few calls a large proportion of the potential. Finally, if the territory is geographically *dispersed*, sales will probably be lower due to time wasted in travel. Past research often centered on *territory workload*—the number of accounts. Ryans and Weinberg report that workload is of questionable value in estimating sales response: "From a managerial standpoint, the recurrent finding of an association between potential and sales results suggests that sales managers should stress territory potential when making sales force decisions." [35]

Sales Resource Opportunity Grid   Deployment analysis matches sales resources to market opportunities. Planning and control units (PCUs) like sales territories or districts are part of an overall portfolio with various units offering different levels of opportunity and requiring different levels of sales resources. A sales resource opportunity grid can be used to classify the industrial firm's portfolio of PCUs.[36] In Figure 16.7 each PCU is classified on the basis of PCU opportunity and sales organization strength.

PCU opportunity is measured by the total potential that the PCU represents for all sellers, while sales organization strength includes the competitive advantages or distinctive competencies that the firm enjoys within the PCU. By positioning all PCUs on the grid, the sales manager can assign sales resources to those PCUs with the greatest level of opportunity that also capitalize on the particular strengths of the sales organization.

The sales resource opportunity grid is important for screening at various points of deployment decision making: size of the sales force,

[35] *Ibid.*, p. 464.
[36] LaForge and Cravens, "Steps in Selling Effort Deployment," pp. 183–194.

Figure 16.7　Sales Resource Opportunity Grid

	High Sales Organization Strength	Low Sales Organization Strength
PCU Opportunity — High	*Opportunity Analysis* PCU offers good opportunity since it has high potential and sales organization has strong position *Sales Resource Assignment* High level of sales resources to take advantage of opportunity	*Opportunity Analysis* PCU may offer good opportunity if sales organization can strengthen its position *Sales Resource Assignment* Either direct a high level of sales resources to improve position and take advantage of opportunity or shift resources to other PCUs
PCU Opportunity — Low	*Opportunity Analysis* PCU offers stable opportunity since sales organization has strong position *Sales Resource Assignment* Moderate level of sales resources to keep current position strength	*Opportunity Analysis* PCU offers little opportunity *Sales Resource Assignment* Minimal level of sales resources; selectively eliminate resource coverage; possible elimination of PCU

Sales Organization Strength

Source: Reprinted by permission of the publisher from "Steps in Selling Effort Deployment," by Raymond LaForge and David W. Cravens, *Industrial Marketing Management*, 11 (July 1982), p. 187. Copyright © 1982 by Elsevier Science Publishing Co., Inc.

territory design, allocation of sales calls to customer segments. This method can isolate deployment problems or opportunities worthy of sales management attention and further data analysis.

A Model for Allocating Sales Effort

Several models that support the decision maker in allocating sales effort[37] can be used in conjunction with the sales resource opportunity grid. As a prototype, let us consider the PAIRS model (Purchase Attitudes and Interactive Response to Salesmen) developed by A. Parasura-

[37] For example, see Leonard M. Lodish, "CALLPLAN: An Interactive Salesman's Call Planning System," *Management Science* 18 (December 1971), pp. 25–40; see also, Lodish, "Sales Territory Alignment to Maximize Profit," *Journal of Marketing Research* 12 (February 1975), pp. 30–36; and James M. Comer, "The Computer, Personal Selling and Sales Management," *Journal of Marketing* 39 (July 1975), pp. 27–33.

man and Ralph Day. The PAIRS model draws upon earlier models—most notably CALLPLAN—and adds some new features: [38]

1. Customers in a territory who are similar in their response to selling effort are classified into mutually exclusive and collectively exhaustive groups of approximately equal potential.

2. Salesperson characteristics that management deems useful to the selling job are defined. Selling ability of a salesperson is dependent on factors like education, knowledge of the company's products, and personal traits.

3. The impact of selling effort on a customer in any period is dependent upon the selling ability of sales personnel as well as on the number of sales calls made.

4. The planning horizon is divided into periods based on the average length of the purchase cycle or a similar criterion.

5. Variations in the time per sales call for different customers are included.

6. The expected total volume of sales from each type of customer is specified in terms of potential dollar revenue.

7. The model produces an estimate of the sales revenue for each customer or customer group for each period in the planning horizon.

The model draws upon the experience and judgment of both sales managers and salespersons. Sales managers participate in the development of a salesperson's *effectiveness index* by defining the selling skills the company considers important. Each salesperson is rated on each skill on a 0 (extremely poor) to 10 (excellent) scale. These skills are then weighted for each customer category the firm serves. This approach recognizes that different skills or qualities may be required to reach different market segments or customer types.

Sales personnel participate in the implementation of the model. They provide three estimates of the potential sales revenues for each customer in each district—a most likely, a pessimistic, and an optimistic estimate. They also estimate the sales response at each of four different call levels to develop a sales response function for each customer.

An additional feature of the PAIRS model is the inclusion of a carry-over effect of past sales effort to a current period. Sales personnel are asked: What share of the customer's business could we obtain next year if *no* sales calls were to be made on the customer after the current period?

[38] A. Parasuraman and Ralph L. Day, "A Management-Oriented Model for Allocating Sales Effort," *Journal of Marketing Research* 14 (February 1977), pp. 22–33. For a comprehensive review and analysis of sales management models, see Gary L. Lilien and Philip Kotler, *Marketing Decision Making: A Model-Building Approach* (New York: Harper & Row, Publishers, 1983), pp. 558–602.

This model illustrates the usefulness of examining salesperson–customer interaction in a particular territory. The model does not replace the seasoned judgment of sales managers or the field experience of sales personnel, but instead relies heavily upon that judgment. Such an approach forces all parties to ask the right questions and think creatively about the factors that influence territory sales response.

Allocating Sales Efforts: A Field Test

A method of allocating sales effort was tested under controlled experimental conditions at United Airlines. CALLPLAN, an interactive salesperson's call planning system, was the focus of the experiment. As with the PAIRS model, the objective of CALLPLAN is to determine call frequency norms for each current customer and each prospect (account not currently buying from the salesperson). The sales force at United Airlines is divided into two groups: one promotes passenger travel, the other air freight operations.

Twenty salespersons participated in the experiment: 16 passenger representatives and 4 cargo representatives. Local management provided 10 pairs of matched salespersons. The 10 CALLPLAN participants were chosen randomly—one from each pair. The remaining 10 salespersons were the control group. The CALLPLAN users realized an 8.1 percent higher increase in sales over the previous year than the control group.

An evaluation committee at United Airlines concluded that CALLPLAN:

- Prepares a formal forecast and builds an account-by-account analysis, giving it authority;
- Formalizes the planning process and gives it a long-range character not now present;
- Redirects calls to more susceptible accounts to increase revenue;
- Highlights selling time versus time spent on other tasks;
- Emphasizes a planned call with predetermined objectives over a drop-in type

Source: W. K. Fudge and L. M. Lodish, "Evaluation of the Effectiveness of a Model Based Salesman's Planning System by Field Experimentation," *Interfaces*, Vol. 8, No. 1, Part 2 (November 1977), p. 105, cited in Gary L. Lilien and Philip Kotler, *Marketing Decision Making: A Model-Building Approach* (New York: Harper & Row Publishers, 1983), pp. 570–571.

**Figure 16.8   The Sales Force as Part of the
Corporation's Marketing System**

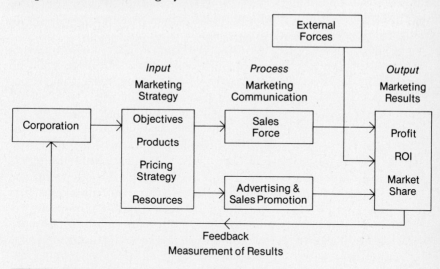

Source: Reprinted by permission of the *Harvard Business Review*. Exhibit from "Manage Your Sales Force as a System," by Porter Henry (March–April 1975). Copyright © 1975 by the President and Fellows of Harvard College; all rights reserved.

Sales Management: A Systems Perspective

To reinforce the strategic role of the sales force in the industrial marketing communications mix, the chapter closes with a systems view of the marketing function. Note (Figure 16.8) that the inputs of the marketing system include the firm's objectives; product, distribution, and pricing strategies; and the resources to be allocated to achieve company objectives in defined market segments. The industrial marketer communicates the existence of the firm's offerings to organizational market segments through: (1) the sales force and (2) advertising and sales promotion. These have been explored in detail. Both types of marketing communication require evaluation and control for maximum effectiveness and efficiency. Essential to a systems perspective is the measurement of output. The goal of marketing strategy is to achieve specific marketing results—for example, profit, return-on-investment, and market share.

Summary

Personal selling is a significant demand-stimulating force in the industrial market. Given the rapidly escalating cost of industrial sales calls and the massive resources invested in personal selling, the industrial marketer must carefully manage this function. Recognizing the needs of organizational customers and the rudiments of organizational buying behavior are fundamental to effective personal selling. Likewise, important insights emerge when the personal selling process is viewed as an exchange process. A satisfactory transaction is more likely when the parties to the buyer–seller relationship are compatible in communication style and content. The increased professionalism of industrial selling is reflected in the increased prominence of four selling styles; consultative selling, negotiation, systems selling, and team selling.

Managing the industrial sales force is a multifaceted task. First, the marketer must clearly define the role of personal selling in overall marketing strategy. Second, the sales organization must be appropriately structured—by geography, product, market, or some combination. Regardless of the method used to organize the sales force, an increasing number of industrial firms are also establishing a national account sales force to profitably serve large customers with complex purchasing requirements. Third, the ongoing process of sales force administration includes recruiting and selection, training, supervision and motivation, and evaluation and control. A particularly challenging sales management task is the deployment of sales effort across products, customer types, and territories. The sales resource opportunity grid is a useful organizing framework for sales deployment decisions. Likewise, the industrial marketer can benefit by examining management-oriented models that deal with sales allocation problems. By capitalizing on advancing computer technology and user-friendly software, the sales manager is better equipped to plan, organize, and control industrial selling strategies.

Discussion Questions

1. In planning a sales call on a particular industrial account, what information would you like concerning the buying center, purchasing requirements, and competition?

2. The members of the selling organization who participate, to some degree, in a particular industrial marketing decision-making process constitute the organizational selling or strategy center. Explain why the composition or functional area representation of the selling center varies from one selling situation to another.

3. Explain how the style and content of communication may strongly influence the quality of interaction between buyer and seller.

4. Some industrial firms organize their sales force around products; others are market-centered. What factors must be considered in selecting the most appropriate organizational arrangement for the sales force?

5. Compare and contrast a *national account* and a *major account*.

6. A successful sales training program can reduce the costs associated with recruiting. Explain.

7. An emerging body of research suggests that role ambiguity and role conflict have a detrimental impact on the job satisfaction of industrial salespersons. What steps can sales managers take to deal with these problems? What role might a management-by-objectives system play in these efforts?

8. To make effective and efficient sales force allocation decisions, the sales manager must analyze sales territories. Describe how the sales manager can profit by examining the (a) potential, (b) concentration, and (c) dispersion of territories.

9. Describe the role of sales managers in operationalizing the PAIRS (Purchase Attitudes and Interactive Response to Salespersons) model. Explain how such decision support models can improve the quality of sales force allocation decisions.

10. What benefits can be derived by examining the industrial marketing communications mix from a systems perspective?

P·A·R·T
V

Evaluating Industrial Marketing Strategy and Performance

C·H·A·P·T·E·R
17

Controlling Industrial Marketing Strategies

Two industrial marketing managers who face identical market conditions and possess equal resources to invest in marketing strategy could generate dramatically different performance results. Why? One manager carefully monitors and controls the performance of industrial marketing strategy; the other does not. The astute marketer evaluates the profitability of alternative segments and examines the effectiveness and efficiency of the components of the marketing mix, so that he or she can isolate problems and opportunities and alter the marketing strategy as market or competitive conditions dictate.

After reading this chapter, you will have an understanding of:

1. *the function and significance of marketing control in industrial marketing management;*
2. *the components of the control process;*
3. *specific methods for evaluating marketing strategy performance;*
4. *trends that will influence the nature of industrial marketing strategy.*

Managing a firm's marketing strategy is very similar to coaching a football team: The excitement and challenge rests in the formulation of strategy. Shall we focus on running or passing? What weaknesses of the opposition can we exploit? How shall we vary our standard plays? So too, the industrial marketer applies managerial talent creatively in developing and implementing unique marketing strategies that not only respond to customer needs but also capitalize on competitive weaknesses.

However, formulating effective strategy is only half of coaching, or management; the other half of the process is control. A truly great coach devotes significant energies to evaluating team performance in last week's game in order to set next week's strategy. Did our strategy work? Why? Where did it break down? Similarly, a successful marketing strategy depends on evaluations of marketing performance. The other half of strategy planning is *marketing control*, the system by which the firm checks actual against planned performance, evaluating the profitability of products, customer segments, and territories.

Information generated by the marketing control system is essential to revising current marketing strategies, formulating new strategies, and allocating funds. The requirements for an effective control system are strict—data must be gathered continuously on the appropriate performance measures. Thus, an effective marketing strategy is rooted in a carefully designed and well-applied control system.

This chapter presents the rudiments of a marketing control system, beginning with a framework incorporating the essential elements of the control process. Next, the types of performance measurement will be examined. Finally, industrial marketing challenges and opportunities in the decade ahead are reviewed.

Marketing Strategy: Allocating Resources

The purpose of any marketing strategy is to yield the best possible results to the company. In this sense, resources are allocated to marketing in general and to individual strategy elements in particular to achieve prescribed objectives. Profit contribution, market share percentage, number of new customers, and level of expenses and sales are typical performance criteria, but regardless of the criteria chosen, four interrelated evaluations are required to design a marketing strategy:

1.   How much should be spent on marketing in the planning period? This is the budget for achieving marketing objectives.

2.   How are marketing dollars to be allocated? For example, how much is to be spent on advertising? On personal selling?

3.   Within each element of the marketing strategy, how should dollars be allocated to best achieve marketing objectives? For example, which advertising media should be selected? How should sales personnel be deployed among customers and prospects?

4. Which market segments, products, and geographic areas will be most profitable? Each market segment may require a different amount of effort as a result of competitive intensity or market potential.

Guiding Strategy Formulation

The integration of market strategy formulation and the marketing control system is highlighted by these four decision areas. First, results in the most recent operating period will show how successful past marketing efforts were in obtaining desired objectives. Second, performance below or above what was expected will signal where funds should be reallocated. If the firm expected to reach 20 percent of the OEM market and actually realized only 12 percent market share, a change in strategy may be required. Performance information provided by the control system might demonstrate that sales personnel in the OEM market were reaching only 45 percent of potential buyers; additional funds could be allocated to expand either the sales force or the advertising budget.

Marketing managers must weigh the interactions among the strategy elements and allocate resources to create effective and efficient marketing strategies. In order to develop successful strategies, a system to monitor past performance is an absolute necessity.[1]

The Marketing Control Process

Marketing control is a process whereby management generates information on marketing performance. Two major forms of control are: (1) control over efficient allocation of marketing effort, and (2) comparison of planned against actual performance.[2] In the first case, the industrial marketer may use past profitability data as a standard against which to evaluate future marketing expenditures. The second form of control alerts management to any differences between planned and actual performance and may also reveal reasons for performance discrepancies. In either case management must have an information system that will provide timely and meaningful data.

Control=Information

The essence of control is information; in fact, a control system is nothing more than an organized body of information which allows management to evaluate how the firm has done and where future opportunities may lie. Industrial marketing strategy requires a vast array of information:

[1] Donald W. Jackson, Jr., Lonnie L. Ostrom, and Kenneth R. Evans, "Measures Used to Evaluate Industrial Marketing Activities," *Industrial Marketing Management* 11 (1982), pp. 269–274.

[2] V. H. Kirpalani and Stanley J. Shapiro, "Financial Dimensions of Marketing Management," *Journal of Marketing* 37 (July 1973), p. 47.

Figure 17.1   The Industrial Marketing Intelligence System

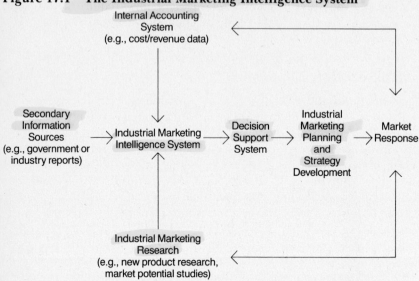

sales, expenses, market share, profits, competitive actions, market trends, and environmental data. The components of the industrial marketing intelligence system were explored in Chapter 5. The internal accounting system (Figure 17.1) provides sales, expense, and other accounting data fundamental to marketing control. The purpose of the industrial marketing research system (see Chapter 5) is to obtain information to solve specific problems or to evaluate particular market opportunities.

The major sectors of the industrial market and important secondary sources of market information were examined in Chapters 2 and 5, and models related to organizational buying, product, pricing, promotion, and distribution were presented in other chapters. The focus of this chapter is on the *use* of the information in controlling the industrial marketing process, especially through accounting systems.

Control at Different Levels

The control process is universal in that it can be applied to any level of marketing analysis. For example, industrial marketers frequently must evaluate whether their general strategies are appropriate and effective. However, it is equally important to know whether the individual elements in the marketing strategy are effectively integrated for a given market. Further, management needs to evaluate resource allocation within a particular element; for example, the effectiveness of direct selling versus the effectiveness of industrial distributors. The control system should work in any of these situations. The four primary levels of marketing control are delineated in Table 17.1.

Table 17.1   Levels of Marketing Control

Type of Control	Primary Responsibility	Purpose of Control	Tools
I. Strategic Control	Top management	To examine whether the company is pursuing its best opportunities with respect to markets, products, and channels	Marketing audit
II. Annual Plan Control	Top management, middle management	To examine whether the planned results are being achieved	Sales analysis Market-share analysis Sales-to-expense ratios Other ratios Attitude tracking
III. Strategic Component Control	Middle management	To examine how well resources have been utilized in each element of the marketing strategy	Expense ratios Advertising effectiveness measures Market potential Contribution margin analysis
IV. Profitability Control	Marketing controller	To examine where the company is making and losing money	Profitability by: product territory, market segment, trade channel, order size

Source: Adapted from: Philip Kotler, *Marketing Management, Analysis Planning and Control*, 4th ed. (Englewood Cliffs, N.J.: Prentice-Hall, Inc., 1980), p. 629. Reprinted by permission of Prentice-Hall, Inc.

Strategic Control

Strategic control is based on a comprehensive evaluation of whether the firm is headed in the right direction. Because the industrial environment is subject to rapid change, existing product-market situations may lose their potential while new product-market match-ups provide important opportunities. Philip Kotler suggests that the firm periodically conduct a *marketing audit*.[3] The marketing audit is a comprehensive, periodic, and systematic evaluation of the firm's marketing operation that specifically analyzes the market environment and the firm's internal marketing activities. An analysis of the environment would assess company image, customer characteristics, competitive activities, regulatory constraints, and economic trends. Evaluation of this information will suggest areas of potential for which the firm may be able to adapt its strategy.

Environmental Analysis   As an example of environmental analysis, Hunkar Labs, a supplier of electrical programmers, analyzed the container market in the late 1960s. The analysis suggested that disposable plastic bottles were the wave of the future. As a result, Hunkar devel-

[3] Philip Kotler, *Marketing Management: Analysis, Planning and Control*, 3rd ed.; (Englewood Cliffs, N.J.: Prentice-Hall, Inc., 1976), p. 447.

oped electrical programmers that could be used to control the flow of plastic into a bottle mold. Because the programmers significantly reduce the quantity of plastic required for a container, Hunkar approached major companies that used significant quantities of plastic containers and convinced them to ask their containers suppliers to use the electrical programmers. Container manufacturers were quick to accept the new programmers; the results of the environmental assessment and its strategic implications had directed the company into a highly profitable market.

An internal evaluation of the marketing system scrutinizes marketing objectives, organization, and implementation. In this way, management may be able to spot situations where existing products could be adapted to new markets or new products developed for existing markets. The regular, systematic marketing audit is a valuable technique for evaluating the direction of marketing strategies.[1]

Competitive Analysis[5]   A thorough assessment of the firm's position vis-a-vis its competitors is fundamental to strategic control. An assessment of an industrial firm's profitability relative to competition includes demand as well as supply factors (Figure 17.2). Consider two alternative paths to a position of competitive strength.

Firm A follows a strategy geared to building volume and reducing production and distribution costs. The strategy exploits the experience effect (see Chapter 14) and scale economies, and thereby achieves cost advantages over competitors. This strategy centers on *supply* factors.

By contrast, firm B follows a strategy that centers on *demand* factors. By providing a high quality product and augmenting the offering with technical services, the firm commands a premium price in certain market segments. The segments served by firm B exhibit low demand elasticity.

Firm A's strategy is to gain a competitive cost advantage (supply factors) while firm B's strategy is to secure a perceived quality advantage (demand factors). Often, however, there is not a clear choice, and the strategic perspective must consider relative competitive position from both the supply and demand sides.

George Day contends that "the relative importance of supply versus demand factors can differ dramatically, depending on perceived differences among products and the ability of competitors to match any cost advantages or provide equivalent customer values."[6] Thus, the marketing control system must consider multiple measures of market share.

---

[1] For example, see Philip Kotler, William Gregor, and William Rogers, "The Marketing Audit Comes of Age," *Sloan Management Review* 18 (Winter 1977), pp. 25–43; Urban T. Kuechle, "A. O. Smith Audits to Sharpen Marketing Teams," *Industrial Marketing* 53 (December 1968), pp. 35–38; and Frank Rotheman, "Intensive Competitive Marketing," *Journal of Marketing* 28 (July 1964), pp. 10–17.

[5] This section is largely based on George Day, "Gaining Insights through Strategy Analysis," *Journal of Business Strategy* 4 (Summer 1983), pp. 51–58.

[6] *Ibid.*, p. 54.

Figure 17.2   Sources of Profitability

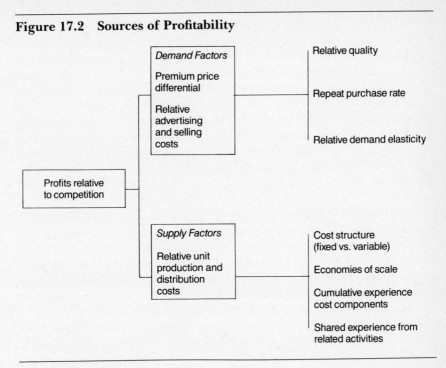

From a supply perspective, the market definition should encompass all related products which influence the size of the production experience base and the ability to achieve economies of scale; the market for the product is broadly defined. A demand perspective, by contrast, has a narrower customer-oriented market definition; it asks: What is the firm's relative share of the profitable segments of the market? Consistent with Figure 17.2, multiple market share measures which isolate key features of the demand and supply environment enrich strategic control.

Annual Plan Control

In annual plan control, the objectives specified in the plan become the performance standards against which actual results are compared. Sales volume, profits, and market share are the typical performance standards for industrial marketers. *Sales analysis* tries to determine why actual sales varied from planned sales. Expected sales may not be realized because of price reductions, inadequate volume, or both. A sales analysis would separate the impact of these variables so that corrective action could be taken.

   Market share analysis asks how the firm is doing relative to competition. A machine tool manufacturer may experience a 10 percent sales gain which, on the surface, appears favorable. However, if total machine tool industry sales are up 25 percent, an analysis of market share would pinpoint that the firm has not fared well relative to competitors.

Finally, *expense-to-sales ratios* analyze the efficiency of marketing operations. In this regard, management is concerned with over- or underspending. Frequently, industry standards or past company ratios are used for standards of comparison. Total marketing expenses and expenses of each strategic marketing element are evaluated in relation to sales. Recall the discussion in Chapter 16 on advertising expenditures, which provided a range of advertising expense-to-sales ratios for industrial firms. These figures provide management with a basis for evaluating the company's performance.

A Framework for Marketing Control   James Hulbert and Norman Toy suggest a comprehensive framework for integrating such measures into a marketing control system.[7] The basic approach is to identify the factors that caused a variance of actual product profitability from planned profitability (Table 17.2). The objective is to isolate the reasons for the differences between planned and actual results (the *variances* displayed in column three), specifically the profit contribution variance.

In this case, management seeks to understand why actual profit contribution was $100,000 less than planned profits. A detailed analysis of the data shows that although total sales were larger than expected (50 million versus 40 million units), the firm failed to achieve its targeted market share. In addition, the firm was unable to maintain its price policy. Management needs to review its forecasting, as the market size was underestimated by 25 percent (40 million vs. 50 million). To the extent

Table 17.2   Operating Results for a Sample Product

Item	Planned	Actual	Variance
Revenues			
Sales (units)	20,000,000	22,000,000	+2,000,000
Price per unit ($)	0.50	0.4773	−0.0227
Total Market (units)	40,000,000	50,000,000	−10,000,000
Share of Market	50%	44%	−6%
Revenues ($)	10,000,000	10,500,000	+500,000
Variable costs ($.30 unit) ($)	6,000,000	6,600,000	−600,000
Profit Contribution ($)	4,000,000	3,900,000	−100,000

Source: Adapted from James M. Hulbert and Norman E. Toy, "A Strategic Framework for Marketing Control," *Journal of Marketing* 41 (April 1977), p. 13.

[7] James M. Hulbert and Norman E. Toy, "A Strategic Framework for Marketing Control," *Journal of Marketing* 41 (April 1977), pp. 12–19.

that marketing strategy allocations are predicated on estimated market size, the firm may have failed to allocate sufficient effort to this market. The variances point to some real weaknesses in the forecasting process.

Because the firm did not share proportionately with its competitors in the market growth, the entire marketing strategy must be reevaluated. Management apparently underestimated the magnitude of price reductions necessary to expand volume. Clearly, *annual plan control* provides valuable insights into where the plan faltered and suggests the type of remedial action that should be taken.

Tracing Losses in Market Share

A standard product that we sell through distributors started to lose market share. Analysis determined that our prices exceeded those of the competition, and that the benefits to the customer did not warrant the higher price. To correct the situation, we required a complete redesign of the product and a new manufacturing area specifically to mass produce it.

Since our objective was to be the dominant producer in the market, all the corrective steps were taken. Today, we *are* the dominant producer and we have competitive prices that offer the customer more features than any of our competitors.

In another market area, association statistics showed we were rapidly losing market share. A more detailed analysis showed that machines based on a different engineering concept than ours were rapidly replacing the type of machine we were building for this market segment.

A plan for corrective action was pulled together. We would have had to design a new machine from the ground up. The plan was rejected because the cost was high. This market was not considered to be of major importance to the corporation, and the monies required for the redesign were needed in other, more important areas.

Our market share continued to slide while alternative solutions were being reviewed. In the meantime, a small manufacturer had entered the field because of technical know-how gained in a different industry. . . . Subsequently it became apparent to him that he had underestimated the cost of entering the market, and that this was a drain on the capital he needed to remain dominant in his normal markets. We were able to acquire the rights to his newly engineered product and thus regain our lost market share.

Meanwhile, our competitors continued to improve their machines to match the performance of ours. However, we failed to allocate sufficient engineering and design funds to remain competitive. In time, we started to lose market share and, once again, we had a product in trouble.

At that point, we had an extreme drain on our engineering groups to provide innovative features and technical steps forward for product lines more important to the well-being of the company. A search was therefore undertaken to locate a foreign manufacturer who did not participate in our market, and who had a machine of proven design that would be applicable to our market. A company was found and a licensing agreement made. Initially, foreign machines were imported while our production facilities were being converted. Unfortunately, neither the imported machines nor those made at our facilities were able to withstand the operating conditions in our market, and our market share continued to slide.

The remaining alternatives were either to redesign our own machines, or to get out of the business. The decision was made to cancel the licensing agreement, and we are now redesigning our machines.—Marketing Services Director from an industrial equipment company.

Source: David S. Hopkins, *Business Strategies for Problem Products* (New York: The Conference Board, 1977), p. 27. Reprinted by permission.

Strategic Component Control

Some of the measures used for annual plan control can be applied to evaluating the performance of individual marketing strategy elements (e.g., pricing). A good control system will provide continuing data on which to evaluate the efficiency of resources used for a given element of marketing strategy. Table 17.3 provides a representative sample of the types of data required. Performance measures and standards will vary by company and situation, according to the goals and objectives delineated in the marketing plan.

Recall the extensive discussion in Chapter 7 which dealt with techniques and procedures for calculating market potential. Because potential represents the *opportunity to sell*, it provides an excellent benchmark against which to measure performance.

Uncovering Strategic Weaknesses The use of potential to evaluate strategic element performance places severe demands on the marketer's information system, but the results are often worth the effort. Perfor-

---

Table 17.3   Illustrative Measures for Strategic Component Control

Product

Sales by market segments
Sales relative to potential
Sales growth rates
Market share
Contribution margin
Percentage of total profits
Return on investment

Distribution

Sales, expenses, and contribution by channel type
Sales and contribution margin by intermediary type and individual intermediaries
Sales relative to market potential by channel, intermediary type, and specific
    intermediaries
Expense to sales ratio by channel, etc.
Order cycle performance by channel, etc.
Logistics cost by logistics activity by channel

Communication

Advertising effectiveness by type of media
Actual audience/target audience ratio
Cost per contact
Number of calls, inquiries, and information requests by type of media
Dollar sales per sales call
Sales per territory relative to potential
Selling expenses to sales ratios
New accounts per time period

Pricing

Price changes relative to sales volume
Discount structure related to sales volume
Bid strategy related to new contracts
Margin structure related to marketing expenses
General price policy related to sales volume
Margins related to channel member performance

---

mance comparisons to market and sales potential facilitate the manager's ability to uncover strategic weaknesses. Consider Table 17.4. On the surface, salesperson A appears to be both more efficient and more effective. A's sales exceeded the historical trend forecast while expenses were relatively low in relation to sales volume. Not only did salesperson B fail to achieve the forecast level of sales, but B's expense ratio is high. However, Table 17.5 adds another dimension to the analysis—sales potential.

Suppose the firm developed sales potential figures for the first time during 1985, and used them as one performance standard. The "real" performance of each salesperson is quite different. Salesperson A's performance is relatively poor given the business available, while salesperson B is coming much closer to realizing all available sales. A's rela-

Table 17.4   Sales Performance—Percentage of Forecast and Expense/Sales Rates

	1985 Sales Volume	1985 Sales Forecast Historical Trend	Percentage of Forecast	Expense/ Sales Ratio
Salesperson A	$500,000	480,000	104%	0.084
Salesperson B	300,000	330,000	91%	0.140

Table 17.5   Sales Performance vs. Sales Potential

	1985 Sales Volume	Estimated Sales Potential 1985	Actual to Potential Sales Ratio
Salesperson A	$500,000	$1,200,000	42%
Salesperson B	300,000	350,000	86%

tively low expense-to-sales ratio may be a result of "skimming" the large accounts and ignoring business that requires significant developmental effort. Salesperson B, by contrast, is working to maximize sales possibilities. Finally, the forecasting system may be suspect. Forecasting on the basis of historical sales volume tends to compound the error.

Similar analysis of performance relative to potential can be made for distribution channels, channel members, and products. The results are sometimes combined with profitability control, the last area of a comprehensive control system.

Profitability Control

The essence of profitability control is to describe where the firm is making or losing money in terms of the important *segments* of its business. A *segment* is the unit of analysis used by management for control purposes; it may be customer segments, product lines, territories, or channel structures. Suppose an industrial firm focuses on three customer segments: machine tools, aircraft parts, and electronics manufacturers. To allocate the marketing budget among the three segments, management must consider the profit contribution associated with each segment and its expected potential. Profitability control, then, provides a methodology for associating marketing costs and revenues to specific segments of the business.

Profitability by Market Segment   Relating sales revenues and marketing costs to market segments improves decision making. More specifically:

For both strategic and tactical decisions, marketing managers may profit by knowing the impact of the marketing mix upon the target segment at which mar-

keting efforts are aimed. If the programs are to be responsive to environmental change, a monitoring system is needed to locate problems and guide adjustments in marketing decisions. Tracing the profitability of segments permits improved pricing, selling, advertising, channel and product management decisions. The success of marketing policies and programs may be appraised by a dollar and cents measure of profitability by segment.[8]

Profitability control, a prerequisite to strategy planning and implementation, has stringent information requirements. To be effective, the firm will need an accounting-marketing information system.

The accounting system must first be able to associate costs with the various marketing functions, and then attach these "functional" costs to the important segments to be analyzed.[9] Thus, as a particular cost is incurred, the cost will be coded as to the function and the segment to which it applies. In the case of, say, warehouse salaries, the distribution function will be debited with the expense. If the salaries can be related to the handling of specific products for specific customer segments, the proportion of expense applicable to each product and customer segment will be coded. Similarly, each sale to customers by product will be coded by segment. The final result is a data base that allows management to evaluate each segment of the business on the basis of its costs and revenues.

Creating Cost Modules   Frank Mossman and his colleagues refer to this type of system as a *modular data base*.[10] By coding costs and revenues as to function and segment, *cost modules* will be created which allow management to regroup costs and revenues for a particular type of analysis. Cost modules can be regrouped in three ways:

1.   Under common responsibilities (i.e., all costs associated with physical distribution), allowing a comparison of estimated and actual costs by function.

2.   By marketing segments, when these costs are added to manufacturing costs of individual products, the total can be deducted from revenues to produce segment profitability.

3.   By expense groupings, for typical external reporting purposes.[11]

Clearly, cost modules cannot be applied universally. Advertising expenses cannot logically be allocated to specific customers; some, however, can be associated with products or territories.

---

[8] Leland L. Beik and Stephen L. Buzby, "Profitability Analysis by Market Segments," *Journal of Marketing* 37 (July 1973), p. 49.

[9] Frank H. Mossman, Paul M. Fischer, and W. J. E. Crissy, "New Approaches to Analyzing Marketing Profitability," *Journal of Marketing* 38 (April 1974), p. 44.

[10] *Ibid.*

[11] *Ibid.*

In summary, profitability control requires a marketing-accounting system that codes expenses, as they are incurred, to the relevant functions and marketing segments. The result is a data base composed of cost modules that can be easily manipulated to determine profit performance by marketing segments—customers, products, and territories. How can the cost and revenue data be combined most effectively to provide a measure of profit performance?

Contribution to Profit   The important concept is *contribution to profit* rather than net profit. To arrive at a net profit figure, certain cost elements that are fixed or not within the control of the marketing manager must be deducted from revenues. For example, administrative and overhead costs do not vary with the level of marketing effort in the short run, and thus no attempt should be made to arbitrarily allocate them. Certain fixed costs assigned to an unprofitable territory would not be eliminated by an elimination of service to that territory. Net profit figures require too many arbitrary allocations to make them suitable for control and performance evaluation purposes.

A more useful and valid measure of performance is controllable profit contribution, that is, revenue associated with a marketing segment (product sales, sales to a particular customer group) minus the costs that can be directly attributed to that segment. Controllable costs are those costs that originate in a particular department (marketing) and over which the manager has some influence.[12] For example, the expenditure of $1500 for a two-page, six-issue advertisement in *Plastics World* is a controllable cost for the marketing department. The expense could not be assigned to customer segments as there is no meaningful basis for allocating the cost, but it can be assigned to one specific product.

Net Segment Margin   The net result of contribution margin analysis is the *segment margin statement* (Table 17.6). Each measure of segment performance permits a different type of analysis. The *segment contribution margin* represents the contribution to profits of the segment based on the revenue generated and the controllable costs; the goal is to maximize revenue with respect to the controllable costs. The *segment controllable margin* includes a subtraction of those costs controllable by the manager, but ones which do not vary directly with the level of sales. For example, if the salespersons who sell to OEM accounts are paid a straight salary, the sales expense does not vary with the level of sales; but if OEM accounts were dropped the expense would disappear. The *controllable margin* represents the net impact (positive or negative) of the segment on the firm's operation during the period. If a longer-term view is desired, the *net segment margin* is determined by subtracting current costs associated with

---

[12] Patrick M. Dunne and Harry I. Wolk, "Marketing Cost Analysis: A Modularized Contribution Approach," *Journal of Marketing* 41 (July 1977), p. 84.

Table 17.6   Segment Margin Statement

Revenue	$800,000
Less: Production and marketing costs directly attributable to the segment	300,000
Segment Contribution Margin	500,000
Less: Nonvariable costs incurred specifically for the segment	180,000
Segment Controllable Margin	320,000
Less: A charge for the use of assets used by the segment, but whose benefits apply over many future periods	80,000
Net Segment Margin	$240,000

Source: Adapted from Frank H. Mossman, Paul M. Fischer, and W. J. E. Crissy, "New Approaches to Analyzing Marketing Profitability," *Journal of Marketing*, 38 (April 1974), p. 46. Reprinted from the *Journal of Marketing*, published by the American Marketing Association.

long-term assets. Net segment margin is not as useful as the other measures for decision-making purposes because it requires some arbitrary cost allocations.

The contribution margin statements can be used for budgeting, performance analysis, short-run decision making, pricing, and evaluating alternatives—for example, whether to keep a territory or to drop it, whether to use a distributor or a direct channel.[13] Because costs are developed first by functional areas and then by segments, the information system can be used to evaluate various marketing functions—for example, personal selling, distribution, and advertising.

In summary, profitability control evaluates the performance of various marketing segments. The key to successful profitability control is the marketing-accounting data base from which the manager develops segmented contribution statements. The controllable contribution margin is the primary segmental performance measure; it relates controllable costs to segment revenues.

Marketing Control Systems: Industry Practices

How do industrial marketing managers evaluate marketing activities? This was the question posed in a study of the control measures used by 146 industrial manufacturers[14] with sales volumes that ranged from $100 million to $500 million, with an average volume of about $150 million. Results are presented in Table 17.7.

---

[13] *Ibid.*, p. 85.

[14] Jackson, Ostrom and Evans, "Measures Used to Evaluate," pp. 269–274.

Table 17.7   Measures Used to Evaluate Industrial Marketing Activities

Measure	Percentage of Responding Firms
Product Performance Measures (n = 142)	
Sales volume by product (units or dollars)	91.5
Sales volume as compared to a predetermined quota by product	54.2
Market share by product	59.9
Expenses incurred by product	40.0
Contributions of product to profit (sales less direct costs)	75.4
Net profit of product (sales less direct costs less indirect costs allocated)	57.0
Return on assets committed to the product	28.9
Customer Performance Measures (n = 116)	
Sales volume by customer (units or dollars)	90.5
Sales volume as compared to a predetermined objective set for the customer	48.3
Contribution of customer profit	41.4
Net profit of customer (sales less direct cost less indirect costs allocated)	24.1
Return on assets committed to the customer	9.5
Geographic Area Performance Measures (n = 110)	
Sales volume by area (units or dollars)	91.8
Sales volume as compared to a predetermined quota set for the area	70.0
Expenses incurred for sales to a particular area	38.2
Contribution of a particular area to profit (sales less direct costs)	25.5
Net profit of each area (sales less direct costs less indirect costs allocated)	11.8
Return on assets committed to a particular area	7.3
Order Size Performance Measures (n = 37)	
Sales volume by order size (units or dollars)	81.1
Sales volume as compared to a predetermined quota set for order sizes	18.9
Expenses incurred in relation to size of order	43.2
Contribution of a particular order size to profit (sales less direct costs)	45.9
Net profit of each order size (sales less direct costs less indirect costs allocated)	35.1

Source: Adapted by permission of the publisher from "Measures Used to Evaluate Industrial Marketing Activities" by Donald W. Jackson, Jr., Lonnie L. Ostrom, and Kenneth R. Evans, *Industrial Marketing Management*, 11 (October 1982), pp. 269–274. Copyright © 1982 by Elsevier Science Publishing Co., Inc.

Sales volume is the most typical measure used to evaluate product performance, followed by contribution of product to profit. Surprisingly, expenses incurred by the product were monitored by only 40 percent of the firms sampled. Sales volume is also the most frequently used measure of customer performance. The net profit from a customer is monitored by relatively few industrial firms.

The same pattern emerged with respect to geographical area performance measures. Again, sales performance was predominant, with only a fraction of the firms monitoring net profit by region. Only one-quarter of the total sample (37 responding firms) used order size performance measures, and most of these used sales volume rather than the net profit by order size. The analysis of order size is useful in developing quantity discounts, alternative forms of shipping, and differentiated sales commission rates.

Improving Efficiency and Effectiveness

The survey of industry marketing control practices suggests that there are significant opportunities for improving industrial marketing efficiency and effectiveness.[15] The control phase continues to be the weak link in marketing management.[16] Given the rising concern about productivity and the sizable asset commitments of many industrial firms, return-on-assets would appear to be a valuable performance measure. Yet it is one used by very few of the industrial firms sampled.

In analyzing profitability by market segment, predominant attention is given to output measures like sales, with only limited attention to inputs, or expenses. By linking sales to expenses by product, customer, territory, and order size, the industrial marketer is better equipped to allocate the marketing budget, establish strategic priorities, and uncover reasons for variations.

Looking Back

Figure 17.3 synthesizes the central components of industrial marketing management and highlights the material presented in this volume. Part One introduced the major classes of customers that constitute the organizational market—commercial enterprises, governmental units, and institutions. The buying behavior of these consumers was considered in Part Two, with particular attention to the myriad forces that act upon organizational decision-makers and decision influencers. Part Three discussed the industrial marketing intelligence system and the tools for assessing industrial market opportunities; it explored techniques for measuring market potential, identifying industrial market segments and forecasting sales. Functionally integrated marketing planning provides a framework for dealing with each component of the industrial marketing mix, as detailed in Part Four.

---

[15] *Ibid.*

[16] Dana Smith Morgan and Fred W. Morgan, "Marketing Cost Controls: A Survey of Industry Practices," *Industrial Marketing Management* 9 (July 1980), pp. 217–221.

Figure 17.3   A Framework for Industrial Marketing Management

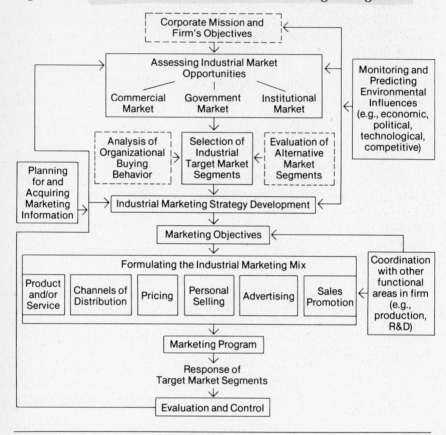

Source: Adapted from David W. Cravens, Gerald E. Hills, and Robert B. Woodruff, *Marketing Decision Making: Concepts and Strategy* (Homewood, IL: Richard D. Irwin, Inc., 1976), p. 20.

Once industrial marketing strategy is formulated, the manager must evaluate the response of target market segments to insure that any discrepancy between planned and actual results is minimized. This chapter, Part Five, explored the critical dimensions of the marketing control process. This process is the final loop in the model presented in Figure 17.3—planning for and acquiring marketing information. Such information forms the core of the firm's management information system; it is derived internally through the marketing-accounting system and externally through the marketing research function. The evaluation and control process enables the marketer to reassess industrial market opportunities and make adjustments as needed in industrial marketing strategy.

Looking Ahead: Future Trends in Industrial Marketing

The strategist seeking to understand the industrial market is dealing with a moving target, with continuous changes in customer require-ments, competitive behavior, technology, economic conditions, and or-ganizational buying behavior. By anticipating and monitoring changes, the industrial marketer is better equipped to capitalize on strategic mar-ket opportunities. This section explores some trends developing in the industrial marketing environment.

A Maturing Strategic Planning Perspective [17]

During the past decade, a growing number of industrial firms adopted formal approaches to strategic planning. Many industrial practitioners became disillusioned when particular strategy analysis methods offered by consulting organizations failed to meet their expectations. Critics charged that the blind acceptance of a particular strategic planning ap-proach can suppress management imagination, depersonalize the re-source allocation process, and lead to strategies which are simplistic and possibly misleading. George Day contends that "there is an unavoidable adjustment period in the life of any management concept or method during which experience is gained and the limitations are appreciated. This is a necessary condition to informed usage and also a useful anti-dote to earlier overselling."[18]

Insightful strategic thinking requires a careful assessment of the underlying premises of a particular strategy analysis method. When properly applied, the General Electric business screen (Chapter 9), prod-uct life cycle analysis, experience curve analysis, product evaluation ma-trix (Chapter 10), and related approaches can enhance the effectiveness of the overall strategic planning process. The strategist must understand the strengths, weaknesses, and underlying premises of each method and its potential relevance.

Since different strategy analysis techniques illuminate different features of the competitive environment, combining several methods is often valuable. For example, in assessing the relationship between mar-ket share and profitability, an industrial firm can often benefit by exam-ining market share from several perspectives—the market share based on conventionally-drawn industry boundaries versus the market share of profitable market segments. A different perspective may emerge when the market boundaries are expanded from domestic to global. A strate-gic planning approach that encompasses alternative perspectives of the

[17] This section is largely based on Day, "Gaining Insights Through Strategy Analysis," pp. 51–58.
[18] *Ibid.*, p. 51.

firm's competitive environment often isolates contradictions. Isolating, evaluating, and resolving these contradictions is fundamental to strategic planning.

Directions in Organizational Buying Behavior

Key trends influencing the purchasing function and organizational buying behavior have been explored throughout this volume. Each has marketing management implications.

Materials Management The growing acceptance of the materials management concept will demand industrial marketing strategies that are precisely synchronized with the service requirements of individual customers or market segments. For example, at selected General Motors assembly plants, parts are now ordered each morning to meet the production requirements of that day. The adoption of "just in time" materials management systems by organizational buyers heightens the need for close buyer–seller coordination and a responsive and reliable supplier logistical system.[19] Sensitive to inventory carrying costs and defective materials and parts, organizational buyers will continue to reward those industrial firms that precisely meet their delivery needs.

Analytical Techniques in Purchasing The application of computer technology to purchasing or materials management will gain further momentum. Rather than restricting computer applications to routine buying situations, purchasing managers will expand their use of the computer for vendor evaluation, value analysis, make-or-buy decisions, price forecasting, and a range of other procurement decisions. The use of more sophisticated purchasing procedures increases the need for industrial marketing strategies that are based on careful analysis of unique customer needs.

Purchasing's Emerging Strategic Role Enjoying rising organizational status during the 1980s, the procurement function will assume a more important role in the strategic planning process. This may provide further impetus for the trend toward the centralization of procurement at the regional, divisional, or headquarters level.

The role of the procurement function in a firm's strategic planning process encompasses the following areas:[20]

- monitoring trends in the supply environment;
- interpreting these trends to the firm;

[19] Michael D. Hutt and Thomas W. Speh, "Realigning Industrial Marketing Channels," *Industrial Marketing Management*, 12 (July 1983), pp. 171–177.

[20] John M. Browning, Noel B. Zabriskie, and Alan B. Huellmantel, "Strategic Purchasing Planning," *Journal of Purchasing and Materials Management*, 19 (Spring 1983), pp. 19–24.

- identifying the materials and services required to support corporate and business unit strategy;
- developing viable supply options.

A marketer who is sensitive to the role and level of influence of the procurement function in a particular organization can more accurately isolate buying influentials, identify buying criteria, and target marketing strategy.

Organizational Buying Behavior Research   Knowledge of the dynamics of organizational buying behavior is crucial to the marketer in identifying profitable market segments, locating buying influences within these segments, and reaching organizational buyers effectively and efficiently. The relevant unit of analysis for the marketing strategist is the buying center.

Significant research attention has been devoted to organizational buying behavior during the past decade. Some argue that the research approaches followed have not led to a coherent attack on the topic. Wesley Johnston, for example, sees a need for new conceptualizations of organizational buying behavior: [21]

Industrial buying and marketing are multidimensional processes. Understanding them must include not only the activities of the buying process, but also the people who initiate and perform these activities and an evaluation of the forces working on the process in specific situations. Emerging approaches should move toward a systems perspective and recognize these complexities.

To increase the managerial usefulness of industrial buying behavior research and to better integrate the area into marketing theory, the search for improved conceptual and methodological approaches to organizational buying behavior research will continue.

Directions in Industrial Marketing Strategy

The industrial market is a dynamic environment shaped by a complex blend of technological, economic, competitive, and political forces. Changing market needs and environmental forces trigger corresponding changes in industrial marketing strategy.

Global Market Focus   The accelerating demand for industrial goods in the international market and the dramatic rise in competition from Japan, Western Europe, and a growing list of Third World multinationals points to the continuing importance of a global market perspective. Igal Ayal and Jehiel Zif contend that the two major and opposing multi-

[21] Wesley J. Johnston, "Industrial Buying Behavior: A State of the Art Review," in Ben M. Enis and Kenneth J. Roering, eds., *Review of Marketing 1981* (Chicago: American Marketing Association, 1981), p. 86; see also, Wesley J. Johnston and Robert E. Spekman, "Industrial Buying Behavior: A Need for an Integrative Approach," *Journal of Business Research*, 10 (June 1982), pp. 135–146.

national expansion strategies are market diversification and market concentration.[22] The key focus here is the rate of entry into new markets and the allocation of efforts among markets. Secondary sources of international market information, highlighted in Chapter 6, can often be valuable in evaluating the relative attractiveness of foreign markets. Market concentration is typified by channeling available marketing resources into a small number of markets in an effort to win a significant share of these markets. Once these goals are attained, the firm may expand the scope of its operations to other locations and segments. A concentration strategy may center on a particular country or only on particular segments within a country.

By contrast, market diversification allocates resources over a large number of markets and segments. Among the factors affecting choice of international market entry strategy are the growth rate of each market, the need for product and communications adaptation, and potential economies of scale in distribution. For example, when the growth rate of each international market is high and there is a need for product and communications adaptation, a concentration strategy is suggested.

To confront these difficult decisions, Yoram Wind and Thomas Robertson recommend that "current marketing concepts and methods be evaluated for their applicability to international operations, modified as necessary, or supplemented with new concepts and methods more appropriate to multinational decisions."[23]

Industrial Market Segmentation   Rapidly advancing marketing intelligence systems, coupled with more sophisticated approaches to industrial marketing research, will allow far more industrial firms to precisely segment the industrial market. Rather than segmenting the market on the basis of broad industrial groupings (e.g., by SIC code), there will be greater opportunities for identifying the smaller micro segments buried within a particular macro segment. Given the concentration of some industrial markets and advancements in marketing information systems, many industrial firms may have no need for market segmentation because they can monitor the needs and purchasing patterns of *each* existing or potential customer.[24]

Product Strategy and the New Manufacturing Technology   By altering the basic tenets of conventional manufacturing, emerging manufacturing technology can alter the nature of industrial marketing strategy.

[22] Igal Ayal and Jehiel Zif, "Market Expansion Strategies in Multinational Marketing," *Journal of Marketing* 43 (Spring 1979), pp. 84–93; see also, Lindsay N. Meredith and Michael D. Hutt, "Toward an International Perspective of Market Analysis in Industrial Marketing," *Journal of Marketing Education* (in press).

[23] Yoram Wind and Thomas S. Robertson, "Marketing Strategy: New Directions for Theory and Research," *Journal of Marketing* 47 (Spring 1983), p. 15.

[24] Yoram Wind, "Industrial Marketing: Present Status and Future Potential," presentation to the American Marketing Association's Second Annual Faculty Consortium on Industrial Marketing, July 5, 1982.

As discussed in Chapter 9, flexible manufacturing systems, the first step toward computer-integrated manufacturing systems, constitute a radical departure from the past, where economies were realized only at high levels of production. Because a flexible manufacturing system can be instantly reprogrammed to make new parts or products, the automation provides the capacity to manufacture goods economically in small volume.

This technology has two strategic implications. First, flexible manufacturing systems allow the industrial firm to efficiently meet the special product requirements of small market segments or large individual customers. Second, flexible manufacturing technology may alter the nature of competition in selected industrial markets by broadening the scope of markets that competitors can serve. While the speed with which the new manufacturing technology will diffuse throughout particular industries is difficult to forecast, computer-integrated manufacturing systems is sure to constitute a potent force in the industrial market.

Reaching Industrial Customers: Evolving Strategies[25]   The rising costs of personal selling, coupled with the desire to improve the efficiency and effectiveness of industrial marketing strategy, have spawned marketing programs that combine traditional and evolving communication methods.

- *National accounts management programs*—the use of a national accounts manager to coordinate relationships with the firm's most important customers.
- *Demonstration centers*—the use of specially designed showrooms where customers can examine complex industrial equipment such as data processing equipment, machine tools, electronic test units, and telecommunications equipment. These centers give the seller the opportunity to custom-design demonstrations that relate directly to the customer's needs.
- *Industrial stores*—the application of conventional retailing strategy to reach selected segments of industrial customers economically. Used successfully in the small business computer industry, the store approach is especially appropriate when (a) personal sales in particular customer segments (e.g., small businesses) would be uneconomical, and (b) the product or process lends itself to demonstration.
- *Telemarketing*—the use of telephone marketing "as a less costly substitute for personal selling, a supplement to personal selling, a higher-impact substitute for direct mail and media advertising, a

---

[25] This section is largely drawn from Benson P. Shapiro and John Wyman, "New Ways to Reach Your Customers," *Harvard Business Review*, 51 (July–August 1981), pp. 103–110.

supplement to direct mail and other media, and a replacement for other slower, less convenient communications techniques."[26]

- *Catalog selling*—a highly cost-effective way to transmit significant amounts of information to selected prospects and customers. Catalog selling is often used in conjunction with telemarketing.

Driven by new technology and the search for increased efficiency and effectiveness, industrial marketers are formulating integrated marketing communications programs. Figure 17.4 illustrates the impact and cost per message of alternative promotional options. By monitoring the relative impact of these options, the industrial marketing strategist can blend the "old" with the "new" to profitably meet changing customer needs.

Strategy Implementation   Industrial firms are giving increased attention to strategy implementation. As emphasized in Chapter 9, a functionally integrated marketing planning approach is fundamental to successful industrial marketing strategy. Here research and development, manufacturing, technical service, physical distribution, and other business functions play fundamental roles.

The enduring buyer–seller relationships are a feature of industrial marketing that demands a sharper interdisciplinary focus. Significant post-transaction exchanges take place between the buyer and seller, often involving representatives from several functional areas in the selling firm, including engineering, manufacturing, and research and development. The industrial salesperson guides the interaction of key members of the client and the selling organization. To insure maximum customer satisfaction and the desired market response, industrial sellers must effectively manage these flows of influence. Thus, the successful industrial marketing manager performs as an integrator by drawing on the collective strengths of the enterprise to profitably satisfy customer needs.

Summary

Central to market strategy is the allocation of resources to each strategy element and the application of marketing efforts to segments. The marketing control system is the process by which the industrial firm generates information to make these decisions. Moreover, the marketing control system is the means by which current performance can be evaluated and steps can be taken to correct deficiencies. An effective control system will have four distinct components. *Strategic control*, which is operationalized through the marketing audit, provides evaluative information

---

[26] *Ibid.*, p. 106.

Figure 17.4   Comparing the Evolving and Traditional Options

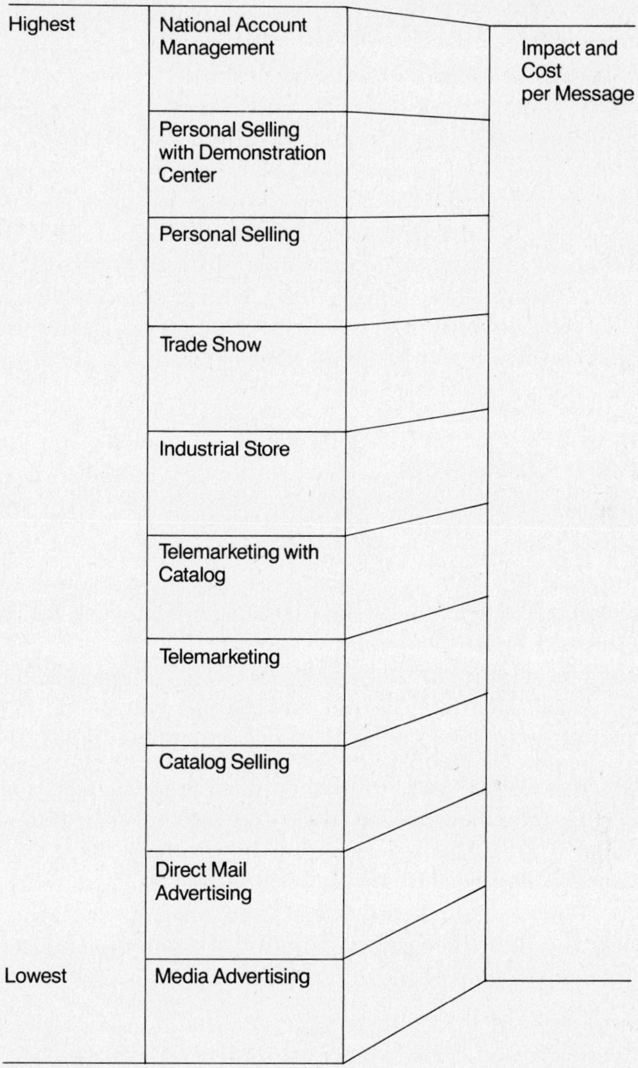

Highest	National Account Management		Impact and Cost per Message
	Personal Selling with Demonstration Center		
	Personal Selling		
	Trade Show		
	Industrial Store		
	Telemarketing with Catalog		
	Telemarketing		
	Catalog Selling		
	Direct Mail Advertising		
Lowest	Media Advertising		

on the present and future course of the firm's basic product-market mission. *Annual plan control* compares annual to planned results to provide input for future planning. *Strategic component control* focuses on the effectiveness of each element in the marketing strategy. Finally, *profitability control* seeks to evaluate profitability by segment.

Several trends emerging in the industrial marketing environment are worthy of particular attention. First, a maturing strategic planning perspective is evident in many industrial firms. Insightful strategic thinking requires a careful assessment of the underlying premises of alternative strategy analysis methods. Second, the growing acceptance of the materials management concept, and the increased application of analytical techniques in purchasing, heighten the need for carefully-designed and integrated industrial marketing strategies. Third, industrial marketers are supplementing traditional promotional tools with a new mix of communications and distribution strategies. These include national accounts management, demonstration centers, industrial stores, telemarketing, and catalog selling. Fourth, the complex nature of buyer–seller relationships demands a functionally integrated marketing planning perspective if industrial marketing strategy is to be successful.

Discussion Questions

1. Last December, Lisa Schmitt, vice president of marketing at Bock Machine Tool, identified four market segments that her firm would attempt to penetrate in the next year. As the year comes to an end, Lisa would like to evaluate the firm's performance in each of these. Of course, Lisa turns to you for assistance. First, what information would you seek from the firm's marketing information system to perform the analysis? Second, how would you know if the firm's performance in a particular market segment was good or bad?

2. Susan Breck, president of Breck Chemical Corporation, added three new products to the firm's line two years ago to serve the needs of five SIC groups. Each of the products has a separate advertising budget, although they are sold by the same salespersons. Susan requests your assistance in determining what type of information the firm should be gathering to monitor and control the performance of these products. Outline your reply.

3. Assume that the information you requested in question 2 has been gathered for you. How would you determine whether advertising or personal selling funds should be shifted from one product to another?

4. Hamilton Tucker, president of Tucker Manufacturing Company, is concerned about the "seat-of-the-pants" approach used by managers in allocating the marketing budget. He cites the Midwest and Eastern regions as examples. The firm increased its demand-stimulating expenditures (e.g., advertising, personal selling) in the Midwest by 20 percent and sales climbed only 6 percent last year. In contrast, demand-stimulating expenditures were cut by 17 percent and sales dropped by 22 percent in the East. Hamilton would

like you to assist the Midwest and Eastern regional managers in allocating their funds next year. Carefully outline the approach that you would follow.

5. Delineate the central components of the marketing control process. Describe the role of the control system in formal marketing planning.

6. Distinguish between *contribution to profit* and *net profit*.

7. Two major and opposing multinational expansion strategies are market diversification and market concentration. Describe the key features of each strategy.

8. Some experts predict that emerging manufacturing technology will alter the nature of industrial marketing strategy. Explain.

P · A · R · T
VI

Cases

Case Planning Guide

Page	Case No.	Case Title	1	2	3	4	5	6	7	8	9	10	11	12	13	14	15	16	17
485	1	Caloway Box Company	■	■															
489	2	EFI—MS	■	■															
495	3	S. C. Johnson and Son, Limited (R)	■	■										■				■	
508	4	Trus Joist Corporation (B)			■	■		■			■	■							
521	5	Boltronics Corporation					■	■			■								■
538	6	Varian Associates, Incorporated					■										■		
543	7	Modern Plastics					■		■	■									
552	8	Duralake Plastics, Inc.									■	■							
557	9	Power Tools, Inc. (B)											■	■				■	
561	10	The McKenzie Company (A)											■	■					
572	11	The McKenzie Company (B)											■	■					
573	12	Hyde-Phillip Chemical Company											■	■				■	
577	13	Transcon Parts													■				
580	14	The Ajax Pump Company													■				
585	15	Caterpillar Tractor Company										■		■		■			
590	16	Midland Industries, Ltd. (B)									■					■			
599	17	Texas Instruments: Electronic Appliance Controls				■					■					■			
607	18	Lectron Corporation			■	■	■	■	■	■	■	■					■	■	■

Relevant Chapters

Caloway Box Company*

The Folding Box Industry

Folding paper boxes are manufactured by die-cutting paper board on equipment similar to a printing press. The board itself typically runs between 0.016 to 0.030 inches in thickness. Depending upon the requirements of the purchaser, the die-cut paper board may be either treated with glue along certain edges or cut with corner locks which allow the purchaser to set up the box without gluing it.

Compared to other packaging items, the folding paper box is relatively inexpensive. One distinct advantage, which it has over competing containers, is the fact that it can be shipped and stored in its flat position thus lowering the cost of handling and transportation.

The firm purchasing the box converts it to its set-up position either by hand or by using automatic equipment. In very large-volume use situations, such as the breakfast food and detergent industries, the folding box may be set up on sophisticated, high-speed equipment. In relatively low-volume situations, such as manufacturers of small hardware items, it may be set-up manually.

There are a wide diversity of end uses for folding boxes including foods, cosmetics, sporting goods, medicinals, toys, tobacco, soap, bakery items, candy, and textiles. In terms of dollar volume, the food category represents the greatest part of the market, accounting for slightly over 50 percent of the usage. In terms of value per ton of shipments, the cosmetic, medicinal, hardware, toy, and sporting goods fields are highest and are thought by some analysts to represent the fastest growing end uses.

Approximately 460 companies in the United States produce folding boxes. The sizes of these firms vary greatly. It has been estimated that the top eight companies hold over one-third of the dollar volume for the total industry. In general, these very big firms concentrate upon large orders. At the opposite end of the field are many small producers, such as Caloway, who serve lower volume accounts. As reported by the Department of Commerce, the dollar value of shipments for the period of 1960–1974 was as follows (in million of dollars):

1960	$ 893
1963	912
1965	950
1967	1109
1970	1225

1971	....	1250
1972	....	1330†
1973	....	1400†
1974	....	1460†

† Estimated

In terms of "value added," the industry average approximates 50 percent of the selling price. As a rough rule of thumb, in estimating the price of a folding carton, one can double the cost of the raw materials used, mainly the paper board. However, this relationship varies with the size of order, quality of materials, and intricacy of design.

Folding carton plants are oriented toward operation on a local or regional basis. Being in or near large-usage areas not only reduces shipping costs but enables firms to respond quickly to changes in customer demand and to supply maximum service. Service and flexibility are considered highly important for successful operation in this field.

In addition to die-cutting paper board into the required shape and providing gluing surfaces where necessary, the folding carton firm generally prints the box as well. Frequently, graphic design work is required in connection with such printing.

Background of the Caloway Box Company

The Caloway Box Company was founded in 1960 by Harold Callahan and Charles Wayman. Each man had had about 10 years of experience as a salesman for box-making firms in the Los Angeles area (company name and location are disguised). For some time they had considered the possibility of establishing their own company to manufacture and sell folding boxes. In order to do so, they estimated that they would require an initial capitalization of roughly $50,000.

To acquire sufficient funds to begin operations, they worked out a loan arrangement with Mr. Richard Foster, who owned two very successful automobile agencies in the area.

By 1963, Callahan and Wayman had fully repaid the loan. While Mr. Foster had never taken an active part in the operation of the firm, he had been designated vice president for finance and director of the corporation. Mr. Callahan served as president and Mr. Wayman as executive vice president. This arrangement was continued after repayment of the loan.

Mr. Foster's role had always been largely of an advisory nature on matters of general business practice. While he had no direct experience in the box industry, he had extensive industrial experience in other areas, stretching over some 35 years. In addition, the office staff at one of Mr. Foster's automobile agencies handled all clerical and bookkeeping activities for Caloway.

Mr. Callahan and Mr. Wayman held an informal luncheon meeting with Mr. Foster each Friday. At that time they discussed the general progress of the company and also turned over the necessary information for Mr. Foster's staff to handle invoicing, payment of bills, and general bookkeeping procedures. For these services, as well as for his services as director and advisor, Mr. Foster received $3,000 per year. The arrangement permitted Caloway to operate with no secretarial or clerical staff.

Caloway employed approximately 15 people, including the two co-owners. Of the 15, only the principals, Harold Callahan and Charles Wayman, were directly engaged in sales and customer contact work. Because of the small size of the organization, Callahan and Wayman were also deeply involved in all other aspects of the firm's operations. One man, Jack Grant, was employed as an assistant reporting to both of the owners. He concerned himself mainly with purchasing and shipping. The company employed a chief pressman, who was responsible for all production activities and who reported to Mr. Wayman. All of the remaining employees were engaged in production.

Sales History of the Company

During its first year of operation, Caloway acquired 19 customers, primarily through previous contacts which Mr. Callahan and Mr. Wayman had made during their years as box salesmen. By 1970, the number of customers had reached 102. Dollar sales volume rose from approximately $125,000 in 1961 to about $650,000 in 1973. The growth rate was heaviest in the first few years of operation but continued at approximately 10 percent per year after 1966. Caloway concentrated upon customers in the Los Angeles area, with a few customers as far away as San Diego. In terms of size, the company's accounts varied from $80,000 per year to very small firms doing less than $500 a year with Caloway. The average run of boxes for current customers was around 20,000 units. Gross profit was about 30 percent.

Promotional Policies

Caloway is relatively inactive in seeking new business through any planned promotional program. The company runs a display advertisement in the yellow pages of the telephone directory and maintains contact with four paper jobbers who refer customers to Caloway on a commission basis. On the average, the company estimates that it gains about two new accounts from the telephone directory listing and 10 to 12 new accounts from the jobbers each year. In addition, new accounts are acquired through referrals by current customers. Occasionally, Mr. Wayman makes unsolicited calls on potential customers, but such activity rarely runs to more than three calls per year.

Essentially, most prospects initiate contact with the company after seeing the yellow page listing or through referral by a paper jobber or present customer. Upon determining the customer's needs, Mr. Wayman, who handles most of the new accounts, prepares a sample box and submits an estimate on the cost. No charge is made for preparation of the sample or for cost estimates. Roughly 50 percent of the prospects for whom samples are prepared become customers of the firm. The usual procedure for the company is to produce only upon receiving an order rather than attempting to anticipate customer requirements. Even though Caloway has not been especially active in seeking new accounts, the growth rate of the company has been consistent, and both Mr. Callahan and Mr. Wayman feel that excellent customer service is at the heart of their success. By remaining relatively small, Caloway has been able to stay close to its customers and to remain flexible in its ability to meet their needs. For example, while the company maintains little or no advance inventory, it is able to rearrange production to meet rush orders whenever necessary.

Company officials regard their competition as coming mainly from about 10 other firms in the area whose sales are under $1 million a year. In general, larger firms are not interested in the low-volume accounts handled by Caloway. By the same token, Caloway feels itself unable to compete on very large orders. In several cases, the company handles small portions of the folding carton business for firms who purchase much larger quantities from other suppliers.

The company's equipment includes three two-color printing presses, three single-color presses, four die-cutting machines, and a machine for glue application.

Expansion Possibilities

In the spring of 1974, Caloway was considering moving from its present location, where it occupied about 15,000 square feet, to a building where it would occupy approximately 20,000 square feet. Given its present equipment, the company could handle an annual volume of $800,000 to $900,000. If the plant is moved to this new location, it would be possible to add additional equipment and to increase output potential substantially.

Callahan and Wayman were also considering the possibility of adding a full-time salesperson. They felt that a good person could be found if they could guarantee earnings of at least $18,000 per year, based on a commission of 5 percent of sales. They estimated that a competent, new person might take about two years to reach a sales level of $360,000. Having a full-time salesperson would place an added workload on Mr. Wayman, since he would be required to have samples prepared and to make job estimates for the increased number of potential customers such a salesperson could be expected to produce. While about half of Caloway's present prospects become customers, the ratio might be much lower should the firm turn to active solicitation of new business.

When they discussed the possibility of expansion with Mr. Foster, he indicated his feeling that, based on the past success of the company, he felt it deserved strong consideration. If necessary, he was prepared to loan the company up to $150,000 for expansion purposes. He also suggested that it might be wise to consider increased promotional activity either in place of or in addition to the hiring of a salesperson.

EFI—MS*

Every January and July, Joe Hinds had to travel to Tulsa to meet with the corporate executives to evaluate his department's performance and review existing guidelines and policies. Throughout the year his department (MS) was granted virtual operational freedom. However, during those two visits, which typically lasted three or four days, Mr. Hinds always felt that the corporation had the intention and the ability to investigate even the slightest problems of MS.

In January 1981, Joe Hinds went confidently to corporate headquarters. He had been managing his department for almost 10 years, and this was the third record profit and sales year in a row. He had accomplished most of his objectives and was able to show an impressive backlog of orders. Nonetheless, he had some hesitations. He wanted to let them know that some policies must be changed, that some practices had become obsolete.

Company History

Engels and Ferrell Industries, Inc. was established in 1894 to manufacture railroad cars in Western Pennsylvania. The company has grown steadily over the years and now has 19 operating divisions in eight states, Canada, Germany, and New Zealand. Engels and Ferrell manufactures several thousand different industrial products in more than 50 plants and had a total corporate 1980 sales volume of approximately $485 million. The company strategy is based on several loosely-controlled autonomous divisions and relatively small plants, most of which are located in small to middle-size communities. Engels and Ferrell stresses product quality and is known for its excellence in engineering and research.

The Military Space (MS) Department, the largest plant of the Electronics Division, is in Johnstown, Indiana. The plant began operation in 1950 as a research facility for vacuum power tubes. A few years later, MS received an army contract to design and develop a battery to launch and guide a classified army weapon. Over the next few years, MS won several more military and then space contracts. Since 1966, almost all of MS's sales have been related to military and space batteries and battery components. Today, MS employs 526 people and is recognized by the free world military and space battery industry as the leader in terms of dollar sales volume, product diversification, and technical expertise.

Recent Information

Rearranging bits and pieces from Mr. Hind's presentation, several tables and charts were constructed to illustrate facts about the MS department's operational potentialities and weaknesses (see Exhibits 1 through 9).

Exhibit 1   Sales Volume (in $000)

Customer (end-user)	1972	1974	1976	1978	1980
U.S. Army	2721	2685	2340	2046	3048
U.S. Navy	860	704	660	2960	3641
U.S. Air Force	2142	2899	3509	3214	4684
Dept. of Energy [1]	820	1490	2631	3140	3966
NASA	1421	1656	2124	2291	1744
U.S. Marine Corps	160	179	130	64	0
Commercial	0	0	0	416	0
Foreign	0	36	424	622	941
Unknown/Other	0	1	71	83	20
Total	8124	9650	11889	14836	18044

[1] Formerly the Atomic Energy Commission and then the Energy Research Development Agency.

Exhibit 2   Sales Volume (in $000)

Product Type	1972	1974	1976	1978	1980
Thermal	2437	2743	3885	5296	7943
Ordnance (fuse)	1114	1222	1464	2024	2788
Silver Zinc	3281	3974	4424	4551	4110
Nickel Cadmium (sealed)	604	911	1142	819	314
Nickel Hydrogen	0	0	0	120	301
Nickel Zinc	196	122	0	40	0
Lithium	332	499	844	1922	2588
Other	160	179	130	64	0
Total	8124	9650	11889	14836	18044

Exhibit 3   Sales Projections for 1981 (in $000)

Thermal	10100	U.S. Army	4600
Ordnance (fuse)	3700	U.S. Navy	4600
Silver Zinc	4600	U.S. Air Force	4600
Nickel Cadmium (sealed)	200	Dept. of Energy	5800
Nickel Hydrogen	800	NASA	2300
Nickel Zinc	0	U.S. Marine Corps	0
Lithium	4300	Commercial	100
Other	0	Foreign	1700
		Unknown/Other	0
Total	23700	Total	23700

Exhibit 4   Current Backlog (in $000) (as of 1 January 1981) [1]

Thermal	3934	U.S. Army	1983
Ordnance (fuse)	160	U.S. Navy	56
Silver Zinc	2114	U.S. Air Force	3280
Nickel Cadmium (sealed)	64	Dept. of Energy	1214
Nickel Hydrogen	588	NASA	896
Lithium	1306	Foreign	631
		Commercial	106
Total	8166	Total	8166

[1] 1 January 1980 backlog was $5981.

Exhibit 5   1981 Projected Production Schedule (in $000) by Product Type

	Jan/Feb/Mar	Apr/May/Jun	Jul/Aug/Sep	Oct/Nov/Dec
Thermal	2384	3080	2600	2000
Ordnance (fuse)	160	420	1400	1700
Silver Zinc	1260	1300	1000	1000
Nickel Cadmium	64	0	0	150
Nickel Hydrogen	588	0	0	240
Lithium	1214	820	1000	1310
Totals	5670	5620	6000	6400

Exhibit 6   1981 Projected Production Schedule (in $000) by Customer Type

	Jan/Feb/Mar	Apr/May/Jun	Jul/Aug/Sep	Oct/Nov/Dec
U.S. Army	920	996	1300	1400
U.S. Navy	600	856	1500	1600
U.S. Air Force	1184	920	1100	1400
Dept. of Energy	1322	1448	1500	1600
NASA	1150	936	200	0
Foreign	398	464	400	400
Commercial	96	0	0	0
Totals	5670	5620	6000	6400

Marketing Dimensions

Three years ago MS recruited Bruce Jacobs, 38, as contract manager (sales responsibilities). He had previously sold automatic guidance systems and microwave tubes for military purposes. His background in sales of military equipment and his extensive marketing studies (Ph.D. in Business Administration with marketing major from Northwestern) had quickly made him a very valuable asset. However, many issues stayed un-

Exhibit 7   1980 Sales Dollar Distribution

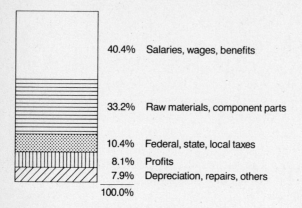

40.4%	Salaries, wages, benefits
33.2%	Raw materials, component parts
10.4%	Federal, state, local taxes
8.1%	Profits
7.9%	Depreciation, repairs, others
100.0%	

Exhibit 8   MS White-Collar Workers

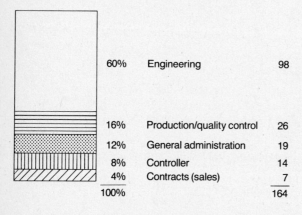

60%	Engineering	98
16%	Production/quality control	26
12%	General administration	19
8%	Controller	14
4%	Contracts (sales)	7
100%		164

Exhibit 9   Organization Chart

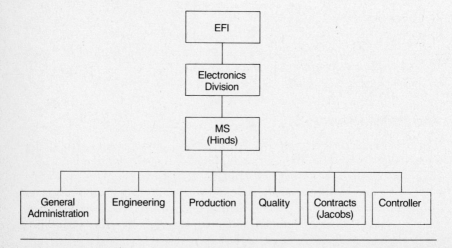

resolved in spite of the contract manager's good intentions, sound and methodical approach, and successful results. In his own words:

MS is a tremendous outfit. We have managed to recruit and keep the best engineers and researchers in the industry. The products we produce are truly the leading ones in our field. There is no single major NASA project that will not get our batteries at our price. There is no major producer of military equipment that will not ask us first for advice with respect to batteries. MS is a research power base. But we do not do any marketing. Of course, industrial marketing and especially for military products is very peculiar. However, with a very small sales department (only seven people), 1,000-plus products, and sales exceeding $18 million, we do have a problem. Each product has a different contribution, different frequency of ordering, different production planning requirement, and is in a different stage of its life cycle. Most of our products have disappeared. They are useless now. Still we cannot see the market needs. We cannot see often the new trends, and I believe that somehow we have to start with a large clean-up job, trim our lines, reposition the department, get ourselves better. . . .

However, in spite of many similar statements Jacobs was continuing his work exactly as had his predecessor (retired). "I do not want to rock the boat" was his usual answer, and he had opted to avoid major conflicts with the rest of the executives, largely of engineering backgrounds, at MS. Nevertheless, everybody knew exactly what he wanted to say. He had cautiously managed to persuade many of his colleagues about the need to stress not only the high quality of their products but also their promotion, price potentials, channels of distribution, product elimination, and product modifications.

Although Jacobs was cautious, there had been a few reactions. The engineering manager, a 60-year-old veteran with MS said:

[Bruce Jacobs] is surely one heck of a nice guy. But I think he overtheorizes. Last week he was talking to me about the "saliency" of our products. Really it's none of his business to comment and especially to develop guidelines with respect to battery heat loss, energy density, peak voltage regulation, deep discharge and the like. It does not make sense. We have been selling successfully the silver-zinc for many years. We've stayed ahead of GE in nickel-cadmium and now nickel-hydrogen for space applications. Sure GE, Mallory, RCA, and others sell a lot to commercial users, but that's not what we here at MS care about. We've been number one in the standard thermal batteries since their development by Sandia's government lab. But sometimes he tries to interfere where there is no place for him.

The 1980 Report

The report that Mr. Hinds and his staff prepared for presentation at headquarters was a real tribute to the MS management. It showed a cost-effective operation that during 1980 undertook many profitable projects and covered production gaps with "fillers" that kept capacity at nearly 100 percent. Additionally, MS had improved or modified 96 of its products, assuring their better performance; also, it was in a very healthy cash position. Given that 1980 was not a good year for military and space projects, MS management felt very good about their performance, record sales and high profits.

However, Mr. Hinds was worried. His contract manager's views had affected his overall thinking. Both men had many opportunities to meet outside the work environment, and Jacobs had shown him many instances where slightly different sales practices could have provided better production planning. But basically, the contract manager was talking about policy issues. For example, he proposed to examine each product individually, to eliminate the slow-moving or unprofitable ones, and to create more room for cost-effective production. On the other hand, Jacobs was also proposing to study market opportunities (he had a comprehensive list), both for military/space uses and for lighter industrial uses that potentially could be marketed autonomously. Mr. Hinds had many questions. It was evident to him that the contract manager had some good ideas. It was also evident that actualizing these ideas was going to create several organizational problems. More than 150 people were presently involved in research, design, and development, and some of them were working on what Jacobs thought to be an "unprofitable cause." But for the general manager, the most important questions had to do with the new orientation that the contract manager proposed. He really did not need to "rock the boat." He could apply those concepts in a very small part of MS operations; then, if they proved successful, they could be gradually extended further. But these questions remained: How can you identify products that might be eliminated? How can you see future market opportunities? How can you make the existing products more salient to the present customers and also expand their market segments? There were many obstacles. At the end, Mr. Hinds decided not to bring up the issue at the January corporate meeting, but opted to work on the concept during the next months and to prepare a proposal for the July meeting.

Questions

1.   Given the information provided, make an evaluation of MS's performance.

2.   Identify MS's potential weaknesses and strengths (make a checklist).

3.   Comment on the approaches and beliefs of the following:
Joe Hinds
Bruce Jacobs
the engineering manager

S. C. Johnson and Son, Limited (R)*

Four months ago, in November 1980, George Styan had been appointed Division Manager of INNOCHEM, at S. C. Johnson & Son, Limited[1] (SCJ), a Canadian subsidiary of S. C. Johnson & Son, Inc. INNOCHEM's sole product line consisted of industrial cleaning chemicals for use by business, institutions, and government. Styan was concerned by the Division's poor market share, particularly in Montreal and Toronto. Together, these two cities represented approximately 35% of Canadian demand for industrial cleaning chemicals, but less than 10% of INNO-CHEM sales. It appeared that SCJ distributors could not match the aggressive discounting practiced by direct selling manufacturers in metropolitan markets.

Recently, Styan had received a rebate proposal from his staff designed to increase the distributor's ability to cut end-user prices by "sharing" part of the total margin with SCJ when competitive conditions demanded discounts of 30 percent or more off the list price to end-users. George had to decide if the rebate plan was the best way to penetrate price-sensitive markets. Moreover, he wondered about the plan's ultimate impact on divisional profit performance. George either had to develop an implementation plan for the rebate plan, or draft an alternative proposal to unveil at the 1981 Distributors' Annual Spring Convention, three weeks away.

The Canadian Market for Industrial Cleaning Chemicals

In 1980, the Canadian market for industrial cleaning chemicals was approximately $100 million at end-user prices. Growth was stable at an overall rate of approximately 3 percent per year.

"Industrial cleaning chemicals" included all chemical products designed to clean, disinfect, sanitize, or protect industrial, commercial, and institutional buildings and equipment. The label was broadly applied to general purpose cleaners, floor maintenance products (strippers, sealers, finishes, and detergents), carpet cleaners and deodorizers, disinfectants, air fresheners, and a host of specialty chemicals such as insecticides, pesticides, drain cleaners, oven cleaners, and sweeping compounds.

Industrial cleaning chemicals were distinct from equivalent consumer products typically sold through grocery stores. Heavy-duty industrial products were packaged in larger containers in bulk and marketed directly by the cleaning chemical manufacturers or sold through distributors to a variety of end users. Exhibit 1 shows market segmentation

*Copyright © 1982, School of Business Administration, The University of Western Ontario. This case was written by Carolyn Vose under the supervision of Associate Professor Roger More. Reprinted with permission.

[1] Popularly known as "Canadian Johnson Wax".

Exhibit 1 Segmentation of the Canadian Market for Industrial Cleaning Chemicals (S. C. Johnson & Son Limited)

(1) By End-User Category

End-User Category	% Total Canadian Market for Industrial Cleaning Chemicals (End-User Value)
Retail Outlets	25%
Contractors	17
Hospitals	15
Industrial and Office	13
Schools, Colleges	8
Hotels, Motels	6
Nursing Homes	5
Recreation	3
Government	3
Fast Food	2
Full Service Restaurants	2
All Others	1
Total	100% = $95 million

(2) By-Product Category

Product Category	% Total Canadian Market for Industrial Cleaning Chemicals
Floor Care Products	40%
General Purpose Cleaners	16
Disinfectants	12
Carpet Care Products	8
Odor Control Products	5
Glass Cleaners	4
All Others	15
Total	100% = $95 million

by primary end-user categories, including janitorial service contractors and the in-house maintenance departments of government, institutions, and companies.

Building Maintenance Contractors

In Canada, maintenance contractors purchased 17% of the industrial cleaning chemicals sold during 1980 (end-user price). The segment was growing at approximately 10–15% a year, chiefly at the expense of other end-user categories. *Canadian Business* reported, "Contract cleaners have made sweeping inroads into the traditional preserve of in-house janitorial staffs, selling themselves on the strength of cost efficiency."[2] Maintenance contract billings reached an estimated $1 billion in 1980.

[2] "Contract Cleaners Want to Whisk Away Ring-Around-the-Office," *Canadian Business*, 00 (1981) p. 22.

Frequently, demand for building maintenance services was highly price-sensitive, and since barriers to entry were low (small capitalization, simple technology), competition squeezed contractor gross margins below 6% (before tax). Variable cost control was a matter of survival and only products bringing compensatory labor savings could command a premium price in this segment of the cleaning chemical market.

A handful of contract cleaners did specialize in higher margin services to prestige office complexes, luxury apartments, art museums, and other "quality-conscious" customers. However, even contractors serving this select clientele did not necessarily buy premium cleaning supplies.

In-House Maintenance Departments

Government   In 1980, cleaning chemical sales to various government offices (federal, provincial, and local) approached $2 million. Typically, a government body solicited bids by formally advertising for quotations for given quantities of particular cleaning chemicals. Although bid requests often named specific brands, suppliers were permitted to offer "equivalent substitutes." Separate competitions were held for each item and normally covered 12 months' supply with provision for delivery "as required." Contracts were frequently awarded solely on the basis of price.

Institutions   Like government bodies, most institutions were price-sensitive owing to restrictive budgets and limited ability to pass on expenses to users. Educational institutions and hospitals were the largest consumers of cleaning chemicals in this segment. School boards used an open bid system patterned on the government model. Heavy sales time requirements, and demands for frequent delivery of small shipments to as many as 100 locations were characteristic.

Colleges and universities tended to be operated somewhat differently. Dan Stalport, purchasing agent responsible for maintenance supplies at The University of Western Ontario, offered the following comments:

Sales reps come to UWO year 'round. If one of us (in the buying group) talks to a salesman who seems to have something—say, a labor-saving feature—we get a sample and test it. . . . Testing can take up to a year. Floor covering, for example, has to be exposed to seasonal changes in weather and traffic.

If we're having problems with a particular item, we'll compare the performance and price of three or four competitors. There are usually plenty of products that do the job. Basically, we want value—acceptable performance at the lowest available price.

Hospitals accounted for 15% of cleaning chemical sales. Procurement policies at University Hospital (UH), a medium-sized (450-bed) facility in London, Ontario, were typical. UH distinguished between "critical" and "non-critical" products. Critical cleaning chemicals (i.e., those significantly affecting patient health, such as phenolic germicide), could be bought only on approval of the staff microbiologist who tested the "kill factor." This measure of effectiveness was regularly retested and any downgrading of product performance could void a supplier's contract. In contrast, non-critical supplies, such as general purpose cleaners, floor finishes, and the like, were the exclusive province of Bob Chandler, purchasing agent attached to the Housekeeping Department. Bob explained that performance of non-critical cleaning chemicals was informally judged and monitored by the housekeeping staff:

Just last year, for example, the cleaners found the floor polish was streaking badly. We (the Housekeeping Department) tested and compared five or six brands —all in the ballpark price-wise—and chose the best.

Business The corporate segment was highly diverse, embracing both service and manufacturing industries. Large-volume users tended to be price-sensitive—particularly when profits were low. Often, however, cleaning products represented such a small percentage of the total operating budget that the cost of searching for the lowest cost supplier would be expected to exceed any realizable saving. Under such conditions, the typical industrial customer sought efficiencies in the purchasing process itself, for example, by dealing with the supplier offering the broadest mix of janitorial products (chemicals, paper supplies, equipment, etc.). Guy Breton, purchasing agent for Securitech, a Montreal-based security systems manufacturer, commented on the time-economies of "one-stop shopping":

With cleaning chemicals, it simply isn't worth the trouble to shop around and stage elaborate product performance tests. . . . I buy all our chemicals, brushes, dusters, towelling—the works—from one or two suppliers . . . buying reputable brands from familiar suppliers saves hassles—backorders are rare and Maintenance seldom complains.

Distribution Channels for Industrial Cleaning Chemicals

The Canadian market for industrial cleaning chemicals was supplied through three main channels, each characterized by a distinctive set of strengths and weaknesses:

a.   Distributor sales of national brands

b.   Distributor sales of private label products

c.   Direct sale by manufacturers

Direct sellers held a 61% share of the Canadian market for industrial cleaning chemicals, while the distributors of national brands and private label products held shares of 25% and 14%, respectively. Relative market shares varied geographically, however. In Montreal and Toronto, for example, the direct marketers' share rose to 70% and private labellers' to 18%, reducing the national brand share to 12%. The pattern shown in Exhibit 2 reflected an interplay of two areas of channel differ-

Exhibit 2   Effect of Geography on Market Share of Different Distribution Channels (S. C. Johnson & Son Limited)

Supplier Type	Share Nationwide	Share in Montreal and Toronto
Direct Marketers	61%[1]	70%
Private Label Distributors	14%	18%
National Brands Distributors	25%[2]	12%

[1]
Dustbane	17%
G. H. Wood	13
All Others	31
Total	61%

[2]
SCJ	8%
N/L	4
Airkem	3
All Others	10
Total	25%

entiation, namely, discount capability at the end-user level, and the cost of serving geographically dispersed customers.

Distributor Sales of National Brand Cleaning Chemicals   National brand manufacturers, such as S. C. Johnson and Son, Airkem, and National Labs, produced a relatively limited range of "high quality" janitorial products, including many special purpose formulations of narrow market interest. Incomplete product range combined with shortage of manpower and limited warehousing made direct distribution infeasible in most cases. Normally, a national brand company would negotiate with distributors who handled a broad array of complementary products (equipment, tools, and supplies) by different manufacturers. "Bundling" of goods brought the distributors' cost efficiencies in selling, warehousing, and delivery by spreading fixed costs over a large sales volume. Distributors were, therefore, better able to absorb the costs of after-hour emergency service, frequent routine sales and service calls to many potential buyers, and shipments of small quantities of cleaning chemicals to multiple destinations. As a rule, the greater the geographic dispersion of customers and the smaller the average order, the greater the relative economies of distributor marketing.

Comparatively high gross margins (approximately 50% of wholesale price) enabled national brand manufacturers to offer distributors strong marketing support and sales training along with liberal terms of payment and freight plus low minimum order requirements. Distributors readily agreed to handle national brand chemicals, and in metropolitan markets, each brand was sold through several distributors. By the same token, most distributors carried several directly competitive product lines. Styan suspected that some distributor salesmen only used national brands to "lead" with and tended to offer private label whenever a customer proved price-sensitive, or a competitor handled the same national brand. Using an industry rule of thumb, he estimated that most distributors needed at least 20% gross margin on retail sales to cover their salesmen's commission of 10% on retail sales, plus delivery and inventory expenses.

Distributor Sales of Private Label Cleaning Chemicals   Direct selling manufacturers were dominating urban markets by aggressively discounting end-user prices—sometimes below the wholesale price national brand manufacturers charged their distributors. To compete against the direct seller, increasing numbers of distributors were adding low-cost private label cleaning chemicals to their product lines. Private labelling also helped differentiate a particular distributor from others carrying the same national brands.

Sizeable minimum order requirements restricted the private label strategy to the largest distributors. Private label manufacturers produced to order, formulating to meet low prices specified by distributors. The relatively narrow margins (30–35% wholesale price) associated with private label manufacture precluded the extensive marketing and sales support national brand manufacturers characteristically provided to distributors. Private label producers pared their expenses further still by requiring distributors to bear the cost of inventory and accept rigid terms of payment as well as delivery (net 30 days, FOB plant).

In addition to absorbing these selling expenses normally assumed by the manufacturer, distributors paid their salesmen higher commissions on private label sales (15% of resale) than national brands (10% of resale). However, the incremental administration and selling expenses associated with private label business were more than offset by the differential savings on private label wholesale goods. By pricing private label chemicals at competitive parity with national brands, the distributor could enjoy approximately a 50% gross margin at resale list, while preserving considerable resale discount capability.

Private label products were seldom sold outside the metropolitan areas where most were manufactured. First, the high costs of moving bulky, low-value freight diminished the relative cost advantage of private label chemicals. Second, generally speaking, it was only in metro areas that distributors dealt in volumes great enough to satisfy the private labeller's minimum order requirement. Finally, outside the city, distributors were less likely to be in direct local competition with others handling the same national brand, reducing value of the private label as a source of supplier differentiation.

For some very large distributors, backward integration into chemical production was a logical extension of the private labelling strategy. Recently, several distributors had become direct marketers through acquisition of captive manufacturers.

Direct Sale by Manufacturers of Industrial Cleaning Chemicals
Manufacturers dealing directly with the end user increased their gross

margins to 60–70% of retail list price. Greater margins increased their ability to discount end-user price—a distinct advantage in the price-competitive urban marketplace. Overall, direct marketers averaged a gross margin of 50%.

Many manufacturers of industrial cleaning chemicals attempted some direct selling, but relatively few relied on this channel exclusively. Satisfactory adoption of a full-time direct selling strategy required the manufacturer to match distributor's sales and delivery capabilities without sacrificing overall profitability. These conflicting demands had been resolved successfully by two types of company, large scale powder chemical manufacturers and full-time janitorial products manufacturers.

Large Scale Powder Chemical Manufacturers   Economies of large-scale production plus experience in the capital-intensive manufacture of powder chemicals enabled a few established firms, such as Diversey-Wyandotte, to dominate the market for powder warewash and vehicle cleansers. Selling through distributors offered these producers few advantages. Direct selling expense was almost entirely commission (i.e., variable). Moreover, powder concentrates were characterized by comparatively high value-to-bulk ratios, and so could absorb delivery costs even where demand was geographically dispersed. Thus, any marginal benefits from using middlemen were more than offset by the higher margins (and associated discount capability) possible through direct distribution. Among these chemicals firms, competition was not limited to price. The provision of dispensing and metering equipment was important, as was 24-hour servicing.

Full-Line Janitorial Products Manufacturers   These manufacturers offered a complete range of maintenance products including paper supplies, janitorial chemicals, tools, and mechanical equipment. Although high margins greatly enhanced retail price flexibility, overall profitability depended on securing a balance of high and low margin business, as well as controlling selling and distribution expenses. This was accomplished in several ways, including:

- focusing on market areas of concentrated demand to minimize costs of warehousing, sales travel, and the like;
- increasing average order size, either by adding product lines which could be sold to existing customers, or by seeking new large-volume customers; and
- tying sales commission to profitability to motivate sales personnel to sell volume, without unnecessary discounting of end-user price.

Direct marketers of maintenance products varied in scale from established nationwide companies to hundreds of regional operators. The two largest direct marketers, G. H. Wood and Dustbane, together supplied almost a third of Canadian demand for industrial cleaning chemicals.

S. C. Johnson and Son, Limited

SCJ was one of 42 foreign subsidiaries owned by the U.S.-based multinational, S. C. Johnson and Son, Inc. It was ranked globally as one of the largest privately held companies. SCJ contributed substantially to worldwide sales and profits and was based in Brantford, Ontario, close to the Canadian urban markets of Hamilton, Kitchener, Toronto, London, and Niagara Falls. About 300 people worked at the head office and plant; another 100 were employed in field sales.

INNOCHEM Division INNOCHEM (Innovative Chemicals for Professional Use) was a special division established to serve corporate, institutional, and government customers of SCJ. The division manufactured an extensive line of industrial cleaning chemicals, including general purpose cleansers, waxes, polishes, and disinfectants, plus a number of specialty products of limited application, as shown in Exhibit 3. In 1980, INNOCHEM sold $4.5 million of industrial cleaning chemicals through distributors and $0.2 million direct to end users. Financial statements for INNOCHEM are shown in Exhibit 4.

INNOCHEM Marketing Strategy Divisional strategy hinged on reliable product performance, product innovation, active promotion, and mixed channel distribution. Steve Remen, market development manager, maintained that "customers know our products are of excellent quality. They know that the products will always perform as expected."

At SCJ, performance requirements were detailed and tolerances precisely defined. The Department of Quality Control routinely inspected and tested raw materials, work in process, packaging, and finished goods. At any phase during the manufacturing cycle, Quality Control was empowered to halt the process and quarantine suspect product or materials. SCJ maintained that nothing left the plant "without approval from Quality Control."

"Keeping the new product shelf well stocked" was central to divisional strategy, as the name INNOCHEM implies. Products launched over the past three years represented 33% of divisional gross sales, 40% of gross profits, and 100% of growth.

INNOCHEM had a sales force of ten that sold and serviced the distributor accounts. These salespeople were paid almost all salary, with some bonus potential up to 10 percent for exceptional sales volume increases. The company had also recently committed one salesperson to work with large direct accounts. The advertising budget of $75,000 was primarily allocated to trade magazines and direct mail advertisements to large segments of end-users such as maintenance contractors. Sales promotions, by contrast, were directed mainly at distributors, and consisted largely of special pricing and packaging deals to get distributors to more aggressively bid Johnson products in their offers to end users.

Exhibit 3   INNOCHEM Product Line (S. C. Johnson & Son Limited)

—for all floors except unsealed wood and unsealed cork
Stripper: **Step-Off** — powerful, fast action
Finish: **Pronto** — fast drying, good gloss, minimum maintenance
Spray-Buff
Solution: **The Shiner Liquid Spray Cleaner**
               or
               The Shiner Aerosol Spray Finish
Maintainer:
Forward — cleans, disinfects, deodorizes, sanitizes

—for all floors except unsealed wood and unsealed cork
Stripper: **Step-Off** — powerful, fast stripper
Finish: **Carefree** — tough, beauty, durable minimum maintenance.
Maintainer: **Forward** — cleans, disinfects, deodorizes, sanitizes

— for all floors except unsealed wood and unsealed cork
Stripper: **Step-Off** — for selective stripping
Sealer: **Over & Under-Plus** — undercoater-sealer
Finish: **Scrubbable Step-Ahead** — Brilliant, Scrubbable
Maintainer: **Forward** — cleans, disinfects, sanitizes, deodorizes.

— for all floors except unsealed word and cork
Stripper: **Step-Off**—powerful, fast stripper
Finish: **Easy Street** — high solids, high gloss, spray buffs to a "wet look" appearance
Maintainer: **Forward** — cleans, disinfects, deodorizes
               Expose — phenolic cleaner disinfectant

— for all floors except unsealed wood and unsealed cork
Stripper: **Step-Off** — for selective stripping
Sealer: **Over & Under-Plus** — undercoater-sealer
Finishes: **Traffic Grade** — heavy-duty, floor wax
               Waxtral — extra tough, high solids
Maintainer: **Forward** — cleans, disinfects, sanitizes, deodorizes

— for all floors except asphalt, mastic and rubber tile. Use sealer and wax finsihes on wood, cork and cured concrete; sealer-finish on terrazzo, marble, clay and ceramic tile; wax finish only on vinyl, linoleum and magnesite.
Sealer: **Johnson Gym Finish**—sealer and top-coater cleans as it waxes
Wax Finishes: **Traffic Wax Paste**—heavy-duty buffing wax
               Beautiflor Traffic Wax—liquid buffing wax
Maintainers: **Forward**—cleans, disinfects, sanitizes, deodorizes
               Conq-r-Dust—mop treatment

Stripper: **Step-Off**—stripper for sealer and finish
Sealer: **Secure**—fast-bonding, smooth, long-lasting
Finish: **Traffic Grade**—heavy-duty floor wax
Maintainer: **Forward, or Big Bare**

Sealer-Finish: **Johnson Gym Finish**—seal and top-coater
Maintainer: **Conq-r-Dust**—mop treatment

General   **Break-Up** — cleans soap and body scum fast
Cleaning: **Forward** — cleans, disinfects, sanitizes, deodorizes.
               Bon Ami — instant cleaner, pressurized, or pump, disinfects
Toilet-Urinals: **Go-Getter** — "Working Foam" cleaner
Glass: **Bon Ami** — spray-on foam or liquid cleaner
Disinfectant
Spray: **End-Bac II** — controls bacteria, odors
Air Freshener: **Glade** — dewy-fresh fragrances
Spot   **Johnson's Pledge** — cleans, waxes, polishes
Cleaning: **Johnson's Lemon Pledge** — refreshing scent
               Bon Ami Stainless Steel Cleaner — cleans, polishes and protects

All-Purpose   **Forward** — cleans, disinfects, sanitizes,
Cleaners: deodorizes
               Break-Up — degreaser for animal and vegetable fats
               Big Bare — heavy-duty industrial cleaner

Carpets: **Rugbee Powder & Liquid Extraction Cleaner** —
               Rugbee Soil Release Concentrate — for pre-spraying and bonnet buffing.
               Rugbee Shampoo — for power shampoo machines
               Rugbee Spotter — spot remover
Furniture: **Johnson's Pledge** — cleans, waxes, polishes
               Johnson's Lemon Pledge — refreshing scent
               Shine-Up Liquid — general purpose cleaning
Disinfectant
Spray   **End-Bac II** — controls bacteria, odors
Air Freshener: **Glade** — dewy-fresh fragrances
Glass: **Bon Ami** — spray-on foam or liquid cleaner

Cleaning: **Break-Up** — special degreaser designed to remove animal and vegetable fats
Equipment: **Break-Up Foamer** — special generator designed to dispense Break-Up Cleaner

General   **Forward** — fast-working germicidal cleaner
Cleaning: for floors, walls — all washable surfaces.
               Expose — phenolic disinfectant cleaner
Sanitizing: **J80 Sanitizer** — liquid for total environmental control of bacteria. No rinse necessary if used as directed
Disinfectant
Spray: **End-Bac II Spray** — controls bacteria, odors

Flying Insects: Bolt Liquid Airborne, or Pressurized Airborne, P3610 through E10 dispenser
Crawling   Bolt Liquid Residual or Pressurized Residual,
Insects: P3610 through E10 dispenser
               Bolt Roach Bait
Rodents: **Bolt Rodenticide** — for effective control of rats and mice, use with Bolt Bait Box

PRODUCTS OF **Johnson·wax** COMMERCIAL PRODUCTS DIVISION

Johnson Wax is a systems innovator. Frequently, a new product leads to a whole new system of doing things—a Johnson system of "matched" products formulated to work together. This makes the most of your time, your effort and your expense. Call today and see how these Johnson systems can give you maximum results at a minimum cost.

Mixed Distribution Strategy   INNOCHEM used a mixed distribution system to broaden market coverage. Eighty-seven percent of divisional sales were handled by a force of 200 distributor salesmen and serviced from 50 distributor warehouses representing 35 distributors. The indirect channel was particularly effective outside Ontario and Quebec. In

---

Exhibit 4   Profit Statement of the Division
(S. C. Johnson & Son Limited)

Profit Statement

	$000
Gross Sales	4,682
Returns	46
Allowances	1
Cash Discounts	18
Net Sales	4,617
Cost of Sales	2,314
Gross Profit	2,303
Advertising	75
Promotions	144
Deals	—
External Marketing Services	2
Sales Freight	292
Other Distribution Expenses	176
Service Fees	184[1]
Total Direct Expenses	873
Sales Force	592
Marketing Administration	147
Provision for Bad Debts	—
Research and Development	30[2]
Financial	68
Information Resource Mgt.	47
Administration Management	56
Total Functional Expenses	940
Total Operating Expenses	1,813
Operating Profit	490

---

[1] Fees paid to SCJ (Corporate) for corporate services.

[2] A portion of a research chemist's cost to conduct R and D specifically for industrial products.

---

part, the tendency for SCJ market penetration to increase with distances from Montreal and Toronto reflected Canadian demographics and the general economics of distribution. Outside the two production centers, demand was dispersed and delivery distances long.

Distributor salesmen were virtually all paid a straight commission on sales, and were responsible for selling a wide variety of products in addition to S. C. Johnson's. Several of the distributors had sales levels much higher than INNOCHEM.

For INNOCHEM, the impact of geography was compounded by a significant freight cost advantage: piggybacking industrial cleaning chemicals with SCJ consumer goods. In Toronto, for example, the cost of SCJ to a distributor was 30% above private label, while the differential in British Columbia was only 8%. On lower value products, the "freight effect" was even more pronounced.

SCJ had neither the salesmen nor the delivery capabilities to reach large volume end users who demanded heavy selling effort or frequent shipments of small quantities. Furthermore, it was unlikely that SCJ could develop the necessary selling and distribution strength economically, given the narrowness of the division's range of janitorial products (i.e., industrial cleaning chemicals only).

Exhibit 5 Distributors' Rebate Pricing Schedule: An Example Using Pronto Floor Wax (S. C. Johnson & Son Limited)

Code 04055	Product Pronto	Description Fast Dry Fin	Size 209 Lit	Pack 1

Eff. Date: 03-31-81
Resale List Price 71   613.750
Distributor Price List 74   349.837
Percent Markup on Cost with Carload & Rebate

Dis- count % 1	Quote (FST) (incl) 2	Rebate % 3	Rebate DLRS 4	2% Net 5	2% MU– % 6	3% Net	3% MU– %	4% Net	4% MU– %	5% Net	5% MU– %
30.0	429.63	8.0	27.99	314.85	36	311.35	38	307.86	40	304.36	41
35.0	398.94	12.0	41.98	300.86	33	297.36	34	293.86	36	290.36	27
40.0	368.25	17.0	59.47	283.37	30	279.87	32	276.37	33	272.87	35
41.0	362.11	17.5	61.22	281.62	29	278.12	30	274.62	32	271.12	34
42.0	355.98	18.0	62.97	279.87	27	276.37	29	272.87	30	269.37	32
43.0	349.84	18.5	64.72	278.12	26	274.62	27	271.12	29	267.63	31
44.0	343.70	19.0	66.47	276.37	24	272.87	26	269.37	28	265.88	29
45.0	337.56	20.0	69.97	272.87	24	269.37	25	265.88	27	262.38	29
46.0	331.43	20.5	71.72	271.12	22	267.63	24	264.13	25	260.63	27
47.0	325.29	21.0	73.47	269.37	21	265.88	22	262.38	24	258.88	26
48.0	319.15	21.5	75.21	267.63	19	264.13	21	260.63	22	257.13	24
49.0	313.01	22.0	76.96	265.88	18	262.38	19	258.88	21	255.38	23
50.0	306.88	23.0	80.46	262.38	17	258.88	19	255.38	20	251.88	22
51.0	300.74	24.0	83.96	258.88	16	255.38	18	251.88	19	248.38	21
52.0	294.60	25.0	87.46	255.38	15	251.88	17	248.38	19	244.89	20
53.0	288.46	26.0	90.96	251.88	15	248.38	16	244.89	18	241.39	19
54.0	282.33	28.0	97.95	244.89	15	241.39	17	237.89	19	234.39	20
55.0	276.19	30.0	104.95	237.89	16	234.39	18	230.89	20	227.39	21

[1] Discount extended to end user on resale list price.

[2] Resale price at given discount level (includes federal sales tax).

[3] Percentage of distributor's price ($613.75) rebated by SCJ.

[4] Actual dollar amount of rebate by SCJ.

[5] Actual net cost to distributor after deduction of rebate and "carload" (quantity) discount.

[6] Effective rate of distributor markup.

The Rebate Plan

The key strategic problem facing INNOCHEM was how best to challenge the direct marketer (and private label distributor) for large-volume, price-sensitive customers with heavy service requirements, particularly in markets where SCJ had no freight advantage. In this connection George had observed:

> Our gravest weakness is our inability to manage the total margin between the manufactured cost and end-user price in a way that is equitable and sufficiently profitable to support the investment and expenses of both the distributors and ourselves.

> Our prime competition across Canada is from direct selling national and regional manufacturers. These companies control both the manufacturing and distribution gross margins. Under our pricing system, the distributors margin at end-user list on sales is 43%. Our margin (the manufacturing margin) is 50% on sales. When these margins are combined, as in the case of direct selling manufacturers, the margin becomes 70% at list. This long margin provides significant price flexibility in a price-competitive marketplace. We must find a way to profitably attack the direct marketer's 61% market share.

The rebate plan Styan was now evaluating had been devised to meet the competition head-on.

"Profitable partnership" between INNOCHEM and the distributors was the underlying philosophy of the plan. Rebates offered a means to "share fairly the margins available between factory cost and consumer

---

Exhibit 6   Effect of Rebate Plan on Manufacturer and Distributor Margins: The Example of One 209-Liter Pack of Pronto Floor Finish Retailed at 40% Below Resale List Price (S. C. Johnson & Son Limited)

I.   Under Present Arrangements

Base Price to Distributor	$349.84
Price to Distributor, Assuming 2% Carload Discount[1]	342.84
SCJ Cost	174.92
∴ SCJ Margin	$167.92
Resale List Price	613.75
Resale List Price Minus 40% Discount	368.25
Distributor Price, Assuming 2% Carload Discount	342.84
∴ Distributor's Margin	$ 25.41

II. Under Rebate Plan

Rebate to Distributor Giving 40% Discount Off Resale Price Amounted to 17% Distributor's Base Price	$ 59.47
SCJ Margin (Minus Rebate)	108.45
Distributor Margin (Plus Rebate)	84.88

III. Competitive Prices

For this example, George estimated that a distributor could buy a private-branded "comparable" product for approximately $244.

---

[1] A form of quantity discount which, in this case, drops the price the distributor pays to SCJ from $349.84 to $342.84.

Exhibit 7 Effect of End-User Discount Level on Manufacturer and Distributor Margins under Proposed Rebate Plan

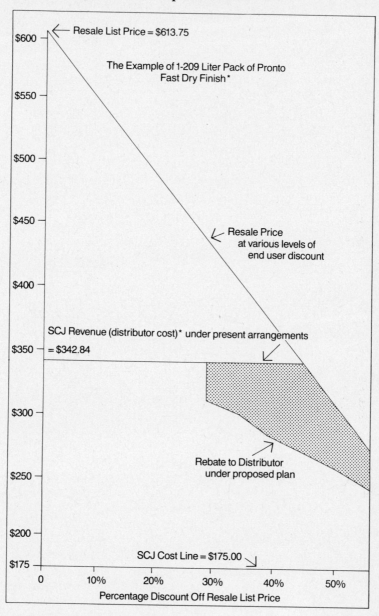

* Assuming 2% quantity ("carload") discount off price to distributor.

price." Whenever competitive conditions required a distributor to discount the resale list price by 30% or more, SCJ would give a certain percentage of the wholesale price back to the distributor. SCJ would sacrifice part of its margin to help offset a heavy end-user discount. Rebate percentages would vary with the rate of discount, following a set schedule. Different schedules were to be established for each product type and size. Exhibits 5, 6, and 7 outline the effect of rebates on both the unit gross margins of SCJ and individual distributors for a specific product example.

The rebate plan was designed for new, "incremental" business only, not for existing distributor accounts. Distributors would be required to seek SCJ approval for end-user discounts of over 30% of resale list. The maximum allowable end-user discount would rarely exceed 50%. To request rebate payments, distributors would send SCJ a copy of the resale invoice along with a written claim. The rebate would then be paid within 60 days.

Proponents of the plan maintained that the resulting resale price flexibility would not only enhance INNOCHEM competitiveness among end users, but would also diminish distributor attraction to private label.

As he studied the plan, George questioned whether all the implications were fully understood and wondered what other strategies, if any, might increase urban market penetration. Any plan he devised would have to be sold to distributors as well as to corporate management. George had only three weeks to develop an appropriate action plan.

Trus Joist Corporation (B)*

Mr. Mike Kalish, salesman for the Micro=Lam® Division of Trus Joist Corporation, had just received another moderately sized order for the product Micro=Lam laminated veneer lumber; however, the order held particular interest for him. The unique feature of the order was that the material Micro=Lam was to be used as a truck trailer bedding material. This represented the second-largest order ever processed for that function.

Earlier in the fall of 1978, Mr. Kalish had spent some time in contacting prospective customers for truck trailer flooring in the Northwest and Midwest; however, the response from manufacturers had been disappointing. Despite this reception, smaller local builders of truck trailers were interested and placed several small orders for Micro=Lam laminated veneer lumber. The order Mr. Kalish had just received was from one of the midwestern companies he had contacted earlier, thus renewing his belief that the trailer manufacturing industry held great potential for Micro=Lam laminated veneer lumber as a flooring material.

* This case is produced with the permission of Dr. Stuart U. Rich, Professor of Marketing and Director, Forest Industries Management Center, College of Business Administration, University of Oregon, Eugene, Oregon.

Company Background

The Trus Joist Corporation, headquartered in Boise, Idaho, is a manufacturer of structural wood products with plants located in the Pacific Northwest, Midwest, Southeast, and Southwest. Annual sales, which totaled over $78 million in 1978, were broken down into three major product categories: the Micro=Lam Division, contributing 7 percent of sales (the majority of Micro=Lam sales were internal); the Commercial Divisions, with 82 percent of sales; and the Residential Sales Program, with 11 percent of sales.

In the late 1950s, Art Troutner and Harold Thomas developed a unique concept in joist design, implemented a manufacturing process for the design, and then founded the Trus Joint Corporation. By 1978, the company employed over 1,000 people, of whom about 180 were sales personnel. The majority of salesmen were assigned to the regional Commercial Division sales offices; four outside salesmen were assigned to the Micro=Lam Division. The functions of selling and manufacturing were performed at each of the five geographically organized Commercial Divisions; therefore, the salesmen concentrated on geographic selling. The Micro=Lam Division was more centralized in nature, conducting all nationwide sales and manufacturing activities from Eugene, Oregon.

In 1971, Trus Joist first introduced and patented Micro=Lam laminated veneer lumber. The product is made of thin $\frac{1}{10}'$- or $\frac{1}{8}'$-thick veneer sheets of Douglas fir glued together by a waterproof phenol formaldehyde adhesive. Under exact and specified conditions, the glued sheets are heated and pressed together. The Micro=Lam lumber, or billet,[1] is "extruded" from specially-made equipment in 80' lengths and 24' widths. The billets can be cut to any customer-desired length or width within those limiting dimensions. The billets come in several thicknesses ranging from $\frac{3}{4}''$ to $2\frac{1}{2}''$; however, $1\frac{1}{2}''$ and $1\frac{3}{4}''$ are the two sizes produced regularly in volume.

Marketing Micro=Lam

When Micro=Lam was first introduced, Trus Joist executives asked an independent research group to perform a study indicating possible industrial applications for the product. The first application for Micro =Lam was to replace the high-quality solid sawn lumber 2″ × 4″ trus chords[2] in its open web joist designs and the solid sawn lumber flanges[3] on its wooden I-beam joist (TJI). Into the fall of 1978, this still represented the majority of Micro=Lam production. The findings of the research report suggested that Micro=Lam could be used as scaffold

---

[1] Micro=Lam is manufactured in units called billets, and the basic unit is one billet foot. The actual dimensions of a billet foot are 1′ × 2′ × 1½″, and one billet is 80′ × 24′ × 1½′.

[2] Trus chords are the top and bottom components in an open web trus incorporating wood chords and tubular steel webs.

[3] Flanges are the top and bottom components in an all-wood I-beam. Refer to Exhibit 1.

Exhibit 1   End View of an All-Wood I-Beam (TJI)

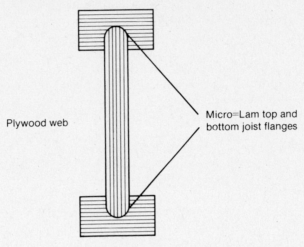

Plywood web

Micro=Lam top and
bottom joist flanges

planking, mobile home trus chords, and housing components. These products accounted for about 25 percent of the Micro=Lam production. Mr. Kalish had also begun to develop new markets for Micro=Lam, including ladder rails and framing material for office partitions.

When marketing Micro=Lam to potential customers, Trus Joist emphasized the superior structural qualities of the product over conventional lumber. Micro=Lam did not possess the undesirable characteristics of warping, checking, and twisting, yet it did show greater bending strength and more structural stability. (One ad claimed, "Testing proves Micro=Lam to be approximately 30% stiffer than #1 dense select structural Douglas fir.") In some applications, Micro=Lam offered distinct price advantages over its competing wood alternatives and this factor always proved to be a good selling point. Manufacturers were often concerned about the lead/delivery time involved in ordering Micro=Lam. Trus Joist promised to deliver within one to three weeks of an order, which was often a full two weeks to two months ahead of other wood manufacturers.

The industrial application report had also suggested using Micro=Lam as a decking material for truck trailers. This use became a reality when Sherman Brothers Trucking, a local trucking firm that frequently transported Micro=Lam, made a request for Micro=Lam to redeck some of its worn-out trailers. To increase the durability of the flooring surface, the manufacturing department of Trus Joist replaced the top two veneer sheets of Douglas fir with apitong. Apitong was a Southeast Asian wood known for its strength, durability, and high specific gravity. This foreign hardwood had been used in the United States for several years because of the diminishing supplies of domestic hardwoods. (See Exhibit 2.)

Exhibit 2   Mechanical Properties of Wood Used for Trailer Decking

Common name of Species	Specific Gravity (percent moisture content)	Modules of Elasticity (million psi)	Compression Parallel to Grain and Fiber Strength Maximum Crush Strength (psi)
Apitong	0.59	2.35	8.540
Douglas fir	0.48	1.95	7.240
Alaska yellow cedar	0.42	1.59	6.640
White oak	0.68	1.78	7.440
Northern red oak	0.63	1.82	6.760
Micro=Lam	0.55	2.20	8.200

*Micro=Lam using Douglas fir as the veneer faces of the lumber.

Source: Wood Handbook: Wood as an Engineering Material, USDA Handbook no. 72, rev. ed., 1974: U.S. Forest Products Laboratory.

The pioneer advertisement for Micro=Lam as a trailer deck material had consisted of one ad in a national trade journal and had depicted the Micro=Lam cut so that the edges were used as the top surface. (See Exhibit 3.) The response from this ad had been dismal and had resulted in only one or two orders. The latest advertisement depicting Micro =Lam as it was currently being used (with apitong as the top veneer layers) had better results. This ad, sent to every major truck or trailer manufacturing journal as a news release on a new product, resulted in 30 to 50 inquiries which turned into 10 to 15 orders. Approximately 15 decks were sold as a result of the promotion.

Everyone at Trus Joist believed that the current price on Micro =Lam was the absolute rock bottom price possible. In fact, most people believed that Micro=Lam was underpriced. The current price of Micro =Lam included a gross margin of 20 percent. The price of 1¼" thick and 1½" thick Micro=Lam was based on the costs of a 1½" billet. The total variable costs of 1½" material were multiplied by ⅚ to estimate the same costs of 1¼" material. There had recently been some discussion over the appropriateness of this ratio. Some of the marketing personnel believed that a more appropriate estimate of the variable costs for the 1¼" Micro=Lam would be the ratio of the number of veneers in a 1¼" billet to the number of veneers in a 1½" billet, or ¹⁴⁄₁₆. At the present time, the costs of veneer represented 55 percent of the selling price. Glue cost was approximately 13 cents/square foot; fixed overhead represented 14 cents/square foot; and other variable costs amounted to approximately 12½ cents/square foot. The total variable costs were divided by 0.80 to cover all selling and administrative expenses and to secure a profit.[4]

[4] All cost figures have been disguised.

Exhibit 3   End View of *Remanufactured* Micro = Lam

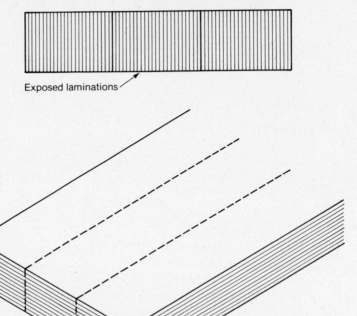

Exposed laminations

Original Micro=Lam billet depicting the cutting path (-------) during the remanufacturing process

In 1977, truck trailer manufacturers ordered and used 46 million square feet for installation in new truck trailer construction. This figure was understated because redecking or replacement of worn-out floors of trailers had not been incorporated, and there was little organized information to determine what this potential could be. As of 1975, 236 truck trailer manufacturers produced $646.7 million worth of trailers. (See Exhibits 4 and 5.)

The problem Mr. Kalish saw with this aggregate data was that it was not broken down into the various segments of trailer builders. For example, not all of the 236 manufacturers produced trailers which used wooden floors. Among those not using wooden floors were tankers and logging trailers. Mr. Kalish believed that the real key to selling Micro =Lam in this industry would be to determine the segment of the trailer industry on which he should concentrate his selling efforts. Mr. Kalish also knew that he somehow had to determine trailer manufacturers' requirements for trailer decking. The Eugene-Portland, Oregon, area offered what he thought to be a good cross section of the type of trailer manufacturers that might be interested in Micro=Lam. He had already contacted some of those firms about buying Micro=Lam.

Exhibit 4 Truck Trailer Shipments and Dollar Value (by calendar year)

	1975	1974	1973	1972	1971
Complete trailers and chassis	67,888	191,262	167,201	141,143	103,784
Value	$613,702,000	$1,198,520,000	$956,708,000	$795,500,000	$585,264,000
Containers	4,183*	10,108*	18,626	18,166	8,734
Value	$18,071,000	$27,343,000	$60,159,000	$51,527,000	$26,514,000
Container chassis	2,936	12,883	12,790	15,498	9,775
Value	$14,898,000	$42,076,000	$33,143,000	$39,028,000	$24,999,000
Total units	75,007	214,253	198,617	174,807	122,293
Value	$646,671,000	$1,267,939,000	$1,050,010,000	$886,055,000	$636,777,000

Source: Ward's Automotive Yearbook, 1978, p. 91.

Truck Trailer Manufacturers Association Data for 1975 preliminary and subject to slight possible change.

*Containers not reported June–October 1974 and January–March 1975.

Exhibit 5   Truck Trailer Manufacturers

Allentown Brake & Wheel Service, Inc., Allentown, Pa.
Allied Products Corp., Chicago, Ill.
Aluminum Body Corp., Montebello, Calif.
American Body & Equipment Co., Grand Prairie, Tex.
American Trailers, Inc., Oklahoma City, Okla.
Anthony Co., Streator, Ill.
Atlantic International Corp., Baltimore, Md.
Atlantic International Marketing Corp., Baltimore, Md.
Atlantic Manufacturing Corp., Baltimore, Md.
Atlantic Mobile Corp., Cockeysville, Md.
Atlas Hoist & Body, Inc., Montreal, Que., Can.
Bartlett Trailer Corp., Chicago, Ill.
Bethlehem Fabricators, Inc., Bethlehem, Pa.
Adam Black & Sons, Inc., Jersey City, N.J.
Black Diamond Enterprises, Inc., Bristol, Va.
Herman Born & Sons, Inc., Baltimore, Md.
Budd Co., Troy, Mich.
Centennial Industries Division, Columbus, Ga.
Copco Trailer Division, South Bend, Ind.
Custom Trailers, Inc., Springfield, Mo.
Delta Truck Trailer Co., Inc., Camden, Ark.
Distribution International Corp., Ft. Washington, Pa.
Dorsey Corp., Chattanooga, Tenn.
Dorsey Trailers, Inc., Elba, Ala.
Dura Corp., Southfield, Mich.
Durobilt Mfg. Co., El Monte, Calif.
Eight Point Trailer Corp., Los Angeles, Calif.
Essick Mfg. Co., Los Angeles, Calif.
Evans Products, Portland, Ore.
Expediter Systems, Inc., Birmingham, Ala.
Firmers Lumber & Supply Co., Sioux City, Iowa
Ford Motor Co., Dearborn, Mich.
Ford Motor Co. of Canada Ltd., Oakville, Ont., Can.
Fruehauf Corp., Detroit, Mich.
Fruehauf Trailer Co. of Canada Ltd., Dixie, Ont., Can.
General Body Mfg. Co., Inc., Kansas City, Mo.
Gerstenslager Co., Wooster, Ohio
Great Dane Trailers, Inc., Savannah, Ga.
Hawker Siddeley Canada Ltd., Toronto, Ont., Can.
Hendrickson Mfg. Co., Lyons, Ill.
Hercules Mfg. Co., Henderson, Ky.

Source: Poor's Register

General Trailer Company

Mr. Jim Walline had been the purchasing agent for General Trailer
Company of Springfield, Oregon, for the past 2½ years. He stated, "The
engineering department makes the decisions on what materials to buy. I
place the orders after the requisition has been placed on my desk."

Hesse Corp., Kansas City, Mo.
Highway Trailers of Canada Ltd., Cooksville, Ont., Can.
Hobbs Trailers, Fort Worth, Tex.
Hyster Co., Portland, Ore.
Leland Equipment Co., Tulsa, Okla.
Lodestar Corp., Niles, Ohio
McCade-Powers Body Co., St. Louis, Mo.
McQuerry Trailer Co., Fort Worth, Tex.
Meyers Industries, Inc., Tecumseh, Mich.
Mindustrial Corp., Ltd., Toronto, Ont., Can.
Mitsubishi Electric Corp., Chiyoda-ku, Tokyo, 100, Japan
Moline Body Co., Moline, Ill.
Montone Mfg. Co., Hazelton, Pa.
Nabors Trailers, Inc., West Palm Beach, Fla.
Noble Division (Waterloo Plant), Waterloo, Iowa
OMC-Lincoln, Lincoln, Neb.
Ohio Body Mfg. Co., New London, Ohio
Olson Trailer & Body Builders Co., Green Bay, Wis.
Pike Trailer Co., Los Angeles, Calif.
Pointer Truck Trailer Co., Renton, Wash.
Polar Manufacturing Co., Holdingford, Minn.
Pullman, Inc., Chicago, Ill.
Pullman Trailmobile, Chicago, Ill.
Ravens-Metal Products, North Parkersburg, W.Va.
Reliance Trailer Manufacturing, Cotati, Calif.
Remke, Inc., Roseville, Mich.
Rogers Bros. Corp., Albion, Pa.
Shetky Equipment Corp., Portland, Ore.
Southwest Truck Body Company, St. Louis, Mo.
Starcraft Corp., Goshen, Ind.
Sterling Precision Corp., West Palm Beach, Fla.
Thiele, Inc., Windber, Pa.
Timpte, Inc., Denver, Colo.
Timpte Industries, Inc., Denver, Colo.
Trailco, Hummels Wharf, Pa.
Transport Trailers, Cedar Rapids, Iowa
Troyler Corp., Scranton, Pa.
Utility Tool & Body Co., Clintonville, Wis.
Valley Tow-Rite, Lodi, Calif.
Peter Wendel & Sons, Inc., Irvington, N.J.
Whitehead & Kales Co., River Rouge, Mich.
Williamsen Truck Equipment Corp., Salt Lake City, Utah

General Trailer Company was a manufacturer of several different types of trailers: low-boys, chip trailers, log trailers, and flatbeds. In 1977, General manufactured five flatbeds and redecked five flatbeds. General did most of its business with the local timber industry; however, it sold three flatbeds in 1977 to local firms in the steel industry.

The flatbeds General Trailer manufactured were 40' to 45' long and approximately 7' wide. Log trailers were approximately 20' to 25' long.

General Trailer manufactured trailers primarily for the West Coast market, although it had sold a few trailers to users in Alaska. On the West Coast, General's major competitors were Peerless, Fruehauf, and Trailmobile, all large-scale manufacturers of truck trailers. Even though General was comparatively small in size, it did not feel threatened, because "we build a top-quality trailer which is not mass-produced," as Mr. Walline put it.

General had been using apitong as a trailer decking material until customers complained of its weight and its expansion/contraction characteristics when exposed to weather. At that time, Mr. Schmidt, the general manager and head of the engineering department, made the decision to switch from apitong to laminated fir.

Laminated fir (consisting of solid sawn lumber strips glued together) was currently being used as the material for decking flatbeds, and Pacific Laminated Company of Vancouver, Washington, supplied all of General's fir decking, so General would only order material when a customer bought a new trailer or needed to have a trailer redecked. Mr. Walline was disappointed with the two- to three-week delivery time, since it often meant that much more time before the customer's trailer was ready.

Laminated fir in 40' lengths, 11¾" widths, and 1¼" thickness was used by General. General paid approximately $2 to $3 per square foot for this decking.

Even though Pacific Laminated could provide customer-cut and edged pieces with no additional lead time, General preferred ship-lapped fir in the previously noted dimensions, with the top two layers treated with a waterproof coating.

The different types of trailers General manufactured required different decking materials. Low-boys required material 2¼" thick and General used 3" × 12" rough-cut fir lumber. Chip trailers required ⅝"-thick MDO (medium density overlay) plywood with a slick surface.

Mr. Walline said General had used Micro=Lam on one trailer; however, the customer had not been expecting it and was very displeased with the job.[5] Therefore, the current policy was to use only laminated fir for the local market unless a customer specifically ordered a different decking material. Trailers headed for Alaska were decked with laminated oak, supplied by a vendor other than Pacific Laminated.

---

[5] After purchasing Micro=Lam, General Trailer modified the material by ripping the billets into 1½" widths and then relaminating these strips back into 12"- or 24"-wide pieces of lumber. This remanufacturing added substantial costs. Also, the laminations were now directly exposed to the weather. Moisture could more easily seep into cracks or voids, causing swells and buckling. (See Exhibit 3.)

Mr. Walline said that if he wanted to make a recommendation to change decking materials, he would need to know price advantages, lead times, moisture content, availability, and industry experience with the material.

Sherman Brothers Trucking

"We already use Micro=Lam on our trailers," was the response of Mr. Sherman, president of Mayflower Moving and Storage Company, when asked about the trailer decking material his company used. He went on to say, "In fact, we had hauled several shipments for Trus Joist when we initiated a call to them asking if they could make a decking material for us."

Mayflower Moving and Storage owned 60 trailers (flatbeds) which it used to haul heavy equipment and machinery. It had been in a dilemma for eight years about the types of materials used to replace the original decks. Nothing seemed to be satisfactory. Solid apitong was tough, but it was too heavy and it did not weather very well. Plywood did not provide adequate weight distribution and had too many joints. Often the small wheels of the forklifts would break through the decking, or heavy equipment with steel legs would punch a hole through the decks. Laminated fir was too expensive.

Mayflower Moving and Storage was currently redecking a trailer per week. It usually patched the decks until the whole bed fell apart; then the trailer would sit in the yard waiting for a major overhaul. By this time the trailers needed to have the crossbeams repaired and new bearings as well as a new deck.

Mr. Sherman went on to say, "The shop mechanic just loves Micro =Lam. This is because it used to take the mechanic and one other employee two days to redeck a trailer, and now it just takes the shop mechanic one day to do the same job." Advantages (over plywood and apitong) of the 2' × 40' Micro=Lam pieces were ease of installation, excellent weight distribution due to the reduced number of seams, and reduced total weight of the bed.

Mr. Sherman explained that Mayflower Moving and Storage usually purchased four or five decks at a time, and warehoused some of the materials until a trailer needed redecking.

Mr. Sherman thought the original decking on flatbeds was some type of hardwood, probably oak, which could last up to five years; however, a similar decking material had not been found for a reasonable price. The plywood and fir decks used in the past 8 to 10 years had lasted anywhere from 1 to 2 years, and some had worn out in as little as six months. After using Micro=Lam for six months, Mr. Sherman expected the decking to last up to three to five years.

When asked about the type of flooring used in the company's moving vans, Mr. Sherman emphasized the top care that those floors received. "We sand, buff, and wax them just like a household floor; in fact, we take such good care of these floors they will occasionally outlast the trailer." The original floors in moving vans were made out of a laminated oak and had to be kept extremely smooth, allowing freight to slide freely without the possibility of damaging items of freight with legs. The local company purchased all of its moving vans through Mayflower Moving Vans. The only problem with floors in moving vans was that the jointed floors would occasionally buckle because of swelling.

The fact that Micro=Lam protruded ⅛" above the metal lip[6] which edged the flatbed trailers posed no problem for Sherman Brothers. "All we had to do was plane the edge at 40 degrees. In fact, the best fit will have the decking protrude a hair above the metal edge," Mr. Sherman said. Just prior to this, Mr. Sherman had recounted an experience which occurred with the first shipment of Micro=Lam. Because the deck was too thick, Mayflower Moving and Storage had about ⅛" planed from one side of the decking material. However, the company shaved off the apitong veneer, exposing the fir. Mr. Sherman said that he laughed about it now, but at the time he wasn't too pleased.

Peerless Trucking Company

"Sure, I've heard of Micro=Lam. They [Trus Joist salesmen] have been in here. . . . but we don't need that good a material." This was the response of Mel Rogers, head of Peerless' Purchasing Department, Tualatin, Oregon, when asked about the use of Micro=Lam as a truck decking material. Mr. Rogers, a 30-year veteran of the trailer manufacturing industry, seemed very skeptical of all laminated decking materials.

The primary products manufactured by Peerless (in Tualatin) required bedding materials very different from Micro=Lam. Chip trailers and rail car dumpers required metal beds to facilitate unloading. Lowboys required a heavy decking material (usually 2" × 12" or 3" × 12" rough planking) as Caterpillar tractors were frequently driven on them. Logging trailers had no beds.

Approximately 60 decks per year were required by Peerless in the manufacture of flatbeds and in redecking jobs. Micro=Lam could have been used in these applications, but fir planking was used exclusively, except for some special overseas jobs. Fir planking was available in full trailer lengths, requiring eight man-hours to install on new equipment. Usually, five or six decks were stocked at a time. The estimated life of a new deck was two to three years.

Fir planking was selected for decking applications on the basis of price and durability. Peerless purchased fir planking for $1,000 per MBF. Tradition supported fir planking in durability, as it was a well-known product.

[6] Refer to Exhibit 6.

**Exhibit 6   Cross-Sectional End View of Trailer
Decking (Tongue and Groove)**

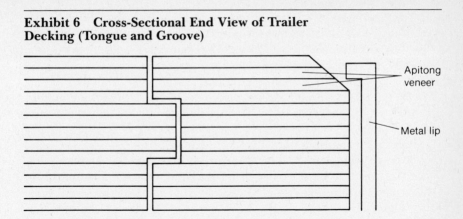

Apitong
veneer

Metal lip

Decking material thickness was critical, according to Mr. Rogers, as any deviation from the industry standard of 1⅜″ required extensive retooling.

Any new decking materials for use in original equipment manufacture had to be approved by the Peerless engineering department. Alternative decking materials could have been used locally if specified by the customer.

Mr. Rogers was certainly going to be a hard person to sell on the use of Micro=Lam. Mr. Kalish felt, "Why use Micro=Lam when I can buy fir planking for less?" Rogers had said.

Fruehauf Trucking Company

"I'd be very happy if someone would come up with a durable [trailer] deck at a reasonable price," was the response of Wayne Peterson when asked about Fruehauf's experience with decking materials. Mr. Peterson was service manager for Fruehauf's factory branch in Milwaukie, Oregon. Fruehauf Corporation, with its principal manufacturing facilities in Detroit, Michigan, was one of the nation's largest manufacturers of truck trailers.

The manufacturing facilities in Milwaukie produced 40-ton low-beds as well as assembled truck bodies manufactured in Detroit. The low-beds were subjected to heavy use, often with forklifts, which required a decking material of extreme strength and durability. Laminated decking materials then available were therefore excluded from this application.

The decking materials used in the truck bodies were specified by the sales department in Detroit, based on customer input. Generally, apitong or laminated oak was installed at the factory. Any new product to be used in original equipment manufacture had to be approved by Fruehauf's well-developed factory engineering department.

The Milwaukie operation also did about 15 redecking jobs per year. The decking material was specified by the customer on the basis of price and weathering characteristics. The materials used were laminated oak (11½″ W × 40′), apitong (7″ × ⅛″—random lengths), Alaska yellow cedar (2″ × 6″ T&G), fir planking (2″ × 6″ T&G), and laminated fir (24″ W × 40′). Alaska yellow cedar was priced below all other decking materials, followed (in order) by fir planking, laminated fir, laminated oak, and apitong.

Fruehauf's suppliers of decking materials were as follows: laminated fir—Pacific Laminating, Vancouver, Washington; Alaska yellow cedar—Al Disdero Lumber Company, Portland, Oregon; and apitong—Builterials, Portland, Oregon. There were no specific suppliers for the other materials.

A minimum inventory of decking materials was kept on hand to allow for immediate repair needs only. Orders were placed for complete decks as needed.

A redecking job typically required 30 man-hours per 7′ × 40′ trailer, including the removal of the old deck and installation of the new one. Decking materials that were available in full trailer lengths were preferred, as they greatly reduced installation time, improved weight distribution, and had fewer joints along which failure could occur.

The use of alternative products, such as composition flooring of wood and aluminum, was not under consideration.

Alaska yellow cedar and fir planking had the best weathering characteristics, while apitong and laminated oak weathered poorly. Oak and apitong did, however, have a hard, nonscratching surface that was desirable in enclosed use. When asked about the weathering characteristics of laminated flooring in general, Mr. Peterson responded, "It's all right for the dry states, but not around here."

Competition

There were a large number of materials with which Micro=Lam competed in the trailer flooring market, ranging from fir plywood to aluminum floors. Trus Joist felt that the greatest obstacles to Micro=Lam's success would be from the old standard products like laminated fir and oak, which had a great deal of industry respect. For years, oak had been the premier flooring material; recently, however, supplies had been short and delivery times long (two months in some cases), and prices were becoming prohibitive. (See Exhibit 7.)

Mr. Kalish had found that in the Northwest, Pacific Laminated Company was one of the major flooring suppliers to local manufacturers. Pacific Laminated produced a Douglas fir laminated product that was highly popular; however, like oak, it was relatively high-priced. Despite the price, Pacific Laminated could cut the product to dimensions up to 2′ wide and 40′ long. Delivery time was excellent for its customers,

Exhibit 7   Decking Material Prices, November 1978

Product	Price	Form
Alaska yellow cedar	$650/MBF	2" × 6" T&B 15' lengths
Apitong	$1.30–$2/lineal foot*	1⅜" × 7" random lengths
Fir planking	$1/bd. ft.	2" × 6" T&G random lengths
Fir laminated	$2.50/sq. ft.	1¼" × 11¾" × 40'
Micro=Lam	$1.30/sq. ft.	1¼" × 24" × 40'
	$1.50/sq. ft.	1½" × 24" × 40'
Oak laminated	$2.20/sq. ft.	1⅜" × 1½" × 40'

*Lineal foot—price per unit length of the product

Sources: Al Disdero Lumber Company, Portland, Oregon, Builterials, Portland, Oregon

even with special milling for shiplapped or tongue and groove edges and manufacturing to user thickness.

Conclusion

Although Mr. Kalish had had limited success marketing Micro=Lam to truck trailer manufacturers, he was concerned with the marketing program for his product. Several trailer manufacturers had raised important questions concerning the price and durability of Micro=Lam compared to alternative decking materials. He knew Micro=Lam had some strong attributes, yet he was hesitant to expand beyond the local market. Mr. Kalish was also wondering about the action he should eventually take in order to determine the additional information he would need to successfully introduce Micro=Lam nationally as a trailer decking material. One thought that crossed his mind was to define the company's marketing strategy for this product. Meanwhile, small orders continued to trickle in.

Boltronics Corporation*

On April 1, 1976, Bob McAfee left his position as a manufacturing manager for W. R. Grace, a large industrial company, to devote his full efforts to Boltronics Corporation, a "panel shop" company he had founded. Presently, Boltronics was primarily an assembler of electrical control panels which started, stopped, or regulated machinery. (Exhibit 1 shows control panels for a piece of production equipment.) Boltronics'

*Copyright 1977, Dan T. Dunn, Jr., Associate Professor, College of Business Administration, Northeastern University, Boston, Massachusetts.

Exhibit 1   Control Panels for a Piece of Production Equipment

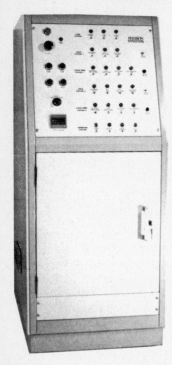

production facilities were now located in the basement of McAfee's home; a spare bedroom served as the president's office. Boltronics had been incorporated six months before, and until April 1 it had been treated as a nighttime and weekend enterprise by Mr. McAfee and several others involved. Sales so far totaled about $12,000.

McAffee wanted to reassess how to make Boltronics grow to a sales level of well over $100,000 annually.[1] Boltronics had already filled or booked several orders, but additional orders would have to be booked soon and, moreover, possibly a whole new marketing strategy developed to provide desired sales. It was possible that the company should move away from serving mainly as an assembly subcontractor for control panels. For example, Boltronics could try to deal more directly with final buyers rather than as a subcontractor for some other supplier. And there were many other possible ways to "grow" Boltronics. McAfee was considering initiating some type of market research project to assess alternative strategies possibly available to Boltronics.

---

[1] McAfee's basement production facility could handle such a sales level. The maximum level was probably $200,000 annually.

Genesis of the Boltronics Enterprise

For at least 10 years McAfee had wanted to start his own company. His dream was some day to own a series of small companies, each with sales probably under $1 million, so that the total operations would be substantial. This desire began while he served as an electrical engineer and afterward as a nuclear engineer for the Navy (1960–70) and extended through his years at W. R. Grace. (McAfee had graduated from the Naval Academy and later had completed two electrical engineering degrees at the Massachusetts Institute of Technology.)

McAfee had joined a W. R. Grace plant in Lexington, Massachusetts, in 1970 as a project engineer, where he defined his initial responsibilities as follows:

Once the decision to build a plant was made, then all responsibilities regarding plant construction and operation were the project engineer's. The function was multifaceted. Areas of responsibility included finance, construction, engineering, and continual contact with all suppliers involved in the operation. In fact, there was as much or more contact with outside suppliers as inside contact with other Grace affiliates.

In 1971 McAfee was promoted to manufacturing manager of the Letterflex Systems Group, which was a part of the company's Polyfibron Division. The Letterflex Systems Group, with sales of about $20 million, was involved primarily in the design of machines used for printing newspapers and commercial products (textbooks, etc.) and the manufacture of the chemicals used in the machine process. Specifically, the Letterflex System developed a Letterflex Plate for printing which utilized a liquid photopolymer curable with photoelectric light. The actual assembly of Letterflex machines was contracted to outside companies, while the chemicals were made by Grace.

At Letterflex, McAfee had supervised 30 people and managed over $750,000 in overhead. Primarily, McAfee said he was accountable for getting "the parts in, the people in, and the production out on schedule." He frequently dealt with outside contractors. Concerning control panels, he managed a group of engineers who designed various pieces of production equipment, many relying upon such controls. Most of this equipment was designed by McAfee and his staff and built by outside electrical-mechanical contractors (subcontractors).

In one instance, he had been responsible for designing and later debugging a new machine built by outside contractors. When the new machine was completed under budget and in one half the time predicted, McAfee said he developed a reputation as "something of an expert with regard to project engineering and research and development."

In addition, experience with this project crystallized some of McAfee's feelings about contracting electrical-mechanical equipment to outside suppliers. Specifically, as a customer, he was distressed that he could not find a reliable supplier to provide a complete "machine controls package." Typically, what happened was that an outside machine

shop, in turn, had to subcontract the design and/or assembly of associated control panels. This procedure, according to McAfee, slowed deliveries of the equipment and at least raised the possibility that the control
panels were more expensive than necessary and/or of rather unknown
quality. However, he had no idea whether buyers at other firms shared
these feelings.

In late 1975, W. R. Grace told McAfee to expect a transfer to Baltimore due to "the recession's effect on Letterflex orders." Considering
the transfer a lateral shift in his career and not anxious to leave New
England, McAfee began to seriously consider starting his own business.
The problems he personally had experienced with suppliers seemed an
obvious area for further investigation.

Market Information Gathered Prior to April 1976

By April 1976, McAfee already knew something about a number of companies which he considered Boltronics' competitors since he had dealt
with them as Grace suppliers. It was common for Grace to let several
outside contractors compete for a job, and part of the screening process
involved asking questions about supplier products, operations, personnel, financial strength, etc. For example, he knew that three or four
panel shops had sales of almost $500,000 in the New England area.

McAfee had tried to organize his thoughts about these suppliers-
turned-competitors. Depending upon how he defined Boltronics' business, McAfee thought that there could be several categories of potential
competitors, performing one or more of the following functions:

1. Parts distribution   According to the Yellow Pages, at least 100 small
and medium-sized Greater Boston concerns were parts distributors
(manufacturer's representatives) for component parts manufacturers
(among electrical parts manufacturers were such well-known companies
as General Electric and Westinghouse and a host of other companies).
Parts distributors carried a variety of parts made by different companies.
(See Exhibit 2 for the products of one "full-line" distributor.)

Electrical parts were used in a wide variety of applications, including control panels. Parts might find themselves in control panels in several ways. McAfee offered the framework shown at top of page 525.

Parts distributors usually received discounts of 49 percent off "list"
prices; those who bought "at wholesale" (e.g., panel shops, contractors,
certain OEMs) from such distributors received 41 percent off list. (Final
users/buyers were normally billed at list prices.)

Some distributors had large parts sales to panel shops, while others
concentrated on self-manufacture, he thought. Parts sales to other contractors and OEMs could also vary substantially between distributors,
McAfee noted, although he was not sure of the actual variation among
the parts distributors in his area.

*Knows about suppliers – how best
to approach them?*

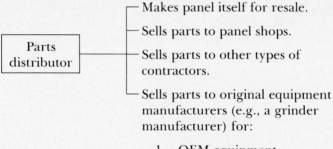

	— Makes panel itself for resale.
Parts distributor	— Sells parts to panel shops.
	— Sells parts to other types of contractors.
	— Sells parts to original equipment manufacturers (e.g., a grinder manufacturer) for:

1. OEM equipment.
2. Resale by OEMs.
3. Repairs on OEM equipment.
4. "House" wiring of OEM.

2. Control panel assembly According to McAfee, many parts distributors also assembled parts into finished control panels, having initially added this operation to support parts sales to certain customers who also demanded assembly. McAfee felt sure that such assembly was much less important to the shops than parts sales, in terms of both revenue and profit. He guessed that control panel assembly accounted for less than 15 percent of most concerns' total sales. Since most concerns were not specialists in assembling control panels, McAfee thought that they were not always the most efficient. For example, he had "priced out" one control panel done by a Grace supplier, and figured that the components cost could have been lowered 20 percent by substituting completely adequate but less expensive components.

There were also an undetermined number of panel assembly operations not owned by a parts distributor, although many assemblers sought to establish some type of long-term relationship with distributors in order to seek price concessions, get referrals, etc.

3. Control panel design According to McAfee, the design work for control panels done by parts distributors and/or assemblers ranged from "very good to homemade and unnecessarily expensive." Few of these concerns employed degreed engineers, and much of the design work was "based on experience with similar designs or was drawn from information supplied by the components manufacturers." It should be noted that many assemblers used designs supplied by customers (for example, at W. R. Grace, McAfee himself had done the design for many control panels that were then assembled by outside companies). McAfee also thought that, regardless of the design source, many control panels also were "not designed with human engineering in mind" and that placement of control buttons, switches, etc., was important to plant workers using them. McAfee believed that most designers, as well as many manufacturing managers, thought too little of such operator needs.

Exhibit 2   Product Brochure of a Parts Distributor

Mount Electric Company
Electrical Distributor
Worcester, Massachusetts

Ballasts
  Advance
  General Electric
  Jefferson
Batteries—flashlights
  Ray-O-Vac
  Union Carbide (Eveready)
*Bells—buzzers—signals
  Edwards
  Federal
  General Electric
*Blocks—terminal
  Buchanan
  Connectron
  Cutler-Hammer
  General Electric
Boxes—enclosures
  Appleton
  Hoffman
  Lee
  Raco
  Red Dot
  Steel City
Cable grips
  Kellems

Fixtures
  Compakett (Photo-Sw)
  Day-O-Lite
  Dazor
  Holophane
  Litecontrol
  Miller
  Stocker & Yale
  Stonco
  Swivelier
  Sylvania
  O. C. White
*Fuses—accessories
  Buss
  Chase-Shawmut
  Connecticut
  General Electric
  Ideal
  Littelfuse
  Marathon
  Mini-Breaker
Greenfield
  American Flexible Conduit
*Heating devices
  Chromalox
  General Electric

Tape
  General Electric
  Minnesota Mining & Manufacturing Co. (3M)
  Plymouth
Testing equipment
  General Electric
  Ideal
  Mueller
  Sperry Instruments
*Transformers
  Acme
  Edwards
  General Electric
  Hevi-Duty
  Jefferson
*Wire
  American Electric Cable
  American Flexible Conduit (Bx)
  Brand Rex
  Carol
  Cornish
  Excel
  General Electric
  PWC
  Rome
  United States Steel

527

Conduit—accessories
  Greenlee
*Conduit—emt
  E.T.P.
  Kaiser
  Republic
*Controls—motor and distribution
  Cutler-Hammer
  General Electric
  Micro Farmer
  Micro Switch
Emergency lighting
  Chloride
  Dual-Lite
  Litecor
Fans
  Airmaster (Diehl)
*Fittings
  Appleton
  Briscon
  Efcor
  O.Z. Gedney
  Russell & Stoll
  Thomas & Betts
  Victor

Lamps
  General Electric
  Sylvania
Meter equipment
  Anchor
Proximity switches
  Cutler-Hammer
  General Electric
  Micro Farmer
  Micro Switch
  Tann Controls
Sealtite
  Anaconda
Solder
  M. W. Dunton
*Switches
  Cutler-Hammer
  General Electric
  Linemaster
  Micro Farmer
  Micro Switch
  McGill
  Tann Controls

Wire clamps, staples, etc.
  Briscon
  Victor
*Wire connectors—lugs
  Atlas-Rattan (Marr)
  Burndy
  Ideal
  Ilsco
  Minnesota Mining & Manufacturing Co. (3M)
  Thomas & Betts
*Wire markers
  W. H. Brady Co.
  Stranco
  T&B (E-Z Line)
Wireway-racks
  ECP Corp.
  Hoffman
  Kindorf (Steel City)
  Power Strut (Power Eng.)
  Taylor
  Wiremold
Wiring devices
  General Electric
  Harvey Hubbell
  McGill
  Daniel Woodhead

Established 1885

Call us for your electrical needs

Manufacturers' catalogs available on request

*Types of parts bought by Boltronics and other panel shops.

Most of the Boston-area concerns with one or more of the above functions (1–3) were local companies, according to McAfee. There was one notable exception, however—the Foxboro Company. Foxboro, a $300 million company with headquarters in New England, made and sold parts and designed and assembled control panels, in addition to other operations.[2] McAfee said, "Maybe I could become a Foxboro."

4. Contractors According to McAfee, competition could also come from certain other concerns:

A. *Electrical-mechanical contractors* (sometimes called machine builders) A few large shops apparently provided a complete machine controls package without subcontracting out any part of the job. A piece of production equipment which automatically blended paint was one example McAfee knew of. The contractor had assembled and fabricated metal and plastic parts and supplied as well the electrical drive and associated control systems. The Greater Boston Yellow Pages listed about 30 companies calling themselves electrical-mechanical contractors. (The Yellow Pages had no separate electrical-mechanical contractor heading; rather, the company names were found under such headings as machine shops and electrical contractors.)

B. *Machine shops* (mechanical contractors) The Yellow Pages listed over 300 shops which designed, assembled, and/or fabricated parts, finished items, installations, etc. McAfee believed that the great majority of shops had to subcontract electrical control systems, if needed, to electrical contractors, control panel shops, etc. An undetermined number of shops had ties with a parts or panel business.

C. *Electrical contractors* The Yellow Pages also listed over 375 electrical contractors ranging from residential electricians to larger companies in the commercial market with a broad line of products and/or services. An unknown number designed and assembled control panels or had subcontractors.

D. *Controls, control systems, and regulator companies* The Yellow Pages also listed over 135 concerns under this heading. (Some were also listed under electrical contractors.) The companies ranged from Digital Equipment, Foxboro, Honeywell, and General Electric to local panel shops and parts distributors. McAfee thought that at least 11 of these concerns

---

[2] The Foxboro Company is a leading worldwide supplier of instruments and systems for process management and control. Its worldwide customers include the chemical, oil and gas, pulp and paper, power, food, metals, minerals, textile, and marine industries. The company's products range from control instruments and accessories to computer-based process management and control systems. The products are used to measure, indicate, record, control, and monitor such process variables as flow temperature, pressure, and liquid level. The company also provides extensive engineering, training, and field service support to its customers.

Exhibit 3   List of Competitors

Company Name	Panel Designer	Panel Assembler	Parts Dealer	Other Known Information as of April, 1976
Control, Inc.			X	Close ties to Componapart; uses Componapart almost exclusively for its customers who need panels
Control Design, Ltd.	X	X	X	Has excellent engineering capabilities, but fortunately for Boltronics, does not use them well
Rustin & Co.		X	X	
Beta Controls	X	X		Formerly an electrician, turned panel builder
Efficiency Controls				—
Systems Service and Controls, Inc.				—
Bell Company, Ltd.	X	X		
Componapart	X	X		Close ties to Control, Inc.; uses Control, Inc., as a parts dealer and a major source for its designer and assembly business
Wyatt Engineering		X	X	Boltronics buys parts from and also competes, in terms of assembly operations, with Wyatt Engineering
Industrionics	?	?	?	Uncertain as to whether a competitor or not
Mekontrol	?	?	?	Uncertain as to whether a competitor or not

would be direct competitors of Boltronics in the eastern Massachusetts area (see Exhibit 3). There might be others, but he was fairly confident that his list of 11 was complete.

Most of the companies involved in the above activities (1–4) relied heavily on previous customer relations as a method of securing sales. Beyond such direct sales activity, the Yellow Pages and catalogs were also considered important. McAfee could not recall any other major forms of promotion used within the controls business.

5. Indirect competition   Many user companies themselves had the capability "in house," if they chose, to design and assemble control panels. Some of these panels controlled production equipment; other panels were incorporated into OEM items (such as the Letterflex System) which were sold to customers. McAfee could not hazard a guess as to the overall size of this market were it to be placed with outside suppliers. (At

Grace's Letterflex operation, about $75,000 of panel business per year was given to outsider suppliers.)

McAfee had also thought about potential customers for Boltronics. Given his present understanding of the market, he chose to place them in several categories:

1. *Machine shops wanting to become electrical-mechanical contractors.* One way for some machine shops to expand their sales was by also supplying associated controls. Boltronics could possibly seek business from these shops, serving as their subcontractor.

2. *Overflow business of other contractors.* Shops supplying controls could at times, and maybe frequently, McAfee speculated, become overloaded with orders. Rather than turn away business, such shops might take the business and subcontract panels to Boltronics.

3. *Chemical companies.* Process-oriented manufacturing companies such as chemical companies (e.g., W. R. Grace) needed various pieces of production equipment requiring controls. According to McAfee, "The chemical companies are always changing their manufacturing processes and thus need to change or add controls. However, the chemical companies are full of chemical engineers, not electrical engineers who can do the control panel design." There were at least 25 large chemical plants in New England, according to McAfee.

4. *Other manufacturing companies needing machine controls panels.* McAfee thought that food, pulp, textile, and paper, rubber, and perhaps other companies could use Boltronics when they needed control panels for production equipment or OEM items.

For chemical and other types of companies, McAfee viewed the design and assembly of machines and/or controls as an important "make-or-buy" decision. However, he was not sure that many companies were very analytical about the economic and quality trade-offs involved, particularly in the design stage. "Design engineers themselves routinely are responsible for the make-or-buy decision, and they like their in-house designs unless the project is clearly beyond their field of expertise or they're swamped with work," he said.

In an attempt to gain some understanding of the needs of various customers, McAfee had conducted a mail survey of 100 companies in early 1976. The companies, all located in Greater Boston, included machine shops and industrial companies in the chemical, food, textile, paper, and rubber industries. Specific company names had been selected from a list provided by the state of Massachusetts to anyone interested. The survey was addressed to the "Chief Design Engineer" at each company since people's names were not given in the state report.

The survey is shown in Exhibit 4. Four replies were received. Three said "no interest"; a fourth requested a visit by a Boltronics representative.

Exhibit 4   McAfee's Mail Survey

Boltronics Corporation is a newly formed company organized to provide a unique combination of service and product. There are many engineering firms that design electrical control systems for a fee, and there are many electrical shops that build to your design. Boltronics Corp. has the capability to both design and build control systems to meet your requirements. Our design costs you nothing—all you pay for is the control system itself, which is guaranteed to work in your application. The control system will be manufactured in strict accordance with all applicable codes and designed to keep costs to an absolute minimum. We will not proliferate parts at your expense.

Boltronics Corp. employs two graduate electrical engineers with a total of 23 years in the design and manufacture of control systems. Rather than hire full-time talent like this, we offer you the alternative of utilizing our expertise when the need arises.

Boltronics Corp. is anxious to give you the chance to use our design and manufacturing capabilities while expanding your own business base in the process. In the past you may have had to turn down attractive OEM contracts because of the lack of necessary electrical capability. No longer—Boltronics Corp. will completely relieve you of all your electrical headaches. We will design the controls, build them in our own shop, wire your machine, and thoroughly test to demonstrate suitability. We do the work, you control the job. Let us become your electrical design engineers and electrical production shop all in one.

Please . . .

take a few minutes of your time to read our advertisement and give us your response. Thank you!

Sincerely,
Boltronics Corp.

1. Is the service described in our advertising flyer of interest to you? ☐ Yes ☐ No
2. Could our service expand your business? ☐ Yes ☐ No
3. Have you turned down jobs because electrical design and/or assembly were required? ☐ Yes ☐ No
4. Would you be able to bid on OEM machines and equipment if you had access to our electrical skills? ☐ Yes ☐ No
5. Would you like more information about us or our service? ☐ Yes ☐ No
6. Would you like our sales engineer to contact you? ☐ Yes ☐ No

If you checked either 5 or 6 yes, please give us your company name and address

---

Boltronics as of April 1976

In April 1976, Boltronics was, according to McAfee, merely a skeleton of the company he anticipated. Presently he employed only a few part-time assemblers, in addition to his wife, who served as a part-time secretary-bookkeeper, and his teenage son, a part-time assembler.

By April, Boltronics had finished $12,000 in orders and was working on an $11,000 order, a $1,500 order, and a small order or two. The largest order had come from a company that McAfee had known while at Grace. This machine shop, Wicker, Inc., had subcontracted to Boltronics the assembly of several control panels which were part of a Grace order. The $1,500 order came from P. B. Hinkle Company, a machine shop which McAfee had "cold-called." A few small orders ($200–$300 each) had come from a small contractor who was a personal friend of McAfee. It also seemed that Wicker, Inc., might give Boltronics a second order for similar equipment, but Wicker, Inc., wanted it at 3 percent below the price on the first order. All of these orders would absorb present production capacity through the early summer. At the present level of operations, the $11,000 order represented about two months' work.

The first order for Wicker, Inc., according to McAfee, had been priced "at the market," although he could have chosen to "cut price, possibly cut costs by redesign, or have done both." For planning purposes, McAfee tried to estimate his gross margin on the order:

Sales	$11,000
Cost of goods sold:	
Components	5,200
Estimated labor at $5 per hour	1,050
Total cost of goods sold	6,250
Gross margin	$ 4,750

Again, for planning purposes, McAfee made a guess at some probable *minimum fixed manufacturing and delivery costs* for Boltronics for the first year:

Truck depreciation and operation	$1,600
Depreciation on tools	200
Salaried personnel: secretarial	2,000
Total	$3,800

Also, McAfee noted that he had placed a $20,000 loss limit for himself on the Boltronics venture should it turn sour. This amount represented his assets other than his house. As of April, he had invested about $2,000 in tools, equipment, and supplies and in trading in one of his cars for a pickup truck.

Possible Marketing Strategy Alternatives

McAfee wanted to generate an overall marketing strategy that would make Boltronics more stable and prosperous. He knew he was going to have to greatly expand his customer base, possibly changing the basic concept of Boltronics in the process. Most important, he would have to concentrate on new customers. Personal contacts from his W. R. Grace days were exhausted, it appeared, and Boltronics would have to seek business from people who knew neither him nor Boltronics.

As for customer groups, the initial thinking was that they could be one or more of the groups previously discussed. How to turn them into actual buyers was basically unresolved, although McAfee said it was time "to brainstorm about various ways of reaching them, selling them, and keeping them sold." Also unresolved was whether Boltronics should be a control panel designer, a control panel assembler, a parts distributor, or some combination of these. Another issue was, should Boltronics deal at arm's length with other contractors and parts distributors, or should it try to formalize some kind of relationship, as many other panel shops had done? Finally, McAfee could deemphasize panel assembly, concentrating on design and becoming a general design consultant.

Possible Market Research Alternatives

Within the New England-based control panel industry, McAfee knew of no company that conducted "formal" market research such as a mail, telephone, or personal survey of customers. McAfee, though, had taken a marketing course during a night MBA program where market research had been discussed, and wondered if market research was appropriate for Boltronics. About five classes had been spent on the topic. The discussions had focused more on the "managerial aspects" of research (purpose of the research, value of the information, and general research methodology) than on "technical aspects" (specific research sample designs, advanced quantitative data analysis techniques, etc.). McAfee was hopeful that his exposure to market research in school would be helpful in picking an appropriate market research strategy for Boltronics.

At a minimum, McAfee knew that he had several possible research alternatives. First, he had already spoken with the professor for the marketing course he had taken concerning the possibility of retaining the professor on a consulting basis. In his files, he had a letter from the professor outlining a possible research project and some very preliminary estimates of costs (see Exhibit 5).

Second, the professor had introduced him to an undergraduate marketing major at the school who needed a project as part of a course requirement. Several weeks ago, McAfee had spoken with the student, Arthur Marshall, about it. Based on a three-hour meeting with McAfee, Marshall had proposed a research strategy for Boltronics. McAfee would pay for Marshall's out-of-pocket expenses in relation to the project, estimated at $50. The basic elements of the proposed research, scheduled for May and June 1976 and to be conducted by the student under McAfee's supervision, were as follows:

1. Telephone survey of sample of 25 potential customers
    Using a list of sample companies provided by McAfee, Marshall proposed to telephone either the company's purchasing agent or the design engineer responsible for controls. The companies would be drawn from SIC (Standard Industrial Classification) groups thought to be prime candidates for Boltronics business (i.e., food, textiles, fibers, pulp, paper, chemicals, rubber, and nonelectrical production machinery).[3]

---

[3] *Major Group 20*, Processed Foods—foods and beverages and certain related products such as vegetable and animal fats and oils, and prepared feeds for animals and fowls. *Major Group 22*, Textiles and Fiber—(1) manufacturing of yarn, thread, braids, twine, and cordage; (2); manufacturing broad woven fabrics, knit fabrics, and carpets and rugs from yarn; (3) dyeing and finishing fiber; (4) the integrated manufacture of knit apparel and other finished articles from yarn; (5) coating, waterproofing, or otherwise treating fabric; (6) the manufacture of felt goods, lace goods, nonwoven fabrics, and miscellaneous textiles. *Major Group 26*, Pulp and Paper—the manufacture of pulps, paper, and paperboard as well as converted products such as paper bags, paper boxes and envelopes. *Major Group 28*, Chemicals—(1) basic chemicals, (2) chemical products to be used in further manufacture, and (3) finished chemical products to be used for ultimate consumption. *Major Group 30*, Rubber—rubber products such as tires, rubber footwear, mechanical rubber goods, hats, soles, and flooring. *Major Group 35*, Nonelectrical production machinery; also, machines powered by built-in or detachable motors, and portable tools, both electrical and pneumatic.

Exhibit 5   Consultant's Research Proposal

February 4, 1976

Mr. Robert McAfee
Whitcomb Road
Bolton, Massachusetts 01740
Dear Bob,

I have enjoyed hearing about Boltronics and believe you have made the right decision to leave W. R. Grace at the end of March to devote your full efforts to this enterprise. As requested, I am outlining a possible market research plan for Boltronics based on our very brief discussion of what you have told me you are trying to do. The project can be initiated immediately, or we can wait until the spring after you have left Grace. Please understand that this is a preliminary proposal that reflects what you told me was your most serious problem—lack of detailed information concerning the market and its various segments and competitors.

What I am proposing is a multistage research project that will begin with an exploratory field survey of customers and competitors. Afterward I would be willing to supervise or conduct additional "library" research of the industry, public data available about competitors, trade association files, government reports and data, etc.

The basic purpose of the customer survey would be to probe the buying motives and habits of various customer groups and their perception of suppliers. If you decide to initiate the project with me, we'll sit down and generate a series of research hypotheses concerning market and competitive behavior that can be tested through the survey.

The library research stage should probably begin with further investigation of competition. There must be public data about them available somewhere in state government files. We'll find it. Or we can get some very basic information from financial rating services.

The survey research part of the project would basically be divided into design and implementation phases. I would be responsible for research design. As for implementation, I suggest a methodology based on personal interviews with potential customers. A less costly approach would be telephone interviews. And of course the total cost of the project will be largely dependent upon how many people you want to interview or call. We'll have to discuss this further.

My fees in relation to designing the survey project would be $150 per day. The library-type research is $80 per day if I do it myself or $40 if I subcontract it. As for someone to actually conduct the personal or phone interviews, I can contract to hire people at $10 per hour for personal interviews, or $3.50 per hour for telephoning (all expenses included). The agencies I have in mind, however, tend to concentrate on consumer products, although they will also research industrial products. An alternative is to use one of my MBA students. He has a bachelor's degree in mechanical engineering and has taken several of our MBA marketing courses. He said he is available for $5 per hour, plus expenses if he has to travel or call long distance.

I hope this very tentative proposal meets your expectations at this stage. If you decide to proceed, we will have to sharpen the general research plan discussed herein. Please call if you have any questions.

Yours truly,
Greg Parker

Marshall proposed a methodology consisting of a few closed-end questions and a series of open-end questions. Closed-end questions required the respondent to pick among several answers supplied by the researcher. Open-end questions did not limit the respondent to any set answer, but required more conversational answers. Marshall said that the open-ended questions could be used for "in-depth probing of customer needs and wants, in addition to their perception of competition, since the objective would be to determine what the buyers would like to see when they consider process controls."

2.   Reports available from the state of Massachusetts
      Several types of secondary (published) data were also antici-
pated. First, McAfee knew that the state government collected at
least some information about companies operating in Massachusetts for tax and legal purposes, although he was not sure of the
exact nature and amount of the information available. Marshall's
plan here was to visit the statehouse and "fish around for interesting information." Second, Marshall proposed to assemble statistics
on industrial growth and capital expenditures for Massachusetts
and New England industry since he believed that industrial growth
or decline in the area would be a prime indicator of Boltronics'
prospects. Finally, Marshall wanted to collect basic demographic
and economic information on the major manufacturing cities in
Massachusetts.

3.   Background information
      Since the research would be part of a class project, for his
term paper Marshall would be required by the professor to gather
additional information from McAfee concerning Boltronics—its
history, corporate objectives, product line, production plan, financial capabilities, employees, marketing policies, etc. Marshall also
planned to interview McAfee to record in as much detail as possible
McAfee's understanding of the market and competition prior to
the research.

4.   Recommendations
      Marshall planned to conclude his report with a set of action rec-
ommendations for Boltronics.

5.   Final report
      Marshall expected the final report to be "about 100 pages."
About one quarter would be comments on the data collected, while
the rest would be photocopies of government reports, completed
survey forms, and other data. Marshall proposed to submit the
finished report to McAfee in late June, the deadline set by his
professor.

      Marshall had asked permission to "pilot-test" one part of the plan
(telephone interviews), and McAfee had agreed, giving him a few names
to call. The answers from one pilot respondent to the *closed-end* questions only are shown in Exhibit 6. Also in Exhibit 7 is a letter from the
professor to McAfee concerning Marshall.

      McAfee knew that other research strategies were possible. For ex-
ample, the sales calls he had already made to a limited number of companies had generated considerable information that was already a part
of his understanding of the market. Thus it was possible that McAfee
himself could continue such informal research in conjunction with sales
calls or perhaps without trying to push for an order during a "research"
visit.

Exhibit 6   Responses in Pilot Test of Marshall's Survey (closed-end questions only)*

1. Name __[a textile mill]__   4. Purchasing agent __Ben Hill__
2. Address __Worcester, Massa-__   5. SIC number __84 041__
    chusetts
3. Phone number __965-5099__
6. Do you use process controls in your manufacturing?
    Yes _____ No _____
7. What do you manufacture? __Textiles__
8. What type of controls do you use presently? Electronic __X__
    Mechanical _____ Computerized _____ Other _____
9. Do you use or have you ever used outside sources to develop and/or implement
    your process controls?   No _____ Yes __X__
10. The following rating system will be used to evaluate the answers to the following
    questions:
    1. Not important.
    2. Very little importance.
    3. Secondary importance.
    4. Very important.
    5. Determining factor, of greatest importance.
11. I would purchase new process controls because:
    1. It would make my operation more efficient. __4__
    2. It would increase my production. __5__
    3. It's the trend in sophisticated manufacturing. __1__
    4. I would have a need for it in the expansion of my operation. __1__
    5. Other reasons. _____
12. The following are how important to you in purchase determination of process
    controls?   Price __4__   Quality of the system __5__   Sophistication of the system
    __1__   Company that makes the system __2__   Principle in the company __1__
    Salesman __3__   Amount of time the company is in business __2__   Company's
    reputation __2__
13. When and if my company purchases process controls:
    1. We develop it and produce it ourselves. _____
    2. We develop it and have an outside source produce it. _____
    3. We have an outside source develop it and we produce it. _____

---

*Marshall also took rough notes on the answers to the open-end questions he raised; he would discuss these with McAfee during a face-to-face meeting.

Also, McAfee knew that he himself might undertake some or most of the research steps proposed by either the professor or the student. And he knew that there were numerous other survey research possibilities concerning his customers and competition. Finally, he could also consider using the test market approach or the observational research method. Possibly, test marketing could be used on a limited number of customers to assess various marketing strategies. In the observational method, market behavior was generally observed without directly questioning the respondent. For example, from the MBA program he remembered how one of the large tire companies had sent an employee into the field to pose as a customer at competitive tire stores.

McAfee also remembered from his class how the professor had concluded one session citing the principle that "good decisions are based on good information about the market." Intuitively, that guideline seemed to make sense, and he wondered to what extent and how the guideline should be applied to Boltronics.

4. We let an outside source handle the whole thing; we just let him know what our needs are, and he takes care of the rest. __X__
5. Other. _____

14. When I have an outside source involved, my selection process in giving out the job would be by:
    1. A competitive bidding process. __X__
    2. Referral. _____
    3. Picking the one I like the best. _____
    4. Just going to the Yellow Pages and picking one. _____
    5. Other. _____

15. What is the time span of planning, purchase, and implementation of the process controls? __72 weeks__

16. Are you using an outside source presently? If so, whom? __No__

17. What does he do for you? _____

18. Do you want your salesman to be:
    1. Highly educated and trained in the field? __Yes__
    2. Somewhat educated and trained? _____
    3. Makes no difference. _____

Company Classification

19. Sales __$26.5__ million
20. Number of factory workers __120__
21. Number of management people other than engineers __4__
22. Number of engineers __0__
23. Have you had any expansion recently in the company, or do you expect to have expansion in the near future? __Yes__
24. How much have you spent on process controls in the past two years? __$10,000__
25. How much will you spend in the next two years? __$30,000__
26. How long has your company been in business? __6 years__
27. Any additional comments: _____

Exhibit 7   Letter Concerning Student

March 20, 1976

Mr. Robert McAfee
Whitcomb Road
Bolton, Massachusetts 01740
Dear Bob,

I am pleased to respond to your request for further information on the student we discussed. As I said, I had him in one of my undergraduate marketing management classes, where he was an able performer and earned the grade of B. He was aggressive in class discussions and also did well on tests on the textbook and notes; his papers were less impressive, although still in the top half of the class.

Other than grades, I will add that the student is known by the faculty as a hard worker. Also, he has told me that he was a "star" on his co-op job, where he worked several quarters for a silverware manufacturer selling to discount jewelry outlets. He says that the company wants to hire him permanently, starting August, for a pile of money but that he wants to go on to graduate business school.

Hope this helps.

Yours truly,
Greg Parker

Varian Associates, Incorporated*

The marketing research director of the Tube Division of Varian Associates, Inc., was faced with the problem of responding to a request made by the manager of the Operations Research Unit to specify exactly what types of decisions could and would be made using data obtained from the media survey now in the field. The media study had been initiated by the advertising manager of the Tube Division to obtain needed information on the readership of selected magazines and journals. At one time or another a variety of interested parties, including the division's advertising agency, the corporate public relations officer, the corporate director of research, and the division's marketing manager had participated in formulating the study of design.

Varian Associates, with headquarters in Palo Alto, California, is one of the largest electronics companies in the world. The company is organized into three major groups:

1. Microwave Tube Group This group is comprised of the Palo Alto Tube Division; the Eimac Division of San Carlos, California; the Bomac Division of Beverly, Massachusetts, S-F-D Laboratories, Inc., of Union, New Jersey; Varian Associates of Canada, Ltd., Georgetown, Ontario; and Semicon Associates, Inc., Lexington, Kentucky. Major products of the group consist of klystron tubes, traveling wave tubes, magnetron tubes, gas switching tubes, microwave components, solid-state devices, crossed-field devices, backward wave oscillators, and klystron amplifiers. The basic applications for these products include early warning radar, radar astronomy, satellite communications, missile guidance, air traffic control, weather radar, UHF television, microwave relay systems, beacons, microwave test equipment, navigation aids, and navigation.

2. Instrument Group This group is comprised of the Analytical Instrument Division of Palo Alto, the Recorder Division also in Palo Alto, and the Quantum Electronics Division of Beverly, Massachusetts and Palo Alto. The major products of the group include spectrometers, laboratory electromagnetics and superconducting magnets, recorders, frequency standards, and magnetometers. The basic applications for these products include quantitative and qualitative nondestructive analysis of chemical compounds, isotope identification, laboratory research, studies of the behavior of matter under the influence of precise magnetic fields, navigation, timekeeping, communications, geophysical exploration, magnetic search, deep space probes, and oceanographic research.

3. Equipment Group This group produced such products as ultrahigh vacuum pumps and systems, vacuum instrumentation, and linear accel-

---

*Reprinted from *Stanford Business Cases* 1966, with permission of the Publishers, Stanford University Graduate School of Business. © 1966, 1984 by the Board of Trustees of the Leland Stanford Junior University.

erators. The basic applications of these products include appendage pumping, vacuum tube processing, mass spectrometers, physics experiments, evaporation and deposition, environmental testing, study of services, metallurgical studies, physical and biological studies, clinical radiation therapy, food irradiation, high energy physics studies, and radiation chemistry studies.

The Tube Group was the largest in sales of the three groups. It sold its products to both military and industrial companies typically on a contract-bid basis. The group employed a total of 40 salesmen and servicemen. In addition, a substantial number of men at the various headquarters offices assisted the field men when the occasion arose. The Tube Group spent several hundred thousands of dollars each year in advertising and promotion including media advertising, trade shows, workshops, publicity, direct mail, and catalogs.

The advertising manager of the Tube Group summed up his request for a media study by saying, "I want to know w hat magazines and journals are the most efficient to use to cover audiences that I specify as needing to receive certain messages." He also indicated that in preparation for a media study of some sort he was revising his master mailing list by omitting individuals who were not influential in the purchase of products produced by the Tube Group. This master list had been compiled over the years through sales reports, inquiries, trade shows, direct mail, and workshops. In order to bring it up to date all tube sales and service people were asked to indicate the names, titles, and addresses of all those people whom they thought were influential in deciding what supplier to use. The specific request read, "We would like to ask that you prepare a list of the ten most influential people in each of your major accounts; these should be people that you feel we should be reaching with our advertising."

After receiving the names from the field force and further culling, the master list contained approximately 3,500 names, of which 600 were indicated as being "prime influentials." It was decided to conduct the survey among all 3,500, but to identify the 600 separately so as to be able to follow up either by phone or mail on them where necessary.

The group's advertising agency was asked what information should be obtained in the media study. The agency's response is shown in Exhibit 1. After evaluating the agency's reply as well as requests from other individuals, a final questionnaire was prepared (see Exhibit 2). Followups were planned on the entire sample to obtain a high rate of returns. The questionnaire was mailed with a stamped first-class return envelope in February and March.

At one of the several conferences held to implement the survey the responsibility for analyzing the returns was given to the Operations Research Unit. Since the same survey approach would likely be used by other Varian groups, the OR Unit was anxious to develop a standardized set of procedures for computerizing and analyzing the data. To do this

Exhibit 1

Hoefer, Dieterich & Brown, Inc.
Advertising and Public Relations
414 Jackson Square,
San Francisco, California 94111   Yukon 1-1811

Mr. Dick Barck
Marketing Department
Varian Associates
611 Hansen Way
Palo Alto, California

Dear Dick:

I enclose an outline of the kinds of information that we would find useful when the media preference survey is completed for the Tube Group.

Taking the groupings in order, we're interested in a breakdown of the company's primary areas of interest because different kinds of products should, obviously, be advertised to different kinds of systems manufacturers. You may be able to provide this information within Varian on most of the companies.

We want some sort of breakdown on job function, because the new Business Publication Association (BPA) figures on circulation by member publication will be broken down in this manner. The functions that I have suggested are those used by Microwaves magazine in their own circulation analysis.

We would like to break the surveys into groupings by (1) specifying function and (2) approving function. In addition, if possible, we would like to have a "rating" as to degree of actual influence in the actual purchase.

As to the publications themselves, I have listed the magazines now under consideration for Tube Group promotion, plus two amateur-oriented publications being used by Eimac. The list should probably be checked with Bob Landon to make sure that we are covering his market adequately. I have consciously excluded questions dealing with the "most useful" editorial or "do you read the advertisements," because I frankly don't know what to do with this type of information after I have it. We don't care, in my opinion, whether he reads the magazine because it contains information pertinent to his job, or because it contributes interdisciplinary information in which he is interested, or because it provides general news about his industry. We do care whether or not he reads it regularly, and whether or not he considers it "must" reading. As to the advertising readership, it's our job to make the ads sufficiently interesting so that he *will* read them.

After the results are in, we will provide cost information which can be related to publication preferences and market coverage. It should be fairly simple to determine a "cost efficiency" rating by comparing the weighted percentage of regular readers to the absolute cost of a single advertising page.

Please call me if you have any questions.

Very truly yours,

Hoefer, Dieterich & Brown, Inc.

/s/Hal

Hal H. Marquis

sh

Enclosure

they had to know *exactly* what decisions the advertising manager planned to make using the survey data, what additional information he wished to correlate with the survey data, and what "operational" measures he wanted to use. As an example of the latter the word "coverage" represented a problem. The term could be used in a variety of ways including the number of people reached by the average issue of a given magazine

cc: Mr. Paul Warner
      Mr. Bill Engel
      Mr. Jim Kirby

(1) Company's primary areas of interest:

      Communications systems manufacturers
      Telemetering and data systems manufacturers
      Electronic countermeasures systems manufacturers
      Navigation and guidance systems manufacturers
      Air traffic control and landing systems manufacturers
      Weapon control systems manufacturers
      Miscellaneous radar systems manufacturers
      Research and development laboratories
      U.S. government and military
      Microwave test equipment manufacturers
      Miscellaneous microwave components manufacturers
      General: materials, plasma, nuclear, magnetics, etc.

(2) Job function of individual answering questionnaire:

      Application engineering
      Development engineering
      Design engineering
      Research
      Engineering management
      Purchasing
      Administrative management
      Production management

(3) Individual's influence in buying decision:

    a. Specify components: (rate 1 to 10)
    b. Review purchase decision: (rate 1 to 10)

(4) Readership of the following publications (rated "read occasionally," "read regularly," and "consider *must* reading"):

PRODUCT: Electronic Design, Electronics, EDN (Electrical Design News), E.E.E., Electro-Technology, Electronic Industries, Signal, Space Aeronautics, Solid State Design, IEEE Proceedings, IEEE Spectrum

PURCHASING: Electronic Procurement, Electronic Specifying and Procurement

MILITARY: Air Force & Space Digest, Armed Forces Management, Army, Ordnance, Data, Journal of the Armed Forces, Naval Institute Proceedings

AMATEUR: CQ and QST

HORIZONTAL: Aviation Week, Astronautics & Aeronautics, Electronic News, Industrial Research, International Science & Technology, Missiles & Rockets, Research/Development, Scientific American

(5) Agency will provide information on circulation, cost-per-thousand-readers, and cost-per-page. Final figures should relate cost-per-page to weighted percentage of regular readers in Varian study.

---

or journal, or it could mean the cumulative audience reached by a given number of issues of a magazine or journal.

The OR Unit requested that the Tube Group marketing research manager get together with the division's advertising manager to respond to numerous suggestions pertaining to the development of a media model which would be made operational through the use of the survey data. The proposed model is described in Exhibit 3.

Exhibit 2

Varian Associates Executive Offices
Palo Alto, California

Robert T. Davis
Vice President, Marketing

Dear Sir:

Would you please help us in solving one of our marketing problems?

We're trying to improve our communications programs. During the next eighteen months, we will, with your permission, be calling on you for your personal advice on the subject of magazine ads.

This survey is the first of the series and asks for your reading preference; the second will follow in about six months and will deal with the effectiveness of our ads; the third questionnaire, later in the year, will give you the opportunity to help us actually write our ads.

We hope you will take a few minutes to answer this questionnaire. Your response will be very meaningful and greatly appreciated.

Very truly yours,
Robert T. Davis

RTD/bb

Inside are photographs of 28 magazines serving our industry. In the spaces provided, please check how often you read each of these magazines. If you do not read a magazine, simply leave the spaces blank. (Note: This part of the questionnaire is not contained in the case.)

Questionnaire*

Which of the 28 mentioned magazines do you find most helpful in your work? (Please list in order of importance)

1. _____   4. _____
2. _____   5. _____
3. _____   6. _____

In addition, we ask you to indicate your job function and the primary area(s) of your work.

My work is primarily concerned with the following:

(Check one only)

Management   Engineering
  ☐ Administrative   ☐ Design/Application
  ☐ Engineering Program   ☐ Manufacturing/Production
Research & Development   ☐ Other _____
  ☐ Basic (No specific end product)   (Specify)
  ☐ Applied (Product development)

The primary technical area(s) of my work is (are) concerned with:

  ☐ Radar   ☐ Test Measurement
    Navigation, Guidance   ☐ Industrial Heating Process & Control
    & Control   ☐ Scientific & Medical
  ☐ ECM/PEN Aids   ☐ Other _____
  ☐ Telemetry   (Specify)
    Communications
    ☐ Broadcast
    ☐ Military
    ☐ Other _____

(Specify)

Thank you for taking the time to answer these questions. Your assistance in this phase of our overall marketing program is sincerely appreciated. All that remains is to fold the questionnaire and return it to me in the enclosed self-addressed envelope.

---

*These questions were asked in addition to those pertaining to the readership (if any) of the 28 magazines.

Exhibit 3

Excerpts from the Proposal by the OR Unit to Set up a Media Model

The proposed model (called MISER) has as its objective among selected audience groups the generation of a weighted readership scale *and* a readership distribution. The former provides a score based on reach and frequency of exposure within specified time periods while the latter consists of two distributions, the first of which yields the percentage of readers exposed once, twice, etc. The second distribution is cumulative. By comparing the weighted scores and the readership distribution of two or more alternative media schedules the user can decide which schedule best suits his objectives.

The media vehicle data which is being obtained by individuals from the survey will be collapsed into the following question—"what is the probability of prospect X being exposed to the *average* issue of each of a variety of print media vehicles?" No attempt will be made to measure the extent or degree of exposure. Thus, exposure is defined operationally as whether a respondent reports reading "something" within a particular vehicle.

The probability statement is used because of the problem of time. Assume a quarterly journal. If one knew that a prospect is exposed on the average to three out of four issues then the probability of exposure to the *average* issue would be .75; if the exposure is two out of four it will be .50; and so on. Obviously, if the prospect is exposed to all four issues then it would be certain (1.0) that he read the average issue.

The problem of how to treat additional exposures (either within a specific vehicle through time or between media vehicles) is not easily solved. The problem is complex because of the need to ascertain at the margin the effect of each additional exposure given certain time intervals between exposures. Naturally, the effect of repetition has to be evaluated differently for different products. In the case at hand it is proposed that the first exposure be rated at .9, the second at 1.0, the third at .9,—all within a two months' interval on the assumption that your advertising will be centered on products which are relatively new and complex; therefore, the "reader" will need exposure to two ads in order to obtain "full" information. A special feature of the model calls for providing you with the opportunity of inserting the "current" media schedule to inoculate individual prospects following which the schedule to be tested can be better evaluated through the weighting of additional exposures.

We estimate the total cost of building MISER at about $4,000 and that each schedule can be "tested" at a cost not to exceed $40.

How should the marketing research manager and advertising manager of the Tube Group respond to the request from the OR Unit?

Modern Plastics*

Institutional Sales Manager Jim Clayton had spent most of Monday morning planning for the rest of the month. It was early July and Jim knew that an extremely busy time was coming with the preparation of the following year's sales plan.

Since starting his current job less than a month ago, Jim had been involved in learning the requirements of the job and making his initial territory visits. Now that he was getting settled, Jim was trying to plan his activities according to priorities. The need for planning had been instilled in him during his college days. As a result of his three years field sales experience and development of time management skills, he felt prepared for the challenge of the sales manager's job.

While sitting at his desk, Jim recalled a conversation that he had a week ago with Bill Hanson, the former manager who had been pro-

*This case was prepared by Thomas Ingram, Danny Bellenger, and Kenneth Bernhardt, Georgia State University, © 1977 by Danny N. Bellenger and Kenneth L. Bernhardt. Reprinted by permission.

moted to another division. Bill told him that the sales forecast (annual and monthly) for plastic trash bags in the Southeast region would be due soon as an initial step toward developing the sales plan for the next year. Bill had laughed as he told him, "Boy, you ought to have a ball doing the forecast being a rookie sales manager!"

When Jim had asked what Bill meant, he explained by saying that the forecast was often "winged" because the headquarters in Chicago already knew what they wanted and would change the forecast to meet their figures, particularly if the forecast was for an increase of less than 10 percent. The experienced sales manager could throw numbers together in a short time that would pass as a serious forecast and ultimately be adjusted to fit the plans of headquarters. However, he felt an inexperienced manager would have a difficult time "winging" a credible forecast.

Bill had also told Jim that the other alternative meant gathering mountains of data and putting together a forecast that could be sold to the various levels of Modern Plastics management. This alternative would prove to be time consuming and could still be changed anywhere along the chain of command before final approval.

Clayton started reviewing pricing and sales volume history (see Exhibit 1). He also looked at the key account performance for the past two and a half years (see Exhibit 2). During the past month Clayton had visited many of the key accounts, and on the average they had indicated that their purchases from Modern would prob; ,ly increase 15 to 20 percent in the coming year.

Schedule for Preparing the Forecast

Jim had received a memo recently from Robert Baxter, the regional marketing manager, detailing the plans for completing the 1978 forecast. The key dates in the memo began in only three weeks:

August 1	Presentation of forecast to regional marketing manager
August 10	Joint presentation with marketing manager to regional general manager
September 1	Regional general manager presents forecast to division vice president
September 1–30	Review of forecast by staff of division vice president
October 1	Review forecast with corporate staff
October 1–15	Revision as necessary
October 15	Final forecast forwarded to division vice president from regional general manager

Company Background

The Plastics Division of Modern Chemical Company was founded in 1965 when Modern Chemical purchased Cordco, a small plastics manufacturer with national sales of $15,000,000. At that time, the chief products of the Plastics Division were sandwich bags, plastic tablecloths, trash cans, and plastic-coated clothesline.

Exhibit 1 Plastic Trash Bags' Sales and Pricing History 1975–1977

	Pricing Dollars per Case			Sales Volume in Cases			Sales Volume in Dollars		
	1975	1976	1977	1975	1976	1977	1975	1976	1977
January	$6.88	$ 7.70	$15.40	33,000	46,500	36,500	$ 227,000	$ 358,000	$ 562,000
February	6.82	7.70	14.30	32,500	52,500	23,000	221,500	404,000	329,000
March	6.90	8.39	13.48	32,000	42,000	22,000	221,000	353,000	296,500
April	6.88	10.18	12.24	45,500	42,500	46,500	313,000	432,500	569,000
May	6.85	12.38	11.58	49,000	41,500	45,500	335,500	514,000	527,000
June	6.85	12.65	10.31	47,500	47,000	42,000	325,500	594,500	443,000
July	7.42	13.48	9.90E	40,000	43,500	47,500E	297,000	586,500	470,000E
August	6.90	13.48	10.18E	48,500	63,500	43,500E	334,500	856,000	443,000E
September	7.70	14.30	10.31E	43,000	49,000	47,500E	331,000	700,500	489,500E
October	7.56	15.12	10.31E	52,500	50,000	51,000E	397,000	756,000	526,000E
November	7.15	15.68	10.72E	62,000	61,500	47,500E	443,500	964,500	509,000E
December	7.42	15.43	10.59E	49,000	29,000	51,000E	363,500	447,500	540,000E
Total	$7.13	$12.25	$11.30	534,500	568,500	503,500	$3,810,000	$6,967,000	$5,694,000

E July–December 1977 figures are forecast of sales manager J. A. Clayton. Other data comes from historical sales information.

Exhibit 2   1977 Key Account Sales History (in cases)

Customer	1975	1976	First 6 Months 1977	1975 Monthly Avg.	1976 Monthly Avg.	First Half 1977 Monthly Avg.	First Qtr. 1977 Monthly Avg.
Transco Paper Company	125774	134217	44970	10481	11185	7495	5823
Callaway Paper	44509	46049	12114	3709	3837	2019	472
Florida Janitorial Supply	34746	36609	20076	2896	3051	3346	2359
Jefferson	30698	34692	25044	2558	2891	4174	1919
Cobb Paper	13259	23343	6414	1105	1945	1069	611
Miami Paper	10779	22287	10938	900	1857	1823	745
Milne Surgical Company	23399	21930		1950	1828		
Graham	8792	15331	1691	733	1278	281	267
Crawford Paper	7776	14132	6102	648	1178	1017	1322
John Steele	8634	13277	6663	720	1106	1110	1517
Henderson Paper	9185	8850	2574	765	738	429	275
Durant Surgical		7766	4356		647	726	953
Master Paper	4221	5634	600	352	470	100	
D.T.A.			2895			482	
Crane Paper	4520	5524	3400	377	460	566	565
Janitorial Service	3292	5361	2722	274	447	453	117
Georgia Paper	5466	5053	2917	456	421	486	297
Paper Supplies, Inc.	5117	5119	1509	426	427	251	97
Southern Supply	1649	3932	531	137	328	88	78
Horizon Hospital Supply	4181	4101	618	348	342	103	206
Total Cases	346007	413217	156134	28835	34436	26018	17623

Since 1965, the Plastics Division has grown to a sales level exceeding $200 million with five regional profit centers covering the United States. Each regional center has manufacturing facilities and a regional sales force. There are three product groups in each region:

1. Food Packaging   PVC meat film, plastic bags for various food products
2. Institutional   Plastic trash bags and disposable tableware (plates, bowls, etc.)
3. Industrial   Case overwrap film, heavy duty fertilizer packaging bags, plastic film for use in pallet overwrap systems

Each product group is supervised jointly by a product manager and a district sales manager, both of whom report to the regional marketing manager. The sales representatives report directly to the district sales manager but also work closely with the product manager on matters concerning pricing and product specifications.

The five regional general managers report to Mr. J. R. Hughes, vice-president of the Plastics Division. Mr. Hughes is located in Chicago. Although Modern Chemical is owned by a multinational paper company, the Plastics Division has been able to operate in a virtually independent manner since its establishment in 1965. The reasons for this include:

1. Limited knowledge of the plastics industry on the part of the paper company management.

2. Excellent growth by the Plastics Division has been possible without management supervision from the paper company.

3. Profitability of the Plastics Division has consistently been higher than that of other divisions of the chemical company.

The Institutional Trash Bag Market

The institutional trash bag is a polyethyelene bag used to collect and transfer refuse to its final disposition point. There are different sizes and colors available to fit the various uses of the bag. For example, a small bag for desk wastebaskets is available as well as a heavier bag for large containers such as a 55-gallon drum. There are 25 sizes in the Modern line; 13 of those sizes are available in three colors—white, buff, and clear. Customers typically buy several different items on an order.

The institutional trash bag is a separate product from the consumer grade trash bag typically sold to homeowners through retail outlets. The institutional trash bag is sold primarily through paper wholesalers, hospital supply companies, and janitorial supply companies to a variety of end users. Since trash bags are used on such a wide scale, the list of end users could include almost any business or institution. The segments include hospitals, hotels, schools, office buildings, transportation facilities, and restaurants.

Based on historical data and a current survey of key wholesalers and end users in the Southeast, the annual market for institutional trash bags in the region was estimated to be 55 million pounds. Translated into cases, the market potential was close to 2 million cases. During the past five years, the market for trash bags has grown at an average rate of 89 percent per year. Now a mature product, future market growth is expected to parallel overall growth in the economy. The 1978 real growth in GNP is forecast to be 4.5 percent.

General Market Conditions

The current market is characterized by a distressing trend. The market is in a position of oversupply, with approximately 20 manufacturers competing for business in the Southeast. Prices have been on the decline for several months, but are expected to level out during the last six months of the year.

This problem arose after a record year in 1976 for Modern Plastics. During 1976, supply was very tight due to raw material shortages. Unlike many of its competitors, Modern had only minor problems securing adequate raw material supplies. As a result, competitors were few in 1976, and all who remained in business were prosperous. By early 1977 raw materials were plentiful and prices began to drop as new competitors tried to buy their way into the market. During the first quarter of 1977 Modern Plastics learned the hard way that a competitive price was a necessity in the current market. Volume fell off drastically in February and March as customers shifted orders to new suppliers when Modern chose to maintain a slightly higher than market price on trash bags.

With the market becoming extremely price competitive and profits declining, the overall quality has dropped to a point of minimum standard. Most suppliers now make a bag "barely good enough to get the job done." It was believed that this quality level is acceptable to most buyers who do not demand high quality for this type of product.

Modern Plastics vs. Competition

A recent study of Modern vs. competition had been conducted by an outside consultant to see how well Modern measured up in several key areas. Each area was weighted according to its importance in the purchase decision, and Modern was compared to its key competitors in each area and on an overall basis. The key factors and their weights are shown below:

	Weight
1. Pricing	0.50
2. Quality	0.15
3. Breadth of Line	0.10
4. Sales Coverage	0.10
5. Packaging	0.05
6. Service	0.10
Total	1.00

Exhibit 3 Competitive Factors Ratings by Competitor*

Weight	Factor	Modern	National Film	Bonanza	South-eastern	PBI	BAGCO	Southwest Bag	Florida Plastics	East Coast Bag Co.
0.50	Price	2	3	2	2	2	2	2	2	3
0.15	Quality	3	2	3	4	3	2	3	3	4
0.10	Breadth	1	2	2	3	3	3	3	3	3
0.10	Sales Coverage	1	3	3	3	4	3	3	4	3
0.05	Packaging	3	3	2	3	3	1	3	3	3
0.10	Service	4	3	3	2	2	2	3	4	3

*Overall Weighed Ranking***

1.	BAGCO	2.15
2.	Modern	2.20
3.	Bonanza	2.25
4.	Southwest Bag (Tie)	2.50
5.	PBI (Tie)	2.50
6.	Southeastern	2.55
7.	Florida Plastics	2.60
8.	National Film	2.65
9.	East Coast Bag	3.15

*Ratings on a 1 to 5 scale with 1 being the best rating and 5 the worst.

**The weighted ranking is the sum of each rank times its weight. The lower the number, the better the overall rating.

As shown in Exhibit 3, Modern compared favorably with its key competitors on an overall basis. None of the other suppliers were as strong as Modern in breadth of line nor did any competitor offer as good sales coverage as that provided by Modern. Clayton knew that sales coverage would be even better next year, since the Florida and North Carolina territories had grown enough to add two salespeople to the current eight in the institutional group by January 1, 1978.

Pricing, quality, and packaging seemed to be neither an advantage nor a disadvantage. However, service was a problem. The main cause for this, Clayton was told, was temporary out of stock situations which occurred occasionally, primarily due to the wide variety of trash bags offered by Modern.

During the past two years, Modern Plastics had maintained approximately 27 percent of the market. Some new competitors had entered the market since 1975; others had left (see Exhibit 4). The previous district sales manager, Bill Hanson, had left Clayton some comments regarding the major competitors. These are reproduced in Exhibit 5.

Developing the Sales Forecast

After a careful study of trade journals, government statistics, and surveys conducted by Modern marketing research personnel, projections for growth potential were formulated by segment and are shown in Ex-

---

Exhibit 4   Market Share by Supplier 1975 and 1976

Supplier	% of Market 1975	% of Market 1976
National Film	11	12
Bertram	16	0*
Bonanza	11	12
Southeastern	5	6
Bay	9	0*
Johnson Graham	8	0*
PBI	2	5
Lewis	2	0*
BAGCO	—	6
Southwest Bag	—	2
Florida Plastics	—	4
East Coast Bag Co.	—	4
Miscellaneous & Unknown	8	22
Modern	28	27
	100	100

*Out of business in 1976.

Source: This information was developed from a field survey conducted by Modern Plastics.

Exhibit 5   Characteristics of Competitors

National Film   Broadest product line in the industry. Quality a definite advantage.
                   Good service. Sales coverage adequate, but not an advantage. Not as
                   aggressive as most suppliers on price. Strong competitor.

Bonanza   Well-established, tough competitor. Very aggressive on pricing. Good
                   packaging, quality okay.

Southeastern   Extremely price competitive in Southern Florida. Dominates Miami
                   market. Limited product line. Not a threat outside of Florida.

PBI   Extremely aggressive on price. Have made inroads into Transco
                   Paper Company during 1977. Good service but poor sales coverage.

BAGCO   New competitor in 1977. Very impressive with a high quality prod-
                   uct, excellent service, and strong sales coverage. A real threat, partic-
                   ularly in Florida.

Southwest Bag   A factor in Louisiana and Mississippi. Their strategy is simple—an
                   acceptable product at a rock bottom price.

Florida Plastics   Active when market is at a profitable level with price cutting. When
                   market declines to a low profit range, Florida manufactures other
                   types of plastic packaging and stays out of the trash bag market. Poor
                   reputation as a reliable supplier, but can still "spot-sell" at low prices.

East Coast Bag   Most of their business is from a state bid which began in January 1976
                   for a two-year period. Not much of a threat to Modern's business in
                   the Southeast, as most of their volume is north of Washington D.C.

Exhibit 6   1978 Real Growth Projections by Segment

Total Industry	+5.0%
Commercial	+5.4%
Restaurant	+6.8%
Hotel/Motel	+2.0%
Transportation	+1.9%
Office Users	+5.0%
Other	+4.2%
Noncommercial	+4.1%
Hospitals	+3.9%
Nursing Homes	+4.8%
Colleges/Universities	+2.4%
Schools	+7.8%
Employee Feeding	+4.3%
Other	+3.9%

Source: Developed from several trade journals.

hibit 6. This data had been compiled by Bill Hanson just before he had
been promoted.

Jim looked back at Baxter's memo giving the time schedule for the
forecast and knew he had to get started. As he left the office at 7:15 he
wrote himself a large note and pinned it on his wall—"Get started on the
sales forecast!"

Duralake Plastics, Inc.*

Duralake Plastics, Inc., is a large producer of plastics sold to industrial concerns for use in making their consumer products. Duralake's productive output is measured in millions of pounds per year, and its customers are located throughout the world.

Duralake has a large research and development laboratory called the Technical Center. The Technical Center pursues both basic and applied research in an attempt to discover and develop new compounds with potentially useful characteristics. In the late 1960s a polymer was discovered by the Technical Center that had some promising properties. With a proper mix of chemical compounds and a suitable catalyst, a highly reactive, low weight polymer could be prepared. The chemical properties of this new polymer were judged by the Technical Center research staff to be of potential value as an intermediate product to other products. Therefore, although the polymer was not typical of Duralake's other products, it was decided to pursue the development of the product. The compound was named Malake, and it was patented by Duralake.

Based upon the characteristics of Malake, it was felt that the product might find use in three areas: the detergent market as a builder, the textile industry as a sizing agent, and the glass industry as a coupling agent. Since Duralake did not produce detergents, textiles, or glass, this developmental research was done in cooperation with firms that did produce those products. At this stage of the product's development, the chemical properties of the product were quite variable. Many variations were developed by the Technical Center either on their own initiative or in response to a participating firm's request.

In order to support the laboratory work and market development, it was necessary to provide a sufficient supply of Malake. Duralake thus developed a manufacturing process which provided enough Malake to meet developmental needs. Malake was produced by the Technical Center in a pilot plant operation using commercially available raw materials.

By the early 1970s it had been concluded that Malake, although a technical success, was not cost competitive in either the detergent or textile industries. Developmental work in those areas was halted. Two other firms cooperating with Duralake did develop proprietary applications of Malake in their production processes. A large chemical firm found that, even with the relatively high price, Malake had significant advantages in a particular type of cleaning compound, and a major glass manufacturer developed a patented manufacturing process based upon Malake. Both of these companies encouraged Duralake to finalize the chemical-property design of Malake and place it in commercial production since that would be of great benefit to these two firms.

Therefore, under external pressure for production of the product and normal internal pressure to recover developmental costs, Duralake decided to proceed with market introduction of Malake. However, production and commercialization of Malake created some problems for the firm.

Production and Commercialization of Malake

The primary products of Duralake were high volume plastic materials. Malake, being a liquid polymer, was quite different from Duralake's normal products, and its manufacture required production equipment that the firm did not have. There was no doubt that the sales volume for the foreseeable future would not justify Duralake's investment in specialized production equipment. The two existing customers demanding Malake represented a very low volume demand. Potential market demand in addition to these two firms was questionable. However, the pricing of Malake did promise a profitable product. More importantly, the two firms which would purchase Malake were important customers for other Duralake products, and Duralake felt some pressure and obligation to meet all of the product demands of these customers.

Since existing production facilities were not available within the Duralake organization, the product commercialization plan that was developed included two elements not typical of the firm's normal operations. First, the product would be manufactured by an outside firm under a custom manufacturing arrangement. A custom manufacturer, called a toller, is a production firm that manufactures a product to the client's specifications. The arrangements are similar to arrangements for private brand production of hard goods for national retailers such as Sears, Roebuck and Company, Inc. The use of a toller by Duralake would allow the firm to meet the current low volume demand for Malake without investing in facilities. The revenue generated from the sale of Malake could be used to support continued market development. If the market was developed to sufficient volume to justify the investment by Duralake in production facilities, manufacturing would ultimately be continued internally rather than through the tolling arrangement. Second, the market development of the product was assigned to a single individual within the marketing department. This would allow overhead to be held to a minimum and at the same time provide the careful, controlled direction necessary if the plan was to succeed.

The use of custom manufacturing is unusual in the chemical industry, but quite popular with other types of industry. For example, in the consumer and industrial cleaner markets, most large firms look to small, independent compounders to provide test market quantities of product. In some cases the custom manufacturer is used to provide a continuous supply of the product in difficult-to-reach market segments. The custom manufacturing arrangement is usually an extremely profitable and flexible relationship for both firms involved. It also involves some potential dangers for both firms. Under customer manufacturing, the larger client firm (the buyer) has the advantage of medium-scale production capability at reasonable cost without the need for capital expenditure. Therefore, the risk of new product introduction is substantially reduced. The client firm, however, retains liability for the product produced by the toller and is also ethically, if not legally, responsible for the safety and good manufacturing practice of the toller. The customer manufacturer, on the other hand, can realize increased plant utilization which will decrease operating costs and improve profits. The toller does have certain responsibilities. It is required by the client firm to produce the correct quality product in the proper volume within a given time. The toller is also normally held responsible to provide the product based upon a specified manufacturing process provided by the client. Legal agreements prevent the toller's selling the product to other than the client firm.

In firms that use custom manufacturing extensively, the relationship between the client and the toller is the responsibility of an identifiable group of the client's employees. This liaison group has three fundamental responsibilities. First, it is charged with providing the manufacturer with the technical and informational support necessary to produce the product. Second, this group is responsible for minimizing the liability of the client firm in connection with both the product and the toller. Third, the group is responsible for the security of trade secrets which may be transferred to the toller. These responsibilities are discharged by the development, coordination, and transfer to the custom manufacturer of a manufacturing "package." This "package" would normally include raw materials specifications, product formula and specifications, and safety information on both raw materials and the final product.

Duralake proceeded to establish a liaison group composed of personnel from the marketing and technical departments. A workable relationship was set up with a custom manufacturer which met the quality and cost requirements of the firm, and Malake was commercialized with initial sales to the two cooperating firms in the chemical and glass industries.

Because of the attractive chemical characteristics of Malake, Duralake felt that there was a large range of possible applications for this product. The potential of a great demand boded well for Malake's future, but the wide range of possible applications made it financially impossible for Duralake's Technical Center to pursue the necessary technical developmental work. It was decided that a new marketing approach would be used instead. Advertisements were placed in chemical trade magazines giving technical information about Malake without specifying applications. The response was very encouraging and literature was followed up with samples of the product as requested.

As a matter of convenience, samples were normally shipped from the Technical Center rather than from the toller's plant. Large drums of the product were shipped by the toller to the Technical Center, where laboratory technicians repackaged the product into sample-sized quantities. Late in 1974 a laboratory technician noticed an unusual condition in one of the drums.

An Unexpected By-Product

The drum in question had a crystallized material on the steel lid. Since the product could not crystallize under reasonable conditions, an investigation was begun to determine the nature of the substance. It was concluded that the substance was probably a by-product of catalyst decomposition. Samples of the crystallized substance and the product itself were sent to the catalyst supplier for further analysis. The report was that the crystals were in fact a by-product of the catalyst and that low levels were present in all of the product. The by-product was identified by the catalyst manufacturer as a highly dangerous toxic compound.

Upon receiving this information Duralake immediately took four actions. First, both existing customers purchasing Malake were notified of the presence and characteristics of the toxic material. They were also provided with recommendations as to how the product could be handled safely. Second, the custom manufacturer was provided with the same information. Third, the Technical Center began a project to find a suitable substitute to replace the offending catalyst. Fourth, an outside consulting firm was contracted to do a toxicological analysis of the product to determine its possible hazard to ultimate consumers.

As a consequence of the toxicity problem, the chemical firm determined that they could no longer use Malake in their cleaning compound. They reformulated their product to exclude Malake, and those sales were lost to Duralake. The glass manufacturer performed an industrial hygiene survey of their facilities using Malake and concluded that the toxic by-product did not present a problem for them and they continued to purchase the product. The Technical Center's effort to replace the catalyst was very successful in the laboratory, but the alternative catalyst could not be made to perform satisfactorily in large-scale production operations. The consulting firm reported that their analysis indicated that Malake was one thousand times less toxic than the crystalized substance. The product was not toxic, they reported, by the standards of the Occupational Safety and Health Administration.

Production of Malake was continued throughout 1975 and 1976 in order to meet the needs of the purchasing customer. Even with the low volume and tolling arrangement, Malake remained a very profitable product.

In January of 1977, as a result of internal organizational changes, a new manager was assigned responsibility for the marketing of Malake. During the transfer of responsibility, the new manager developed several concerns about the handling of the toxicity problem with Malake.

A review of the history of the toxicity situation uncovered many related problems. The glass manufacturer, for example, had been notified of the toxicity problem (in 1974) only by a telephone call. Without any written record of Duralake's having informed the glass company, Duralake's liability concerning any legal action caused by the toxicity could not be defined.

It was further discovered that Duralake's internal product control procedures had been unintentionally bypassed by the custom manufacturing operation. The normal control procedure required that every product be internally reviewed every year to insure that all formulas, specifications, safety information sheets, and manufacturing processes complied with all federal and state regulations on safety and pollution control. In the case of Malake these responsibilities were supposed to have been assumed by the liaison group formed to oversee the custom manufacturing arrangement. In early 1977 it was determined that many of the internal control procedures for Malake were never implemented or else, in some cases, review forms were signed in a perfunctory manner after a brief or no review.

It was also determined that only the two original customers for Malake were told of the toxicity problem. No information on the safety or toxicity of the product had been given to any of the hundreds of firms which had been sent samples of the material.

Action by Duralake

The status of Duralake's relationship with the toller was also questionable. No contractual agreement had ever been made between the two firms. The product was ordered and produced on the basis of a simple purchase order system. The lack of a contractual agreement raised the question of legal liability concerning the toller's treatment of toxic by-products removed from Malake as it was being manufactured. The by-product is removed with a solvent, which the toller then uses as a cooling agent in his plant before it is discharged into his normal waste treatment system. Additionally, the toller did not, nor was he required to, test the products for the level of toxic contaminant. The new manager of the Malake product developed a program to minimize the liability of the firm while providing for the adequate protection of both customers and the custom manufacturer. The basic premise was that any product could be sold as long as it was properly represented to the customers, the manufacturer, and the firm. However, the manager went one step further: the overriding objective of the manager was to insure that not only minimal but complete safety and health information was provided to all who were involved with the project. This was a significant decision since it meant that the firm was committed to complete disclosure of the problem to the customer, those who had received samples, and to the custom manufacturer. Clearly, the concern was for principle, not profit. The first action to be taken was to set up a central clearing point for information to insure that accurate and consistent information was disseminated. Next, the corporate legal department was notified of the many problems involved and it was requested to provide a recommendation as to the quality of all historical actions and to propose a course of future action. Based upon their recommendation and under the guidance of the manager, an action plan was developed to resolve the toxicity question. The plan was made up of three sections. The first involved the immediate, proper representation of the products and problems, both internally and externally, while corrective action was being taken. This was done by renotification of the customer of the present status, placing all sample and literature requests on "hold," and notifying all customers or potential customers who had received significant quantities of the product about the problem. The manufacturer was also notified of the potential disposal problem associated with the toxic by-product. Action was also taken to insure that all internal controls (formulas, manufacturing, package, etc.) were consistent.

The second and third sections of the action plan were contingency plans based upon the continued use of either the offending or the alternate catalyst system. These plans involved revision of the product literature, development of internal procedures to insure that both literature and samples were accompanied by correct safety information, etc. Based upon the work to be completed it was anticipated that all problems would be resolved by June 1, 1977.

The firm's legal department made three interesting recommendations. First, it decided that it was in the best interest of the firm to continue to manufacture outside without a contract. Their opinion was that common business law was sufficient to protect both parties regardless of the toxicity and waste disposal problems. They also decided that Duralake was only required to inform the manufacturer that his waste disposal system was probably insufficient and that Duralake was not required to provide an adequate disposal method. Finally, after a review of all information, the legal department concluded that the alternate catalyst should not be used under any conditions. This was based on the fact that this catalyst, as received, was potentially explosive. The firm would be liable for any accident regardless of negligence or circumstances. The risk of using the toxic material was substantially less, and the legal liability could be controlled by proper documentation.

Power Tools, Inc. (B)*

Harvey Beeson had just been named president of the United States Operations Group of Power Tools, Inc., the largest branch of this worldwide company. He was justifiably proud of his new appointment. It meant that he would now sit on the board of directors of this corporation, which was listed in the *Fortune* 500. He believed the promotion was merited because he had overseen the impressive growth of the Consumer Products Division over the last several years. Beeson had started out as a company salesman about twenty years earlier and later became the head of the Asian-Pacific Division of the organization. Although born in the United States, he was a Canadian citizen. His office was in one of the company's older establishments in the Middle Atlantic states.

Sales of the Consumer Products Division had risen at a compound annual rate that approached 15 per cent during the last several years. Beeson had been at the helm of the division while all this rapid growth had occurred. Although the profitability of this division was not as impressive as its sales, profitability too had grown rapidly over the last several years.

However, Beeson knew that all was not well in the other units under his control. Principally, Beeson was concerned about the serious situation that prevailed in the Air Products Division. He knew that the Air Products Division was not performing profitably and for three years had not met its goals. It was the only unprofitable division in the company.

Beeson asked the Air Products Division general manager, Arthur Molnar, to meet with him to give him a summary of the current situation.

In order to comply with Beeson's request, Molnar first met with two Air Products Division officers, comptroller Bob Roberts and marketing manager Tom Solow. At this conference, Molnar saw a very displeasing picture. The following two viewpoints emerged at the conference.

Marketing's View

Molnar asked Solow to summarize how marketing saw the situation. Solow thought of it as a problem thrust upon the Air Products Division from corporate headquarters, which in Solow's view clearly failed to understand the economic characteristics and problems of air-powered tools. A successful small maker of precision power tools located in Ohio, the General Precision Pneumatic Corporation, had been taken over by the much larger Power Tools, Inc., about three years ago. As the marketing manager saw it, the subsidiary had been asked to perform as if it were a rapid growth company. Solow related how the General Precision Pneumatic product line had been stripped of all specialty items and forced to streamline its product offerings. Worse yet, in Solow's view, General Precision Pneumatic had been forced to drop its established direct-to-the-user method of selling in favor of selling through industrial distributors. The traditional strength of General Precision Pneumatic had been its highly capable sales engineers, who could meet directly with users and potential users and custom design products to suit their desires. These sales engineers had been redirected by management to cover the entire nation through a type of middleman, the industrial distributors serving the Electric Tool Division of Power Tools, Inc. In addition, the parent company was so confident that it approximately doubled the capacity of the Ohio plant. Solow stated that he had certainly been able to foresee the disaster that followed. He then explained somberly that division sales dropped rapidly. Solow related that the remaining employees at General Precision Pneumatic, now renamed the Air Products Division of Power Tools, Inc., were disappointed with the entire merger.

Finally, Solow remarked that in his view the marketing policies of a consumer-products-oriented organization would not work when applied to the industrial customers served by the Air Products Division. Solow advocated a return to the limited number of customers who had been served previously by General Precision Pneumatic and to the high profit products that were better suited to the customers' needs.

The Corporate View

Bob Roberts had grown up with the parent company and was clearly an unofficial emissary from headquarters. Roberts took the opportunity to present his view with apparent relish.

The Air Products comptroller related that he understood the problem quite differently from Solow. Roberts stated that the major source of growth in the parent company had been the concept of positive price elasticity of demand for power tools. As Roberts put it, "This concept means that as prices drop, volume in units will increase rapidly, and subsequent dollar sales will increase even faster." Roberts explained that the Consumer Products Division was a clear example of this valuable principle at work.

Roberts related that in the Consumer Products Division, as prices were reduced, great economies of scale in production and marketing generated rapid growth in profits. In addition, there was a greatly expanded market for power tools. In fact, prices for power tools were about half the level they had been ten years ago, whereas the dollar market was easily two to three times as large.

The Air Products comptroller then explained that the parent firm believed that if the very expensive air products were reduced in price and marketed through a channel of distribution that would reach many new users, the same principle would operate. In his eyes, this would have occured had there been cooperation on the part of General Precision Pneumatic employees. Instead, Roberts related, there had been a small strike, and this difficulty had been followed by considerable administrative personnel turnover.

A Telephone Conversation

While Roberts and Solow were presenting their points of view to Molnar, a very important telephone call came in for Molnar that contributed further to his perplexing situation.

Paul Fitzgerald, the sales manager for the Automotive Products Division, called to confirm a last-minute plan to increase the production for the division's half-inch air impact wrench. In Fitzgerald's view, the success or failure of his division depended upon the Air Products Division's ability to supply that organization with a reliable and inexpensive air wrench with which he could offer the broader product line that wholesale distributors of automotive products demanded.

The Automotive Products Division sales manager envisaged a sales campaign that would reverse earlier failures on the part of Power Tools, Inc., to consolidate its position in the automotive products market. Just as Power Tools, Inc., had been gaining an important market share in the automotive marketplace, the Japanese had invaded the air wrench market with very inexpensive products that Fitzgerald described as "inferior or perhaps even cheap." Undeniably, the Jananese had been able to price their products well below the current prices of domestic manufacturers. Worse, they had captured an important part of the market. Fitzgerald was telephoning to be sure that there would be no delay in the latest product redesigns, which would allow costs to be reduced to a level at which the Automotive Products Division would be able at least to meet the prices of the Japanese competition, even if it could not beat this formidable competition.

Molnar's Conference with Beeson

As Beeson had requested, Molnar put together a summary of what he thought of the current situation in the Air Products Division. It was not really a pretty picture to present to his new boss, Molnar thought.

Molnar agreed with Solow that marketing policies that worked with a consumer product would not always work with industrial products. However, Molnar had to agree with Roberts that the considerably reduced prices instituted by Power Tools, Inc., had not been given a real chance to have an impact. There had been great friction between the employees of the General Precision Pneumatic Company and the employees of the new parent company. This had subsided, Molnar thought, as time had progressed. He thought that it really could not be considered a problem today.

In his conference with Beeson, Molnar outlined the situation in simple terms. The concept of altering the General Precision Pneumatic way of distributing the product from custom representatives to the idea of industrial distributors most likely would not work. He suggested a return to a sales engineer calling upon an industrial user. Molnar also suggested that the pricing strategy put forth by the parent company should be given a chance to work in the Automotive Products Division. He stated, however, that the prices for the Air Products Division output sold directly to industrial users should be increased to reflect the new costs of marketing directly.

Beeson listened intently, but he was not pleased. He knew that any substantial reduction in the sales of the Air Products Division would most likely mean that division's demise, and that would mean a large loss to the parent company. In his first year as president, Beeson did not want to incur a new loss. On the other hand, Beeson did not need to be told that the situation as it stood could not be sustained for any long period of time. Something simply had to be done. Beeson viewed the Automotive Division's pursuit of the air wrench market as a good idea. Perhaps it was the only action that would increase the demand on the Air Products Division's factory and thus reduce losses there while stimulating sales in the lagging Automotive Products Division. Advise Power Tools, Inc.

The McKenzie Company (A)*

Martin McKenzie waited impatiently in the service department of the Mercedes dealership. He was anxious to return to his office, for later that afternoon he would have to tell the sales manager of Hosunwa America whether he had chosen either to continue to represent Hosunwa or Elm Grove Capacitor. Elm Grove had introduced a new product line that had brought the two companies into competition.

As owner of an electronics sales representative company, McKenzie could sell only noncompeting products. The conflict of interest that had arisen between two of his largest principals required that McKenzie choose between them. As each had contributed about 20% of his firm's 1981 revenues, loss of either was going to have a significant impact on McKenzie's income. Even in a good year the choice would have been unpleasant, but in the spring of 1982 it was especially onerous. For the last 18 months McKenzie had felt like the Red Queen in *Alice in Wonderland*—running as fast as he could to stay in the same place.

Background

A tall man whose sandy hair and complexion reflected his Scottish ancestry, McKenzie had come to California from the Midwest to go to college. After receiving an electrical engineering degree from Cal Tech, he had gone to work for a small engineering firm that had a defense subcontract from Honeywell. When the contract ended, McKenzie chose not to return to the laboratory. He moved into one of Honeywell's sales divisions and within three years was made a sales manager. Shortly thereafter, his division was reorganized. The resulting policy changes were not to his liking, so when he was offered a job by an electronics sales representative firm in Los Angeles, he gladly accepted.

Smith Associates, founded seven years earlier by Richard Smith, 44, had three other employees: Smith's son-in-law, Andrew Edwards, a

---

*The McKenzie Company does not exist. Issues presented herein for classroom discussion were drawn from the composite experiences of a number of electronics sales representative firms and are typical problems faced within their industry. © 1982 Dan R. E. Thomas & Company, Palo Alto, California.

bookkeeper, and a sales secretary who also handled customer calls. The firm represented eight small component manufacturers or "principals" including three Japanese lines. Taken on three years before, the Japanese lines had, to Smith's surprise, come to account for approximately 60% of the firm's sales. Smith had begun to receive some pressure from several of the manufacturers to increase his sales staff to provide them with better market coverage in the Los Angeles territory, so he offered McKenzie a job.

Smith's selection of McKenzie was a good one, for McKenzie learned the business quickly. Finding himself in a position to substantially increase his previous income through commissions, McKenzie was highly motivated. He was well organized in his sales efforts and did not neglect the American lines. He soon built a good rapport with the sales managers of two of the American principals who had wanted Smith to add staff, and through McKenzie's efforts, sales of those two lines increased significantly.

Within three years McKenzie was generating 40% of the firm's revenues. In spite of the "easy sales" of the Japanese components, which enjoyed a sole-source position in several specialized markets, McKenzie continued to generate 60% of his sales from the American lines. In contrast, sales made by Smith and his son-in-law were about 60% Japanese components. Sales percentages for the firm are illustrated in Exhibit 1.

McKenzie began to feel that the firm should be more aggressive. While Smith was content with the status quo, his American principals were again pushing him to enlarge the sales force. Fully realizing his own role in the growth of the firm's revenues, McKenzie approached Smith, asking to be made a partner. Smith's response did not satisfy McKenzie. Smith intimated that he had been considering offering 25% of the firm to his son-in-law, and 25% to McKenzie "in a few more years." Smith's son-in-law, Edwards, was a low-key man with a lackluster sales record; he had assumed most of the office management chores for which Smith was grateful, but Edwards' sales contribution was below average.

Several months after McKenzie suggested partnership, the sales manager of Elm Grove Capacitor Company, one of Smith Associates' American principals, asked McKenzie to have lunch with him. Elm Grove had acquired a film capacitor manufacturer. The addition of film to Elm Grove's ceramic and tantalum capacitor product line brought the com-

Exhibit 1   Smith Associates' Revenue by Salesperson and Manufacturers

	Total	Japanese Manufacturers	American Manufacturers
McKenzie	40%	16%	24%
Smith & Son-in-Law	60%	36%	24%
Total	100%	52%	48%

pany into direct competition with Smith's largest principal, Misan Electronics. Pleased with McKenzie's past performance, the sales manager offered him Elm Grove's account and encouraged him to start his own firm. After thinking it over for two weeks, McKenzie decided to go ahead.

McKenzie had signed a strict noncompete agreement with Smith Associates that prohibited him from becoming a direct competitor of Smith's and/or from working for any of Smith's principals for one year after leaving Smith's employ. However, McKenzie's lawyer advised him that the courts were unlikely to uphold the agreement because it prohibited him from pursuing his livelihood. McKenzie felt that Smith would be unlikely to undertake litigation, in part because of Smith's intense dislike of lawyers. In addition, the conflict of interest between the Japanese product and Elm Grove would cause Smith to drop the smaller American line which had accounted for less than 16% of Smith's revenues in the preceding year.

The McKenzie Company

Eight weeks later, in January 1978, the McKenzie Company was formed. McKenzie hired a part-time secretary and subleased an office from Circuit Specialists, a new business started by two former employees of the engineering firm that had been McKenzie's first employer.

In addition to Elm Grove's line of electrolytic capacitors, McKenzie began to represent the custom-designed hybrid circuits that his landlords were manufacturing.

In March 1978, McKenzie answered three ads in a trade journal and was successful in adding all three lines. He was interviewed and hired by Genesis Gate Array, a small local company that did semi-custom circuit design. Genesis's founders had contacts in the aerospace industry which had generated enough business to get them established. Recent advances in software tools had made it possible for Genesis to serve a broader set of customers. They had concluded that it was time for them to enlarge their market and that hiring a sales representative made more sense than hiring their own direct sales force.

McKenzie also was hired by two New England-based manufacturers, Waltham Resistor Inc., which made resistor networks, and Pronto Circuit Company, which made two-sided and multi-layer printed circuit boards.

Hybrid circuit sales generally involved a long lead time for development. Commission on sales could lag behind orders by up to 18 months. Gate array technology was just emerging in 1978. However, McKenzie's three other product lines—capacitors, resistor networks, and printed circuits—began to produce steady revenues. McKenzie completed his first year in business slightly ahead of the goal he had targeted for himself. His 1978 revenues were $70,000, and his target had been $60,000. Sixty percent of his revenues came from the sale of Elm Grove's capacitors.

Exhibit 2   Percentages of Revenue/Principal

	1979
Elm Grove Capacitor	40.0%
Circuit Specialists	15.0%
Genesis Gate Array	14.0%
Waltham Resistor	16.0%
Pronto Circuit	14.0%
Flexico (10/79)	1.0%
	100%

In August 1979, McKenzie was approached by Flexico, another small printed circuit board manufacturer that specialized in flexible circuits. McKenzie happily accepted Flexico's line.

McKenzie's second year went well. He hired a bookkeeper who also handled customers' telephone orders. His revenues were $115,000 in 1979. His revenues per principal are shown in Exhibit 2.

At lunch to celebrate his second anniversary with Elm Grove's sales manager, McKenzie was introduced to Donald Monroe. Monroe had been the sales manager in Elm Grove's Boston office for three years. When Monroe's wife was offered a job in Los Angeles, the couple decided to relocate. Monroe had decided to find an outside sales job, believing it would offer both greater independence and more money. Following lunch, Elm Grove's sales manager spent an hour with McKenzie. He gave Monroe glowing references and urged McKenzie to hire him, "to give us better sales coverage in this territory."

At dinner with Monroe and his wife two days later, McKenzie discovered that they had mutual friends from college, and that Monroe also loved sailing. After dinner McKenzie gave the Monroes an office tour, then took them to see his sailboat. Over drinks at a bar overlooking the marina, McKenzie offered Monroe a job.

Monroe accompanied McKenzie on sales calls for four weeks, emphasizing the northern end of Los Angeles County which would be Monroe's territory. The men had lunch or dinner with each of the company's principals and McKenzie spent time explaining the "politics" of each principal.

McKenzie had anticipated that within about nine months Monroe would be paying his own way. He was delighted when Monroe was able to write orders for Elm Grove's product line on his first solo sales call. However, McKenzie's expectations proved unrealistic. He had thoroughly underestimated how long it would take a person to learn how to effectively sell multiple lines of electronic components. Since McKenzie's engineering experience had made him familiar with most electronic technologies, he had assumed that Monroe had as diverse a background as he had. However, Monroe's experience was much more specific, de-

Exhibit 3

1/80–12/80	Cost to McKenzie (Salary, Car Expenses)	Incremental Commission Revenues on Sales*
1st Quarter	$15,000	$ 1,000
2nd Quarter	$15,000	$ 2,500
3rd Quarter	$15,000	$ 5,500
4th Quarter	$15,000	$ 8,500
	$60,000	$17,500

*Commission revenues from Monroe's new accounts.

rived from working with Elm Grove. He tended to emphasize the products and technologies he knew best and to avoid any appearance of ignorance before McKenzie or a customer.

McKenzie did not speak directly to Monroe about his sales performance. He did, however, grumble about what Monroe was costing him to a few friends who were also in the sales business. Their response surprised McKenzie for they all supported Monroe, told McKenzie he had to give a new man at least 12 to 18 months to pay his way, and suggested he spend more time with Monroe. McKenzie, feeling he had to increase his own sales to cover his additional expenses, did not take their advice.

Exhibit 3 shows Monroe's performance during his first year with McKenzie.

In June 1980, McKenzie added the line of Alba Electronics, an integrated circuit socket manufacturer. In November 1980, McKenzie's firm was one of three to be interviewed by the new American subsidiary of Hosunwa Electronics of Japan. Hosunwa manufactured aluminum electrolytic capacitors. The line went to McKenzie in part because Hosunwa America's new sales manager was as avid a sailor as McKenzie and Monroe. Exhibit 4 shows McKenzie's revenues per principal for 1980.

Exhibit 4   Percentage of Revenue/Principal

	1979	1980
Elm Grove Capacitor	40.0%	33.0%
Circuit Specialists	15.0%	15.0%
Genesis Gate Array	14.0%	19.5%
Waltham Resistor	16.0%	12.0%
Pronto Circuit	14.0%	14.0%
Flexico	1.0%	5.5%
Alba Electronics (8/80)	—	1.0%
Hosunwa America (12/80)	—	
	100%	100%

1981

Between 1978 and 1980, the price of tantalite ore had risen approximately 270%. In keeping with industry trends, the price of Elm Grove's tantalum electrolytic capacitors had been driven up 115% in 1980. Many of McKenzie's customers had begun to switch to cheaper aluminum electrolytic capacitors.

The McKenzie Company's sales of Elm Grove's capacitors were flat in the first two quarters of 1981. Increased supply caused the price of tantalum powder to drop, allowing Elm Grove to reduce its prices. By the third quarter of 1981, prices of tantalum electrolytic capacitors were down 25%, but this effort to hold market share only served to hold the company's sales in this segment at 1980 levels.

Elm Grove was also forced to drop prices for its ceramic monolythic capacitors in an effort to maintain sales in the face of significant industry overcapacity. Rising material costs forced Elm Grove's film capacitor prices up 5%.

By the end of the third quarter, Elm Grove's sales were 4% below 1980 levels, with some sales regions posting 8% declines. McKenzie and Monroe had managed to hold sales at 1980 levels within the Los Angeles territory, which was not feeling the effects of the recession quite as sharply as other regions.

Many of McKenzie's accounts began to switch to cheaper aluminum capacitors. The Hosunwa line not only allowed McKenzie to maintain sales that would otherwise have been lost, but opened avenues to new markets. Although aluminum electrolytic capacitors were manufactured throughout the Far East, the Japanese product was judged to be superior in quality and technology. McKenzie gained market share from other aluminum electrolytic capacitor manufacturers as well as from former tantalum users.

The Hosunwa line experienced rapid sales growth at the expense of their competitors. The company was very price competitive and anxious to gain share quickly. McKenzie's revenues from Hosunwa sales equalled market revenues from Elm Grove sales by the end of the second quarter of 1981. However, the Hosunwa sales manager was working toward a quota determined by Hosunwa of Japan's five-year strategic plan, which did not anticipate the 1980–1981 recession. He was often critical of The McKenzie Company's performance even though McKenzie's sales were 10% to 30% above those of the other Hosunwa representatives' quotas in the western region. He developed the habit of calling the office to suggest that McKenzie or Monroe be sure to see, "so-and-so as soon as possible this week," using a tone of voice that quickly raised the listener's anger.

After 18 months with The McKenzie Company, Donald Monroe had hit full stride. He had become comfortable with all the company's lines and the rising sales volumes for Hosunwa America products were as much his doing as McKenzie's. Although McKenzie was slow to praise

Monroe directly, he emphasized the man's abilities to the company's principals.

In June of 1981, McKenzie hired a second salesman, James Hadinata, who was a Los Angeles native. He had spent his senior year in high school as an exchange student in Japan, and after graduating from UCLA had gone to work for Nippon Electric Company's first U.S. subsidiary. Starting in sales, he had received several promotions during his four years with the firm and was a marketing manager for Nippon's 16 K RAM when Nippon's president's daughter abruptly broke their engagement and Hadinata elected to leave the company.

McKenzie had known Hadinata casually for two years (their boats were in adjacent moorings) and Monroe and Hadinata had raced against each other in several local regattas. When Monroe mentioned that Hadinata was job hunting, McKenzie reached for the phone, asked Hadinata to join them for dinner, and the following Monday, Hadinata joined the firm.

The entire passive components/semiconductor industry experienced a sales slump in the first half of 1981. Waltham Resistor, Pronto Circuit, Flexico, and Alba Electronics all had flat sales through the first two quarters. Only Genesis Gate Array and Circuit Specialists were immune to the recession. Their sales doubled from the same period the previous year.

During good times McKenzie had been diligent in communicating with his principals, sending short notes with competitive information or market forecasts at least bimonthly. Now McKenzie went to greater lengths, calling and/or writing at least every four weeks to trace the extent of the recession, identify any bright spots, and assure his principals that the drop in orders in no way reflected the amount of service they were receiving.

As the recession deepened in the third quarter of 1981, an anti-Japanese feeling appeared to be growing within the electronic components industry as imports continued to take share from American products. Several of McKenzie's American principals, and in particular Elm Grove, made comments about McKenzie's Japanese line. These ranged from small jokes to unusually hostile remarks about supporting American-made products during hard times. This attitude on the part of the American principals made it even more difficult for McKenzie to keep his temper with Hosunwa's sales manager. Whenever possible he had Hadinata take the calls that were briefer and less vitriolic when Japanese was spoken.

Ironically Hosunwa's sales continued to increase beyond expectation. The company had a product of superior quality, an American service staff that gave extremely prompt and courteous customer service plus low prices. By the end of 1981 revenues from McKenzie's sales of Hosunwa's line exceeded revenues of Elm Grove. Exhibit 5 shows McKenzie's revenue per principal for 1981.

Exhibit 5   Percentage of Revenue/Principal

	1979	1980	1981
Elm Grove Capacitor	40.0%	33.5%	20.5%
Circuit Specialists	15.0%	15.0%	16.0%
Genesis Gate Array	14.0%	19.0%	22.0%
Waltham Resistor	16.0%	12.0%	6.0%
Pronto Circuit	14.0%	14.0%	9.0%
Flexico	1.0%	5.5%	4.0%
Alba Electronics	—	1.0%	2.0%
Hosunwa America	—	—	20.5%
	100%	100%	100%

1982

In December 1981, Circuit Specialists was acquired by the Roundy Corporation, a Boston-based semiconductor manufacturer. Circuit Specialists was Roundy's seventh acquisition in three years. The aggressive, rapid-growth company had developed a diversification plan that hinged on its acquisition of small companies with leading-edge technologies within the semiconductor industry.

As more than 60% of Roundy's sales were made in New England, the company maintained a direct sales force in the east. The balance of the company sales were made through electronic sales representative firms. In January 1982, Roundy fired Circuit Specialists' New England representative and added the line to their own sales portfolio. Circuit Specialists' president invited McKenzie to lunch January 5 to tell him of the new arrangements and, "to assure you that Roundy has no intention of extending their direct sales force outside New England." However, as a matter of company policy, McKenzie was given a copy of Roundy's standard contract which would supercede Circuit Specialists contract with McKenzie Company in 90 days. While commission rates were not affected, the new contract had a 30-day cancellation clause, with commission paid on outstanding orders for only 60 days. In contrast, Circuit Specialists' contract had had a 90-day termination clause with commission to be paid on all outstanding backlog. Given the long development time associated with custom circuit design, only a very small percentage of outstanding commissions would be collected in 60 days.

Roundy's main line of semiconductors was presently under contract with the largest sales representative firm in Los Angeles. McKenzie wondered if Roundy would also wish to consolidate their subsidiaries' lines with one firm. In spite of the personal assurances from his old friend at Circuit Specialists, McKenzie was troubled.

Even more alarming news came from Elm Grove's sales manager on January 10, 1982. Elm Grove had adopted a strategic plan to improve its performance in the capacitor marketplace. In order to try to recapture sales volume lost to aluminum electrolytic capacitors, Elm Grove had decided to add an aluminum capacitor manufactured in Taiwan to their product line. This addition would become effective April 1, and at that time McKenzie would probably have to choose between his two major principals.

Elm Grove had also decided that the company must now move to avoid further erosion of the market share. IC chips had displaced discrete capacitors and resistors in many electronics applications between 1978–1981. The decline in market share was offset slightly by technological constraints that limited the amount of capacitance that could be incorporated into an IC chip. To bridge this gap, discrete capacitors could be mounted externally on a printed circuit board supporting the IC. Elm Grove had quietly invested the lion's share of their 1981 R&D money in the development of capacitor chips. Some industry observers had predicted that the chip format could gain 20% of the capacitor market by the mid-1980s. Elm Grove's sales manager expected that the company would have their new product ready for market within eight months, by August 1982, although no date for official introduction had been announced.

For McKenzie's customers the choice between Hosunwa's line and the Taiwanese capacitor would be equivalant to choosing between an unknown generic product and a well-advertised major name brand. As McKenzie knew only too well, the Hosunwa line had an enthusiastic clientele who would not be easily persuaded to switch to an unknown product particularly when cost was equal and the quality of the Taiwanese capacitor was unproven.

McKenzie, Monroe, and Hadinata met to objectively evaluate the two principals. Monroe supported Elm Grove. He argued that the company was mature, reliable, prompt to pay commissions, and its sales manager was a friend. Although not a market leader in the past, its new strategy could signal a more aggressive approach that might generate larger sales if the company's predictions for capacitor chips and its new products proved sound. The contract with Elm Grove had a 90-day cancellation clause and commission would be paid on all outstanding orders.

Hosunwa was certainly the more dynamic company. It was aggressively pursuing market share. Its R&D expenditures were believed to be high. The company had suffered some growing pains; its policies kept changing with its management as people moved up. The present sales manager was a pain in the neck, but the man's ambition was such that Hadinata predicted that he would seek promotion successfully and move on within the company. There were rumors that the company planned to expand its product line. Twice Hosunwa's sales manager had cut McKenzie's commission rate on large sales. In addition, as the recession had continued, Hosunwa had dropped its maximum commission for sales to a single customer.

Exhibit 6   The McKenzie Company

Time Line for Personnel and Principals Added

Personnel (Date of Hire)	1978 Jan Mar Jun Oct	1979 Jan Mar Jun Oct	1980 Jan Mar Jun Oct	1981 Jan Mar Jun Oct	1982 Jan Mar Jun Oct
McKenzie					
Secretary					
Bookkeeper	(part time 1978)				
Monroe				*	
Hadinata					
Principals:					
Elm Grove	60%	40%	33%	20.5%	
Circuit Specialists	4%	15%	15%	16%	
Genesis G. A.	6%	14%	19.5%	22%	
Waltham Resistor	15%	16%	12%	6%	
Pronto P. C.	13%	14%	14%	9%	
Flexico		1%	5.5%	4%	
Alba			1%	2%	
Hosunwa				20.5%	

*Monroe now fully productive.

McKenzie found it hard to assess the anti-Japanese sentiments so recently surfacing among his Amercan principals and the electronics industry as a whole. There had been talk in Washington about raising tariffs or imposing quotas on Japanese imports. McKenzie wondered if his possession of one major Japanese line might attract others. Remembering Smith Associates' experience with Japanese products, McKenzie thought of them as "money in the bank," assuming they did not grow so big that they found it more profitable to move away from sales reps into direct sales.

Conclusion

Back in his office, McKenzie again weighed Elm Grove against Hosunwa. He realized that whatever course he chose, he could expect a substantial drop in revenue in 1982. After nine months with McKenzie, Hadinata was performing beyond any expectation and would show a profit above his costs to the company within three months if he continued at his present pace. McKenzie knew that with the loss of either principal, the McKenzie Company's sales would probably be off at least 20%. In the short run he would be hard pressed to keep Hadinata, yet in the long run he had no choice if the firm were to grow. And if McKenzie's firm were to grow as he wished, he knew he needed to take a long look at his principals and their futures (see Exhibits 6–8).

Exhibit 7　The McKenzie Company's Income Statement 1978–1981

Commission Revenue	1978 $70,000	1979 $115,000	1980 $153,900	1981 $263,000
Expenses				
Business Meals & Entertainment	3,640	5,980	8,003	13,676
Dues & Subs.	70	115	154	263
Group Insurance	1,750	2,875	3,847	6,575
Insurance	378	621	831	1,420
Payroll Taxes	3,211	5,155	7,002	11,902
Postage	189	310	416	710
Professional Services	2,800	4,600	6,156	10,520
Rent and Office Expenses	3,570	5,865	7,849	13,413
Salaries and Commissions	49,394	79,312	107,730	183,112
Telephone and Telegraph	3,241	5,324	7,126	12,177
Travel	1,407	2,312	3,093	5,286
Total Operating Expenses	69,650	112,470	152,207	259,055
Net Income Before Tax	350	2,530	1,693	3,945
Taxes	168	1,214	813	1,894
Net Income after Tax	$182	$1,316	$880	$2,051

**Exhibit 8   The McKenzie Company:
Percentage of Revenue per Principal per Year**

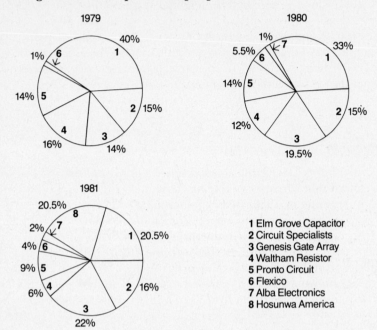

1979

1980

1981

1 Elm Grove Capacitor
2 Circuit Specialists
3 Genesis Gate Array
4 Waltham Resistor
5 Pronto Circuit
6 Flexico
7 Alba Electronics
8 Hosunwa America

The McKenzie Company (B)*

In May 1982, one of the McKenzie Company's former principals, Hosunwa of Japan, reached a cooperative agreement with two other Japanese passive component manufacturers. The three merged to form a new corporation. Hosunwa America was to be enlarged. Its management staff would take responsibility for introducing the other product lines in the United States.

Hosunwa America's sales manager, Bill Tanabe, was given responsibility for all three product lines. He immediately exercised a 30-day termination clause with all Hosunwa's U.S. sales representatives and began to set up a direct sales force. One of his first job offers went to James Hadinata, to whom he offered a sales position in Hosunwa's Western Region. Tanabe implied that he expected a promotion soon, and that Hadinata would be in line for his job as sales manager.

Hadinata received Hosunwa's offer on May 28. Unexpected and unsolicited, it nevertheless appeared to be an extraordinary opportunity. Hadinata spent the Memorial Day weekend trying to evaluate the offer from all perspectives. On Tuesday, June 1, he came into the office early to catch McKenzie before he could leave to make sales calls, and bluntly outlined Hosunwa's offer and its apparent advantages, which included a $4,000 raise and bonus/commission potential that appeared likely to increase his present income by about 30% within twelve months.

It's a great opportunity for me, Mac. The only really negative thing about it is that I'd report directly to Tanabe. But I've managed to work with him from here, even though I don't like him. If his market projections are sound Hosunwa offers real potential for advancement. I told him I'd give him my answer on Friday after I had a chance to think about it and talk to you.

McKenzie suggested Hadinata join him for dinner the following evening, and Hadinata left the office. With effort McKenzie restrained himself from putting his fist through the wall. He immediately called his lawyer to determine whether he could legally prevent Hadinata from taking the job through the noncompete agreement Hadinata had signed.

McKenzie's lawyer was immediately pessimistic. McKenzie had terminated the Hosunwa contract in April 1982 when a conflict of interest between Elm Grove Capacitor and Hosunwa had arisen. In general, McKenzie's lawyer felt that noncompete contracts were difficult to enforce. Likely costs of litigation, in time and energy as well as money, could be high.

Once his anger cooled, McKenzie began to consider what other options he had available. Hadinata was a superb salesman and he worked well with McKenzie and Monroe. It would be difficult to attract another large principal with only one salesman besides himself to cover the territory and even Hadinata who was far from typical had taken 12 months of training to begin to pay his way.

Hyde-Phillip Chemical Company

*Alternative Forms of Sales Representation**

Michael Claxton, a recent marketing graduate of a well-known college, has been assigned the task of evaluating Hyde-Phillip Chemical Company's methods of selling the firm's products. Hyde-Phillip currently uses a mix of company salespersons, merchant wholesalers, and agent wholesalers to present its products to present and potential users. While this combination of selling forces is somewhat usual, it reflects the orientation of management over time as to the relative values of alternative forms of sales representation. Claxton's challenge is to review the data that has been gathered on the three types of sales efforts, determine if additional information is needed, and make recommendations as to what changes, if any, should be made in the firm's sales representation.

*From W. Wayne Talarzyk, *Cases for Analysis in Marketing* (Hinsdale, Il.: The Dryden Press, 1977), pp. 70–74. © 1977 by The Dryden Press. Reprinted by permission of The Dryden Press, CBS College Publishing.

Information on the Company

Hyde-Phillip was formed in the early 1960s through the merger of Hyde Industrial Chemicals and Phillip Laboratories. Both firms had a broad range of experience in the development and production of certain types of chemicals and related supplies for a variety of industrial users. While the two firms had a few overlapping product lines, each brought to the merger some exclusive product offerings. The combination yielded a new organization capable of marketing a complete line of chemicals for industrial use.

Prior to the merger, Hyde Industrial Chemicals had utilized a group of industrial distributors (merchant wholesalers) to market its products. Phillip Laboratories, on the other hand, had several manufacturers' agents (agent wholesalers) who sold its product offering. The new firm, after the merger, retained some of the industrial distributors and some of the manufacturing agents and then began to develop its own sales force.

Today, Hyde-Phillip serves 30 sales territories in states east of the Mississippi through its own sales force of 50 individuals (6 women and 44 men), 9 industrial distributors, and 9 manufacturers' agents. The 50 salespeople are allocated about evenly across 12 of the sales territories. Each of the industrial distributors and manufacturers' agents has exclusive selling rights in one of the 18 remaining sales territories. Individual distributors and agents have from 5 to 30 people working for them and many represent other noncompeting manufacturers. The 30 sales territories were originally established to represent areas of approximately equal sales potential for Hyde-Phillip's products.

Many types of sales support are made available to each sales territory by the company. Territory managers have the option of using such sales support. Sales support items currently available include: (1) a variety of descriptive brochures to supplement the information given in the firm's product catalog, (2) study programs with cassette tapes to enable sales representatives to be more familiar with the firm's products and current market situations and developments, (3) a program to provide generous product samples to potential customers for test purposes, and (4) direct-mail programs aimed at prospective customers to solicit inquiries for descriptive materials and product samples.

Data on Sales Territories

As a first step in beginning his analysis, Claxton asked his assistant to compile the information available on each of the 30 sales territories. This information is coded in Exhibit 1.

In terms of level of sales, nine territories have annual sales in excess of $2 million, 15 have sales between $1 million and $2 million, and six have sales less than $1 million. As already indicated, in 12 of the territo-

Exhibit 1   Available Data on Sales Territories

Territory Number	Level of Sales	Type of Representation	Use of Sales Support	Geographic Location
1	2	1	2	3
2	3	1	3	3
3	2	2	1	1
4	1	1	1	1
5	2	3	1	1
6	2	1	2	1
7	3	3	2	3
8	1	2	1	1
9	2	1	2	2
10	2	1	2	3
11	1	2	1	1
12	1	1	1	2
13	2	2	2	2
14	2	3	2	1
15	1	1	2	3
16	2	3	2	2
17	2	1	3	1
18	1	2	1	2
19	2	3	2	2
20	3	1	3	2
21	1	3	1	3
22	2	2	1	3
23	3	3	1	1
24	3	1	3	2
25	3	2	3	1
26	1	2	1	2
27	2	1	2	2
28	1	2	1	3
29	2	3	3	3
30	2	3	2	3

Codes:
Level of sales: 1   over $2 million; 2 $1–2 million; 3   under $1 million.
Type of representation: 1   company sales force; 2   industrial distributor; 3   manufacturers' agent.
Use of sales support: 1   extensive user; 2   moderate user; 3   light user.
Geographic location: 1   Northern; 2   Southern; 3   Eastern.

ries the firm is represented by its own sales force, and industrial distributors and manufacturers' agents each represent the company in nine territories.

Based on estimates provided by the sales support department, 12 of the territories make extensive use of the sales support programs, 12 are moderate users, and six are light users. Each of the sales territories is also divided into one of three geographic divisions: Northern, Southern, or Eastern, each with 10 sales territories.

Initial Analysis

Using the information in Exhibit 1, Claxton constructed the cross-tabulation of sales versus type of representation as shown in Exhibit 2. He first set up the cross-tabulation using raw numbers and then calculated the conditional probabilities for each row and column.

Exhibit 2   Cross-Tabulation of Level of Sales versus Type of Representation

			Company Sales Force (1)	Industrial Distrib- utor (2)	Manu- facturers' Agent (3)	Totals
	Over $2 million	(1)	3.	5	1	9
Level of Sales	$1–2 million	(2)	6	3	6	15 A
	Under $1 million	(3)	3	1	2	6
	Totals		12	9	9	

			Company Sales Force (1)	Industrial Distrib- utor (2)	Manu- facturers' Agent (3)	
	Over $2 million	(1)	33.3	55.6	11.1	100.0
Level of Sales	$1–2 million	(2)	40.0	20.0	40.0	100.0 B
	Under $1 million	(3)	50.0	16.7	33.3	100.0
	Totals		40.0	30.0	30.0	100.0

			Company Sales Force (1)	Industrial Distrib- utor (2)	Manu- facturers' Agent (3)	
	Over $2 million	(1)	25.0	55.6	11.1	30.0
Level of Sales	$1–2 million	(2)	50.0	33.3	66.7	50.0 C
	Under $1 million	(3)	25.0	11.1	22.2	20.0
	Totals		100.0	100.0	100.0	

Code: A—raw numbers
B—row conditional probabilities
C—column conditional probabilities.

As seen in part B of Exhibit 2, 30.0 percent of Hyde-Phillip's territories with sales over $2 million were served by industrial distributors. Only 11.1 percent of the largest sales territories were represented by manufacturers' agents and 33.3 percent were served by the company sales force. Stated differently, as shown in part C of Exhibit 2, 25 percent of territories served by the company's sales force had sales over $2 million, while 55.6 percent of the industrial distributors and 11.1 percent of the manufacturers' agents served territories with sales over $2 million.

Claxton's initial reaction was that the firm should consider replacing part of its own sales force and the manufacturers' agents with industrial distributors. He was concerned, however, with what other variables should be taken into account to more fully analyze and evaluate Hyde-Phillip's current approach to sales representation.

Transcon Parts*

Interoffice
Memorandum

To: Mr. Leo Sarns, Distribution Manager

From: George Kall, Warehouse Manager, Aurora

Subject: Parts Delivery

Date: January 12, 1977

Ref: P.O. Nos. 11-76-328C
                11-76-012C
                11-76-921C

Routing: TX

I must call to your attention that to date the back-ordered items on these P.O.s have not been received as follows:

21 NE 040	3 gross
2100-0125-0050	7 dozen
19 NTE 080	4 gross

Customers are jumping up and down. Please advise immediately re current status by return TX.

Mr. Sarns hesitated outside Norman Jane's office while he mulled the contents of the memo. He could predict Mr. Jane's reaction to it, but there seemed to be no alternative but to bring the matter before his boss, who was vice president of marketing and customer service.

---

*"Transcon Parts" was authored by William B. Ayars, Ph.D., and Howard F. Rudd, Jr., D.B.A., of California State College, Bakersfield.

"Come in, Leo what's on your mind today?"

"Hi, Norm. Another one just came in on the Telex, this time from Aurora, Illinois. Here, take a look at it. I have checked with shipping and those backorders were shipped on December 20 out of our Anaheim plant. The fleet manager has traced two of them, which were misrouted to Mobile. He can't pin down the other one . . . I've tried, Norm. I guess we all have. Two of those customers are Cone Brothers and Kennecott Copper. I guess you know that heads will roll if we lose either one of them."

"Yeah, Leo, I know. How many complaints like this are we getting?"

"This makes the eleventh since the first of the year."

"Wow. Say, I have an appointment in 15 minutes with John Seamon, why don't you join me? I want to bring this thing up, and I need you to help me on the details."

The Company

Mr. Seamon was actually not very surprised that this matter was brought to his attention. In fact, he had foreseen it years before he became president of Transcon Parts. He had joined the company in 1942, shortly after it had been formed in response to government demand for tank tracks, sprockets, axles, and pins during World War II. The company had done very well until 1946, as it had just one customer, which bought all it could produce.

After the war, the company had switched over to making replacement tractor and loader parts and attachments. While the production operation required relatively little modification, the company had soon found itself serving many diverse markets, and the distribution function had taken on a whole new and constantly changing complexion.

By 1965 the original plant in Joliet, Illinois, had been supplemented with plants in Anaheim, California, Pittsburgh, Pennsylvania, Mobile, Alabama, and Portland, Oregon. In addition, the company operated 18 storage and distribution warehouses in large cities in Arizona, Utah, Colorado, Texas (2), Oklahoma, Kansas, Iowa, Louisiana, Tennessee, Ohio (3), Georgia, Florida (2), New Jersey, and Massachusetts.

Each plant and warehouse provided full multistate service to customers either through their own facilities or through dealers, distributors, manufacturers' representatives, or jobbing contractors in every state of the Union.

Iron and steel were purchased from steel mills for motor transportation to the plants. Each plant had distinctly different production patterns. One plant might do rough castings and finished tracks, where another would finish rough castings and produce rough forgings. Still another plant reclaimed and converted used track. Thus, one plant was dependent to some extent for its raw materials upon the output of another plant.

Additions to the product mix included rollers, shafts, lifting devices, bushings, seals, and lugs. By 1972, Mr. Seamon had the impression that the augmented product lines were in line with customer expectations.

Mr. Seamon knew that Transcon's price structure was slightly above that of the competition, but his decision has been made at the request of the sales force. In this way they could argue that the company provided superior service in exchange for premium prices. Most customer purchasing agents had seemed more interested in service than in shaving the prices.

This strategy had been effective over the years as the company grew larger. However, now that it was a nationwide operation there was some question about the company's continuing ability to meet expected levels of service.

The permanent fleet at present includes 15 tractors and 35 trailers. Six tractors and 15 trailers are stationed at Joliet, and four tractors and nine trailers are stationed in Anaheim and Pittsburgh, and the remainder in Mobile. All vehicles are dispatched by the fleet manager's office in Joliet.

An individual truck might typically be routed as follows: Loaded at Joliet with track and finished castings, it would proceed toward Pittsburgh, stopping en route for partial unloadings at warehouses in Ohio and for on-site deliveries to contractors in Michigan, Indiana, Kentucky, and West Virginia. At Pittsburgh the vehicle might reload with stock destined for dealers, wholesalers, and contractors in New York, Vermont, New Hampshire, Maine, Connecticut, and Rhode Island. The vehicle might return via Pittsburgh with imported goods loaded in Boston and Hoboken, New Jersey, partially unloading en route in states as far south as Virginia. Some of this lading might be destined for finishing in Anaheim; therefore, additional loadings would take place at Pittsburgh and Joliet, and the truck would be routed westward in a similar manner.

The Industry

Mr. Seamon knew that customer service always had been of paramount importance in the business. Customers depended on quality of steel and workmanship in casting, forging, milling, grinding, and fabrication to be sure, but they were even more concerned about on-time deliveries and minimizing loss, damage, and misroutings.

On the other hand, competition keeps the company's net margin to 25–30 percent. This constraint requires that warehouse stock turn an average of four times per year. Just a few years ago, when inflation was not as serious, three times a year was sufficient.

Top Management Meets

Mr. Seamon greeted Mr. Jane and Mr. Sarns as they walked into his office. He studied the memo and ventured an opinion.

"Gentlemen, it looks like we have outgrown private carriage as our best method of distribution. Let's explore the other feasible alternatives. What is our competition using?"
Mr. Sarns responded.
"Well, Topper Corp. operates east of the Mississippi, as you know. They have been using common carriers and UPS blue label* for four years that I know of. Apparently, they have

*This is United Parcel Service combined with air freight.

found this satisfactory. Then there is Trans-United. They are nationwide, and they recently switched over from private carriage to a contract surface carrier. I imagine that they supplement this with air freight. It is too early to say just how well this arrangement is working out. There is also the Abel Speeder Corp. which has been a West Coast firm and appears to be going nationwide. They have been using common carriers and bus package express. Earthworm Tractor uses rail freight in combination with regular air cargo service nationwide, but they're not into replacement parts like we are."

Mr. Jane was next to comment.

"That's a good rundown on the competition, Leo, but I don't see that it helps us very much. How can we get a good handle on the types of services these carriers can provide for us, and how good are they?"

"Well, an interstate common motor carrier may tell you seven days delivery time from pick-up anywhere in the country. But you don't know when he will pick up and how often the lading must be interlined.** Therefore, you really cannot tell when your lading will arrive at destination. In practice, intrastate hauls can arrive two days after pickup, which is pretty good. In any case, they will not haul without a full load.

"Contract carriers vary quite a lot. If you can get one to make regularly scheduled runs between our plants and maybe warehouses, you can depend on his delivery dates. On the other hand, you may not have much lading for a particular run, but you will need to pay him in full for the run anyhow. In that case he may fill up with other shipper's stuff or he may not. You must share this risk with him, and his terms will reflect this. Regarding on-site contractor deliveries, I don't know. I imagine that this is negotiable, perhaps on a cost-plus basis.

"Rail freight is similar to common motor carriers, but you never do have much of an idea when it will get there. Heavy loads are cheaper, but you have to haul it to the rail head. You also have to load it onto a spotted rail car to the carrier's specifications.

"Bus and air freight both require packages no longer than six feet, and each shipment must be no heavier than 100 pounds in two or more cartons. Bus will take three days from the West Coast to, say, St. Louis and five days to Boston. Air freight will get it there in one to two days portal to portal, but it'll cost you.

"Now you wanted to know how good these carriers are. Here are the results of a recent survey done by *Purchasing* magazine. (See Exhibit 1.) Looks like the Postal Service is not competitive, but the rest of the data may help us."

Mr. Seamon replied.

"Thank you, Leo. It looks like we have something to work with here. Norm, I'd like you to come up with a recommendation. Keep in mind that it may still be possible to revamp our private carriage to handle the job, althouth I realize that you have already tried several different arrangements. At any rate, we'll have to move on this so our company image doesn't go straight down the tubes. Let's have a preliminary recommendation by next Wednesday. Thank you, gentlemen, and good day."

Back in his office, Mr. Jane cancelled his Saturday morning golf date and glanced through a sheaf of memos similar to the one that brought Leo Sarns into his office. It now occurred to him that during the past few months the number of phone calls he had received from dissatisfied customers had increased dramatically. Also, most of them dealt with promised delivery dates not kept. Apparently, customers still liked the quality of Transcon products, but this was of little consolation when they were not getting them when and where they needed them.

The Ajax Pump Company *

The Ajax Pump Company is the number two supplier of small pumps and valves to industrial replacement markets. The company's early success (1940s and 1950s) was built on local availability of virtually all

---

** Interlining means unloading from a truck belonging to a carrier who does not have ICC authority to haul farther, and loading onto one that does. Each interline requires an extra 1–2 days.

* This case was prepared by James D. Blaser, director, Cleveland Consulting Associates. Reprinted by permission.

Exhibit 1 Survey by the Editors of *Purchasing* Magazine, May–June, 1976: How Buyers Rate Carriers

Buyers surveyed were asked to rate carriers for each factor on a scale from 1 to 10, where 10 indicates the best possible performance and 1, the worst possible.

	Strongest Points (7.0 or higher)		Weakest Points (5.0 or lower)			
	Reliability of Service	Reasonable Rates	Assistance, Advice, Other Aid	Careful Handling	Claims Handling	Overall Performance
Air						
United Parcel Service (air)	8.0	7.8	6.9	7.6	6.4	7.5
Air Express	7.1	5.4	7.0	7.3	5.8	7.0
Air freight forwarder	7.5	6.1	7.6	7.2	6.4	6.6
Air Taxi Commuter	7.7	5.7	7.0	7.3	5.9	6.6
Regular air service	7.0	5.8	6.7	6.7	5.8	6.6
Air Parcel Post	5.5	5.8	5.1	4.5	4.2	5.0
Surface						
United Parcel Service (surface)	8.3	8.3	6.9	7.6	6.4	7.9
Bus package express	7.6	7.7	6.3	7.1	6.1	6.9
Water carriers (inland & intercoastal)	6.6	6.6	6.4	6.6	6.4	6.7
Motor carrier (trucks)	7.0	6.3	7.4	6.3	5.6	6.6
Water carriers (ocean)	6.5	6.8	6.4	6.6	5.4	6.4
Rail freight forwarder (carloading companies)	5.9	6.0	7.0	6.3	5.2	6.1
Rail	4.9	6.0	6.3	5.2	5.2	5.3
Parcel Post	4.3	5.5	4.5	4.0	4.2	4.2

replacement pumps and valves. In response to that market need, Ajax developed a strong distributor network, backed up by 23 small field warehouses under the direct control of the local marketing managers.

Two plants, one in New York and one in Chicago, ship to the field warehouses direct through small plant warehouses. Warehouse replenishment orders are generated by warehouse clerks using a manual system. Clerks record sales and shipments received and therefore determine actual inventory levels continuously. Orders for replenishing the inventory are placed when a predetermined level of on-hand inventory is reached. Manual order records are mailed to headquarters for billing and accumulation of sales statistics.

Several important market trends developed in the 1960s:

1. Ajax's distributors, after being caught in the first modern credit crunch (1966) became much less willing to hold inventory. They carry most of the line but now rely more heavily on the Ajax field warehouse for backup stock and all fringe items.

2. The company's marketing department has successfully developed national service contracts with major industrial concerns to be administered directly. These accounts are served from the regional warehouses, and their demand is more difficult to predict than the demand generated through the local distributors.

3. The product line has proliferated: In 1960, the line amounted to 1575 separate items or stock-keeping units: now the product offering has 5320 separate items.

4. Manufacturing completed a three-year program to reconfigure the production facilities and integrate foundry and aluminum die casting capabilities. While costs are lower, economic run sizes are now substantially larger and flexibility has been reduced from when most components were purchased outside.

During the chaotic 1973–1975 economic period, Ajax was thrown into a loss position for the first time in 36 years. Inventories skyrocketed and, coupled with funding requirements associated with the manufacturing program, forced the company to borrow up to the limit of its financial ability. Market conditions have stabilized but inventory remains too high by traditional standards. In spite of high inventories, Ajax's customer service level is below customer expectations and industry standards. In fact, marketing has gone on record that Ajax has lost market share because of poor service.

A new distribution manager has been hired and been given responsibility for the warehouses, finished goods inventory control, order processing, and traffic. His first job is to develop a plan to restore Ajax's distribution position for presentation to top management within the next three months. To facilitate this task, he examined key financial and distribution data (see Exhibits 1–3).

Exhibit 1   Ajax Pump Company: Summary Financial Statements, 1976

Profit and Loss Statement

	Thousands
Sales	$75,000
Cost of Goods	42,220
Gross Profit	$32,780
Distribution Costs	$12,760
Selling and Administrative	5,750
Depreciation	9,000
Interest	2,520
Income Taxes	1,250
Net Income	$ 1,500

Balance Sheet

Assets		Liabilities and Capital	
Cash	$ 400	Current Liabilities	$ 5,600
Receivables	8,000	Long Term Debt	26,500
Inventories	20,000		
Manufacturing Facilities[1]	38,200	Total Debt	$32,100
Distribution Facilities[1]	12,900		
Other	500	Shareholder Equity	$47,900
Total	$80,000	Total	$80,000

[1] Net of accumulated depreciation

Exhibit 2   Key Financial Relationships and Ratios (Dollars in Thousands)

Incremental Pretax Profit Contribution:

	Total % of sales	Variable % of sales	% of Sales
Reported gross margin			43.7%
Other variable costs:			
Distribution	17%	38%	−6.5
Selling and administrative	8	15	−1.2
Contribution Margin			36.0%

Finished Goods Inventory Turns:

Cost of goods	$42,220		
Average f.g. inventory	16,000		2.6

Exhibit 3.   Key Distribution Data

Analysis of Distribution Cost	Thousands	Percent of Sales
Inbound transportation	$ 3,150	4.2%
Outbound transportation	2,100	2.8%
Warehouse operating costs		
fixed	3,345	4.5
variable	1,380	1.8
Order entry/billing system	1,100	1.5
Packaging	535	0.7
Logistics administration	100	0.1
Traffic, receiving, and shipping	600	0.8
Taxes, obsolescence, and insurances	450	0.6
Total	$12,760	17.0%

Shipment Profile

	Truckload	LTL	Other
Inbound replenishment	73%	27%	0%
Outbound	3	96	1

	Dollars	Pounds
Average Shipment Size:	$700	800

Order Cycle Time

	Average	95% Confidence
Order mail in	2	4
Internal processing	4	10
Outbound shipment	1	3
Total	7	17

Customer Service Level

% of items filled	83%

The new distribution manager has been through an improvement effort like the one required at Ajax before and, after becoming thoroughly familiar with the situation, has developed a shopping list of major projects and programs he would like to evaluate and perhaps implement:

1. Evaluate a consolidated distribution network with five to seven new modern distribution centers to take the place of the present 23 warehouses.

2. Design a new order entry/inventory control billing system that would automatically update inventory records and have extensive order and stock inquiry capabilities.

3. Develop a shipment consolidation program to accumulate a greater share of outbound shipments into truckloads.

4.   Evaluate the possibility of pulling back the fringe items into a master warehouse and provide rapid-response national service for those items, using premium transportation.

Over lunch one day, the distribution manager bounced these ideas off the president and vice president of marketing. The president was very interested but reminded the distribution manager that these appeared to be major long-term projects, requiring considerable analysis and capital to implement. He reiterated his wish that the distribution improvement plan include detailed financial evaluations and justification.

In view of his objective to restore a sound financial position, the president asked that less capital intense improvements be looked at first. The vice president of marketing added that Ajax's major competitors were delivering orders within a three-day turnaround time and achieving a reported 92 percent initial order fill level. As a result, the company was losing sales and market share every day.

With those facts in mind, the distribution manager set about designing the improvement plan.

Caterpillar Tractor Company*

Background

Caterpillar Tractor Company is a large industrial manufacturing firm headquartered in Peoria, Illinois. Its familiar "CAT" logo and yellow paint are known throughout the world. Indeed, in its business Caterpillar has an estimated 37% of the world market; its closest rival, Japan's Komatsu, has an estimated 15%.

A multinational company, Caterpillar has manufacturing and dealer representatives throughout the world. The products which the firm designs, manufactures, and markets can be classified into two basic categories:

1.   Earthmoving, Construction and Materials Handling equipment—track-type tractors, bulldozers, rippers, track and wheel-type loaders, pipelayers, wheel dozers, compactors, wheel tractor-scrapers, off-highway trucks and tractors, motor graders, hydraulic excavators, log skidders, lift trucks, and related parts and equipment.

2.   Engines—for earthmoving and construction machines, on-highway trucks, marine petroleum, agricultural, industrial and electric power generation systems. Engines, either diesel or natural gas, have power ranges from 85 to 1600 horsepower, or, in generator

*This case was prepared by Dr. George B. Glisan, Illinois State University. Copyright 1984.

set versions, from 55 to 1200 kilowatts. Turbines range from 25 to 10,600 horsepower, and, in generator set configurations, from 10 to 7900 kilowatts.

Strategy

Caterpillar's market success is based upon two areas of strategic importance—product and after-sale support. The guiding principles of the CAT product strategy are fourfold. First, advanced technology is incorporated into machines so that users derive optimal productivity and efficiency. To maintain the flow of product applications, the organization commits hundreds of millions of dollars each year to research and development. A second product guideline is quality. Within the last ten years several billion dollars have been spent on plant and equipment to ensure the quality of Caterpillar products. Customers demand quality to avoid costly downtime, and to ensure reliability in the hostile operating environments the machines endure.

Another aspect of the product strategy is to offer a full line of products. This implies machines capable of performing on jobsites as small as a residential lot or as large as the Alaskan pipeline, and on jobsites as forebidding as the Amazon jungle, the Sahara Desert, or the Arctic tundra. The CAT product line offers over 100 different machines with a nearly infinite number of options/modifications. A final principle of the product strategy is to design and build only machines that can be produced on an assembly line, to take advantage of the manufacturing expertise and efficiency of the Caterpillar plants, and to provide significant economies of scale.

The other key area of strategic importance to Caterpillar's market success is after-sale support. The core of this effort is the network of 248 independent industrial distributors that represent the firm in the United States (93) and 140 other countries (155). The typical CAT dealer is a very large organization. The combined capitalization of all dealers, in fact, nearly equals the $3+ billion net worth of Caterpillar.

The dealer organization offers after-sale support in two ways—services and parts supply. All Caterpillar dealers are staffed with highly trained technicians and have well-equiped facilities for servicing customer machines. A typical dealer will offer:

1. Customer Track Service—dealer technicians examine the track of track-type machines to detect signs of unusual wear and potential failure before they shut down the machine.

2. Field Service—dealers, through a fleet of specially equipped trucks, can perform many repairs for customers at the jobsite.

3. Technical Analysis—a field check of major mechanical, electrical, cooling, and hydraulic systems as a means of preventive maintenance.

4.   Scheduled Oil Sampling—customers can have samples of the
motor oil in their machines subjected to sophisticated chemical
analysis to detect signs of internal engine wear.

Caterpillar facilitates the quality of this service by providing training
clinics for technicians at the dealership, and by conducting schools at the
Service Training Center in East Peoria, Illinois.

Servicing ablity is moot without the necessary parts. Furthermore,
many customers service their own machines, requiring only parts from
their CAT dealer. As a result a well-stocked inventory of parts is essential. Caterpillar first analyzes the population of machines within a
dealer's sales territory and, based upon this analysis, recommends the
appropriate parts to inventory, as well as the quantity. This minimizes
the inventory cost to the dealer by eliminating unneeded and slow-
moving parts, as well as maximizing service to users. With this suggested
inventory configuration, slightly more than 90% of all parts requests can
be filled from the dealer's inventory.

Caterpillar also facilitates parts supply by providing a way to meet
the unfilled parts requests. All U.S. dealers of Caterpillar are linked by
computer terminal to a parts distribution system. First, a dealer checks
to determine if nearby CAT dealers have the needed parts. If not, a
dealer then searches the inventory of the nearest Caterpillar parts depot
(there are eleven depots in the United States to back up dealers for
emergency parts needs). Routine orders placed by dealers (typically
weekly) are supplied by one of four regional parts distribution departments. Exhibit 1 shows how this system is structured. The system assures
a customer of receiving a part within 48 hours.

Oil Filters

Part of Caterpillar's after-sale system of support is its line of supply
items. These are parts that preserve and maintain the operating efficiency of machines and engines. The engine oil filter plays a critical
maintenance role. While Caterpillar does not actually manufacture oil
filters, it does design and engineer filters, and prescribe to suppliers the
performance parameters that filters must meet. All such filters carry the
Caterpillar label.

One of Caterpillar's procurement policies is to have multiple suppliers for its oil filters. These suppliers are given the design specifications for the filters, and a commitment by Caterpillar to purchase all filters ordered that meet performance standards. Most suppliers produce
and market filters for Caterpillar equipment under their own brand as
well. These filters, however, enter each supplier's own channel of distribution, and are not available at the Caterpillar dealer.

After suppliers manufacture the CAT filters they are shipped to
Caterpillar's main parts distribution center at Morton, Illinois. There filters are randomly selected from shipments and sent to the metallurgical

Exhibit 1   Caterpillar Parts Distribution System

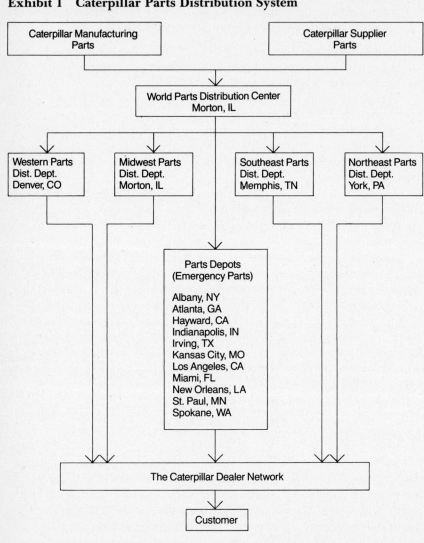

laboratory for testing to determine their acceptability. If a shipment is accepted, the filters are packaged in Caterpillar containers and placed in inventory, ready for shipment through the distribution system.

The New Filter

Recently several problems associated with oil filters have surfaced at Caterpillar. One concerns a new filter design. Initial reports showed sales to be far lower than expected. Optimism for the new design was based upon several improvements over the older design that provide extended protection of users' engines. Specific improvements in the new filter design included full rubber grommets and metal end caps to provide better sealing for maximum oil filtration, a helical coil spring to keep the filter firmly in place under all operating conditions, a superior bypass valve that operates under low- as well as high-pressure conditions to prevent oil starvation to the engine, and a larger filtration element.

Parts marketing representatives have investigated the situation to determine the reasons for the sales resistance, and have found that dealers' and customers' resistance is due to the price of the new filter. There are nearly a dozen competitive brands of oil filters for Caterpillar diesel engines. The mean unit price of these competitive filters is $2.71, whereas the Caterpillar filter is priced at $3.08. With the distinct design advantages of the new filter, as well as the quality assurance of the CAT name, management felt that the 10% price premium was more than justified.

Confirming the reduced sales of filters have been the reports coming from the engine remanufacturing facility at Bettendorf, Iowa. The engines sent to the facility originate from customers who trade their used engine for one that has been remanufactured by Caterpillar. During the inspection of customers' trade-in engines, personnel record the brand of oil filter on the engines. Recent reports show that competitors' oil filters outnumber the Caterpillar brand on the traded engines.

The Dirty Filter

While assessing the situation of the new design filter, management has been notified of the discovery of defective filters during routine testing at the metallurgical laboratory in Morton. Technicians report that one of the tests performed on a sample of filters show that they are "dirty." This means that during the manufacturing process foreign contaminants were trapped inside the filters. If such a filter was to be used by a customer, these contaminants would enter the engine oil unfiltered. The result would be premature engine damage leading to repairs costing several thousand dollars, as well as lost income due to downtime on the job site. Additional testing by the lab has revealed that the scope of the problem is much larger than first thought, and that several hundred thousand filters may be defective. The lab also reports that the filters in question came from only one supplier. The dilemma is double edged for management. Although the decision to return the rejected oil filters to the supplier in question is obvious, because there are so many filters involved there will be a filter shortage in the distribution system. Not only will lost sales result, but competitors will have an opportunity to sell to CAT filter buyers at a time when it is difficult to maintain loyalty due to the price differential.

Supplier Difficulties

A final disturbing problem has emerged. The rejected oil filters that were returned to the supplier have started turning up in customer engines. The rejected filters were simply relabeled by the supplier with their own brand, and placed into their own distribution system. Additionally, close inspection of the relabeled filters reveal that it is not difficult to detect the CAT logo on the filters, which were simply spray painted. Such an action violates one of the covenants of the supplier agreement, that all rejected filters will be destroyed. An interview with the president of the filter supplier reveals that this action was done against company policy, and without his personal knowledge. An immediate dilemma is that customers think they are buying, in effect, an equivalent quality Caterpillar filter. Dealers report that unsuspecting customers using the rejected/relabeled filters have been suffering severe engine damage, and are asking that Caterpillar stand behind the engines under warranty repair.

Needless to say, management is confronted with several difficulties. At this point they have not made any final decisions. They would like to attack all their problems with a coordinated strategy.

Midland Industries, Ltd. (B)*

Midland Industries Limited was a custom plastics molding company located in Midland, Ontario, north of Toronto. In January 1980, Lin Love, the President and General Manager of Midland, was concerned about the declining profitability of the Harris Products account. Since 1978, Harris Products, a U.S. marketer of garden accessories, had supplied its Canadian customers with injection-molded flowerpots purchased from Midland. In the first year, Midland sold 188,000 units to Harris for gross sales of $86,253, yielding an average gross margin of 10.3%. The following year, Midland sold $216,504 on sales of 366,000 units to Harris but gross margin slipped below 5%. Lin had to decide whether Midland should increase the markup on future Harris orders, and if so, by how much. The market for plastic flowerpots was highly price sensitive at the wholesale level, and Lin realized that a large sudden increase could prompt Harris to move to other suppliers.

Midland Industries

Midland Industries claimed to "custom mold plastics of every type into every variety of shape, size and form utilizing every modern (plastics) manufacturing process." Annual company revenues totalled $3.9 mil-

*Copyright © 1982, School of Business Administration, The University of Western Ontario. This case was written by Carolyn Vose under the supervision of Associate Professor Roger More. Reprinted with permission.

Exhibit 1 Midland Injection Molding: Operating Statistics

	1978	1979
Theoretical injection molding capacity/year	114,000 (machine hours)	114,000 (machine hours)
Actual utilization of available injection molding capacity	45%	65%
Total annual revenue	$3,900,000	$5,400,000
Revenue from injection molding only	$2,730,000	$3,780,000
Revenue from Harris account	$ 96,760	$ 216,504
Actual unit sales to Harris	188,000	372,000
Annual average gross margin on all injection molding	15%	11%
Average gross margin on Harris account— opening quarter	11%	7%
Average gross margin on Harris account— closing quarter	7%	3.6%

Note: There is no direct comparison between revenue and number of molding hours. Once molded, products may undergo a variety of secondary operations, each adding value.

lion in 1978 and $5.4 million in 1979, of which 70% came from manufacturing injection molded parts. Over the same period, capacity utilization of injection molding equipment rose from 45% to 65%,[1] as shown on Exhibit 1. Midland operated as a job shop. Goods were produced to custom-bid orders, shipped on completion, and billed net 30 days from delivery.

Operations at Midland were well-suited to the specialty molding market (e.g., automotive parts, appliance components). In this segment, success depended on engineering and technical expertise, secondary finishing capability, and the ability to meet tight specifications. Midland had up-to-date equipment for injection compression and transfer molding, as well as for a variety of secondary operations (e.g., spray painting, silk screening, hot stamping, sonic welding, and punching). In addition, advanced quality control facilities enabled Midland to guarantee exact customer specifications within tolerances of .002 inch for many molded parts.

Typically, custom specialty molding was characterized by short runs (72 machine hours or less), high per unit variable manufacturing costs, substantial investment in raw materials inventory, and complicated production scheduling with frequent work in process delays. According to the Canadian Society of Plastics Industries, gross contribution margins on specialty jobs generally ranged between 14 and 18 percent.

Midland's operation was generally less competitive than the high volume "commodities" segment, such as buttons, bottle closures, house-

[1] Midland operated on a 5-day week, 24 hours per day. Together, the 19 injection molding machines had an annual theoretical capacity of 114,000 machine hours (i.e., 19 machines × 50 work weeks per year × 120 work hours per week).

wares, combs, and similar standard design items that were relatively simple to produce. Low barriers to entry encouraged heavy price competition from small "basement molders" following a low investment, high capacity utilization strategy. Aggressive price cutting kept gross margins below 14%, thereby limiting competition from high-overhead molding operations like Midland.

The Initial Order

Harris Products, a U.S. company, marketed a 23-item line of plastic flowerpots available in 4 colors. The line was sold through department stores, discount houses, hardware stores, and other large volume merchandisers in both the U.S. and Canada.

The demand for plastic flowerpots was highly price sensitive at the wholesale level. Plastic pots competed directly against clay and ceramic pots. At the consumer level, clay flowerpots sold for about $1.00, plastic pots around $1.50 and ceramic pots over $2.00. Retailers exerted careful cost control to preserve gross margins at 40% or more.

Late in 1977, Harris had entered the Canadian market, hiring a domestic sales agent to promote and sell the line. Initially, the agent had estimated that Canadian sales of the pots could exceed one million units in 1978. Harris had considered supplying the entire Canadian market from their U.S. molder, but were discouraged by the 15% duty imposed on imported plastic flowerpots. Furthermore, exportation involved operating a warehouse and shipping department in Canada at an estimated cost of $150,000 per year (largely fixed costs).[2]

Harris had sought bids from Canadian custom molders to make, package, warehouse, and ship flowerpots for an all-inclusive unit price less than, or equal to, the "laid-down" cost of U.S. imports. Since new molds would cost around $15,000 (Canadian dollars) each, Harris had planned to shuttle the flowerpot molds between the U.S. and Canadian molders at a cost of $50.00/mold (return).

At Harris' request, Midland had submitted a bid quotation ($ Cdn.) on an initial flowerpot order for three items of 5,000 units each. The quotation was based on factory cost estimates plus gross margin:

	Item 1	Item 2	Item 3
Estimated factory cost/1000 units	$416.80	$407.50	$499.24
Initial quotation/1000 units	$500.00	$497.00	$595.00

Midland and Harris finally agreed to a pricing schedule which reduced Midland's expected gross margin to between 13% and 15%:

	Item 1	Item 2	Item 3
Estimated factory cost/1000 units	$416.80	$407.50	$499.24
Negotiated price/1000 units	$490.00	$487.00	$567.00

[2] Large-volume buyers insisted on frequent delivery of small shipments, often to dispersed locations, so servicing these customers from a Canadian warehouse would have improved delivery speed and reduced overall transport costs.

However, actual factory costs proved higher than expected, further squeezing Midland's gross margin:

	Item 1	Item 2	Item 3
Actual factory cost/1000 units	$434.24	$433.31	$501.06
Negotiated price/1000 units	$490.00	$487.00	$567.00

The unfavorable variance resulted mainly from underestimating molding time. Midland's calculations had been based on cycle times reported by Harris' supplier. In retrospect, Lin suspected that customer-provided cost information had shown an understandable bias toward understatement. This tendency was somewhat tempered by Harris' desire to develop a long-term business relationship with a Canadian molder.

Although Midland and Harris had signed a binding contract for the initial order, no formal agreement had been undertaken concerning future business. Lin explained:

We have an understanding that Midland will be the molder in Canada for any items which can be costed on a mutually acceptable basis. Midland submits prices on a quotation form and Harris negotiates by item, depending on market conditions and competitive laid-down U.S. price.

Recent Cost and Pricing History at Midland

Canadian sales of the Harris product line had fallen short of early expectations, as shown in Exhibit 2. Midland had sold Harris 188,000 flowerpots in 1978 and 366,000 the following year. As a result, the sales to Harris more than doubled from $96,760 to $216,504. Molding time increased accordingly from 2100 machine hours to 4135 machine hours.

Profits had not kept pace with sales, however. In January 1978, the average gross margin on the Harris account was 11%. The average gross margin dropped to 7% by January 1979 and continued to fall, reaching 3.6% eleven months later. The deterioration of gross margins was attributable to mounting cost and Harris's resistance to price increases in negotiation. The effect of the changes in the product mix was not significant.

Exhibit 3 traces the pricing histories of the three items which constituted the initial order. The cost structure of this order was representative. Actual factory costs are recorded in detail in Exhibit 4.

Exhibit 2   Canadian Sales Projections for Harris Planterware* (Number of Flowerpots)

	Projected Sales	Actual Sales
1978	1,072,000 units	188,000 units
1979	656,000 units	366,000 units
1980	1,250,000 units	—

*Forecast by Canadian sales agent for Harris Planterware.

Exhibit 3   Actual Pricing and Costing History of Three Representative Items Molded by Midland for Harris (Canadian dollars)

	January 1978			January 1979			December 1979		
	Item 1	Item 2	Item 3	Item 1	Item 2	Item 3	Item 1	Item 2	Item 3
Midland's estimated factory cost/1000 units	$416.80	$407.50	$499.24	$465.00	$450.60	$527.00	$511.00	$495.00	$589.00
Midland's initial quotation/1000 units	$500.00	$497.00	$595.00	$567.00	$550.00	$636.00	$608.00	$580.00	$695.00
Negotiated price/1000 units	$490.00	$487.00	$567.00	$544.00	$535.00	$622.00	$584.00	$562.00	$653.00
Midland's actual factory cost/1000 units	$434.24	$433.31	$501.06	$495.74	$500.80	$580.66	$551.50	$549.88	$631.26
Midland's actual gross margin (%)	11.4%	11%	11.7%	8.8%	6.3%	6.6%	5.5%	2.1%	3.3%
Midland's actual selling and administrative expense/1000 units	$ 19.60	$ 19.40	$ 22.70	$ 21.76	$ 21.40	$ 24.90	$ 23.40	$ 22.50	$ 26.10
Midland's profit (loss) before tax/1000 units	$ 36.16	$ 34.30	$ 43.24	$ 26.50	$ 12.80	$ 16.44	$ 9.10	$ (10.38)	$ (4.10)

Average run assumed to be 5000 units. Excludes cost of mold transportation (borne by Harris).

Exhibit 4 Midland's Actual Factory Costs of Items 1, 2, and 3 (Canadian dollars)

	January 1978			January 1979			December 1979		
	Item 1	Item 2	Item 3	Item 1	Item 2	Item 3	Item 1	Item 2	Item 3
Resin cost per pound	$ .323	$ .323	$ .323	$ .388	$ .388	$ .388	$ .440	$ .440	$ .440
Pounds of resin/1000 units[1]	580	604	620	580	604	620	580	604	620
Resin cost/1000 units	$187.34	$195.10	$200.26	$225.04	$234.35	$240.56	$255.20	$265.76	$272.80
Number of units/cycle	2	1	1	2	1	1	2	1	1
Avg. cycle time (seconds)	48	44	47	47	44	47	47	44	47
Molding hours/1000 units	7	12.8	13	6.8	12.8	13	6.8	12.8	13
Machine hour rate[2]	$ 29.10	$ 15.20	$ 19.20	$ 32.65	$ 17.00	$ 21.75	$ 35.90	$ 18.15	$ 22.91
Machine hour cost/1000 units	$203.70	$194.56	$249.60	$222.02	$217.60	$282.75	$244.12	$232.32	$297.70
Preparation time per run (hours)[3]	1	1	1	1	1	1	2	1	1
Preparation cost/1000 units	$ 5.80	$ 3.05	$ 3.80	$ 6.53	$ 3.40	$ 4.35	$ 7.18	$ 3.63	$ 4.58
Packaging cost/1000 units	$ 37.40	$ 40.60	$ 47.40	$ 42.15	$ 45.45	$ 53.00	$ 45.00	$ 48.17	$ 56.18
Total factory cost/1000 units	$434.24	$433.31	$501.06	$495.70	$500.80	$580.66	$551.50	$549.88	$631.26

	Item 1	Item 2	Item 3	Item 1	Item 2	Item 3	Item 1	Item 2	Item 3
Machine hour rates:									
Variable costs	$10.15	$ 7.40	$ 8.25	$11.77	$ 8.51	$ 9.16	$12.72	$ 9.10	$10.26
Fixed costs	$18.95	$ 7.80	$10.95	$21.49	$ 8.79	$12.59	$23.18	$ 9.05	$12.65
Total machine hour rate	$29.10	$15.20	$19.20	$32.65	$17.00	$21.75	$35.90	$18.15	$22.91

[1] Includes 5% scrap allowance

[2] *Machine hour rates:*

[3] Assuming an average run length of 5000 units.

Exhibit 5 Midland's Estimate of the Costs Associated with Harris's Export Alternative (Canadian dollars)

	January 1978			January 1979			December 1979		
	Item 1	Item 2	Item 3	Item 1	Item 2	Item 3	Item 1	Item 2	Item 3
Estimated factory costs of U.S. molder									
Resin cost/lb	$ .265	$ .265	$ .265	$ .318	$ .318	$ .318	$ .360	$ .360	$ .360
Lbs. of resin/1000 units	580 lb	604 lb	620 lb	580 lb	604 lb	620 lb	580 lb	604 lb	620 lb
Total resin cost/1000 units	$153.70	$160.06	$164.30	$184.44	$192.07	$197.16	$208.80	$217.44	$223.20
Molding hours/1000 units	7 hr	12.8 hr	13 hr	7 hr	12.8 hr	13 hr	7 hr	12.8 hr	13 hr
Machine-hour rate	$ 26.00	$ 13.50	$ 16.50	$ 29.00	$ 15.00	$ 18.50	$ 31.90	$ 16.50	$ 20.30
Total machine cost/1000 units	$182.00	$172.80	$214.00	$203.00	$192.00	$240.50	$223.30	$211.20	$263.90
Preparation time (set up & purge)/run	1 hr.	1 hr	1 hr	1 hr	1 hr	1 hr	1 hr	1 hr	1 hr
Preparation cost/hour	$ 26.00	$ 13.50	$ 16.50	$ 29.00	$ 15.10	$ 18.50	$ 31.90	$ 16.50	$ 20.30
Preparation cost/1000 units	$ 1.70	$ .90	$ 1.10	$ 1.90	$ 1.00	$ 1.20	$ 2.10	$ 1.10	$ 1.35

Packaging cost/1000 units	$ 29.00	$ 34.50	$ 40.00	$ 32.70	$ 39.00	$ 44.80	$ 34.00	$ 40.56	$ 46.60
Total factory costs of U.S. molder/1000 units	$366.40	$368.00	$419.40	$422.04	$424.07	$483.66	$468.20	$470.30	$535.05
Selling and administration costs of U.S. molder/ 1000 units	$ 17.00	$ 17.20	$ 16.75	$ 19.40	$ 19.70	$ 22.50	$ 21.50	$ 21.60	$ 24.60
Profit of U.S. molder, before tax/1000 units	$ 41.60	$ 44.90	$ 43.85	$ 42.69	$ 49.23	$ 55.84	$ 48.30	$ 48.10	$ 55.35
U.S. molder's selling price to Harris/1000 units	$425.00	$430.00	$480.00	$485.00	$493.00	$562.00	$538.00	$540.00	$615.00
Cost to Harris/1000 units (U.S. molder's selling price plus 15% import duty)	$488.75	$494.50	$552.00	$557.75	$567.00	$646.30	$618.70	$621.00	$707.25

Assumptions

—Calculations were based on cycle times clocked at Midland rather than those reported by Harris. Lin Love assumed that Midland operated at maximum efficiency and that Harris had understated the actual molding times achieved by their U.S. supplier.

—Average run for molder supplying U.S. and Canada would be 15,000 units.

—Transportation costs would be passed on to Harris customers. Overall there would be no significant freight cost difference whether the pots were shipped from Bartlett, Illinois or from Midland, Ontario.

—The export strategy would require leasing a shipping and warehouse operation costing Harris an additional $150,000 per year.

Unfavorable cost variances were largely caused by escalating resin prices. OPEC-inspired shortages of raw material feedstocks had increased the price of polypropylene from 32.3 cents/pound in January 1978 to 38.8 cents/pound by January 1979 and 44.0 cents/pound by December 1979. In January 1978, resin had accounted for about 45% of the factory cost of Harris flowerpots.[3] Over the same period, inflation increased machine hour rates and packaging costs between 18% and 20%.

Midland's incremental costs of producing for Harris extended beyond factory expenses. Midland was given temporary use of the molds, which were owned by Harris and normally held in custody of Harris's U.S. supplier. The various flowerpot molds made 37 round trips between the United States and Canada in 1978, and 68 trips, the following year.[4] Almost 50% of the time, Midland's scheduling was disrupted by the late arrival of a mold, anywhere from 3 to 10 days overdue. A third of the Harris runs were "rushed" because molds were recalled on short notice. Often, on these occasions, Midland would stop another customer's order mid-run to use the Harris mold immediately. The additional set-up and purge costs were borne by Midland. Lin believed that the delays and disruptions "undoubtedly created some problems with their clients, although it was difficult to assess the value of any lost goodwill."

Harris's Other Option: U.S. Manufacture and Export

Midland's chief rival for the flowerpot business was Harris's U.S. supplier. Lin had a fair idea of production costs and selling prices south of the border. Several years earlier, Lin had organized a study sponsored by the Society of Plastics Industries of Canada to prove "the Canadian molder had to deal with higher costs in molding a given part than his U.S. counterpart." This report to the Canadian Trade and Tariffs Committee on the GATT talks had demonstrated that Canadians paid approximately 22% more for resin, 18% more for packaging and 12% more for processing (machine-hour rate).

Aware that inflation had increased costs at the same rate in Canada as the United States, Lin was able to estimate costs of U.S. manufacture and exportation for the three examples shown in Exhibit 5. Lin hoped that comparative study of cost/price history in the United States and Canada would suggest an appropriate strategy for future negotiations.

Lin had assumed the U.S. custom molder's actual cycle times were equal to Midland's and that the average U.S. run would be three times as

---

[3] At Midland, this was considered a relatively high proportion. Generally, Midland molded products required extensive secondary finishing, decreasing resin as a percentage of factory value.

[4] Harris paid the freight costs associated with shuttling the molds between U.S. and Canada. The cost of shipping the molds totalled $1850 (Canadian dollars) in 1978, and $3750 (Canadian dollars) the following year.

long (i.e., 15,000 units). Even after allowing the United States molder a margin of 15–16% (before tax), the U.S. selling price to Harris would be lower than Midland's costs of production. Customs duty would have raised Harris's cost of importation by 15%. Additionally the import strategy would have cost Harris an incremental $150,000 per year in leased Canadian warehousing (fixed cost).

Lin wondered how much Midland could raise the price without losing the Harris account. He questioned whether an increase acceptable to Harris would adequately protect Midland from further cost escalation and assure his firm reasonable return. Within a week, Lin had to decide if Midland should continue to mold flowerpots for Harris, and if so, under what terms.

Texas Instruments:
Electronic Appliance Controls*

The telephone was ringing as Charles Ames, Manager of Appliance Controls Engineering, entered his office on the morning of June 21, 1976. The call was from the Director of Engineering for Electronic Cooking Incorporated (ECI), who told Ames that a competitor had underbid Texas Instruments for an order of electronic controls for microwave ovens. Mr. Ames was confident that the competitor's bid price was unrealistically low since Texas Instruments, with its accumulated experience, could meet the bid only by pricing with profit margins significantly less than the TI model for this product line.

While assembling his staff to discuss the ramifications of the competitive bid, Ames realized that a decision of this importance would significantly affect the direction of TI market growth. Accordingly, a meeting time that afternoon was set to bring together Ames, his staff, and their group vice president to formulate a course of action.

The Company

Texas Instruments Incorporated (TI) is a world leader in electronic technology innovation, production, and applications. In 1975, 84 percent of TI's total business was electronics-based. TI is a major producer of handheld calculators in terms of dollar volume.

Past and Future Performance   TI has experienced almost a threefold increase in net sales in the last decade. Net sales volume in 1975 was approximately $1.4 billion compared with net sales of about $580 million

* From Roger A. Kerin and Robert A. Peterson, *Strategic Marketing Problems: Cases and Comments*, Third Edition. Copyright © 1984 by Allyn and Bacon, Inc.

Exhibit 1   Abbreviated Texas Instruments' Consolidated Financial Statements for the Year Ended December 31, 1975 (in thousands of dollars)

Income Statement

Net Sales		$1,367,621
Operating Costs and Expenses		
Cost of goods and services sold	1,004,133	
General, administrative, and marketing	227,515	
Employees' retirement and profit sharing plans	21,185	
Total		1,252,833
Profit from Operations		$ 114,788
Other Income (Net)		11,971
Interest on Loans		(10,822)
Income Before Provision for Income Taxes		$ 115,937
Provision for Income Taxes		53,795
Net Income		$ 62,142

Balance Sheet

Current Assets	
Cash and Short-term Investments	$ 266,578
Accounts Receivable	245,785
Inventories (net of progress billings)	142,880
Prepaid Expenses	7,322
Total	$ 662,565
Property, Plant and Equipment (Net)	253,709
Other Assets and Deferred Charges	25,203
Total assets	$ 941,477
Liabilities and Stockholders' Equity	
Current liabilities	$ 301,843
Deferred liabilities	54,346
Stockholders' equity	585,288
Total liabilities and stockholders' equity	$ 941,477

Source: Annual Report.

---

in 1966. TI was ranked 152 in the *Fortune* 500 in 1975. Abbreviated TI 1976 financial statements are shown in Exhibit 1.

Two years ago, TI announced its goal to grow to $10 billion in net sales by the late 1980s. The guidelines for achieving the $10-billion goal were articulated in the *First Quarter and Stockholders Meeting Report, 1976:*

- We will model TI's business to self-fund growth.
- We intend to rely primarily on internal growth rather than on major acquisitions.

- We will optimize our resources to improve TI's share position.
- We will emphasize expansion of served markets into contiguous new segments, taking advantage of intra-TI shared experience.
- We will rely primarily on opportunities related to electronics, particularly those in which our semi-conductor skills can be decisive.

The operating guidelines for reaching the $10-billion goal were also outlined in the 1976 document:

- We must meet TI's return on assets goals to allow the growth to be self-funded.
- We must meet the operating model parameters to generate adequate OST[1] funds.
- OST funds must be invested in TI's major growth thrusts, that is, products that serve markets with a high growth rate and in which TI can develop a profitable position.
- We must retain and build upon TI philosophies and methods to manage profitable growth. This is why the institutionalism of TI's management culture has been emphasized through mechanisms such as the OST system, People and Asset Effectiveness, and Design-to-Cost.[2]
- TI must continue to increase its basic technological strength, especially in semiconductors. This includes not only the design and development of key components but also the application of these components to advanced systems and services.
- We must make Success Sharing[3] work because it is the key to increased productivity.

OST Budgetary Procedure   An OST program—Objectives, Strategies, and Tactics—is the action plan for a particular endeavor. An OST program states not only what a particular endeavor expects to achieve, but also how it will be achieved and the actions necessary to achieve it, including the costs of engineering, marketing, and production. OST funding is derived from a portion of operating profits intended to support a new business strategy and is controlled at the department (profit and loss center) level. Funding for OST programs is competitive in that division managers obtain inputs from each of the department managers and subsequently submit funding requests to a budget committee. OST programs are ranked according to their growth and profitability potential by the budget committee, with funds allocated accordingly.

---

[1] The TI Objectives, Strategies, and Tactics (OTS) system is described briefly in the OST budgetary procedure section of this case.

[2] Design-to-Cost is described briefly in the text.

[3] Success Sharing is a term used to designate the total package of TI employees' pension, profit sharing, and stock option purchase plans.

The annual budgeting procedure is highly refined and well-controlled. Flexibility is retained, however, to modify a product or program definition operating within the OST system. Programs are defined in the fourth quarter for the coming calendar year and are reviewed monthly and quarterly. The flexibility of the process is illustrated by Mr. Ames' reflection on the Electronic Controls program:

In 1973, the Oven Temp Sensor Program was funded $50,000 and the Electronic Control Program was allocated $10,000. In 1974, Oven Temp was allocated $60,000 while the Electronic Controls Department was allocated nothing. Then, in December 1974, a group of vice-presidents from a microwave oven manufacturer visited TI. The prospects outlined by these executives allowed for an improved Electronic Control Program to be developed. Funds from another program were immediately diverted to Electronic Controls, which marked the beginning of the program as it now stands.

Mr. Ames noted that this episode was not uncommon, given TI's corporate position that OST funds should be invested in products that serve growth markets and in which TI could develop a profitable position. Existing programs exhibiting poor performance could lose funding. Mr. Ames was very much aware of this fact: "The sequence of events that benefited the Electronic Controls Program could work against it unless the program could be made profitable."

Tactical Action Program: Electronic Controls

Pre-1975   Texas Instruments executives had decided to examine the electronic control market for microwave ovens in late 1972 in order to utilize and expand TI's semiconductor expertise. Microwave oven volume had grown substantially in the late 1960s and early 1970s. According to industry estimates, total industry sales in 1972 were 320,000 units compared with 20,000 units in 1968. Total industry sales in 1974 were approximately 785,000 units. During this period, ECI held the major share of the market, accounting for about 40 percent of the microwave oven units sold.

Controls for microwave ovens prior to 1975 were produced by electro-mechanical companies. However, industry sources indicated that these companies were experimenting with electronic controls. Other firms with semiconductor technology were showing signs of interest in producing electronic controls; yet, no firm had openly entered the market. "But TI had the right product at the right time, the capacity to support the potential demand, and the recognized technological expertise from calculators and related products to enter the market," Ames noted.

January–June 1975   On January 27, 1975, Charles Ames was assigned as manager of TI's Electronic Controls Program, then called the Tactical Action Program (TAP). Ames was responsible for both the engineering and marketing functions. He had responsibility for designing the product in addition to developing proposals for microwave oven producers.

Within two weeks of his appointment, Ames made his first presentation to ECI. The proposal was rejected in March. In April, he presented a proposal to AMEX Ovens for electronic controls with a unit sales price of $55.00. AMEX made a verbal commitment in June for 50,000 units.

During this period, Ames' energies were devoted to designing the electronic controls to cost requirements imposed by the cost-conscious appliance industry. The idea of Design-to-Cost (DTC) is central to TI's production and marketing thrust. Briefly, this concept involves designing a product from the start to achieve specific performance, cost, and profit goals. This practice involves the reduction in product cost necessary to perform a function due to a lower material and labor content. The impact of the DTC process for a TI handheld calculator serves as a typical illustration. In 1974, forty-seven total parts (including sixteen electronic parts) were required to build the TI19 model calculator. By 1976, the TI1200 calculator, identical in function, required twenty-three parts, and only two parts were electronic. Mr. Ames' efforts were focused on similar DTC activities for electronic controls.

The guide used by Ames in charting cost reductions was the learning or experience curve phenomenon. In effect, Ames hoped that he could realize a 20-percent reduction in electronic control assembly labor cost each time his volume doubled for a new design. Similar curves would be developed for each proposal to microwave oven producers and would reflect Ames' ability to economize on material and labor content for each succeeding generation of controls. Mr. Ames realized, however, that a practical limit existed in how much he could reduce overall costs.

July–December 1975 On July 2, Mr. Ames received a call from a Superior Cooking Products (SCP) executive requesting that he prepare a proposal for them. This proposal included a bid price per unit of $45.00. On August 14, SCP placed the first confirmed order for 50,000 units.

Mr. Ames received a call from ECI on November 28 asking for a proposal. A new proposal was developed to the ECI specifications and a price of $36.00 per unit was bid. The difference in prices between the AMEX, SCP, and ECI prices arose from TI manufacturing cost savings due to order size (250,000 per year for ECI) and different control specifications.

During this period, Ames consolidated and generated a variety of data pertaining to the appliance market and the electronic controls market for the purpose of forecasting TI's potential market growth and identifying possible areas of product superiority. These data would serve as inputs for his OST funding requests and preparation of financial planning and control indices.

Appliance Market and Microwave Ovens   Frequent discussions with marketing executives of appliance manufacturers revealed that technological innovation was the single most distinguishable factor separating competing products. Accordingly, appliance manufacturers were constantly seeking out new product features, provided the costs of product innovation were commensurate with the benefits. One reason for the search for new product designs was the saturation level of appliances in American homes. According to industry estimates, about 70 percent of the 72.7 million electrically-wired homes in the United States had electric ranges in 1975. Approximately six of ten electric ranges sold in 1975 were replacement purchases rather than net new purchases.

Microwave oven unit volume had grown substantially since the early 1970s, in spite of unfavorable publicity regarding the potential for radiation emission. Exhibit 2 shows Ames' forecast of microwave oven unit sales and penetration of electronic controls in the total market through 1980 based on discussions with appliance manufacturer executives. Ames believed that these estimates might be optimistic because some industry observers were forecasting a 17 percent saturation level among American homes by 1980. The annual rate of increase in the number of homes was about 2.3 percent, and the replacement cycle of microwave ovens had not been determined.

Also of interest to Ames was potential market share of major microwave oven producers. ECI had been a major supplier in the market prior to 1975. However, Home Appliance, Inc. (HAI), Superior Appliance, and AMEX had made competitive inroads and would continue to do so, according to industry sources. Despite some disagreement among microwave oven producers as to their respective market shares, Exhibit 3 shows the market share ranges described by industry observers.

Microwave Oven Controls Competition   Two major suppliers of electro-mechanical controls existed in late 1975, Relays and Wire, Inc. (R&W) and the Contact-Switch Company (C-S). Both firms had made progress in designing electro-mechanical controls at competitive prices. However,

---

Exhibit 2   Forecast of Microwave and Electric Range Unit Volume and Penetration of Electronic Controls (unit volume in millions)

	1977	1978	1979	1980
Microwave units	2	2.8	3.5	4
Percentage of microwave units with electronic controls	30%	45%	60%	80%
Electric ranges	2.9	2.87	2.85	2.8
Percentage of electric ranges with electronic controls	0%	3%	5%	10%

Exhibit 3   Estimated Market Shares of Microwave Producers, 1975, 1976, 1980

	1975 (%)	1976 (%)	1980 (%)
Electronic Cooking Inc.	25–33	25–30	15
Superior Appliance	16–25	20–25	15
Amex Ovens	10–18	15–25	12–20
Home Appliance Inc.	10	10–12	20–25
Other U.S. Producers	5–7	7–8	15–20
Japanese Producers	8–18	8–15	5–8

Ames believed that inherent limitations in the electro-mechanical technology would prohibit them from making major cost reductions or offering the innovative control features possible through semiconductor technology in the future. Nevertheless, in 1975, electro-mechanical technology was able to supply controls at a lower cost than semiconductor technology and this competitive advantage was forecast to exist until 1979. This would happen "provided semiconductor producers could penetrate the market, the microwave oven growth potential was realized, and so on and so forth," Ames opined. "A lot depends on how long semiconductor firms will stay with it, given very limited profit margins in the short run of maybe four to five years."

January–June 1976 On February 26, 1976, Ames was notified that ECI had accepted his bid price. During the remaining spring months, Ames directed an increasing amount of his time toward DTC efforts for second generation controls for TI customers and the ensuing production of first generation controls. Time was also spent preparing OST funding and planning schedules.

On April 19, 1976, Ames was asked to bid on a second-generation control for ECI. Given the nature of the bid, including the specifications and quantity (150,000 units), Ames proposed a price of $44.00 (see the cost schedule in Exhibit 4 and supplementary material). Shortly thereafter, Ames was advised that the competitive bid level was $42.00 per unit, which TI met after considerable discussion. Then, on June 21, 1976 Ames was informed that TI had been underbid by a major semiconductor manufacturing company at a price of $37.00. He assembled his staff to discuss the ramifications of the bid.

Ames had forecast an 80 percent labor learning curve for his bid, as shown in the exhibit. The labor estimate early in the process was about 1.75 hours/unit, but would decrease to about 0.36 hours/u   at the 150,000th unit. The midpoint at 75,000 units was 0.45 hours/unit. Hence, one-half of the unit volume would require more than 0.45 hours/unit to build and one-half would require less.

Exhibit 4   ECI Second Generation Control Cost Estimate

The cost estimate developed by Ames is shown below:

$26.50	Yielded material cost
6.50	(.45 hours/unit @ $14.45/hour)*
$33.00	Total material, labor and overhead or "manufactured cost"
11.00	25% Gross margin objective
$44.00	Control selling price at 150,000 unit volume

Estimated Labor Learning Curve for the ECI Second Generation Control

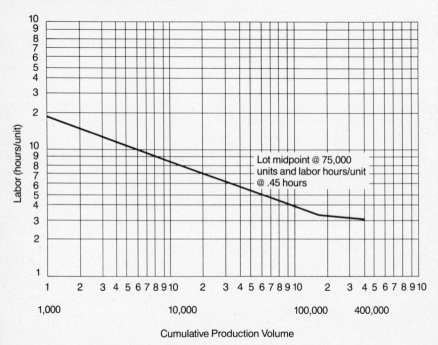

Cumulative Production Volume

---

*.45 Hours = lot mid-point of the 150,000 unit lot;
  $14.45 = hourly rate including factory overhead.

The 90 percent labor learning curve corresponded to the doubling of unit volume from 150,000 to 300,000. The flattening of the curve was a fact of life: learning gains would be less dramatic beyond 150,000 units without redesign and major change to the configuration. The labor hours/unit of the 300,000th unit would be 0.325, with the midpoint being approximately 0.34 labor hours/unit at the 225,000th unit produced.

Ames did not forecast reductions in material or yield cost, since he did not plan an interim design change that would be fruitful in the short run. Furthermore, labor cost/unit reductions, assuming that he would bid for an additional 150,000 second-generation ECI controls, did not look promising.

Overshadowing the entire situation was the question of whether the competitor was also forecasting prices and costs on an 80 percent labor learning curve. If so, then Ames would have to consider how long his group would stay in the electronic range control business. This factor was critical if volume doubled again for the ECI account.

Ames was also plagued by other considerations. First, the future of cumulative microwave sales volume remained a question. Second, even if Ames received the contract, all 150,000 units might not be shipped since the customer could stop shipment of controls at any time. In other words, as few as 50,000 to 75,000 units could be shipped and the order could be stopped. Third, TI policy held that every contract must achieve profit from operation objectives consistent with total company operations. Future OST funding for electronic appliance controls would depend, to a significant degree, on his ability to meet these objectives.

Lectron Corporation*

The Lectron Corporation was founded in the early 1970s by William Patton, to develop new electrical products for industrial and commercial markets. Prior to founding Lectron, Mr. Patton was executive vice president of a leading electrical products manufacturing company and had 20 years successful experience in the industry.

After two years of extensive research and development at a cost of approximately $300,000, the Lectron control was developed. Although the product was being marketed primarily as a motor control, the general design of this unit is suitable for many electrical switching applications, including temperature controls, lighting controls, and as a motor control. During the development stage, sales were minimal and usually to selected industries for special applications which served to prove the product under normal operating conditions.

Recently Mr. Patton has shifted his emphasis from development and field testing to consideration of how best to market the product with limited funds. The product by all estimates fits a market need, is technically sound and priced competitively, and has superior performance characteristics, yet it is far from reaching its full market potential, estimated to be in the millions of dollars. As a result, a great deal of planning is being done to identify the type of marketing program that would lead to increased sales growth and the "take off" stage in the product life cycle.

---

*This case prepared by Professor David McConaughy of the University of Southern California. Reprinted by permission.

Product

The Lectron motor control was a completely solid-state device: that is, it was totally electronic and had no mechanical moving parts. Its design was well tested and used only top quality components, such as those manufactured by RCA and Westinghouse. It met appropriate National Electrical Manufacturers Association standards and was the first such device approved for switching applications by Underwriter's Laboratory, a safety and circuit certification company. Underwriter's approvals are accepted and often required by state and industry safety departments and insurance companies.

The primary function of the Lectron control was to provide a "soft start," i.e., to reduce the heavy current inrush and starting torque of an electric motor. By avoiding the high initial current flow and torque, the following benefits occurred:

1. Reduced starting power requirements.

2. Reduced line voltage drop during motor starts.

3. Reduced possibility of damage to the motor and equipment that it drives.

4. Reduced thermal and electrical stress on motor and electrical circuits.

The Lectron control was more trouble-free, provided smoother operation, was quieter, operated in a wider range of environments, and was less expensive than alternative "soft-start" equipment. Because of its solid state design, the Lectron control did not cause the electromagnetic interference that was common with mechanical types of switching and thus it reduced "electromagnetic pollution," which was of growing concern to the FCC. Exhibits 1 and 2 show the product, and an example of the relevant data and benefits. Exhibit 3 gives the background on a highly successful application on a Coast Guard cutter which created a great deal of interest in the marine industry and received widespread publicity in new product and new application sections of trade publications.

Competition

At the time, there was no direct competition, and the Lectron control was the only effective solid state product on the market. This probably will change, as many solid state control circuits were being developed and published by component manufacturers and the Institute of Electrical Engineers. However, Mr. Patton does hold several comprehensive patents on the Lectron circuit. Electromechanical starters that provided a similar function produced by GE, Westinghouse, Allen-Bradley, and other firms were, of course, competition because they were an accepted method of "soft-start" control. Of these, the principal control being used

Exhibit 1   The Lectron Control

was the auto-transformer. While this device limited initial power surge, it made a jerky shift to each power level as the current was increased. This jerky movement had a high burn-out risk compared to the Lectron control, which was smooth throughout the entire starting cycle. Other "soft-start" controls were the part winding starter, which may require a specially designed (thus costly) motor, and the primary resistor starter, which mechanically switched an electrical resistor bank in series with the

Exhibit 2   The Lectron Control: Features and Applications

Lectron Soft-Start Controls

General Description:

Lectron soft-start controls are general-purpose devices for remote, automatic, or manual starting of three phase squirrel cage induction motors.

Starting characteristics, both torque and acceleration, are readily adjustable by access to simple adjustment screws through the top of the control module.

Switching options include low voltage, three wire momentary start/stop, 110 low voltage on/off or by contactor for reversing or dual speed operation.

The low voltage digital logic design, encompassing state of the art technology, insures perfect balance, reliability, long life, and easy interface with other control systems.

Applications:

☐Conveyor lines, both high-speed and heavy duty.
☐Bridge cranes and monorail systems.
☐Stackers, balancers, unloaders, etc.
☐Centrifugal blowers and pumps.
☐Other high-inertia starting loads.
☐Any belt, gear, or chain connected load.

Features:

Adjustable starting torque—limits inrush and mechanical shock.
☐Adjustable rate of acceleration—1 to 30 seconds— standard (other by request).
☐Noiseless, maintenance-free operation.
Fully encapsulated affected by difficult environmental conditions.
Eliminates switching transients common to electromechanical devices—the prime cause of motor failure.
Smooth, stepless transition from start to full-on.
☐Compact size—lightweight.
☐Guaranteed performance.

Exhibit 3   Case History: Solid State, Reduced Voltage Motor Controls Give the Coast Guard a Low Cost Cure for Electronic Failure

Environment:

Coast Guard Cutter Point Carrew, operating out of the Eleventh Coast Guard District.

Problem:

The addition of electrical and electronic equipment on ocean-going vessels, generally, and small craft, particularly, has taxed the generator and distribution system beyond its capacity to supply constant voltage. The condition becomes critical on start up of three-phase induction motors.

The voltage drop on normal starting of a three horsepower motor reduced line voltage below the tolerance of electronic equipment such as Radar, thus creating a potential hazard and, at best, an interruption in communications.

Test Duration:

Device installed June 14, 1972 and still operating as of this date, November 24, 1972.

Solution:

Repeated tests using the Lectron Motor Control showed no visible effect on the Radar performance. There was no detectable radio interference on AM and FM receivers. The test installation was considered 100% satisfactory and seems an attractive cure for electronic failure caused by voltage fluctuations that exist on many cutters and boats. It appears more cost-effective than the alternatives of individual voltage regulators and rewiring to provide a separate, quiet ship's distribution system.

Comparative Cost:

	Autotransformer Reduced Voltage Starter	Lectron Solid-State Control
Material Cost (Note)	$1,100	$265
Installation Cost	$100 (est)	$20
Weight	80 lbs (est)	3.5 lbs
Volume	7060 cu in.	64 cu in.
Moving Parts	17	0

Note: The Autotransformer consisted of a total replacement of existing controls, whereas, the Lectron device was a retrofit unit installed within and compatible with the existing system.

Comparative Performance:

	Before Installation	After Installation
Bus Volts (steady state)	450 Volts	450 Volts
Bus Volts—max drop	20 Volts	5 Volts
Current Starting Surge	28 Amps	8 Amps
Current—Steady State	4.3 Amps	4.3 Amps

The material contained herein was furnished by the United States Coast Guard, Eleventh Coast Guard District. It should not be considered as Coast Guard approval nor a recommendation of the Lectron Solid State Motor Control.

motor as it was started. Exhibit 4 gives a brief comparison among the costs and features of the various starting devices. Exhibit 10 describes these different devices.

Market Potential

The exact market potential for Lectron control was unknown because it could be used in a large number of industrial equipment and electrical control applications. The total market for motor and related controls of

Exhibit 4   Comparison among Features and Prices for Selected 10-Horsepower Motor Starters

Type of Control	Type of Start	Size	Weight	List Price	Comments
Magnetic Starter	On-Off Only	12″ × 7″ × 6″	15 lbs.	$ 162	Switches full power only.
Primary Resistor	Stepped-Smooth	29″ × 18″ × 10″	120 lbs.	$ 839	Low efficiency.
Autotransformer	Stepped-Smooth	35″ × 24″ × 12″	450 lbs.	$1139	Most widely used reduced voltage starter.
Part Winding	Stepped-Smooth	21″ × 14″ × 7″	100 lbs.	$ 448	Requires special motor with winding taps.
Star-Delta	One-Step Start	35″ × 35″ × 12″	210 lbs.	$ 695	Three-phase motors only.
Lectron	Continuous-Smooth	12″ × 10″ × 5¾″	15 lbs.	$ 875	Solid state—no moving parts.

Source: Company records.

Exhibit 5   Value of Shipments of Selected Switchgear and Control Apparatus 1974

SIC	Product	Number of Producing Companies	Shipments (Mil$)	Growth 1973–74
3613 701	Magnetic Control Circuit Relays	56	$256.5	9.3%
3613 704	Starter Accessories, Inc., Overload Relays	25	17.2	3.6%
3622 012	A.C. Full Voltage Starters 600 Volts or Less	42	182.9	27.4%
3622 013	A.C. Contactors 600 Volts or Less	30	37.5	−6.0%
3622 011	A.C. Reduced Voltage Controls	19	25.2	NA
3622 015	Synchronous Motor Starters	6	NA	NA
3622 016	Motor Control Centers	55	145.1	54.0%
3622 018	Starters and Contractors for Motors over 600 Volts	21	37.3	33.2%
3622 081	Rheostats and Resistors	17	20.1	39.6%
3622 097	All Other General Industry Devices	48	268.1	28.5%
3622 045	Marine and Navy Auxiliary Controls and Accessories	18	27.0	.4%
3622 048	Metal Mill, Crane and Hoist Controls, Constant and Adjustable Voltage	30	66.3	11.6%
3622 049	Definite Purpose Contractors and Starters for Refrigeration and Air Conditioning	9	23.5	NA

Source: U.S. Department of Commerce.

all types was in excess of $1 billion a year with the relevant control market perhaps as large as $800 million a year.

To aid in market planning, Mr. Patton collected available market data and developed a list of potential industrial applications where he felt that the Lectron control offered distinct advantages. Exhibit 5 lists the value of shipments of switchgear and control apparatus. Exhibit 6 lists the shipment of selected industries where the Lectron control could be used, and Exhibit 7 is a list of possible applications.

While the demand and shipments for industry equipment were clearly derived from capital investment plans of industry, even when such spending declined, the demand for labor-saving devices and motors rarely declined. Thus, Mr. Patton thought that general economic conditions should not affect the need for the Lectron control very much. On the other hand, developing a marketing program to sell to an industry having rapid growth, such as the pump and compressor industry (due to energy-related capital expansion and the growth of food processing), mining, and pulp and paper mills, might produce built-in growth once the Lectron control was adopted.

Exhibit 6   Selected Industry Data

Industry Category	SIC	1975 Shipments (Mil$)	Establish-ments	Average Annual Growth Rate 1967–75		Major Producing Areas
				Shipments	Exports	
Pumps and Compressors	3561 3563	$4,700	643	10.8%	15.6%	North Central Northeast
Material Handling Equipment	3534 3535 3536 3537	$3,720	1,250	5.7%	17.9%	Middle Atlantic North Central Western
Mining Machinery	3532	$1,550	240	14.5%	16.4%	Pennsylvania West Virginia Ohio
Oil Machinery	3533	$3,250	314	20.6%	28.6%	Texas Oklahoma California Louisiana
Food Products Machinery	3551	$1,745	675	10.8%	16.1%	North Central California New York
Textile Machinery	3552	$ 845	578	1.8%	12.7%	Northeast Southeast
Switchgear	3613	$2,760	898	5.0%	NA	NA
Motors and Generators	3621	$3,125	775	4.0%	NA	NA
Industrial Controls	3622	$2,093	1,173	6.0%	NA	NA
Shipbuilding	3731	$4,710	455	8.6%	NA	Great Lakes East, West, and Gulf Coasts

Source: U.S. Department of Commerce.

Exhibit 7   Potential Applications

Blowers
Centrifugal
Constant Pressure
Brick Plants
Augers
Conveyors
Dry Pans
Pug Mills
By-Product Coke Plants
Door Machines
Leveler Rams
Pusher Bars
Valve Reversing Machines
Cement Mills
Conveyors
Crushers
Dryers—Rotary
Elevators
Grinders, Pulverizers
Kilns
Coal Mines
Car Hauls
Conveyors
Cutters
Fans
Hoists—Slope
Hoists—Vertical
Jigs
Picking Tables
Rotary Car Dumpers
Shaker Screens
Compressors
Constant Speed
Varying Speed
   Centrifugal
   Plunger Type
Cranes—General Purpose
Hoist
Bridge or Trolley—Sleeve Bearing
Bridge or Trolley—Roller Bearing
Concrete Mixers

Flour Mills
Line Shafting
Food Plants
Butter Churns
Dough Mixers
Hoists
Mine Hoists—Slope
Mine Hoists—Vertical
Contractors Hoist
Winch
Larry Car
Lift Bridges
Machine Tools
Bending Rolls
Boring Mills
Bull Dozers
Drills
Gear Cutters
Grinders
Hobbing Machines
Lathes
Milling Machines
Presses
Punches
Saws
Shapers
Material Handling
Coal and Ore Bridges:
   Holding
   Closing
   Trolley
   Bridge
Metal Mining
Ball, Rod, or Tube Mills
Car Dumpers—Rotary
Converters—Copper
Conveyers
Crushers
Tilting Furnace
Paper Mills
Beaters

Current Lectron customers seem unrelated by product or industry, and usually purchase the Lectron control for very limited and unusual applications where no other starter would work. Two major crane manufacturing companies were in the process of testing the Lectron control, and Mr. Patton hoped to sell 2,000 to 3,000 units in this market. Several brewing and bottling companies had successfully tested the Lectron device to control pumping operations and had expressed great enthusiasm for the product, although no formal commitments from either of these markets had yet been forthcoming. At a volume of 2,000 units the manufacturing margin was estimated to be about 75 percent.

In addition to his own efforts, Mr. Patton used six sales representatives in the major industrial areas of the country. Most orders, however, ended up being placed directly with the company as a result of several

Calendars
Pipe Working
Cutting and Threading
Expanding and Flanging
Power Plants
Clinker Grinders
Coal Crushers
Conveyors—Belt
Conveyors—Screw
Pulverized Fuel Feeders
Pulverizers, Ball Type
Pulverizers, Centrifugal Type
Stokers
Pumps
Centrifugal
Plunger
Rubber Mills
Calendars
Crackers
Mixing Mills
Washers
Steel Mills
Accumulators
Casting Machines—Pig
Charging Machines
  Bridge
  Peel Revolving
  Trolley
Coiling Machines
Conveyors
Converters—Metal
Cranes
  Hoist
  Bridge and Trolleys, Sleeve Bearing
  Bridge Trolleys, Roller Bearing
Crushers
Furnace Doors
Gas Valves
Gas Washers
Hot Metal Mixers
Ingot Buggy

Kick Off
Levelers
Manipulator Fingers
Pickling Machine
Pliers—Slab
Racks
Reelers
Saws—Hot or Cold
Screw Downs
Shears
Shuffle Bars
Side Guards
Sizing Rolls
Slab Buggy
Soaking Pit Covers
Straighteners
Tables
  Approach
  Roll
  Shear Approach
  Lift
  Main Roll
  Transfer
  Tilting Furnaces
  Wiring Stranding Machines
Textiles
Weaving
Knitting
Throwing
Winding
Tufting
Wood Working Plants
Boring Machines
Lathe
Mortiser
Moulder
Planers
Power Trimmer and Mitre
Sanders
Saws
Shapers
Shingle Machines

press releases describing the Lectron control, or as a result of Mr. Patton's work with selected customers. Orders were typically for one or only a few controls and were shipped by United Parcel Service after being built to order by the small production department.

Marketing Strategy

After five years of directing his attention to problems of product development and manufacturing, Mr. Patton has become increasingly aware of the need for a comprehensive marketing plan if Lectron is to reach its full business potential. He was not sure that his sales representatives were effective in developing new markets, although his sales cost was only 8 percent with this approach. Company-employed salespersons

Exhibit 8   Productivity and Costs for Selected Types of Salespersons

Type of Salesperson	Metropolitan Area			Suburban Area	
	Average Direct Cost	Calls/ Year	Cost/ Call	Calls/ Year	Cost/ Call
Account Representative—calls on already established customers; selling is low key with minimal pressure to develop new business.	$23,500	1,195	$20	598	$39
Detail Salesperson—performs promotional activities and introduces new products; actual sale is ultimately made through a wholesaler.	$20,500	1,912	$11	1,195	$17
Sales Engineer—sells products where technical know-how and technical aspects are important to sale; experience in identifying and solving customers' problems is required.	$29,750	1,030	$29	665	$45
Industrial Products Salesperson—sells a tangible product to industrial or commercial purchasers; a high degree of technical knowledge is not required.	$25,000	1,673	$15	956	$26
Intangibles/Service Salesperson—must be able to sell effectively intangible benefits such as design services or application concepts.	$24,250	2,153	$11	1,195	$20

Source: *Sales and Marketing* magazine, February 9, 1976.

would be more committed to sell the product, except that they are expensive, and Mr. Patton was not sure which companies and market areas to direct them to. Exhibit 8 lists some typical sales costs, but he recognized that selling costs were higher in major metropolitan areas, such as New York, Chicago, and San Francisco, where costs were 40 to 60 percent higher than average. In the smaller cities of the Southeast, such as Greenville, near the textile industry, costs were 15 to 20 percent below average.

Mr. Patton has also developed a list of possible trade publications where Lectron advertising might be placed. Before he does any advertising, he wonders if he should get wholesale distribution so that customers can get local service and delivery of the product. He was not strongly in favor of distribution through wholesalers, as his earlier experience with electrical wholesalers led him to the conclusion that: (1) wholesalers didn't make an effort to push the product; (2) wholesalers carry too many other products; and (3) wholesalers really lacked the technical knowledge to understand potential applications. It seemed to him that some form of personal selling would be required, and if this were done properly, perhaps he might not have to advertise until he could better afford it, as the costs for advertising in many trade publications seemed quite high. Exhibit 9 lists the publications Mr. Patton was considering.

Exhibit 9   Cost and Circulation Data on Selected Trade Publications

Magazine	Circulation	Cost of B & W Page	Comments
Automation	90,223	$2,280	Production engineering emphasis; trade show issues.
Control Engineering	70,627	$1,925	Instrumentation and automatic control emphasis.
Design News	123,189	$2,760	Design engineer's idea magazine.
Electrical Apparatus	15,031	$ 750	Magazine of electromechanical operation and maintenance, edited for the after-market.
Electrical Contractor	40,004	$1,350	Electrical construction and maintenance industry.
Electrical Construction and Maintenance	70,521	$2,295	
Electrical Equipment	75,060	$3,053	Edited for electrical and electromechanical engineers who research, design, and install electrical or electromechanical products.
Electrified Industry	32,600	$1,110	Edited for electrically responsible engineers; covers automation, electric controls, material handling, and electrical maintenance.
Electrical Wholesaling	16,114	$1,350	Controlled circulation to electrical distributors; sourcebook of electrical wholesaling, marketing, and selling.
Factory	91,086	$2,590	General interest manufacturing magazine.
Food Processing	56,031	$1,420	New product reports, case histories; covers processing equipment, material handling, etc.
Industrial Equipment News	142,735	$7,915	What's new in equipment, parts, and materials; covers literature and catalogs that are available.
Industrial Maintenance and Plant Operation	105,581	$3,390	News tabloid magazine for those responsible for maintenance and operation of industrial plants.
Machine Design	127,419	$2,554	
Marine Engineering/ Log	22,490	$ 800	Covers new developments in marine engineering and naval construction.
Materials Handling Engineering	76,733	$2,090	Technical magazine for material handling, packaging, and shipping specialists.
New Equipment Digest	139,120	$2,340	Covers equipment, materials, processes, and design literature and catalogs.
Pit and Quarry	22,242	$1,085	Directed to management who specify and buy equipment, supplies, and services for mining, quarrying, and processing non-metallic minerals.
Purchasing	74,498	$2,385	News magazine for industrial buyers.

Source: Standard Rate and Data Service, June 24, 1976.

Exhibit 10   Starting Devices: Product Description

Auto-Transformer Control

Auto-transformer-type starters are the most widely used reduced voltage starter because of their efficiency and flexibility. All power taken from the line, except transformer losses, is transmitted to the motor to accelerate the load. Taps on the transformer allow adjustment of the starting torque and inrush to meet the requirements of most applications. The following characteristics are produced by the three voltage taps:

Tap	Starting Torque % Locked Torque	Line Inrush % Locked Ampere
50%	25%	28%
65%	42%	45%
80%	64%	67%

Part Winding Controls

Part winding starting provides convenient economical one-step acceleration at reduced current where the power company specifies a maximum, or limits the increments of current drawn from the line. These starters can be used with standard dual-voltage motors on the lower voltage and with special part-winding motors designed for any voltage. When used with standard dual-voltage motors, it should be established that the torque produced by the first half-winding will accelerate the load sufficiently so as not to produce a second undesirable inrush when the second half-winding is connected to the line. Most motors will produce a starting torque equal to between ½ to ⅔ of NEMA standard values with half of the winding energized and draw about ⅔ of normal line current inrush.

Primary Resistor

Primary resistor-type starters, sometimes known as "cushion-type" starters, will reduce the motor torque and starting inrush current to produce a smooth, cushioned acceleration with closed transition. Although not as efficient as other methods of reduced voltage starting, primary resistor-type starters are ideally suited to applications such as conveyors, textile machines, or other delicate machinery where reduction of starting torque is of prime consideration. Starters through size 5 will limit inrush to approximately 80% of lock rotor current and starting torque to approximately 64% of locked torque. Larger sizes are custom designed to the application.

Star-Delta Control

Star-Delta-type starters have been applied extensively to industrial air conditioning installations because they are particularly applicable to starting motors driving high inertia loads with resulting long acceleration times. They are not, however, limited to this application. When six or twelve lead delta-connected motors are started star-connected, approximately 58% of full line voltage is applied to each winding and the motor develops 33% of normal locked rotor current from the line. When the motor has accelerated, it is reconnected for normal delta operation.

Mr. Patton had identified three possible marketing strategies he felt had some promise for success:

1.   Sell product concept to electrical design engineers and OEM equipment manufacturers and encourage them to specify the Lectron Control, include it with their products, or at least recommend it to their customers.

2.   Sell control services by selling the control, including wiring and connecting equipment, to end users of equipment or possibly to OEM equipment manufacturers.

3. Sell control to manufacturing and maintenance buyers to solve a specific application problem or to reduce maintenance costs and breakage.

Other possible market considerations were selling to government agencies, such as the Coast Guard, or other manufacturers of controls, even though there seemed to be little interest among the major manufacturers. Also, he wondered if he might be more successful if he sold the complete control package including possibly the motor rather than just the control alone.

As Mr. Patton cleared a space on his desk he wondered to himself if Thomas Edison and other pioneers in the electrical industry had gone through this process.

He then carefully began considering how to choose an appropriate marketing strategy that would hasten the success of the Lectron control.

Subject Index

Name Index